PRINCIPLES OF MICROECONOMICS

Eighth Edition

N. GREGORY MANKIW

HARVARD UNIVERSITY

CENGAGE

Australia • Brazil • Canada • India • Mexico • Singapore • United Kingdom • United States

Cengage

Principles of Microeconomics, 8e

N. Gregory Mankiw

For product information and technology assistance, contact us at
asia.infoindia@cengage.com

For permission to use material from this text or product, submit all requests online at
www.cengage.com/permissions

ISBN-13: 978-93-5573-415-0
ISBN-10: 93-5573-415-8

Cengage Learning India Pvt. Ltd.
T-303, 3rd Floor
DAV Complex, Plot 3
Mayur Vihar Phase 1
Delhi-110091

Cengage is a leading provider of customized learning solutions with employees residing in nearl 40 different countries and sales in more than 125 countries around the world. Find your loca representative at **www.cengage.com**

Cengage is committed to creating inclusive and diverse products, including perspectives that represent th diversity of people across all backgrounds, identities, opinions, and experiences. If you have any feedbac related to this, please contact us at **support.cengage.com**

To learn more about Cengage products, platforms and services, visit at **www.cengage.co.in**

Disclaimer:
This book contains link to resources which are a part of the imported edition. The same may not b available with the Indian edition. The buyer needs to purchase a copy of the imported edition to hav full access to those resources. In no event the publisher shall be liable for any limitation or performanc due to unavailability of these resources.

Printed by:
Rajiv Book Binding House
D-1518, DSIIDC Industrial Complex, Narela, New Delhi-110040.

Printed in India
Print Number: 07 Print Year: 2024

To Catherine, Nicholas, and Peter,
my other contributions to the next generation

About the Author

Jordi Cabré

N. Gregory Mankiw is the Robert M. Beren Professor of Economics at Harvard University. As a student, he studied economics at Princeton University and MIT. As a teacher, he has taught macroeconomics, microeconomics, statistics, and principles of economics. He even spent one summer long ago as a sailing instructor on Long Beach Island.

Professor Mankiw is a prolific writer and a regular participant in academic and policy debates. His work has been published in scholarly journals, such as the *American Economic Review, Journal of Political Economy,* and *Quarterly Journal of Economics*, and in more popular forums, such as the *New York Times* and *The Wall Street Journal*. He is also author of the best-selling intermediate-level textbook *Macroeconomics* (Worth Publishers). In addition to his teaching, research, and writing, Professor Mankiw has been a research associate of the National Bureau of Economic Research, an adviser to the Congressional Budget Office and the Federal Reserve Banks of Boston and New York, and a member of the ETS test development committee for the Advanced Placement exam in economics. From 2003 to 2005, he served as chairman of the President's Council of Economic Advisers.

Professor Mankiw lives in Wellesley, Massachusetts, with his wife, Deborah, three children, Catherine, Nicholas, and Peter, and their border terrier, Tobin.

Brief Contents

PART I Introduction 1

1 Ten Principles of Economics 3
2 Thinking Like an Economist 19
3 Interdependence and the Gains from Trade 47

PART II How Markets Work 61

4 The Market Forces of Supply and Demand 63
5 Elasticity and Its Application 87
6 Supply, Demand, and Government Policies 109

PART III Markcts and Welfare 129

7 Consumers, Producers, and the Efficiency of Markets 131
8 Application: The Costs of Taxation 151
9 Application: International Trade 165

PART IV The Economics of the Public Sector 183

10 Externalities 185
11 Public Goods and Common Resources 205
12 The Design of the Tax System 221

PART V Firm Behavior and the Organization of Industry 239

13 The Costs of Production 241
14 Firms in Competitive Markets 261
15 Monopoly 283
16 Monopolistic Competition 313
17 Oligopoly 331

PART VI The Economics of Labor Markets 353

18 The Markets for the Factors of Production 355
19 Earnings and Discrimination 377
20 Income Inequality and Poverty 395

PART VII Topics for Further Study 413

21 The Theory of Consumer Choice 415
22 Frontiers of Microeconomics 441

Preface: To the Student

"Economics is a study of mankind in the ordinary business of life." So wrote Alfred Marshall, the great 19th-century economist, in his textbook, *Principles of Economics*. We have learned much about the economy since Marshall's time, but this definition of economics is as true today as it was in 1890, when the first edition of his text was published.

Why should you, as a student in the 21st century, embark on the study of economics? There are three reasons.

The first reason to study economics is that it will help you understand the world in which you live. There are many questions about the economy that might spark your curiosity. Why are apartments so hard to find in New York City? Why do airlines charge less for a round-trip ticket if the traveler stays over a Saturday night? Why is Robert Downey, Jr., paid so much to star in movies? Why are living standards so meager in many African countries? Why do some countries have high rates of inflation while others have stable prices? Why are jobs easy to find in some years and hard to find in others? These are just a few of the questions that a course in economics will help you answer.

The second reason to study economics is that it will make you a more astute participant in the economy. As you go about your life, you make many economic decisions. While you are a student, you decide how many years to stay in school. Once you take a job, you decide how much of your income to spend, how much to save, and how to invest your savings. Someday you may find yourself running a small business or a large corporation, and you will decide what prices to charge for your products. The insights developed in the coming chapters will give you a new perspective on how best to make these decisions. Studying economics will not by itself make you rich, but it will give you some tools that may help in that endeavor.

The third reason to study economics is that it will give you a better understanding of both the potential and the limits of economic policy. Economic questions are always on the minds of policymakers in mayors' offices, governors' mansions, and the White House. What are the burdens associated with alternative forms of taxation? What are the effects of free trade with other countries? What is the best way to protect the environment? How does a government budget deficit affect the economy? As a voter, you help choose the policies that guide the allocation of society's resources. An understanding of economics will help you carry out that responsibility. And who knows: Perhaps someday you will end up as one of those policymakers yourself.

Thus, the principles of economics can be applied in many of life's situations. Whether the future finds you following the news, running a business, or sitting in the Oval Office, you will be glad that you studied economics.

N. Gregory Mankiw
December 2016

Video Application

Video application features the book's author introducing chapter content. Author Greg Mankiw introduces the important themes in every chapter by delivering a highly relevant deposition on the real-world context to the economic principles that will be appearing in the upcoming chapter. These videos are intended to motivate students to better understand how economics relates to their day-to-day lives and in the world around them.

ConceptClip Videos

ConceptClip videos help students master economics terms. These high-energy videos, embedded throughout the interactive book, address the known student challenge of understanding economics terminology when initially introduced to the subject matter. Developed by Professor Mike Brandl of The Ohio State University, these concept-based animations provide students with memorable context to the key terminology required for your introductory economics course.

> *"I have always wanted supplemental material such as this to help me understand certain concepts in economics."*

Graph Builder

Graph Builder allows students to move step-by-step through complex graphical figures. Designed specifically for introductory economics students, Graph Builder interactive exercises help students first understand complex graphs by deconstructing a graph into finite steps that build upon one another, then practice graphing by drawing out a similar scenario from scratch. This drawing method supports the kinesthetic learning approach valued by instructors, like you— all within the context of the interactive book!

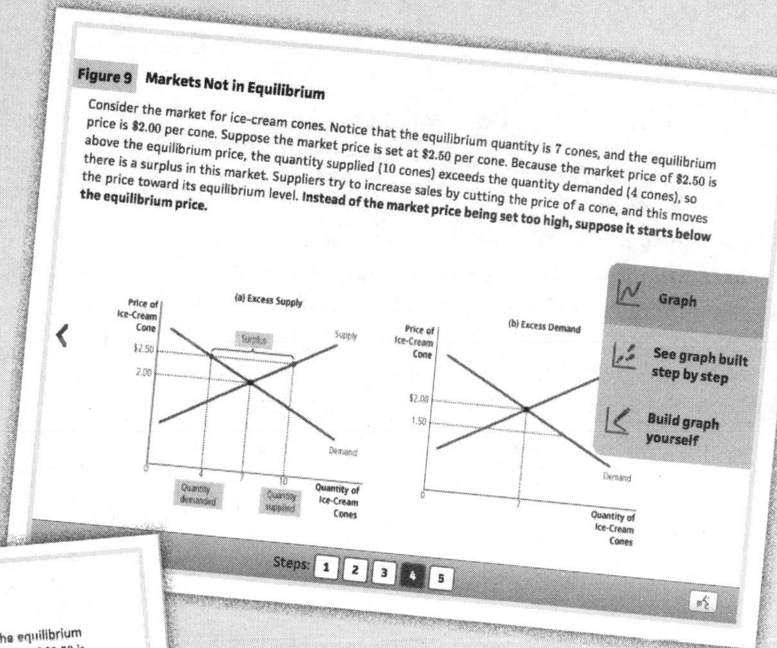

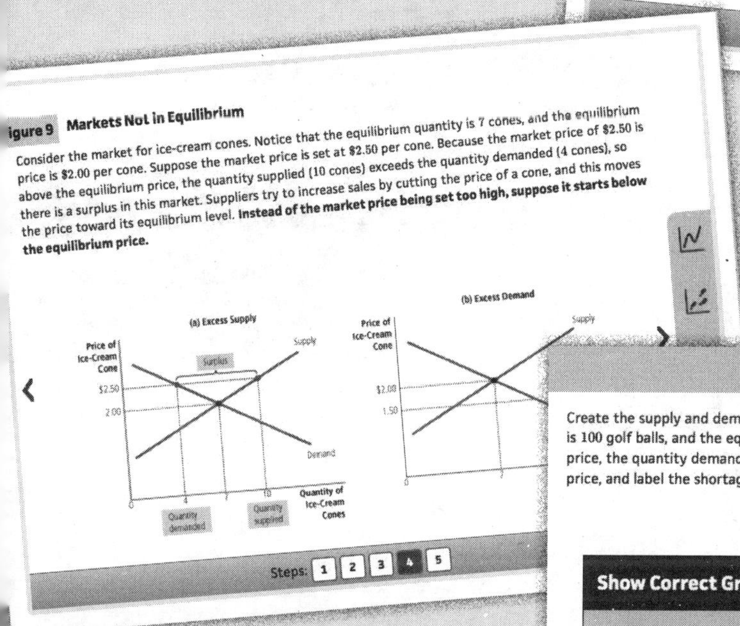

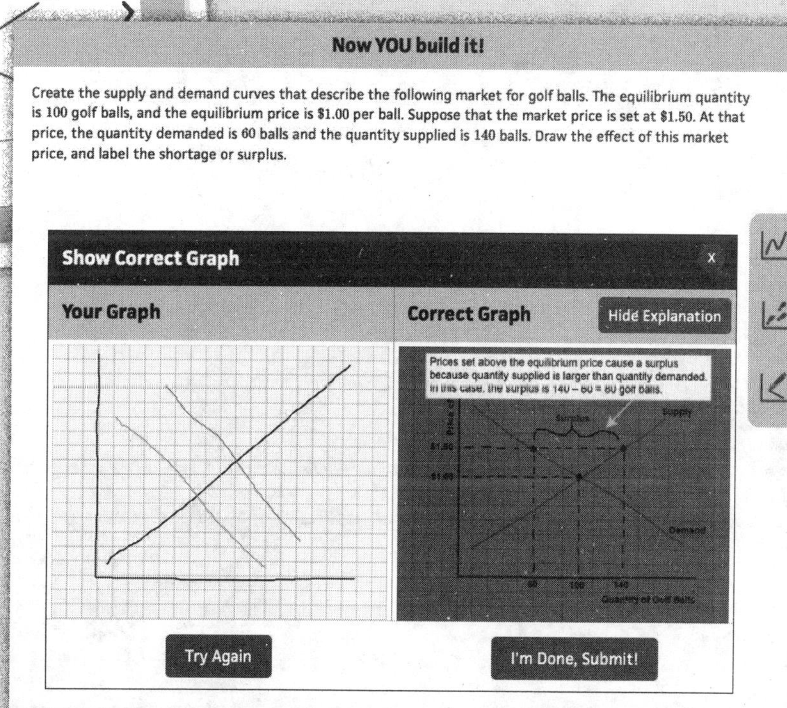

"I have not used anything like this before."

"The Graph Builder is amazing! This would help me a lot and the concept is great. I think all students should have access to this feature because it would better their knowledge of how to make graphs."

Study and Test Prep

The Mankiw Study Guide is now a part of MindTap!

The study guide by David Hakes for Mankiw's *Principles of Economics* has long been the standard of what a print study guide could be. Students like how it reinforces the text and improves understanding of the chapter content. Now for the eighth edition, the study guide is integrated right into the MindTap course at no additional charge!

For each chapter, students get the same great resources that users of the print Study Guide have always received:

- The Chapter Overview
- Problems and Short Answers
- Self-Test
- Advanced Critical Thinking
- Solutions for All Study Guide Questions

David Hakes and Greg Mankiw

MindTap®

"Additional practice with problems is extremely helpful, especially when combined with the immediate feedback that I received via the online server."

"The adaptive feedback system was incredibly useful, because by the time the test rolled around I didn't always remember what I had struggled with in previous weeks."

Adaptive Test Prep Prepares Your Students for High-Stakes Testing

Are your students constantly asking you for more practice questions as exam time comes closer? Do your students complain because the test bank-type questions in the exam do not have the same look and feel as their homework assignments?

Adaptive Test Prep is a powerful tool that uses 4,000 new test bank-like questions to give students almost unlimited practice for each chapter and section. They can take as many tests as they like that are immediately graded for them. Students see how they did and the program gives them immediate remediation in the form of very robust feedback, a link right back into the text where the question topic resides, and for about 2,000 questions, they get a brief Quick Coach video with an instructor walking them through the exact question they missed!

Students can generate reports that show them which chapters and sections they need the most help on so they can tailor future practice tests just on the areas they are struggling with.

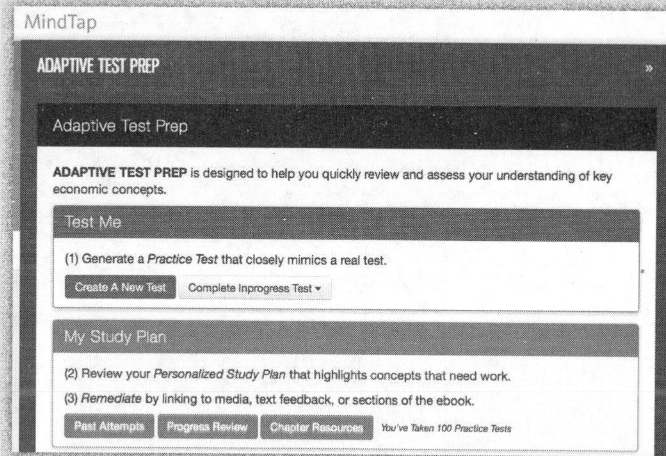

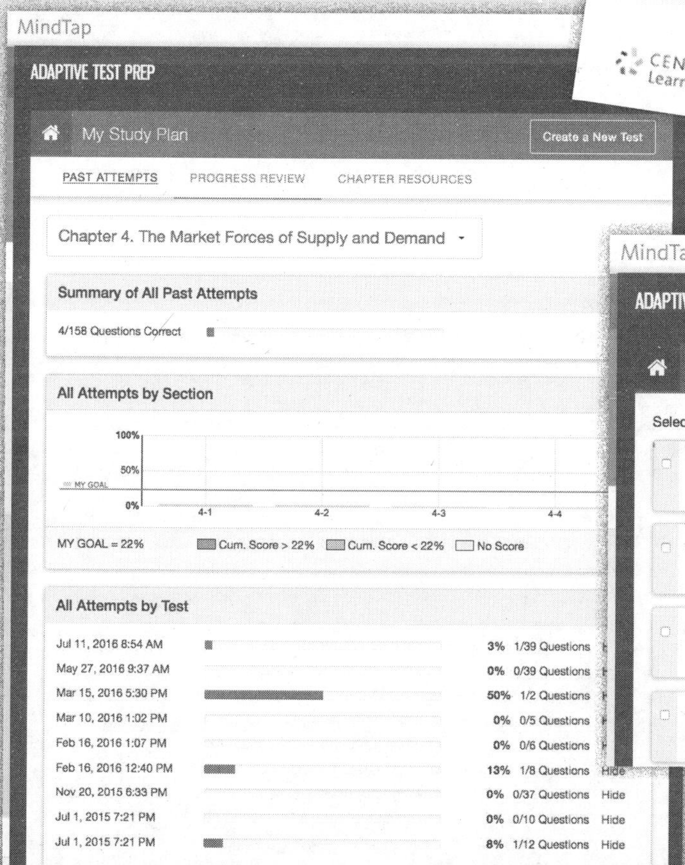

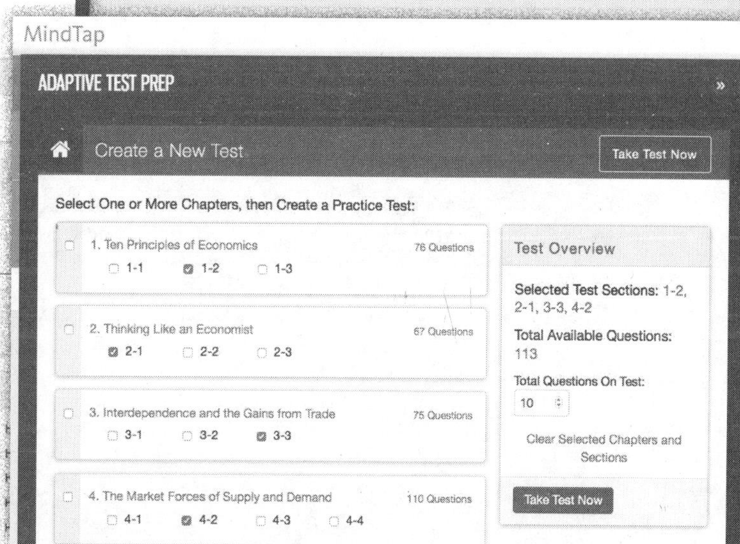

Acknowledgments

In writing this book, I benefited from the input of many talented people. Indeed, the list of people who have contributed to this project is so long, and their contributions so valuable, that it seems an injustice that only a single name appears on the cover.

Let me begin with my colleagues in the economics profession. The many editions of this text and its supplemental materials have benefited enormously from their input. In reviews and surveys, they have offered suggestions, identified challenges, and shared ideas from their own classroom experience. I am indebted to them for the perspectives they have brought to the text. Unfortunately, the list has become too long to thank those who contributed to previous editions, even though students reading the current edition are still benefiting from their insights.

Most important in this process has been David Hakes (University of Northern Iowa). David, a dedicated teacher, has served as a reliable sounding board for ideas and is a hardworking partner with me in putting together the superb package of supplements. In addition, a special thanks to Ron Cronovich, an insightful instructor and trusted advisor, for his many years of consultation.

A special thanks to the team of teaching economists who worked on the test bank and ancillaries for this edition, many of whom have been working on the Mankiw ancillaries from the beginning. To Ken McCormick for vetting the entire test bank (with 17,000 questions) for correctness, and to Ken Brown, Sarah Cosgrove, Harold Elder, Michael Enz, Lisa Jepsen, Bryce Kanago, Daniel Marburger, Amanda Nguyen, Alicia Rosburg, Forrest Spence, and Kelvin Wong for authoring new questions and updating existing ones.

The following reviewers of the seventh edition provided suggestions for refining the content, organization, and approach in the eighth.

Mark Abajian, *San Diego Mesa College*
Rahi Abouk, *University of Wisconsin Milwaukee*
Mathew Abraham, *Indiana University – Purdue University Indianapolis*
Nathanael Adams, *Cardinal Stritch University*
Seemi Ahmad, *Dutchess Community College*
May Akabogu-Collins, *Mira Costa College–Oceanside*
Ercument Aksoy, *Los Angeles Valley College*
Basil Al-Hashimi, *Mesa Community College*
Rashid Al-Hmoud, *Texas Tech University*
William Aldridge, *University of Alabama–Tuscaloosa*
Donald L. Alexander, *Western Michigan University*
Hassan Aly, *Ohio State University*
Michelle Amaral, *University of the Pacific*
Shahina Amin, *University of Northern Iowa*
Catalina Amuedo-Dorantes, *San Diego State University*
Vivette Ancona, *Hunter College–CUNY*
Aba Anil, *University of Utah*
Diane Anstine, *North Central College*
Carolyn Arcand, *University of Massachusetts Boston*
Becca Arnold, *San Diego Community College*
Ali Ataiifar, *Delaware County Community College*
Shannon Aucoin, *University of Louisiana Lafayette*
Lisa Augustyniak, *Lake Michigan College*
Wesley Austin, *University of Louisiana Lafayette*
Dennis Avola, *Framingham State University*
Regena M. Aye, *Allen Community College*
Sang Hoo Bae, *Clark University*
Karen Baehler, *Hutchinson Community College*
Sahar Bahmani, *University of Wisconsin-Parkside*
Mohsen Bahmani-Oskooee, *University of Wisconsin Milwaukee*

Richard Baker, *Copiah-Lincoln Community College*
Stephen Baker, *Capital University*
Tannista Banerjee, *Auburn University*
Bob Barnes, *DePaul University*
Hamid Bastin, *Shippensburg University*
James Bathgate, *Western Nevada College*
Leon Battista, *Albertus Magnus College*
Gerald Baumgardner, *Susquehanna University*
Christoph Bauner, *University of Massachusetts–Amherst*
Elizabeth Bayley, *University of Delaware*
Ergin Bayrak, *University of Southern California*
Nihal Bayraktar, *Pennsylvania State University*
Mike Belleman, *St. Clair County Community College*
Audrey Benavidez, *Del Mar College*
Cynthia Benelli, *University of California Santa Barbara*
Charles Bennett, *Gannon University*
Bettina Berch, *Borough of Manhattan Community College*
Stacey Bertke, *Owensboro Community & Technical College*
Tibor Besedes, *Georgia Institute of Technology*
Abhijeet Bhattacharya, *Illinois Valley Community College*
Ronald Bishop, *Lake Michigan College*
Thomas Bishop, *California State Channel Islands*
Nicole Bissessar, *Kent State University-Ashtabula*
Janet Blackburn, *San Jacinto South College*
Jeanne Boeh, *Augsburg College*
Natalia Boliari, *Manhattan College*
Antonio Bos, *Tusculum College*
Jennifer Bossard, *Doane College*
James Boudreau, *University of Texas–Pan American*
Mike Bowyer, *Montgomery Community College*
William Brennan, *Minnesota State University–Mankato*
Genevieve Briand, *Washington State University*
Scott Broadbent, *Western Kentucky University*
Greg Brock, *Georgia Southern University*
Ivy Broder, *American University*
Todd Broker, *Murray State University*
Stacey Brook, *University of Iowa*
Keith Brouhle, *Grinnell College*
Byron Brown, *Michigan State University*
Crystal Brown, *Anderson University*
Kris Bruckerhoff, *University of Minnesota-Crookston*
Christopher Brunt, *Lake Superior State University*
Laura Bucila, *Texas Christian University*
Donna Bueckman, *University of Tennessee–Knoxville*
Don Bumpass, *Sam Houston State University*
Joe Bunting, *St. Andrews University*
Benjamin Burden, *Temple College*
Mariya Burdina, *University of Central Oklahoma*
Rob Burrus, *University of North Carolina–Wilmington*
James Butkiewicz, *University of Delaware*
William Byrd, *Troy University*
Anna Cai, *University of Alabama–Tuscaloosa*
Samantha Cakir, *Macalester College*
Michael Carew, *Baruch College*
William Carner, *Westminster College*
Craig Carpenter, *Albion College*
John Carter, *California State University-Stanislaus*
Ginette Carvalho, *Fordham University*
Onur Celik, *Quinnipiac University*
Avik Chakrabarti, *University of Wisconsin–Milwaukee*
Kalyan Chakraborty, *Emporia State University*
Suparna Chakraborty, *Baruch College–CUNY*
Dustin Chambers, *Salisbury University*
Silvana Chambers, *Salisbury University*
Krishnamurti Chandrasekar, *New York Institute of Technology*
Yong Chao, *University of Louisville*
David Chaplin, *Northwest Nazarene University*
Xudong Chen, *Baldwin-Wallace College*
Yi-An Chen, *University of Washington, Seattle*
Kirill Chernomaz, *San Francisco State University*
Ron Cheung, *Oberlin College*
Hui-Chu Chiang, *University of Central Oklahoma*
Mainul Chowdhury, *Northern Illinois University*
Dmitriy Chulkov, *Indiana University Kokomo*
Lawrence Cima, *John Carroll University*
Cindy Clement, *University of Maryland*
Matthew Clements, *St. Edward's University*
Sondra Collins, *University of Southern Mississippi*
Tina Collins, *San Joaquin Valley College*
Scott Comparato, *Southern Illinois University*
Kathleen Conway, *Carnegie Mellon University*
Stephen Cotten, *University of Houston Clear Lake*
Jim Cox, *Georgia Perimeter College*
Michael Craig, *University of Tennessee–Knoxville*
Matt Critcher, *University of Arkansas Community College at Batesville*
George Crowley, *Troy University, Troy*
David Cullipher, *Arkansas State University-Mountain Home*
Dusan Curcic, *University of Virginia*
Norman Cure, *Macomb Community College*
Maria DaCosta, *University of Wisconsin–EauClaire*
Bruce Dalgaard, *St. Olaf College*
Anusua Datta, *Philadelphia University*
Earl Davis, *Nicholls State University*
Amanda Dawsey, *University of Montana*
Prabal De, *City College of New York*
Rooj Debasis, *Kishwaukee College*
Dennis Debrecht, *Carroll University*
William DeFrance, *University of Michigan-Flint*
Theresa J. Devine, *Brown University*
Paramita Dhar, *Central Connecticut State University*
Ahrash Dianat, *George Mason University*
Stephanie Dieringer, *University of South Florida St. Petersburg*
Du Ding, *Northern Arizona University*
Liang Ding, *Macalester College*
Parks Dodd, *Georgia Institute of Technology*
Veronika Dolar, *Long Island University*
Zachary Donohew, *University of Central Arkansas*
Kirk Doran, *University of Notre Dame*
Craig Dorsey, *College of DuPage*

Caf Dowlah, *Queensborough Community College–CUNY*
Tanya Downing, *Cuesta College*
Michael J. Driscoll, *Adelphi University*
Ding Du, *Northern Arizona University*
Kevin Dunagan, *Oakton community college*
Nazif Durmaz, *University of Houston–Victoria*
Tomas Dvorak, *Union College*
Eva Dziadula, *Lake Forest College*
Dirk Early, *Southwestern University*
Ann Eike, *University of Kentucky*
Harold Elder, *University of Alabama–Tuscaloosa*
Lynne Elkes, *Loyola University Maryland*
Diantha Ellis, *Abraham Baldwin College*
Noha Emara, *Columbia University*
Michael Enz, *Framingham State University*
David Epstein, *The College of New Jersey*
Lee Erickson, *Taylor University*
Sarah Estelle, *Hope College*
Pat Euzent, *University of Central Florida–Orlando*
Timothy Ewest, *Wartburg College*
Yang Fan, *University of Washington*
Amir Farmanesh, *University of Maryland*
MohammadMahdi Farsiabi, *Wayne State University*
Julie Finnegan, *Mendocino College*
Ryan Finseth, *University of Montana*
Donna Fisher, *Georgia Southern University*
Nikki Follis, *Chadron State College*
Joseph Franklin, *Newberry College*
Matthew Freeman, *Mississippi State University*
Gary Frey, *City College of New York*
Ted Fu, *Shenandoah University*
Winnie Fung, *Wheaton College*
Marc Fusaro, *Arkansas Tech University*
Todd Gabe, *University of Maine*
Mary Gade, *Oklahoma State University*
Jonathan Gafford, *Columbia State Community College*
Iris Geisler, *Austin Community College*
Jacob Gelber, *University of Alabama at Birmingham*
Robert Gentenaar, *Pima Downtown Community College*
Soma Ghosh, *Albright College*
Edgar Ghossoub, *University of Texas at San Antonio*
Alex Gialanella, *Manhattanville College*
Bill Gibson, *University of Vermont*
Kenneth Gillingham, *Yale University*
Gregory Gilpin, *Montana State University*
Robert Godby, *University of Wyoming*
Jayendra Gokhale, *Oregon State University*
Joel Goldhar, *IIT/Stuart School of Business*
Michael Goode, *Central Piedmont Community College*
Michael J Gootzeit, *University of Memphis*
Jackson Grant, *US Air Force Academy*
Jeremy Groves, *Northern Illinois University*
Ilhami Gunduz, *Brooklyn College–CUNY*
Roberts Halsey, *Indiana University*
Michele Hampton, *Cuyahoga Community College Eastern*
James Hartley, *Mount Holyoke College*
Mike Haupert, *University of Wisconsin LaCrosse*
David Hedrick, *Central Washington University*
Evert Van Der Heide, *Calvin College*
Sara Helms, *Samford University*
Jessica Hennessey, *Furman University*
Thomas Henry, *Mississippi State University*
Alexander Hill, *University of Colorado-Boulder*
Bob Holland, *Purdue University*
Paul Holmes, *Ashland University*
Kim Hoolda, *Fordham University*
Aaron Hoshide, *University of Maine*
Michael Hoyte, *York College*
Glenn Hsu, *University of Central Oklahoma*
Kuang-Chung Hsu, *University of Central Oklahoma*
Jim Hubert, *Seattle Central Community College*
George Hughes, *University of Hartford*
Andrew Hussey, *University of Memphis*
Christopher Hyer, *University of New Mexico*
Kent Hymel, *California State University–Northridge*
Miren Ivankovic, *Anderson University*
Eric Jacobson, *University of Delaware*
Bolormaa Jamiyansuren, *Augsburg College*
Justin Jarvis, *Orange Coast College*
Andres Jauregui, *Columbus State University*
Ricot Jean, *Valencia College*
Michal Jerzmanowski, *Clemson University*
Bonnie Johnson, *California Lutheran University*
Bruce Johnson, *Centre College*
Paul Johnson, *University of Alaska Anchorage*
Philipp Jonas, *KV Community College*
Adam Jones, *University of North Carolina–Wilmington*
Jason Jones, *Furman University*
Roger Jordan, *Baker College*
James Jozefowicz, *Indiana University of Pennsylvania*
Sujana Kabiraj, *Louisiana State University*
Simran Kahai, *John Carroll University*
Leo Kahane, *Providence College*
Venoo Kakar, *San Francisco State University*
David Kalist, *Shippensburg University*
Lillian Kamal, *University of Hartford*
Willie Kamara, *North Lake College*
Robert Kane, *State University of New York-Fredonia*
David Karemera, *St. Cloud State University*
Logan Kelly, *University of Wisconsin*
Craig Kerr, *California State Polytechnic University-Pomona*
Wahhab Khandker, *University of Wisconsin–LaCrosse*
Jongsung Kim, *Bryant University*
Kihwan Kim, *Rutgers*
Elsy Kizhakethalackal, *Bowling Green State University*
Todd Knoop, *Cornell College*
Fred Kolb, *University of Wisconsin–EauClaire*
Oleg Korenok, *Virginia Commonwealth University*
Janet Koscianski, *Shippensburg University*
Kafui Kouakou, *York College*
Mikhail Kouliavtsev, *Stephen F. Austin State University*
Maria Kula, *Roger Williams University*
Nakul Kumar, *Bloomsburg University*
Ben Kyer, *Francis Marion University*

Yuexing Lan, *Auburn Montgomery*
Daniel Lawson, *Oakland Community College*
Elena Lazzari, *Marygrove College*
Quan Le, *Seattle University*
Chun Lee, *Loyola Marymount, University*
Daniel Lee, *Shippensburg University*
Jihoon Lee, *Northeastern University*
Jim Lee, *Texas A&M–Corpus Christi*
Junghoon Lee, *Emory University*
Ryan Lee, *Indiana University*
Sang Lee, *Southeastern Louisiana University*
James Leggette, *Belhaven University*
Bozena Leven, *The College of New Jersey*
Qing Li, *College of the Mainland*
Zhen Li, *Albion College*
Carlos Liard-Muriente, *Central Connecticut State University*
Larry Lichtenstein, *Canisius College*
Jenny Liu, *Portland State University*
Jialu Liu, *Allegheny College*
Sam Liu, *West Valley College*
Xuepeng Liu, *Kennesaw State University*
Jie Ma, *Indiana University*
Michael Machiorlatti, *Oklahoma City Community College*
Bruce Madariaga, *Montgomery College and Northwestern University*
Brinda Mahalingam, *University of Alabama-Huntsville*
C. Lucy Malakar, *Lorain County Community College*
Paula Manns, *Atlantic Cape Community College*
Gabriel Manrique, *Winona State University*
Dan Marburger, *Arizona State University*
Hardik Marfatia, *Northeastern Illinois University*
Christina Marsh, *Wake Forest University*
William McAndrew, *Gannon University*
Katherine McClain, *University of Georgia*
Michael McIlhon, *Century College*
Steven McMullen, *Hope College*
Jennifer McNiece, *Howard Payne University*
Robert Menafee, *Sinclair Community College*
Fabio Mendez, *Loyola University Maryland*
Charles Meyrick, *Housatonic Community College*
Heather Micelli, *Mira Costa College*
Laura Middlesworth, *University of Wisconsin–Eau Claire*
Meghan Mihal, *St. Thomas Aquinas College*
Eric Miller, *Oakton Community College*
Phillip Mixon, *Troy University–Troy*
Evan Moore, *Auburn University–Montgomery*
Francis Mummery, *California State University–Fullerton*
John Mundy, *St. Johns River State University*
Charles Murray, *The College of Saint Rose*
James Murray, *University of Wisconsin–LaCrosse*
Christopher Mushrush, *Illinois State University*
John Nader, *Davenport University*
Max Grunbaum Nagiel, *Daytona State College*
Mihai Nica, *University of Central Oklahoma*
Scott Niederjohn, *Lakeland College*
Mark Nixon, *Fordham University*
George Norman, *Tufts University*
David O'Hara, *Metropolitan State University*
Brian O'Roark, *Robert Morris University*
Yanira Ogrodnik, *Post University*
Wafa Orman, *University of Alabama in Huntsville*
Glenda Orosco, *Oklahoma State University Institute of Technology*
Orgul Ozturk, *University of South Carolina*
Jennifer Pakula, *Saddleback College*
Maria Papapavlou, *San Jacinto Central College*
Nitin Paranjpe, *Wayne State University*
Irene Parietti, *Felician College*
Jooyoun Park, *Kent State University*
Dodd Parks, *Georgia Institute of Technology*
Jason Patalinghug, *University of New Haven*
Michael Patton, *St. Louis Community College–Wildwood*
Wesley Pech, *Wofford College*
Josh Phillips, *Iowa Central Community College*
Germain Pichop, *Oklahoma City Community College*
Lodovico Pizzati, *University of Southern California*
Florenz Plassmann, *Binghamton University*
Lana Podolak, *Community College of Beaver County*
Gyan Pradhan, *Eastern Kentucky University*
Curtis Price, *University of Southern Indiana*
Silvia Prina, *Case Western Reserve University*
Thomas Prusa, *Rutgers University*
Conrad Puozaa, *University of Mississippi*
John Stuart Rabon, *Missouri State University*
Mark Reavis, *Arkansas Tech University*
Robert Rebelein, *Vassar College*
Agne Reizgeviciute, *California State University-Chico*
Matt Rendleman, *Southern Illinois University*
Judith Ricks, *Onondaga Community College*
Chaurey Ritam, *Binghamton University*
Jared Roberts, *North Carolina State University*
Josh Robinson, *University of Alabama-Birmingham*
Kristen Roche, *Mount Mary College*
Antonio Rodriguez, *Texas A&M International University*
Debasis Rooj, *Kishwaukee College*
Larry Ross, *University of Alaska*
Subhasree Basu Roy, *Missouri State University*
Jeff Rubin, *Rutgers University–New Brunswick*
Jason C. Rudbeck, *University of Georgia*
Jeff Ruggiero, *University of Dayton*
Robert Rycroft, *University of Mary Washington*
Allen Sanderson, *University of Chicago*
Malkiat Sandhu, *San Jose City College*
Lisle Sanna, *Ursinus College*
Nese Sara, *University of Cincinnati*
Naveen Sarna, *Northern Virginia Community College–Alexandria*
Eric Sartell, *Whitworth University*
Martin Schonger, *Princeton University*
Andy Schuchart, *Iowa Central Community College*

Michael Schultz, *Menlo College*
Jessica Schuring, *Central College*
Danielle Schwarzmann, *Towson University*
Gerald Scott, *Florida Atlantic University*
Elan Segarra, *San Francisco State University*
Bhaswati Sengupta, *Iona College*
Reshmi Sengupta, *Northern Illinois University*
Dan Settlage, *University of Arkansas-Fort Smith*
David Shankle, *Blue Mountain College*
Alex Shiu, *McLennan Community College*
Robert Shoffner, *Central Piedmont Community College*
Mark Showalter, *Brigham Young University*
Sanchit Shrivastava, *University of Utah*
Johnny Shull, *Wake Tech Community College*
Suann Shumaker, *Las Positas College*
Nicholas Shunda, *University of Redlands*
Milan Sigetich, *Southern Oregon University*
Jonathan Silberman, *Oakland University*
Joe Silverman, *Mira Costa College–Oceanside*
Silva Simone, *Murray State University*
Harmeet Singh, *Texas A&M University–Kingsville*
Catherine Skura, *Sandhills Community College*
Gary Smith, *Canisius College*
Richard Smith, *University of South Florida–St. Petersburg*
Joe Sobieralski, *Southwestern Illinois College–Belleville*
Mario Solis-Garcia, *Macalester College*
Arjun Sondhi, *Wayne State University*
Soren Soumbatiants, *Franklin University*
Matt Souza, *Indiana University – Purdue University Columbus*
Nekeisha Spencer, *Binghamton University*
Dean Stansel, *Florida Gulf Coast University*
Sylwia Starnawska, *D'Youville College*
Keva Steadman, *Augustana College*
Rebecca Stein, *University of Pennsylvania*
Dale Steinreich, *Drury University*
Paul Stock, *University of Mary Hardin-Baylor*
Michael Stroup, *Stephen F. Austin State University*
Edward Stuart, *Northeastern Illinois University*
Yang Su, *University of Washington*
Yu-hsuan Su, *University of Washington*
Samanta Subarna, *The College of New Jersey*
Abdul Sukar, *Cameron University*
Burak Sungu, *Miami University*
John Susenburger, *Utica College*
James Swofford, *University of South Alabama*
Vera Tabakova, *East Carolina U niversity*
Ariuna Taivan, *University of Minnesota-Duluth*
Eftila Tanellari, *Radford University*
Eric Taylor, *Central Piedmont Community College*
Erdal Tekin, *Georgia State University*
Noreen Templin, *Butler Community College*
Thomas Tenerelli, *Central Washington University*
Anna Terzyan, *California State University-Los Angeles*
Petros Tesfazion, *Ithaca College*
Charles Thompson, *Brunswick Community College*
Flint Thompson, *Chippewa Valley Technical College*
Deborah Thorsen, *Palm Beach State College–Central*
James Tierney, *University of California Irvine*
Julie Trivitt, *Arkansas Tech University*
Arja Turunen-Red, *University of New Orleans*
Mark Tuttle, *Sam Houston State University*
Jennifer VanGilder, *Ursinus College*
Ross vanWassenhove, *University of Houston*
Ben Vaughan, *Trinity University*
Roumen Vesselinov, *Queens College, City University of New York*
Rubina Vohra, *St. Peter's College*
Will Walsh, *Samford University*
Chih-Wei Wang, *Pacific Lutheran University*
Jingjing Wang, *University of New Mexico*
Chad Wassell, *Central Washington University*
Christine Wathen, *Middlesex Community College*
J. Douglas Wellington, *Husson University*
Adam Werner, *California Polytechnic State University*
Sarah West, *Macalester College*
Elizabeth Wheaton, *Southern Methodist University*
Oxana Wieland, *University of Minnesota, Crookston*
Christopher Wimer, *Bowling Green State University–Firelands College*
Do Youn Won, *University of Utah*
Kelvin Wong, *University of Minnesota*
Ken Woodward, *Saddleback College*
Irena Xhurxhi, *York College*
Xu Xu, *Mississippi state university*
Ying Yang, *University of Rhode Island*
Young-Ro Yoon, *Wayne State University*
Eric Zemjic, *Kent State University*
Yongchen Zhao, *Towson University*
Zhen Zhu, *University of Central Oklahoma*
Kent Zirlott, *University of Alabama–Tuscaloosa*
Joseph Zwiller, *Lake Michigan College*

The team of editors who worked on this book improved it tremendously. Jane Tufts, developmental editor, provided truly spectacular editing—as she always does. Michael Parthenakis, senior product manager, did a splendid job of overseeing the many people involved in such a large project. Anita Verma, senior content developer, was crucial in assembling an extensive and thoughtful group of reviewers to give me feedback on the previous edition, while putting together an excellent team to revise the supplements. Colleen Farmer, senior content project manager, had the patience and dedication necessary to turn my manuscript into this book. Kasie Jean, digital content designer and a trained economist, designed and implemented all of the valuable student resources in MindTap. Michelle Kunkler, senior art director, gave this book its clean, friendly look. Bruce Morser, the illustrator, helped make the book more visually appealing and the economics in it less abstract. Pamela Rockwell, copyeditor, refined my prose, and Lumina Datamatic's indexer, prepared a careful and thorough index. John Carey, executive marketing manager, worked long hours getting the word out to potential users of this book. The rest of the Cengage team has, as always, been consistently professional, enthusiastic, and dedicated.

I am grateful also to Denis Fedin and Nina Vendhan, two star Harvard undergraduates, who helped me refine the manuscript and check the page proofs for this edition.

As always, I must thank my "in-house" editor Deborah Mankiw. As the first reader of most things I write, she continued to offer just the right mix of criticism and encouragement.

Finally, I would like to mention my three children Catherine, Nicholas, and Peter. Their contribution to this book was putting up with a father spending too many hours in his study. The four of us have much in common—not least of which is our love of ice cream (which becomes apparent in Chapter 4).

N. Gregory Mankiw
December 2016

Contents

Preface: To the Student ix

Acknowledgments xv

PART I Introduction 1

CHAPTER 1

Ten Principles of Economics 3

1-1 How People Make Decisions 4
- 1-1a Principle 1: People Face Trade-offs 4
- 1-1b Principle 2: The Cost of Something Is What You Give Up to Get It 5
- 1-1c Principle 3: Rational People Think at the Margin 6
- 1-1d Principle 4: People Respond to Incentives 7

1-2 How People Interact 8
- 1-2a Principle 5: Trade Can Make Everyone Better Off 8
- 1-2b Principle 6: Markets Are Usually a Good Way to Organize Economic Activity 9
- **FYI:** Adam Smith and the Invisible Hand 10
- **CASE STUDY:** Adam Smith Would Have Loved Uber 11
- 1-2c Principle 7: Governments Can Sometimes Improve Market Outcomes 11

1-3 How the Economy as a Whole Works 13
- 1-3a Principle 8: A Country's Standard of Living Depends on Its Ability to Produce Goods and Services 13
- 1-3b Principle 9: Prices Rise When the Government Prints Too Much Money 13
- 1-3c Principle 10: Society Faces a Short-Run Trade-off between Inflation and Unemployment 14

1-4 Conclusion 15

Summary 16

Key Concepts 16

Questions for Review 16

Problems and Applications 17

CHAPTER 2

Thinking Like an Economist 19

2-1 The Economist as Scientist 20
- 2-1a The Scientific Method: Observation, Theory, and More Observation 20
- 2-1b The Role of Assumptions 21
- 2-1c Economic Models 22
- 2-1d Our First Model: The Circular-Flow Diagram 22
- 2-1e Our Second Model: The Production Possibilities Frontier 24
- 2-1f Microeconomics and Macroeconomics 26

2-2 The Economist as Policy Adviser 27
- 2-2a Positive versus Normative Analysis 27
- 2-2b Economists in Washington 28
- 2-2c Why Economists' Advice Is Not Always Followed 29

2-3 Why Economists Disagree 30
- 2-3a Differences in Scientific Judgments 30
- 2-3b Differences in Values 30
- 2-3c Perception versus Reality 31
- **ASK THE EXPERTS:** Ticket Resale 32

2-4 Let's Get Going 32

Summary 34

Key Concepts 34

Questions for Review 34

Problems and Applications 35

Appendix Graphing: A Brief Review 37

CHAPTER 3

Interdependence and the Gains from Trade 47

3-1 A Parable for the Modern Economy 48
- 3-1a Production Possibilities 49
- 3-1b Specialization and Trade 50

3-2 Comparative Advantage: The Driving Force of Specialization 52
3-2a Absolute Advantage 52
3-2b Opportunity Cost and Comparative Advantage 52
3-2c Comparative Advantage and Trade 53
3-2d The Price of the Trade 54
FYI: The Legacy of Adam Smith and David Ricardo 55

3-3 Applications of Comparative Advantage 55
3-3a Should Serena Williams Mow Her Own Lawn? 55
3-3b Should the United States Trade with Other Countries? 56
ASK THE EXPERTS: Trade between China and the United States 56

3-4 Conclusion 57
Summary 58
Key Concepts 58
Questions for Review 58
Problems and Applications 58

PART II How Markets Work 61

CHAPTER 4

The Market Forces of Supply and Demand 63

4-1 Markets and Competition 64
4-1a What Is a Market? 64
4-1b What Is Competition? 64

4-2 Demand 65
4-2a The Demand Curve: The Relationship between Price and Quantity Demanded 65
4-2b Market Demand versus Individual Demand 66
4-2c Shifts in the Demand Curve 67
CASE STUDY: Two Ways to Reduce the Quantity of Smoking Demanded 69

4-3 Supply 71
4-3a The Supply Curve: The Relationship between Price and Quantity Supplied 71
4-3b Market Supply versus Individual Supply 72
4-3c Shifts in the Supply Curve 73

4-4 Supply and Demand Together 74
4-4a Equilibrium 74
4-4b Three Steps to Analyzing Changes in Equilibrium 76

4-5 Conclusion: How Prices Allocate Resources 81
ASK THE EXPERTS: Price Gouging 81
Summary 83
Key Concepts 83
Questions for Review 83
Problems and Applications 84

CHAPTER 5

Elasticity and Its Application 87

5-1 The Elasticity of Demand 88
5-1a The Price Elasticity of Demand and Its Determinants 88
5-1b Computing the Price Elasticity of Demand 89
5-1c The Midpoint Method: A Better Way to Calculate Percentage Changes and Elasticities 90
5-1d The Variety of Demand Curves 91
FYI: A Few Elasticities from the Real World 91
5-1e Total Revenue and the Price Elasticity of Demand 93
5-1f Elasticity and Total Revenue along a Linear Demand Curve 94
5-1g Other Demand Elasticities 96

5-2 The Elasticity of Supply 97
5-2a The Price Elasticity of Supply and Its Determinants 97
5-2b Computing the Price Elasticity of Supply 97
5-2c The Variety of Supply Curves 98

5-3 Three Applications of Supply, Demand, and Elasticity 100
5-3a Can Good News for Farming Be Bad News for Farmers? 100
5-3b Why Did OPEC Fail to Keep the Price of Oil High? 102
5-3c Does Drug Interdiction Increase or Decrease Drug-Related Crime? 103

5-4 Conclusion 105
Summary 106
Key Concepts 106
Questions for Review 107
Problems and Applications 107

CHAPTER 6

Supply, Demand, and Government Policies 109

6-1 Controls on Prices 110
6-1a How Price Ceilings Affect Market Outcomes 110
CASE STUDY: Lines at the Gas Pump 112

CASE STUDY: Rent Control in the Short Run and the Long Run 113
6-1b How Price Floors Affect Market Outcomes 116
ASK THE EXPERTS: Rent Control 114
CASE STUDY: The Minimum Wage 116
ASK THE EXPERTS: The Minimum Wage 117
6-1c Evaluating Price Controls 118

6-2 Taxes 118
6-2a How Taxes on Sellers Affect Market Outcomes 119
6-2b How Taxes on Buyers Affect Market Outcomes 120
CASE STUDY: Can Congress Distribute the Burden of a Payroll Tax? 122
6-2c Elasticity and Tax Incidence 122
CASE STUDY: Who Pays the Luxury Tax? 124

6-3 Conclusion 125
Summary 126
Key Concepts 126
Questions for Review 126
Problems and Applications 127

PART III Markets and Welfare 129

CHAPTER 7

Consumers, Producers, and the Efficiency of Markets 131

7-1 Consumer Surplus 132
7-1a Willingness to Pay 132
7-1b Using the Demand Curve to Measure Consumer Surplus 133
7-1c How a Lower Price Raises Consumer Surplus 134
7-1d What Does Consumer Surplus Measure? 135

7-2 Producer Surplus 137
7-2a Cost and the Willingness to Sell 137
7-2b Using the Supply Curve to Measure Producer Surplus 138
7-2c How a Higher Price Raises Producer Surplus 139

7-3 Market Efficiency 140
7-3a The Benevolent Social Planner 141
7-3b Evaluating the Market Equilibrium 142
CASE STUDY: Should There Be a Market for Organs? 144
ASK THE EXPERTS: Supplying Kidneys 145

7-4 Conclusion: Market Efficiency and Market Failure 145
Summary 147
Key Concepts 147
Questions for Review 147
Problems and Applications 147

CHAPTER 8

Application: The Costs of Taxation 151

8-1 The Deadweight Loss of Taxation 152
8-1a How a Tax Affects Market Participants 153
8-1b Deadweight Losses and the Gains from Trade 155

8-2 The Determinants of the Deadweight Loss 156
CASE STUDY: The Deadweight Loss Debate 158

8-3 Deadweight Loss and Tax Revenue as Taxes Vary 159
CASE STUDY: The Laffer Curve and Supply-Side Economics 160
ASK THE EXPERTS: The Laffer Curve 161

8-4 Conclusion 162
Summary 163
Key Concept 163
Questions for Review 163
Problems and Applications 163

CHAPTER 9

Application: International Trade 165

9-1 The Determinants of Trade 166
9-1a The Equilibrium without Trade 166
9-1b The World Price and Comparative Advantage 167

9-2 The Winners and Losers from Trade 168
9-2a The Gains and Losses of an Exporting Country 168
9-2b The Gains and Losses of an Importing Country 169
9-2c Effects of a Tariff 171
FYI: Import Quotas: Another Way to Restrict Trade 173
9-2d The Lessons for Trade Policy 173
9-2e Other Benefits of International Trade 174

9-3 The Arguments for Restricting Trade 175
9-3a The Jobs Argument 175
9-3b The National-Security Argument 176
9-3c The Infant-Industry Argument 176
9-3d The Unfair-Competition Argument 177
9-3e The Protection-as-a-Bargaining-Chip Argument 177
CASE STUDY: Trade Agreements and the World Trade Organization 177
ASK THE EXPERTS: Trade Deals 178

9-4 Conclusion 178
Summary 180
Key Concepts 180
Questions for Review 180
Problems and Applications 181

PART IV The Economics of the Public Sector 183

CHAPTER 10

Externalities 185

10-1 Externalities and Market Inefficiency 187
- 10-1a Welfare Economics: A Recap 187
- 10-1b Negative Externalities 188
- 10-1c Positive Externalities 189
- **CASE STUDY:** Technology Spillovers, Industrial Policy, and Patent Protection 190

10-2 Public Policies toward Externalities 191
- 10-2a Command-and-Control Policies: Regulation 191
- 10-2b Market-Based Policy 1: Corrective Taxes and Subsidies 192
- **ASK THE EXPERTS:** Vaccines 192
- **CASE STUDY:** Why Is Gasoline Taxed So Heavily? 193
- 10-2c Market-Based Policy 2: Tradable Pollution Permits 195
- **ASK THE EXPERTS:** Carbon Taxes 195
- 10-2d Objections to the Economic Analysis of Pollution 197

10-3 Private Solutions to Externalities 197
- 10-3a The Types of Private Solutions 197
- 10-3b The Coase Theorem 198
- 10-3c Why Private Solutions Do Not Always Work 199

10-4 Conclusion 200
Summary 201
Key Concepts 201
Questions for Review 201
Problems and Applications 202

CHAPTER 11

Public Goods and Common Resources 205

11-1 The Different Kinds of Goods 206

11-2 Public Goods 208
- 11-2a The Free-Rider Problem 208
- 11-2b Some Important Public Goods 208
- **CASE STUDY:** Are Lighthouses Public Goods? 210
- 11-2c The Difficult Job of Cost–Benefit Analysis 210
- **CASE STUDY:** How Much Is a Life Worth? 211

11-3 Common Resources 212
- 11-3a The Tragedy of the Commons 212
- 11-3b Some Important Common Resources 213
- **ASK THE EXPERTS:** Congesting Pricing 213
- **IN THE NEWS:** The Case for Toll Roads 214
- **CASE STUDY:** Why the Cow Is Not Extinct 216

11-4 Conclusion: The Importance of Property Rights 217
Summary 218
Key Concepts 218
Questions for Review 218
Problems and Applications 218

CHAPTER 12

The Design of the Tax System 221

12-1 An Overview of U.S. Taxation 222
- 12-1a Taxes Collected by the Federal Government 222
- 12-1b Taxes Collected by State and Local Governments 225

12-2 Taxes and Efficiency 226
- 12-2a Deadweight Losses 226
- **CASE STUDY:** Should Income or Consumption Be Taxed? 227
- 12-2b Administrative Burden 228
- 12-2c Marginal Tax Rates versus Average Tax Rates 229
- 12-2d Lump-Sum Taxes 229

12-3 Taxes and Equity 230
- 12-3a The Benefits Principle 230
- 12-3b The Ability-to-Pay Principle 231
- **CASE STUDY:** How the Tax Burden Is Distributed 232
- 12-3c Tax Incidence and Tax Equity 233
- **CASE STUDY:** Who Pays the Corporate Income Tax? 234

12-4 Conclusion: The Trade-off between Equity and Efficiency 234
Summary 236
Key Concepts 236
Questions for Review 236
Problems and Applications 237

PART V Firm Behavior and the Organization of Industry 239

CHAPTER 13

The Costs of Production 241

13-1 What Are Costs? 242
13-1a Total Revenue, Total Cost, and Profit 242
13-1b Costs as Opportunity Costs 243
13-1c The Cost of Capital as an Opportunity Cost 243
13-1d Economic Profit versus Accounting Profit 244

13-2 Production and Costs 245
13-2a The Production Function 245
13-2b From the Production Function to the Total-Cost Curve 247

13-3 The Various Measures of Cost 248
13-3a Fixed and Variable Costs 249
13-3b Average and Marginal Cost 249
13-3c Cost Curves and Their Shapes 250
13-3d Typical Cost Curves 252

13-4 Costs in the Short Run and in the Long Run 253
13-4a The Relationship between Short-Run and Long-Run Average Total Cost 254
13-4b Economies and Diseconomies of Scale 255
FYI: Lessons from a Pin Factory 255

13-5 Conclusion 256
Summary 257
Key Concepts 258
Questions for Review 258
Problems and Applications 258

CHAPTER 14

Firms in Competitive Markets 261

14-1 What Is a Competitive Market? 262
14-1a The Meaning of Competition 262
14-1b The Revenue of a Competitive Firm 263

14-2 Profit Maximization and the Competitive Firm's Supply Curve 264
14-2a A Simple Example of Profit Maximization 264
14-2b The Marginal-Cost Curve and the Firm's Supply Decision 265
14-2c The Firm's Short-Run Decision to Shut Down 267
14-2d Spilt Milk and Other Sunk Costs 269
CASE STUDY: Near-Empty Restaurants and Off-Season Miniature Golf 269
14-2e The Firm's Long-Run Decision to Exit or Enter a Market 270
14-2f Measuring Profit in Our Graph for the Competitive Firm 271

14-3 The Supply Curve in a Competitive Market 273
14-3a The Short Run: Market Supply with a Fixed Number of Firms 273
14-3b The Long Run: Market Supply with Entry and Exit 273
14-3c Why Do Competitive Firms Stay in Business If They Make Zero Profit? 274
14-3d A Shift in Demand in the Short Run and Long Run 275
14-3e Why the Long-Run Supply Curve Might Slope Upward 276

14-4 Conclusion: Behind the Supply Curve 278
Summary 279
Key Concepts 279
Questions for Review 279
Problems and Applications 280

CHAPTER 15

Monopoly 283

15-1 Why Monopolies Arise 284
15-1a Monopoly Resources 285
15-1b Government-Created Monopolies 285
15-1c Natural Monopolies 286

15-2 How Monopolies Make Production and Pricing Decisions 287
15-2a Monopoly versus Competition 287
15-2b A Monopoly's Revenue 288
15-2c Profit Maximization 290
15-2d A Monopoly's Profit 292
FYI: Why a Monopoly Does Not Have a Supply Curve 292
CASE STUDY: Monopoly Drugs versus Generic Drugs 293

15-3 The Welfare Cost of Monopolies 294
15-3a The Deadweight Loss 295
15-3b The Monopoly's Profit: A Social Cost? 297

15-4 Price Discrimination 297
15-4a A Parable about Pricing 298
15-4b The Moral of the Story 299
15-4c The Analytics of Price Discrimination 299
15-4d Examples of Price Discrimination 300
IN THE NEWS: Price Discrimination in Higher Education 302

15-5 Public Policy toward Monopolies 302
15-5a Increasing Competition with Antitrust Laws 302
15-5b Regulation 303
ASK THE EXPERTS: Airline Mergers 303
15-5c Public Ownership 304
15-5d Doing Nothing 305

15-6 Conclusion: The Prevalence of Monopolies 305
Summary 307
Key Concepts 307
Questions for Review 308
Problems and Applications 308

CHAPTER 16
Monopolistic Competition 313

16-1 Between Monopoly and Perfect Competition 314

16-2 Competition with Differentiated Products 316
16-2a The Monopolistically Competitive Firm in the Short Run 316
16-2b The Long-Run Equilibrium 317
16-2c Monopolistic versus Perfect Competition 318
16-2d Monopolistic Competition and the Welfare of Society 321

16-3 Advertising 322
16-3a The Debate over Advertising 322
CASE STUDY: Advertising and the Price of Eyeglasses 323
16-3b Advertising as a Signal of Quality 324
16-3c Brand Names 325

16-4 Conclusion 326
Summary 327
Key Concepts 328
Questions for Review 328
Problems and Applications 328

CHAPTER 17
Oligopoly 331

17-1 Markets with Only a Few Sellers 332
17-1a A Duopoly Example 332
17-1b Competition, Monopolies, and Cartels 333
17-1c The Equilibrium for an Oligopoly 334
17-1d How the Size of an Oligopoly Affects the Market Outcome 335
ASK THE EXPERTS: Nash Equilibrium 335

17-2 The Economics of Cooperation 336
17-2a The Prisoners' Dilemma 337
17-2b Oligopolies as a Prisoners' Dilemma 338
CASE STUDY: OPEC and the World Oil Market 339
17-2c Other Examples of the Prisoners' Dilemma 340
17-2d The Prisoners' Dilemma and the Welfare of Society 341
17-2e Why People Sometimes Cooperate 342
CASE STUDY: The Prisoners' Dilemma Tournament 342

17-3 Public Policy toward Oligopolies 343
17-3a Restraint of Trade and the Antitrust Laws 344
CASE STUDY: An Illegal Phone Call 344
17-3b Controversies over Antitrust Policy 344
CASE STUDY: The Microsoft Case 346
IN THE NEWS: Europe versus Google 348

17-4 Conclusion 349
Summary 350
Key Concepts 350
Questions for Review 350
Problems and Applications 350

PART VI The Economics of Labor Markets 353

CHAPTER 18
The Markets for the Factors of Production 355

18-1 The Demand for Labor 356
18-1a The Competitive Profit-Maximizing Firm 357
18-1b The Production Function and the Marginal Product of Labor 357
18-1c The Value of the Marginal Product and the Demand for Labor 359
18-1d What Causes the Labor-Demand Curve to Shift? 360
FYI: Input Demand and Output Supply: Two Sides of the Same Coin 361

18-2 The Supply of Labor 362
18-2a The Trade-off between Work and Leisure 362

18-2b What Causes the Labor-Supply Curve to Shift? 362
ASK THE EXPERTS: Immigration 363

18-3 Equilibrium in the Labor Market 363
18-3a Shifts in Labor Supply 364
18-3b Shifts in Labor Demand 365
IN THE NEWS: The Economics of Immigration 366
CASE STUDY: Productivity and Wages 367
FYI: Monopsony 368

18-4 The Other Factors of Production: Land and Capital 369
18-4a Equilibrium in the Markets for Land and Capital 369
FYI: What Is Capital Income? 370
18-4b Linkages among the Factors of Production 371
CASE STUDY: The Economics of the Black Death 371

18-5 Conclusion 372
Summary 373
Key Concepts 373
Questions for Review 373
Problems and Applications 374

CHAPTER 19

Earnings and Discrimination 377

19-1 Some Determinants of Equilibrium Wages 378
19-1a Compensating Differentials 378
19-1b Human Capital 379
CASE STUDY: The Increasing Value of Skills 379
ASK THE EXPERTS: Inequality and Skills 380
IN THE NEWS: Schooling as a Public Investment 381
19-1c Ability, Effort, and Chance 382
CASE STUDY: The Benefits of Beauty 382
19-1d An Alternative View of Education: Signaling 383
19-1e The Superstar Phenomenon 384
19-1f Above-Equilibrium Wages: Minimum-Wage Laws, Unions, and Efficiency Wages 384

19-2 The Economics of Discrimination 385
19-2a Measuring Labor-Market Discrimination 385
CASE STUDY: Is Emily More Employable than Lakisha? 387
19-2b Discrimination by Employers 387
CASE STUDY: Segregated Streetcars and the Profit Motive 388
19-2c Discrimination by Customers and Governments 389
CASE STUDY: Discrimination in Sports 389

19-3 Conclusion 390
Summary 391
Key Concepts 392
Questions for Review 392
Problems and Applications 392

CHAPTER 20

Income Inequality and Poverty 395

20-1 The Measurement of Inequality 396
20-1a U.S. Income Inequality 396
20-1b Inequality around the World 397
20-1c The Poverty Rate 399
20-1d Problems in Measuring Inequality 400
CASE STUDY: Alternative Measures of Inequality 401
20-1e Economic Mobility 402

20-2 The Political Philosophy of Redistributing Income 402
20-2a Utilitarianism 403
20-2b Liberalism 404
20-2c Libertarianism 405

20-3 Policies to Reduce Poverty 406
20-3a Minimum-Wage Laws 406
20-3b Welfare 407
20-3c Negative Income Tax 407
20-3d In-Kind Transfers 408
20-3e Antipoverty Programs and Work Incentives 408

20-4 Conclusion 409
Summary 411
Key Concepts 411
Questions for Review 411
Problems and Applications 412

PART VII Topics for Further Study 412

CHAPTER 21

The Theory of Consumer Choice 415

21-1 The Budget Constraint: What the Consumer Can Afford 416

21-2 Preferences: What the Consumer Wants 418
21-2a Representing Preferences with Indifference Curves 418
21-2b Four Properties of Indifference Curves 419
21-2c Two Extreme Examples of Indifference Curves 420

21-3 Optimization: What the Consumer Chooses 422
21-3a The Consumer's Optimal Choices 422

FYI: Utility: An Alternative Way to Describe Preferences and Optimization 423
21-3b How Changes in Income Affect the Consumer's Choices 424
21-3c How Changes in Prices Affect the Consumer's Choices 425
21-3d Income and Substitution Effects 426
21-3e Deriving the Demand Curve 428

21-4 Three Applications 429
21-4a Do All Demand Curves Slope Downward? 429
CASE STUDY: The Search for Giffen Goods 430
21-4b How Do Wages Affect Labor Supply? 430
CASE STUDY: Income Effects on Labor Supply: Historical Trends, Lottery Winners, and the Carnegie Conjecture 433
21-4c How Do Interest Rates Affect Household Saving? 434

21-5 Conclusion: Do People Really Think This Way? 436
Summary 437
Key Concepts 438
Questions for Review 438
Problems and Applications 438

CHAPTER 22

Frontiers of Microeconomics 441

22-1 Asymmetric Information 442
22-1a Hidden Actions: Principals, Agents, and Moral Hazard 442
FYI: Corporate Management 443
22-1b Hidden Characteristics: Adverse Selection and the Lemons Problem 444
22-1c Signaling to Convey Private Information 445
CASE STUDY: Gifts as Signals 445
22-1d Screening to Uncover Private Information 446
22-1e Asymmetric Information and Public Policy 446

22-2 Political Economy 447
22-2a The Condorcet Voting Paradox 447
22-2b Arrow's Impossibility Theorem 448
22-2c The Median Voter Is King 449
22-2d Politicians Are People Too 450

22-3 Behavioral Economics 451
22-3a People Aren't Always Rational 451
22-3b People Care about Fairness 453
22-3c People Are Inconsistent over Time 454

22-4 Conclusion 455
Summary 456
Key Concepts 456
Questions for Review 456
Problems and Applications 456

Glossary 459
Index 465

PART I

Introduction

Ten Principles of Economics

CHAPTER 1

The word *economy* comes from the Greek word *oikonomos*, which means "one who manages a household." At first, this origin might seem peculiar. But in fact, households and economies have much in common.

A household faces many decisions. It must decide which household members do which tasks and what each member receives in return: Who cooks dinner? Who does the laundry? Who gets the extra dessert at dinner? Who gets to drive the car? In short, a household must allocate its scarce resources (time, dessert, car mileage) among its various members, taking into account each member's abilities, efforts, and desires.

Like a household, a society faces many decisions. It must find some way to decide what jobs will be done and who will do them. It needs some people to grow food, other people to make clothing, and still others to design computer software. Once society has allocated people (as well as land, buildings, and machines) to various jobs, it must also allocate the goods and services they produce. It must decide who will eat caviar and who will eat potatoes. It must decide who will drive a Tesla and who will take the bus.

scarcity
the limited nature of society's resources

The management of society's resources is important because resources are scarce. **Scarcity** means that society has limited resources and therefore cannot produce all the goods and services people wish to have. Just as each member of a household cannot get everything she wants, each individual in a society cannot attain the highest standard of living to which she might aspire.

economics
the study of how society manages its scarce resources

Economics is the study of how society manages its scarce resources. In most societies, resources are allocated not by an all-powerful dictator but through the combined choices of millions of households and firms. Economists, therefore, study how people make decisions: how much they work, what they buy, how much they save, and how they invest their savings. Economists also study how people interact with one another. For instance, they examine how the multitude of buyers and sellers of a good together determine the price at which the good is sold and the quantity that is sold. Finally, economists analyze the forces and trends that affect the economy as a whole, including the growth in average income, the fraction of the population that cannot find work, and the rate at which prices are rising.

The study of economics has many facets, but it is unified by several central ideas. In this chapter, we look at *Ten Principles of Economics*. Don't worry if you don't understand them all at first or if you aren't completely convinced. We explore these ideas more fully in later chapters. The ten principles are introduced here to give you an overview of what economics is all about. Consider this chapter a "preview of coming attractions."

1-1 How People Make Decisions

There is no mystery to what an economy is. Whether we are talking about the economy of Los Angeles, the United States, or the whole world, an economy is just a group of people dealing with one another as they go about their lives. Because the behavior of an economy reflects the behavior of the individuals who make up the economy, we begin our study of economics with four principles about individual decision making.

1-1a Principle 1: People Face Trade-offs

You may have heard the old saying, "There ain't no such thing as a free lunch." Grammar aside, there is much truth to this adage. To get something that we like, we usually have to give up something else that we also like. Making decisions requires trading off one goal against another.

Consider a student who must decide how to allocate her most valuable resource—her time. She can spend all of her time studying economics, spend all of it studying psychology, or divide it between the two fields. For every hour she studies one subject, she gives up an hour she could have used studying the other. And for every hour she spends studying, she gives up an hour she could have spent napping, bike riding, watching TV, or working at her part-time job for some extra spending money.

Consider parents deciding how to spend their family income. They can buy food, clothing, or a family vacation. Or they can save some of the family income for retirement or the children's college education. When they choose to spend an extra dollar on one of these goods, they have one less dollar to spend on some other good.

When people are grouped into societies, they face different kinds of trade-offs. One classic trade-off is between "guns and butter." The more a society spends on national defense (guns) to protect its shores from foreign aggressors, the less it can spend on consumer goods (butter) to raise the standard of living at home. Also important in modern society is the trade-off between a clean environment and a high level of income. Laws that require firms to reduce pollution raise the cost of producing goods and services. Because of these higher costs, the firms end up earning smaller profits, paying lower wages, charging higher prices, or some combination of these three. Thus, while pollution regulations yield the benefit of a cleaner environment and the improved health that comes with it, they come at the cost of reducing the incomes of the regulated firms' owners, workers, and customers.

Another trade-off society faces is between efficiency and equality. **Efficiency** means that society is getting the maximum benefits from its scarce resources. **Equality** means that those benefits are distributed uniformly among society's members. In other words, efficiency refers to the size of the economic pie, and equality refers to how the pie is divided into individual slices.

efficiency
the property of society getting the most it can from its scarce resources

equality
the property of distributing economic prosperity uniformly among the members of society

When government policies are designed, these two goals often conflict. Consider, for instance, policies aimed at equalizing the distribution of economic well-being. Some of these policies, such as the welfare system or unemployment insurance, try to help the members of society who are most in need. Others, such as the individual income tax, ask the financially successful to contribute more than others to support the government. Though they achieve greater equality, these policies reduce efficiency. When the government redistributes income from the rich to the poor, it reduces the reward for working hard; as a result, people work less and produce fewer goods and services. In other words, when the government tries to cut the economic pie into more equal slices, the pie gets smaller.

Recognizing that people face trade-offs does not by itself tell us what decisions they will or should make. A student should not abandon the study of psychology just because doing so would increase the time available for the study of economics. Society should not stop protecting the environment just because environmental regulations reduce our material standard of living. The poor should not be ignored just because helping them distorts work incentives. Nonetheless, people are likely to make good decisions only if they understand the options that are available to them. Our study of economics, therefore, starts by acknowledging life's trade-offs.

1-1b Principle 2: The Cost of Something Is What You Give Up to Get It

Because people face trade-offs, making decisions requires comparing the costs and benefits of alternative courses of action. In many cases, however, the cost of an action is not as obvious as it might first appear.

Consider the decision to go to college. The main benefits are intellectual enrichment and a lifetime of better job opportunities. But what are the costs? To answer this question, you might be tempted to add up the money you spend on tuition, books, room, and board. Yet this total does not truly represent what you give up to spend a year in college.

There are two problems with this calculation. First, it includes some things that are not really costs of going to college. Even if you quit school, you need a place to sleep and food to eat. Room and board are costs of going to college only to the extent that they are more expensive at college than elsewhere. Second, this calculation ignores the largest cost of going to college—your time. When you spend a year listening to lectures, reading textbooks, and writing papers, you cannot spend that time working at a job. For most students, the earnings they give up to attend school are the single largest cost of their education.

opportunity cost
whatever must be given up to obtain some item

The **opportunity cost** of an item is what you give up to get that item. When making any decision, decision makers should be aware of the opportunity costs that accompany each possible action. In fact, they usually are. College athletes who can earn millions if they drop out of school and play professional sports are well aware that their opportunity cost of attending college is very high. It is not surprising that they often decide that the benefit of a college education is not worth the cost.

1-1c Principle 3: Rational People Think at the Margin

rational people
people who systematically and purposefully do the best they can to achieve their objectives

Economists normally assume that people are rational. **Rational people** systematically and purposefully do the best they can to achieve their objectives, given the available opportunities. As you study economics, you will encounter firms that decide how many workers to hire and how much of their product to manufacture and sell to maximize profits. You will also encounter individuals who decide how much time to spend working and what goods and services to buy with the resulting income to achieve the highest possible level of satisfaction.

Rational people know that decisions in life are rarely black and white but usually involve shades of gray. At dinnertime, the question you face is not "Should I fast or eat like a pig?" More likely, you will be asking yourself "Should I take that extra spoonful of mashed potatoes?" When exams roll around, your decision is not between blowing them off and studying 24 hours a day but whether to spend an extra hour reviewing your notes instead of watching TV. Economists use the term **marginal change** to describe a small incremental adjustment to an existing plan of action. Keep in mind that *margin* means "edge," so marginal changes are adjustments around the edges of what you are doing. Rational people often make decisions by comparing *marginal benefits* and *marginal costs*.

marginal change
a small incremental adjustment to a plan of action

For example, suppose you are considering calling a friend on your cell phone. You decide that talking with her for 10 minutes would give you a benefit that you value at about $7. Your cell phone service costs you $40 per month plus $0.50 per minute for whatever calls you make. You usually talk for 100 minutes a month, so your total monthly bill is $90 ($0.50 per minute times 100 minutes, plus the $40 fixed fee). Under these circumstances, should you make the call? You might be tempted to reason as follows: "Because I pay $90 for 100 minutes of calling each month, the average minute on the phone costs me $0.90. So a 10-minute call costs $9. Because that $9 cost is greater than the $7 benefit, I am going to skip the call." That conclusion is wrong, however. Although the *average* cost of a 10-minute call is $9, the *marginal* cost—the amount your bill increases if you make the extra call—is only $5. You will make the right decision only by comparing the marginal benefit and the marginal cost. Because the marginal benefit of $7 is greater than the marginal cost of $5, you should make the call. This is a principle that people innately understand: Cell phone users with unlimited minutes (that is, minutes that are free at the margin) are often prone to making long and frivolous calls.

Thinking at the margin works for business decisions as well. Consider an airline deciding how much to charge passengers who fly standby. Suppose that flying a 200-seat plane across the United States costs the airline $100,000. In this case, the average cost of each seat is $100,000/200, which is $500. One might be tempted to conclude that the airline should never sell a ticket for less than $500. But a rational airline can increase its profits by thinking at the margin. Imagine that a plane is about to take off with 10 empty seats and a standby passenger waiting at the gate is willing to pay $300 for a seat. Should the airline sell the ticket? Of course it should. If the plane has empty seats, the cost of adding one more passenger is tiny. The *average* cost of flying a passenger is $500, but the *marginal* cost is merely the cost of the can of soda that the extra passenger will consume. As long as the standby passenger pays more than the marginal cost, selling the ticket is profitable.

Marginal decision making can help explain some otherwise puzzling economic phenomena. Here is a classic question: Why is water so cheap, while diamonds are so expensive? Humans need water to survive, while diamonds are unnecessary. Yet people are willing to pay much more for a diamond than for a cup of water. The reason is that a person's willingness to pay for a good is based on the marginal benefit that an extra unit of the good would yield. The marginal benefit, in turn, depends on how many units a person already has. Water is essential, but the marginal benefit of an extra cup is small because water is plentiful. By contrast, no one needs diamonds to survive, but because diamonds are so rare, people consider the marginal benefit of an extra diamond to be large.

A rational decision maker takes an action if and only if the marginal benefit of the action exceeds the marginal cost. This principle explains why people use their cell phones as much as they do, why airlines are willing to sell tickets below average cost, and why people are willing to pay more for diamonds than for water. It can take some time to get used to the logic of marginal thinking, but the study of economics will give you ample opportunity to practice.

BLEND IMAGES / ALAMY

"Is the marginal benefit of this call greater than the marginal cost?"

1-1d Principle 4: People Respond to Incentives

An **incentive** is something (such as the prospect of a punishment or reward) that induces a person to act. Because rational people make decisions by comparing costs and benefits, they respond to incentives. You will see that incentives play a central role in the study of economics. One economist went so far as to suggest that the entire field could be summarized as simply "People respond to incentives. The rest is commentary."

incentive
something that induces a person to act

Incentives are key to analyzing how markets work. For example, when the price of an apple rises, people decide to eat fewer apples. At the same time, apple orchards decide to hire more workers and harvest more apples. In other words, a higher price in a market provides an incentive for buyers to consume less and an incentive for sellers to produce more. As we will see, the influence of prices on the behavior of consumers and producers is crucial to how a market economy allocates scarce resources.

Public policymakers should never forget about incentives: Many policies change the costs or benefits that people face and, as a result, alter their behavior. A tax on gasoline, for instance, encourages people to drive smaller, more fuel-efficient cars. That is one reason people drive smaller cars in Europe, where gasoline taxes are high, than in the United States, where gasoline taxes are low. A higher gasoline tax also encourages people to carpool, take public transportation, and live closer to where they work. If the tax were larger, more people would be driving hybrid cars, and if it were large enough, they would switch to electric cars.

When policymakers fail to consider how their policies affect incentives, they often end up facing unintended consequences. For example, consider public policy regarding auto safety. Today, all cars have seat belts, but this was not true

60 years ago. In 1965, Ralph Nader's book *Unsafe at Any Speed* generated much public concern over auto safety. Congress responded with laws requiring seat belts as standard equipment on new cars.

How does a seat belt law affect auto safety? The direct effect is obvious: When a person wears a seat belt, the probability of surviving an auto accident rises. But that's not the end of the story because the law also affects behavior by altering incentives. The relevant behavior here is the speed and care with which drivers operate their cars. Driving slowly and carefully is costly because it uses the driver's time and energy. When deciding how safely to drive, rational people compare, perhaps unconsciously, the marginal benefit from safer driving to the marginal cost. As a result, they drive more slowly and carefully when the benefit of increased safety is high. For example, when road conditions are icy, people drive more attentively and at lower speeds than they do when road conditions are clear.

Consider how a seat belt law alters a driver's cost–benefit calculation. Seat belts make accidents less costly because they reduce the likelihood of injury or death. In other words, seat belts reduce the benefits of slow and careful driving. People respond to seat belts as they would to an improvement in road conditions—by driving faster and less carefully. The result of a seat belt law, therefore, is a larger number of accidents. The decline in safe driving has a clear, adverse impact on pedestrians, who are more likely to find themselves in an accident but (unlike the drivers) don't have the benefit of added protection.

At first, this discussion of incentives and seat belts might seem like idle speculation. Yet in a classic 1975 study, economist Sam Peltzman argued that auto-safety laws have had many of these effects. According to Peltzman's evidence, these laws give rise to fewer deaths per accident but also to more accidents. He concluded that the net result is little change in the number of driver deaths and an increase in the number of pedestrian deaths.

Peltzman's analysis of auto safety is an offbeat and controversial example of the general principle that people respond to incentives. When analyzing any policy, we must consider not only the direct effects but also the less obvious indirect effects that work through incentives. If the policy changes incentives, it will cause people to alter their behavior.

QuickQuiz *Describe an important trade-off you recently faced. • Give an example of some action that has both a monetary and nonmonetary opportunity cost. • Describe an incentive your parents offered to you in an effort to influence your behavior.*

1-2 How People Interact

The first four principles discussed how individuals make decisions. As we go about our lives, many of our decisions affect not only ourselves but other people as well. The next three principles concern how people interact with one another.

1-2a Principle 5: Trade Can Make Everyone Better Off

You may have heard on the news that the Chinese are our competitors in the world economy. In some ways, this is true because American and Chinese firms produce many of the same goods. Companies in the United States and China compete for the same customers in the markets for clothing, toys, solar panels, automobile tires, and many other items.

Yet it is easy to be misled when thinking about competition among countries. Trade between the United States and China is not like a sports contest in which one side wins and the other side loses. In fact, the opposite is true: Trade between two countries can make each country better off.

To see why, consider how trade affects your family. When a member of your family looks for a job, she competes against members of other families who are looking for jobs. Families also compete against one another when they go shopping because each family wants to buy the best goods at the lowest prices. In a sense, each family in an economy competes with all other families.

Despite this competition, your family would not be better off isolating itself from all other families. If it did, your family would need to grow its own food, make its own clothes, and build its own home. Clearly, your family gains much from its ability to trade with others. Trade allows each person to specialize in the activities she does best, whether it is farming, sewing, or home building. By trading with others, people can buy a greater variety of goods and services at lower cost.

"For $5 a week you can watch baseball without being nagged to cut the grass!"

Like families, countries also benefit from the ability to trade with one another. Trade allows countries to specialize in what they do best and to enjoy a greater variety of goods and services. The Chinese, as well as the French, Egyptians, and Brazilians, are as much our partners in the world economy as they are our competitors.

1-2b Principle 6: Markets Are Usually a Good Way to Organize Economic Activity

The collapse of communism in the Soviet Union and Eastern Europe in the late 1980s and early 1990s was one of the last century's most transformative events. Communist countries operated on the premise that government officials were in the best position to allocate the economy's scarce resources. These central planners decided what goods and services were produced, how much was produced, and who produced and consumed these goods and services. The theory behind central planning was that only the government could organize economic activity in a way that promoted economic well-being for the country as a whole.

Most countries that once had centrally planned economies have abandoned the system and are instead developing market economies. In a **market economy**, the decisions of a central planner are replaced by the decisions of millions of firms and households. Firms decide whom to hire and what to make. Households decide which firms to work for and what to buy with their incomes. These firms and households interact in the marketplace, where prices and self-interest guide their decisions.

market economy
an economy that allocates resources through the decentralized decisions of many firms and households as they interact in markets for goods and services

At first glance, the success of market economies is puzzling. In a market economy, no one is looking out for the economic well-being of society as a whole. Free markets contain many buyers and sellers of numerous goods and services, and all of them are interested primarily in their own well-being. Yet despite decentralized decision making and self-interested decision makers, market economies have proven remarkably successful in organizing economic activity to promote overall economic well-being.

In his 1776 book *An Inquiry into the Nature and Causes of the Wealth of Nations*, economist Adam Smith made the most famous observation in all of economics: Households and firms interacting in markets act as if they are guided by an "invisible hand" that leads them to desirable market outcomes. One of our goals in this book is to understand how this invisible hand works its magic.

As you study economics, you will learn that prices are the instrument with which the invisible hand directs economic activity. In any market, buyers look at the price when determining how much to demand, and sellers look at the price when deciding how much to supply. As a result of the decisions that buyers and sellers make, market prices reflect both the value of a good to society and the cost to society of making the good. Smith's great insight was that prices adjust to guide these individual buyers and sellers to reach outcomes that, in many cases, maximize the well-being of society as a whole.

Smith's insight has an important corollary: When a government prevents prices from adjusting naturally to supply and demand, it impedes the invisible hand's ability to coordinate the decisions of the households and firms that make up an economy. This corollary explains why taxes adversely affect the allocation of resources: They distort prices and thus the decisions of households and firms. It also explains the great harm caused by policies that directly control prices, such as rent control. And it explains the failure of communism. In communist countries, prices were not determined in the marketplace but were dictated by central planners. These planners lacked the necessary information about consumers' tastes and producers' costs, which in a market economy is reflected in prices. Central planners failed because they tried to run the economy with one hand tied behind their backs—the invisible hand of the marketplace.

FYI

Adam Smith and the Invisible Hand

It may be only a coincidence that Adam Smith's great book *The Wealth of Nations* was published in 1776, the exact year in which American revolutionaries signed the Declaration of Independence. But the two documents share a point of view that was prevalent at the time: Individuals are usually best left to their own devices, without the heavy hand of government guiding their actions. This political philosophy provides the intellectual basis for the market economy and for free society more generally.

Why do decentralized market economies work so well? Is it because people can be counted on to treat one another with love and kindness? Not at all. Here is Adam Smith's description of how people interact in a market economy:

> *Man has almost constant occasion for the help of his brethren, and it is in vain for him to expect it from their benevolence only. He will be more likely to prevail if he can interest their self-love in his favour, and show them that it is for their own advantage to do for him what he requires of them. . . . Give me that which I want, and you shall have this which you want, is the meaning of every such offer; and it is in this manner that we obtain from one another the far greater part of those good offices which we stand in need of.*

BETTMANN/CORBIS

Adam Smith

> *It is not from the benevolence of the butcher, the brewer, or the baker that we expect our dinner, but from their regard to their own interest. We address ourselves, not to their humanity but to their self-love, and never talk to them of our own necessities but of their advantages. Nobody but a beggar chooses to depend chiefly upon the benevolence of his fellow-citizens. . . .*
>
> *Every individual . . . neither intends to promote the public interest, nor knows how much he is promoting it. . . . He intends only his own gain, and he is in this, as in many other cases, led by an invisible hand to promote an end which was no part of his intention. Nor is it always the worse for the society that it was no part of it. By pursuing his own interest he frequently promotes that of the society more effectually than when he really intends to promote it.*

Smith is saying that participants in the economy are motivated by self-interest and that the "invisible hand" of the marketplace guides this self-interest into promoting general economic well-being.

Many of Smith's insights remain at the center of modern economics. Our analysis in the coming chapters will allow us to express Smith's conclusions more precisely and to analyze more fully the strengths and weaknesses of the market's invisible hand. ■

CASE STUDY

ADAM SMITH WOULD HAVE LOVED UBER

You have probably never lived in a centrally planned economy, but if you have ever tried to hail a cab in a major city, you have likely experienced a highly regulated market. In many cities, the local government imposes strict controls in the market for taxis. The rules usually go well beyond regulation of insurance and safety. For example, the government may limit entry into the market by approving only a certain number of taxi medallions or permits. It may determine the prices that taxis are allowed to charge. The government uses its police powers—that is, the threat of fines or jail time—to keep unauthorized drivers off the streets and to prevent all drivers from charging unauthorized prices.

RICHARD LEVINE / ALAMY

Technology can improve this market.

Recently, however, this highly controlled market has been invaded by a disruptive force: Uber. Launched in 2009, this company provides an app for smartphones that connects passengers and drivers. Because Uber cars do not roam the streets looking for taxi-hailing pedestrians, they are technically not taxis and so are not subject to the same regulations. But they offer much the same service. Indeed, rides from Uber cars are often more convenient. On a cold and rainy day, who wants to stand on the side of the road waiting for an empty cab to drive by? It is more pleasant to remain inside, use your smartphone to arrange for a ride, and stay warm and dry until the car arrives.

Uber cars often charge less than taxis, but not always. Uber allows drivers to raise their prices significantly when there is a surge in demand, such as during a sudden rainstorm or late on New Year's Eve, when numerous tipsy partiers are looking for a safe way to get home. By contrast, regulated taxis are typically prevented from surge pricing.

Not everyone is fond of Uber. Drivers of traditional taxis complain that this new competition eats into their source of income. This is hardly a surprise: Suppliers of goods and services usually dislike new competitors. But vigorous competition among producers makes a market work well for consumers.

That is why economists love Uber. A 2014 survey of several dozen prominent economists asked whether car services such as Uber increased consumer well-being. Yes, said every single economist. The economists were also asked whether surge pricing increased consumer well-being. Yes, said 85 percent of them. Surge pricing makes consumers pay more at times, but because Uber drivers respond to incentives, it also increases the quantity of car services supplied when they are most needed. Surge pricing also helps allocate the services to those consumers who value them most highly and reduces the costs of searching and waiting for a car.

If Adam Smith were alive today, he would surely have the Uber app on his phone. ●

1-2c Principle 7: Governments Can Sometimes Improve Market Outcomes

If the invisible hand of the market is so great, why do we need government? One purpose of studying economics is to refine your view about the proper role and scope of government policy.

One reason we need government is that the invisible hand can work its magic only if the government enforces the rules and maintains the institutions that are key to a market economy. Most important, market economies need institutions to enforce **property rights** so individuals can own and control scarce resources.

property rights
the ability of an individual to own and exercise control over scarce resources

A farmer won't grow food if she expects her crop to be stolen; a restaurant won't serve meals unless it is assured that customers will pay before they leave; and a film company won't produce movies if too many potential customers avoid paying by making illegal copies. We all rely on government-provided police and courts to enforce our rights over the things we produce—and the invisible hand counts on our ability to enforce those rights.

Another reason we need government is that, although the invisible hand is powerful, it is not omnipotent. There are two broad rationales for a government to intervene in the economy and change the allocation of resources that people would choose on their own: to promote efficiency or to promote equality. That is, most policies aim either to enlarge the economic pie or to change how the pie is divided.

market failure
a situation in which a market left on its own fails to allocate resources efficiently

externality
the impact of one person's actions on the well-being of a bystander

market power
the ability of a single economic actor (or small group of actors) to have a substantial influence on market prices

Consider first the goal of efficiency. Although the invisible hand usually leads markets to allocate resources to maximize the size of the economic pie, this is not always the case. Economists use the term **market failure** to refer to a situation in which the market on its own fails to produce an efficient allocation of resources. As we will see, one possible cause of market failure is an **externality,** which is the impact of one person's actions on the well-being of a bystander. The classic example of an externality is pollution. When the production of a good pollutes the air and creates health problems for those who live near the factories, the market left to its own devices may fail to take this cost into account. Another possible cause of market failure is **market power,** which refers to the ability of a single person or firm (or a small group) to unduly influence market prices. For example, if everyone in town needs water but there is only one well, the owner of the well is not subject to the rigorous competition with which the invisible hand normally keeps self-interest in check; she may take advantage of this opportunity by restricting the output of water so she can charge a higher price. In the presence of externalities or market power, well-designed public policy can enhance economic efficiency.

Now consider the goal of equality. Even when the invisible hand yields efficient outcomes, it can nonetheless leave sizable disparities in economic well-being. A market economy rewards people according to their ability to produce things that other people are willing to pay for. The world's best basketball player earns more than the world's best chess player simply because people are willing to pay more to watch basketball than chess. The invisible hand does not ensure that everyone has sufficient food, decent clothing, and adequate healthcare. This inequality may, depending on one's political philosophy, call for government intervention. In practice, many public policies, such as the income tax and the welfare system, aim to achieve a more equal distribution of economic well-being.

To say that the government *can* improve on market outcomes does not mean that it always *will*. Public policy is made not by angels but by a political process that is far from perfect. Sometimes policies are designed simply to reward the politically powerful. Sometimes they are made by well-intentioned leaders who are not fully informed. As you study economics, you will become a better judge of when a government policy is justifiable because it promotes efficiency or equality and when it is not.

QuickQuiz *Why is a country better off not isolating itself from all other countries? • Why do we have markets, and according to economists, what roles should government play in them?*

1-3 How the Economy as a Whole Works

We started by discussing how individuals make decisions and then looked at how people interact with one another. All these decisions and interactions together make up "the economy." The last three principles concern the workings of the economy as a whole.

1-3a Principle 8: A Country's Standard of Living Depends on Its Ability to Produce Goods and Services

The differences in living standards around the world are staggering. In 2014, the average American had an income of about $55,000. In the same year, the average Mexican earned about $17,000, the average Chinese about $13,000, and the average Nigerian only $6,000. Not surprisingly, this large variation in average income is reflected in various measures of quality of life. Citizens of high-income countries have more TV sets, more cars, better nutrition, better healthcare, and a longer life expectancy than citizens of low-income countries.

Changes in living standards over time are also large. In the United States, incomes have historically grown about 2 percent per year (after adjusting for changes in the cost of living). At this rate, average income doubles every 35 years. Over the past century, average U.S. income has risen about eightfold.

What explains these large differences in living standards among countries and over time? The answer is surprisingly simple. Almost all variation in living standards is attributable to differences in countries' **productivity**—that is, the amount of goods and services produced by each unit of labor input. In nations where workers can produce a large quantity of goods and services per hour, most people enjoy a high standard of living; in nations where workers are less productive, most people endure a more meager existence. Similarly, the growth rate of a nation's productivity determines the growth rate of its average income.

productivity
the quantity of goods and services produced from each unit of labor input

The fundamental relationship between productivity and living standards is simple, but its implications are far-reaching. If productivity is the primary determinant of living standards, other explanations must be of secondary importance. For example, it might be tempting to credit labor unions or minimum-wage laws for the rise in living standards of American workers over the past century. Yet the real hero of American workers is their rising productivity. As another example, some commentators have claimed that increased competition from Japan and other countries explained the slow growth in U.S. incomes during the 1970s and 1980s. Yet the real villain was not competition from abroad but flagging productivity growth in the United States.

The relationship between productivity and living standards also has profound implications for public policy. When thinking about how any policy will affect living standards, the key question is how it will affect our ability to produce goods and services. To boost living standards, policymakers need to raise productivity by ensuring that workers are well educated, have the tools they need to produce goods and services, and have access to the best available technology.

1-3b Principle 9: Prices Rise When the Government Prints Too Much Money

In January 1921, a daily newspaper in Germany cost 0.30 marks. Less than two years later, in November 1922, the same newspaper cost 70,000,000 marks. All other prices in the economy rose by similar amounts. This episode is one of history's most spectacular examples of **inflation,** an increase in the overall level of prices in the economy.

inflation
an increase in the overall level of prices in the economy

"Well it may have been 68 cents when you got in line, but it's 74 cents now!"

Although the United States has never experienced inflation even close to that of Germany in the 1920s, inflation has at times been an economic problem. During the 1970s, for instance, when the overall level of prices more than doubled, President Gerald Ford called inflation "public enemy number one." By contrast, inflation in the first decade of the 21st century ran about 2½ percent per year; at this rate, it would take almost 30 years for prices to double. Because high inflation imposes various costs on society, keeping inflation at a low level is a goal of economic policymakers around the world.

What causes inflation? In almost all cases of large or persistent inflation, the culprit is growth in the quantity of money. When a government creates large quantities of the nation's money, the value of the money falls. In Germany in the early 1920s, when prices were on average tripling every month, the quantity of money was also tripling every month. Although less dramatic, the economic history of the United States points to a similar conclusion: The high inflation of the 1970s was associated with rapid growth in the quantity of money, and the return of low inflation in the 1980s was associated with slower growth in the quantity of money.

1-3c Principle 10: Society Faces a Short-Run Trade-off between Inflation and Unemployment

Although a higher level of prices is, in the long run, the primary effect of increasing the quantity of money, the short-run story is more complex and controversial. Most economists describe the short-run effects of monetary injections as follows:

- Increasing the amount of money in the economy stimulates the overall level of spending and thus the demand for goods and services.
- Higher demand may over time cause firms to raise their prices, but in the meantime, it also encourages them to hire more workers and produce a larger quantity of goods and services.
- More hiring means lower unemployment.

This line of reasoning leads to one final economy-wide trade-off: a short-run trade-off between inflation and unemployment.

Although some economists still question these ideas, most accept that society faces a short-run trade-off between inflation and unemployment. This simply means that, over a period of a year or two, many economic policies push inflation and unemployment in opposite directions. Policymakers face this trade-off regardless of whether inflation and unemployment both start out at high levels (as they did in the early 1980s), at low levels (as they did in the late 1990s), or someplace in between. This short-run trade-off plays a key role in the analysis of the **business cycle**—the irregular and largely unpredictable fluctuations in economic activity, as measured by the production of goods and services or the number of people employed.

business cycle
fluctuations in economic activity, such as employment and production

Policymakers can exploit the short-run trade-off between inflation and unemployment using various policy instruments. By changing the amount that the government spends, the amount it taxes, and the amount of money it prints, policymakers can influence the overall demand for goods and services. Changes in demand in turn influence the combination of inflation and unemployment that the economy experiences in the short run. Because these instruments of economic policy are potentially so powerful, how policymakers should use them to control the economy, if at all, is a subject of continuing debate.

This debate heated up in the early years of Barack Obama's presidency. In 2008 and 2009, the U.S. economy, as well as many other economies around the world, experienced a deep economic downturn. Problems in the financial system, caused by bad bets on the housing market, spilled over into the rest of the economy, causing incomes to fall and unemployment to soar. Policymakers responded in various ways to increase the overall demand for goods and services. President Obama's first major initiative was a stimulus package of reduced taxes and increased government spending. At the same time, the nation's central bank, the Federal Reserve, increased the supply of money. The goal of these policies was to reduce unemployment. Some feared, however, that these policies might over time lead to an excessive level of inflation.

QuickQuiz *List and briefly explain the three principles that describe how the economy as a whole works.*

1-4 Conclusion

You now have a taste of what economics is all about. In the coming chapters, we develop many specific insights about people, markets, and economies. Mastering these insights will take some effort, but it is not an overwhelming task. The field of economics is based on a few big ideas that can be applied in many different situations.

Throughout this book, we will refer back to the *Ten Principles of Economics* highlighted in this chapter and summarized in Table 1. Keep these building blocks in mind: Even the most sophisticated economic analysis is founded on the ten principles introduced here.

TABLE 1

Ten Principles of Economics

How People Make Decisions
1: People Face Trade-offs
2: The Cost of Something Is What You Give Up to Get It
3: Rational People Think at the Margin
4: People Respond to Incentives

How People Interact
5: Trade Can Make Everyone Better Off
6: Markets Are Usually a Good Way to Organize Economic Activity
7: Governments Can Sometimes Improve Market Outcomes

How the Economy as a Whole Works
8: A Country's Standard of Living Depends on Its Ability to Produce Goods and Services
9: Prices Rise When the Government Prints Too Much Money
10: Society Faces a Short-Run Trade-off between Inflation and Unemployment

CHAPTER QuickQuiz

1. Economics is best defined as the study of
   a. how society manages its scarce resources.
   b. how to run a business most profitably.
   c. how to predict inflation, unemployment, and stock prices.
   d. how the government can stop the harm from unchecked self-interest.

2. Your opportunity cost of going to a movie is
   a. the price of the ticket.
   b. the price of the ticket plus the cost of any soda and popcorn you buy at the theater.
   c. the total cash expenditure needed to go to the movie plus the value of your time.
   d. zero, as long as you enjoy the movie and consider it a worthwhile use of time and money.

3. A marginal change is one that
   a. is not important for public policy.
   b. incrementally alters an existing plan.
   c. makes an outcome inefficient.
   d. does not influence incentives.
4. Adam Smith's "invisible hand" refers to
   a. the subtle and often hidden methods that businesses use to profit at consumers' expense.
   b. the ability of free markets to reach desirable outcomes, despite the self-interest of market participants.
   c. the ability of government regulation to benefit consumers, even if the consumers are unaware of the regulations.
   d. the way in which producers or consumers in unregulated markets impose costs on innocent bystanders.
5. Governments may intervene in a market economy in order to
   a. protect property rights.
   b. correct a market failure due to externalities.
   c. achieve a more equal distribution of income.
   d. All of the above.
6. If a nation has high and persistent inflation, the most likely explanation is
   a. the central bank creating excessive amounts of money.
   b. unions bargaining for excessively high wages.
   c. the government imposing excessive levels of taxation.
   d. firms using their monopoly power to enforce excessive price hikes.

SUMMARY

- The fundamental lessons about individual decision making are that people face trade-offs among alternative goals, that the cost of any action is measured in terms of forgone opportunities, that rational people make decisions by comparing marginal costs and marginal benefits, and that people change their behavior in response to the incentives they face.
- The fundamental lessons about interactions among people are that trade and interdependence can be mutually beneficial, that markets are usually a good way of coordinating economic activity among people, and that the government can potentially improve market outcomes by remedying a market failure or by promoting greater economic equality.
- The fundamental lessons about the economy as a whole are that productivity is the ultimate source of living standards, that growth in the quantity of money is the ultimate source of inflation, and that society faces a short-run trade-off between inflation and unemployment.

KEY CONCEPTS

scarcity, p. 4
economics, p. 4
efficiency, p. 5
equality, p. 5
opportunity cost, p. 6
rational people, p. 6
marginal change, p. 6
incentive, p. 7
market economy, p. 9
property rights, p. 11
market failure, p. 12
externality, p. 12
market power, p. 12
productivity, p. 13
inflation, p. 13
business cycle, p. 14

QUESTIONS FOR REVIEW

1. Give three examples of important trade-offs that you face in your life.
2. What items would you include to figure out the opportunity cost of a vacation to Disney World?
3. Water is necessary for life. Is the marginal benefit of a glass of water large or small?
4. Why should policymakers think about incentives?
5. Why isn't trade among countries like a game with some winners and some losers?
6. What does the "invisible hand" of the marketplace do?

7. What are the two main causes of market failure? Give an example of each.
8. Why is productivity important?
9. What is inflation and what causes it?
10. How are inflation and unemployment related in the short run?

PROBLEMS AND APPLICATIONS

1. Describe some of the trade-offs faced by each of the following:
   a. a family deciding whether to buy a new car
   b. a member of Congress deciding how much to spend on national parks
   c. a company president deciding whether to open a new factory
   d. a professor deciding how much to prepare for class
   e. a recent college graduate deciding whether to go to graduate school
2. You are trying to decide whether to take a vacation. Most of the costs of the vacation (airfare, hotel, and forgone wages) are measured in dollars, but the benefits of the vacation are psychological. How can you compare the benefits to the costs?
3. You were planning to spend Saturday working at your part-time job, but a friend asks you to go skiing. What is the true cost of going skiing? Now suppose you had been planning to spend the day studying at the library. What is the cost of going skiing in this case? Explain.
4. You win $100 in a basketball pool. You have a choice between spending the money now and putting it away for a year in a bank account that pays 5 percent interest. What is the opportunity cost of spending the $100 now?
5. The company that you manage has invested $5 million in developing a new product, but the development is not quite finished. At a recent meeting, your salespeople report that the introduction of competing products has reduced the expected sales of your new product to $3 million. If it would cost $1 million to finish development and make the product, should you go ahead and do so? What is the most that you should pay to complete development?
6. A 1996 bill reforming the federal government's antipoverty programs limited many welfare recipients to only two years of benefits.
   a. How does this change affect the incentives for working?
   b. How might this change represent a trade-off between equality and efficiency?
7. Explain whether each of the following government activities is motivated by a concern about equality or a concern about efficiency. In the case of efficiency, discuss the type of market failure involved.
   a. regulating cable TV prices
   b. providing some poor people with vouchers that can be used to buy food
   c. prohibiting smoking in public places
   d. breaking up Standard Oil (which once owned 90 percent of all oil refineries) into several smaller companies
   e. imposing higher personal income tax rates on people with higher incomes
   f. instituting laws against driving while intoxicated
8. Discuss each of the following statements from the standpoints of equality and efficiency.
   a. "Everyone in society should be guaranteed the best healthcare possible."
   b. "When workers are laid off, they should be able to collect unemployment benefits until they find a new job."
9. In what ways is your standard of living different from that of your parents or grandparents when they were your age? Why have these changes occurred?
10. Suppose Americans decide to save more of their incomes. If banks lend this extra saving to businesses, which use the funds to build new factories, how might this lead to faster growth in productivity? Who do you suppose benefits from the higher productivity? Is society getting a free lunch?
11. During the Revolutionary War, the American colonies could not raise enough tax revenue to fully fund the war effort. To make up the difference, the colonies decided to print more money. Printing money to cover expenditures is sometimes referred to as an "inflation tax." Who do you think is being "taxed" when more money is printed? Why?

To find additional study resources, visit cengagebrain.com, and search for "Mankiw."

CHAPTER 2

Thinking Like an Economist

Every field of study has its own language and its own way of thinking. Mathematicians talk about axioms, integrals, and vector spaces. Psychologists talk about ego, id, and cognitive dissonance. Lawyers talk about venue, torts, and promissory estoppel.

Economics is no different. Supply, demand, elasticity, comparative advantage, consumer surplus, deadweight loss—these terms are part of the economist's language. In the coming chapters, you will encounter many new terms and some familiar words that economists use in specialized ways. At first, this new language may seem needlessly arcane. But as you will see, its value lies in its ability to provide you with a new and useful way of thinking about the world in which you live.

The purpose of this book is to help you learn the economist's way of thinking. Just as you cannot become a mathematician, psychologist, or lawyer overnight, learning to think like an economist will take some time. Yet with a combination of theory, case studies, and examples of economics in the news, this book will give you ample opportunity to develop and practice this skill.

Before delving into the substance and details of economics, it is helpful to have an overview of how economists approach the world. This chapter discusses the field's methodology. What is distinctive about how economists confront a question? What does it mean to think like an economist?

2-1 The Economist as Scientist

Economists try to address their subject with a scientist's objectivity. They approach the study of the economy in much the same way a physicist approaches the study of matter and a biologist approaches the study of life: They devise theories, collect data, and then analyze these data in an attempt to verify or refute their theories.

"I'm a social scientist, Michael. That means I can't explain electricity or anything like that, but if you ever want to know about people, I'm your man."

To beginners, the claim that economics is a science can seem odd. After all, economists do not work with test tubes or telescopes. The essence of science, however, is the *scientific method*—the dispassionate development and testing of theories about how the world works. This method of inquiry is as applicable to studying a nation's economy as it is to studying the earth's gravity or a species' evolution. As Albert Einstein once put it, "The whole of science is nothing more than the refinement of everyday thinking."

Although Einstein's comment is as true for social sciences such as economics as it is for natural sciences such as physics, most people are not accustomed to looking at society through a scientific lens. Let's discuss some of the ways economists apply the logic of science to examine how an economy works.

2-1a The Scientific Method: Observation, Theory, and More Observation

Isaac Newton, the famous 17th-century scientist and mathematician, allegedly became intrigued one day when he saw an apple fall from a tree. This observation motivated Newton to develop a theory of gravity that applies not only to an apple falling to the earth but to any two objects in the universe. Subsequent testing of Newton's theory has shown that it works well in many circumstances (albeit not in all circumstances, as Einstein would later show). Because Newton's theory has been so successful at explaining observation, it is still taught in undergraduate physics courses around the world.

This interplay between theory and observation also occurs in economics. An economist might live in a country experiencing rapidly increasing prices and be moved by this observation to develop a theory of inflation. The theory might assert that high inflation arises when the government prints too much money. To test this theory, the economist could collect and analyze data on prices and money from many different countries. If growth in the quantity of money were completely unrelated to the rate of price increase, the economist would start to doubt the validity of this theory of inflation. If money growth and inflation were strongly correlated in international data, as in fact they are, the economist would become more confident in the theory.

Although economists use theory and observation like other scientists, they face an obstacle that makes their task especially challenging: In economics, conducting experiments is often impractical. Physicists studying gravity can drop many objects in their laboratories to generate data to test their theories. By contrast, economists studying inflation are not allowed to manipulate a nation's monetary policy simply to generate useful data. Economists, like astronomers and evolutionary biologists, usually have to make do with whatever data the world happens to give them.

To find a substitute for laboratory experiments, economists pay close attention to the natural experiments offered by history. When a war in the Middle East interrupts the supply of crude oil, for instance, oil prices skyrocket around the world. For consumers of oil and oil products, such an event depresses living standards. For economic policymakers, it poses a difficult choice about how best to respond. But for economic scientists, the event provides an opportunity to study the effects of a key natural resource on the world's economies. Throughout this book, therefore, we consider many historical episodes. These episodes are valuable to study because they give us insight into the economy of the past and, more important, because they allow us to illustrate and evaluate economic theories of the present.

2-1b The Role of Assumptions

If you ask a physicist how long it would take a marble to fall from the top of a ten-story building, he will likely answer the question by assuming that the marble falls in a vacuum. Of course, this assumption is false. In fact, the building is surrounded by air, which exerts friction on the falling marble and slows it down. Yet the physicist will point out that the friction on the marble is so small that its effect is negligible. Assuming the marble falls in a vacuum simplifies the problem without substantially affecting the answer.

Economists make assumptions for the same reason: Assumptions can simplify the complex world and make it easier to understand. To study the effects of international trade, for example, we might assume that the world consists of only two countries and that each country produces only two goods. In reality, there are numerous countries, each of which produces thousands of different types of goods. But by considering a world with only two countries and two goods, we can focus our thinking on the essence of the problem. Once we understand international trade in this simplified imaginary world, we are in a better position to understand international trade in the more complex world in which we live.

The art in scientific thinking—whether in physics, biology, or economics—is deciding which assumptions to make. Suppose, for instance, that instead of dropping a marble from the top of the building, we were dropping a beach ball of the same weight. Our physicist would realize that the assumption of no friction is less accurate in this case: Friction exerts a greater force on the beach ball because it is much larger than a marble. The assumption that gravity works in a vacuum is reasonable when studying a falling marble but not when studying a falling beach ball.

Similarly, economists use different assumptions to answer different questions. Suppose that we want to study what happens to the economy when the government changes the number of dollars in circulation. An important piece of this analysis, it turns out, is how prices respond. Many prices in the economy change infrequently: The newsstand prices of magazines, for instance, change only once every few years. Knowing this fact may lead us to make different assumptions when studying the effects of the policy change over different time horizons. For studying the short-run effects of the policy, we may assume that prices do not change much. We may even make the extreme and artificial assumption that all prices are completely fixed. For studying the long-run effects of the policy, however, we may assume that all prices are completely flexible. Just as a physicist uses different assumptions when studying falling marbles and falling beach balls, economists use different assumptions when studying the short-run and long-run effects of a change in the quantity of money.

2-1c Economic Models

High school biology teachers teach basic anatomy with plastic replicas of the human body. These models have all the major organs—the heart, the liver, the kidneys, and so on—which allow teachers to show their students very simply how the important parts of the body fit together. Because these plastic models are stylized and omit many details, no one would mistake one of them for a real person. Despite this lack of realism—indeed, because of this lack of realism—studying these models is useful for learning how the human body works.

Economists also use models to learn about the world, but unlike plastic manikins, their models mostly consist of diagrams and equations. Like a biology teacher's plastic model, economic models omit many details to allow us to see what is truly important. Just as the biology teacher's model does not include all the body's muscles and capillaries, an economist's model does not include every feature of the economy.

As we use models to examine various economic issues throughout this book, you will see that all the models are built with assumptions. Just as a physicist begins the analysis of a falling marble by assuming away the existence of friction, economists assume away many details of the economy that are irrelevant to the question at hand. All models—in physics, biology, and economics—simplify reality to improve our understanding of it.

2-1d Our First Model: The Circular-Flow Diagram

The economy consists of millions of people engaged in many activities—buying, selling, working, hiring, manufacturing, and so on. To understand how the economy works, we must find some way to simplify our thinking about all these activities. In other words, we need a model that explains, in general terms, how the economy is organized and how participants in the economy interact with one another.

circular-flow diagram
a visual model of the economy that shows how dollars flow through markets among households and firms

Figure 1 presents a visual model of the economy called a **circular-flow diagram.** In this model, the economy is simplified to include only two types of decision makers—firms and households. Firms produce goods and services using inputs, such as labor, land, and capital (buildings and machines). These inputs are called the *factors of production*. Households own the factors of production and consume all the goods and services that the firms produce.

Households and firms interact in two types of markets. In the *markets for goods and services*, households are buyers, and firms are sellers. In particular, households buy the output of goods and services that firms produce. In the *markets for the factors of production*, households are sellers, and firms are buyers. In these markets, households provide the inputs that firms use to produce goods and services. The circular-flow diagram offers a simple way of organizing the economic transactions that occur between households and firms in the economy.

The two loops of the circular-flow diagram are distinct but related. The inner loop represents the flows of inputs and outputs. The households sell the use of their labor, land, and capital to the firms in the markets for the factors of production. The firms then use these factors to produce goods and services, which in turn are sold to households in the markets for goods and services. The outer

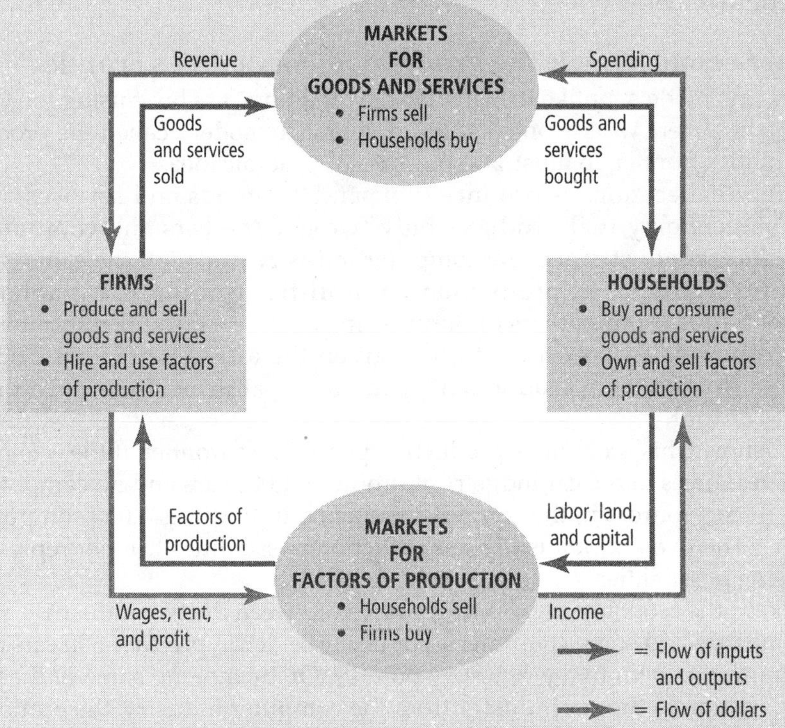

FIGURE 1

The Circular Flow

This diagram is a schematic representation of the organization of the economy. Decisions are made by households and firms. Households and firms interact in the markets for goods and services (where households are buyers and firms are sellers) and in the markets for the factors of production (where firms are buyers and households are sellers). The outer set of arrows shows the flow of dollars, and the inner set of arrows shows the corresponding flow of inputs and outputs.

loop of the diagram represents the corresponding flow of dollars. The households spend money to buy goods and services from the firms. The firms use some of the revenue from these sales to pay for the factors of production, such as the wages of their workers. What's left is the profit of the firm owners, who are themselves members of households.

Let's take a tour of the circular flow by following a dollar bill as it makes its way from person to person through the economy. Imagine that the dollar begins at a household—say, in your wallet. If you want to buy a cup of coffee, you take the dollar (along with a few of its brothers and sisters) to one of the economy's markets for goods and services, such as your local Starbucks coffee shop. There, you spend it on your favorite drink. When the dollar moves into the Starbucks cash register, it becomes revenue for the firm. The dollar doesn't stay at Starbucks for long, however, because the firm uses it to buy inputs in the markets for the factors of production. Starbucks might use the dollar to pay rent to its landlord for the space it occupies or to pay the wages of its workers. In either case, the dollar enters the income of some household and, once again, is back in someone's wallet. At that point, the story of the economy's circular flow starts once again.

The circular-flow diagram in Figure 1 is a very simple model of the economy. A more complex and realistic circular-flow model would include, for instance, the roles of government and international trade. (A portion of that dollar you gave to Starbucks might be used to pay taxes or to buy coffee beans from a farmer in Brazil.) Yet these details are not crucial for a basic understanding of how the economy is organized. Because of its simplicity, this circular-flow diagram is useful to keep in mind when thinking about how the pieces of the economy fit together.

2-1e Our Second Model: The Production Possibilities Frontier

Most economic models, unlike the circular-flow diagram, are built using the tools of mathematics. Here we use one of the simplest such models, called the production possibilities frontier, to illustrate some basic economic ideas.

production possibilities frontier
a graph that shows the combinations of output that the economy can possibly produce given the available factors of production and the available production technology

Although real economies produce thousands of goods and services, let's consider an economy that produces only two goods—cars and computers. Together, the car industry and the computer industry use all of the economy's factors of production. The **production possibilities frontier** is a graph that shows the various combinations of output—in this case, cars and computers—that the economy can possibly produce given the available factors of production and the available production technology that firms use to turn these factors into output.

Figure 2 shows this economy's production possibilities frontier. If the economy uses all its resources in the car industry, it produces 1,000 cars and no computers. If it uses all its resources in the computer industry, it produces 3,000 computers and no cars. The two endpoints of the production possibilities frontier represent these extreme possibilities.

More likely, the economy divides its resources between the two industries, producing some cars and some computers. For example, it can produce 600 cars and 2,200 computers, shown in the figure by point A. Or, by moving some of the factors of production to the car industry from the computer industry, the economy can produce 700 cars and 2,000 computers, represented by point B.

Because resources are scarce, not every conceivable outcome is feasible. For example, no matter how resources are allocated between the two industries, the economy cannot produce the amount of cars and computers represented by point C. Given the technology available for manufacturing cars and computers, the economy does not have enough of the factors of production to support that level of output. With the resources it has, the economy can produce at any point on or

FIGURE 2

The Production Possibilities Frontier
The production possibilities frontier shows the combinations of output—in this case, cars and computers—that the economy can possibly produce. The economy can produce any combination on or inside the frontier. Points outside the frontier are not feasible given the economy's resources. The slope of the production possibilities frontier measures the opportunity cost of a car in terms of computers. This opportunity cost varies, depending on how much of the two goods the economy is producing.

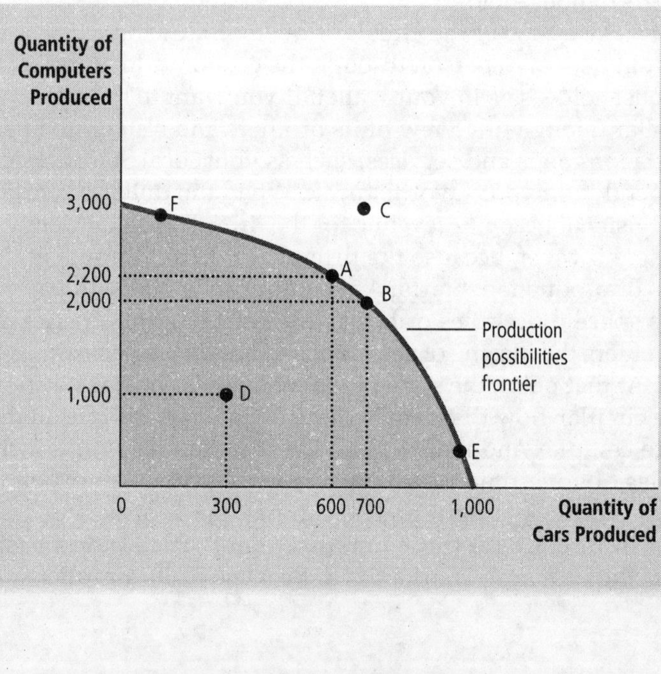

inside the production possibilities frontier, but it cannot produce at points outside the frontier.

An outcome is said to be *efficient* if the economy is getting all it can from the scarce resources it has available. Points on (rather than inside) the production possibilities frontier represent efficient levels of production. When the economy is producing at such a point, say point A, there is no way to produce more of one good without producing less of the other. Point D represents an *inefficient* outcome. For some reason, perhaps widespread unemployment, the economy is producing less than it could from the resources it has available: It is producing only 300 cars and 1,000 computers. If the source of the inefficiency is eliminated, the economy can increase its production of both goods. For example, if the economy moves from point D to point A, its production of cars increases from 300 to 600, and its production of computers increases from 1,000 to 2,200.

One of the *Ten Principles of Economics* discussed in Chapter 1 is that people face trade-offs. The production possibilities frontier shows one trade-off that society faces. Once we have reached an efficient point on the frontier, the only way of producing more of one good is to produce less of the other. When the economy moves from point A to point B, for instance, society produces 100 more cars at the expense of producing 200 fewer computers.

This trade-off helps us understand another of the *Ten Principles of Economics:* The cost of something is what you give up to get it. This is called the *opportunity cost*. The production possibilities frontier shows the opportunity cost of one good as measured in terms of the other good. When society moves from point A to point B, it gives up 200 computers to get 100 additional cars. That is, at point A, the opportunity cost of 100 cars is 200 computers. Put another way, the opportunity cost of each car is two computers. Notice that the opportunity cost of a car equals the slope of the production possibilities frontier. (If you don't recall what slope is, you can refresh your memory with the graphing appendix to this chapter.)

The opportunity cost of a car in terms of the number of computers is not constant in this economy but depends on how many cars and computers the economy is producing. This is reflected in the shape of the production possibilities frontier. Because the production possibilities frontier in Figure 2 is bowed outward, the opportunity cost of a car is highest when the economy is producing many cars and few computers, such as at point E, where the frontier is steep. When the economy is producing few cars and many computers, such as at point F, the frontier is flatter, and the opportunity cost of a car is lower.

Economists believe that production possibilities frontiers often have this bowed shape. When the economy is using most of its resources to make computers, the resources best suited to car production, such as skilled autoworkers, are being used in the computer industry. Because these workers probably aren't very good at making computers, increasing car production by one unit will cause only a slight reduction in the number of computers produced. Thus, at point F, the opportunity cost of a car in terms of computers is small, and the frontier is relatively flat. By contrast, when the economy is using most of its resources to make cars, such as at point E, the resources best suited to making cars are already at work in the car industry. Producing an additional car means moving some of the best computer technicians out of the computer industry and turning them into autoworkers. As a result, producing an additional car requires a substantial loss of computer output. The opportunity cost of a car is high, and the frontier is steep.

The production possibilities frontier shows the trade-off between the outputs of different goods at a given time, but the trade-off can change over time. For

FIGURE 3

A Shift in the Production Possibilities Frontier
A technological advance in the computer industry enables the economy to produce more computers for any given number of cars. As a result, the production possibilities frontier shifts outward. If the economy moves from point A to point G, then the production of both cars and computers increases.

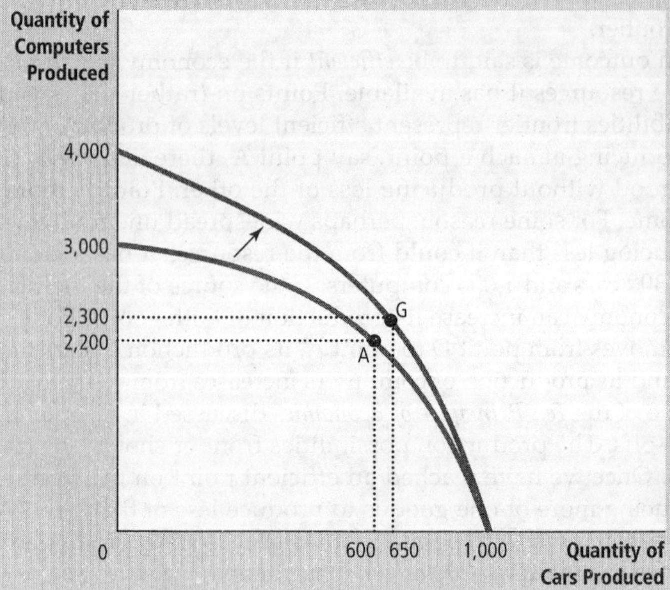

example, suppose a technological advance in the computer industry raises the number of computers that a worker can produce per week. This advance expands society's set of opportunities. For any given number of cars, the economy can now make more computers. If the economy does not produce any computers, it can still produce 1,000 cars, so one endpoint of the frontier stays the same. But if the economy devotes some of its resources to the computer industry, it will produce more computers from those resources. As a result, the production possibilities frontier shifts outward, as in Figure 3.

This figure illustrates what happens when an economy grows. Society can move production from a point on the old frontier to a point on the new frontier. Which point it chooses depends on its preferences for the two goods. In this example, society moves from point A to point G, enjoying more computers (2,300 instead of 2,200) and more cars (650 instead of 600).

The production possibilities frontier simplifies a complex economy to highlight some basic but powerful ideas: scarcity, efficiency, trade-offs, opportunity cost, and economic growth. As you study economics, these ideas will recur in various forms. The production possibilities frontier offers one simple way of thinking about them.

2-1f Microeconomics and Macroeconomics

Many subjects are studied on various levels. Consider biology, for example. Molecular biologists study the chemical compounds that make up living things. Cellular biologists study cells, which are made up of many chemical compounds and, at the same time, are themselves the building blocks of living organisms. Evolutionary biologists study the many varieties of animals and plants and how species change gradually over the centuries.

Economics is also studied on various levels. We can study the decisions of individual households and firms. Or we can study the interaction of households and firms in markets for specific goods and services. Or we can study the operation of the economy as a whole, which is the sum of the activities of all these decision makers in all these markets.

The field of economics is traditionally divided into two broad subfields. **Microeconomics** is the study of how households and firms make decisions and how they interact in specific markets. **Macroeconomics** is the study of economy-wide phenomena. A microeconomist might study the effects of rent control on housing in New York City, the impact of foreign competition on the U.S. auto industry, or the effects of compulsory school attendance on workers' earnings. A macroeconomist might study the effects of borrowing by the federal government, the changes over time in the economy's rate of unemployment, or alternative policies to promote growth in national living standards.

microeconomics
the study of how households and firms make decisions and how they interact in markets

macroeconomics
the study of economy-wide phenomena, including inflation, unemployment, and economic growth

Microeconomics and macroeconomics are closely intertwined. Because changes in the overall economy arise from the decisions of millions of individuals, it is impossible to understand macroeconomic developments without considering the associated microeconomic decisions. For example, a macroeconomist might study the effect of a federal income tax cut on the overall production of goods and services. But to analyze this issue, he must consider how the tax cut affects households' decisions about how much to spend on goods and services.

Despite the inherent link between microeconomics and macroeconomics, the two fields are distinct. Because they address different questions, each field has its own set of models, which are often taught in separate courses.

QuickQuiz *In what sense is economics like a science? • Draw a production possibilities frontier for a society that produces food and clothing. Show an efficient point, an inefficient point, and an infeasible point. Show the effects of a drought. • Define* microeconomics *and* macroeconomics.

2-2 The Economist as Policy Adviser

Often, economists are asked to explain the causes of economic events. Why, for example, is unemployment higher for teenagers than for older workers? Sometimes, economists are asked to recommend policies to improve economic outcomes. What, for instance, should the government do to improve the economic well-being of teenagers? When economists are trying to explain the world, they are scientists. When they are trying to help improve it, they are policy advisers.

2-2a Positive versus Normative Analysis

To help clarify the two roles that economists play, let's examine the use of language. Because scientists and policy advisers have different goals, they use language in different ways.

For example, suppose that two people are discussing minimum-wage laws. Here are two statements you might hear:

PORTIA: Minimum-wage laws cause unemployment.
NOAH: The government should raise the minimum wage.

Ignoring for now whether you agree with these statements, notice that Portia and Noah differ in what they are trying to do. Portia is speaking like a scientist: She is making a claim about how the world works. Noah is speaking like a policy adviser: He is making a claim about how he would like to change the world.

positive statements
claims that attempt to describe the world as it is

normative statements
claims that attempt to prescribe how the world should be

In general, statements about the world come in two types. One type, such as Portia's, is positive. **Positive statements** are descriptive. They make a claim about how the world *is*. A second type of statement, such as Noah's, is normative. **Normative statements** are prescriptive. They make a claim about how the world *ought to be*.

A key difference between positive and normative statements is how we judge their validity. We can, in principle, confirm or refute positive statements by examining evidence. An economist might evaluate Portia's statement by analyzing data on changes in minimum wages and changes in unemployment over time. By contrast, evaluating normative statements involves values as well as facts. Noah's statement cannot be judged using data alone. Deciding what is good or bad policy is not just a matter of science. It also involves our views on ethics, religion, and political philosophy.

Positive and normative statements are fundamentally different, but within a person's set of beliefs, they are often intertwined. In particular, positive views about how the world works affect normative views about what policies are desirable. Portia's claim that the minimum wage causes unemployment, if true, might lead her to reject Noah's conclusion that the government should raise the minimum wage. Yet normative conclusions cannot come from positive analysis alone; they involve value judgments as well.

As you study economics, keep in mind the distinction between positive and normative statements because it will help you stay focused on the task at hand. Much of economics is positive: It just tries to explain how the economy works. Yet those who use economics often have normative goals: They want to learn how to improve the economy. When you hear economists making normative statements, you know they are speaking not as scientists but as policy advisers.

2-2b Economists in Washington

President Harry Truman once said that he wanted to find a one-armed economist. When he asked his economists for advice, they always answered, "On the one hand, ... On the other hand, ..."

"Let's switch. I'll make the policy, you implement it, and he'll explain it."

Truman was right in realizing that economists' advice is not always straightforward. This tendency is rooted in one of the *Ten Principles of Economics*: People face trade-offs. Economists are aware that trade-offs are involved in most policy decisions. A policy might increase efficiency at the cost of equality. It might help future generations but hurt current generations. An economist who says that all policy decisions are easy or clear-cut is an economist not to be trusted.

Truman was not the only president who relied on the advice of economists. Since 1946, the president of the United States has received guidance from the Council of Economic Advisers, which consists of three members and a staff of a few dozen economists. The council, whose offices are just a few steps from the White House, has no duty other than to advise the president and to write the annual *Economic Report of the President*, which discusses recent developments in the economy and presents the council's analysis of current policy issues.

The president also receives input from economists in many administrative departments. Economists at the Office of Management and Budget help formulate spending plans and regulatory policies. Economists at the Department of the Treasury help design tax policy. Economists at the Department of Labor analyze data on workers and those looking for work to help formulate labor-market policies. Economists at the Department of Justice help enforce the nation's antitrust laws.

Economists are also found outside the administrative branch of government. To obtain independent evaluations of policy proposals, Congress relies on the advice of the Congressional Budget Office, which is staffed by economists. The Federal Reserve, the institution that sets the nation's monetary policy, employs hundreds of economists to analyze economic developments in the United States and throughout the world.

The influence of economists on policy goes beyond their role as advisers: Their research and writings often affect policy indirectly. Economist John Maynard Keynes offered this observation:

> The ideas of economists and political philosophers, both when they are right and when they are wrong, are more powerful than is commonly understood. Indeed, the world is ruled by little else. Practical men, who believe themselves to be quite exempt from intellectual influences, are usually the slaves of some defunct economist. Madmen in authority, who hear voices in the air, are distilling their frenzy from some academic scribbler of a few years back.

These words were written in 1935, but they remain true today. Indeed, the "academic scribbler" now influencing public policy is often Keynes himself.

2-2c Why Economists' Advice Is Not Always Followed

Any economist who advises presidents or other elected leaders knows that his recommendations are not always heeded. Frustrating as this can be, it is easy to understand. The process by which economic policy is actually made differs in many ways from the idealized policy process assumed in economics textbooks.

Throughout this text, whenever we discuss economic policy, we often focus on one question: What is the best policy for the government to pursue? We act as if policy were set by a benevolent king. Once the king figures out the right policy, he has no trouble putting his ideas into action.

In the real world, figuring out the right policy is only part of a leader's job, sometimes the easiest part. After a president hears from his economic advisers about what policy is best from their perspective, he turns to other advisers for related input. His communications advisers will tell him how best to explain the proposed policy to the public, and they will try to anticipate any misunderstandings that might make the challenge more difficult. His press advisers will tell him how the news media will report on his proposal and what opinions will likely be expressed on the nation's editorial pages. His legislative affairs advisers will tell him how Congress will view the proposal, what amendments members of Congress will suggest, and the likelihood that Congress will pass some version of the president's proposal into law. His political advisers will tell him which groups will organize to support or oppose the proposed policy, how this proposal will affect his standing among different groups in the electorate, and whether it will change support for any of the president's other policy initiatives. After hearing and weighing all this advice, the president then decides how to proceed.

Making economic policy in a representative democracy is a messy affair—and there are often good reasons why presidents (and other politicians) do not advance the policies that economists advocate. Economists offer crucial input to the policy process, but their advice is only one ingredient of a complex recipe.

QuickQuiz *Give an example of a positive statement and an example of a normative statement that somehow relates to your daily life. • Name three parts of government that regularly rely on advice from economists.*

2-3 Why Economists Disagree

"If all economists were laid end to end, they would not reach a conclusion." This quip from George Bernard Shaw is revealing. Economists as a group are often criticized for giving conflicting advice to policymakers. President Ronald Reagan once joked that if the game Trivial Pursuit were designed for economists, it would have 100 questions and 3,000 answers.

Why do economists so often appear to give conflicting advice to policymakers? There are two basic reasons:

- Economists may disagree about the validity of alternative positive theories of how the world works.
- Economists may have different values and therefore different normative views about what government policy should aim to accomplish.

Let's discuss each of these reasons.

2-3a Differences in Scientific Judgments

Several centuries ago, astronomers debated whether the earth or the sun was at the center of the solar system. More recently, climatologists have debated whether the earth is experiencing global warming and, if so, why. Science is an ongoing search to understand the world around us. It is not surprising that as the search continues, scientists sometimes disagree about the direction in which truth lies.

Economists often disagree for the same reason. Economics is a young science, and there is still much to be learned. Economists sometimes disagree because they have different hunches about the validity of alternative theories or about the size of important parameters that measure how economic variables are related.

For example, economists disagree about whether the government should tax a household's income or its consumption (spending). Advocates of a switch from the current income tax to a consumption tax believe that the change would encourage households to save more because income that is saved would not be taxed. Higher saving, in turn, would free resources for capital accumulation, leading to more rapid growth in productivity and living standards. Advocates of the current income tax system believe that household saving would not respond much to a change in the tax laws. These two groups of economists hold different normative views about the tax system because they have different positive views about saving's responsiveness to tax incentives.

2-3b Differences in Values

Suppose that Peter and Paula both take the same amount of water from the town well. To pay for maintaining the well, the town taxes its residents. Peter has income of $150,000 and is taxed $15,000, or 10 percent of his income. Paula has income of $30,000 and is taxed $6,000, or 20 percent of her income.

Is this policy fair? If not, who pays too much and who pays too little? Does it matter whether Paula's low income is due to a medical disability or to her decision to pursue an acting career? Does it matter whether Peter's high income is due to a large inheritance or to his willingness to work long hours at a dreary job?

These are difficult questions about which people are likely to disagree. If the town hired two experts to study how it should tax its residents to pay for the well, we would not be surprised if they offered conflicting advice.

This simple example shows why economists sometimes disagree about public policy. As we know from our discussion of normative and positive analysis, policies cannot be judged on scientific grounds alone. Sometimes, economists give conflicting advice because they have different values. Perfecting the science of economics will not tell us whether Peter or Paula pays too much.

2-3c Perception versus Reality

Because of differences in scientific judgments and differences in values, some disagreement among economists is inevitable. Yet one should not overstate the amount of disagreement. Economists agree with one another to a much greater extent than is sometimes understood.

Table 1 contains twenty propositions about economic policy. In surveys of professional economists, these propositions were endorsed by an overwhelming

TABLE 1

Propositions about Which Most Economists Agree

Proposition (and percentage of economists who agree)

1. A ceiling on rents reduces the quantity and quality of housing available. (93%)
2. Tariffs and import quotas usually reduce general economic welfare. (93%)
3. Flexible and floating exchange rates offer an effective international monetary arrangement. (90%)
4. Fiscal policy (for example, tax cut and/or government expenditure increase) has a significant stimulative impact on a less than fully employed economy. (90%)
5. The United States should not restrict employers from outsourcing work to foreign countries. (90%)
6. Economic growth in developed countries like the United States leads to greater levels of well-being. (88%)
7. The United States should eliminate agricultural subsidies. (85%)
8. An appropriately designed fiscal policy can increase the long-run rate of capital formation. (85%)
9. Local and state governments should eliminate subsidies to professional sports franchises. (85%)
10. If the federal budget is to be balanced, it should be done over the business cycle rather than yearly. (85%)
11. The gap between Social Security funds and expenditures will become unsustainably large within the next 50 years if current policies remain unchanged. (85%)
12. Cash payments increase the welfare of recipients to a greater degree than do transfers-in-kind of equal cash value. (84%)
13. A large federal budget deficit has an adverse effect on the economy. (83%)
14. The redistribution of income in the United States is a legitimate role for the government. (83%)
15. Inflation is caused primarily by too much growth in the money supply. (83%)
16. The United States should not ban genetically modified crops. (82%)
17. A minimum wage increases unemployment among young and unskilled workers. (79%)
18. The government should restructure the welfare system along the lines of a "negative income tax." (79%)
19. Effluent taxes and marketable pollution permits represent a better approach to pollution control than the imposition of pollution ceilings. (78%)
20. Government subsidies on ethanol in the United States should be reduced or eliminated. (78%)

Source: Richard M. Alston, J. R. Kearl, and Michael B. Vaughn, "Is There Consensus among Economists in the 1990s?" *American Economic Review* (May 1992): 203–209; Dan Fuller and Doris Geide-Stevenson, "Consensus among Economists Revisited," *Journal of Economics Education* (Fall 2003): 369–387; Robert Whaples, "Do Economists Agree on Anything? Yes!" *Economists' Voice* (November 2006): 1–6; Robert Whaples, "The Policy Views of American Economic Association Members: The Results of a New Survey," *Econ Journal Watch* (September 2009): 337–348.

majority of respondents. Most of these propositions would fail to command a similar consensus among the public.

The first proposition in the table is about rent control, a policy that sets a legal maximum on the amount landlords can charge for their apartments. Almost all economists believe that rent control adversely affects the availability and quality of housing and is a costly way of helping the neediest members of society. Nonetheless, many city governments ignore the advice of economists and place ceilings on the rents that landlords may charge their tenants.

The second proposition in the table concerns tariffs and import quotas, two policies that restrict trade among nations. For reasons we discuss more fully later in this text, almost all economists oppose such barriers to free trade. Nonetheless, over the years, presidents and Congress have chosen to restrict the import of certain goods.

Why do policies such as rent control and trade barriers persist if the experts are united in their opposition? It may be that the realities of the political process stand as immovable obstacles. But it also may be that economists have not yet convinced enough of the public that these policies are undesirable. One purpose of this book is to help you understand the economist's view on these and other subjects and, perhaps, to persuade you that it is the right one.

ASK THE EXPERTS

Ticket Resale

"Laws that limit the resale of tickets for entertainment and sports events make potential audience members for those events worse off on average."

What do economists say?

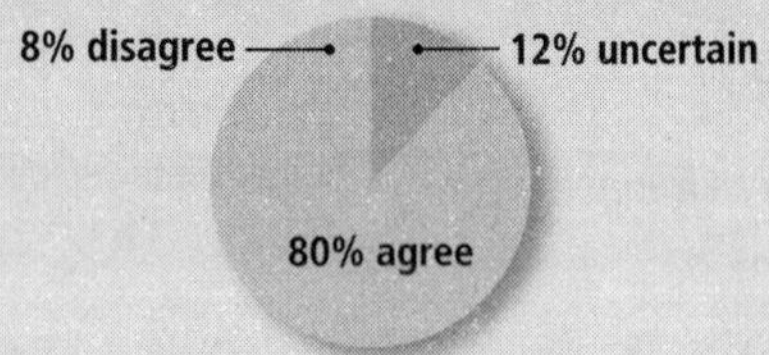

Source: IGM Economic Experts Panel, April 16, 2012.

As you read the book, you will occasionally see small boxes called "Ask the Experts." These are based on the IGM Economics Experts Panel, an ongoing survey of several dozen of the world's most prominent economists. Every few weeks, these experts are offered a proposition and then asked whether they agree with it, disagree with it, or are uncertain. The results in these boxes will give you a sense of when economists are united, when they are divided, and when they just don't know what to think.

You can see an example here regarding the resale of tickets to entertainment and sporting events. Lawmakers sometimes try to prohibit reselling tickets, or "scalping" as it is sometimes called. The survey results show that many economists side with the scalpers rather than the lawmakers.

QuickQuiz *Why might economic advisers to the president disagree about a question of policy?*

2-4 Let's Get Going

The first two chapters of this book have introduced you to the ideas and methods of economics. We are now ready to get to work. In the next chapter, we start learning in more detail the principles of economic behavior and economic policy.

As you proceed through this book, you will be asked to draw on many of your intellectual skills. You might find it helpful to keep in mind some advice from the great economist John Maynard Keynes:

> The study of economics does not seem to require any specialized gifts of an unusually high order. Is it not . . . a very easy subject compared with the higher branches of philosophy or pure science? An easy subject, at which very few excel! The paradox finds its explanation, perhaps, in that the master-economist must possess a rare *combination* of gifts. He must be mathematician, historian, statesman, philosopher—in some degree. He must understand symbols and speak in words. He must contemplate the particular in terms of the general, and touch abstract and concrete in the same flight of thought. He must study the present in the light of the past for the purposes of the future. No part of man's nature or his institutions must lie entirely outside his regard. He must be purposeful and disinterested in a simultaneous mood; as aloof and incorruptible as an artist, yet sometimes as near the earth as a politician.

This is a tall order. But with practice, you will become more and more accustomed to thinking like an economist.

Chapter QuickQuiz

1. An economic model is
   a. a mechanical machine that replicates the functioning of the economy.
   b. a fully detailed, realistic description of the economy.
   c. a simplified representation of some aspect of the economy.
   d. a computer program that predicts the future of the economy.
2. The circular-flow diagram illustrates that, in markets for the factors of production,
   a. households are sellers, and firms are buyers.
   b. households are buyers, and firms are sellers.
   c. households and firms are both buyers.
   d. households and firms are both sellers.
3. A point inside the production possibilities frontier is
   a. efficient but not feasible.
   b. feasible but not efficient.
   c. both efficient and feasible.
   d. neither efficient nor feasible.
4. An economy produces hot dogs and hamburgers. If a discovery of the remarkable health benefits of hot dogs were to change consumers' preferences, it would
   a. expand the production possibilities frontier.
   b. contract the production possibilities frontier.
   c. move the economy along the production possibilities frontier.
   d. move the economy inside the production possibilities frontier.
5. All of the following topics fall within the study of microeconomics EXCEPT
   a. the impact of cigarette taxes on the smoking behavior of teenagers.
   b. the role of Microsoft's market power in the pricing of software.
   c. the effectiveness of antipoverty programs in reducing homelessness.
   d. the influence of the government budget deficit on economic growth.
6. Which of the following is a positive, rather than a normative, statement?
   a. Law X will reduce national income.
   b. Law X is a good piece of legislation.
   c. Congress ought to pass law X.
   d. The president should veto law X.

SUMMARY

- Economists try to address their subject with a scientist's objectivity. Like all scientists, they make appropriate assumptions and build simplified models to understand the world around them. Two simple economic models are the circular-flow diagram and the production possibilities frontier.
- The field of economics is divided into two subfields: microeconomics and macroeconomics. Microeconomists study decision making by households and firms and the interactions among households and firms in the marketplace. Macroeconomists study the forces and trends that affect the economy as a whole.
- A positive statement is an assertion about how the world *is*. A normative statement is an assertion about how the world *ought to be*. When economists make normative statements, they are acting more as policy advisers than as scientists.
- Economists who advise policymakers sometimes offer conflicting advice either because of differences in scientific judgments or because of differences in values. At other times, economists are united in the advice they offer, but policymakers may choose to ignore the advice because of the many forces and constraints imposed by the political process.

KEY CONCEPTS

circular-flow diagram, p. 22
production possibilities frontier, p. 24
microeconomics, p. 27
macroeconomics, p. 27
positive statements, p. 28
normative statements, p. 28

QUESTIONS FOR REVIEW

1. In what ways is economics a science?
2. Why do economists make assumptions?
3. Should an economic model describe reality exactly?
4. Name a way that your family interacts in the factor market and a way that it interacts in the product market.
5. Name one economic interaction that isn't covered by the simplified circular-flow diagram.
6. Draw and explain a production possibilities frontier for an economy that produces milk and cookies. What happens to this frontier if a disease kills half of the economy's cows?
7. Use a production possibilities frontier to describe the idea of "efficiency."
8. What are the two subfields into which economics is divided? Explain what each subfield studies.
9. What is the difference between a positive and a normative statement? Give an example of each.
10. Why do economists sometimes offer conflicting advice to policymakers?

PROBLEMS AND APPLICATIONS

1. Draw a circular-flow diagram. Identify the parts of the model that correspond to the flow of goods and services and the flow of dollars for each of the following activities.
   a. Selena pays a storekeeper $1 for a quart of milk.
   b. Stuart earns $8 per hour working at a fast-food restaurant.
   c. Shanna spends $40 to get a haircut.
   d. Salma earns $20,000 from her 10 percent ownership of Acme Industrial.
2. Imagine a society that produces military goods and consumer goods, which we'll call "guns" and "butter."
   a. Draw a production possibilities frontier for guns and butter. Using the concept of opportunity cost, explain why it most likely has a bowed-out shape.
   b. Show a point that is impossible for the economy to achieve. Show a point that is feasible but inefficient.
   c. Imagine that the society has two political parties, called the Hawks (who want a strong military) and the Doves (who want a smaller military). Show a point on your production possibilities frontier that the Hawks might choose and a point that the Doves might choose.
   d. Imagine that an aggressive neighboring country reduces the size of its military. As a result, both the Hawks and the Doves reduce their desired production of guns by the same amount. Which party would get the bigger "peace dividend," measured by the increase in butter production? Explain.
3. The first principle of economics discussed in Chapter 1 is that people face trade-offs. Use a production possibilities frontier to illustrate society's trade-off between two "goods"—a clean environment and the quantity of industrial output. What do you suppose determines the shape and position of the frontier? Show what happens to the frontier if engineers develop a new way of producing electricity that emits fewer pollutants.
4. An economy consists of three workers: Larry, Moe, and Curly. Each works 10 hours a day and can produce two services: mowing lawns and washing cars. In an hour, Larry can either mow one lawn or wash one car; Moe can either mow one lawn or wash two cars; and Curly can either mow two lawns or wash one car.
   a. Calculate how much of each service is produced under the following circumstances, which we label A, B, C, and D:
      - All three spend all their time mowing lawns. (A)
      - All three spend all their time washing cars. (B)
      - All three spend half their time on each activity. (C)
      - Larry spends half his time on each activity, while Moe only washes cars and Curly only mows lawns. (D)
   b. Graph the production possibilities frontier for this economy. Using your answers to part *a*, identify points A, B, C, and D on your graph.
   c. Explain why the production possibilities frontier has the shape it does.
   d. Are any of the allocations calculated in part *a* inefficient? Explain.
5. Classify the following topics as relating to microeconomics or macroeconomics.
   a. a family's decision about how much income to save
   b. the effect of government regulations on auto emissions
   c. the impact of higher national saving on economic growth
   d. a firm's decision about how many workers to hire
   e. the relationship between the inflation rate and changes in the quantity of money
6. Classify each of the following statements as positive or normative. Explain.
   a. Society faces a short-run trade-off between inflation and unemployment.
   b. A reduction in the rate of money growth will reduce the rate of inflation.
   c. The Federal Reserve should reduce the rate of money growth.
   d. Society ought to require welfare recipients to look for jobs.
   e. Lower tax rates encourage more work and more saving.

To find additional study resources, visit cengagebrain.com, and search for "Mankiw."

Appendix

Graphing: A Brief Review

Many of the concepts that economists study can be expressed with numbers—the price of bananas, the quantity of bananas sold, the cost of growing bananas, and so on. Often, these economic variables are related to one another: When the price of bananas rises, people buy fewer bananas. One way of expressing the relationships among variables is with graphs.

Graphs serve two purposes. First, when developing economic theories, graphs offer a visual way to express ideas that might be less clear if described with equations or words. Second, when analyzing economic data, graphs provide a powerful way of finding and interpreting patterns. Whether we are working with theory or with data, graphs provide a lens through which a recognizable forest emerges from a multitude of trees.

Numerical information can be expressed graphically in many ways, just as there are many ways to express a thought in words. A good writer chooses words that will make an argument clear, a description pleasing, or a scene dramatic. An effective economist chooses the type of graph that best suits the purpose at hand.

In this appendix, we discuss how economists use graphs to study the mathematical relationships among variables. We also discuss some of the pitfalls that can arise in the use of graphical methods.

Graphs of a Single Variable

Three common graphs are shown in Figure A-1. The *pie chart* in panel (a) shows how total income in the United States is divided among the sources of income, including compensation of employees, corporate profits, and so on. A slice of the pie represents each source's share of the total. The *bar graph* in panel (b) compares income in four countries. The height of each bar represents the average income in each country. The *time-series graph* in panel (c) traces the rising productivity in the U.S. business sector over time. The height of the line shows output per hour in each year. You have probably seen similar graphs in newspapers and magazines.

Graphs of Two Variables: The Coordinate System

The three graphs in Figure A-1 are useful in showing how a variable changes over time or across individuals, but they are limited in how much they can tell us. These graphs display information only about a single variable. Economists are often concerned with the relationships between variables. Thus, they need to display two variables on a single graph. The *coordinate system* makes this possible.

Suppose you want to examine the relationship between study time and grade point average. For each student in your class, you could record a pair of numbers: hours per week spent studying and grade point average. These numbers could then be placed in parentheses as an *ordered pair* and appear as a single point on the graph. Albert E., for instance, is represented by the ordered pair (25 hours/week, 3.5 GPA),

FIGURE A-1

Types of Graphs

The pie chart in panel (a) shows how U.S. national income is derived from various sources. The bar graph in panel (b) compares the average income in four countries. The time-series graph in panel (c) shows the productivity of labor in U.S. businesses over time.

(a) Pie Chart **(b) Bar Graph** **(c) Time-Series Graph**

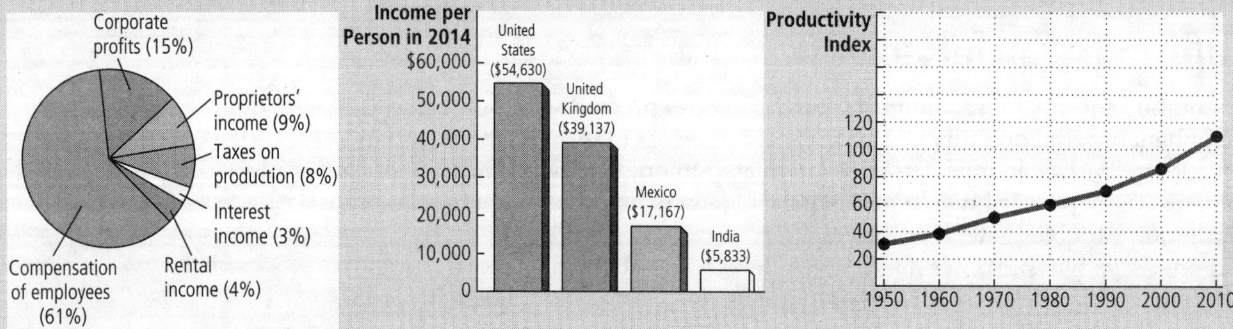

while his "what-me-worry?" classmate Alfred E. is represented by the ordered pair (5 hours/week, 2.0 GPA).

We can graph these ordered pairs on a two-dimensional grid. The first number in each ordered pair, called the *x-coordinate*, tells us the horizontal location of the point. The second number, called the *y-coordinate*, tells us the vertical location of the point. The point with both an x-coordinate and a y-coordinate of zero is known as the *origin*. The two coordinates in the ordered pair tell us where the point is located in relation to the origin: x units to the right of the origin and y units above it.

Figure A-2 graphs grade point average against study time for Albert E., Alfred E., and their classmates. This type of graph is called a *scatter plot* because it plots

FIGURE A-2

Using the Coordinate System

Grade point average is measured on the vertical axis and study time on the horizontal axis. Albert E., Alfred E., and their classmates are represented by various points. We can see from the graph that students who study more tend to get higher grades.

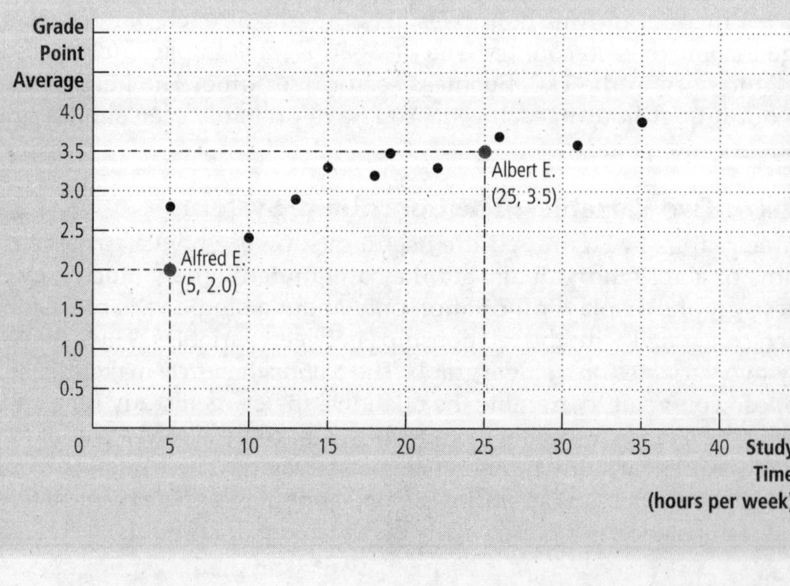

scattered points. Looking at this graph, we immediately notice that points farther to the right (indicating more study time) also tend to be higher (indicating a better grade point average). Because study time and grade point average typically move in the same direction, we say that these two variables have a *positive correlation*. By contrast, if we were to graph party time and grades, we would likely find that higher party time is associated with lower grades. Because these variables typically move in opposite directions, we say that they have a *negative correlation*. In either case, the coordinate system makes the correlation between two variables easy to see.

Curves in the Coordinate System

Students who study more do tend to get higher grades, but other factors also influence a student's grades. Previous preparation is an important factor, for instance, as are talent, attention from teachers, even eating a good breakfast. A scatter plot like Figure A-2 does not attempt to isolate the effect that studying has on grades from the effects of other variables. Often, however, economists prefer looking at how one variable affects another, holding everything else constant.

To see how this is done, let's consider one of the most important graphs in economics: the *demand curve*. The demand curve traces out the effect of a good's price on the quantity of the good consumers want to buy. Before showing a demand curve, however, consider Table A-1, which shows how the number of novels that Emma buys depends on her income and on the price of novels. When novels are cheap, Emma buys them in large quantities. As they become more expensive, she instead borrows books from the library or chooses to go to the movies rather than read. Similarly, at any given price, Emma buys more novels when she has a higher income. That is, when her income increases, she spends part of the additional income on novels and part on other goods.

We now have three variables—the price of novels, income, and the number of novels purchased—which is more than we can represent in two dimensions. To put the information from Table A-1 in graphical form, we need to hold one of the three variables constant and trace out the relationship between the other two. Because the demand curve represents the relationship between price and quantity demanded, we hold Emma's income constant and show how the number of novels she buys varies with the price of novels.

Price	For $30,000 Income:	For $40,000 Income:	For $50,000 Income:
$10	2 novels	5 novels	8 novels
9	6	9	12
8	10	13	16
7	14	17	20
6	18	21	24
5	22	25	28
	Demand curve, D_3	Demand curve, D_1	Demand curve, D_2

TABLE A-1

Novels Purchased by Emma

This table shows the number of novels Emma buys at various incomes and prices. For any given level of income, the data on price and quantity demanded can be graphed to produce Emma's demand curve for novels, as shown in Figures A-3 and A-4.

FIGURE A-3

Demand Curve

The line D_1 shows how Emma's purchases of novels depend on the price of novels when her income is held constant. Because the price and the quantity demanded are negatively related, the demand curve slopes downward.

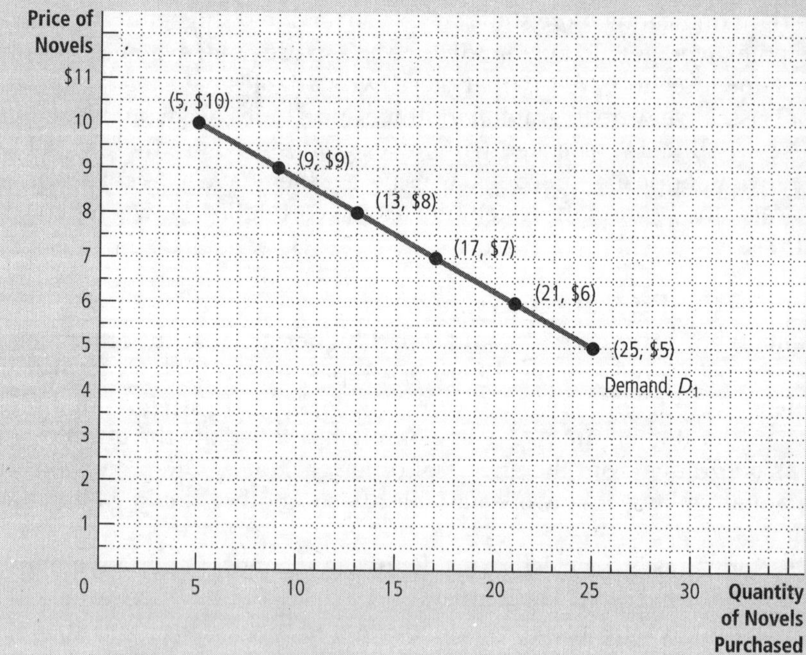

Suppose that Emma's income is $40,000 per year. If we place the number of novels Emma purchases on the *x*-axis and the price of novels on the *y*-axis, we can graphically represent the middle column of Table A-1. When the points that represent these entries from the table—(5 novels, $10), (9 novels, $9), and so on—are connected, they form a line. This line, pictured in Figure A-3, is known as Emma's demand curve for novels; it tells us how many novels Emma purchases at any given price, holding income constant. The demand curve is downward-sloping, indicating that a higher price reduces the quantity of novels demanded. Because the quantity of novels demanded and the price move in opposite directions, we say that the two variables are *negatively related*. (Conversely, when two variables move in the same direction, the curve relating them is upward-sloping, and we say that the variables are *positively related*.)

Now suppose that Emma's income rises to $50,000 per year. At any given price, Emma will purchase more novels than she did at her previous level of income. Just as earlier we drew Emma's demand curve for novels using the entries from the middle column of Table A-1, we now draw a new demand curve using the entries from the right column of the table. This new demand curve (curve D_2) is pictured alongside the old one (curve D_1) in Figure A-4; the new curve is a similar line drawn farther to the right. We therefore say that Emma's demand curve for novels *shifts* to the right when her income increases. Likewise, if Emma's income were to fall to $30,000 per year, she would buy fewer novels at any given price and her demand curve would shift to the left (to curve D_3).

In economics, it is important to distinguish between *movements along a curve* and *shifts of a curve*. As we can see from Figure A-3, if Emma earns $40,000 per year and novels cost $8 apiece, she will purchase 13 novels per year. If the price of

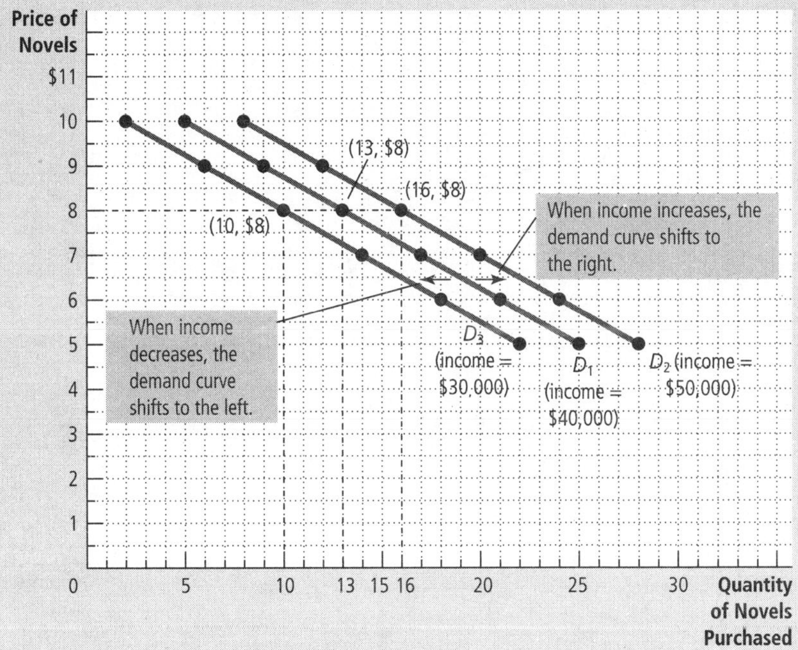

FIGURE A-4

Shifting Demand Curves

The location of Emma's demand curve for novels depends on how much income she earns. The more she earns, the more novels she will purchase at any given price, and the farther to the right her demand curve will lie. Curve D_1 represents Emma's original demand curve when her income is $40,000 per year. If her income rises to $50,000 per year, her demand curve shifts to D_2. If her income falls to $30,000 per year, her demand curve shifts to D_3.

novels falls to $7, Emma will increase her purchases of novels to 17 per year. The demand curve, however, stays fixed in the same place. Emma still buys the same number of novels *at each price*, but as the price falls, she moves along her demand curve from left to right. By contrast, if the price of novels remains fixed at $8 but her income rises to $50,000, Emma increases her purchases of novels from 13 to 16 per year. Because Emma buys more novels *at each price*, her demand curve shifts out, as shown in Figure A-4.

There is a simple way to tell when it is necessary to shift a curve: *When a relevant variable that is not named on either axis changes, the curve shifts*. Income is on neither the *x*-axis nor the *y*-axis of the graph, so when Emma's income changes, her demand curve must shift. The same is true for any change that affects Emma's purchasing habits, with the sole exception of a change in the price of novels. If, for instance, the public library closes and Emma must buy all the books she wants to read, she will demand more novels at each price, and her demand curve will shift to the right. Or if the price of movies falls and Emma spends more time at the movies and less time reading, she will demand fewer novels at each price, and her demand curve will shift to the left. By contrast, when a variable on an axis of the graph changes, the curve does not shift. We read the change as a movement along the curve.

Slope

One question we might want to ask about Emma is how much her purchasing habits respond to price. Look at the demand curve pictured in Figure A-5. If this curve is very steep, Emma purchases nearly the same number of novels regardless

FIGURE A-5

Calculating the Slope of a Line

To calculate the slope of the demand curve, we can look at the changes in the *x*- and *y*-coordinates as we move from the point (21 novels, \$6) to the point (13 novels, \$8). The slope of the line is the ratio of the change in the *y*-coordinate (–2) to the change in the *x*-coordinate (+8), which equals –¼.

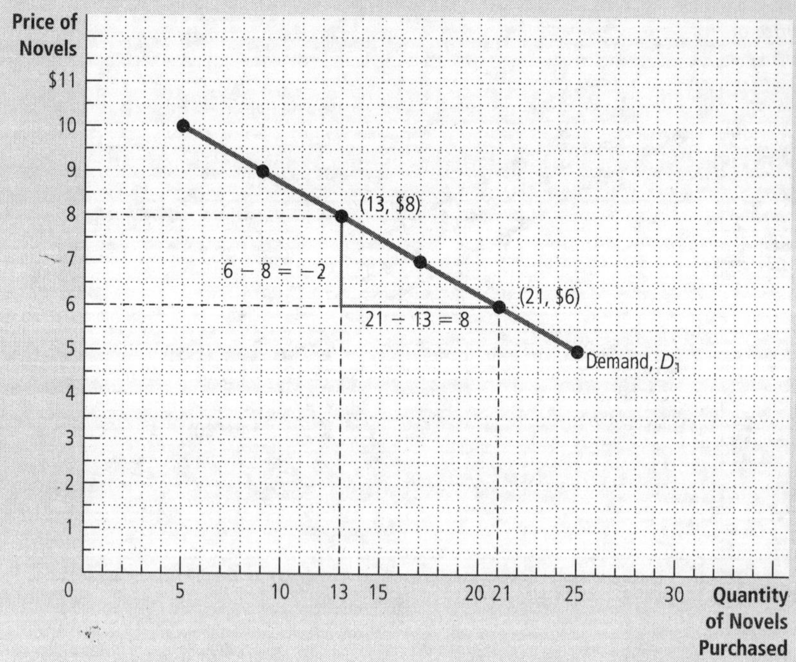

of whether they are cheap or expensive. If this curve is much flatter, the number of novels Emma purchases is more sensitive to changes in the price. To answer questions about how much one variable responds to changes in another variable, we can use the concept of *slope*.

The slope of a line is the ratio of the vertical distance covered to the horizontal distance covered as we move along the line. This definition is usually written out in mathematical symbols as follows:

$$\text{slope} = \frac{\Delta y}{\Delta x},$$

where the Greek letter Δ (delta) stands for the change in a variable. In other words, the slope of a line is equal to the "rise" (change in y) divided by the "run" (change in x). The slope will be a small positive number for a fairly flat upward-sloping line, a large positive number for a steep upward-sloping line, and a negative number for a downward-sloping line. A horizontal line has a slope of zero because in this case the y-variable never changes; a vertical line is said to have an infinite slope because the y-variable can take any value without the x-variable changing at all.

What is the slope of Emma's demand curve for novels? First of all, because the curve slopes down, we know the slope will be negative. To calculate a numerical value for the slope, we must choose two points on the line. With Emma's income at \$40,000, she will purchase 21 novels at a price of \$6 or 13 novels at a price of \$8. When we apply the slope formula, we are concerned with the change between these two points. In other words, we are concerned with the difference between them, which lets us know that we will have to subtract one set of values from the other, as follows:

$$\text{slope} = \frac{\Delta y}{\Delta x} = \frac{\text{first } y\text{-coordinate} - \text{second } y\text{-coordinate}}{\text{first } x\text{-coordinate} - \text{second } x\text{-coordinate}} = \frac{6-8}{21-13} = \frac{-2}{8} = \frac{-1}{4}$$

Figure A-5 shows graphically how this calculation works. Try computing the slope of Emma's demand curve using two different points. You should get exactly the same result, –¼. One of the properties of a straight line is that it has the same slope everywhere. This is not true of other types of curves, which are steeper in some places than in others.

The slope of Emma's demand curve tells us something about how responsive her purchases are to changes in the price. A small slope (a number close to zero) means that Emma's demand curve is relatively flat; in this case, she adjusts the number of novels she buys substantially in response to a price change. A larger slope (a number farther from zero) means that Emma's demand curve is relatively steep; in this case, she adjusts the number of novels she buys only slightly in response to a price change.

Cause and Effect

Economists often use graphs to advance an argument about how the economy works. In other words, they use graphs to argue about how one set of events *causes* another set of events. With a graph like the demand curve, there is no doubt about cause and effect. Because we are varying price and holding all other variables constant, we know that changes in the price of novels cause changes in the quantity Emma demands. Remember, however, that our demand curve came from a hypothetical example. When graphing data from the real world, it is often more difficult to establish how one variable affects another.

The first problem is that it is difficult to hold everything else constant when studying the relationship between two variables. If we are not able to hold other variables constant, we might decide that one variable on our graph is causing changes in the other variable when those changes are actually being caused by a third *omitted variable* not pictured on the graph. Even if we have identified the correct two variables to look at, we might run into a second problem—*reverse causality*. In other words, we might decide that A causes B when in fact B causes A. The omitted-variable and reverse-causality traps require us to proceed with caution when using graphs to draw conclusions about causes and effects.

Omitted Variables To see how omitting a variable can lead to a deceptive graph, let's consider an example. Imagine that the government, spurred by public

COURTESY OF RANDALL MUNROE/XKCD.COM

FIGURE A-6

Graph with an Omitted Variable

The upward-sloping curve shows that members of households with more cigarette lighters are more likely to develop cancer. Yet we should not conclude that ownership of lighters causes cancer because the graph does not take into account the number of cigarettes smoked.

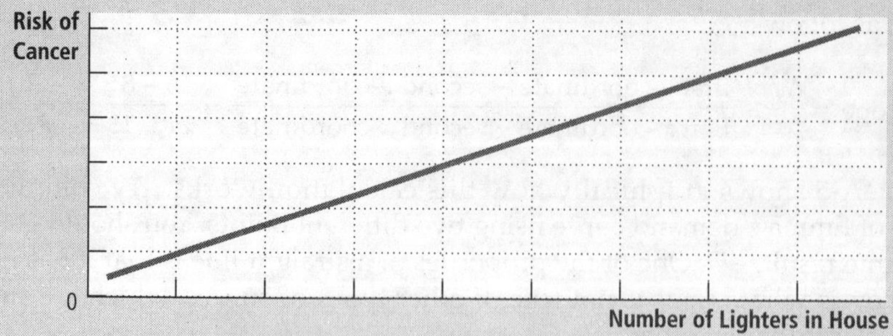

concern about the large number of deaths from cancer, commissions an exhaustive study from Big Brother Statistical Services, Inc. Big Brother examines many of the items found in people's homes to see which of them are associated with the risk of cancer. Big Brother reports a strong relationship between two variables: the number of cigarette lighters that a household owns and the probability that someone in the household will develop cancer. Figure A-6 shows this relationship.

What should we make of this result? Big Brother advises a quick policy response. It recommends that the government discourage the ownership of cigarette lighters by taxing their sale. It also recommends that the government require warning labels: "Big Brother has determined that this lighter is dangerous to your health."

In judging the validity of Big Brother's analysis, one question is key: Has Big Brother held constant every relevant variable except the one under consideration? If the answer is no, the results are suspect. An easy explanation for Figure A-6 is that people who own more cigarette lighters are more likely to smoke cigarettes and that cigarettes, not lighters, cause cancer. If Figure A-6 does not hold constant the amount of smoking, it does not tell us the true effect of owning a cigarette lighter.

This story illustrates an important principle: When you see a graph used to support an argument about cause and effect, it is important to ask whether the movements of an omitted variable could explain the results you see.

Reverse Causality Economists can also make mistakes about causality by misreading its direction. To see how this is possible, suppose the Association of American Anarchists commissions a study of crime in America and arrives at Figure A-7, which plots the number of violent crimes per thousand people in major cities against the number of police officers per thousand people. The anarchists note the curve's upward slope and argue that because police increase rather than decrease the amount of urban violence, law enforcement should be abolished.

If we could run a controlled experiment, we would avoid the danger of reverse causality. To run an experiment, we would randomly assign different numbers of police to different cities and then examine the correlation between police and crime. Figure A-7, however, is not based on such an experiment. We simply

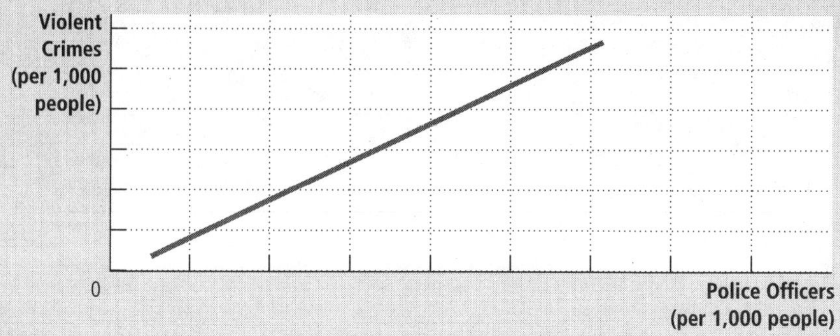

FIGURE A-7

Graph Suggesting Reverse Causality

The upward-sloping curve shows that cities with a higher concentration of police are more dangerous. Yet the graph does not tell us whether police cause crime or crime-plagued cities hire more police.

observe that more dangerous cities have more police officers. The explanation for this may be that more dangerous cities hire more police. In other words, rather than police causing crime, crime may cause police. Nothing in the graph itself allows us to establish the direction of causality.

It might seem that an easy way to determine the direction of causality is to examine which variable moves first. If we see crime increase and then the police force expand, we reach one conclusion. If we see the police force expand and then crime increase, we reach the other. This approach, however, is also flawed: Often, people change their behavior not in response to a change in their present conditions but in response to a change in their *expectations* of future conditions. A city that expects a major crime wave in the future, for instance, might hire more police now. This problem is even easier to see in the case of babies and minivans. Couples often buy a minivan in anticipation of the birth of a child. The minivan comes before the baby, but we wouldn't want to conclude that the sale of minivans causes the population to grow!

There is no complete set of rules that says when it is appropriate to draw causal conclusions from graphs. Yet just keeping in mind that cigarette lighters don't cause cancer (omitted variable) and that minivans don't cause larger families (reverse causality) will keep you from falling for many faulty economic arguments.

Interdependence and the Gains from Trade

CHAPTER 3

Consider your typical day. You wake up in the morning and pour yourself juice from oranges grown in Florida and coffee from beans grown in Brazil. Over breakfast, you read a newspaper written in New York on a tablet made in China. You get dressed in clothes made of cotton grown in Georgia and sewn in factories in Thailand. You drive to class in a car made of parts manufactured in more than a dozen countries around the world. Then you open up your economics textbook written by an author living in Massachusetts, published by a company located in Ohio, and printed on paper made from trees grown in Oregon.

Every day, you rely on many people, most of whom you have never met, to provide you with the goods and services that you enjoy. Such interdependence is possible because people trade with one another. Those people providing you with goods and services are not acting out of generosity. Nor is some government agency directing them to satisfy your desires. Instead, people provide you and other consumers with the goods and services they produce because they get something in return.

In subsequent chapters, we examine how an economy coordinates the activities of millions of people with varying tastes and abilities. As a starting point for this analysis, in this chapter we consider the reasons for economic interdependence. One of the *Ten Principles of Economics* highlighted in Chapter 1 is that trade can make everyone better off. We now examine this principle more closely. What exactly do people gain when they trade with one another? Why do people choose to become interdependent?

The answers to these questions are key to understanding the modern global economy. Most countries today import from abroad many of the goods and services they consume, and they export to foreign customers many of the goods and services they produce. The analysis in this chapter explains interdependence not only among individuals but also among nations. As we will see, the gains from trade are much the same whether you are buying a haircut from your local barber or a T-shirt made by a worker on the other side of the globe.

3-1 A Parable for the Modern Economy

To understand why people choose to depend on others for goods and services and how this choice improves their lives, let's examine a simple economy. Imagine that there are only two goods in the world: meat and potatoes. And there are only two people in the world: a cattle rancher named Ruby and a potato farmer named Frank. Both Ruby and Frank would like to eat a diet of both meat and potatoes.

The gains from trade are most obvious if Ruby can produce only meat and Frank can produce only potatoes. In one scenario, Frank and Ruby could choose to have nothing to do with each other. But after several months of eating beef roasted, boiled, broiled, and grilled, Ruby might decide that self-sufficiency is not all it's cracked up to be. Frank, who has been eating potatoes mashed, fried, baked, and scalloped, would likely agree. It is easy to see that trade would allow both of them to enjoy greater variety: Each could then have a steak with a baked potato or a burger with fries.

Although this scene illustrates most simply how everyone can benefit from trade, the gains would be similar if Frank and Ruby were each capable of producing the other good, but only at great cost. Suppose, for example, that Ruby is able to grow potatoes but her land is not very well suited for it. Similarly, suppose that Frank is able to raise cattle and produce meat but is not very good at it. In this case, Frank and Ruby can each benefit by specializing in what he or she does best and then trading with the other person.

The gains from trade are less obvious, however, when one person is better at producing *every* good. For example, suppose that Ruby is better at raising cattle *and* better at growing potatoes than Frank. In this case, should Ruby choose to remain self-sufficient? Or is there still reason for her to trade with Frank? To answer this question, we need to look more closely at the factors that affect such a decision.

3-1a Production Possibilities

Suppose that Frank and Ruby each work 8 hours per day and can devote this time to growing potatoes, raising cattle, or a combination of the two. The table in Figure 1 shows the amount of time each person requires to produce 1 ounce of each good. Frank can produce an ounce of potatoes in 15 minutes and an ounce of meat in 60 minutes. Ruby, who is more productive in both activities, can produce an ounce of potatoes in 10 minutes and an ounce of meat in 20 minutes. The last two columns in the table show the amounts of meat or potatoes Frank and Ruby can produce if they devote all 8 hours to producing only that good.

Panel (b) of Figure 1 illustrates the amounts of meat and potatoes that Frank can produce. If Frank devotes all 8 hours of his time to potatoes, he produces 32 ounces of potatoes (measured on the horizontal axis) and no meat. If he devotes all of his time to meat, he produces 8 ounces of meat (measured on the vertical axis) and no potatoes. If Frank divides his time equally between the two activities, spending 4 hours on each, he produces 16 ounces of potatoes and 4 ounces of meat. The figure shows these three possible outcomes and all others in between.

This graph is Frank's production possibilities frontier. As we discussed in Chapter 2, a production possibilities frontier shows the various mixes of output

FIGURE 1

The Production Possibilities Frontier

Panel (a) shows the production opportunities available to Frank the farmer and Ruby the rancher. Panel (b) shows the combinations of meat and potatoes that Frank can produce. Panel (c) shows the combinations of meat and potatoes that Ruby can produce. Both production possibilities frontiers are derived assuming that Frank and Ruby each work 8 hours per day. If there is no trade, each person's production possibilities frontier is also his or her consumption possibilities frontier.

(a) Production Opportunities

	Minutes Needed to Make 1 Ounce of:		Amount Produced in 8 Hours	
	Meat	**Potatoes**	**Meat**	**Potatoes**
Frank the farmer	60 min/oz	15 min/oz	8 oz	32 oz
Ruby the rancher	20 min/oz	10 min/oz	24 oz	48 oz

(b) Frank's Production Possibilities Frontier **(c) Ruby's Production Possibilities Frontier**

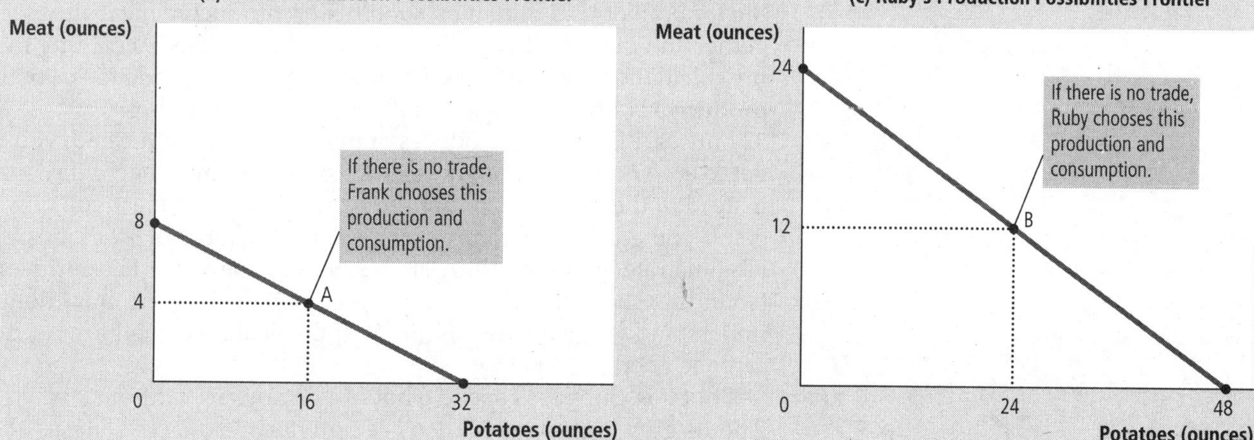

that an economy can produce. It illustrates one of the *Ten Principles of Economics* in Chapter 1: People face trade-offs. Here Frank faces a trade-off between producing meat and producing potatoes.

You may recall that the production possibilities frontier in Chapter 2 was drawn bowed out. In that case, the rate at which society could trade one good for the other depended on the amounts that were being produced. Here, however, Frank's technology for producing meat and potatoes (as summarized in Figure 1) allows him to switch between the two goods at a constant rate. Whenever Frank spends 1 hour less producing meat and 1 hour more producing potatoes, he reduces his output of meat by 1 ounce and raises his output of potatoes by 4 ounces—and this is true regardless of how much he is already producing. As a result, the production possibilities frontier is a straight line.

Panel (c) of Figure 1 shows the production possibilities frontier for Ruby. If Ruby devotes all 8 hours of her time to potatoes, she produces 48 ounces of potatoes and no meat. If she devotes all of her time to meat, she produces 24 ounces of meat and no potatoes. If Ruby divides her time equally, spending 4 hours on each activity, she produces 24 ounces of potatoes and 12 ounces of meat. Once again, the production possibilities frontier shows all the possible outcomes.

If Frank and Ruby choose to be self-sufficient rather than trade with each other, then each consumes exactly what he or she produces. In this case, the production possibilities frontier is also the consumption possibilities frontier. That is, without trade, Figure 1 shows the possible combinations of meat and potatoes that Frank and Ruby can each produce and then consume.

These production possibilities frontiers are useful in showing the trade-offs that Frank and Ruby face, but they do not tell us what Frank and Ruby will actually choose to do. To determine their choices, we need to know the tastes of Frank and Ruby. Let's suppose they choose the combinations identified by points A and B in Figure 1. Based on his production opportunities and food preferences, Frank decides to produce and consume 16 ounces of potatoes and 4 ounces of meat, while Ruby decides to produce and consume 24 ounces of potatoes and 12 ounces of meat.

3-1b Specialization and Trade

After several years of eating combination B, Ruby gets an idea and goes to talk to Frank:

RUBY: Frank, my friend, have I got a deal for you! I know how to improve life for both of us. I think you should stop producing meat altogether and devote all your time to growing potatoes. According to my calculations, if you work 8 hours a day growing potatoes, you'll produce 32 ounces of potatoes. If you give me 15 of those 32 ounces, I'll give you 5 ounces of meat in return. In the end, you'll get to eat 17 ounces of potatoes and 5 ounces of meat every day, instead of the 16 ounces of potatoes and 4 ounces of meat you now get. If you go along with my plan, you'll have more of *both* foods. [To illustrate her point, Ruby shows Frank panel (a) of Figure 2.]

FRANK: (sounding skeptical) That seems like a good deal for me. But I don't understand why you are offering it. If the deal is so good for me, it can't be good for you too.

RUBY: Oh, but it is! Suppose I spend 6 hours a day raising cattle and 2 hours growing potatoes. Then I can produce 18 ounces of meat and 12 ounces of potatoes. After I give you 5 ounces of my meat in exchange for 15 ounces of your potatoes, I'll end up with 13 ounces

FIGURE 2

How Trade Expands the Set of Consumption Opportunities

The proposed trade between Frank the farmer and Ruby the rancher offers each of them a combination of meat and potatoes that would be impossible in the absence of trade. In panel (a), Frank gets to consume at point A* rather than point A. In panel (b), Ruby gets to consume at point B* rather than point B. Trade allows each to consume more meat and more potatoes.

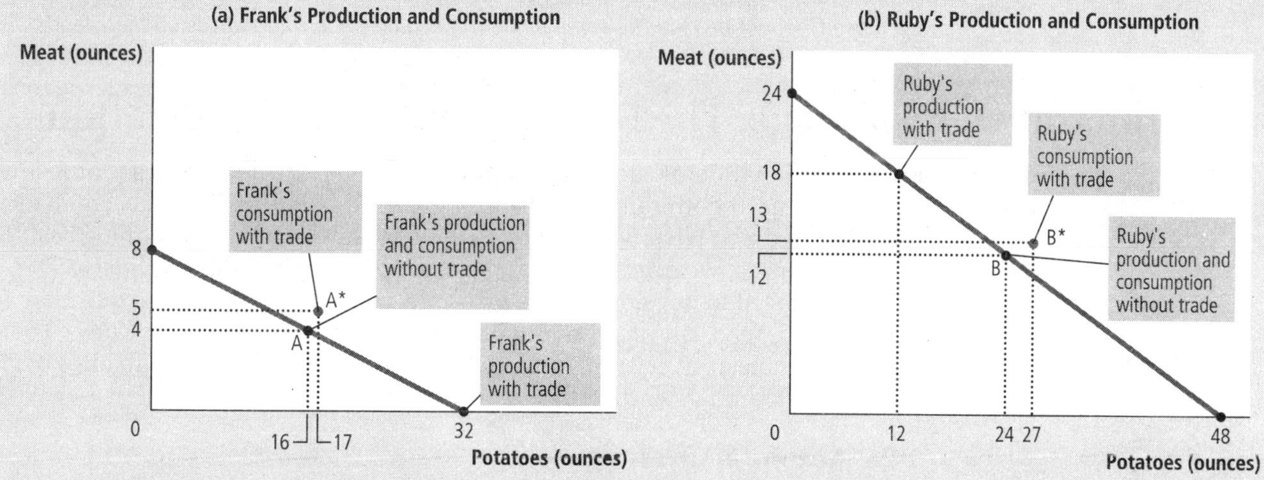

(c) The Gains from Trade: A Summary

	Frank		Ruby	
	Meat	**Potatoes**	**Meat**	**Potatoes**
Without Trade:				
Production and Consumption	4 oz	16 oz	12 oz	24 oz
With Trade:				
Production	0 oz	32 oz	18 oz	12 oz
Trade	Gets 5 oz	Gives 15 oz	Gives 5 oz	Gets 15 oz
Consumption	5 oz	17 oz	13 oz	27 oz
GAINS FROM TRADE:				
Increase in Consumption	+1 oz	+1 oz	+1 oz	+3 oz

of meat and 27 ounces of potatoes, instead of the 12 ounces of meat and 24 ounces of potatoes that I now get. So I will also consume more of both foods than I do now. [She points out panel (b) of Figure 2.]

FRANK: I don't know. . . . This sounds too good to be true.

RUBY: It's really not as complicated as it first seems. Here—I've summarized my proposal for you in a simple table. [Ruby shows Frank a copy of the table at the bottom of Figure 2.]

FRANK: (after pausing to study the table) These calculations seem correct, but I am puzzled. How can this deal make us both better off?

RUBY: We can both benefit because trade allows each of us to specialize in doing what we do best. You will spend more time growing potatoes and less time raising cattle. I will spend more time raising cattle and less time growing potatoes. As a result of specialization and trade, each of us can consume more meat and more potatoes without working any more hours.

QuickQuiz *Draw an example of a production possibilities frontier for Robinson Crusoe, a shipwrecked sailor who spends his time gathering coconuts and catching fish. Does this frontier limit Crusoe's consumption of coconuts and fish if he lives by himself? Would he face the same limits if he could trade with natives on the island?*

3-2 Comparative Advantage: The Driving Force of Specialization

Ruby's explanation of the gains from trade, though correct, poses a puzzle: If Ruby is better at both raising cattle and growing potatoes, how can Frank ever specialize in doing what he does best? Frank doesn't seem to do anything best. To solve this puzzle, we need to look at the principle of *comparative advantage*.

As a first step in developing this principle, consider the following question: In our example, who can produce potatoes at a lower cost—Frank or Ruby? There are two possible answers, and in these two answers lie the solution to our puzzle and the key to understanding the gains from trade.

3-2a Absolute Advantage

absolute advantage
the ability to produce a good using fewer inputs than another producer

One way to answer the question about the cost of producing potatoes is to compare the inputs required by the two producers. Economists use the term **absolute advantage** when comparing the productivity of one person, firm, or nation to that of another. The producer that requires a smaller quantity of inputs to produce a good is said to have an absolute advantage in producing that good.

In our example, time is the only input, so we can determine absolute advantage by looking at how much time each type of production takes. Ruby has an absolute advantage in producing both meat and potatoes because she requires less time than Frank to produce a unit of either good. Ruby needs to input only 20 minutes to produce an ounce of meat, whereas Frank needs 60 minutes. Similarly, Ruby needs only 10 minutes to produce an ounce of potatoes, whereas Frank needs 15 minutes. Thus, if we measure cost in terms of the quantity of inputs, Ruby has the lower cost of producing potatoes.

3-2b Opportunity Cost and Comparative Advantage

opportunity cost
whatever must be given up to obtain some item

There is another way to look at the cost of producing potatoes. Rather than comparing inputs required, we can compare opportunity costs. Recall from Chapter 1 that the **opportunity cost** of some item is what we give up to get that item. In our example, we assumed that Frank and Ruby each spend 8 hours a day working. Time spent producing potatoes, therefore, takes away from time available for producing meat. When reallocating time between the two goods, Ruby and Frank give up units of one good to produce units of the other, thereby moving along the production possibilities frontier. The opportunity cost measures the trade-off between the two goods that each producer faces.

Let's first consider Ruby's opportunity cost. According to the table in panel (a) of Figure 1, producing 1 ounce of potatoes takes 10 minutes of work. When Ruby spends those 10 minutes producing potatoes, she spends 10 fewer minutes producing meat. Because Ruby needs 20 minutes to produce 1 ounce of meat, 10 minutes of work would yield ½ ounce of meat. Hence, Ruby's opportunity cost of producing 1 ounce of potatoes is ½ ounce of meat.

TABLE 1

The Opportunity Cost of Meat and Potatoes

	Opportunity Cost of:	
	1 oz of Meat	**1 oz of Potatoes**
Frank the farmer	4 oz potatoes	¼ oz meat
Ruby the rancher	2 oz potatoes	½ oz meat

Now consider Frank's opportunity cost. Producing 1 ounce of potatoes takes him 15 minutes. Because he needs 60 minutes to produce 1 ounce of meat, 15 minutes of work would yield ¼ ounce of meat. Hence, Frank's opportunity cost of 1 ounce of potatoes is ¼ ounce of meat.

Table 1 shows the opportunity costs of meat and potatoes for the two producers. Notice that the opportunity cost of meat is the inverse of the opportunity cost of potatoes. Because 1 ounce of potatoes costs Ruby ½ ounce of meat, 1 ounce of meat costs Ruby 2 ounces of potatoes. Similarly, because 1 ounce of potatoes costs Frank ¼ ounce of meat, 1 ounce of meat costs Frank 4 ounces of potatoes.

comparative advantage the ability to produce a good at a lower opportunity cost than another producer

Economists use the term **comparative advantage** when describing the opportunity costs faced by two producers. The producer who gives up less of other goods to produce Good X has the smaller opportunity cost of producing Good X and is said to have a comparative advantage in producing it. In our example, Frank has a lower opportunity cost of producing potatoes than Ruby: An ounce of potatoes costs Frank only ¼ ounce of meat, but it costs Ruby ½ ounce of meat. Conversely, Ruby has a lower opportunity cost of producing meat than Frank: An ounce of meat costs Ruby 2 ounces of potatoes, but it costs Frank 4 ounces of potatoes. Thus, Frank has a comparative advantage in growing potatoes, and Ruby has a comparative advantage in producing meat.

Although it is possible for one person to have an absolute advantage in both goods (as Ruby does in our example), it is impossible for one person to have a comparative advantage in both goods. Because the opportunity cost of one good is the inverse of the opportunity cost of the other, if a person's opportunity cost of one good is relatively high, the opportunity cost of the other good must be relatively low. Comparative advantage reflects the relative opportunity cost. Unless two people have the same opportunity cost, one person will have a comparative advantage in one good, and the other person will have a comparative advantage in the other good.

3-2c Comparative Advantage and Trade

The gains from specialization and trade are based not on absolute advantage but on comparative advantage. When each person specializes in producing the good for which he or she has a comparative advantage, total production in the economy rises. This increase in the size of the economic pie can be used to make everyone better off.

In our example, Frank spends more time growing potatoes, and Ruby spends more time producing meat. As a result, the total production of potatoes rises from 40 to 44 ounces, and the total production of meat rises from 16 to 18 ounces. Frank and Ruby share the benefits of this increased production.

We can also view the gains from trade in terms of the price that each party pays the other. Because Frank and Ruby have different opportunity costs, they can both get a bargain. That is, each of them benefits from trade by obtaining a good at a price that is lower than his or her opportunity cost of that good.

Consider the proposed deal from Frank's viewpoint. Frank receives 5 ounces of meat in exchange for 15 ounces of potatoes. In other words, Frank buys each ounce of meat for a price of 3 ounces of potatoes. This price of meat is lower than his opportunity cost for an ounce of meat, which is 4 ounces of potatoes. Thus, Frank benefits from the deal because he gets to buy meat at a good price.

Now consider the deal from Ruby's viewpoint. Ruby buys 15 ounces of potatoes at a cost of 5 ounces of meat. That is, the price for an ounce of potatoes is ⅓ ounce of meat. This price of potatoes is lower than her opportunity cost of an ounce of potatoes, which is ½ ounce of meat. Ruby benefits because she gets to buy potatoes at a good price.

The story of Ruby the rancher and Frank the farmer has a simple moral, which should now be clear: *Trade can benefit everyone in society because it allows people to specialize in activities in which they have a comparative advantage.*

3-2d The Price of the Trade

The principle of comparative advantage establishes that there are gains from specialization and trade, but it raises a couple of related questions: What determines the price at which trade takes place? How are the gains from trade shared between the trading parties? The precise answers to these questions are beyond the scope of this chapter, but we can state one general rule: *For both parties to gain from trade, the price at which they trade must lie between the two opportunity costs.*

In our example, Frank and Ruby agreed to trade at a rate of 3 ounces of potatoes for each ounce of meat. This price is between Ruby's opportunity cost (2 ounces of potatoes per ounce of meat) and Frank's opportunity cost (4 ounces of potatoes per ounce of meat). The price need not be exactly in the middle for both parties to gain, but it must be somewhere between 2 and 4.

To see why the price has to be in this range, consider what would happen if it were not. If the price of meat were below 2 ounces of potatoes, both Frank and Ruby would want to buy meat, because the price would be below each of their opportunity costs. Similarly, if the price of meat were above 4 ounces of potatoes, both would want to sell meat, because the price would be above their opportunity costs. But there are only two members of this economy. They cannot both be buyers of meat, nor can they both be sellers. Someone has to take the other side of the deal.

A mutually advantageous trade can be struck at a price between 2 and 4. In this price range, Ruby wants to sell meat to buy potatoes, and Frank wants to sell potatoes to buy meat. Each party can buy a good at a price that is lower than his or her opportunity cost. In the end, each person specializes in the good for which he or she has a comparative advantage and, as a result, is better off.

QuickQuiz *Robinson Crusoe can gather 10 coconuts or catch 1 fish per hour. His friend Friday can gather 30 coconuts or catch 2 fish per hour. What is Crusoe's opportunity cost of catching 1 fish? What is Friday's? Who has an absolute advantage in catching fish? Who has a comparative advantage in catching fish?*

FYI

The Legacy of Adam Smith and David Ricardo

Economists have long understood the gains from trade. Here is how the great economist Adam Smith put the argument:

> *It is a maxim of every prudent master of a family, never to attempt to make at home what it will cost him more to make than to buy. The tailor does not attempt to make his own shoes, but buys them of the shoemaker. The shoemaker does not attempt to make his own clothes but employs a tailor. The farmer attempts to make neither the one nor the other, but employs those different artificers. All of them find it for their interest to employ their whole industry in a way in which they have some advantage over their neighbors, and to purchase with a part of its produce, or what is the same thing, with the price of part of it, whatever else they have occasion for.*

BETTMANN/CORBIS

David Ricardo

This quotation is from Smith's 1776 book *An Inquiry into the Nature and Causes of the Wealth of Nations*, which was a landmark in the analysis of trade and economic interdependence.

Smith's book inspired David Ricardo, a millionaire stockbroker, to become an economist. In his 1817 book *Principles of Political Economy and Taxation*, Ricardo developed the principle of comparative advantage as we know it today. He considered an example with two goods (wine and cloth) and two countries (England and Portugal). He showed that both countries can gain by opening up trade and specializing based on comparative advantage.

Ricardo's theory is the starting point of modern international economics, but his defense of free trade was not a mere academic exercise. Ricardo put his beliefs to work as a member of the British Parliament, where he opposed the Corn Laws, which restricted the import of grain.

The conclusions of Adam Smith and David Ricardo on the gains from trade have held up well over time. Although economists often disagree on questions of policy, they are united in their support of free trade. Moreover, the central argument for free trade has not changed much in the past two centuries. Even though the field of economics has broadened its scope and refined its theories since the time of Smith and Ricardo, economists' opposition to trade restrictions is still based largely on the principle of comparative advantage. ■

3-3 Applications of Comparative Advantage

The principle of comparative advantage explains interdependence and the gains from trade. Because interdependence is so prevalent in the modern world, the principle of comparative advantage has many applications. Here are two examples, one fanciful and one of great practical importance.

ALLSTAR PICTURE LIBRARY / ALAMY

"They did a nice job with this grass."

3-3a Should Serena Williams Mow Her Own Lawn?

When Serena Williams plays at the Wimbledon tennis tournament, she spends a lot of time running around on grass. One of the most talented tennis players of all time, she can hit a ball with a speed and accuracy that most casual athletes can only dream of. Most likely, she is talented at other physical activities as well. For example, let's imagine that Serena can mow her lawn faster than anyone else. But just because she *can* mow her lawn fast, does this mean she *should*?

To answer this question, we can use the concepts of opportunity cost and comparative advantage. Let's say that Serena can mow her lawn in 2 hours. In that same 2 hours, she could film a television commercial and earn $30,000. By contrast, Forrest Gump, the boy next door, can mow Serena's lawn in 4 hours. In that same 4 hours, Forrest could work at McDonald's and earn $50.

In this example, Serena has an absolute advantage in mowing lawns because she can do the work with a lower input of time. Yet because Serena's opportunity cost of mowing the lawn is $30,000 and Forrest's opportunity cost is only $50, Forrest has a comparative advantage in mowing lawns.

The gains from trade in this example are tremendous. Rather than mowing her own lawn, Serena should make the commercial and hire Forrest to mow the lawn. As long as Serena pays Forrest more than $50 and less than $30,000, both of them are better off.

3-3b Should the United States Trade with Other Countries?

imports
goods produced abroad and sold domestically

exports
goods produced domestically and sold abroad

Just as individuals can benefit from specialization and trade with one another, so can populations of people in different countries. Many of the goods that Americans enjoy are produced abroad, and many of the goods produced in the United States are sold abroad. Goods produced abroad and sold domestically are called **imports.** Goods produced domestically and sold abroad are called **exports.**

To see how countries can benefit from trade, suppose there are two countries, the United States and Japan, and two goods, food and cars. Imagine that the two countries produce cars equally well: An American worker and a Japanese worker can each produce one car per month. By contrast, because the United States has more and better land, it is better at producing food: A U.S. worker can produce 2 tons of food per month, whereas a Japanese worker can produce only 1 ton of food per month.

The principle of comparative advantage states that each good should be produced by the country that has the smaller opportunity cost of producing that good. Because the opportunity cost of a car is 2 tons of food in the United States but only 1 ton of food in Japan, Japan has a comparative advantage in producing cars. Japan should produce more cars than it wants for its own use and export some of them to the United States. Similarly, because the opportunity cost of a ton of food is 1 car in Japan but only 1/2 car in the United States, the United States has a comparative advantage in producing food. The United States should produce more food than it wants to consume and export some to Japan. Through specialization and trade, both countries can have more food and more cars.

In reality, of course, the issues involved in trade among nations are more complex than this example suggests. Most important among these issues is that each country has many citizens with different interests. International trade can make some individuals worse off, even as it makes the country as a whole better off. When the United States exports food and imports cars, the impact on an American farmer is not the same as the impact on an American autoworker. Yet, contrary to the opinions sometimes voiced by politicians and pundits, international trade is not like war, in which some countries win and others lose. Trade allows all countries to achieve greater prosperity.

QuickQuiz *Suppose that a skilled brain surgeon also happens to be the world's fastest typist. Should she do her own typing or hire a secretary? Explain.*

ASK THE EXPERTS

Trade between China and the United States

"Trade with China makes most Americans better off because, among other advantages, they can buy goods that are made or assembled more cheaply in China."

What do economists say?

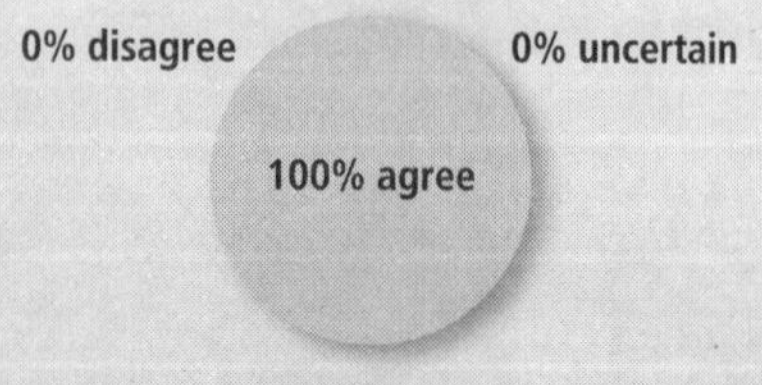

"Some Americans who work in the production of competing goods, such as clothing and furniture, are made worse off by trade with China."

What do economists say?

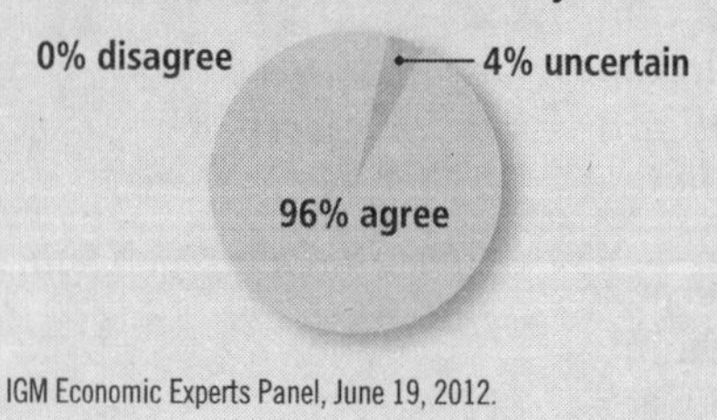

Source: IGM Economic Experts Panel, June 19, 2012.

3-4 Conclusion

You should now understand more fully the benefits of living in an interdependent economy. When Americans buy tube socks from China, when residents of Maine drink orange juice from Florida, and when a homeowner hires the kid next door to mow her lawn, the same economic forces are at work. The principle of comparative advantage shows that trade can make everyone better off.

Having seen why interdependence is desirable, you might naturally ask how it is possible. How do free societies coordinate the diverse activities of all the people involved in their economies? What ensures that goods and services will get from those who should be producing them to those who should be consuming them? In a world with only two people, such as Ruby the rancher and Frank the farmer, the answer is simple: These two people can bargain and allocate resources between themselves. In the real world with billions of people, the answer is less obvious. We take up this issue in the next chapter, where we see that free societies allocate resources through the market forces of supply and demand.

CHAPTER QuickQuiz

1. In an hour, Mateo can wash 2 cars or mow 1 lawn, and Tyler can wash 3 cars or mow 1 lawn. Who has the absolute advantage in car washing, and who has the absolute advantage in lawn mowing?
   a. Mateo in washing, Tyler in mowing.
   b. Tyler in washing, Mateo in mowing.
   c. Mateo in washing, neither in mowing.
   d. Tyler in washing, neither in mowing.
2. Once again, in an hour, Mateo can wash 2 cars or mow 1 lawn, and Tyler can wash 3 cars or mow 1 lawn. Who has the comparative advantage in car washing, and who has the comparative advantage in lawn mowing?
   a. Mateo in washing, Tyler in mowing.
   b. Tyler in washing, Mateo in mowing.
   c. Mateo in washing, neither in mowing.
   d. Tyler in washing, neither in mowing.
3. When two individuals produce efficiently and then make a mutually beneficial trade based on comparative advantage,
   a. they both obtain consumption outside their production possibilities frontier.
   b. they both obtain consumption inside their production possibilities frontier.
   c. one individual consumes inside her production possibilities frontier, while the other consumes outside hers.
   d. each individual consumes a point on her own production possibilities frontier.
4. Which goods will a nation typically import?
   a. those goods in which the nation has an absolute advantage
   b. those goods in which the nation has a comparative advantage
   c. those goods in which other nations have an absolute advantage
   d. those goods in which other nations have a comparative advantage
5. Suppose that in the United States, producing an aircraft takes 10,000 hours of labor and producing a shirt takes 2 hours of labor. In China, producing an aircraft takes 40,000 hours of labor and producing a shirt takes 4 hours of labor. What will these nations trade?
   a. China will export aircraft, and the United States will export shirts.
   b. China will export shirts, and the United States will export aircraft.
   c. Both nations will export shirts.
   d. There are no gains from trade in this situation.
6. Kayla can cook dinner in 30 minutes and wash the laundry in 20 minutes. Her roommate takes half as long to do each task. How should the roommates allocate the work?
   a. Kayla should do more of the cooking based on her comparative advantage.
   b. Kayla should do more of the washing based on her comparative advantage.
   c. Kayla should do more of the washing based on her absolute advantage.
   d. There are no gains from trade in this situation.

SUMMARY

- Each person consumes goods and services produced by many other people both in the United States and around the world. Interdependence and trade are desirable because they allow everyone to enjoy a greater quantity and variety of goods and services.
- There are two ways to compare the ability of two people to produce a good. The person who can produce the good with the smaller quantity of inputs is said to have an *absolute advantage* in producing the good. The person who has the smaller opportunity cost of producing the good is said to have a *comparative advantage*. The gains from trade are based on comparative advantage, not absolute advantage.
- Trade makes everyone better off because it allows people to specialize in those activities in which they have a comparative advantage.
- The principle of comparative advantage applies to countries as well as to people. Economists use the principle of comparative advantage to advocate free trade among countries.

KEY CONCEPTS

absolute advantage, p. 52
opportunity cost, p. 52
comparative advantage, p. 53
imports, p. 57
exports, p. 57

QUESTIONS FOR REVIEW

1. Under what conditions is the production possibilities frontier linear rather than bowed out?
2. Explain how absolute advantage and comparative advantage differ.
3. Give an example in which one person has an absolute advantage in doing something but another person has a comparative advantage.
4. Is absolute advantage or comparative advantage more important for trade? Explain your reasoning using the example in your answer to question 3.
5. If two parties trade based on comparative advantage and both gain, in what range must the price of the trade lie?
6. Why do economists oppose policies that restrict trade among nations?

PROBLEMS AND APPLICATIONS

1. Maria can read 20 pages of economics in an hour. She can also read 50 pages of sociology in an hour. She spends 5 hours per day studying.
   a. Draw Maria's production possibilities frontier for reading economics and sociology.
   b. What is Maria's opportunity cost of reading 100 pages of sociology?
2. American and Japanese workers can each produce 4 cars a year. An American worker can produce 10 tons of grain a year, whereas a Japanese worker can produce 5 tons of grain a year. To keep things simple, assume that each country has 100 million workers.
   a. For this situation, construct a table analogous to the table in Figure 1.
   b. Graph the production possibilities frontiers for the American and Japanese economies.
   c. For the United States, what is the opportunity cost of a car? Of grain? For Japan, what is the opportunity cost of a car? Of grain? Put this information in a table analogous to Table 1.
   d. Which country has an absolute advantage in producing cars? In producing grain?
   e. Which country has a comparative advantage in producing cars? In producing grain?
   f. Without trade, half of each country's workers produce cars and half produce grain. What quantities of cars and grain does each country produce?
   g. Starting from a position without trade, give an example in which trade makes each country better off.
3. Pat and Kris are roommates. They spend most of their time studying (of course), but they leave some time for their favorite activities: making pizza and brewing root beer. Pat takes 4 hours to brew a gallon of root beer and 2 hours to make a pizza. Kris takes 6 hours to brew a gallon of root beer and 4 hours to make a pizza.

a. What is each roommate's opportunity cost of making a pizza? Who has the absolute advantage in making pizza? Who has the comparative advantage in making pizza?
b. If Pat and Kris trade foods with each other, who will trade away pizza in exchange for root beer?
c. The price of pizza can be expressed in terms of gallons of root beer. What is the highest price at which pizza can be traded that would make both roommates better off? What is the lowest price? Explain.

4. Suppose that there are 10 million workers in Canada and that each of these workers can produce either 2 cars or 30 bushels of wheat in a year.
   a. What is the opportunity cost of producing a car in Canada? What is the opportunity cost of producing a bushel of wheat in Canada? Explain the relationship between the opportunity costs of the two goods.
   b. Draw Canada's production possibilities frontier. If Canada chooses to consume 10 million cars, how much wheat can it consume without trade? Label this point on the production possibilities frontier.
   c. Now suppose that the United States offers to buy 10 million cars from Canada in exchange for 20 bushels of wheat per car. If Canada continues to consume 10 million cars, how much wheat does this deal allow Canada to consume? Label this point on your diagram. Should Canada accept the deal?

5. England and Scotland both produce scones and sweaters. Suppose that an English worker can produce 50 scones per hour or 1 sweater per hour. Suppose that a Scottish worker can produce 40 scones per hour or 2 sweaters per hour.
   a. Which country has the absolute advantage in the production of each good? Which country has the comparative advantage?
   b. If England and Scotland decide to trade, which commodity will Scotland export to England? Explain.
   c. If a Scottish worker could produce only 1 sweater per hour, would Scotland still gain from trade? Would England still gain from trade? Explain.

6. The following table describes the production possibilities of two cities in the country of Baseballia:

	Pairs of Red Socks per Worker per Hour	Pairs of White Socks per Worker per Hour
Boston	3	3
Chicago	2	1

   a. Without trade, what is the price of white socks (in terms of red socks) in Boston? What is the price in Chicago?
   b. Which city has an absolute advantage in the production of each color sock? Which city has a comparative advantage in the production of each color sock?
   c. If the cities trade with each other, which color sock will each export?
   d. What is the range of prices at which trade can occur?

7. A German worker takes 400 hours to produce a car and 2 hours to produce a case of wine. A French worker takes 600 hours to produce a car and *X* hours to produce a case of wine.
   a. For what values of *X* will gains from trade be possible? Explain.
   b. For what values of *X* will Germany export cars and import wine? Explain.

8. Suppose that in a year an American worker can produce 100 shirts or 20 computers and a Chinese worker can produce 100 shirts or 10 computers.
   a. For each country, graph the production possibilities frontier. Suppose that without trade the workers in each country spend half their time producing each good. Identify this point in your graphs.
   b. If these countries were open to trade, which country would export shirts? Give a specific numerical example and show it on your graphs. Which country would benefit from trade? Explain.
   c. Explain at what price of computers (in terms of shirts) the two countries might trade.
   d. Suppose that China catches up with American productivity so that a Chinese worker can produce 100 shirts or 20 computers. What pattern of trade would you predict now? How does this advance in Chinese productivity affect the economic well-being of the two countries' citizens?

9. Are the following statements true or false? Explain in each case.
   a. "Two countries can achieve gains from trade even if one of the countries has an absolute advantage in the production of all goods."
   b. "Certain talented people have a comparative advantage in everything they do."
   c. "If a certain trade is good for one person, it can't be good for the other one."
   d. "If a certain trade is good for one person, it is always good for the other one."
   e. "If trade is good for a country, it must be good for everyone in the country."

To find additional study resources, visit cengagebrain.com, and search for "Mankiw."

BROS.

PART II
How Markets Work

The Market Forces of Supply and Demand

CHAPTER 4

When a cold snap hits Florida, the price of orange juice rises in supermarkets throughout the country. When the weather turns warm in New England every summer, the price of hotel rooms in the Caribbean plummets. When a war breaks out in the Middle East, the price of gasoline in the United States rises and the price of a used Cadillac falls. What do these events have in common? They all show the workings of supply and demand.

Supply and *demand* are the two words economists use most often—and for good reason. Supply and demand are the forces that make market economies work. They determine the quantity of each good produced and the price at which it

is sold. If you want to know how any event or policy will affect the economy, you must think first about how it will affect supply and demand.

This chapter introduces the theory of supply and demand. It considers how buyers and sellers behave and how they interact with one another. It shows how supply and demand determine prices in a market economy and how prices, in turn, allocate the economy's scarce resources.

4-1 Markets and Competition

The terms *supply* and *demand* refer to the behavior of people as they interact with one another in competitive markets. Before discussing how buyers and sellers behave, let's first consider more fully what we mean by the terms *market* and *competition*.

4-1a What Is a Market?

market
a group of buyers and sellers of a particular good or service

A **market** is a group of buyers and sellers of a particular good or service. The buyers as a group determine the demand for the product, and the sellers as a group determine the supply of the product.

Markets take many forms. Some markets are highly organized, such as the markets for many agricultural commodities. In these markets, buyers and sellers meet at a specific time and place where an auctioneer helps set prices and arrange sales.

More often, markets are less organized. For example, consider the market for ice cream in a particular town. Buyers of ice cream do not meet together at any one time. The sellers of ice cream are in different locations and offer somewhat different products. There is no auctioneer calling out the price of ice cream. Each seller posts a price for an ice-cream cone, and each buyer decides how much ice cream to buy at each store. Nonetheless, these consumers and producers of ice cream are closely connected. The ice-cream buyers are choosing from the various ice-cream sellers to satisfy their cravings, and the ice-cream sellers are all trying to appeal to the same ice-cream buyers to make their businesses successful. Even though it is not as organized, the group of ice-cream buyers and ice-cream sellers forms a market.

4-1b What Is Competition?

The market for ice cream, like most markets in the economy, is highly competitive. Each buyer knows that there are several sellers from which to choose, and each seller is aware that his product is similar to that offered by other sellers. As a result, the price and quantity of ice cream sold are not determined by any single buyer or seller. Rather, price and quantity are determined by all buyers and sellers as they interact in the marketplace.

competitive market
a market in which there are many buyers and many sellers so that each has a negligible impact on the market price

Economists use the term **competitive market** to describe a market in which there are so many buyers and so many sellers that each has a negligible impact on the market price. Each seller of ice cream has limited control over the price because other sellers are offering similar products. A seller has little reason to charge less than the going price, and if he charges more, buyers will make their purchases elsewhere. Similarly, no single buyer of ice cream can influence the price of ice cream because each buyer purchases only a small amount.

In this chapter, we assume that markets are *perfectly competitive*. To reach this highest form of competition, a market must have two characteristics: (1) The goods offered for sale are all exactly the same, and (2) the buyers and sellers are so numerous that no single buyer or seller has any influence over the market price.

Because buyers and sellers in perfectly competitive markets must accept the price the market determines, they are said to be *price takers*. At the market price, buyers can buy all they want, and sellers can sell all they want.

There are some markets in which the assumption of perfect competition applies perfectly. In the wheat market, for example, there are thousands of farmers who sell wheat and millions of consumers who use wheat and wheat products. Because no single buyer or seller can influence the price of wheat, each takes the market price as given.

Not all goods and services, however, are sold in perfectly competitive markets. Some markets have only one seller, and this seller sets the price. Such a seller is called a *monopoly*. Your local cable television company, for instance, may be a monopoly. Residents of your town probably have only one company from which to buy cable service. Other markets fall between the extremes of perfect competition and monopoly.

Despite the diversity of market types we find in the world, assuming perfect competition is a useful simplification and, therefore, a natural place to start. Perfectly competitive markets are the easiest to analyze because everyone participating in the market takes the price as given by market conditions. Moreover, because some degree of competition is present in most markets, many of the lessons that we learn by studying supply and demand under perfect competition apply in more complicated markets as well.

QuickQuiz *What is a market? • What are the characteristics of a perfectly competitive market?*

4-2 Demand

We begin our study of markets by examining the behavior of buyers. To focus our thinking, let's keep in mind a particular good—ice cream.

4-2a The Demand Curve: The Relationship between Price and Quantity Demanded

The **quantity demanded** of any good is the amount of the good that buyers are willing and able to purchase. As we will see, many things determine the quantity demanded of any good, but in our analysis of how markets work, one determinant plays a central role: the price of the good. If the price of ice cream rose to $20 per scoop, you would buy less ice cream. You might buy frozen yogurt instead. If the price of ice cream fell to $0.20 per scoop, you would buy more. This relationship between price and quantity demanded is true for most goods in the economy and, in fact, is so pervasive that economists call it the **law of demand**: Other things being equal, when the price of a good rises, the quantity demanded of the good falls, and when the price falls, the quantity demanded rises.

quantity demanded
the amount of a good that buyers are willing and able to purchase

law of demand
the claim that, other things being equal, the quantity demanded of a good falls when the price of the good rises

The table in Figure 1 shows how many ice-cream cones Catherine buys each month at different prices. If ice cream is free, Catherine eats 12 cones per month. At $0.50 per cone, Catherine buys 10 cones each month. As the price rises further, she buys fewer and fewer cones. When the price reaches $3.00, Catherine doesn't buy any cones at all. This table is a **demand schedule**, a table that shows the relationship between the price of a good and the quantity demanded, holding constant everything else that influences how much of the good consumers want to buy.

demand schedule
a table that shows the relationship between the price of a good and the quantity demanded

The graph in Figure 1 uses the numbers from the table to illustrate the law of demand. By convention, the price of ice cream is on the vertical axis, and the

FIGURE 1

Catherine's Demand Schedule and Demand Curve

The demand schedule is a table that shows the quantity demanded at each price. The demand curve, which graphs the demand schedule, illustrates how the quantity demanded of the good changes as its price varies. Because a lower price increases the quantity demanded, the demand curve slopes downward.

Price of Ice-Cream Cone	Quantity of Cones Demanded
$0.00	12 cones
0.50	10
1.00	8
1.50	6
2.00	4
2.50	2
3.00	0

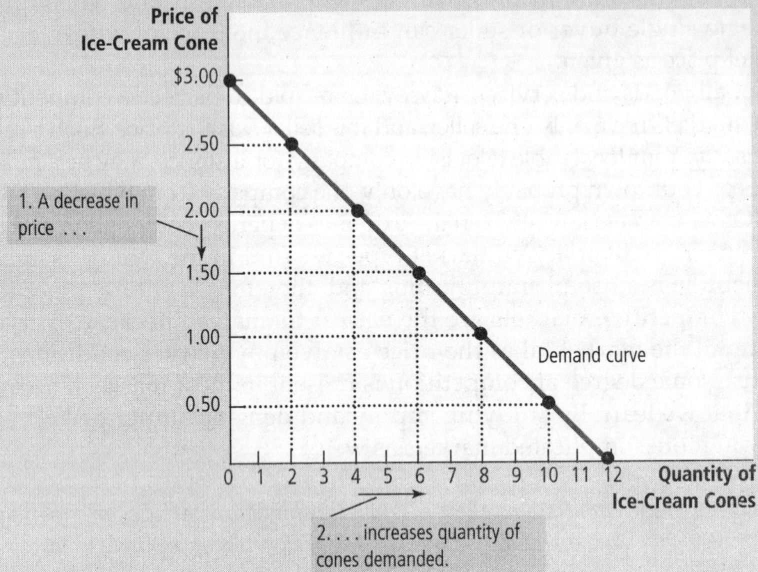

quantity of ice cream demanded is on the horizontal axis. The line relating price and quantity demanded is called the **demand curve**. The demand curve slopes downward because, other things being equal, a lower price means a greater quantity demanded.

demand curve
a graph of the relationship between the price of a good and the quantity demanded

4-2b Market Demand versus Individual Demand

The demand curve in Figure 1 shows an individual's demand for a product. To analyze how markets work, we need to determine the *market demand*, the sum of all the individual demands for a particular good or service.

The table in Figure 2 shows the demand schedules for ice cream of the two individuals in this market—Catherine and Nicholas. At any price, Catherine's demand schedule tells us how much ice cream she buys, and Nicholas's demand schedule tells us how much ice cream he buys. The market demand at each price is the sum of the two individual demands.

The graph in Figure 2 shows the demand curves that correspond to these demand schedules. Notice that we sum the individual demand curves *horizontally* to obtain the market demand curve. That is, to find the total quantity demanded at any price, we add the individual quantities, which are found on the horizontal axis of the individual demand curves. Because we are interested in analyzing how markets function, we work most often with the market demand curve. The market demand curve shows how the total quantity demanded of a good varies as the price of the good varies, while all other factors that affect how much consumers want to buy are held constant.

FIGURE 2

Market Demand as the Sum of Individual Demands

The quantity demanded in a market is the sum of the quantities demanded by all the buyers at each price. Thus, the market demand curve is found by adding horizontally the individual demand curves. At a price of $2.00, Catherine demands 4 ice-cream cones and Nicholas demands 3 ice-cream cones. The quantity demanded in the market at this price is 7 cones.

Price of Ice-Cream Cone	Catherine		Nicholas		Market
$0.00	12	+	7	=	19 cones
0.50	10		6		16
1.00	8		5		13
1.50	6		4		10
2.00	4		3		7
2.50	2		2		4
3.00	0		1		1

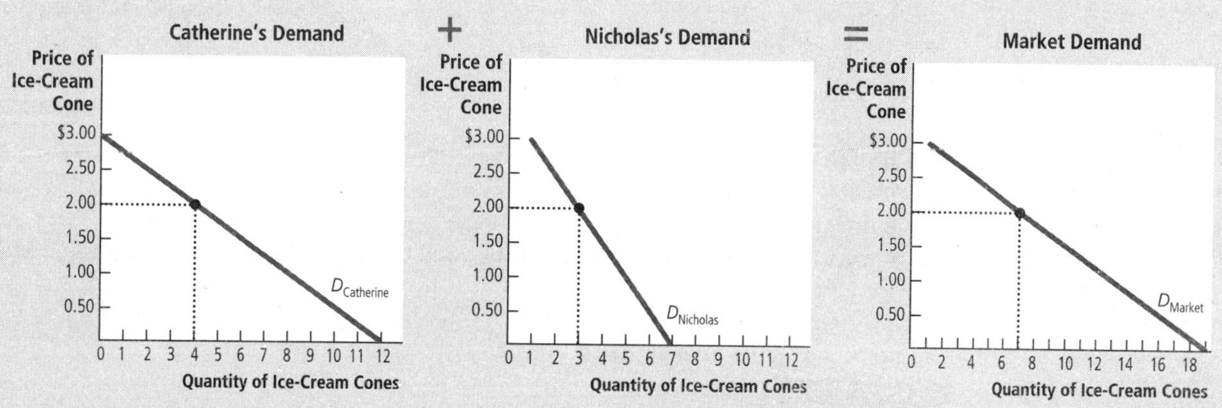

4-2c Shifts in the Demand Curve

Because the market demand curve holds other things constant, it need not be stable over time. If something happens to alter the quantity demanded at any given price, the demand curve shifts. For example, suppose the American Medical Association discovered that people who regularly eat ice cream live longer, healthier lives. The discovery would raise the demand for ice cream. At any given price, buyers would now want to purchase a larger quantity of ice cream, and the demand curve for ice cream would shift.

Figure 3 illustrates shifts in demand. Any change that increases the quantity demanded at every price, such as our imaginary discovery by the American Medical Association, shifts the demand curve to the right and is called an *increase in demand*. Any change that reduces the quantity demanded at every price shifts the demand curve to the left and is called a *decrease in demand*.

There are many variables that can shift the demand curve. Let's consider the most important.

Income What would happen to your demand for ice cream if you lost your job one summer? Most likely, it would fall. A lower income means that you have

FIGURE 3

Shifts in the Demand Curve
Any change that raises the quantity that buyers wish to purchase at any given price shifts the demand curve to the right. Any change that lowers the quantity that buyers wish to purchase at any given price shifts the demand curve to the left.

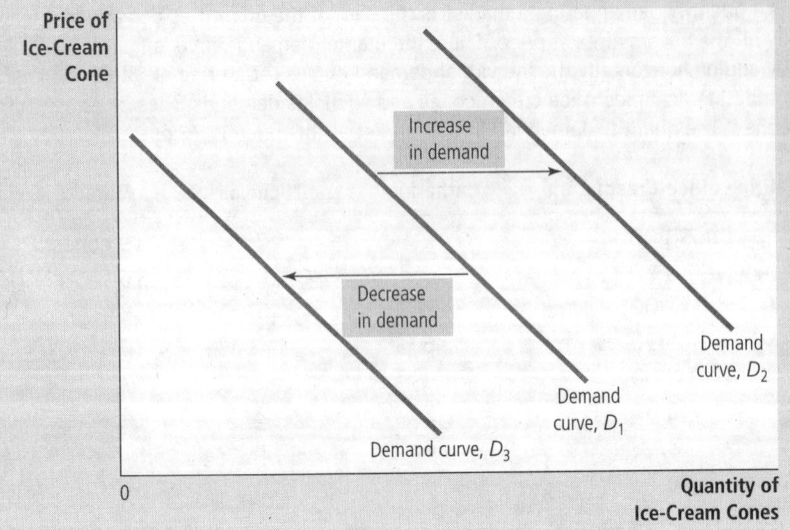

less to spend in total, so you would have to spend less on some—and probably most—goods. If the demand for a good falls when income falls, the good is called a **normal good**.

normal good
a good for which, other things being equal, an increase in income leads to an increase in demand

inferior good
a good for which, other things being equal, an increase in income leads to a decrease in demand

Normal goods are the norm, but not all goods are normal goods. If the demand for a good rises when income falls, the good is called an **inferior good**. An example of an inferior good might be bus rides. As your income falls, you are less likely to buy a car or take a cab and more likely to ride a bus.

substitutes
two goods for which an increase in the price of one leads to an increase in the demand for the other

Prices of Related Goods Suppose that the price of frozen yogurt falls. The law of demand says that you will buy more frozen yogurt. At the same time, you will probably buy less ice cream. Because ice cream and frozen yogurt are both cold, sweet, creamy desserts, they satisfy similar desires. When a fall in the price of one good reduces the demand for another good, the two goods are called **substitutes**. Substitutes are often pairs of goods that are used in place of each other, such as hot dogs and hamburgers, sweaters and sweatshirts, and cinema tickets and film streaming services.

complements
two goods for which an increase in the price of one leads to a decrease in the demand for the other

Now suppose that the price of hot fudge falls. According to the law of demand, you will buy more hot fudge. Yet in this case, you will likely buy more ice cream as well because ice cream and hot fudge are often used together. When a fall in the price of one good raises the demand for another good, the two goods are called **complements**. Complements are often pairs of goods that are used together, such as gasoline and automobiles, computers and software, and peanut butter and jelly.

Tastes The most obvious determinant of your demand is your tastes. If you like ice cream, you buy more of it. Economists normally do not try to explain people's tastes because tastes are based on historical and psychological forces that are beyond the realm of economics. Economists do, however, examine what happens when tastes change.

Expectations Your expectations about the future may affect your demand for a good or service today. If you expect to earn a higher income next month, you may choose to save less now and spend more of your current income buying ice cream. If you expect the price of ice cream to fall tomorrow, you may be less willing to buy an ice-cream cone at today's price.

Number of Buyers In addition to the preceding factors, which influence the behavior of individual buyers, market demand depends on the number of these buyers. If Peter were to join Catherine and Nicholas as another consumer of ice cream, the quantity demanded in the market would be higher at every price, and market demand would increase.

Summary The demand curve shows what happens to the quantity demanded of a good when its price varies, holding constant all the other variables that influence buyers. When one of these other variables changes, the demand curve shifts. Table 1 lists the variables that influence how much of a good consumers choose to buy.

If you have trouble remembering whether you need to shift or move along the demand curve, it helps to recall a lesson from the appendix to Chapter 2. A curve shifts when there is a change in a relevant variable that is not measured on either axis. Because the price is on the vertical axis, a change in price represents a movement along the demand curve. By contrast, income, the prices of related goods, tastes, expectations, and the number of buyers are not measured on either axis, so a change in one of these variables shifts the demand curve.

Variable	A Change in This Variable . . .
Price of the good itself	Represents a movement along the demand curve
Income	Shifts the demand curve
Prices of related goods	Shifts the demand curve
Tastes	Shifts the demand curve
Expectations	Shifts the demand curve
Number of buyers	Shifts the demand curve

TABLE 1

Variables That Influence Buyers
This table lists the variables that affect how much of any good consumers choose to buy. Notice the special role that the price of the good plays: A change in the good's price represents a movement along the demand curve, whereas a change in one of the other variables shifts the demand curve.

CASE STUDY

TWO WAYS TO REDUCE THE QUANTITY OF SMOKING DEMANDED

Because smoking can lead to various illnesses, public policymakers often want to reduce the amount that people smoke. There are two ways that they can attempt to achieve this goal.

One way to reduce smoking is to shift the demand curve for cigarettes and other tobacco products. Public service announcements, mandatory health warnings on cigarette packages, and the prohibition of cigarette advertising on television are all policies aimed at reducing the quantity of cigarettes demanded at any given price. If successful, these policies shift the demand curve for cigarettes to the left, as in panel (a) of Figure 4.

Alternatively, policymakers can try to raise the price of cigarettes. If the government taxes the manufacture of cigarettes, for example, cigarette companies pass much of this tax on to consumers in the form of higher prices. A higher price encourages smokers to reduce the numbers of cigarettes they smoke. In this case, the reduced amount of smoking does not represent a shift in the demand curve.

FIGURE 4

Shifts in the Demand Curve versus Movements along the Demand Curve

If warnings on cigarette packages convince smokers to smoke less, the demand curve for cigarettes shifts to the left. In panel (a), the demand curve shifts from D_1 to D_2. At a price of $4.00 per pack, the quantity demanded falls from 20 to 10 cigarettes per day, as reflected by the shift from point A to point B. By contrast, if a tax raises the price of cigarettes, the demand curve does not shift. Instead, we observe a movement to a different point on the demand curve. In panel (b), when the price rises from $4.00 to $8.00, the quantity demanded falls from 20 to 12 cigarettes per day, as reflected by the movement from point A to point C.

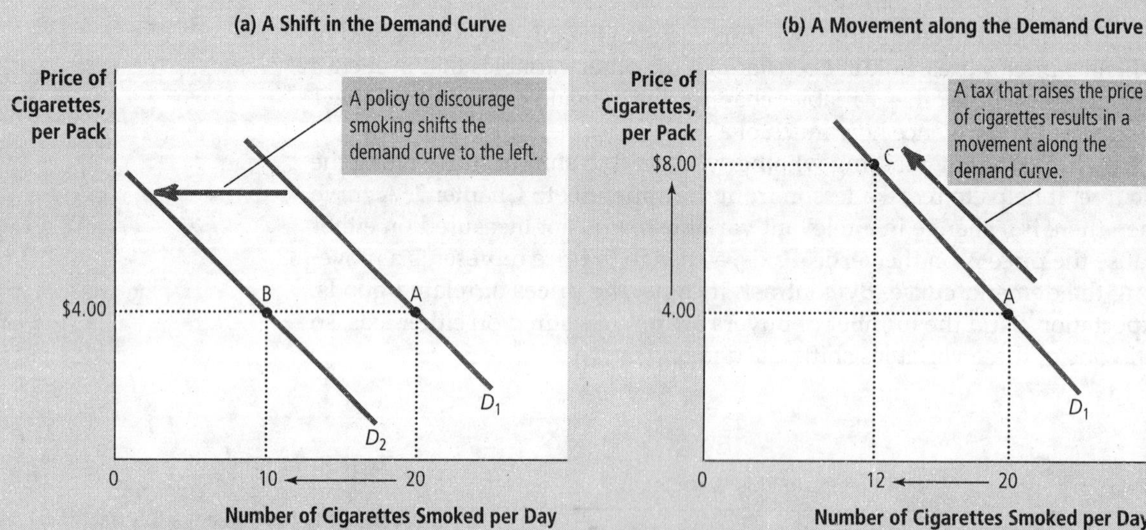

EDYTA PAWLOWSKA/SHUTTERSTOCK.COM

What is the best way to stop this?

Instead, it represents a movement along the same demand curve to a point with a higher price and lower quantity, as in panel (b) of Figure 4.

How much does the amount of smoking respond to changes in the price of cigarettes? Economists have attempted to answer this question by studying what happens when the tax on cigarettes changes. They have found that a 10 percent increase in the price causes a 4 percent reduction in the quantity demanded. Teenagers are especially sensitive to the price of cigarettes: A 10 percent increase in the price causes a 12 percent drop in teenage smoking.

A related question is how the price of cigarettes affects the demand for illicit drugs, such as marijuana. Opponents of cigarette taxes often argue that tobacco and marijuana are substitutes so that high cigarette prices encourage marijuana use. By contrast, many experts on substance abuse view tobacco as a "gateway drug" leading young people to experiment with other harmful substances. Most studies of the data are consistent with this latter view: They find that lower cigarette prices are associated with greater use of marijuana. In other words, tobacco and marijuana appear to be complements rather than substitutes. ●

QuickQuiz *Make up an example of a monthly demand schedule for pizza, and graph the implied demand curve. Give an example of something that would shift this demand curve, and briefly explain your reasoning. Would a change in the price of pizza shift this demand curve?*

4-3 Supply

We now turn to the other side of the market and examine the behavior of sellers. Once again, to focus our thinking, let's consider the market for ice cream.

4-3a The Supply Curve: The Relationship between Price and Quantity Supplied

The **quantity supplied** of any good or service is the amount that sellers are willing and able to sell. There are many determinants of quantity supplied, but once again, price plays a special role in our analysis. When the price of ice cream is high, selling ice cream is profitable, and so the quantity supplied is large. Sellers of ice cream work long hours, buy many ice-cream machines, and hire many workers. By contrast, when the price of ice cream is low, the business is less profitable, so sellers produce less ice cream. At a low price, some sellers may even choose to shut down, and their quantity supplied falls to zero. This relationship between price and quantity supplied is called the **law of supply**: Other things being equal, when the price of a good rises, the quantity supplied of the good also rises, and when the price falls, the quantity supplied falls as well.

quantity supplied
the amount of a good that sellers are willing and able to sell

law of supply
the claim that, other things being equal, the quantity supplied of a good rises when the price of the good rises

The table in Figure 5 shows the quantity of ice-cream cones supplied each month by Ben, an ice-cream seller, at various prices of ice cream. At a price below $1.00, Ben does not supply any ice cream at all. As the price rises, he supplies a greater and greater quantity. This is the **supply schedule**, a table that shows the relationship between the price of a good and the quantity supplied, holding constant everything else that influences how much of the good producers want to sell.

supply schedule
a table that shows the relationship between the price of a good and the quantity supplied

FIGURE 5

Ben's Supply Schedule and Supply Curve

The supply schedule is a table that shows the quantity supplied at each price. This supply curve, which graphs the supply schedule, illustrates how the quantity supplied of the good changes as its price varies. Because a higher price increases the quantity supplied, the supply curve slopes upward.

Price of Ice-Cream Cone	Quantity of Cones Demanded
$0.00	0 cones
0.50	0
1.00	1
1.50	2
2.00	3
2.50	4
3.00	5

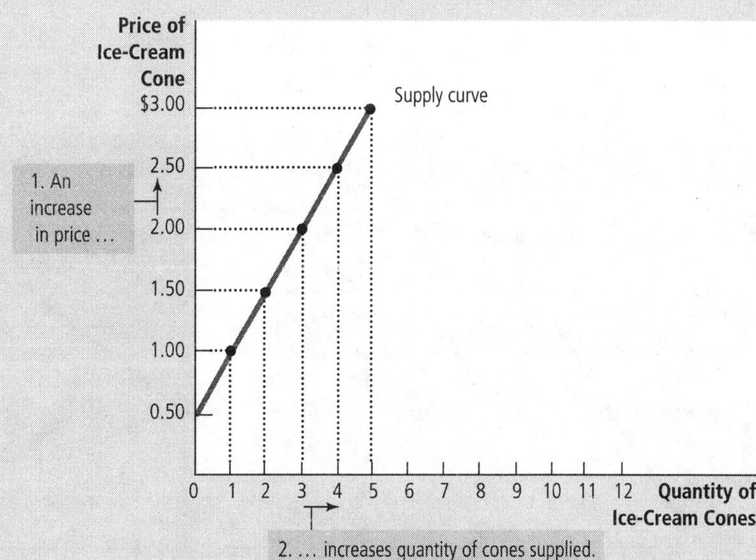

supply curve
a graph of the relationship between the price of a good and the quantity supplied

The graph in Figure 5 uses the numbers from the table to illustrate the law of supply. The curve relating price and quantity supplied is called the **supply curve.** The supply curve slopes upward because, other things being equal, a higher price means a greater quantity supplied.

4-3b Market Supply versus Individual Supply

Just as market demand is the sum of the demands of all buyers, market supply is the sum of the supplies of all sellers. The table in Figure 6 shows the supply schedules for the two ice-cream producers in the market—Ben and Jerry. At any price, Ben's supply schedule tells us the quantity of ice cream that Ben supplies, and Jerry's supply schedule tells us the quantity of ice cream that Jerry supplies. The market supply is the sum of the two individual supplies.

The graph in Figure 6 shows the supply curves that correspond to the supply schedules. As with demand curves, we sum the individual supply curves *horizontally* to obtain the market supply curve. That is, to find the total quantity supplied at any price, we add the individual quantities, which are found on the horizontal axis of the individual supply curves. The market supply curve shows how the total quantity supplied varies as the price of the good varies, holding constant all other factors that influence producers' decisions about how much to sell.

FIGURE 6

Market Supply as the Sum of Individual Supplies

The quantity supplied in a market is the sum of the quantities supplied by all the sellers at each price. Thus, the market supply curve is found by adding horizontally the individual supply curves. At a price of $2.00, Ben supplies 3 ice-cream cones and Jerry supplies 4 ice-cream cones. The quantity supplied in the market at this price is 7 cones.

Price of Ice-Cream Cone	Ben		Jerry		Market
$0.00	0	+	0	=	0 cones
0.50	0		0		0
1.00	1		0		1
1.50	2		2		4
2.00	3		4		7
2.50	4		6		10
3.00	5		8		13

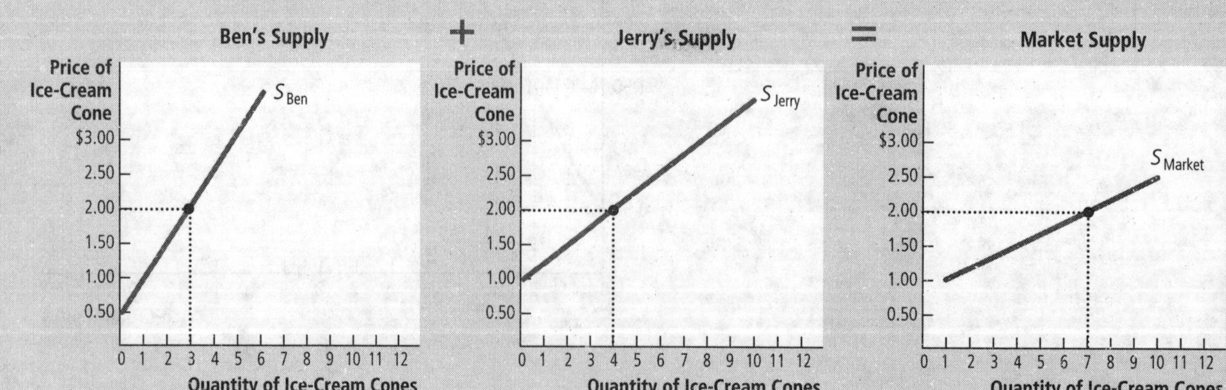

4-3c Shifts in the Supply Curve

Because the market supply curve is drawn holding other things constant, when one of these factors changes, the supply curve shifts. For example, suppose the price of sugar falls. Sugar is an input in the production of ice cream, so the fall in the price of sugar makes selling ice cream more profitable. This raises the supply of ice cream: At any given price, sellers are now willing to produce a larger quantity. As a result, the supply curve for ice cream shifts to the right.

Figure 7 illustrates shifts in supply. Any change that raises quantity supplied at every price, such as a fall in the price of sugar, shifts the supply curve to the right and is called an *increase in supply*. Any change that reduces the quantity supplied at every price shifts the supply curve to the left and is called a *decrease in supply*.

There are many variables that can shift the supply curve. Let's consider the most important.

Input Prices To produce their output of ice cream, sellers use various inputs: cream, sugar, flavoring, ice-cream machines, the buildings in which the ice cream is made, and the labor of workers who mix the ingredients and operate the machines. When the price of one or more of these inputs rises, producing ice cream is less profitable, and firms supply less ice cream. If input prices rise substantially, a firm might shut down and supply no ice cream at all. Thus, the supply of a good is negatively related to the price of the inputs used to make the good.

Technology The technology for turning inputs into ice cream is another determinant of supply. The invention of the mechanized ice-cream machine, for example, reduced the amount of labor necessary to make ice cream. By reducing firms' costs, the advance in technology raised the supply of ice cream.

Expectations The amount of ice cream a firm supplies today may depend on its expectations about the future. For example, if a firm expects the price of ice cream to rise in the future, it will put some of its current production into storage and supply less to the market today.

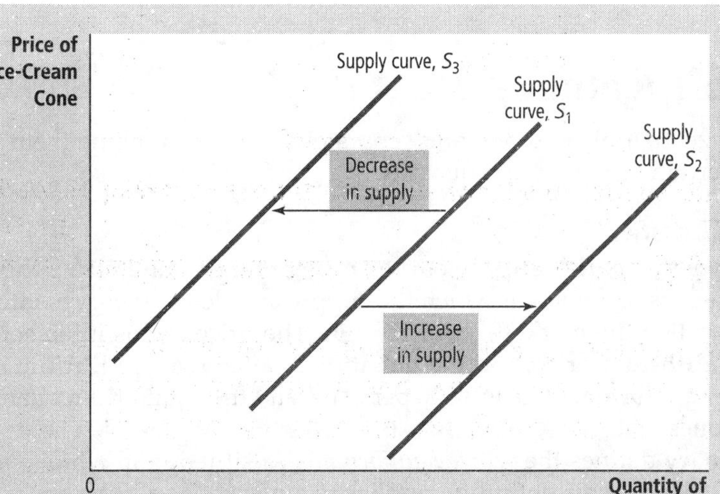

FIGURE 7

Shifts in the Supply Curve
Any change that raises the quantity that sellers wish to produce at any given price shifts the supply curve to the right. Any change that lowers the quantity that sellers wish to produce at any given price shifts the supply curve to the left.

TABLE 2

Variables That Influence Sellers
This table lists the variables that affect how much of any good producers choose to sell. Notice the special role that the price of the good plays: A change in the good's price represents a movement along the supply curve, whereas a change in one of the other variables shifts the supply curve.

Variable	A Change in This Variable . . .
Price of the good itself	Represents a movement along the supply curve
Input prices	Shifts the supply curve
Technology	Shifts the supply curve
Expectations	Shifts the supply curve
Number of sellers	Shifts the supply curve

Number of Sellers In addition to the preceding factors, which influence the behavior of individual sellers, market supply depends on the number of these sellers. If Ben or Jerry were to retire from the ice-cream business, the supply in the market would fall.

Summary The supply curve shows what happens to the quantity supplied of a good when its price varies, holding constant all the other variables that influence sellers. When one of these other variables changes, the supply curve shifts. Table 2 lists the variables that influence how much of a good producers choose to sell.

Once again, to remember whether you need to shift or move along the supply curve, keep in mind that a curve shifts only when there is a change in a relevant variable that is not named on either axis. The price is on the vertical axis, so a change in price represents a movement along the supply curve. By contrast, because input prices, technology, expectations, and the number of sellers are not measured on either axis, a change in one of these variables shifts the supply curve.

QuickQuiz *Make up an example of a monthly supply schedule for pizza, and graph the implied supply curve. Give an example of something that would shift this supply curve, and briefly explain your reasoning. Would a change in the price of pizza shift this supply curve?*

4-4 Supply and Demand Together

equilibrium
a situation in which the market price has reached the level at which quantity supplied equals quantity demanded

equilibrium price
the price that balances quantity supplied and quantity demanded

equilibrium quantity
the quantity supplied and the quantity demanded at the equilibrium price

Having analyzed supply and demand separately, we now combine them to see how they determine the price and quantity of a good sold in a market.

4-4a Equilibrium

Figure 8 shows the market supply curve and market demand curve together. Notice that there is one point at which the supply and demand curves intersect. This point is called the market's **equilibrium**. The price at this intersection is called the **equilibrium price**, and the quantity is called the **equilibrium quantity**. Here the equilibrium price is \$2.00 per cone, and the equilibrium quantity is 7 ice-cream cones.

The dictionary defines the word *equilibrium* as a situation in which various forces are in balance. This definition applies to a market's equilibrium as well. *At the equilibrium price, the quantity of the good that buyers are willing and able to buy exactly balances the quantity that sellers are willing and able to sell.* The equilibrium price is sometimes called the *market-clearing price* because, at this price, everyone

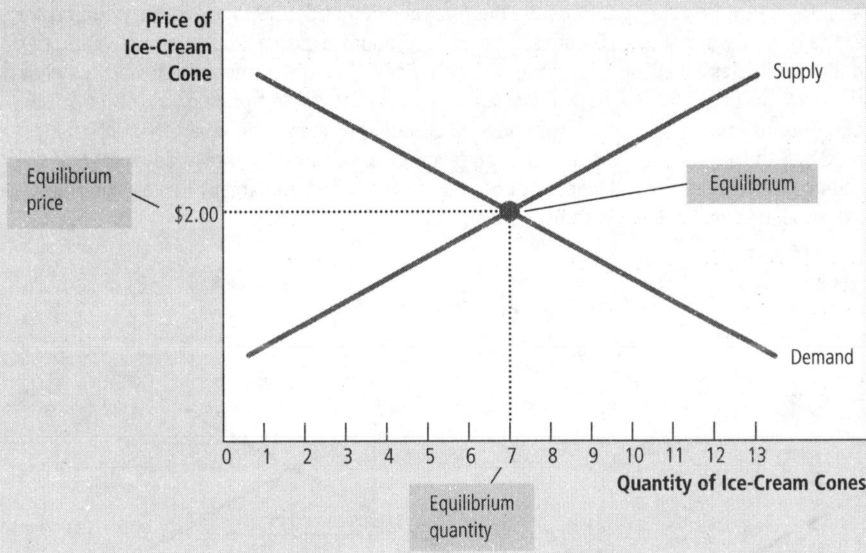

FIGURE 8

The Equilibrium of Supply and Demand
The equilibrium is found where the supply and demand curves intersect. At the equilibrium price, the quantity supplied equals the quantity demanded. Here the equilibrium price is $2.00: At this price, 7 ice-cream cones are supplied and 7 ice-cream cones are demanded.

in the market has been satisfied: Buyers have bought all they want to buy, and sellers have sold all they want to sell.

The actions of buyers and sellers naturally move markets toward the equilibrium of supply and demand. To see why, consider what happens when the market price is not equal to the equilibrium price.

Suppose first that the market price is above the equilibrium price, as in panel (a) of Figure 9. At a price of $2.50 per cone, the quantity of the good supplied (10 cones) exceeds the quantity demanded (4 cones). There is a **surplus** of the good: Suppliers are unable to sell all they want at the going price. A surplus is sometimes called a situation of *excess supply*. When there is a surplus in the ice-cream market, sellers of ice cream find their freezers increasingly full of ice cream they would like to sell but cannot. They respond to the surplus by cutting their prices. Falling prices, in turn, increase the quantity demanded and decrease the quantity supplied. These changes represent movements *along* the supply and demand curves, not shifts in the curves. Prices continue to fall until the market reaches the equilibrium.

surplus
a situation in which quantity supplied is greater than quantity demanded

Suppose now that the market price is below the equilibrium price, as in panel (b) of Figure 9. In this case, the price is $1.50 per cone, and the quantity of the good demanded exceeds the quantity supplied. There is a **shortage** of the good: Demanders are unable to buy all they want at the going price. A shortage is sometimes called a situation of *excess demand*. When a shortage occurs in the ice-cream market, buyers have to wait in long lines for a chance to buy one of the few cones available. With too many buyers chasing too few goods, sellers can respond to the shortage by raising their prices without losing sales. These price increases cause the quantity demanded to fall and the quantity supplied to rise. Once again, these changes represent movements *along* the supply and demand curves, and they move the market toward the equilibrium.

shortage
a situation in which quantity demanded is greater than quantity supplied

Thus, regardless of whether the price starts off too high or too low, the activities of the many buyers and sellers automatically push the market price toward the equilibrium price. Once the market reaches its equilibrium, all buyers and sellers

FIGURE 9

Markets Not in Equilibrium

In panel (a), there is a surplus. Because the market price of $2.50 is above the equilibrium price, the quantity supplied (10 cones) exceeds the quantity demanded (4 cones). Suppliers try to increase sales by cutting the price of a cone, and this moves the price toward its equilibrium level. In panel (b), there is a shortage. Because the market price of $1.50 is below the equilibrium price, the quantity demanded (10 cones) exceeds the quantity supplied (4 cones). With too many buyers chasing too few goods, suppliers can take advantage of the shortage by raising the price. Hence, in both cases, the price adjustment moves the market toward the equilibrium of supply and demand.

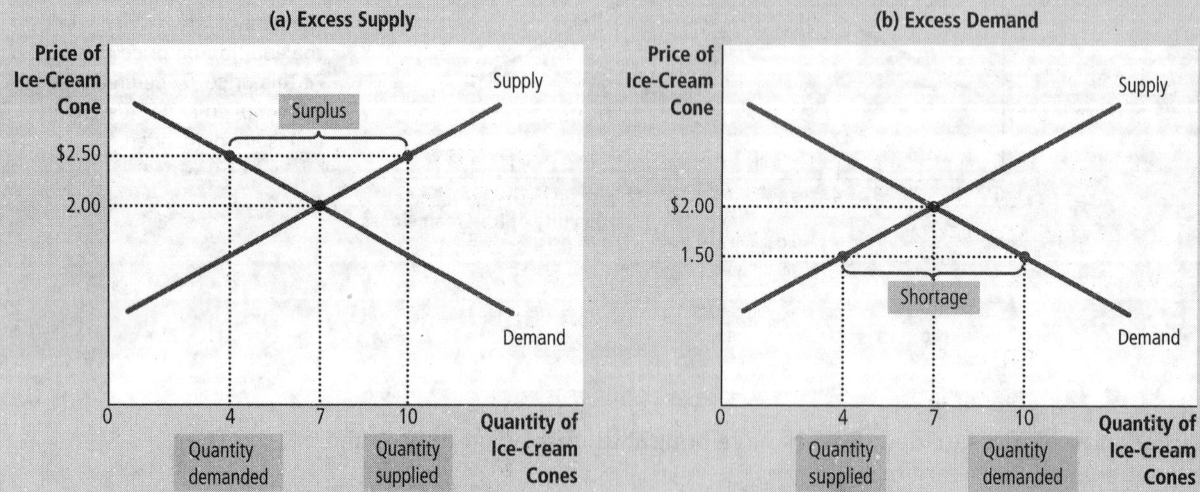

law of supply and demand
the claim that the price of any good adjusts to bring the quantity supplied and the quantity demanded for that good into balance

are satisfied, and there is no upward or downward pressure on the price. How quickly equilibrium is reached varies from market to market depending on how quickly prices adjust. In most free markets, surpluses and shortages are only temporary because prices eventually move toward their equilibrium levels. Indeed, this phenomenon is so pervasive that it is called the **law of supply and demand**: The price of any good adjusts to bring the quantity supplied and quantity demanded for that good into balance.

4-4b Three Steps to Analyzing Changes in Equilibrium

So far, we have seen how supply and demand together determine a market's equilibrium, which in turn determines the price and quantity of the good that buyers

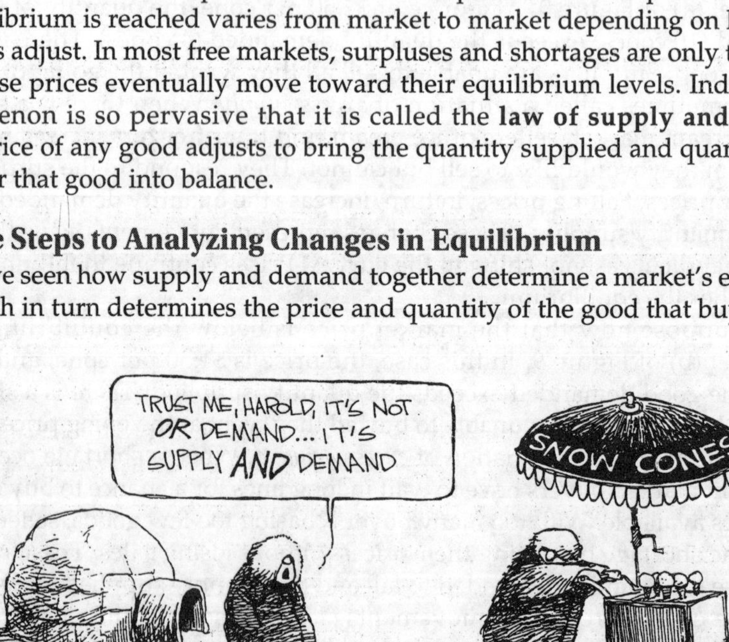

purchase and sellers produce. The equilibrium price and quantity depend on the position of the supply and demand curves. When some event shifts one of these curves, the equilibrium in the market changes, resulting in a new price and a new quantity exchanged between buyers and sellers.

When analyzing how some event affects the equilibrium in a market, we proceed in three steps. First, we decide whether the event shifts the supply curve, the demand curve, or, in some cases, both. Second, we decide whether the curve shifts to the right or to the left. Third, we use the supply-and-demand diagram to compare the initial equilibrium with the new one, which shows how the shift affects the equilibrium price and quantity. Table 3 summarizes these three steps. To see how this recipe is used, let's consider various events that might affect the market for ice cream.

TABLE 3

Three Steps for Analyzing Changes in Equilibrium

1. Decide whether the event shifts the supply or demand curve (or perhaps both).
2. Decide in which direction the curve shifts.
3. Use the supply-and-demand diagram to see how the shift changes the equilibrium price and quantity.

Example: A Change in Market Equilibrium Due to a Shift in Demand Suppose that one summer the weather is very hot. How does this event affect the market for ice cream? To answer this question, let's follow our three steps.

1. The hot weather affects the demand curve by changing people's taste for ice cream. That is, the weather changes the amount of ice cream that people want to buy at any given price. The supply curve is unchanged because the weather does not directly affect the firms that sell ice cream.
2. Because hot weather makes people want to eat more ice cream, the demand curve shifts to the right. Figure 10 shows this increase in demand as a shift in the demand curve from D_1 to D_2. This shift indicates that the quantity of ice cream demanded is higher at every price.
3. At the old price of $2, there is now an excess demand for ice cream, and this shortage induces firms to raise the price. As Figure 10 shows, the increase in demand raises the equilibrium price from $2.00 to $2.50 and the equilibrium quantity from 7 to 10 cones. In other words, the hot weather increases both the price of ice cream and the quantity of ice cream sold.

Shifts in Curves versus Movements along Curves Notice that when hot weather increases the demand for ice cream and drives up the price, the quantity of ice cream that firms supply rises, even though the supply curve remains the same. In this case, economists say there has been an increase in "quantity supplied" but no change in "supply."

Supply refers to the position of the supply curve, whereas the *quantity supplied* refers to the amount suppliers wish to sell. In this example, supply does not change because the weather does not alter firms' desire to sell at any given price. Instead, the hot weather alters consumers' desire to buy at any given price and thereby shifts the demand curve to the right. The increase in demand

FIGURE 10

How an Increase in Demand Affects the Equilibrium
An event that raises quantity demanded at any given price shifts the demand curve to the right. The equilibrium price and the equilibrium quantity both rise. Here an abnormally hot summer causes buyers to demand more ice cream. The demand curve shifts from D_1 to D_2, which causes the equilibrium price to rise from \$2.00 to \$2.50 and the equilibrium quantity to rise from 7 to 10 cones.

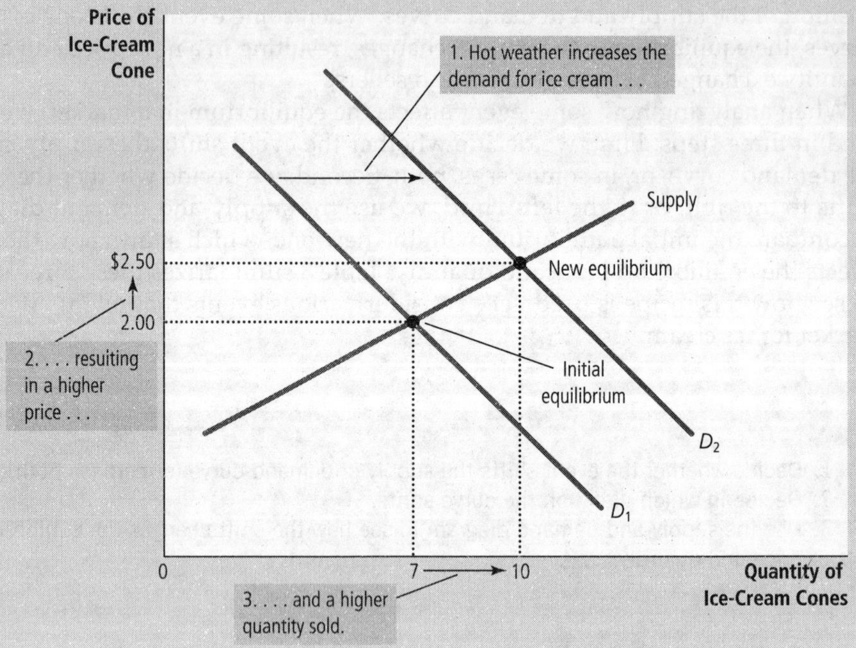

causes the equilibrium price to rise. When the price rises, the quantity supplied rises. This increase in quantity supplied is represented by the movement along the supply curve.

To summarize, a shift *in* the supply curve is called a "change in supply," and a shift *in* the demand curve is called a "change in demand." A movement *along* a fixed supply curve is called a "change in the quantity supplied," and a movement *along* a fixed demand curve is called a "change in the quantity demanded."

Example: A Change in Market Equilibrium Due to a Shift in Supply Suppose that during another summer, a hurricane destroys part of the sugarcane crop and drives up the price of sugar. How does this event affect the market for ice cream? Once again, to answer this question, we follow our three steps.

1. The change in the price of sugar, an input for making ice cream, affects the supply curve. By raising the costs of production, it reduces the amount of ice cream that firms produce and sell at any given price. The demand curve does not change because the higher cost of inputs does not directly affect the amount of ice cream consumers wish to buy.
2. The supply curve shifts to the left because, at every price, the total amount that firms are willing and able to sell is reduced. Figure 11 illustrates this decrease in supply as a shift in the supply curve from S_1 to S_2.
3. At the old price of \$2, there is now an excess demand for ice cream, and this shortage causes firms to raise the price. As Figure 11 shows, the shift in the supply curve raises the equilibrium price from \$2.00 to \$2.50 and

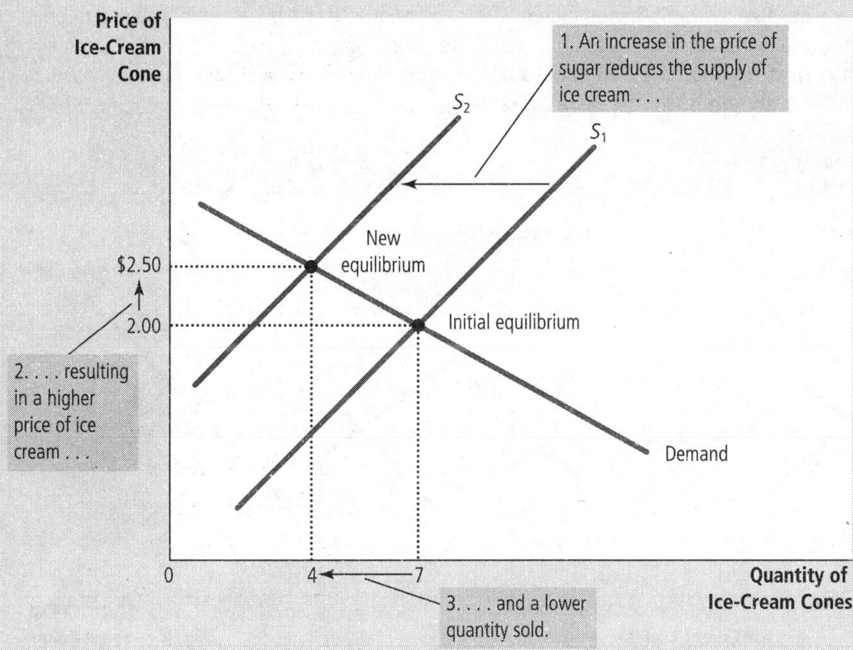

FIGURE 11

How a Decrease in Supply Affects the Equilibrium
An event that reduces quantity supplied at any given price shifts the supply curve to the left. The equilibrium price rises, and the equilibrium quantity falls. Here an increase in the price of sugar (an input) causes sellers to supply less ice cream. The supply curve shifts from S_1 to S_2, which causes the equilibrium price of ice cream to rise from \$2.00 to \$2.50 and the equilibrium quantity to fail from 7 to 4 cones.

lowers the equilibrium quantity from 7 to 4 cones. As a result of the sugar price increase, the price of ice cream rises, and the quantity of ice cream sold falls.

Example: Shifts in Both Supply and Demand Now suppose that the heat wave and the hurricane occur during the same summer. To analyze this combination of events, we again follow our three steps.

1. We determine that both curves must shift. The hot weather affects the demand curve because it alters the amount of ice cream that consumers want to buy at any given price. At the same time, when the hurricane drives up sugar prices, it alters the supply curve for ice cream because it changes the amount of ice cream that firms want to sell at any given price.
2. The curves shift in the same directions as they did in our previous analysis: The demand curve shifts to the right, and the supply curve shifts to the left. Figure 12 illustrates these shifts.
3. As Figure 12 shows, two possible outcomes might result depending on the relative size of the demand and supply shifts. In both cases, the equilibrium price rises. In panel (a), where demand increases substantially while supply falls just a little, the equilibrium quantity also rises. By contrast, in panel (b), where supply falls substantially while demand rises just a little, the equilibrium quantity falls. Thus, these events certainly raise the price of ice cream, but their impact on the amount of ice cream sold is ambiguous (that is, it could go either way).

FIGURE 12

A Shift in Both Supply and Demand

Here we observe a simultaneous increase in demand and decrease in supply. Two outcomes are possible. In panel (a), the equilibrium price rises from P_1 to P_2, and the equilibrium quantity rises from Q_1 to Q_2. In panel (b), the equilibrium price again rises from P_1 to P_2, but the equilibrium quantity falls from Q_1 to Q_2.

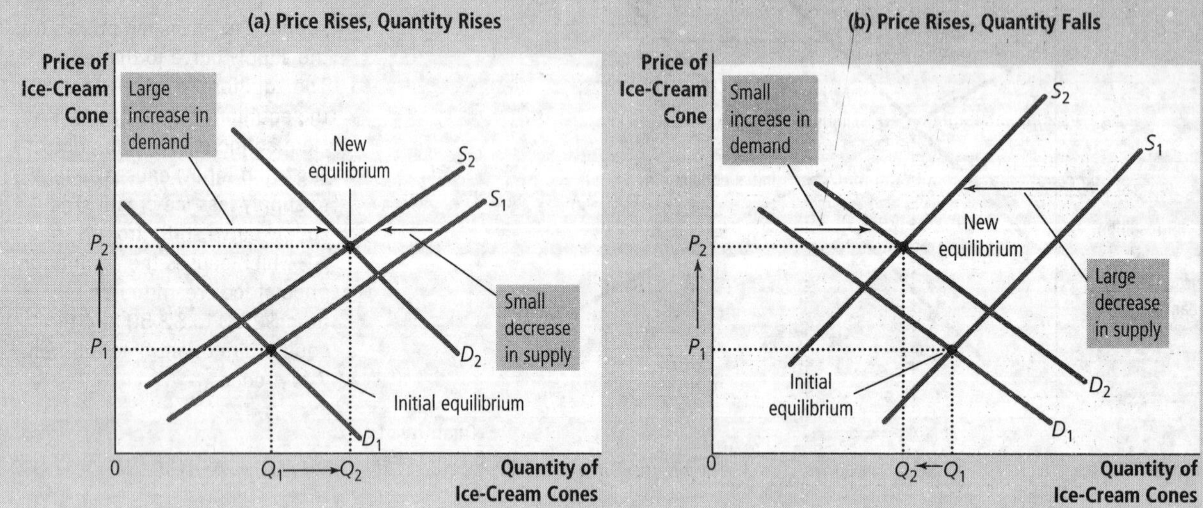

Summary We have just seen three examples of how to use supply and demand curves to analyze a change in equilibrium. Whenever an event shifts the supply curve, the demand curve, or perhaps both curves, you can use these tools to predict how the event will alter the price and quantity sold in equilibrium. Table 4 shows the predicted outcome for any combination of shifts in the two curves. To make sure you understand how to use the tools of supply and demand, pick a few entries in this table and make sure you can explain to yourself why the table contains the prediction that it does. •

TABLE 4

What Happens to Price and Quantity When Supply or Demand Shifts?

As a quick quiz, make sure you can explain at least a few of the entries in this table using a supply-and-demand diagram.

	No Change in Supply	An Increase in Supply	A Decrease in Supply
No Change in Demand	*P* same *Q* same	*P* down *Q* up	*P* up *Q* down
An Increase in Demand	*P* up *Q* up	*P* ambiguous *Q* up	*P* up *Q* ambiguous
A Decrease in Demand	*P* down *Q* down	*P* down *Q* ambiguous	*P* ambiguous *Q* down

QuickQuiz *On the appropriate diagram, show what happens to the market for pizza if the price of tomatoes rises. • On a separate diagram, show what happens to the market for pizza if the price of hamburgers falls.*

4-5 Conclusion: How Prices Allocate Resources

This chapter has analyzed supply and demand in a single market. Our discussion has centered on the market for ice cream, but the lessons learned here apply to most other markets as well. Whenever you go to a store to buy something, you are contributing to the demand for that item. Whenever you look for a job, you are contributing to the supply of labor services. Because supply and demand are such pervasive economic phenomena, the model of supply and demand is a powerful tool for analysis. We use this model repeatedly in the following chapters.

One of the *Ten Principles of Economics* discussed in Chapter 1 is that markets are usually a good way to organize economic activity. Although it is still too early to judge whether market outcomes are good or bad, in this chapter we have begun to see how markets work. In any economic system, scarce resources have to be allocated among competing uses. Market economies harness the forces of supply and demand to serve that end. Supply and demand together determine the prices of the economy's many different goods and services; prices in turn are the signals that guide the allocation of resources.

For example, consider the allocation of beachfront land. Because the amount of this land is limited, not everyone can enjoy the luxury of living by the beach. Who gets this resource? The answer is whoever is willing and able to pay the price. The price of beachfront land adjusts until the quantity of land demanded exactly balances the quantity supplied. Thus, in market economies, prices are the mechanism for rationing scarce resources.

ASK THE EXPERTS

Price Gouging

"Connecticut should pass its Senate Bill 60, which states that during a 'severe weather event emergency, no person within the chain of distribution of consumer goods and services shall sell or offer to sell consumer goods or services for a price that is unconscionably excessive.'"

What do economists say?

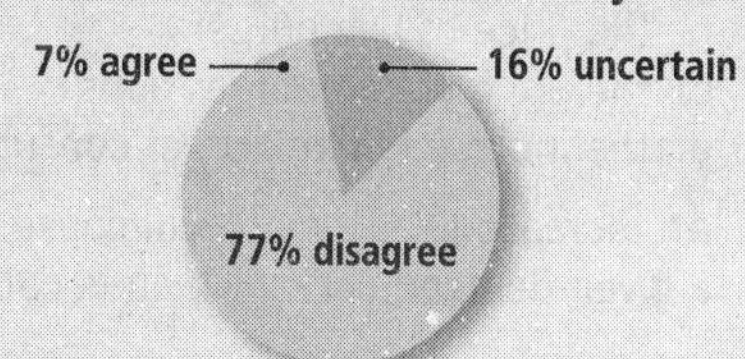

Source: IGM Economic Experts Panel, May 2, 2012.

"Two dollars" *"—and seventy-five cents."*

© ROBERT J. DAY/THE NEW YORKER COLLECTION/ WWW.CARTOONBANK.COM

Similarly, prices determine who produces each good and how much is produced. For instance, consider farming. Because we need food to survive, it is crucial that some people work on farms. What determines who is a farmer and who is not? In a free society, there is no government planning agency making this decision and ensuring an adequate supply of food. Instead, the allocation of workers to farms is based on the job decisions of millions of workers. This decentralized system works well because these decisions depend on prices. The prices of food and the wages of farmworkers (the price of their labor) adjust to ensure that enough people choose to be farmers.

If a person had never seen a market economy in action, the whole idea might seem preposterous. Economies are enormous groups of people engaged in a multitude of interdependent activities. What prevents decentralized decision making from degenerating into chaos? What coordinates the actions of the millions of people with their varying abilities and desires? What ensures that what needs to be done is in fact done? The answer, in a word, is *prices*. If an invisible hand guides market economies, as Adam Smith famously suggested, then the price system is the baton that the invisible hand uses to conduct the economic orchestra.

CHAPTER QuickQuiz

1. A change in which of the following will NOT shift the demand curve for hamburgers?
   a. the price of hot dogs
   b. the price of hamburgers
   c. the price of hamburger buns
   d. the income of hamburger consumers

2. An increase in _______ will cause a movement along a given demand curve, which is called a change in _______.
   a. supply, demand
   b. supply, quantity demanded
   c. demand, supply
   d. demand, quantity supplied

3. Movie tickets and film streaming services are substitutes. If the price of film streaming increases, what happens in the market for movie tickets?
   a. The supply curve shifts to the left.
   b. The supply curve shifts to the right.
   c. The demand curve shifts to the left.
   d. The demand curve shifts to the right.

4. The discovery of a large new reserve of crude oil will shift the _______ curve for gasoline, leading to a _______ equilibrium price.
   a. supply, higher
   b. supply, lower
   c. demand, higher
   d. demand, lower

5. If the economy goes into a recession and incomes fall, what happens in the markets for inferior goods?
   a. Prices and quantities both rise.
   b. Prices and quantities both fall.
   c. Prices rise and quantities fall.
   d. Prices fall and quantities rise.

6. Which of the following might lead to an increase in the equilibrium price of jelly and a decrease in the equilibrium quantity of jelly sold?
   a. an increase in the price of peanut better, a complement to jelly
   b. an increase in the price of Marshmallow Fluff, a substitute for jelly
   c. an increase in the price of grapes, an input into jelly
   d. an increase in consumers' incomes, as long as jelly is a normal good

SUMMARY

- Economists use the model of supply and demand to analyze competitive markets. In a competitive market, there are many buyers and sellers, each of whom has little or no influence on the market price.
- The demand curve shows how the quantity of a good demanded depends on the price. According to the law of demand, as the price of a good falls, the quantity demanded rises. Therefore, the demand curve slopes downward.
- In addition to price, other determinants of how much consumers want to buy include income, the prices of substitutes and complements, tastes, expectations, and the number of buyers. If one of these factors changes, the demand curve shifts.
- The supply curve shows how the quantity of a good supplied depends on the price. According to the law of supply, as the price of a good rises, the quantity supplied rises. Therefore, the supply curve slopes upward.
- In addition to price, other determinants of how much producers want to sell include input prices, technology, expectations, and the number of sellers. If one of these factors changes, the supply curve shifts.
- The intersection of the supply and demand curves determines the market equilibrium. At the equilibrium price, the quantity demanded equals the quantity supplied.
- The behavior of buyers and sellers naturally drives markets toward their equilibrium. When the market price is above the equilibrium price, there is a surplus of the good, which causes the market price to fall. When the market price is below the equilibrium price, there is a shortage, which causes the market price to rise.
- To analyze how any event influences a market, we use the supply-and-demand diagram to examine how the event affects the equilibrium price and quantity. To do this, we follow three steps. First, we decide whether the event shifts the supply curve or the demand curve (or both). Second, we decide in which direction the curve shifts. Third, we compare the new equilibrium with the initial equilibrium.
- In market economies, prices are the signals that guide economic decisions and thereby allocate scarce resources. For every good in the economy, the price ensures that supply and demand are in balance. The equilibrium price then determines how much of the good buyers choose to consume and how much sellers choose to produce.

KEY CONCEPTS

market, p. 66
competitive market, p. 66
quantity demanded, p. 67
law of demand, p. 67
demand schedule, p. 67
demand curve, p. 68
normal good, p. 70
inferior good, p. 70
substitutes, p. 70
complements, p. 70
quantity supplied, p. 73
law of supply, p. 73
supply schedule, p. 73
supply curve, p. 74
equilibrium, p. 76
equilibrium price, p. 76
equilibrium quantity, p. 76
surplus, p. 77
shortage, p. 77
law of supply and demand, p. 78

QUESTIONS FOR REVIEW

1. What is a competitive market? Briefly describe a type of market that is *not* perfectly competitive.
2. What are the demand schedule and the demand curve, and how are they related? Why does the demand curve slope downward?
3. Does a change in consumers' tastes lead to a movement along the demand curve or to a shift in the demand curve? Does a change in price lead to a movement along the demand curve or to a shift in the demand curve? Explain your answers.

4. Harry's income declines, and as a result, he buys more pumpkin juice. Is pumpkin juice an inferior or a normal good? What happens to Harry's demand curve for pumpkin juice?
5. What are the supply schedule and the supply curve, and how are they related? Why does the supply curve slope upward?
6. Does a change in producers' technology lead to a movement along the supply curve or to a shift in the supply curve? Does a change in price lead to a movement along the supply curve or to a shift in the supply curve?
7. Define the equilibrium of a market. Describe the forces that move a market toward its equilibrium.
8. Beer and pizza are complements because they are often enjoyed together. When the price of beer rises, what happens to the supply, demand, quantity supplied, quantity demanded, and price in the market for pizza?
9. Describe the role of prices in market economies.

PROBLEMS AND APPLICATIONS

1. Explain each of the following statements using supply-and-demand diagrams.
   a. "When a cold snap hits Florida, the price of orange juice rises in supermarkets throughout the country."
   b. "When the weather turns warm in New England every summer, the price of hotel rooms in Caribbean resorts plummets."
   c. "When a war breaks out in the Middle East, the price of gasoline rises and the price of a used Cadillac falls."
2. "An increase in the demand for notebooks raises the quantity of notebooks demanded but not the quantity supplied." Is this statement true or false? Explain.
3. Consider the market for minivans. For each of the events listed here, identify which of the determinants of demand or supply are affected. Also indicate whether demand or supply increases or decreases. Then draw a diagram to show the effect on the price and quantity of minivans.
   a. People decide to have more children.
   b. A strike by steelworkers raises steel prices.
   c. Engineers develop new automated machinery for the production of minivans.
   d. The price of sports utility vehicles rises.
   e. A stock market crash lowers people's wealth.
4. Consider the markets for film streaming services, TV screens, and tickets at movie theaters.
   a. For each pair, identify whether they are complements or substitutes:
      - Film streaming and TV screens
      - Film streaming and movie tickets
      - TV screens and movie tickets
   b. Suppose a technological advance reduces the cost of manufacturing TV screens. Draw a diagram to show what happens in the market for TV screens.
   c. Draw two more diagrams to show how the change in the market for TV screens affects the markets for film streaming and movie tickets.
5. Over the past 40 years, technological advances have reduced the cost of computer chips. How do you think this has affected the market for computers? For computer software? For typewriters?
6. Using supply-and-demand diagrams, show the effect of the following events on the market for sweatshirts.
   a. A hurricane in South Carolina damages the cotton crop.
   b. The price of leather jackets falls.
   c. All colleges require morning exercise in appropriate attire.
   d. New knitting machines are invented.
7. Ketchup is a complement (as well as a condiment) for hot dogs. If the price of hot dogs rises, what happens in the market for ketchup? For tomatoes? For tomato juice? For orange juice?
8. The market for pizza has the following demand and supply schedules:

Price	Quantity Demanded	Quantity Supplied
$4	135 pizzas	26 pizzas
5	104	53
6	81	81
7	68	98
8	53	110
9	39	121

   a. Graph the demand and supply curves. What are the equilibrium price and quantity in this market?
   b. If the actual price in this market were *above* the equilibrium price, what would drive the market toward the equilibrium?

c. If the actual price in this market were *below* the equilibrium price, what would drive the market toward the equilibrium?

9. Consider the following events: Scientists reveal that eating oranges decreases the risk of diabetes, and at the same time, farmers use a new fertilizer that makes orange trees produce more oranges. Illustrate and explain what effect these changes have on the equilibrium price and quantity of oranges.

10. Because bagels and cream cheese are often eaten together, they are complements.
    a. We observe that both the equilibrium price of cream cheese and the equilibrium quantity of bagels have risen. What could be responsible for this pattern—a fall in the price of flour or a fall in the price of milk? Illustrate and explain your answer.
    b. Suppose instead that the equilibrium price of cream cheese has risen but the equilibrium quantity of bagels has fallen. What could be responsible for this pattern—a rise in the price of flour or a rise in the price of milk? Illustrate and explain your answer.

11. Suppose that the price of basketball tickets at your college is determined by market forces. Currently, the demand and supply schedules are as follows:

Price	Quantity Demanded	Quantity Supplied
$4	10,000 tickets	8,000 tickets
8	8,000	8,000
12	6,000	8,000
16	4,000	8,000
20	2,000	8,000

    a. Draw the demand and supply curves. What is unusual about this supply curve? Why might this be true?
    b. What are the equilibrium price and quantity of tickets?
    c. Your college plans to increase total enrollment next year by 5,000 students. The additional students will have the following demand schedule:

Price	Quantity Demanded
$4	4,000 tickets
8	3,000
12	2,000
16	1,000
20	0

Now add the old demand schedule and the demand schedule for the new students to calculate the new demand schedule for the entire college. What will be the new equilibrium price and quantity?

To find additional study resources, visit cengagebrain.com, and search for "Mankiw."

CHAPTER

5

Elasticity and Its Application

Imagine that some event drives up the price of gasoline in the United States. It could be a war in the Middle East that disrupts the world supply of oil, a booming Chinese economy that boosts the world demand for oil, or a new tax on gasoline passed by Congress. How would U.S. consumers respond to the higher price?

It is easy to answer this question in a broad fashion: Consumers would buy less. This conclusion follows from the law of demand, which we learned in the previous chapter. But you might want a precise answer. By how much would consumption of gasoline fall? This question can be answered using a concept called *elasticity*, which we develop in this chapter.

Elasticity is a measure of how much buyers and sellers respond to changes in market conditions. When studying how some event or policy affects a market, we can discuss not only the direction of the effects but also their magnitude. Elasticity is useful in many applications, as we see toward the end of this chapter.

Before proceeding, however, you might be curious about the answer to the gasoline question. Many studies have examined consumers' response to changes in gasoline prices, and they typically find that the quantity demanded responds more in the long run than it does in the short run. A 10 percent increase in gasoline prices reduces gasoline consumption by about 2.5 percent after a year and by about 6 percent after 5 years. About half of the long-run reduction in quantity demanded arises because people drive less, and half arises because they switch to more fuel-efficient cars. Both responses are reflected in the demand curve and its elasticity.

5-1 The Elasticity of Demand

When we introduced demand in Chapter 4, we noted that consumers usually buy more of a good when its price is lower, when their incomes are higher, when the prices of its substitutes are higher, or when the prices of its complements are lower. Our discussion of demand was qualitative, not quantitative. That is, we discussed the direction in which quantity demanded moves but not the size of the change. To measure how much consumers respond to changes in these variables, economists use the concept of **elasticity**.

elasticity
a measure of the responsiveness of quantity demanded or quantity supplied to a change in one of its determinants

5-1a The Price Elasticity of Demand and Its Determinants

The law of demand states that a fall in the price of a good raises the quantity demanded. The **price elasticity of demand** measures how much the quantity demanded responds to a change in price. Demand for a good is said to be *elastic* if the quantity demanded responds substantially to changes in the price. Demand is said to be *inelastic* if the quantity demanded responds only slightly to changes in the price.

price elasticity of demand
a measure of how much the quantity demanded of a good responds to a change in the price of that good, computed as the percentage change in quantity demanded divided by the percentage change in price

The price elasticity of demand for any good measures how willing consumers are to buy less of the good as its price rises. Because a demand curve reflects the many economic, social, and psychological forces that shape consumer preferences, there is no simple, universal rule for what determines a demand curve's elasticity. Based on experience, however, we can state some rules of thumb about what influences the price elasticity of demand.

Availability of Close Substitutes Goods with close substitutes tend to have more elastic demand because it is easier for consumers to switch from that good to others. For example, butter and margarine are easily substitutable. A small increase in the price of butter, assuming the price of margarine is held fixed, causes the quantity of butter sold to fall by a large amount. By contrast, because eggs are a food without a close substitute, the demand for eggs is less elastic than the demand for butter. A small increase in the price of eggs does not cause a sizable drop in the quantity of eggs sold.

Necessities versus Luxuries Necessities tend to have inelastic demands, whereas luxuries have elastic demands. When the price of a doctor's visit rises, people do not dramatically reduce the number of times they go to the doctor, although they might go somewhat less often. By contrast, when the price of sailboats rises, the quantity of sailboats demanded falls substantially. The reason is that most people view doctor visits as a necessity and sailboats as a luxury. Whether a good is a necessity or a luxury depends not on the intrinsic properties of the good but on the preferences of the buyer. For avid sailors with little concern about their health, sailboats might be a necessity with inelastic demand and doctor visits a luxury with elastic demand.

Definition of the Market The elasticity of demand in any market depends on how we draw the boundaries of the market. Narrowly defined markets tend to have more elastic demand than broadly defined markets because it is easier to find close substitutes for narrowly defined goods. For example, food, a broad category, has a fairly inelastic demand because there are no good substitutes for food. Ice cream, a narrower category, has a more elastic demand because it is easy to substitute other desserts for ice cream. Vanilla ice cream, a very narrow category, has a very elastic demand because other flavors of ice cream are almost perfect substitutes for vanilla.

Time Horizon Goods tend to have more elastic demand over longer time horizons. When the price of gasoline rises, the quantity of gasoline demanded falls only slightly in the first few months. Over time, however, people buy more fuel-efficient cars, switch to public transportation, and move closer to where they work. Within several years, the quantity of gasoline demanded falls more substantially.

5-1b Computing the Price Elasticity of Demand

Now that we have discussed the price elasticity of demand in general terms, let's be more precise about how it is measured. Economists compute the price elasticity of demand as the percentage change in the quantity demanded divided by the percentage change in the price. That is,

$$\text{price elasticity of demand} = \frac{\text{percentage change in quantity demanded}}{\text{percentage change in price}}$$

For example, suppose that a 10 percent increase in the price of an ice-cream cone causes the amount of ice cream you buy to fall by 20 percent. We calculate your elasticity of demand as

$$\text{price elasticity of demand} = \frac{20 \text{ percent}}{10 \text{ percent}} = 2$$

In this example, the elasticity is 2, reflecting that the change in the quantity demanded is proportionately twice as large as the change in the price.

Because the quantity demanded of a good is negatively related to its price, the percentage change in quantity will always have the opposite sign as the percentage change in price. In this example, the percentage change in price is a *positive* 10 percent (reflecting an increase), and the percentage change in quantity demanded is a *negative* 20 percent (reflecting a decrease). For this reason, price elasticities of demand are sometimes reported as negative numbers. In this book, we follow the common practice of dropping the minus sign and reporting all price elasticities of demand as positive numbers. (Mathematicians call this the *absolute value.*) With this convention, a larger price elasticity implies a greater responsiveness of quantity demanded to changes in price.

5-1c The Midpoint Method: A Better Way to Calculate Percentage Changes and Elasticities

If you try calculating the price elasticity of demand between two points on a demand curve, you will quickly notice an annoying problem: The elasticity from point A to point B seems different from the elasticity from point B to point A. For example, consider these numbers:

point A:	price = \$4	quantity = 120
point B:	price = \$6	quantity = 80

Going from point A to point B, the price rises by 50 percent and the quantity falls by 33 percent, indicating that the price elasticity of demand is 33/50, or 0.66. Going from point B to point A, the price falls by 33 percent and the quantity rises by 50 percent, indicating that the price elasticity of demand is 50/33, or 1.5. This difference arises because the percentage changes are calculated from a different base.

One way to avoid this problem is to use the *midpoint method* for calculating elasticities. The standard procedure for computing a percentage change is to divide the change by the initial level. By contrast, the midpoint method computes a percentage change by dividing the change by the midpoint (or average) of the initial and final levels. For instance, \$5 is the midpoint between \$4 and \$6. Therefore, according to the midpoint method, a change from \$4 to \$6 is considered a 40 percent rise because $(6 - 4) / 5 \times 100 = 40$. Similarly, a change from \$6 to \$4 is considered a 40 percent fall.

Because the midpoint method gives the same answer regardless of the direction of change, it is often used when calculating the price elasticity of demand between two points. In our example, the midpoint between point A and point B is:

midpoint: price = \$5 quantity = 100

According to the midpoint method, when going from point A to point B, the price rises by 40 percent and the quantity falls by 40 percent. Similarly, when going from point B to point A, the price falls by 40 percent and the quantity rises by 40 percent. In both directions, the price elasticity of demand equals 1.

The following formula expresses the midpoint method for calculating the price elasticity of demand between two points, denoted (Q_1, P_1) and (Q_2, P_2):

$$\text{price elasticity of demand} = \frac{(Q_2 - Q_1) / [(Q_2 + Q_1) / 2]}{(P_2 - P_1) / [(P_2 + P_1) / 2]}$$

The numerator is the percentage change in quantity computed using the midpoint method, and the denominator is the percentage change in price computed using the midpoint method. If you ever need to calculate elasticities, you should use this formula.

In this book, however, we rarely perform such calculations. For most of our purposes, what elasticity represents—the responsiveness of quantity demanded to a change in price—is more important than how it is calculated.

5-1d The Variety of Demand Curves

Economists classify demand curves according to their elasticity. Demand is considered *elastic* when the elasticity is greater than 1, which means the quantity moves proportionately more than the price. Demand is considered *inelastic* when the elasticity is less than 1, which means the quantity moves proportionately less than the price. If the elasticity is exactly 1, the percentage change in quantity equals the percentage change in price, and demand is said to have *unit elasticity*.

Because the price elasticity of demand measures how much quantity demanded responds to changes in the price, it is closely related to the slope of the demand curve. The following rule of thumb is a useful guide: The flatter the demand curve that passes through a given point, the greater the price elasticity of demand. The steeper the demand curve that passes through a given point, the smaller the price elasticity of demand.

Figure 1 shows five cases. In the extreme case of a zero elasticity, shown in panel (a), demand is *perfectly inelastic*, and the demand curve is vertical. In this case, regardless of the price, the quantity demanded stays the same. As the elasticity rises, the demand curve gets flatter and flatter, as shown in panels (b), (c), and (d). At the opposite extreme, shown in panel (e), demand is *perfectly elastic*. This occurs as the price elasticity of demand approaches infinity and the demand curve becomes horizontal, reflecting the fact that very small changes in the price lead to huge changes in the quantity demanded.

Finally, if you have trouble keeping straight the terms *elastic* and *inelastic*, here's a memory trick for you: *I*nelastic curves, such as in panel (a) of Figure 1, look like the letter I. This is not a deep insight, but it might help on your next exam.

FYI

A Few Elasticities from the Real World

We have talked about what elasticity means, what determines it, and how it is calculated. Beyond these general ideas, you might ask for a specific number. How much, precisely, does the price of a particular good influence the quantity demanded?

To answer such a question, economists collect data from market outcomes and apply statistical techniques to estimate the price elasticity of demand. Here are some price elasticities of demand, obtained from various studies, for a range of goods:

Eggs	0.1
Healthcare	0.2
Cigarettes	0.4
Rice	0.5
Housing	0.7
Beef	1.6
Peanut Butter	1.7
Restaurant Meals	2.3
Mountain Dew	4.4

These kinds of numbers are fun to think about, and they can be useful when comparing markets.

Nonetheless, one should take these estimates with a grain of salt. One reason is that the statistical techniques used to obtain them require some assumptions about the world, and these assumptions might not be true in practice. (The details of these techniques are beyond the scope of this book, but you will encounter them if you take a course in econometrics.) Another reason is that the price elasticity of demand need not be the same at all points on a demand curve, as we will see shortly in the case of a linear demand curve. For both reasons, you should not be surprised if different studies report different price elasticities of demand for the same good. ■

FIGURE 1

The Price Elasticity of Demand

The price elasticity of demand determines whether the demand curve is steep or flat. Note that all percentage changes are calculated using the midpoint method.

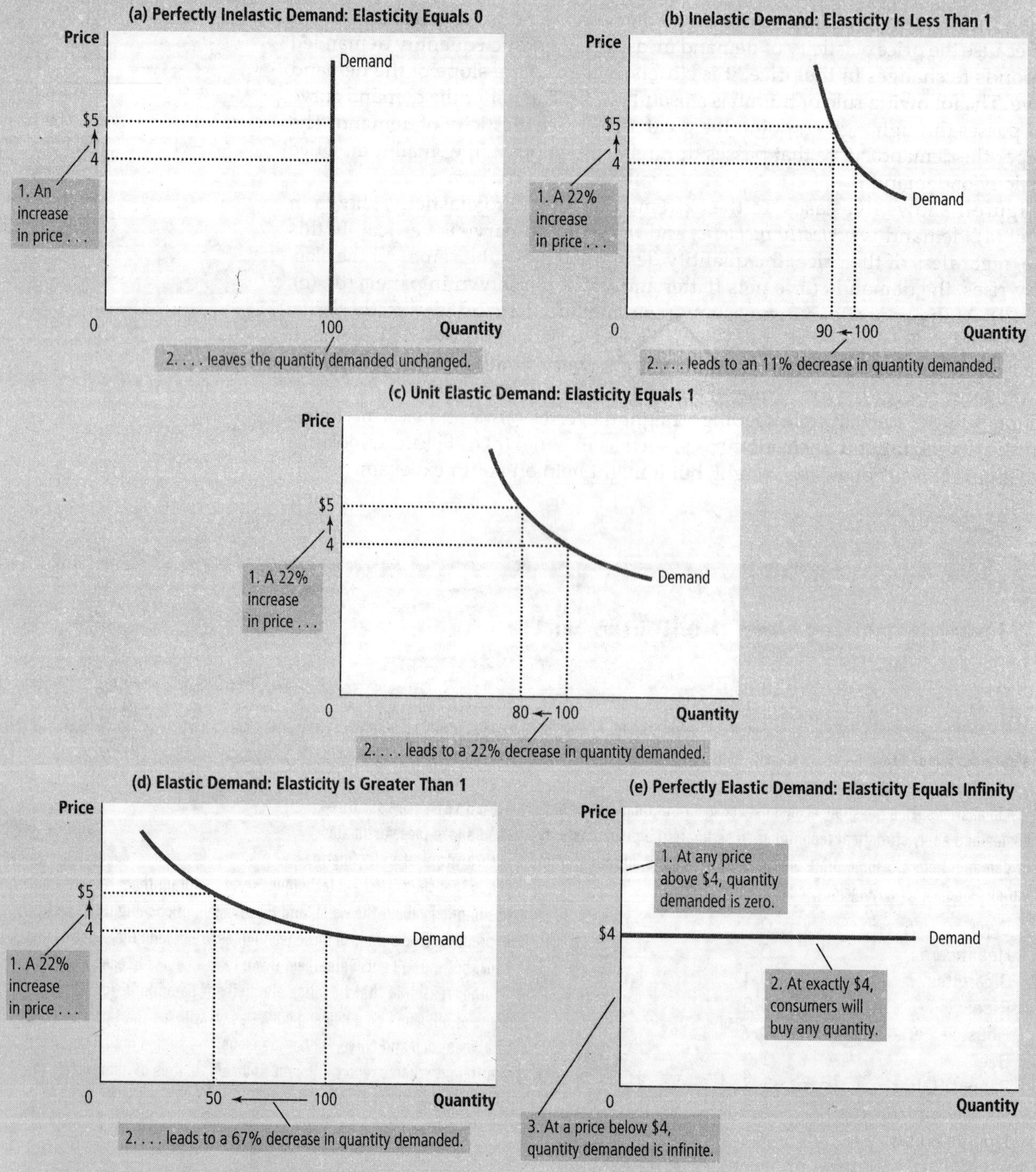

5-1e Total Revenue and the Price Elasticity of Demand

When studying changes in supply or demand in a market, one variable we often want to study is **total revenue**, the amount paid by buyers and received by sellers of a good. In any market, total revenue is $P \times Q$, the price of the good times the quantity of the good sold. We can show total revenue graphically, as in Figure 2. The height of the box under the demand curve is P, and the width is Q. The area of this box, $P \times Q$, equals the total revenue in this market. In Figure 2, where $P = \$4$ and $Q = 100$, total revenue is $\$4 \times 100$, or $400.

total revenue
the amount paid by buyers and received by sellers of a good, computed as the price of the good times the quantity sold

How does total revenue change as one moves along the demand curve? The answer depends on the price elasticity of demand. If demand is inelastic, as in panel (a) of Figure 3, then an increase in the price causes an increase in total revenue. Here an increase in price from $4 to $5 causes the quantity demanded to fall from 100 to 90, so total revenue rises from $400 to $450. An increase in price raises $P \times Q$ because the fall in Q is proportionately smaller than the rise in P. In other words, the extra revenue from selling units at a higher price (represented by area A in the figure) more than offsets the decline in revenue from selling fewer units (represented by area B).

We obtain the opposite result if demand is elastic: An increase in the price causes a decrease in total revenue. In panel (b) of Figure 3, for instance, when the price rises from $4 to $5, the quantity demanded falls from 100 to 70, so total revenue falls from $400 to $350. Because demand is elastic, the reduction in the quantity demanded is so great that it more than offsets the increase in the price. That is, an increase in price reduces $P \times Q$ because the fall in Q is proportionately greater than the rise in P. In this case, the extra revenue from selling units at a higher price (area A) is smaller than the decline in revenue from selling fewer units (area B).

The examples in this figure illustrate some general rules:

- When demand is inelastic (a price elasticity less than 1), price and total revenue move in the same direction: If the price increases, total revenue also increases.

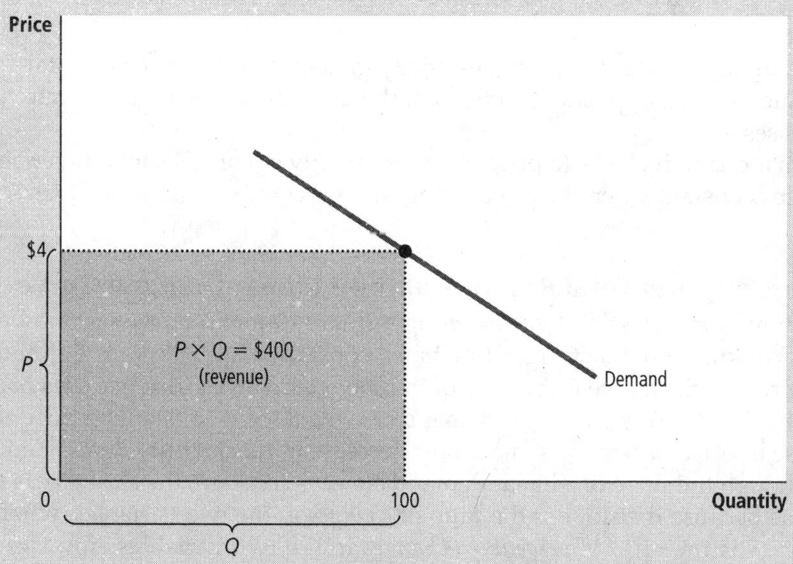

FIGURE 2

Total Revenue
The total amount paid by buyers, and received as revenue by sellers, equals the area of the box under the demand curve, $P \times Q$. Here, at a price of $4, the quantity demanded is 100 and total revenue is $400.

FIGURE 3

How Total Revenue Changes When Price Changes

The impact of a price change on total revenue (the product of price and quantity) depends on the elasticity of demand. In panel (a), the demand curve is inelastic. In this case, an increase in the price leads to a decrease in quantity demanded that is proportionately smaller, so total revenue increases. Here an increase in the price from $4 to $5 causes the quantity demanded to fall from 100 to 90. Total revenue rises from $400 to $450. In panel (b), the demand curve is elastic. In this case, an increase in the price leads to a decrease in quantity demanded that is proportionately larger, so total revenue decreases. Here an increase in the price from $4 to $5 causes the quantity demanded to fall from 100 to 70. Total revenue falls from $400 to $350.

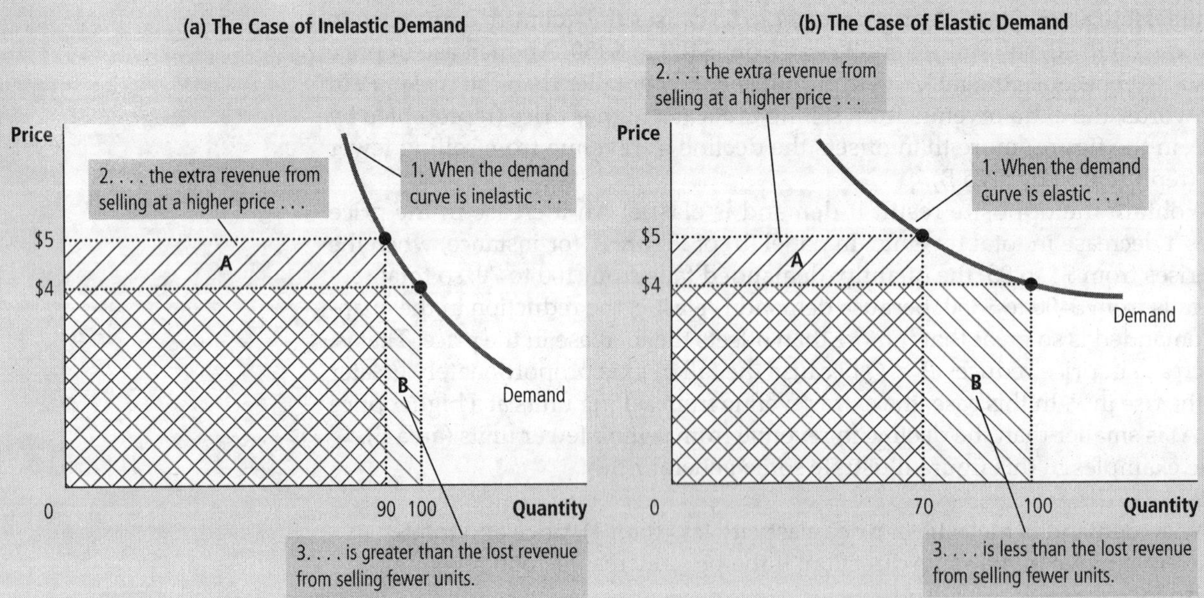

- When demand is elastic (a price elasticity greater than 1), price and total revenue move in opposite directions: If the price increases, total revenue decreases.
- If demand is unit elastic (a price elasticity exactly equal to 1), total revenue remains constant when the price changes.

5-1f Elasticity and Total Revenue along a Linear Demand Curve

Let's examine how elasticity varies along a linear demand curve, as shown in Figure 4. We know that a straight line has a constant slope. Slope is defined as "rise over run," which here is the ratio of the change in price ("rise") to the change in quantity ("run"). This particular demand curve's slope is constant because each $1 increase in price causes the same 2-unit decrease in the quantity demanded.

Even though the slope of a linear demand curve is constant, the elasticity is not. This is true because the slope is the ratio of *changes* in the two variables, whereas the elasticity is the ratio of *percentage changes* in the two variables. You can see this by looking at the table in Figure 4, which shows the demand schedule for the

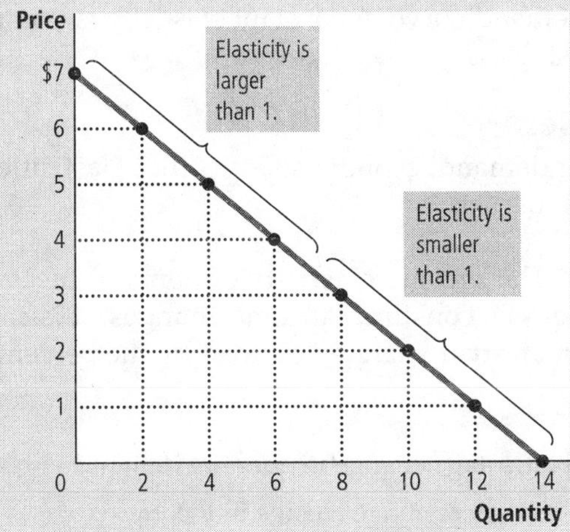

FIGURE 4

Elasticity along a Linear Demand Curve

The slope of a linear demand curve is constant, but its elasticity is not. The price elasticity of demand is calculated using the demand schedule in the table and the midpoint method. At points with a low price and high quantity, the demand curve is inelastic. At points with a high price and low quantity, the demand curve is elastic.

Price	Quantity	Total Revenue (Price × Quantity)	Percentage Change in Price	Percentage Change in Quantity	Elasticity	Description
$7	0	$0				
			15	200	13.0	Elastic
6	2	12				
			18	67	3.7	Elastic
5	4	20				
			22	40	1.8	Elastic
4	6	24				
			29	29	1.0	Unit elastic
3	8	24				
			40	22	0.6	Inelastic
2	10	20				
			67	18	0.3	Inelastic
1	12	12				
			200	15	0.1	Inelastic
0	14	0				

linear demand curve in the graph. The table uses the midpoint method to calculate the price elasticity of demand. The table illustrates the following: *At points with a low price and high quantity, the demand curve is inelastic. At points with a high price and low quantity, the demand curve is elastic.*

The explanation for this fact comes from the arithmetic of percentage changes. When the price is low and consumers are buying a lot, a $1 price increase and 2-unit reduction in quantity demanded constitute a large percentage increase in the price and a small percentage decrease in quantity demanded, resulting in a small elasticity. When the price is high and consumers are not buying much, the same $1 price increase and 2-unit reduction in quantity demanded constitute a small percentage increase in the price and a large percentage decrease in quantity demanded, resulting in a large elasticity.

The table also presents total revenue at each point on the demand curve. These numbers illustrate the relationship between total revenue and elasticity. When the price is $1, for instance, demand is inelastic and a price increase to $2 raises total revenue. When the price is $5, demand is elastic and a price increase to $6 reduces total revenue. Between $3 and $4, demand is exactly unit elastic and total revenue is the same at these two prices.

The linear demand curve illustrates that the price elasticity of demand need not be the same at all points on a demand curve. A constant elasticity is possible, but it is not always the case.

5-1g Other Demand Elasticities

In addition to the price elasticity of demand, economists use other elasticities to describe the behavior of buyers in a market.

income elasticity of demand
a measure of how much the quantity demanded of a good responds to a change in consumers' income, computed as the percentage change in quantity demanded divided by the percentage change in income

The Income Elasticity of Demand The **income elasticity of demand** measures how the quantity demanded changes as consumer income changes. It is calculated as the percentage change in quantity demanded divided by the percentage change in income. That is,

$$\text{income elasticity of demand} = \frac{\text{percentage change in quantity demanded}}{\text{percentage change in income}}$$

As we discussed in Chapter 4, most goods are *normal goods*: Higher income raises the quantity demanded. Because quantity demanded and income move in the same direction, normal goods have positive income elasticities. A few goods, such as bus rides, are *inferior goods*: Higher income lowers the quantity demanded. Because quantity demanded and income move in opposite directions, inferior goods have negative income elasticities.

Even among normal goods, income elasticities vary substantially in size. Necessities, such as food and clothing, tend to have small income elasticities because consumers choose to buy some of these goods even when their incomes are low. Luxuries, such as caviar and diamonds, tend to have large income elasticities because consumers feel that they can do without these goods altogether if their incomes are too low.

cross-price elasticity of demand
a measure of how much the quantity demanded of one good responds to a change in the price of another good, computed as the percentage change in quantity demanded of the first good divided by the percentage change in price of the second good

The Cross-Price Elasticity of Demand The **cross-price elasticity of demand** measures how the quantity demanded of one good responds to a change in the price of another good. It is calculated as the percentage change in quantity demanded of good 1 divided by the percentage change in the price of good 2. That is,

$$\text{cross-price elasticity of demand} = \frac{\text{percentage change in quantity demanded of good 1}}{\text{percentage change in the price of good 2}}$$

Whether the cross-price elasticity is a positive or negative number depends on whether the two goods are substitutes or complements. As we discussed in Chapter 4, *substitutes* are goods that are typically used in place of one another, such as hamburgers and hot dogs. An increase in hot dog prices induces people to grill hamburgers instead. Because the price of hot dogs and the quantity of hamburgers demanded move in the same direction, the cross-price elasticity is positive. Conversely, *complements* are goods that are typically used together, such as computers and software. In this case, the cross-price elasticity is negative, indicating that an increase in the price of computers reduces the quantity of software demanded.

QuickQuiz *Define the price elasticity of demand. • Explain the relationship between total revenue and the price elasticity of demand.*

5-2 The Elasticity of Supply

When we introduced supply in Chapter 4, we noted that producers of a good offer to sell more of it when the price of the good rises. To turn from qualitative to quantitative statements about quantity supplied, we once again use the concept of elasticity.

5-2a The Price Elasticity of Supply and Its Determinants

The law of supply states that higher prices raise the quantity supplied. The **price elasticity of supply** measures how much the quantity supplied responds to changes in the price. Supply of a good is said to be *elastic* if the quantity supplied responds substantially to changes in the price. Supply is said to be *inelastic* if the quantity supplied responds only slightly to changes in the price.

price elasticity of supply
a measure of how much the quantity supplied of a good responds to a change in the price of that good, computed as the percentage change in quantity supplied divided by the percentage change in price

The price elasticity of supply depends on the flexibility of sellers to change the amount of the good they produce. For example, beachfront land has an inelastic supply because it is almost impossible to produce more of it. Manufactured goods, such as books, cars, and televisions, have elastic supplies because firms that produce them can run their factories longer in response to a higher price.

In most markets, a key determinant of the price elasticity of supply is the time period being considered. Supply is usually more elastic in the long run than in the short run. Over short periods of time, firms cannot easily change the size of their factories to make more or less of a good. Thus, in the short run, the quantity supplied is not very responsive to the price. Over longer periods of time, firms can build new factories or close old ones. In addition, new firms can enter a market, and old firms can exit. Thus, in the long run, the quantity supplied can respond substantially to price changes.

5-2b Computing the Price Elasticity of Supply

Now that we have a general understanding about the price elasticity of supply, let's be more precise. Economists compute the price elasticity of supply as the percentage change in the quantity supplied divided by the percentage change in the price. That is,

$$\text{price elasticity of supply} = \frac{\text{percentage change in quantity supplied}}{\text{percentage change in price}}$$

For example, suppose that an increase in the price of milk from \$2.85 to \$3.15 a gallon raises the amount that dairy farmers produce from 9,000 to 11,000 gallons per month. Using the midpoint method, we calculate the percentage change in price as

$$\text{percentage change in price} = (3.15 - 2.85) / 3.00 \times 100 = 10 \text{ percent}$$

Similarly, we calculate the percentage change in quantity supplied as:

$$\text{Percentage change in quantity supplied} = (11{,}000 - 9{,}000) / 10{,}000 \times 100 = 20 \text{ percent.}$$

In this case, the price elasticity of supply is

$$\text{price elasticity of supply} = \frac{20 \text{ percent}}{10 \text{ percent}} = 2$$

In this example, the elasticity of 2 indicates that the quantity supplied changes proportionately twice as much as the price.

5-2c The Variety of Supply Curves

Because the price elasticity of supply measures the responsiveness of quantity supplied to changes in price, it is reflected in the appearance of the supply curve. Figure 5 (on the facing page) shows five cases. In the extreme case of zero elasticity, as shown in panel (a), supply is *perfectly inelastic* and the supply curve is vertical. In this case, the quantity supplied is the same regardless of the price. As the elasticity rises, the supply curve gets flatter, which shows that the quantity supplied responds more to changes in the price. At the opposite extreme, shown in panel (e), supply is *perfectly elastic*. This occurs as the price elasticity of supply approaches infinity and the supply curve becomes horizontal, meaning that very small changes in the price lead to very large changes in the quantity supplied.

In some markets, the elasticity of supply is not constant but varies over the supply curve. Figure 6 (presented below) shows a typical case for an industry in which firms have factories with a limited capacity for production. For low levels of quantity supplied, the elasticity of supply is high, indicating that firms respond substantially to changes in the price. In this region, firms have capacity for production that is not being used, such as plants and equipment that are idle for all or part of the day. Small increases in price make it profitable for firms to begin using this idle capacity. As the quantity supplied rises, firms begin to reach capacity. Once capacity is fully used, further increases in production require the construction of new plants. To induce firms to incur this extra expense, the price must rise substantially, so supply becomes less elastic.

Figure 6 presents a numerical example of this phenomenon. When the price rises from \$3 to \$4 (a 29 percent increase, according to the midpoint method), the quantity supplied rises from 100 to 200 (a 67 percent increase). Because quantity supplied changes proportionately more than the price, the supply curve has an elasticity greater than 1. By contrast, when the price rises from \$12 to \$15 (a 22 percent increase), the quantity supplied rises from 500 to 525 (a 5 percent increase). In this case, quantity supplied moves proportionately less than the price, so the elasticity is less than 1.

QuickQuiz *Define the price elasticity of supply. • Explain why the price elasticity of supply might be different in the long run than in the short run.*

FIGURE 6

How the Price Elasticity of Supply Can Vary

Because firms often have a maximum capacity for production, the elasticity of supply may be very high at low levels of quantity supplied and very low at high levels of quantity supplied. Here an increase in price from \$3 to \$4 increases the quantity supplied from 100 to 200. Because the 67 percent increase in quantity supplied (computed using the midpoint method) is larger than the 29 percent increase in price, the supply curve is elastic in this range. By contrast, when the price rises from \$12 to \$15, the quantity supplied rises only from 500 to 525. Because the 5 percent increase in quantity supplied is smaller than the 22 percent increase in price, the supply curve is inelastic in this range.

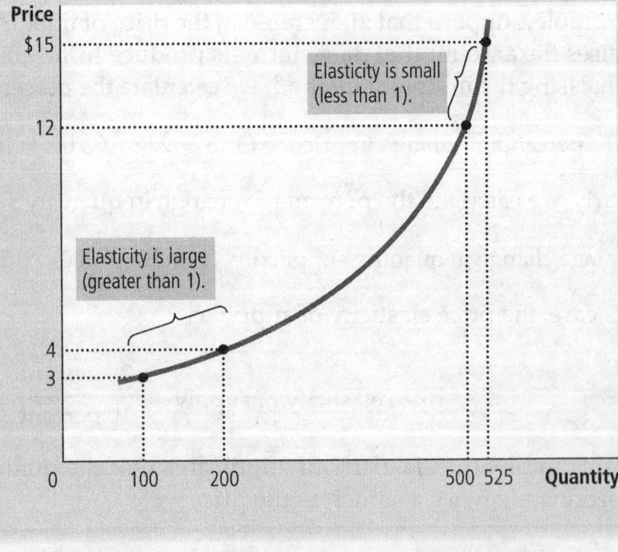

The price elasticity of supply determines whether the supply curve is steep or flat. Note that all percentage changes are calculated using the midpoint method.

FIGURE 5

The Price Elasticity of Supply

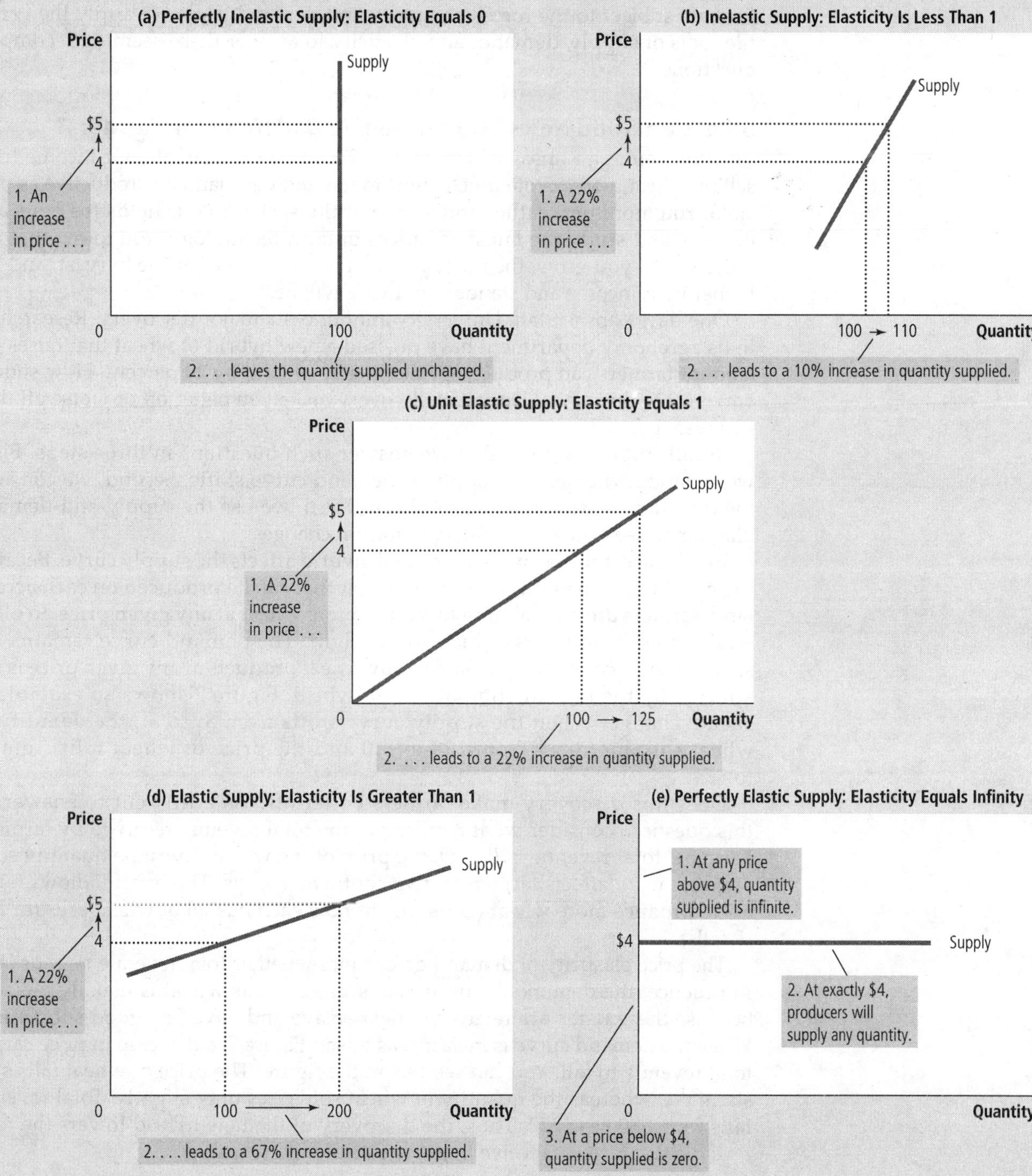

5-3 Three Applications of Supply, Demand, and Elasticity

Can good news for farming be bad news for farmers? Why did OPEC, the international oil cartel, fail to keep the price of oil high? Does drug interdiction increase or decrease drug-related crime? At first, these questions might seem to have little in common. Yet all three questions are about markets, and all markets are subject to the forces of supply and demand. Here we apply the versatile tools of supply, demand, and elasticity to answer these seemingly complex questions.

5-3a Can Good News for Farming Be Bad News for Farmers?

Imagine you're a Kansas wheat farmer. Because you earn all your income from selling wheat, you devote much effort to making your land as productive as possible. You monitor weather and soil conditions, check your fields for pests and disease, and study the latest advances in farm technology. You know that the more wheat you grow, the more you will have to sell after the harvest, and the higher your income and standard of living will be.

One day, Kansas State University announces a major discovery. Researchers in its agronomy department have devised a new hybrid of wheat that raises the amount farmers can produce from each acre of land by 20 percent. How should you react to this news? Does this discovery make you better off or worse off than you were before?

Recall from Chapter 4 that we answer such questions in three steps. First, we examine whether the supply or demand curve shifts. Second, we consider the direction in which the curve shifts. Third, we use the supply-and-demand diagram to see how the market equilibrium changes.

In this case, the discovery of the new hybrid affects the supply curve. Because the hybrid increases the amount of wheat that can be produced on each acre of land, farmers are now willing to supply more wheat at any given price. In other words, the supply curve shifts to the right. The demand curve remains the same because consumers' desire to buy wheat products at any given price is not affected by the introduction of a new hybrid. Figure 7 shows an example of such a change. When the supply curve shifts from S_1 to S_2, the quantity of wheat sold increases from 100 to 110 and the price of wheat falls from \$3 to \$2.

Does this discovery make farmers better off? As a first cut to answering this question, consider what happens to the total revenue received by farmers. Farmers' total revenue is $P \times Q$, the price of the wheat times the quantity sold. The discovery affects farmers in two conflicting ways. The hybrid allows farmers to produce more wheat (Q rises), but now each bushel of wheat sells for less (P falls).

The price elasticity of demand determines whether total revenue rises or falls. In practice, the demand for basic foodstuffs such as wheat is usually inelastic because these items are relatively inexpensive and have few good substitutes. When the demand curve is inelastic, as it is in Figure 7, a decrease in price causes total revenue to fall. You can see this in the figure: The price of wheat falls substantially, whereas the quantity of wheat sold rises only slightly. Total revenue falls from \$300 to \$220. Thus, the discovery of the new hybrid lowers the total revenue that farmers receive from the sale of their crops.

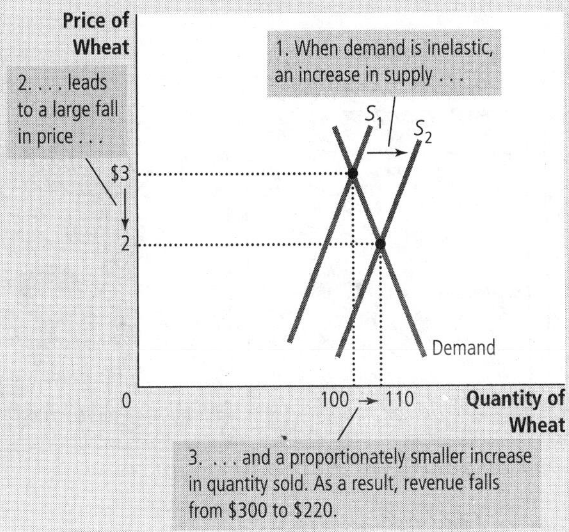

FIGURE 7

An Increase in Supply in the Market for Wheat
When an advance in farm technology increases the supply of wheat from S_1 to S_2, the price of wheat falls. Because the demand for wheat is inelastic, the increase in the quantity sold from 100 to 110 is proportionately smaller than the decrease in the price from \$3 to \$2. As a result, farmers' total revenue falls from \$300 (\$3 × 100) to \$220 (\$2 × 110).

If farmers are made worse off by the discovery of this new hybrid, one might wonder why they adopt it. The answer goes to the heart of how competitive markets work. Because each farmer is only a small part of the market for wheat, she takes the price of wheat as given. For any given price of wheat, it is better to use the new hybrid to produce and sell more wheat. Yet when all farmers do this, the supply of wheat increases, the price falls, and farmers are worse off.

This example may at first seem hypothetical, but it helps to explain a major change in the U.S. economy over the past century. Two hundred years ago, most Americans lived on farms. Knowledge about farm methods was sufficiently primitive that most Americans had to be farmers to produce enough food to feed the nation's population. But over time, advances in farm technology increased the amount of food that each farmer could produce. This increase in food supply, together with the inelastic demand for food, caused farm revenues to fall, which in turn encouraged people to leave farming.

A few numbers show the magnitude of this historic change. As recently as 1950, 10 million people worked on farms in the United States, representing 17 percent of the labor force. Today, fewer than 3 million people work on farms, or 2 percent of the labor force. This change coincided with tremendous advances in farm productivity: Despite the large drop in the number of farmers, U.S. farms now produce about five times as much output as they did in 1950.

This analysis of the market for farm products also explains a seeming paradox of public policy: Certain farm programs try to help farmers by inducing them *not* to plant crops on all of their land. The purpose of these programs is to reduce the supply of farm products and thereby raise prices. With inelastic demand for their products, farmers as a group receive greater total revenue if they supply a smaller crop to the market. No single farmer would choose to leave her land fallow on her own because each takes the market price as given. But if all farmers do so together, they can all be better off.

When analyzing the effects of farm technology or farm policy, it is important to keep in mind that what is good for farmers is not necessarily good for society as a whole. Improvement in farm technology can be bad for farmers because it makes farmers increasingly unnecessary, but it is surely good for consumers who pay less for food. Similarly, a policy aimed at reducing the supply of farm products may raise the incomes of farmers, but it does so at the expense of consumers.

5-3b Why Did OPEC Fail to Keep the Price of Oil High?

Many of the most disruptive events for the world's economies over the past several decades have originated in the world market for oil. In the 1970s, members of the Organization of the Petroleum Exporting Countries (OPEC) decided to raise the world price of oil to increase their incomes. These countries accomplished this goal by agreeing to jointly reduce the amount of oil they supplied. As a result, the price of oil (adjusted for overall inflation) rose more than 50 percent from 1973 to 1974. Then, a few years later, OPEC did the same thing again. From 1979 to 1981, the price of oil approximately doubled.

Yet OPEC found it difficult to maintain such a high price. From 1982 to 1985, the price of oil steadily declined about 10 percent per year. Dissatisfaction and disarray soon prevailed among the OPEC countries. In 1986, cooperation among OPEC members completely broke down, and the price of oil plunged 45 percent. In 1990, the price of oil (adjusted for overall inflation) was back to where it began in 1970, and it stayed at that low level throughout most of the 1990s. (In the first decade and a half of the 21st century, the price of oil fluctuated substantially once again, but the main driving force was not OPEC supply restrictions. Instead, booms and busts in economies around the world caused demand to fluctuate, while advances in fracking technology caused large increases in supply.)

The OPEC episodes of the 1970s and 1980s show how supply and demand can behave differently in the short run and in the long run. In the short run, both the supply and demand for oil are relatively inelastic. Supply is inelastic because the quantity of known oil reserves and the capacity for oil extraction cannot be changed quickly. Demand is inelastic because buying habits do not respond immediately to changes in price. Thus, as panel (a) of Figure 8 shows, the short-run

When the supply of oil falls, the response depends on the time horizon. In the short run, supply and demand are relatively inelastic, as in panel (a). Thus, when the supply curve shifts from S_1 to S_2, the price rises substantially. In the long run, however, supply and demand are relatively elastic, as in panel (b). In this case, the same size shift in the supply curve (S_1 to S_2) causes a smaller increase in the price.

FIGURE 8

A Reduction in Supply in the World Market for Oil

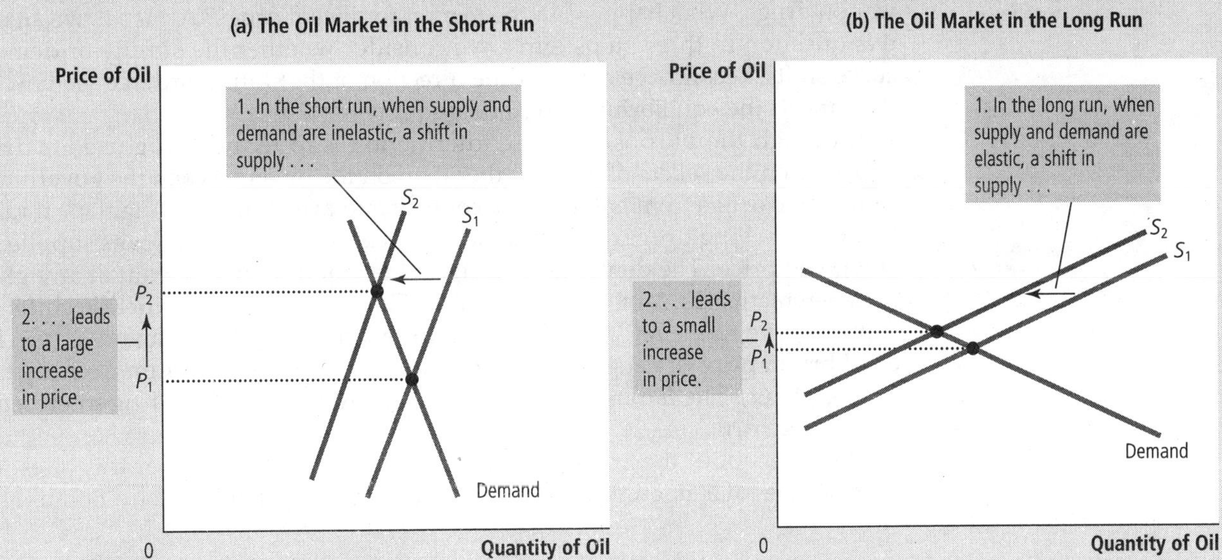

supply and demand curves are steep. When the supply of oil shifts from S_1 to S_2, the price increase from P_1 to P_2 is large.

The situation is very different in the long run. Over long periods of time, producers of oil outside OPEC respond to high prices by increasing oil exploration and by building new extraction capacity. Consumers respond with greater conservation, such as by replacing old inefficient cars with newer efficient ones. Thus, as panel (b) of Figure 8 shows, the long-run supply and demand curves are more elastic. In the long run, the shift in the supply curve from S_1 to S_2 causes a much smaller increase in the price.

This analysis shows why OPEC succeeded in maintaining a high price of oil only in the short run. When OPEC countries agreed to reduce their production of oil, they shifted the supply curve to the left. Even though each OPEC member sold less oil, the price rose by so much in the short run that OPEC incomes rose. In the long run, however, supply and demand are more elastic. As a result, the same reduction in supply, measured by the horizontal shift in the supply curve, caused a smaller increase in the price. Thus, OPEC's coordinated reduction in supply proved less profitable in the long run. The cartel learned that raising prices is easier in the short run than in the long run.

5-3c Does Drug Interdiction Increase or Decrease Drug-Related Crime?

A persistent problem facing our society is the use of illegal drugs, such as heroin, cocaine, ecstasy, and methamphetamine. Drug use has several adverse effects. One is that drug dependence can ruin the lives of drug users and their families.

Another is that drug addicts often turn to robbery and other violent crimes to obtain the money needed to support their habit. To discourage the use of illegal drugs, the U.S. government devotes billions of dollars each year to reducing the flow of drugs into the country. Let's use the tools of supply and demand to examine this policy of drug interdiction.

Suppose the government increases the number of federal agents devoted to the war on drugs. What happens in the market for illegal drugs? As usual, we answer this question in three steps. First, we consider whether the supply or demand curve shifts. Second, we consider the direction of the shift. Third, we see how the shift affects the equilibrium price and quantity.

Although the purpose of drug interdiction is to reduce drug use, its direct impact is on the sellers of drugs rather than on the buyers. When the government stops some drugs from entering the country and arrests more smugglers, it raises the cost of selling drugs and, therefore, reduces the quantity of drugs supplied at any given price. The demand for drugs—the amount buyers want at any given price—remains the same. As panel (a) of Figure 9 shows, interdiction shifts the supply curve to the left from S_1 to S_2 without changing the demand curve. The equilibrium price of drugs rises from P_1 to P_2, and the equilibrium quantity falls from Q_1 to Q_2. The fall in the equilibrium quantity shows that drug interdiction does reduce drug use.

But what about the amount of drug-related crime? To answer this question, consider the total amount that drug users pay for the drugs they buy. Because few

FIGURE 9

Policies to Reduce the Use of Illegal Drugs

Drug interdiction reduces the supply of drugs from S_1 to S_2, as in panel (a). If the demand for drugs is inelastic, then the total amount paid by drug users rises, even as the amount of drug use falls. By contrast, drug education reduces the demand for drugs from D_1 to D_2, as in panel (b). Because both price and quantity fall, the amount paid by drug users falls.

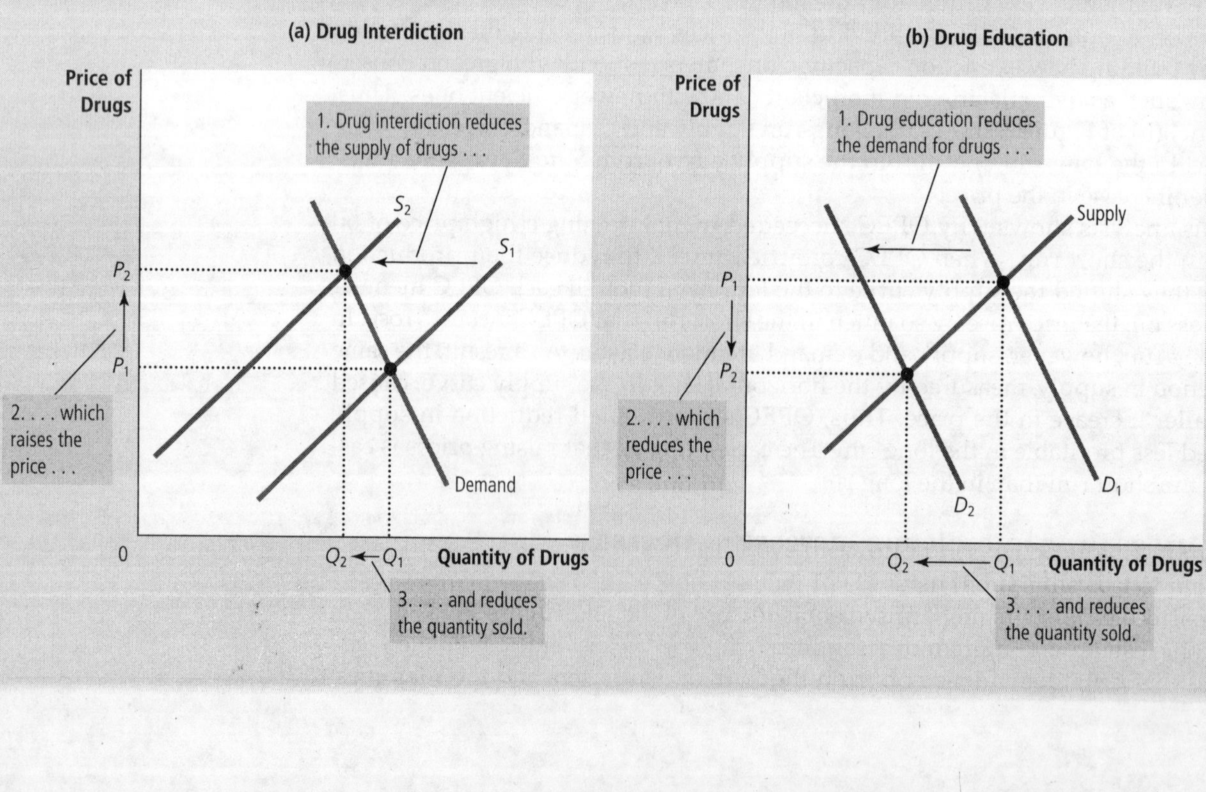

drug addicts are likely to break their destructive habits in response to a higher price, it is likely that the demand for drugs is inelastic, as it is drawn in the figure. If demand is inelastic, then an increase in price raises total revenue in the drug market. That is, because drug interdiction raises the price of drugs proportionately more than it reduces drug use, it raises the total amount of money that drug users pay for drugs. Addicts who already had to steal to support their habits would have an even greater need for quick cash. Thus, drug interdiction could increase drug-related crime.

Because of this adverse effect of drug interdiction, some analysts argue for alternative approaches to the drug problem. Rather than trying to reduce the supply of drugs, policymakers might try to reduce the demand by pursuing a policy of drug education. Successful drug education has the effects shown in panel (b) of Figure 9. The demand curve shifts to the left from D_1 to D_2. As a result, the equilibrium quantity falls from Q_1 to Q_2, and the equilibrium price falls from P_1 to P_2. Total revenue, $P \times Q$, also falls. Thus, in contrast to drug interdiction, drug education can reduce both drug use and drug-related crime.

Advocates of drug interdiction might argue that the long-run effects of this policy are different from the short-run effects because the elasticity of demand depends on the time horizon. The demand for drugs is probably inelastic over short periods because higher prices do not substantially affect drug use by established addicts. But demand may be more elastic over longer periods because higher prices would discourage experimentation with drugs among the young and, over time, lead to fewer drug addicts. In this case, drug interdiction would increase drug-related crime in the short run but decrease it in the long run.

QuickQuiz *How might a drought that destroys half of all farm crops be good for farmers? If such a drought is good for farmers, why don't farmers destroy their own crops in the absence of a drought?*

5-4 Conclusion

According to an old quip, even a parrot can become an economist simply by learning to say "supply and demand." These last two chapters should have convinced you that there is much truth to this statement. The tools of supply and demand allow you to analyze many of the most important events and policies that shape the economy. You are now well on your way to becoming an economist (or at least a well-educated parrot).

CHAPTER QuickQuiz

1. A life-saving medicine without any close substitutes will tend to have
   a. a small elasticity of demand.
   b. a large elasticity of demand.
   c. a small elasticity of supply.
   d. a large elasticity of supply.

2. The price of a good rises from $8 to $12, and the quantity demanded falls from 110 to 90 units. Calculated with the midpoint method, the price elasticity of demand is
   a. 1/5.
   b. 1/2.
   c. 2.
   d. 5.

3. A linear, downward-sloping demand curve is
   a. inelastic
   b. unit elastic.
   c. elastic.
   d. inelastic at some points, and elastic at others.
4. The ability of firms to enter and exit a market over time means that, in the long run,
   a. the demand curve is more elastic.
   b. the demand curve is less elastic.
   c. the supply curve is more elastic.
   d. the supply curve is less elastic.
5. An increase in the supply of a good will decrease the total revenue producers receive if
   a. the demand curve is inelastic.
   b. the demand curve is elastic.
   c. the supply curve is inelastic.
   d. the supply curve is elastic.
6. Over time, technological advance increases consumers' incomes and reduces the price of smartphones. Each of these forces increases the amount consumers spend on smartphones if the income elasticity of demand is greater than _______ and if the price elasticity of demand is greater than _______.
   a. zero, zero
   b. zero, one
   c. one, zero
   d. one, one

SUMMARY

- The price elasticity of demand measures how much the quantity demanded responds to changes in the price. Demand tends to be more elastic if close substitutes are available, if the good is a luxury rather than a necessity, if the market is narrowly defined, or if buyers have substantial time to react to a price change.
- The price elasticity of demand is calculated as the percentage change in quantity demanded divided by the percentage change in price. If quantity demanded moves proportionately less than the price, then the elasticity is less than 1 and demand is said to be inelastic. If quantity demanded moves proportionately more than the price, then the elasticity is greater than 1 and demand is said to be elastic.
- Total revenue, the total amount paid for a good, equals the price of the good times the quantity sold. For inelastic demand curves, total revenue moves in the same direction as the price. For elastic demand curves, total revenue moves in the opposite direction as the price.
- The income elasticity of demand measures how much the quantity demanded responds to changes in consumers' income. The cross-price elasticity of demand measures how much the quantity demanded of one good responds to changes in the price of another good.
- The price elasticity of supply measures how much the quantity supplied responds to changes in the price. This elasticity often depends on the time horizon under consideration. In most markets, supply is more elastic in the long run than in the short run.
- The price elasticity of supply is calculated as the percentage change in quantity supplied divided by the percentage change in price. If quantity supplied moves proportionately less than the price, then the elasticity is less than 1 and supply is said to be inelastic. If quantity supplied moves proportionately more than the price, then the elasticity is greater than 1 and supply is said to be elastic.
- The tools of supply and demand can be applied in many different kinds of markets. This chapter uses them to analyze the market for wheat, the market for oil, and the market for illegal drugs.

KEY CONCEPTS

elasticity, p. 90
price elasticity of demand, p. 90
total revenue, p. 95
income elasticity of demand, p. 98
cross-price elasticity of demand, p. 98
price elasticity of supply, p. 99

QUESTIONS FOR REVIEW

1. Define the price elasticity of demand and the income elasticity of demand.
2. List and explain the four determinants of the price elasticity of demand discussed in the chapter.
3. If the elasticity is greater than 1, is demand elastic or inelastic? If the elasticity equals zero, is demand perfectly elastic or perfectly inelastic?
4. On a supply-and-demand diagram, show equilibrium price, equilibrium quantity, and the total revenue received by producers.
5. If demand is elastic, how will an increase in price change total revenue? Explain.
6. What do we call a good with an income elasticity less than zero?
7. How is the price elasticity of supply calculated? Explain what it measures.
8. If a fixed quantity of a good is available, and no more can be made, what is the price elasticity of supply?
9. A storm destroys half the fava bean crop. Is this event more likely to hurt fava bean farmers if the demand for fava beans is very elastic or very inelastic? Explain.

PROBLEMS AND APPLICATIONS

1. For each of the following pairs of goods, which good would you expect to have more elastic demand and why?
   a. required textbooks or mystery novels
   b. Beethoven recordings or classical music recordings in general
   c. subway rides during the next 6 months or subway rides during the next 5 years
   d. root beer or water
2. Suppose that business travelers and vacationers have the following demand for airline tickets from New York to Boston:

Price	Quantity Demanded (business travelers)	Quantity Demanded (vacationers)
$150	2,100 tickets	1,000 tickets
200	2,000	800
250	1,900	600
300	1,800	400

   a. As the price of tickets rises from $200 to $250, what is the price elasticity of demand for (i) business travelers and (ii) vacationers? (Use the midpoint method in your calculations.)
   b. Why might vacationers have a different elasticity from business travelers?
3. Suppose the price elasticity of demand for heating oil is 0.2 in the short run and 0.7 in the long run.
   a. If the price of heating oil rises from $1.80 to $2.20 per gallon, what happens to the quantity of heating oil demanded in the short run? In the long run? (Use the midpoint method in your calculations.)
   b. Why might this elasticity depend on the time horizon?
4. A price change causes the quantity demanded of a good to decrease by 30 percent, while the total revenue of that good increases by 15 percent. Is the demand curve elastic or inelastic? Explain.
5. Cups of coffee and donuts are complements. Both have inelastic demand. A hurricane destroys half the coffee bean crop. Use appropriately labeled diagrams to answer the following questions.
   a. What happens to the price of coffee beans?
   b. What happens to the price of a cup of coffee? What happens to total expenditure on cups of coffee?
   c. What happens to the price of donuts? What happens to total expenditure on donuts?
6. The price of coffee rose sharply last month, while the quantity sold remained the same. Five people suggest various explanations:

LEONARD: Demand increased, but supply was perfectly inelastic.
SHELDON: Demand increased, but it was perfectly inelastic.
PENNY: Demand increased, but supply decreased at the same time.
HOWARD: Supply decreased, but demand was unit elastic.
RAJ: Supply decreased, but demand was perfectly inelastic.

Who could possibly be right? Use graphs to explain your answer.

7. Suppose that your demand schedule for pizza is as follows:

Price	Quantity Demanded (income = $20,000)	Quantity Demanded (income = $24,000)
$8	40 pizza	50 pizza
10	32	45
12	24	30
14	16	20
16	8	12

   a. Use the midpoint method to calculate your price elasticity of demand as the price of pizza increases from $8 to $10 if (i) your income is $20,000 and (ii) your income is $24,000.
   b. Calculate your income elasticity of demand as your income increases from $20,000 to $24,000 if (i) the price is $12 and (ii) the price is $16.

8. The *New York Times* reported (Feb. 17, 1996) that subway ridership declined after a fare increase: "There were nearly four million fewer riders in December 1995, the first full month after the price of a token increased 25 cents to $1.50, than in the previous December, a 4.3 percent decline."
   a. Use these data to estimate the price elasticity of demand for subway rides.
   b. According to your estimate, what happens to the Transit Authority's revenue when the fare rises?
   c. Why might your estimate of the elasticity be unreliable?

9. Two drivers, Walt and Jessie, each drive up to a gas station. Before looking at the price, each places an order. Walt says, "I'd like 10 gallons of gas." Jessie says, "I'd like $10 worth of gas." What is each driver's price elasticity of demand?

10. Consider public policy aimed at smoking.
    a. Studies indicate that the price elasticity of demand for cigarettes is about 0.4. If a pack of cigarettes currently costs $5 and the government wants to reduce smoking by 20 percent, by how much should it increase the price?
    b. If the government permanently increases the price of cigarettes, will the policy have a larger effect on smoking 1 year from now or 5 years from now?
    c. Studies also find that teenagers have a higher price elasticity of demand than adults. Why might this be true?

11. You are the curator of a museum. The museum is running short of funds, so you decide to increase revenue. Should you increase or decrease the price of admission? Explain.

12. Explain why the following might be true: A drought around the world raises the total revenue that farmers receive from the sale of grain, but a drought only in Kansas reduces the total revenue that Kansas farmers receive.

To find additional study resources, visit cengagebrain.com, and search for "Mankiw."

Supply, Demand, and Government Policies

CHAPTER 6

Economists have two roles. As scientists, they develop and test theories to explain the world around them. As policy advisers, they use these theories to help change the world for the better. The focus of the preceding two chapters has been scientific. We have seen how supply and demand determine the price of a good and the quantity of the good sold. We have also seen how various events shift supply and demand, thereby changing the equilibrium price and quantity. And we have developed the concept of elasticity to gauge the size of these changes.

This chapter offers our first look at policy. Here we analyze various types of government policy using only the tools of supply and demand. As you will see, the analysis yields some surprising insights. Policies often have effects that their architects did not intend or anticipate.

We begin by considering policies that directly control prices. For example, rent-control laws set a maximum rent that landlords may charge tenants. Minimum-wage laws set the lowest wage that firms may pay workers. Price controls are usually enacted when policymakers believe that the market price of a good or service is unfair to buyers or sellers. Yet, as we will see, these policies can generate inequities of their own.

After discussing price controls, we consider the impact of taxes. Policymakers use taxes to raise revenue for public purposes and to influence market outcomes. Although the prevalence of taxes in our economy is obvious, their effects are not. For example, when the government levies a tax on the amount that firms pay their workers, do the firms or the workers bear the burden of the tax? The answer is not at all clear—until we apply the powerful tools of supply and demand.

6-1 Controls on Prices

To see how price controls affect market outcomes, let's look once again at the market for ice cream. As we saw in Chapter 4, if ice cream is sold in a competitive market free of government regulation, the price of ice cream adjusts to balance supply and demand: At the equilibrium price, the quantity of ice cream that buyers want to buy exactly equals the quantity that sellers want to sell. To be concrete, let's suppose that the equilibrium price is $3 per cone.

Some people may not be happy with the outcome of this free-market process. The American Association of Ice-Cream Eaters complains that the $3 price is too high for everyone to enjoy a cone a day (their recommended daily allowance). Meanwhile, the National Organization of Ice-Cream Makers complains that the $3 price—the result of "cutthroat competition"—is too low and is depressing the incomes of its members. Each of these groups lobbies the government to pass laws that alter the market outcome by directly controlling the price of an ice-cream cone.

Because buyers of any good always want a lower price while sellers want a higher price, the interests of the two groups conflict. If the Ice-Cream Eaters are successful in their lobbying, the government imposes a legal maximum on the price at which ice-cream cones can be sold. Because the price is not allowed to rise above this level, the legislated maximum is called a **price ceiling**. By contrast, if the Ice-Cream Makers are successful, the government imposes a legal minimum on the price. Because the price cannot fall below this level, the legislated minimum is called a **price floor**. Let us consider the effects of these policies in turn.

price ceiling
a legal maximum on the price at which a good can be sold

price floor
a legal minimum on the price at which a good can be sold

6-1a How Price Ceilings Affect Market Outcomes

When the government, moved by the complaints and campaign contributions of the Ice-Cream Eaters, imposes a price ceiling in the market for ice cream, two outcomes are possible. In panel (a) of Figure 1, the government imposes a price ceiling of $4 per cone. In this case, because the price that balances supply and demand ($3) is below the ceiling, the price ceiling is *not binding*. Market forces naturally move the economy to the equilibrium, and the price ceiling has no effect on the price or the quantity sold.

In panel (a), the government imposes a price ceiling of $4. Because the price ceiling is above the equilibrium price of $3, the price ceiling has no effect, and the market can reach the equilibrium of supply and demand. In this equilibrium, quantity supplied and quantity demanded both equal 100 cones. In panel (b), the government imposes a price ceiling of $2. Because the price ceiling is below the equilibrium price of $3, the market price equals $2. At this price, 125 cones are demanded and only 75 are supplied, so there is a shortage of 50 cones.

FIGURE 1

A Market with a Price Ceiling

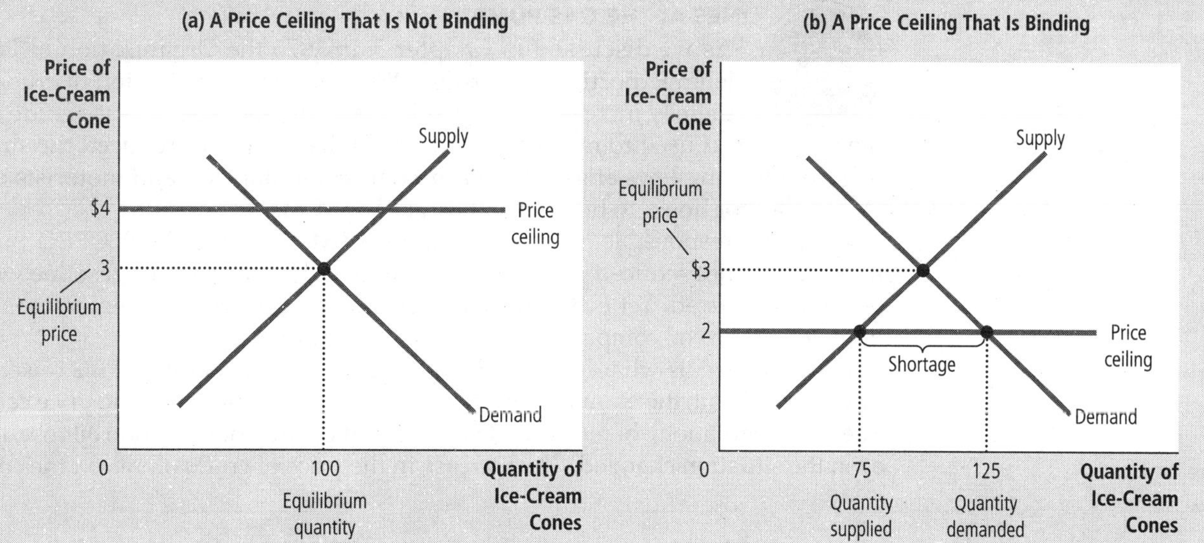

Panel (b) of Figure 1 shows the other, more interesting, possibility. In this case, the government imposes a price ceiling of $2 per cone. Because the equilibrium price of $3 is above the price ceiling, the ceiling is a *binding constraint* on the market. The forces of supply and demand tend to move the price toward the equilibrium price, but when the market price hits the ceiling, it cannot, by law, rise any further. Thus, the market price equals the price ceiling. At this price, the quantity of ice cream demanded (125 cones in the figure) exceeds the quantity supplied (75 cones). Because of this excess demand of 50 cones, some people who want to buy ice cream at the going price are unable to do so. In other words, there is a shortage of ice cream.

In response to this shortage, some mechanism for rationing ice cream will naturally develop. The mechanism could be long lines: Buyers who are willing to arrive early and wait in line get a cone, while those unwilling to wait do not. Alternatively, sellers could ration ice-cream cones according to their own personal biases, selling them only to friends, relatives, or members of their own racial or ethnic group. Notice that even though the price ceiling was motivated by a desire to help buyers of ice cream, not all buyers benefit from the policy. Some buyers do get to pay a lower price, although they may have to wait in line to do so, but other buyers cannot get any ice cream at all.

This example in the market for ice cream shows a general result: *When the government imposes a binding price ceiling on a competitive market, a shortage of the good arises, and sellers must ration the scarce goods among the large number of potential buyers*. The rationing mechanisms that develop under price ceilings are rarely desirable. Long lines are inefficient because they waste buyers' time. Discrimination according to seller bias is both inefficient (because the good may not go to the buyer who values it most highly) and often unfair. By contrast, the rationing mechanism in a free, competitive market is both efficient and impersonal. When the market for ice cream reaches its equilibrium, anyone who wants to pay the market price can get a cone. Free markets ration goods with prices.

CASE STUDY

LINES AT THE GAS PUMP

As we discussed in Chapter 5, in 1973 the Organization of Petroleum Exporting Countries (OPEC) reduced production of crude oil, thereby increasing its price in world oil markets. Because crude oil is the major input used to make gasoline, the higher oil prices reduced the supply of gasoline. Long lines at gas stations became commonplace, and motorists often had to wait for hours to buy only a few gallons of gas.

What was responsible for the long gas lines? Most people blame OPEC. Surely, if OPEC had not reduced production of crude oil, the shortage of gasoline would not have occurred. Yet economists blame the U.S. government regulations that limited the price oil companies could charge for gasoline.

Figure 2 reveals what happened. As panel (a) shows, before OPEC raised the price of crude oil, the equilibrium price of gasoline, P_1, was below the price ceiling. The price regulation, therefore, had no effect. When the price of crude oil rose, however, the situation changed. The increase in the price of crude oil raised the cost of

FIGURE 2

The Market for Gasoline with a Price Ceiling

Panel (a) shows the gasoline market when the price ceiling is not binding because the equilibrium price, P_1, is below the ceiling. Panel (b) shows the gasoline market after an increase in the price of crude oil (an input into making gasoline) shifts the supply curve to the left from S_1 to S_2. In an unregulated market, the price would have risen from P_1 to P_2. The price ceiling, however, prevents this from happening. At the binding price ceiling, consumers are willing to buy Q_D, but producers of gasoline are willing to sell only Q_S. The difference between quantity demanded and quantity supplied, $Q_D - Q_S$, measures the gasoline shortage.

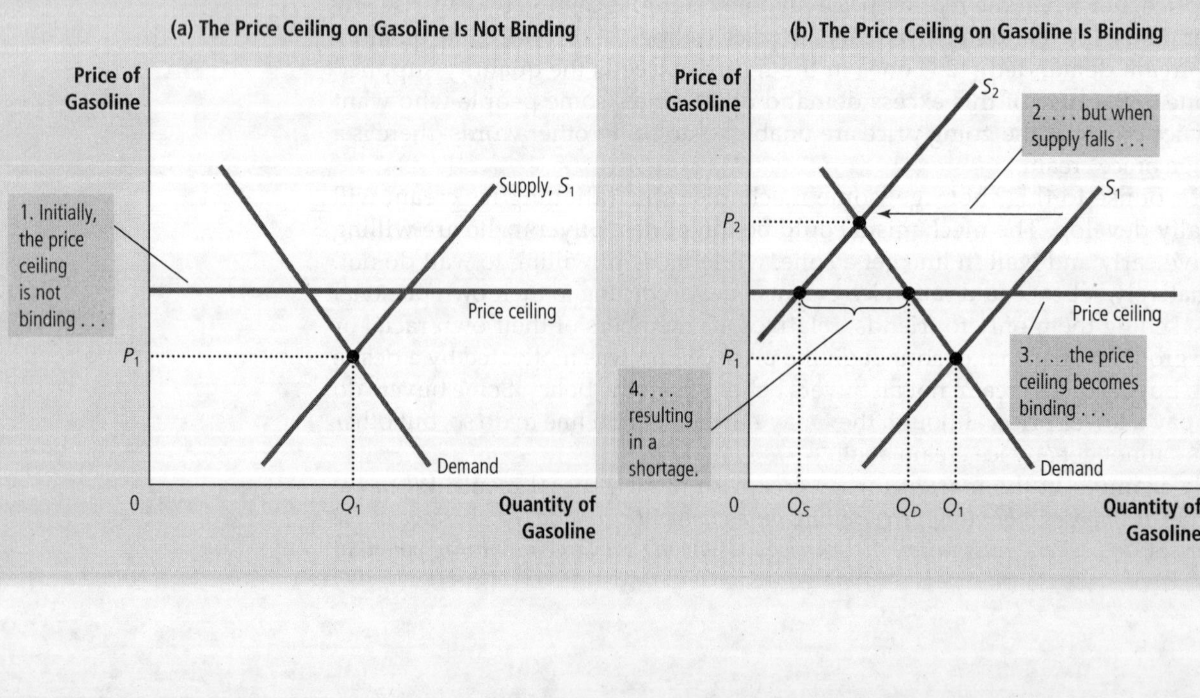

producing gasoline, and this reduced the supply of gasoline. As panel (b) shows, the supply curve shifted to the left from S_1 to S_2. In an unregulated market, this shift in supply would have raised the equilibrium price of gasoline from P_1 to P_2, and no shortage would have resulted. Instead, the price ceiling prevented the price from rising to the equilibrium level. At the price ceiling, producers were willing to sell Q_S, but consumers were willing to buy Q_D. Thus, the shift in supply caused a severe shortage at the regulated price.

Eventually, the laws regulating the price of gasoline were repealed. Lawmakers came to understand that they were partly responsible for the many hours Americans lost waiting in line to buy gasoline. Today, when the price of crude oil changes, the price of gasoline can adjust to bring supply and demand into equilibrium. ●

CASE STUDY

RENT CONTROL IN THE SHORT RUN AND THE LONG RUN

One common example of a price ceiling is rent control. In many cities, the local government places a ceiling on rents that landlords may charge their tenants. The goal of this policy is to help the poor by making housing more affordable. Economists often criticize rent control, arguing that it is a highly inefficient way to help the poor raise their standard of living. One economist called rent control "the best way to destroy a city, other than bombing."

The adverse effects of rent control are less apparent to the general population because these effects occur over many years. In the short run, landlords have a fixed number of apartments to rent, and they cannot adjust this number quickly as market conditions change. Moreover, the number of people searching for housing in a city may not be highly responsive to rents in the short run because people take time to adjust their housing arrangements. Therefore, the short-run supply and demand for housing are relatively inelastic.

Panel (a) of Figure 3 shows the short-run effects of rent control on the housing market. As with any binding price ceiling, rent control causes a shortage. But because supply and demand are inelastic in the short run, the initial shortage caused by rent control is small. The primary effect in the short run is to reduce rents.

The long-run story is very different because the buyers and sellers of rental housing respond more to market conditions as time passes. On the supply side, landlords respond to low rents by not building new apartments and by failing to maintain existing ones. On the demand side, low rents encourage people to find their own apartments (rather than living with their parents or sharing apartments with roommates) and induce more people to move into the city. Therefore, both supply and demand are more elastic in the long run.

Panel (b) of Figure 3 illustrates the housing market in the long run. When rent control depresses rents below the equilibrium level, the quantity of apartments supplied falls substantially and the quantity of apartments demanded rises substantially. The result is a large shortage of housing.

In cities with rent control, landlords use various mechanisms to ration housing. Some landlords keep long waiting lists. Others give preference to tenants without children. Still others discriminate on the basis of race. Sometimes apartments are allocated to those willing to offer under-the-table payments to building superintendents. In essence, these bribes bring the total price of an apartment closer to the equilibrium price.

To understand fully the effects of rent control, we have to remember one of the *Ten Principles of Economics* from Chapter 1: People respond to incentives. In free

FIGURE 3

Rent Control in the Short Run and in the Long Run

Panel (a) shows the short-run effects of rent control: Because the supply and demand curves for apartments are relatively inelastic, the price ceiling imposed by a rent-control law causes only a small shortage of housing. Panel (b) shows the long-run effects of rent control: Because the supply and demand curves for apartments are more elastic, rent control causes a large shortage.

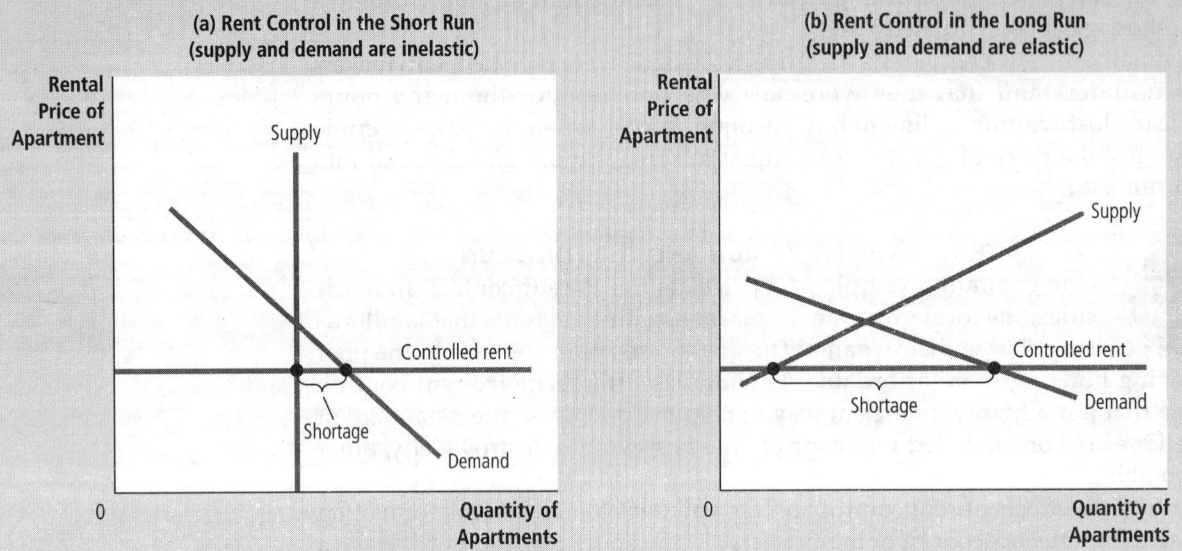

ASK THE EXPERTS

Rent Control

"Local ordinances that limit rent increases for some rental housing units, such as in New York and San Francisco, have had a positive impact over the past three decades on the amount and quality of broadly affordable rental housing in cities that have used them."

What do economists say?

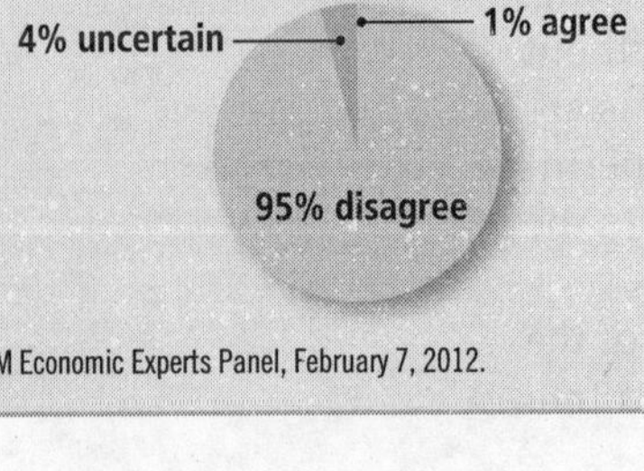

Source: IGM Economic Experts Panel, February 7, 2012.

markets, landlords try to keep their buildings clean and safe because desirable apartments command higher prices. By contrast, when rent control creates shortages and waiting lists, landlords lose their incentive to respond to tenants' concerns. Why should a landlord spend money to maintain and improve the property when people are waiting to move in as it is? In the end, tenants get lower rents, but they also get lower-quality housing.

Policymakers often react to the effects of rent control by imposing additional regulations. For example, various laws make racial discrimination in housing illegal and require landlords to provide minimally adequate living conditions. These laws, however, are difficult and costly to enforce. By contrast, when rent control is eliminated and a market for housing is regulated by the forces of competition, such laws are less necessary. In a free market, the price of housing adjusts to eliminate the shortages that give rise to undesirable landlord behavior. ●

6-1b How Price Floors Affect Market Outcomes

To examine the effects of another kind of government price control, let's return to the market for ice cream. Imagine now that the government is persuaded by the pleas of the National Organization of Ice-Cream Makers whose members feel that the $3 equilibrium price is too low. In this case, the government might institute a price floor. Price floors, like price ceilings, are an attempt by the government to maintain prices at other than equilibrium levels. Whereas a price ceiling places a legal maximum on prices, a price floor places a legal minimum.

When the government imposes a price floor on the ice-cream market, two outcomes are possible. If the government imposes a price floor of $2 per cone when the equilibrium price is $3, we obtain the outcome in panel (a) of Figure 4. In this case, because the equilibrium price is above the floor, the price floor is not binding. Market forces naturally move the economy to the equilibrium, and the price floor has no effect.

Panel (b) of Figure 4 shows what happens when the government imposes a price floor of $4 per cone. In this case, because the equilibrium price of $3 is below the floor, the price floor is a binding constraint on the market. The forces of supply and demand tend to move the price toward the equilibrium price, but when the market price hits the floor, it can fall no further. The market price equals the price floor. At this floor, the quantity of ice cream supplied (120 cones) exceeds the quantity demanded (80 cones). Because of this excess supply of 40 cones, some people who want to sell ice cream at the going price are unable to. *Thus, a binding price floor causes a surplus.*

Just as the shortages resulting from price ceilings can lead to undesirable rationing mechanisms, so can the surpluses resulting from price floors. The sellers who appeal to the personal biases of the buyers, perhaps due to racial or familial ties, may be better able to sell their goods than those who do not. By contrast, in a free market, the price serves as the rationing mechanism, and sellers can sell all they want at the equilibrium price.

In panel (a), the government imposes a price floor of $2. Because this is below the equilibrium price of $3, the price floor has no effect. The market price adjusts to balance supply and demand. At the equilibrium, quantity supplied and quantity demanded both equal 100 cones. In panel (b), the government imposes a price floor of $4, which is above the equilibrium price of $3. Therefore, the market price equals $4. Because 120 cones are supplied at this price and only 80 are demanded, there is a surplus of 40 cones.

FIGURE 4

A Market with a Price Floor

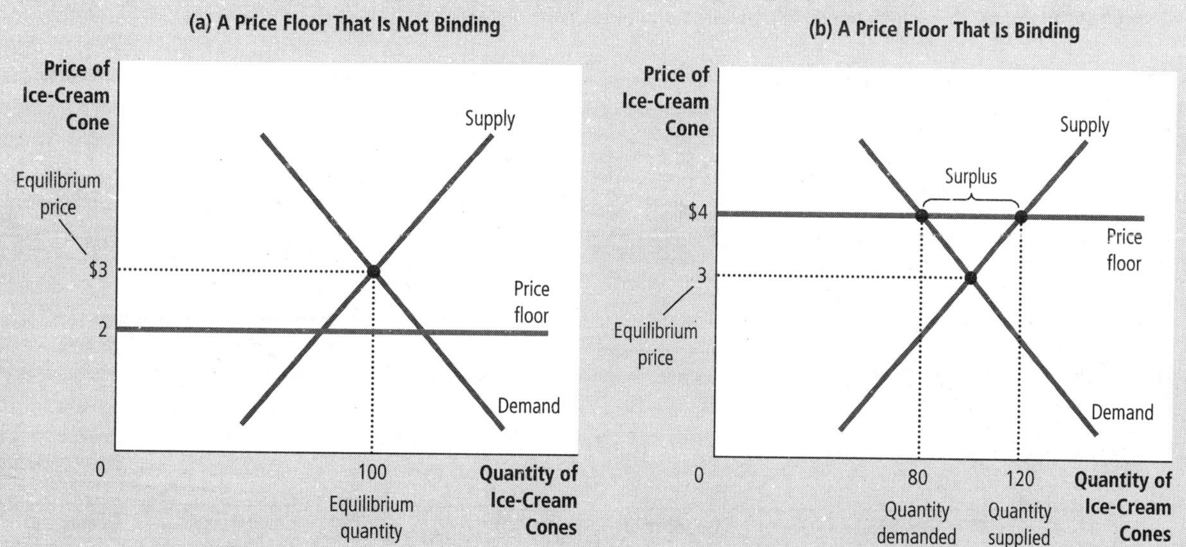

CASE STUDY

THE MINIMUM WAGE

An important example of a price floor is the minimum wage. Minimum-wage laws dictate the lowest price for labor that any employer may pay. The U.S. Congress first instituted a minimum wage with the Fair Labor Standards Act of 1938 to ensure workers a minimally adequate standard of living. In 2015, the minimum wage according to federal law was $7.25 per hour. (Some states mandate minimum wages above the federal level.) Many European nations have minimum-wage laws as well, sometimes significantly higher than in the United States. For example, even though the average income in France is almost 30 percent lower than it is in the United States, the French minimum wage is more than 30 percent higher.

To examine the effects of a minimum wage, we must consider the market for labor. Panel (a) of Figure 5 shows the labor market, which, like all markets, is subject to the forces of supply and demand. Workers determine the supply of labor, and firms determine the demand. If the government doesn't intervene, the wage normally adjusts to balance labor supply and labor demand.

Panel (b) of Figure 5 shows the labor market with a minimum wage. If the minimum wage is above the equilibrium level, as it is here, the quantity of labor supplied exceeds the quantity demanded. The result is unemployment. Thus, while the minimum wage raises the incomes of those workers who have jobs, it lowers the incomes of workers who cannot find jobs.

To fully understand the minimum wage, keep in mind that the economy contains not a single labor market but many labor markets for different types of workers. The impact of the minimum wage depends on the skill and experience of the worker. Highly skilled and experienced workers are not affected because their equilibrium wages are well above the minimum. For these workers, the minimum wage is not binding.

FIGURE 5

How the Minimum Wage Affects the Labor Market

Panel (a) shows a labor market in which the wage adjusts to balance labor supply and labor demand. Panel (b) shows the impact of a binding minimum wage. Because the minimum wage is a price floor, it causes a surplus: The quantity of labor supplied exceeds the quantity demanded. The result is unemployment.

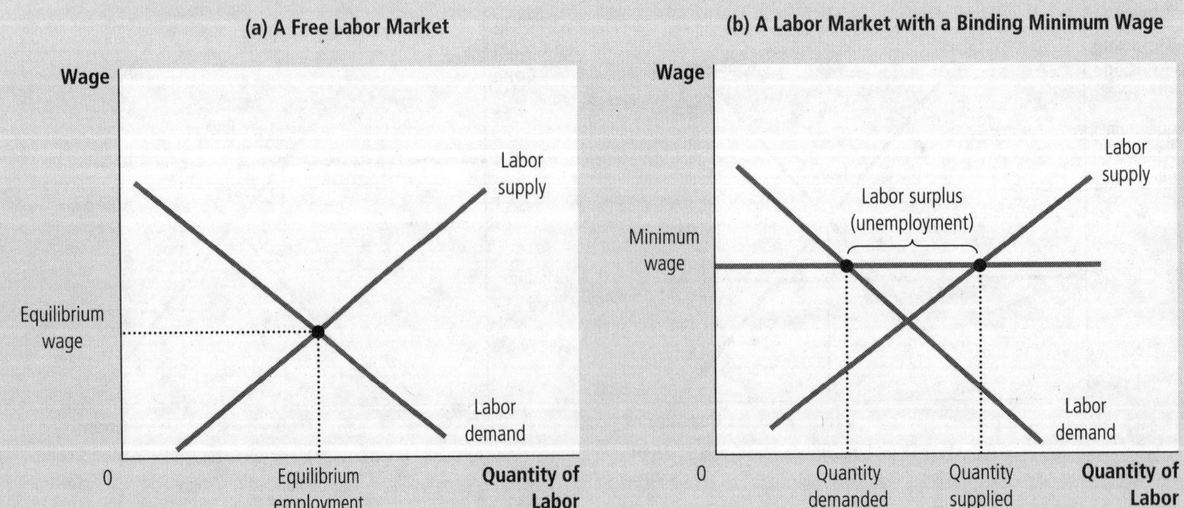

The minimum wage has its greatest impact on the market for teenage labor. The equilibrium wages of teenagers are low because teenagers are among the least skilled and least experienced members of the labor force. In addition, teenagers are often willing to accept a lower wage in exchange for on-the-job training. (Some teenagers, including many college students, are willing to work as interns for no pay at all. Because internships pay nothing, minimum-wage laws often do not apply to them. If they did, these internship opportunities might not exist.) As a result, the minimum wage is binding more often for teenagers than for other members of the labor force.

Many economists have studied how minimum-wage laws affect the teenage labor market. These researchers compare the changes in the minimum wage over time with the changes in teenage employment. Although there is some debate about how much the minimum wage affects employment, the typical study finds that a 10 percent increase in the minimum wage depresses teenage employment by 1 to 3 percent. In interpreting this estimate, note that a 10 percent increase in the minimum wage does not raise the average wage of teenagers by 10 percent. A change in the law does not directly affect those teenagers who are already paid well above the minimum, and enforcement of minimum-wage laws is not perfect. Thus, the estimated drop in employment of 1 to 3 percent is significant.

In addition to altering the quantity of labor demanded, the minimum wage alters the quantity supplied. Because the minimum wage raises the wage that teenagers can earn, it increases the number of teenagers who choose to look for jobs. Studies have found that a higher minimum wage influences which teenagers are employed. When the minimum wage rises, some teenagers who are still attending high school choose to drop out and take jobs. With more people vying for the available jobs, some of these new dropouts displace other teenagers who had already dropped out of school and now become unemployed.

The minimum wage is a frequent topic of debate. Advocates of the minimum wage view the policy as one way to raise the income of the working poor. They correctly point out that workers who earn the minimum wage can afford only a meager standard of living. In 2015, for instance, when the minimum wage was $7.25 per hour, two adults working 40 hours a week for every week of the year at minimum-wage jobs had a total annual income of only $30,160. This amount was 24 percent above the official poverty line for a family of four but was less than half of the median family income in the United States. Many advocates of the minimum wage admit that it has some adverse effects, including unemployment, but they believe that these effects are small and that, all things considered, a higher minimum wage makes the poor better off.

Opponents of the minimum wage contend that it is not the best way to combat poverty. They note that a high minimum wage causes unemployment, encourages teenagers to drop out of school, and prevents some unskilled workers from getting on-the-job training. Moreover, opponents of the minimum wage point out that it is a poorly targeted policy. Not all minimum-wage workers are heads of households trying to help their families escape poverty. In fact, less than a third of minimum-wage earners are in families with incomes below the

ASK THE EXPERTS

The Minimum Wage

"If the federal minimum wage is raised gradually to $15-per-hour by 2020, the employment rate for low-wage U.S. workers will be substantially lower than it would be under the status quo."

What do economists say?

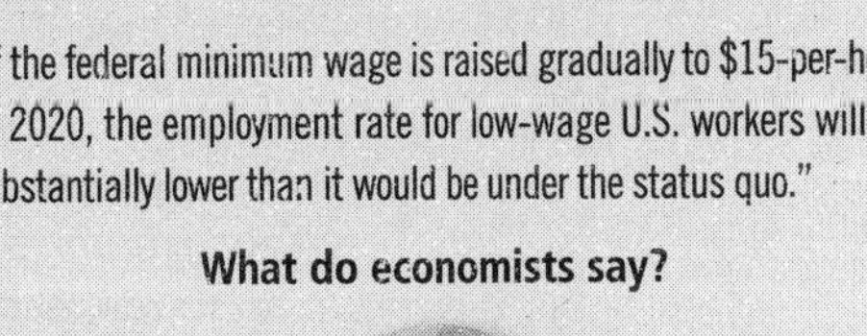

Source: IGM Economic Experts Panel, September 22, 2015.

poverty line. Many are teenagers from middle-class homes working at part-time jobs for extra spending money. ●

6-1c Evaluating Price Controls

One of the *Ten Principles of Economics* discussed in Chapter 1 is that markets are usually a good way to organize economic activity. This principle explains why economists usually oppose price ceilings and price floors. To economists, prices are not the outcome of some haphazard process. Prices, they contend, are the result of the millions of business and consumer decisions that lie behind the supply and demand curves. Prices have the crucial job of balancing supply and demand and, thereby, coordinating economic activity. When policymakers set prices by legal decree, they obscure the signals that normally guide the allocation of society's resources.

Another one of the *Ten Principles of Economics* is that governments can sometimes improve market outcomes. Indeed, policymakers are motivated to control prices because they view the market's outcome as unfair. Price controls are often aimed at helping the poor. For instance, rent-control laws try to make housing affordable for everyone, and minimum-wage laws try to help people escape poverty.

Yet price controls often hurt those they are trying to help. Rent control may keep rents low, but it also discourages landlords from maintaining their buildings and makes housing hard to find. Minimum-wage laws may raise the incomes of some workers, but they also cause other workers to become unemployed.

Helping those in need can be accomplished in ways other than controlling prices. For instance, the government can make housing more affordable by paying a fraction of the rent for poor families. Unlike rent control, such rent subsidies do not reduce the quantity of housing supplied and, therefore, do not lead to housing shortages. Similarly, wage subsidies raise the living standards of the working poor without discouraging firms from hiring them. An example of a wage subsidy is the *earned income tax credit*, a government program that supplements the incomes of low-wage workers.

Although these alternative policies are often better than price controls, they are not perfect. Rent and wage subsidies cost the government money and, therefore, require higher taxes. As we see in the next section, taxation has costs of its own.

QuickQuiz *Define price ceiling and price floor and give an example of each. Which leads to a shortage? Which leads to a surplus? Why?*

6-2 Taxes

All governments—from national governments around the world to local governments in small towns—use taxes to raise revenue for public projects, such as roads, schools, and national defense. Because taxes are such an important policy instrument and affect our lives in many ways, we return to the study of taxes several times throughout this book. In this section, we begin our study of how taxes affect the economy.

To set the stage for our analysis, imagine that a local government decides to hold an annual ice-cream celebration—with a parade, fireworks, and speeches by town officials. To raise revenue to pay for the event, the town decides to place a $0.50 tax on the sale of ice-cream cones. When the plan is announced, our two lobbying groups swing into action. The American Association of Ice-Cream Eaters claims that consumers of ice cream are having trouble making ends meet, and it argues that *sellers* of ice cream should pay the tax. The National Organization of Ice-Cream Makers claims that its members are struggling to survive in a competitive market, and it argues that *buyers* of ice cream should pay the tax. The town mayor, hoping to reach a compromise, suggests that half the tax be paid by the buyers and half be paid by the sellers.

To analyze these proposals, we need to address a simple but subtle question: When the government levies a tax on a good, who actually bears the burden of the tax? The people buying the good? The people selling the good? Or if buyers and sellers share the tax burden, what determines how the burden is divided? Can the government simply legislate the division of the burden, as the mayor is suggesting, or is the division determined by more fundamental market forces? The term **tax incidence** refers to how the burden of a tax is distributed among the various people who make up the economy. As we will see, some surprising lessons about tax incidence can be learned by applying the tools of supply and demand.

tax incidence
the manner in which the burden of a tax is shared among participants in a market

6-2a How Taxes on Sellers Affect Market Outcomes

We begin by considering a tax levied on sellers of a good. Suppose the local government passes a law requiring sellers of ice-cream cones to send \$0.50 to the government for every cone they sell. How does this law affect the buyers and sellers of ice cream? To answer this question, we can follow the three steps in Chapter 4 for analyzing supply and demand: (1) We decide whether the law affects the supply curve or the demand curve. (2) We decide which way the curve shifts. (3) We examine how the shift affects the equilibrium price and quantity.

Step One The immediate impact of the tax is on the sellers of ice cream. Because the tax is not levied on buyers, the quantity of ice cream demanded at any given price is the same; thus, the demand curve does not change. By contrast, the tax on sellers makes the ice-cream business less profitable at any given price, so it shifts the supply curve.

Step Two Because the tax on sellers raises the cost of producing and selling ice cream, it reduces the quantity supplied at every price. The supply curve shifts to the left (or, equivalently, upward).

In addition to determining the direction in which the supply curve moves, we can also be precise about the size of the shift. For any market price of ice cream, the effective price to sellers—the amount they get to keep after paying the tax—is \$0.50 lower. For example, if the market price of a cone happened to be \$2.00, the effective price received by sellers would be \$1.50. Whatever the market price, sellers will supply a quantity of ice cream as if the price were \$0.50 lower than it is. Put differently, to induce sellers to supply any given quantity, the market price must now be \$0.50 higher to compensate for the effect of the tax. Thus, as shown in Figure 6, the supply curve shifts *upward* from S_1 to S_2 by the exact size of the tax (\$0.50).

Step Three Having determined how the supply curve shifts, we can now compare the initial and the new equilibriums. Figure 6 shows that the equilibrium price of ice cream rises from \$3.00 to \$3.30, and the equilibrium quantity falls from 100 to 90 cones. Because sellers sell less and buyers buy less in the new equilibrium, the tax reduces the size of the ice-cream market.

FIGURE 6

A Tax on Sellers

When a tax of $0.50 is levied on sellers, the supply curve shifts up by $0.50 from S_1 to S_2. The equilibrium quantity falls from 100 to 90 cones. The price that buyers pay rises from $3.00 to $3.30. The price that sellers receive (after paying the tax) falls from $3.00 to $2.80. Even though the tax is levied on sellers, buyers and sellers share the burden of the tax.

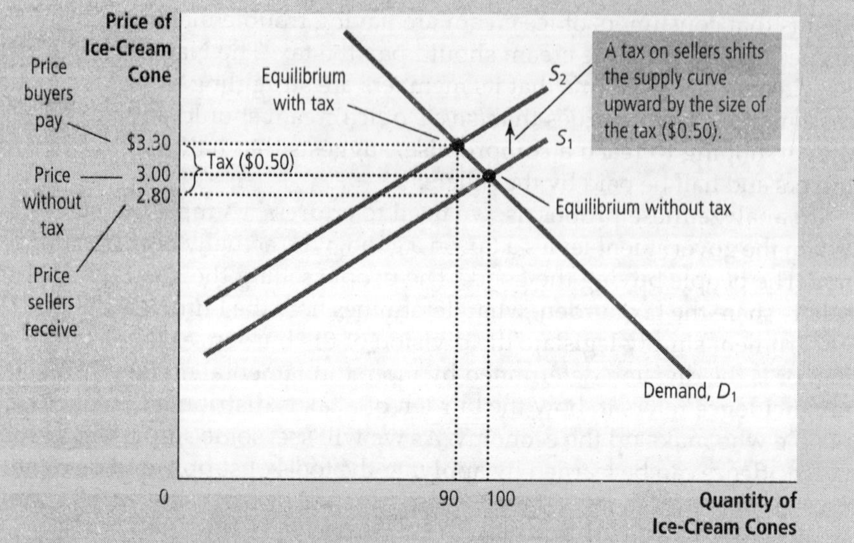

Implications We can now return to the question of tax incidence: Who pays the tax? Although sellers send the entire tax to the government, buyers and sellers share the burden. Because the market price rises from $3.00 to $3.30 when the tax is introduced, buyers pay $0.30 more for each ice-cream cone than they did without the tax. Thus, the tax makes buyers worse off. Sellers get a higher price ($3.30) from buyers than they did previously, but what they get to keep after paying the tax is only $2.80 ($3.30 – $0.50 = $2.80), compared with $3.00 before the tax. Thus, the tax also makes sellers worse off.

To sum up, this analysis yields two lessons:

- Taxes discourage market activity. When a good is taxed, the quantity of the good sold is smaller in the new equilibrium.
- Buyers and sellers share the burden of taxes. In the new equilibrium, buyers pay more for the good, and sellers receive less.

6-2b How Taxes on Buyers Affect Market Outcomes

Now consider a tax levied on buyers of a good. Suppose that our local government passes a law requiring buyers of ice-cream cones to send $0.50 to the government for each ice-cream cone they buy. What are the effects of this law? Again, we apply our three steps.

Step One The initial impact of the tax is on the demand for ice cream. The supply curve is not affected because, for any given price of ice cream, sellers have the same incentive to provide ice cream to the market. By contrast, buyers now have to pay a tax to the government (as well as the price to the sellers) whenever they buy ice cream. Thus, the tax shifts the demand curve for ice cream.

Step Two Next, we determine the direction of the shift. Because the tax on buyers makes buying ice cream less attractive, buyers demand a smaller quantity of ice cream at every price. As a result, the demand curve shifts to the left (or, equivalently, downward), as shown in Figure 7.

Once again, we can be precise about the size of the shift. Because of the \$0.50 tax levied on buyers, the effective price to buyers is now \$0.50 higher than the market price (whatever the market price happens to be). For example, if the market price of a cone happened to be \$2.00, the effective price to buyers would be \$2.50. Because buyers look at their total cost including the tax, they demand a quantity of ice cream as if the market price were \$0.50 higher than it actually is. In other words, to induce buyers to demand any given quantity, the market price must now be \$0.50 lower to make up for the effect of the tax. Thus, the tax shifts the demand curve *downward* from D_1 to D_2 by the exact size of the tax (\$0.50).

Step Three Having determined how the demand curve shifts, we can now see the effect of the tax by comparing the initial equilibrium and the new equilibrium. You can see in Figure 7 that the equilibrium price of ice cream falls from \$3.00 to \$2.80, and the equilibrium quantity falls from 100 to 90 cones. Once again, the tax on ice cream reduces the size of the ice-cream market. And once again, buyers and sellers share the burden of the tax. Sellers get a lower price for their product; buyers pay a lower market price to sellers than they did previously, but the effective price (including the tax buyers have to pay) rises from \$3.00 to \$3.30.

Implications If you compare Figures 6 and 7, you will notice a surprising conclusion: *Taxes levied on sellers and taxes levied on buyers are equivalent.* In both cases, the tax places a wedge between the price that buyers pay and the price that sellers receive. The wedge between the buyers' price and the sellers' price is the same, regardless of whether the tax is levied on buyers or sellers. In either case, the wedge shifts the relative position of the supply and demand curves. In the new equilibrium, buyers and sellers share the burden of the tax. The only difference between a tax levied on sellers and a tax levied on buyers is who sends the money to the government.

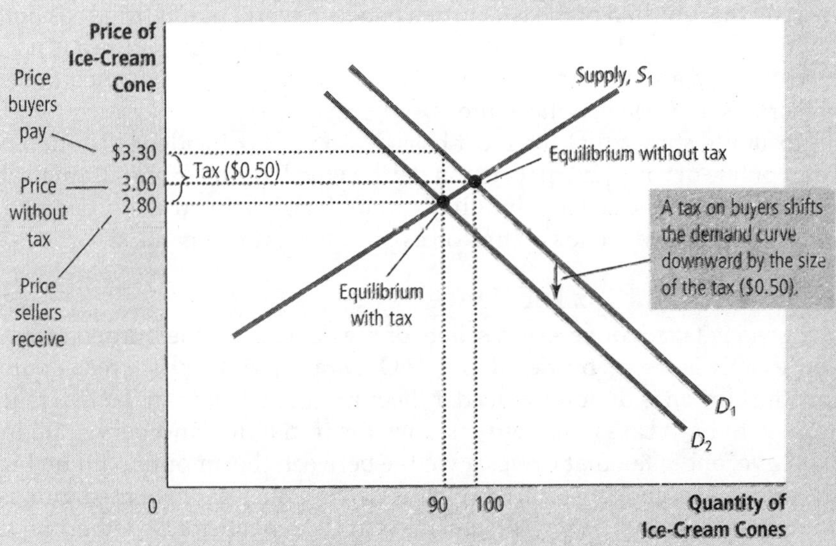

FIGURE 7

A Tax on Buyers

When a tax of \$0.50 is levied on buyers, the demand curve shifts down by \$0.50 from D_1 to D_2. The equilibrium quantity falls from 100 to 90 cones. The price that sellers receive falls from \$3.00 to \$2.80. The price that buyers pay (including the tax) rises from \$3.00 to \$3.30. Even though the tax is levied on buyers, buyers and sellers share the burden of the tax.

The equivalence of these two taxes is easy to understand if we imagine that the government collects the $0.50 ice-cream tax in a bowl on the counter of each ice-cream store. When the government levies the tax on sellers, the seller is required to place $0.50 in the bowl after the sale of each cone. When the government levies the tax on buyers, the buyer is required to place $0.50 in the bowl every time a cone is bought. Whether the $0.50 goes directly from the buyer's pocket into the bowl, or indirectly from the buyer's pocket into the seller's hand and then into the bowl, does not matter. Once the market reaches its new equilibrium, buyers and sellers share the burden, regardless of how the tax is levied.

CASE STUDY

CAN CONGRESS DISTRIBUTE THE BURDEN OF A PAYROLL TAX?

If you have ever received a paycheck, you probably noticed that taxes were deducted from the amount you earned. One of these taxes is called FICA, an acronym for the Federal Insurance Contributions Act. The federal government uses the revenue from the FICA tax to pay for Social Security and Medicare, the income support and healthcare programs for the elderly. FICA is an example of a *payroll tax*, which is a tax on the wages that firms pay their workers. In 2015, the total FICA tax for the typical worker was 15.3 percent of earnings.

Who do you think bears the burden of this payroll tax—firms or workers? When Congress passed this legislation, it tried to mandate a division of the tax burden. According to the law, half of the tax is paid by firms, and half is paid by workers. That is, half of the tax is paid out of firms' revenues, and half is deducted from workers' paychecks. The amount that shows up as a deduction on your pay stub is the worker contribution.

Our analysis of tax incidence, however, shows that lawmakers cannot dictate the distribution of a tax burden so easily. To illustrate, we can analyze a payroll tax as merely a tax on a good, where the good is labor and the price is the wage. The key feature of the payroll tax is that it places a wedge between the wage that firms pay and the wage that workers receive. Figure 8 shows the outcome. When a payroll tax is enacted, the wage received by workers falls, and the wage paid by firms rises. In the end, workers and firms share the burden of the tax, much as the legislation requires. Yet this division of the tax burden between workers and firms has nothing to do with the legislated division: The division of the burden in Figure 8 is not necessarily fifty-fifty, and the same outcome would prevail if the law levied the entire tax on workers or if it levied the entire tax on firms.

This example shows that the most basic lesson of tax incidence is often overlooked in public debate. Lawmakers can decide whether a tax comes from the buyer's pocket or from the seller's, but they cannot legislate the true burden of a tax. Rather, tax incidence depends on the forces of supply and demand. ●

6-2c Elasticity and Tax Incidence

When a good is taxed, buyers and sellers of the good share the burden of the tax. But how exactly is the tax burden divided? Only rarely will it be shared equally. To see how the burden is divided, consider the impact of taxation in the two markets in Figure 9. In both cases, the figure shows the initial demand curve, the initial supply curve, and a tax that drives a wedge between the amount paid by buyers and the amount received by sellers. (Not drawn in either panel of the figure is the new supply or demand curve. Which curve shifts depends on whether the tax is levied on buyers or sellers. As we have seen, this is irrelevant for determining the

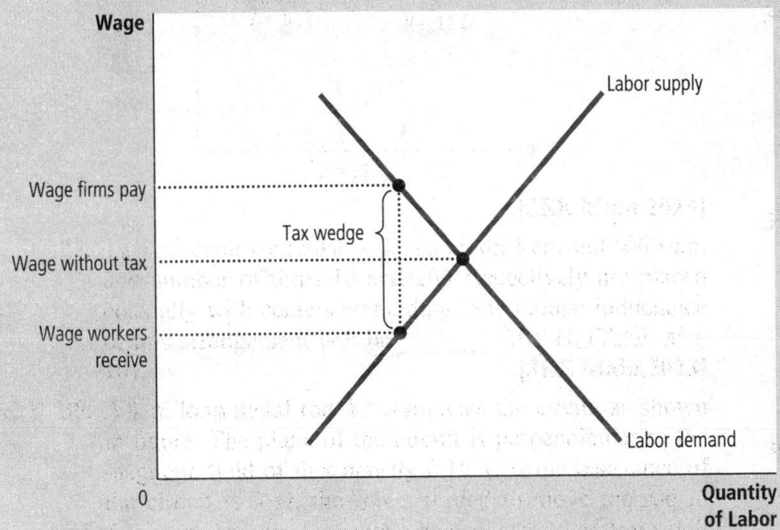

FIGURE 8

A Payroll Tax
A payroll tax places a wedge between the wage that workers receive and the wage that firms pay. Comparing wages with and without the tax, you can see that workers and firms share the tax burden. This division of the tax burden between workers and firms does not depend on whether the government levies the tax on workers, levies the tax on firms, or divides the tax equally between the two groups.

incidence of the tax.) The difference in the two panels is the relative elasticity of supply and demand.

Panel (a) of Figure 9 shows a tax in a market with very elastic supply and relatively inelastic demand. That is, sellers are very responsive to changes in the price of the good (so the supply curve is relatively flat), whereas buyers are not very responsive (so the demand curve is relatively steep). When a tax is imposed on a market with these elasticities, the price received by sellers does not fall by much, so sellers bear only a small burden. By contrast, the price paid by buyers rises substantially, indicating that buyers bear most of the burden of the tax.

Panel (b) of Figure 9 shows a tax in a market with relatively inelastic supply and very elastic demand. In this case, sellers are not very responsive to changes in the price (so the supply curve is steeper), whereas buyers are very responsive (so the demand curve is flatter). The figure shows that when a tax is imposed, the price paid by buyers does not rise by much, but the price received by sellers falls substantially. Thus, sellers bear most of the burden of the tax.

The two panels of Figure 9 show a general lesson about how the burden of a tax is divided: *A tax burden falls more heavily on the side of the market that is less elastic.* Why is this true? In essence, the elasticity measures the willingness of buyers or sellers to leave the market when conditions become unfavorable. A small elasticity of demand means that buyers do not have good alternatives to consuming this particular good. A small elasticity of supply means that sellers do not have good alternatives to producing this particular good. When the good is taxed, the side of the market with fewer good alternatives is less willing to leave the market and, therefore, bears more of the burden of the tax.

We can apply this logic to the payroll tax discussed in the previous case study. Most labor economists believe that the supply of labor is much less elastic than the demand. This means that workers, rather than firms, bear most of the burden of the payroll tax. In other words, the distribution of the tax burden is far from the fifty-fifty split that lawmakers intended.

FIGURE 9

How the Burden of a Tax Is Divided
In panel (a), the supply curve is elastic, and the demand curve is inelastic. In this case, the price received by sellers falls only slightly, while the price paid by buyers rises substantially. Thus, buyers bear most of the burden of the tax. In panel (b), the supply curve is inelastic, and the demand curve is elastic. In this case, the price received by sellers falls substantially, while the price paid by buyers rises only slightly. Thus, sellers bear most of the burden of the tax.

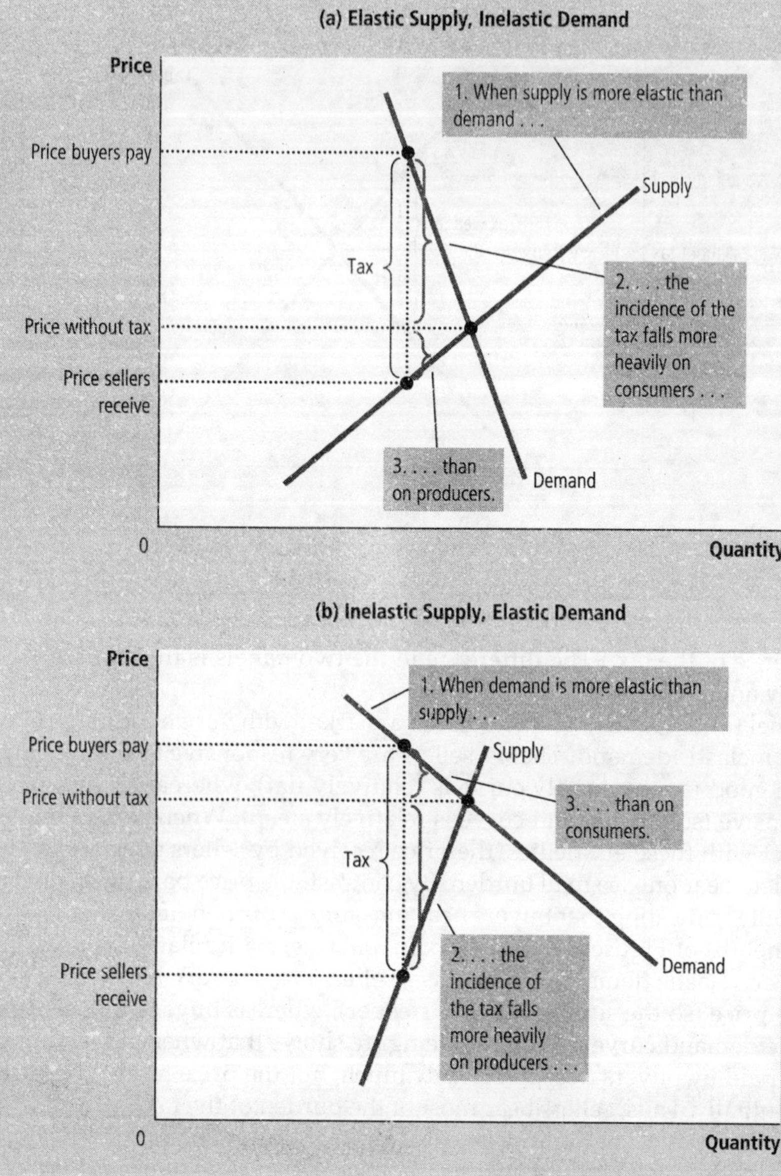

CASE STUDY

WHO PAYS THE LUXURY TAX?

In 1990, Congress adopted a new luxury tax on items such as yachts, private airplanes, furs, jewelry, and expensive cars. The goal of the tax was to raise revenue from those who could most easily afford to pay. Because only the rich could afford to buy such extravagances, taxing luxuries seemed a logical way of taxing the rich.

Yet, when the forces of supply and demand took over, the outcome was quite different from the one Congress intended. Consider, for example, the market for yachts. The demand for yachts is quite elastic. A millionaire can easily not buy a yacht; he can use the money to buy a bigger house, take a European vacation, or leave a larger bequest to his heirs. By contrast, the supply of yachts is relatively inelastic, at least in the short run. Yacht factories are not easily converted to alternative uses, and workers who build yachts are not eager to change careers in response to changing market conditions.

Our analysis makes a clear prediction in this case. With elastic demand and inelastic supply, the burden of a tax falls largely on the suppliers. That is, a tax on yachts places a burden largely on the firms and workers who build yachts because they end up getting a significantly lower price for their product. The workers, however, are not wealthy. Thus, the burden of a luxury tax falls more on the middle class than on the rich.

BLEND IMAGES/GETTY IMAGES

"If this boat were any more expensive, we'd be playing golf."

The mistaken assumptions about the incidence of the luxury tax quickly became apparent after the tax went into effect. Suppliers of luxuries made their congressional representatives well aware of the economic hardship they experienced, and Congress repealed most of the luxury tax in 1993. ●

QuickQuiz *In a supply-and-demand diagram, show how a tax on car buyers of $1,000 per car affects the quantity of cars sold and the price of cars. In another diagram, show how a tax on car sellers of $1,000 per car affects the quantity of cars sold and the price of cars. In both of your diagrams, show the change in the price paid by car buyers and the change in the price received by car sellers.*

6-3 Conclusion

The economy is governed by two kinds of laws: the laws of supply and demand and the laws enacted by governments. In this chapter, we have begun to see how these laws interact. Price controls and taxes are common in various markets in the economy, and their effects are frequently debated in the press and among policymakers. Even a little bit of economic knowledge can go a long way toward understanding and evaluating these policies.

In subsequent chapters, we analyze many government policies in greater detail. We examine the effects of taxation more fully and consider a broader range of policies than we considered here. Yet the basic lessons of this chapter will not change: When analyzing government policies, supply and demand are the first and most useful tools of analysis.

CHAPTER QuickQuiz

1. When the government imposes a binding price floor, it causes
   a. the supply curve to shift to the left.
   b. the demand curve to shift to the right.
   c. a shortage of the good to develop.
   d. a surplus of the good to develop.

2. In a market with a binding price ceiling, an increase in the ceiling will ________ the quantity supplied, ________ the quantity demanded, and reduce the ________.
   a. increase, decrease, surplus
   b. decrease, increase, surplus
   c. increase, decrease, shortage
   d. decrease, increase, shortage

3. A $1 per unit tax levied on consumers of a good is equivalent to
   a. a $1 per unit tax levied on producers of the good.
   b. a $1 per unit subsidy paid to producers of the good.
   c. a price floor that raises the good's price by $1 per unit.
   d. a price ceiling that raises the good's price by $1 per unit.
4. Which of the following would increase quantity supplied, decrease quantity demanded, and increase the price that consumers pay?
   a. the imposition of a binding price floor
   b. the removal of a binding price floor
   c. the passage of a tax levied on producers
   d. the repeal of a tax levied on producers
5. Which of the following would increase quantity supplied, increase quantity demanded, and decrease the price that consumers pay?
   a. the imposition of a binding price floor
   b. the removal of a binding price floor
   c. the passage of a tax levied on producers
   d. the repeal of a tax levied on producers
6. When a good is taxed, the burden of the tax falls mainly on consumers if
   a. the tax is levied on consumers.
   b. the tax is levied on producers.
   c. supply is inelastic, and demand is elastic.
   d. supply is elastic, and demand is inelastic.

SUMMARY

- A price ceiling is a legal maximum on the price of a good or service. An example is rent control. If the price ceiling is below the equilibrium price, then the price ceiling is binding, and the quantity demanded exceeds the quantity supplied. Because of the resulting shortage, sellers must in some way ration the good or service among buyers.
- A price floor is a legal minimum on the price of a good or service. An example is the minimum wage. If the price floor is above the equilibrium price, then the price floor is binding, and the quantity supplied exceeds the quantity demanded. Because of the resulting surplus, buyers' demands for the good or service must in some way be rationed among sellers.
- When the government levies a tax on a good, the equilibrium quantity of the good falls. That is, a tax on a market shrinks the size of the market.
- A tax on a good places a wedge between the price paid by buyers and the price received by sellers. When the market moves to the new equilibrium, buyers pay more for the good and sellers receive less for it. In this sense, buyers and sellers share the tax burden. The incidence of a tax (that is, the division of the tax burden) does not depend on whether the tax is levied on buyers or sellers.
- The incidence of a tax depends on the price elasticities of supply and demand. Most of the burden falls on the side of the market that is less elastic because that side of the market cannot respond as easily to the tax by changing the quantity bought or sold.

KEY CONCEPTS

price ceiling, p. 112 | price floor, p. 112 | tax incidence, p. 121

QUESTIONS FOR REVIEW

1. Give an example of a price ceiling and an example of a price floor.
2. Which causes a shortage of a good—a price ceiling or a price floor? Justify your answer with a graph.
3. What mechanisms allocate resources when the price of a good is not allowed to bring supply and demand into equilibrium?
4. Explain why economists usually oppose controls on prices.
5. Suppose the government removes a tax on buyers of a good and levies a tax of the same size on sellers of the good. How does this change in tax policy affect the price that buyers pay sellers for this good, the amount buyers are out of pocket (including any tax payments they

make), the amount sellers receive (net of any tax payments they make), and the quantity of the good sold?

6. How does a tax on a good affect the price paid by buyers, the price received by sellers, and the quantity sold?

7. What determines how the burden of a tax is divided between buyers and sellers? Why?

PROBLEMS AND APPLICATIONS

1. Lovers of classical music persuade Congress to impose a price ceiling of $40 per concert ticket. As a result of this policy, do more or fewer people attend classical music concerts? Explain.

2. The government has decided that the free-market price of cheese is too low.
   a. Suppose the government imposes a binding price floor in the cheese market. Draw a supply-and-demand diagram to show the effect of this policy on the price of cheese and the quantity of cheese sold. Is there a shortage or surplus of cheese?
   b. Producers of cheese complain that the price floor has reduced their total revenue. Is this possible? Explain.
   c. In response to cheese producers' complaints, the government agrees to purchase all the surplus cheese at the price floor. Compared to the basic price floor, who benefits from this new policy? Who loses?

3. A recent study found that the demand-and-supply schedules for Frisbees are as follows:

Price per Frisbee	Quantity Demanded	Quantity Supplied
$11	1 million Frisbees	15 million Frisbees
10	2	12
9	4	9
8	6	6
7	8	3
6	10	1

   a. What are the equilibrium price and quantity of Frisbees?
   b. Frisbee manufacturers persuade the government that Frisbee production improves scientists' understanding of aerodynamics and thus is important for national security. A concerned Congress votes to impose a price floor $2 above the equilibrium price. What is the new market price? How many Frisbees are sold?
   c. Irate college students march on Washington and demand a reduction in the price of Frisbees. An even more concerned Congress votes to repeal the price floor and impose a price ceiling $1 below the former price floor. What is the new market price? How many Frisbees are sold?

4. Suppose the federal government requires beer drinkers to pay a $2 tax on each case of beer purchased. (In fact, both the federal and state governments impose beer taxes of some sort.)
   a. Draw a supply-and-demand diagram of the market for beer without the tax. Show the price paid by consumers, the price received by producers, and the quantity of beer sold. What is the difference between the price paid by consumers and the price received by producers?
   b. Now draw a supply-and-demand diagram for the beer market with the tax. Show the price paid by consumers, the price received by producers, and the quantity of beer sold. What is the difference between the price paid by consumers and the price received by producers? Has the quantity of beer sold increased or decreased?

5. A senator wants to raise tax revenue and make workers better off. A staff member proposes raising the payroll tax paid by firms and using part of the extra revenue to reduce the payroll tax paid by workers. Would this accomplish the senator's goal? Explain.

6. If the government places a $500 tax on luxury cars, will the price paid by consumers rise by more than $500, less than $500, or exactly $500? Explain.

7. Congress and the president decide that the United States should reduce air pollution by reducing its use of gasoline. They impose a $0.50 tax on each gallon of gasoline sold.
   a. Should they impose this tax on producers or consumers? Explain carefully using a supply-and-demand diagram.
   b. If the demand for gasoline were more elastic, would this tax be more effective or less effective in reducing the quantity of gasoline consumed? Explain with both words and a diagram.
   c. Are consumers of gasoline helped or hurt by this tax? Why?
   d. Are workers in the oil industry helped or hurt by this tax? Why?

8. A case study in this chapter discusses the federal minimum-wage law.
   a. Suppose the minimum wage is above the equilibrium wage in the market for unskilled labor. Using a supply-and-demand diagram of the market for unskilled labor, show the market wage, the number of workers who are employed, and the number of workers who are unemployed. Also show the total wage payments to unskilled workers.
   b. Now suppose the secretary of labor proposes an increase in the minimum wage. What effect would this increase have on employment? Does the change in employment depend on the elasticity of demand, the elasticity of supply, both elasticities, or neither?
   c. What effect would this increase in the minimum wage have on unemployment? Does the change in unemployment depend on the elasticity of demand, the elasticity of supply, both elasticities, or neither?
   d. If the demand for unskilled labor were inelastic, would the proposed increase in the minimum wage raise or lower total wage payments to unskilled workers? Would your answer change if the demand for unskilled labor were elastic?
9. At Fenway Park, home of the Boston Red Sox, seating is limited to about 38,000. Hence, the number of tickets issued is fixed at that figure. Seeing a golden opportunity to raise revenue, the City of Boston levies a per ticket tax of $5 to be paid by the ticket buyer. Boston sports fans, a famously civic-minded lot, dutifully send in the $5 per ticket. Draw a well-labeled graph showing the impact of the tax. On whom does the tax burden fall—the team's owners, the fans, or both? Why?
10. A market is described by the following supply and demand curves:

$$Q^S = 2P$$
$$Q^D = 300 - P$$

   a. Solve for the equilibrium price and quantity.
   b. If the government imposes a price ceiling of $90, does a shortage or surplus (or neither) develop? What are the price, quantity supplied, quantity demanded, and size of the shortage or surplus?
   c. If the government imposes a price floor of $90, does a shortage or surplus (or neither) develop? What are the price, quantity supplied, quantity demanded, and size of the shortage or surplus?
   d. Instead of a price control, the government levies a tax on producers of $30. As a result, the new supply curve is:

$$Q^S = 2(P - 30).$$

   Does a shortage or surplus (or neither) develop? What are the price, quantity supplied, quantity demanded, and size of the shortage or surplus?

To find additional study resources, visit cengagebrain.com, and search for "Mankiw."

PART III

Markets and Welfare

Consumers, Producers, and the Efficiency of Markets

CHAPTER 7

When consumers go to grocery stores to buy food for Thanksgiving dinner, they may be disappointed see the high price of turkey. At the same time, when farmers bring to market the turkeys they have raised, they probably wish that the price of turkey were even higher. These views are not surprising: Buyers always want to pay less, and sellers always want to be paid more. But is there a "right price" for turkey from the standpoint of society as a whole?

In previous chapters, we saw how, in market economies, the forces of supply and demand determine the prices of goods and services and the quantities sold.

So far, however, we have described the way markets allocate scarce resources without directly addressing the question of whether these market allocations are desirable. In other words, our analysis has been *positive* (what is) rather than *normative* (what should be). We know that the price of turkey adjusts to ensure that the quantity of turkey supplied equals the quantity of turkey demanded. But at this equilibrium, is the quantity of turkey produced and consumed too small, too large, or just right?

welfare economics
the study of how the allocation of resources affects economic well-being

In this chapter, we take up the topic of **welfare economics**, the study of how the allocation of resources affects economic well-being. We begin by examining the benefits that buyers and sellers receive from engaging in market transactions. We then examine how society can make these benefits as large as possible. This analysis leads to a profound conclusion: In any market, the equilibrium of supply and demand maximizes the total benefits received by all buyers and sellers combined.

As you may recall from Chapter 1, one of the *Ten Principles of Economics* is that markets are usually a good way to organize economic activity. The study of welfare economics explains this principle more fully. It also answers our question about the right price of turkey: The price that balances the supply and demand for turkey is, in a particular sense, the best one because it maximizes the total welfare of turkey consumers and turkey producers. No consumer or producer of turkeys aims to achieve this goal, but their joint action directed by market prices moves them toward a welfare-maximizing outcome, as if led by an invisible hand.

7-1 Consumer Surplus

We begin our study of welfare economics by looking at the benefits buyers receive from participating in a market.

7-1a Willingness to Pay

Imagine that you own a mint-condition recording of Elvis Presley's first album. Because you are not an Elvis Presley fan, you decide to sell it. One way to do so is to hold an auction.

willingness to pay
the maximum amount that a buyer will pay for a good

Four Elvis fans show up for your auction: Taylor, Carrie, Rihanna, and Gaga. They would all like to own the album, but each of them has a limit on the amount she is willing to pay for it. Table 1 shows the maximum price that each of the four possible buyers would pay. A buyer's maximum is called her **willingness to pay**, and it measures how much that buyer values the good. Each buyer would be eager to buy the album at a price less than her willingness to pay, and she would refuse to buy the album at a price greater than her willingness to pay. At a price

TABLE 1

Four Possible Buyers' Willingness to Pay

Buyer	Willingness to Pay
Taylor	$100
Carrie	80
Rihanna	70
Gaga	50

equal to her willingness to pay, the buyer would be indifferent about buying the good: If the price is exactly the same as the value she places on the album, she would be equally happy buying it or keeping her money.

To sell your album, you begin the bidding process at a low price, say, $10. Because all four buyers are willing to pay much more, the price rises quickly. The bidding stops when Taylor bids $80 (or slightly more). At this point, Carrie, Rihanna, and Gaga have all dropped out of the bidding because they are unwilling to bid any more than $80. Taylor pays you $80 and gets the album. Note that the album has gone to the buyer who values it most highly.

What benefit does Taylor receive from buying the Elvis Presley album? In a sense, Taylor has found a real bargain: She is willing to pay $100 for the album but pays only $80. We say that Taylor receives *consumer surplus* of $20. **Consumer surplus** is the amount a buyer is willing to pay for a good minus the amount the buyer actually pays for it.

consumer surplus
the amount a buyer is willing to pay for a good minus the amount the buyer actually pays for it

Consumer surplus measures the benefit buyers receive from participating in a market. In this example, Taylor receives a $20 benefit from participating in the auction because she pays only $80 for a good she values at $100. Carrie, Rihanna, and Gaga get no consumer surplus from participating in the auction because they left without the album and without paying anything.

Now consider a somewhat different example. Suppose that you had two identical Elvis Presley albums to sell. Again, you auction them off to the four possible buyers. To keep things simple, we assume that both albums are to be sold for the same price and that no one is interested in buying more than one album. Therefore, the price rises until two buyers are left.

In this case, the bidding stops when Taylor and Carrie bid $70 (or slightly higher). At this price, Taylor and Carrie are each happy to buy an album, and Rihanna and Gaga are not willing to bid any higher. Taylor and Carrie each receive consumer surplus equal to her willingness to pay minus the price. Taylor's consumer surplus is $30, and Carrie's is $10. Taylor's consumer surplus is higher now than in the previous example because she gets the same album but pays less for it. The total consumer surplus in the market is $40.

7-1b Using the Demand Curve to Measure Consumer Surplus

Consumer surplus is closely related to the demand curve for a product. To see how they are related, let's continue our example and consider the demand curve for this rare Elvis Presley album.

We begin by using the willingness to pay of the four possible buyers to find the market demand schedule for the album. The table in Figure 1 shows the demand schedule that corresponds to Table 1. If the price is above $100, the quantity demanded in the market is 0 because no buyer is willing to pay that much. If the price is between $80 and $100, the quantity demanded is 1 because only Taylor is willing to pay such a high price. If the price is between $70 and $80, the quantity demanded is 2 because both Taylor and Carrie are willing to pay the price. We can continue this analysis for other prices as well. In this way, the demand schedule is derived from the willingness to pay of the four possible buyers.

The graph in Figure 1 shows the demand curve that corresponds to this demand schedule. Note the relationship between the height of the demand curve and the buyers' willingness to pay. At any quantity, the price given by the demand curve shows the willingness to pay of the *marginal buyer*, the buyer who would leave the market first if the price were any higher. At a quantity of 4 albums, for instance, the demand curve has a height of $50, the price that Gaga

FIGURE 1

The Demand Schedule and the Demand Curve

The table shows the demand schedule for the buyers (listed in Table 1) of the mint-condition copy of Elvis Presley's first album. The graph shows the corresponding demand curve. Note that the height of the demand curve reflects the buyers' willingness to pay.

Price	Buyers	Quantity Demanded
More than $100	None	0
$80 to $100	Taylor	1
$70 to $80	Taylor, Carrie	2
$50 to $70	Taylor, Carrie, Rihanna	3
$50 or less	Taylor, Carrie, Rihanna, Gaga	4

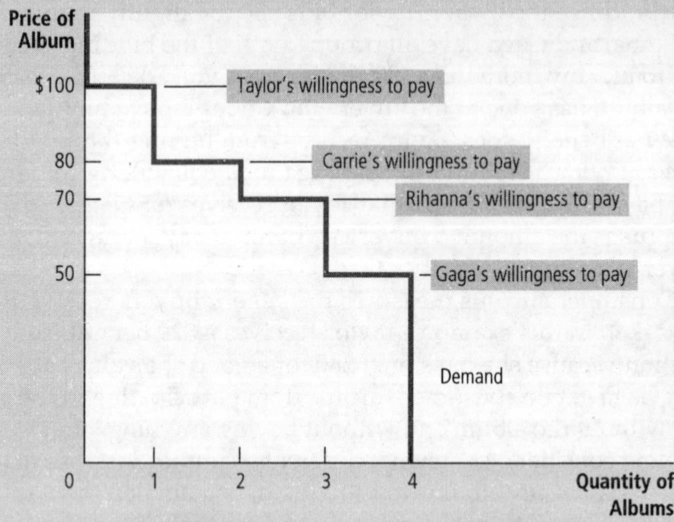

(the marginal buyer) is willing to pay for an album. At a quantity of 3 albums, the demand curve has a height of $70, the price that Rihanna (who is now the marginal buyer) is willing to pay.

Because the demand curve reflects buyers' willingness to pay, we can also use it to measure consumer surplus. Figure 2 uses the demand curve to compute consumer surplus in our two examples. In panel (a), the price is $80 (or slightly above) and the quantity demanded is 1. Note that the area above the price and below the demand curve equals $20. This amount is exactly the consumer surplus we computed earlier when only 1 album is sold.

Panel (b) of Figure 2 shows consumer surplus when the price is $70 (or slightly above). In this case, the area above the price and below the demand curve equals the total area of the two rectangles: Taylor's consumer surplus at this price is $30 and Carrie's is $10. This area equals a total of $40. Once again, this amount is the consumer surplus we computed earlier.

The lesson from this example holds for all demand curves: *The area below the demand curve and above the price measures the consumer surplus in a market.* This is true because the height of the demand curve represents the value buyers place on the good, as measured by their willingness to pay for it. The difference between this willingness to pay and the market price is each buyer's consumer surplus. Thus, the total area below the demand curve and above the price is the sum of the consumer surplus of all buyers in the market for a good or service.

7-1c How a Lower Price Raises Consumer Surplus

Because buyers always want to pay less for the goods they buy, a lower price makes buyers of a good better off. But how much does buyers' well-being rise in response to a lower price? We can use the concept of consumer surplus to answer this question precisely.

In panel (a), the price of the good is $80 and the consumer surplus is $20. In panel (b), the price of the good is $70 and the consumer surplus is $40.

FIGURE 2

Measuring Consumer Surplus with the Demand Curve

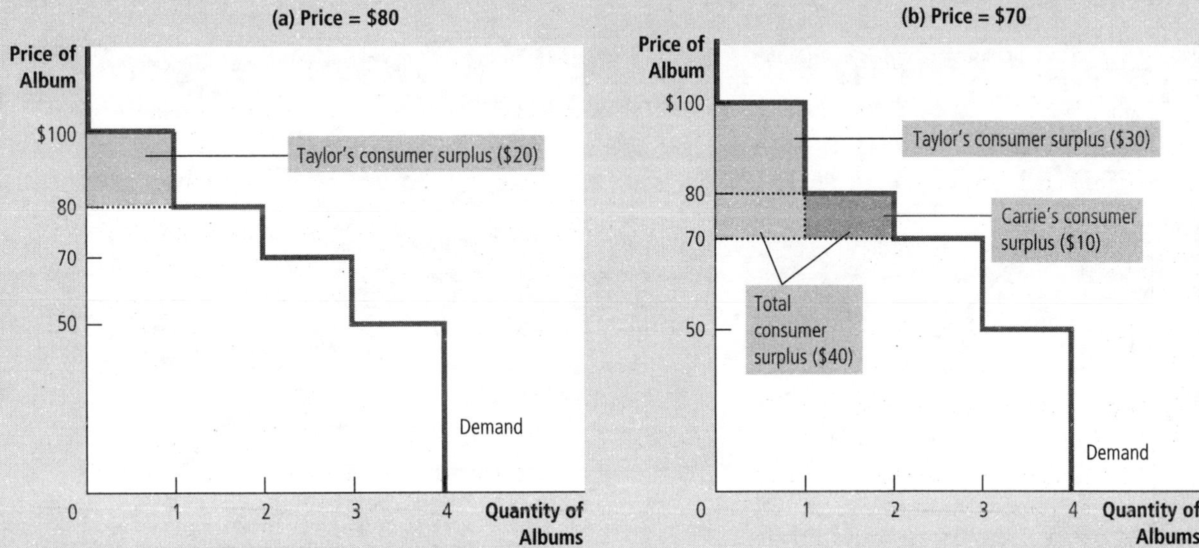

Figure 3 shows a typical demand curve. You may notice that this curve gradually slopes downward instead of taking discrete steps as in the previous two figures. In a market with many buyers, the resulting steps from each buyer dropping out are so small that they form a smooth curve. Although this curve has a different shape, the ideas we have just developed still apply: Consumer surplus is the area above the price and below the demand curve. In panel (a), consumer surplus at a price of P_1 is the area of triangle ABC.

Now suppose that the price falls from P_1 to P_2, as shown in panel (b). The consumer surplus now equals area ADF. The increase in consumer surplus attributable to the lower price is the area BCFD.

This increase in consumer surplus is composed of two parts. First, those buyers who were already buying Q_1 of the good at the higher price P_1 are better off because now they pay less. The increase in consumer surplus of existing buyers is the reduction in the amount they pay; it equals the area of the rectangle BCED. Second, some new buyers enter the market because they are willing to buy the good at the lower price. As a result, the quantity demanded in the market increases from Q_1 to Q_2. The consumer surplus these newcomers receive is the area of the triangle CEF.

7-1d What Does Consumer Surplus Measure?

Our goal in developing the concept of consumer surplus is to make judgments about the desirability of market outcomes. Now that you have seen what consumer surplus is, let's consider whether it is a good measure of economic well-being.

Imagine that you are a policymaker trying to design a good economic system. Would you care about the amount of consumer surplus? Consumer

FIGURE 3

How Price Affects Consumer Surplus

In panel (a), the price is P_1, the quantity demanded is Q_1, and consumer surplus equals the area of the triangle ABC. When the price falls from P_1 to P_2, as in panel (b), the quantity demanded rises from Q_1 to Q_2 and the consumer surplus rises to the area of the triangle ADF. The increase in consumer surplus (area BCFD) occurs in part because existing consumers now pay less (area BCED) and in part because new consumers enter the market at the lower price (area CEF).

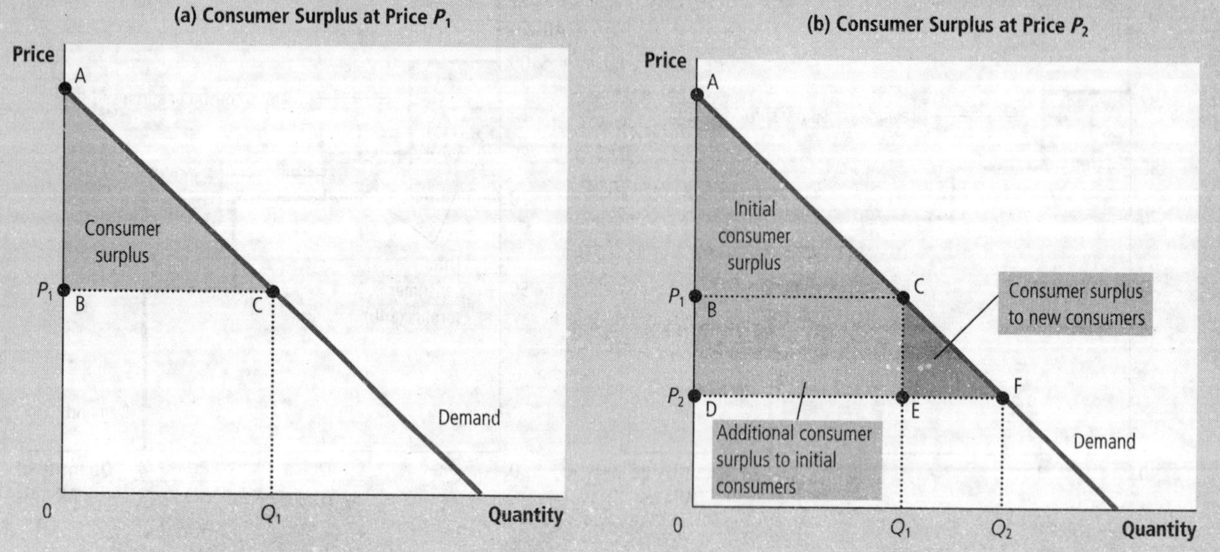

surplus, the amount that buyers are willing to pay for a good minus the amount they actually pay for it, measures the benefit that buyers receive from a good *as the buyers themselves perceive it*. Thus, consumer surplus is a good measure of economic well-being if policymakers want to satisfy the preferences of buyers.

In some circumstances, policymakers might choose to disregard consumer surplus because they do not respect the preferences that drive buyer behavior. For example, drug addicts are willing to pay a high price for heroin. Yet we would not say that addicts get a large benefit from being able to buy heroin at a low price (even though addicts might say they do). From the standpoint of society, willingness to pay in this instance is not a good measure of the buyers' benefit, and consumer surplus is not a good measure of economic well-being, because addicts are not looking after their own best interests.

In most markets, however, consumer surplus does reflect economic well-being. Economists normally assume that buyers are rational when they make decisions. Rational people do the best they can to achieve their objectives, given their opportunities. Economists also normally assume that people's preferences should be respected. In this case, consumers are the best judges of how much benefit they receive from the goods they buy.

QuickQuiz *Draw a demand curve for turkey. In your diagram, show a price of turkey and the consumer surplus at that price. Explain in words what this consumer surplus measures.*

7-2 Producer Surplus

We now turn to the other side of the market and consider the benefits sellers receive from participating in a market. As you will see, our analysis of sellers' welfare is similar to our analysis of buyers' welfare.

7-2a Cost and the Willingness to Sell

Imagine now that you are a homeowner and want to get your house painted. You turn to four sellers of painting services: Vincent, Claude, Pablo, and Andy. Each painter is willing to do the work for you if the price is right. You decide to take bids from the four painters and auction off the job to the painter who will do the work for the lowest price.

Each painter is willing to take the job if the price he would receive exceeds his cost of doing the work. Here the term **cost** should be interpreted as the painters' opportunity cost: It includes the painters' out-of-pocket expenses (for paint, brushes, and so on) as well as the value that the painters place on their own time. Table 2 shows each painter's cost. Because a painter's cost is the lowest price he would accept for his work, cost is a measure of his willingness to sell his services. Each painter would be eager to sell his services at a price greater than his cost and would refuse to sell his services at a price less than his cost. At a price exactly equal to his cost, he would be indifferent about selling his services: He would be equally happy getting the job or using his time and energy for another purpose.

cost
the value of everything a seller must give up to produce a good

When you take bids from the painters, the price might start high, but it quickly falls as the painters compete for the job. Once Andy has bid $600 (or slightly less), he is the sole remaining bidder. Andy is happy to do the job for this price because his cost is only $500. Vincent, Claude, and Pablo are unwilling to do the job for less than $600. Note that the job goes to the painter who can do the work at the lowest cost.

What benefit does Andy receive from getting the job? Because he is willing to do the work for $500 but gets $600 for doing it, we say that he receives *producer surplus* of $100. **Producer surplus** is the amount a seller is paid minus the cost of production. Producer surplus measures the benefit sellers receive from participating in a market.

producer surplus
the amount a seller is paid for a good minus the seller's cost of providing it

Now consider a somewhat different example. Suppose that you have two houses that need painting. Again, you auction off the jobs to the four painters. To keep things simple, let's assume that no painter is able to paint both houses and that you will pay the same amount to paint each house. Therefore, the price falls until two painters are left.

In this case, the bidding stops when Andy and Pablo each offer to do the job for a price of $800 (or slightly less). Andy and Pablo are willing to do the work at this price, while Vincent and Claude are not willing to bid a lower price. At a price of

TABLE 2

The Costs of Four Possible Sellers

Seller	Cost
Vincent	$900
Claude	800
Pablo	600
Andy	500

FIGURE 4

The Supply Schedule and the Supply Curve

The table shows the supply schedule for the sellers (listed in Table 2) of painting services. The graph shows the corresponding supply curve. Note that the height of the supply curve reflects the sellers' costs.

Price	Sellers	Quantity Demanded
$900 or more	Vincent, Claude, Pablo, Andy	4
$800 to $900	Claude, Pablo, Andy	3
$600 to $800	Pablo, Andy	2
$500 to $600	Andy	1
Less than $500	None	0

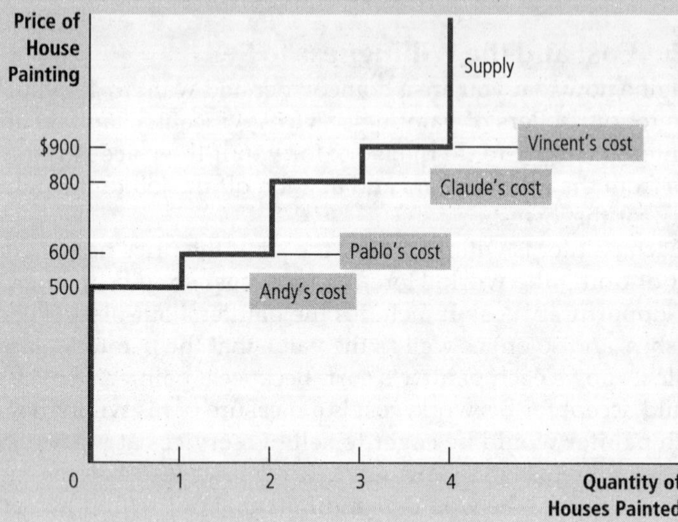

$800, Andy receives producer surplus of $300 and Pablo receives producer surplus of $200. The total producer surplus in the market is $500.

7-2b Using the Supply Curve to Measure Producer Surplus

Just as consumer surplus is closely related to the demand curve, producer surplus is closely related to the supply curve. To see how, let's continue with our example.

We begin by using the costs of the four painters to find the supply schedule for painting services. The table in Figure 4 shows the supply schedule that corresponds to the costs in Table 2. If the price is below $500, none of the four painters is willing to do the job, so the quantity supplied is zero. If the price is between $500 and $600, only Andy is willing to do the job, so the quantity supplied is 1. If the price is between $600 and $800, Andy and Pablo are willing to do the job, so the quantity supplied is 2, and so on. Thus, the supply schedule is derived from the costs of the four painters.

The graph in Figure 4 shows the supply curve that corresponds to this supply schedule. Note that the height of the supply curve is related to the sellers' costs. At any quantity, the price given by the supply curve shows the cost of the *marginal seller*, the seller who would leave the market first if the price were any lower. At a quantity of 4 houses, for instance, the supply curve has a height of $900, the cost that Vincent (the marginal seller) incurs to provide his painting services. At a quantity of 3 houses, the supply curve has a height of $800, the cost that Claude (who is now the marginal seller) incurs.

Because the supply curve reflects sellers' costs, we can use it to measure producer surplus. Figure 5 uses the supply curve to compute producer surplus in our two examples. In panel (a), we assume that the price is $600 (or slightly less). In this case, the quantity supplied is 1. Note that the area below the price and above

In panel (a), the price of the good is $600 and the producer surplus is $100. In panel (b), the price of the good is $800 and the producer surplus is $500.

FIGURE 5

Measuring Producer Surplus with the Supply Curve

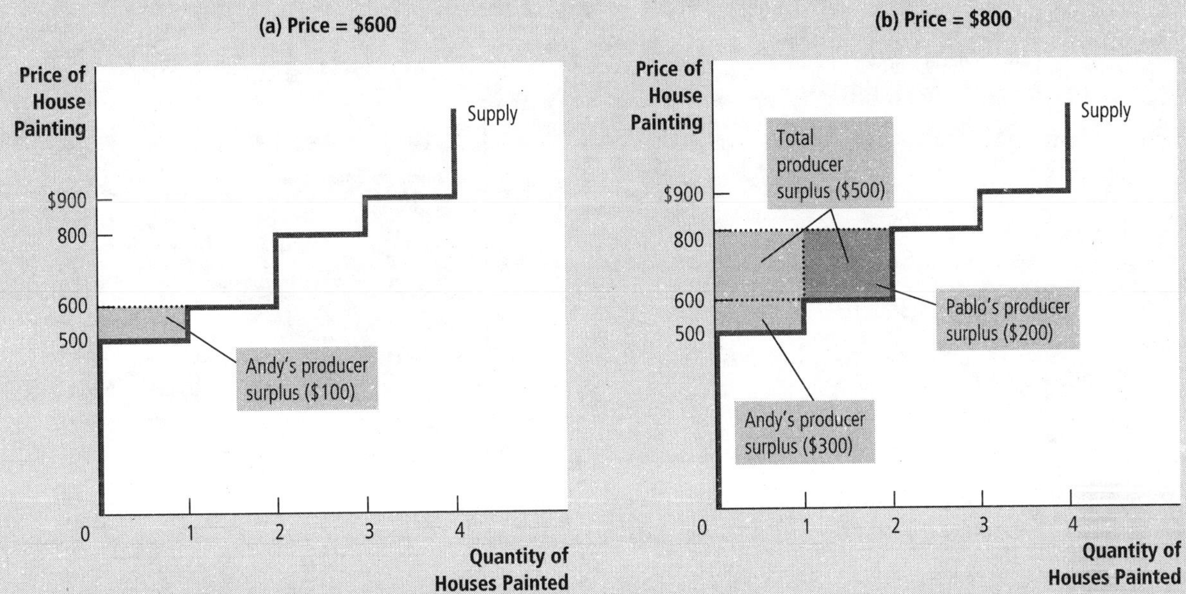

the supply curve equals $100. This amount is exactly the producer surplus we computed earlier for Andy.

Panel (b) of Figure 5 shows producer surplus at a price of $800 (or slightly less). In this case, the area below the price and above the supply curve equals the total area of the two rectangles. This area equals $500, the producer surplus we computed earlier for Pablo and Andy when two houses needed painting.

The lesson from this example applies to all supply curves: *The area below the price and above the supply curve measures the producer surplus in a market.* The logic is straightforward: The height of the supply curve measures sellers' costs, and the difference between the price and the cost of production is each seller's producer surplus. Thus, the total area is the sum of the producer surplus of all sellers.

7-2c How a Higher Price Raises Producer Surplus

You will not be surprised to hear that sellers always want to receive a higher price for the goods they sell. But how much does sellers' well-being rise in response to a higher price? The concept of producer surplus offers a precise answer to this question.

Figure 6 shows a typical upward-sloping supply curve that would arise in a market with many sellers. Although this supply curve differs in shape from the previous figure, we measure producer surplus in the same way: Producer surplus is the area below the price and above the supply curve. In panel (a), the price is P_1 and producer surplus is the area of triangle ABC.

FIGURE 6

How Price Affects Producer Surplus

In panel (a), the price is P_1, the quantity supplied is Q_1, and producer surplus equals the area of the triangle ABC. When the price rises from P_1 to P_2, as in panel (b), the quantity supplied rises from Q_1 to Q_2 and the producer surplus rises to the area of the triangle ADF. The increase in producer surplus (area BCFD) occurs in part because existing producers now receive more (area BCED) and in part because new producers enter the market at the higher price (area CEF).

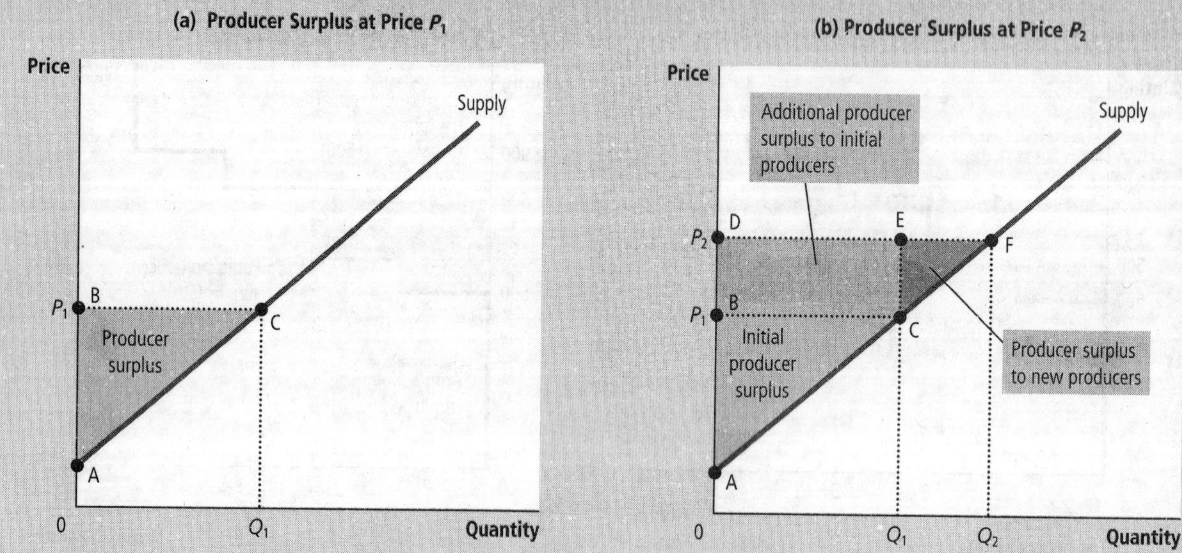

Panel (b) shows what happens when the price rises from P_1 to P_2. Producer surplus now equals area ADF. This increase in producer surplus has two parts. First, those sellers who were already selling Q_1 of the good at the lower price P_1 are better off because they now get more for what they sell. The increase in producer surplus for existing sellers equals the area of the rectangle BCED. Second, some new sellers enter the market because they are willing to produce the good at the higher price, resulting in an increase in the quantity supplied from Q_1 to Q_2. The producer surplus of these newcomers is the area of the triangle CEF.

As this analysis shows, we use producer surplus to measure the well-being of sellers in much the same way as we use consumer surplus to measure the well-being of buyers. Because these two measures of economic welfare are so similar, it is natural to use them together. Indeed, that is exactly what we do in the next section.

QuickQuiz *Draw a supply curve for turkey. In your diagram, show a price of turkey and the producer surplus at that price. Explain in words what this producer surplus measures.*

7-3 Market Efficiency

Consumer surplus and producer surplus are the basic tools that economists use to study the welfare of buyers and sellers in a market. These tools can help us address a fundamental economic question: Is the allocation of resources determined by free markets desirable?

7-3a The Benevolent Social Planner

To evaluate market outcomes, we introduce into our analysis a new, hypothetical character called the benevolent social planner. The benevolent social planner is an all-knowing, all-powerful, well-intentioned dictator. The planner wants to maximize the economic well-being of everyone in society. What should this planner do? Should she just leave buyers and sellers at the equilibrium that they reach naturally on their own? Or can she increase economic well-being by altering the market outcome in some way?

To answer this question, the planner must first decide how to measure the economic well-being of a society. One possible measure is the sum of consumer and producer surplus, which we call *total surplus*. Consumer surplus is the benefit that buyers receive from participating in a market, and producer surplus is the benefit that sellers receive. It is therefore natural to use total surplus as a measure of society's economic well-being.

To better understand this measure of economic well-being, recall how we measure consumer and producer surplus. We define consumer surplus as

Consumer surplus = Value to buyers − Amount paid by buyers.

Similarly, we define producer surplus as

Producer surplus = Amount received by sellers − Cost to sellers.

When we add consumer and producer surplus together, we obtain

Total surplus = (Value to buyers − Amount paid by buyers)
+ (Amount received by sellers − Cost to sellers).

The amount paid by buyers equals the amount received by sellers, so the middle two terms in this expression cancel each other. As a result, we can write total surplus as

Total surplus = Value to buyers − Cost to sellers.

Total surplus in a market is the total value to buyers of the goods, as measured by their willingness to pay, minus the total cost to sellers of providing those goods.

If an allocation of resources maximizes total surplus, we say that the allocation exhibits **efficiency**. If an allocation is not efficient, then some of the potential gains from trade among buyers and sellers are not being realized. For example, an allocation is inefficient if a good is not being produced by the sellers with lowest cost. In this case, moving production from a high-cost producer to a low-cost producer will lower the total cost to sellers and raise total surplus. Similarly, an allocation is inefficient if a good is not being consumed by the buyers who value it most highly. In this case, moving consumption of the good from a buyer with a low valuation to a buyer with a high valuation will raise total surplus.

efficiency
the property of a resource allocation of maximizing the total surplus received by all members of society

In addition to efficiency, the social planner might also care about **equality**—that is, whether the various buyers and sellers in the market have a similar level of economic well-being. In essence, the gains from trade in a market are like a pie to be shared among the market participants. The question of efficiency concerns whether the pie is as big as possible. The question of equality concerns how

equality
the property of distributing economic prosperity uniformly among the members of society

FIGURE 7

Consumer and Producer Surplus in the Market Equilibrium
Total surplus—the sum of consumer and producer surplus—is the area between the supply and demand curves up to the equilibrium quantity.

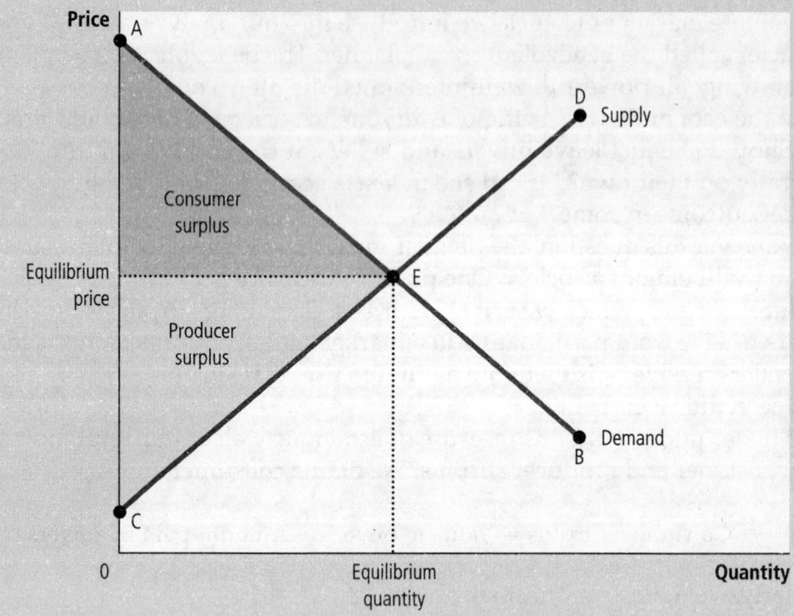

the pie is sliced and how the portions are distributed among members of society. In this chapter, we concentrate on efficiency as the social planner's goal. Keep in mind, however, that real policymakers often care about equality as well.

7-3b Evaluating the Market Equilibrium

Figure 7 shows consumer and producer surplus when a market reaches the equilibrium of supply and demand. Recall that consumer surplus equals the area above the price and under the demand curve and producer surplus equals the area below the price and above the supply curve. Thus, the total area between the supply and demand curves up to the point of equilibrium represents the total surplus in this market.

Is this equilibrium allocation of resources efficient? That is, does it maximize total surplus? To answer this question, recall that when a market is in equilibrium, the price determines which buyers and sellers participate in the market. Those buyers who value the good more than the price (represented by the segment AE on the demand curve) choose to buy the good; buyers who value it less than the price (represented by the segment EB) do not. Similarly, those sellers whose costs are less than the price (represented by the segment CE on the supply curve) choose to produce and sell the good; sellers whose costs are greater than the price (represented by the segment ED) do not.

These observations lead to two insights about market outcomes:

1. Free markets allocate the supply of goods to the buyers who value them most highly, as measured by their willingness to pay.

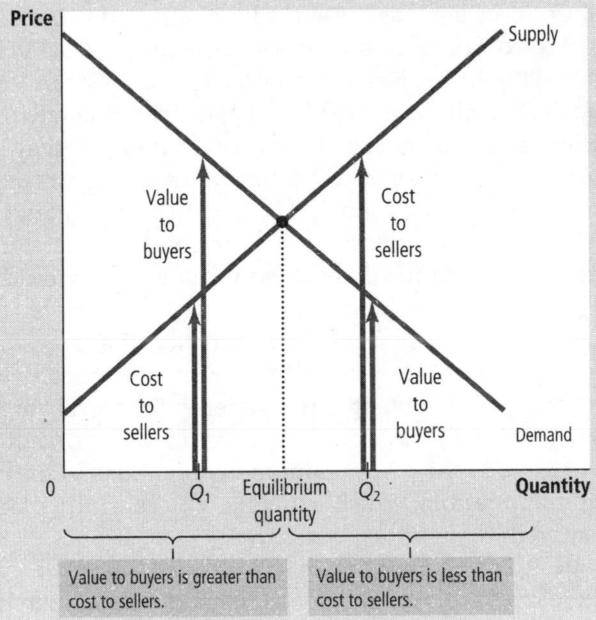

FIGURE 8

The Efficiency of the Equilibrium Quantity
At quantities less than the equilibrium quantity, such as Q_1, the value to buyers exceeds the cost to sellers. At quantities greater than the equilibrium quantity, such as Q_2, the cost to sellers exceeds the value to buyers. Therefore, the market equilibrium maximizes the sum of producer and consumer surplus.

2. Free markets allocate the demand for goods to the sellers who can produce them at the lowest cost.

Thus, given the quantity produced and sold in a market equilibrium, the social planner cannot increase economic well-being by changing the allocation of consumption among buyers or the allocation of production among sellers.

But can the social planner raise total economic well-being by increasing or decreasing the quantity of the good? The answer is no, as stated in this third insight about market outcomes:

3. Free markets produce the quantity of goods that maximizes the sum of consumer and producer surplus.

Figure 8 illustrates why this is true. To interpret this figure, keep in mind that the demand curve reflects the value to buyers and the supply curve reflects the cost to sellers. At any quantity below the equilibrium level, such as Q_1, the value to the marginal buyer exceeds the cost to the marginal seller. As a result, increasing the quantity produced and consumed raises total surplus. This continues to be true until the quantity reaches the equilibrium level. Similarly, at any quantity beyond the equilibrium level, such as Q_2, the value to the marginal buyer is less than the cost to the marginal seller. In this case, decreasing the quantity raises total surplus, and this continues to be true until quantity falls to the equilibrium level. To maximize total surplus, the social planner would choose the quantity where the supply and demand curves intersect.

Together, these three insights tell us that the market outcome makes the sum of consumer and producer surplus as large as it can be. In other words, the equilibrium outcome is an efficient allocation of resources. The benevolent social planner can, therefore, leave the market outcome just as she finds it. This policy of leaving well enough alone goes by the French expression *laissez faire*, which literally translates to "leave to do" but is more broadly interpreted as "let people do as they will."

Society is lucky that the planner doesn't need to intervene. Although it has been a useful exercise imagining what an all-knowing, all-powerful, well-intentioned dictator would do, let's face it: Such characters are hard to come by. Dictators are rarely benevolent, and even if we found someone so virtuous, she would lack crucial information.

Suppose our social planner tried to choose an efficient allocation of resources on her own, instead of relying on market forces. To do so, she would need to know the value of a particular good to every potential consumer in the market and the cost for every potential producer. And she would need this information not only for this market but for every one of the many thousands of markets in the economy. The task is practically impossible, which explains why centrally planned economies never work very well.

The planner's job becomes easy, however, once she takes on a partner: Adam Smith's invisible hand of the marketplace. The invisible hand takes all the information about buyers and sellers into account and guides everyone in the market to the best outcome as judged by the standard of economic efficiency. It is a truly remarkable feat. That is why economists so often advocate free markets as the best way to organize economic activity.

CASE STUDY

SHOULD THERE BE A MARKET FOR ORGANS?

Some years ago, the front page of *The Boston Globe* ran the headline "How a Mother's Love Helped Save Two Lives." The newspaper told the story of Susan Stephens, a woman whose son needed a kidney transplant. When the doctor learned that the mother's kidney was not compatible, he proposed a novel solution: If Stephens donated one of her kidneys to a stranger, her son would move to the top of the kidney waiting list. The mother accepted the deal, and soon two patients had the transplants they were waiting for.

The ingenuity of the doctor's proposal and the nobility of the mother's act cannot be doubted. But the story raises some intriguing questions. If the mother could trade a kidney for a kidney, would the hospital allow her to trade a kidney for an expensive, experimental cancer treatment that she could not otherwise afford? Should she be allowed to exchange her kidney for free tuition for her son at the hospital's medical school? Should she be able to sell her kidney and use the cash to trade in her old Chevy for a new Lexus?

As a matter of public policy, our society makes it illegal for people to sell their organs. In essence, in the market for organs, the government has imposed a price ceiling of zero. The result, as with any binding price ceiling, is a shortage of the good. The deal in the Stephens case did not fall under this prohibition because no cash changed hands.

Many economists believe that there would be large benefits to allowing a free market for organs. People are born with two kidneys, but they usually need only one. Meanwhile, some people suffer from illnesses that leave them without any working kidney. Despite the obvious gains from trade, the current situation is dire: The typical patient has to wait several years for a kidney transplant, and every year thousands of people die because a compatible kidney cannot be found. If those needing a kidney were allowed to buy one from those who have two, the price would rise to balance supply and demand. Sellers would be better off with the extra cash in their pockets. Buyers would be better off with the organ they need to save their lives. The shortage of kidneys would disappear.

Such a market would lead to an efficient allocation of resources, but critics of this plan worry about fairness. A market for organs, they argue, would benefit the rich at the expense of the poor because organs would then be allocated to those most willing and able to pay. But you can also question the fairness of the current system. Now, most of us walk around with an extra organ that we don't really need, while some of our fellow citizens are dying to get one. Is that fair? ●

ASK THE EXPERTS

Supplying Kidneys

"A market that allows payment for human kidneys should be established on a trial basis to help extend the lives of patients with kidney disease."

What do economists say?

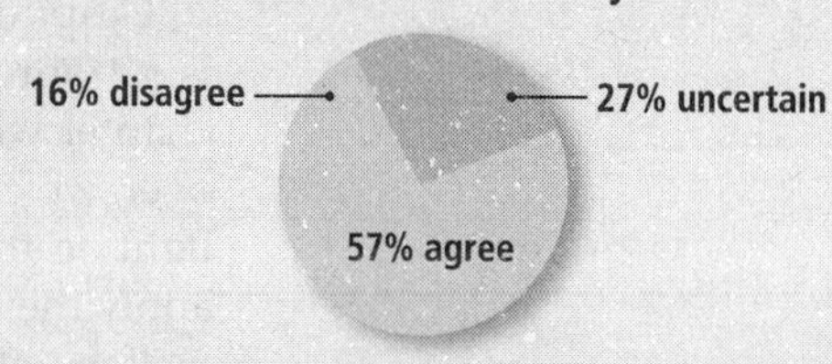

Source: IGM Economic Experts Panel, March 11, 2014.

QuickQuiz *Draw the supply and demand curves for turkey. In the equilibrium, show producer and consumer surplus. Explain why producing more turkeys would lower total surplus.*

7-4 Conclusion: Market Efficiency and Market Failure

This chapter introduced the basic tools of welfare economics—consumer and producer surplus—and used them to evaluate the efficiency of free markets. We showed that the forces of supply and demand allocate resources efficiently. That is, even though each buyer and seller in a market is concerned only about her own welfare, together they are guided by an invisible hand to an equilibrium that maximizes the total benefits to buyers and sellers.

A word of warning is in order. To conclude that markets are efficient, we made several assumptions about how markets work. When these assumptions do not hold, our conclusion that the market equilibrium is efficient may no longer be true. As we close this chapter, let's briefly consider two of the most important assumptions we made.

First, our analysis assumed that markets are perfectly competitive. In actual economies, however, competition is sometimes far from perfect. In some markets, a single buyer or seller (or a small group of them) may be able to control market prices. This ability to influence prices is called *market power*. Market power can cause markets to be inefficient because it keeps the price and quantity away from the levels determined by the equilibrium of supply and demand.

Second, our analysis assumed that the outcome in a market matters only to the buyers and sellers who participate in that market. Yet sometimes the decisions of buyers and sellers affect people who are not participants in the market at all. Pollution is the classic example. The use of agricultural pesticides, for instance, affects not only the manufacturers who make them and the farmers who use them but also many others who breathe the air or drink the water contaminated by these pesticides. When a market exhibits such side effects, called *externalities*, the welfare implications of market activity depend on more than just the value obtained by the buyers and the cost incurred by the sellers. Because buyers and sellers may ignore these side effects when deciding how much to consume and produce, the equilibrium in a market can be inefficient from the standpoint of society as a whole.

Market power and externalities are examples of a general phenomenon called *market failure*—the inability of some unregulated markets to allocate resources efficiently. When markets fail, public policy can potentially remedy the problem and increase economic efficiency. Microeconomists devote much effort to studying when market failures are likely and how they are best corrected. As you continue your study of economics, you will see that the tools of welfare economics developed here are readily adapted to that endeavor.

Despite the possibility of market failure, the invisible hand of the marketplace is extraordinarily important. In many markets, the assumptions we made in this chapter work well and the conclusion of market efficiency applies directly. Moreover, we can use our analysis of welfare economics and market efficiency to shed light on the effects of various government policies. In the next two chapters, we apply the tools we have just developed to study two important policy issues—the welfare effects of taxation and of international trade.

CHAPTER QuickQuiz

1. Jen values her time at $60 an hour. She spends 2 hours giving Colleen a massage. Colleen was willing to pay as much at $300 for the massage, but they negotiate a price of $200. In this transaction,
   a. consumer surplus is $20 larger than producer surplus.
   b. consumer surplus is $40 larger than producer surplus.
   c. producer surplus is $20 larger than consumer surplus.
   d. producer surplus is $40 larger than consumer surplus.
2. The demand curve for cookies is downward-sloping. When the price of cookies is $2, the quantity demanded is 100. If the price rises to $3, what happens to consumer surplus?
   a. It falls by less than $100.
   b. It falls by more than $100.
   c. It rises by less than $100.
   d. It rises by more than $100.
3. John has been working as a tutor for $300 a semester. When the university raises the price it pays tutors to $400, Jasmine enters the market and begins tutoring as well. How much does producer surplus rise as a result of this price increase?
   a. by less than $100
   b. between $100 and $200
   c. between $200 and $300
   d. by more than $300
4. An efficient allocation of resources maximizes
   a. consumer surplus.
   b. producer surplus.
   c. consumer surplus plus producer surplus.
   d. consumer surplus minus producer surplus.
5. When a market is in equilibrium, the buyers are those with the ________ willingness to pay and the sellers are those with the ________ costs.
   a. highest, highest
   b. highest, lowest
   c. lowest, highest
   d. lowest, lowest
6. Producing a quantity larger than the equilibrium of supply and demand is inefficient because the marginal buyer's willingness to pay is
   a. negative.
   b. zero.
   c. positive but less than the marginal seller's cost.
   d. positive and greater than the marginal seller's cost.

SUMMARY

- Consumer surplus equals buyers' willingness to pay for a good minus the amount they actually pay, and it measures the benefit buyers get from participating in a market. Consumer surplus can be computed by finding the area below the demand curve and above the price.
- Producer surplus equals the amount sellers receive for their goods minus their costs of production, and it measures the benefit sellers get from participating in a market. Producer surplus can be computed by finding the area below the price and above the supply curve.
- An allocation of resources that maximizes total surplus (the sum of consumer and producer surplus) is said to be efficient. Policymakers are often concerned with the efficiency, as well as the equality, of economic outcomes.
- The equilibrium of supply and demand maximizes total surplus. That is, the invisible hand of the marketplace leads buyers and sellers to allocate resources efficiently.
- Markets do not allocate resources efficiently in the presence of market failures such as market power or externalities.

KEY CONCEPTS

welfare economics, p. 134
willingness to pay, p. 134
consumer surplus, p. 135
cost, p. 139
producer surplus, p. 139
efficiency, p. 143
equality, p. 143

QUESTIONS FOR REVIEW

1. Explain how buyers' willingness to pay, consumer surplus, and the demand curve are related.
2. Explain how sellers' costs, producer surplus, and the supply curve are related.
3. In a supply-and-demand diagram, show producer and consumer surplus at the market equilibrium.
4. What is efficiency? Is it the only goal of economic policymakers?
5. Name two types of market failure. Explain why each may cause market outcomes to be inefficient.

PROBLEMS AND APPLICATIONS

1. Melissa buys an iPhone for $240 and gets consumer surplus of $160.
   a. What is her willingness to pay?
   b. If she had bought the iPhone on sale for $180, what would her consumer surplus have been?
   c. If the price of an iPhone were $500, what would her consumer surplus have been?
2. An early freeze in California sours the lemon crop. Explain what happens to consumer surplus in the market for lemons. Explain what happens to consumer surplus in the market for lemonade. Illustrate your answers with diagrams.
3. Suppose the demand for French bread rises. Explain what happens to producer surplus in the market for French bread. Explain what happens to producer surplus in the market for flour. Illustrate your answers with diagrams.
4. It is a hot day, and Bert is thirsty. Here is the value he places on each bottle of water:

Value of first bottle	$7
Value of second bottle	$5
Value of third bottle	$3
Value of fourth bottle	$1

a. From this information, derive Bert's demand schedule. Graph his demand curve for bottled water.
b. If the price of a bottle of water is $4, how many bottles does Bert buy? How much consumer surplus does Bert get from his purchases? Show Bert's consumer surplus in your graph.
c. If the price falls to $2, how does quantity demanded change? How does Bert's consumer surplus change? Show these changes in your graph.

5. Ernie owns a water pump. Because pumping large amounts of water is harder than pumping small amounts, the cost of producing a bottle of water rises as he pumps more. Here is the cost he incurs to produce each bottle of water:

Cost of first bottle	$1
Cost of second bottle	$3
Cost of third bottle	$5
Cost of fourth bottle	$7

a. From this information, derive Ernie's supply schedule. Graph his supply curve for bottled water.
b. If the price of a bottle of water is $4, how many bottles does Ernie produce and sell? How much producer surplus does Ernie get from these sales? Show Ernie's producer surplus in your graph.
c. If the price rises to $6, how does quantity supplied change? How does Ernie's producer surplus change? Show these changes in your graph.

6. Consider a market in which Bert from problem 4 is the buyer and Ernie from problem 5 is the seller.
a. Use Ernie's supply schedule and Bert's demand schedule to find the quantity supplied and quantity demanded at prices of $2, $4, and $6. Which of these prices brings supply and demand into equilibrium?
b. What are consumer surplus, producer surplus, and total surplus in this equilibrium?
c. If Ernie produced and Bert consumed one fewer bottle of water, what would happen to total surplus?
d. If Ernie produced and Bert consumed one additional bottle of water, what would happen to total surplus?

7. The cost of producing flat-screen TVs has fallen over the past decade. Let's consider some implications of this fact.
a. Draw a supply-and-demand diagram to show the effect of falling production costs on the price and quantity of flat-screen TVs sold.
b. In your diagram, show what happens to consumer surplus and producer surplus.
c. Suppose the supply of flat-screen TVs is very elastic. Who benefits most from falling production costs—consumers or producers of these TVs?

8. There are four consumers willing to pay the following amounts for haircuts:

Gloria: $35 Jay: $10 Claire: $40 Phil: $25

There are four haircutting businesses with the following costs:

Firm A: $15 Firm B: $30 Firm C: $20 Firm D: $10

Each firm has the capacity to produce only one haircut. To achieve efficiency, how many haircuts should be given? Which businesses should cut hair and which consumers should have their hair cut? How large is the maximum possible total surplus?

9. One of the largest changes in the economy over the past several decades is that technological advances have reduced the cost of making computers.
a. Draw a supply-and-demand diagram to show what happened to price, quantity, consumer surplus, and producer surplus in the market for computers.
b. Forty years ago, students used typewriters to prepare papers for their classes; today they use computers. Does that make computers and typewriters complements or substitutes? Use a supply-and-demand diagram to show what happened to price, quantity, consumer surplus, and producer surplus in the market for typewriters. Should typewriter producers have been happy or sad about the technological advance in computers?
c. Are computers and software complements or substitutes? Draw a supply-and-demand diagram to show what happened to price, quantity, consumer surplus, and producer surplus in the market for software. Should software producers have been happy or sad about the technological advance in computers?
d. Does this analysis help explain why software producer Bill Gates is one of the world's richest people?

10. A friend of yours is considering two cell phone service providers. Provider A charges $120 per month for the service regardless of the number of phone calls made. Provider B does not have a fixed service fee but instead charges $1 per minute for calls. Your friend's

monthly demand for minutes of calling is given by the equation $Q^D = 150 - 50P$, where P is the price of a minute.

a. With each provider, what is the cost to your friend of an extra minute on the phone?
b. In light of your answer to (a), how many minutes with each provider would your friend talk on the phone?
c. How much would she end up paying each provider every month?
d. How much consumer surplus would she obtain with each provider? (*Hint*: Graph the demand curve and recall the formula for the area of a triangle.)
e. Which provider would you recommend that your friend choose? Why?

11. Consider how health insurance affects the quantity of healthcare services performed. Suppose that the typical medical procedure has a cost of \$100, yet a person with health insurance pays only \$20 out of pocket. Her insurance company pays the remaining \$80. (The insurance company recoups the \$80 through premiums, but the premium a person pays does not depend on how many procedures that person chooses to undertake.)
    a. Draw the demand curve in the market for medical care. (In your diagram, the horizontal axis should represent the number of medical procedures.) Show the quantity of procedures demanded if each procedure has a price of \$100.
    b. On your diagram, show the quantity of procedures demanded if consumers pay only \$20 per procedure. If the cost of each procedure to society is truly \$100, and if individuals have health insurance as described above, will the number of procedures performed maximize total surplus? Explain.
    c. Economists often blame the health insurance system for excessive use of medical care. Given your analysis, why might the use of care be viewed as "excessive"?
    d. What sort of policies might prevent this excessive use?

To find additional study resources, visit cengagebrain.com, and search for "Mankiw."

CHAPTER

8

Application: The Costs of Taxation

Taxes are often a source of heated political debate. In 1776, the anger of the American colonists over British taxes sparked the American Revolution. More than two centuries later, the American political parties still debate the proper size and shape of the tax system. Yet no one would deny that some level of taxation is necessary. As Oliver Wendell Holmes, Jr., once said, "Taxes are what we pay for civilized society."

Because taxation has such a major impact on the modern economy, we return to the topic several times throughout this book as we expand the set of tools we have

at our disposal. We began our study of taxes in Chapter 6. There we saw how a tax on a good affects its price and quantity sold and how the forces of supply and demand divide the burden of a tax between buyers and sellers. In this chapter, we extend this analysis and look at how taxes affect welfare, the economic well-being of participants in a market. In other words, we see how high the price of civilized society can be.

The effects of taxes on welfare might at first seem obvious. The government enacts taxes to raise revenue, and this revenue must come out of someone's pocket. As we saw in Chapter 6, both buyers and sellers are worse off when a good is taxed: A tax raises the price buyers pay and lowers the price sellers receive. Yet to fully understand how taxes affect economic well-being, we must compare the reduced welfare of buyers and sellers to the amount of revenue the government raises. The tools of consumer and producer surplus allow us to make this comparison. Our analysis will show that the cost of taxes to buyers and sellers typically exceeds the revenue raised by the government.

8-1 The Deadweight Loss of Taxation

We begin by recalling one of the surprising lessons from Chapter 6: The impact of a tax on a market outcome is the same whether the tax is levied on buyers or sellers of a good. When a tax is levied on buyers, the demand curve shifts downward by the size of the tax; when it is levied on sellers, the supply curve shifts upward by that amount. In either case, when the tax is enacted, the price paid by buyers rises, and the price received by sellers falls. In the end, the elasticities of supply and demand determine how the tax burden is distributed between producers and consumers. This distribution is the same regardless of how the tax is levied.

Figure 1 shows these effects. To simplify our discussion, this figure does not show a shift in either the supply or demand curve, although one curve must shift. Which curve shifts depends on whether the tax is levied on sellers (the supply

FIGURE 1

The Effects of a Tax
A tax on a good places a wedge between the price that buyers pay and the price that sellers receive. The quantity of the good sold falls.

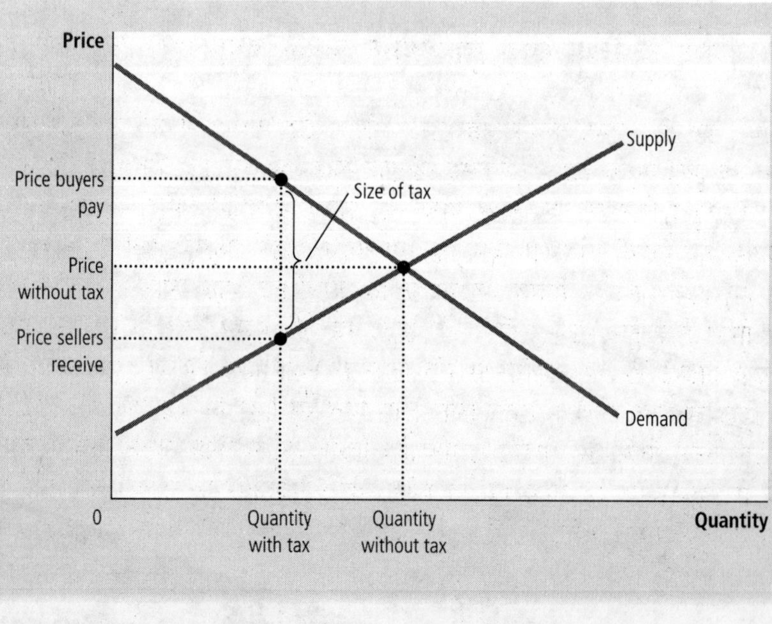

curve shifts) or buyers (the demand curve shifts). In this chapter, we keep the analysis general and simplify the graphs by not showing the shift. For our purposes here, the key result is that the tax places a wedge between the price buyers pay and the price sellers receive. Because of this tax wedge, the quantity sold falls below the level that would be sold without a tax. In other words, a tax on a good causes the size of the market for the good to shrink. These results should be familiar from Chapter 6.

"You know, the idea of taxation with representation doesn't appeal to me very much, either."

8-1a How a Tax Affects Market Participants

Let's use the tools of welfare economics to measure the gains and losses from a tax on a good. To do this, we must take into account how the tax affects buyers, sellers, and the government. The benefit received by buyers in a market is measured by consumer surplus—the amount buyers are willing to pay for the good minus the amount they actually pay for it. The benefit received by sellers in a market is measured by producer surplus—the amount sellers receive for the good minus their costs. These are precisely the measures of economic welfare we used in Chapter 7.

What about the third interested party, the government? If T is the size of the tax and Q is the quantity of the good sold, then the government gets total tax revenue of $T \times Q$. It can use this tax revenue to provide services, such as roads, police, and public education, or to help the needy. Therefore, to analyze how taxes affect economic well-being, we use the government's tax revenue to measure the public benefit from the tax. Keep in mind, however, that this benefit actually accrues not to the government but to those on whom the revenue is spent.

Figure 2 shows that the government's tax revenue is represented by the rectangle between the supply and demand curves. The height of this rectangle is the size of the tax, T, and the width of the rectangle is the quantity of the good sold, Q. Because a rectangle's area is its height multiplied by its width, this rectangle's area is $T \times Q$, which equals the tax revenue.

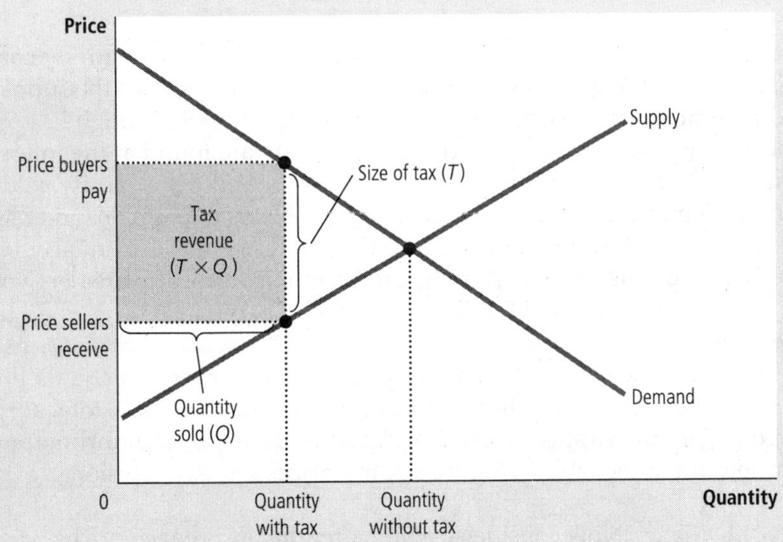

FIGURE 2

Tax Revenue

The tax revenue that the government collects equals $T \times Q$, the size of the tax T times the quantity sold Q. Thus, tax revenue equals the area of the rectangle between the supply and demand curves.

FIGURE 3

How a Tax Affects Welfare

A tax on a good reduces consumer surplus (by the area B + C) and producer surplus (by the area D + E). Because the fall in producer and consumer surplus exceeds tax revenue (area B + D), the tax is said to impose a deadweight loss (area C + E).

	Without Tax	With Tax	Change
Consumer Surplus	A + B + C	A	− (B + C)
Producer Surplus	D + E + F	F	− (D + E)
Tax Revenue	None	B + D	+ (B + D)
Total Surplus	A + B + C + D + E + F	A + B + D + F	− (C + E)

The area C + E shows the fall in total surplus and is the deadweight loss of the tax.

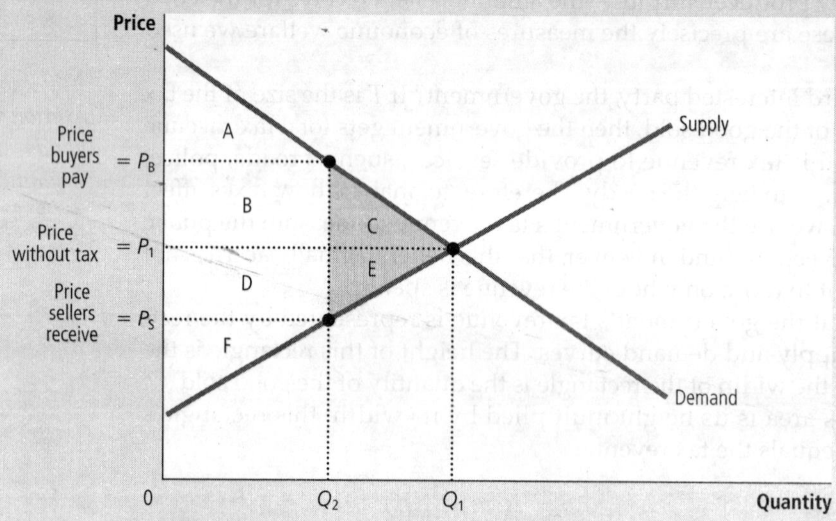

Welfare without a Tax To see how a tax affects welfare, we begin by considering welfare before the government imposes a tax. Figure 3 shows the supply-and-demand diagram with the key areas marked by the letters A through F.

Without a tax, the equilibrium price and quantity are found at the intersection of the supply and demand curves. The price is P_1, and the quantity sold is Q_1. Because the demand curve reflects buyers' willingness to pay, consumer surplus is the area between the demand curve and the price, A + B + C. Similarly, because the supply curve reflects sellers' costs, producer surplus is the area between the supply curve and the price, D + E + F. In this case, because there is no tax, tax revenue is zero.

Total surplus, the sum of consumer and producer surplus, equals the area A + B + C + D + E + F. In other words, as we saw in Chapter 7, total surplus is the area between the supply and demand curves up to the equilibrium quantity. The first column of the table in Figure 3 summarizes these conclusions.

Welfare with a Tax Now consider welfare after the tax is enacted. The price paid by buyers rises from P_1 to P_B, so consumer surplus now equals only area A (the area below the demand curve and above the buyers' price). The price received by sellers falls from P_1 to P_S, so producer surplus now equals only area F (the area above the supply curve and below the sellers' price). The quantity sold falls from Q_1 to Q_2, and the government collects tax revenue equal to the area B + D.

To compute total surplus with the tax, we add consumer surplus, producer surplus, and tax revenue. Thus, we find that total surplus is area A + B + D + F. The second column of the table summarizes these results.

Changes in Welfare We can now see the effects of the tax by comparing welfare before and after the tax is enacted. The third column of the table in Figure 3 shows the changes. Consumer surplus falls by the area B + C, and producer surplus falls by the area D + E. Tax revenue rises by the area B + D. Not surprisingly, the tax makes buyers and sellers worse off and the government better off.

The change in total welfare includes the change in consumer surplus (which is negative), the change in producer surplus (which is also negative), and the change in tax revenue (which is positive). When we add these three pieces together, we find that total surplus in the market falls by the area C + E. *Thus, the losses to buyers and sellers from a tax exceed the revenue raised by the government.* The fall in total surplus that results when a tax (or some other policy) distorts a market outcome is called a **deadweight loss**. The area C + E measures the size of the deadweight loss.

deadweight loss
the fall in total surplus that results from a market distortion, such as a tax

To understand why taxes cause deadweight losses, recall one of the *Ten Principles of Economics* in Chapter 1: People respond to incentives. In Chapter 7, we saw that free markets normally allocate scarce resources efficiently. That is, in the absence of any tax, the equilibrium of supply and demand maximizes the total surplus of buyers and sellers in a market. When the government imposes a tax, it raises the price buyers pay and lowers the price sellers receive, giving buyers an incentive to consume less and sellers an incentive to produce less. As buyers and sellers respond to these incentives, the size of the market shrinks below its optimum (as shown in the figure by the movement from Q_1 to Q_2). Thus, because taxes distort incentives, they cause markets to allocate resources inefficiently.

8-1b Deadweight Losses and the Gains from Trade

To better understand why taxes cause deadweight losses, consider an example. Imagine that Mike cleans Mei's house each week for $100. The opportunity cost of Mike's time is $80, and the value of a clean house to Mei is $120. Thus, Mike and Mei each receive a $20 benefit from their deal. The total surplus of $40 measures the gains from trade in this particular transaction.

Now suppose that the government levies a $50 tax on the providers of cleaning services. There is now no price that Mei can pay Mike that will leave both of them better off. The most Mei would be willing to pay is $120, but then Mike would be left with only $70 after paying the tax, which is less than his $80 opportunity cost. Conversely, for Mike to receive his opportunity cost of $80, Mei would need to pay $130, which is above the $120 value she places on a clean house. As a result, Mei and Mike cancel their arrangement. Mike loses the income, and Mei lives in a dirtier house.

The tax has made Mike and Mei worse off by a total of $40 because they have each lost $20 of surplus. But note that the government collects no revenue from Mike and Mei because they decide to cancel their arrangement. The $40 is pure deadweight loss: It is a loss to buyers and sellers in a market that is not offset by an increase in government revenue. From this example, we can see the ultimate source of deadweight losses: *Taxes cause deadweight losses because they prevent buyers and sellers from realizing some of the gains from trade.*

FIGURE 4

The Source of a Deadweight Loss
When the government imposes a tax on a good, the quantity sold falls from Q_1 to Q_2. At every quantity between Q_1 and Q_2, the potential gains from trade among buyers and sellers are not realized. These lost gains from trade create the deadweight loss.

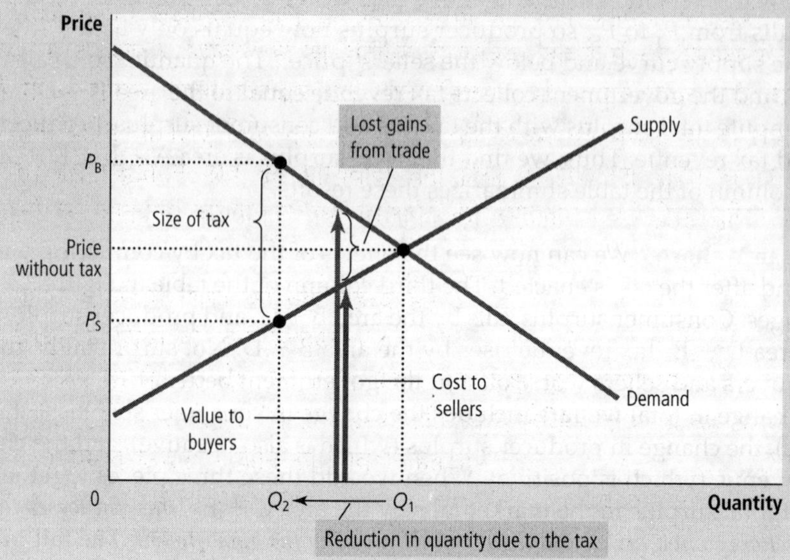

The area of the triangle between the supply and demand curves created by the tax wedge (area C + E in Figure 3) measures these losses. This conclusion can be seen more easily in Figure 4 by recalling that the demand curve reflects the value of the good to consumers and that the supply curve reflects the costs of producers. When the tax raises the price buyers pay to P_B and lowers the price sellers receive to P_S, the marginal buyers and sellers leave the market, so the quantity sold falls from Q_1 to Q_2. Yet as the figure shows, the value of the good to these buyers still exceeds the cost to these sellers. At every quantity between Q_1 and Q_2, the situation is the same as in our example with Mike and Mei. The gains from trade—the difference between buyers' value and sellers' cost—are less than the tax. As a result, these trades are not made once the tax is imposed. The deadweight loss is the surplus that is lost because the tax discourages these mutually advantageous trades.

QuickQuiz *Draw the supply and demand curves for cookies. If the government imposes a tax on cookies, show what happens to the price paid by buyers, the price received by sellers, and the quantity of cookies sold. In your diagram, show the deadweight loss from the tax. Explain the meaning of the deadweight loss.*

8-2 The Determinants of the Deadweight Loss

What determines whether the deadweight loss from a tax is large or small? The answer is the price elasticities of supply and demand, which measure how much the quantity supplied and quantity demanded respond to changes in the price.

Let's consider first how the elasticity of supply affects the size of the deadweight loss. In the top two panels of Figure 5, the demand curve and the size of the tax are the same. The only difference in these figures is the elasticity of the supply curve. In panel (a), the supply curve is relatively inelastic: Quantity supplied responds only slightly to changes in the price. In panel (b), the supply curve is relatively elastic: Quantity supplied responds substantially to changes in the

FIGURE 5

Tax Distortions and Elasticities

In panels (a) and (b), the demand curve and the size of the tax are the same, but the price elasticity of supply is different. Notice that the more elastic the supply curve, the larger the deadweight loss of the tax. In panels (c) and (d), the supply curve and the size of the tax are the same, but the price elasticity of demand is different. Notice that the more elastic the demand curve, the larger the deadweight loss of the tax.

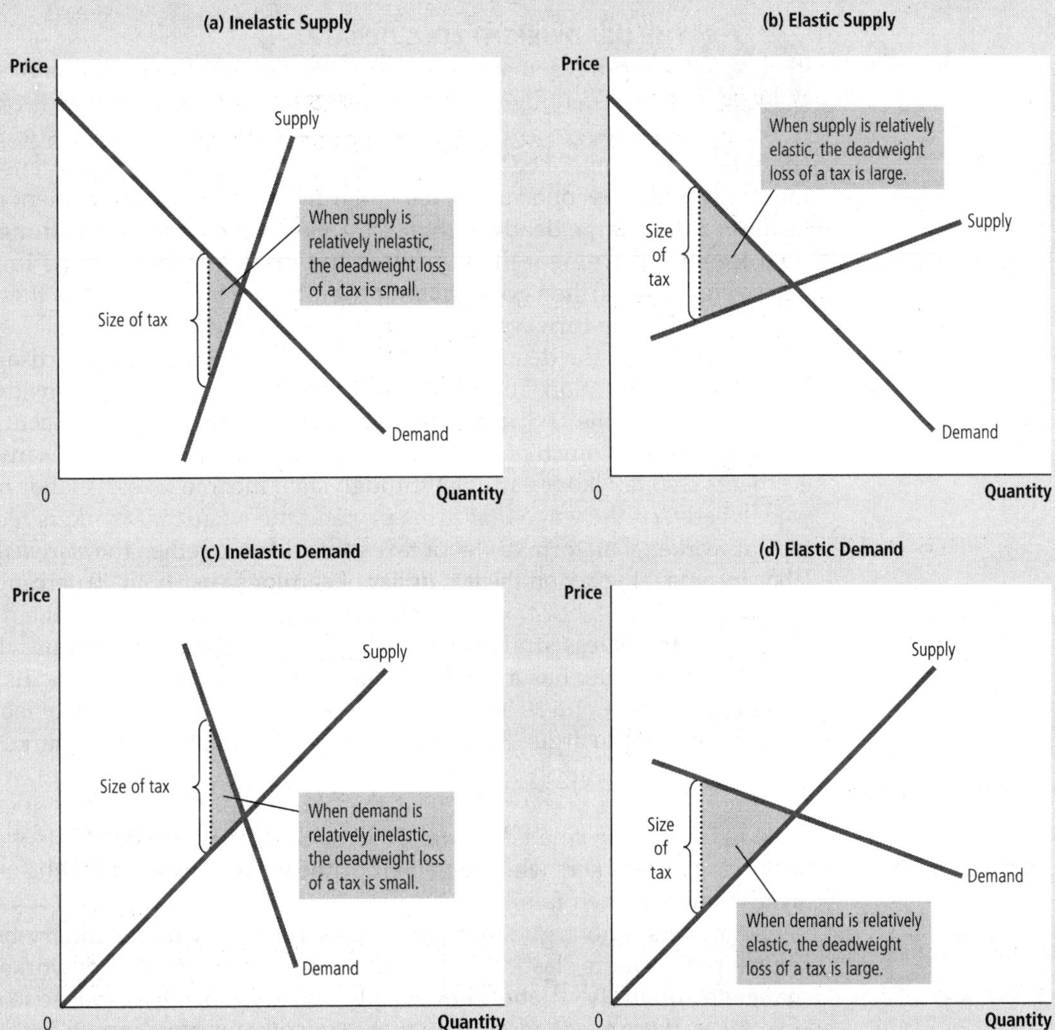

price. Notice that the deadweight loss, the area of the triangle between the supply and demand curves, is larger when the supply curve is more elastic.

Similarly, the bottom two panels of Figure 5 show how the elasticity of demand affects the size of the deadweight loss. Here the supply curve and the size of the tax are held constant. In panel (c), the demand curve is relatively inelastic, and the deadweight loss is small. In panel (d), the demand curve is more elastic, and the deadweight loss from the tax is larger.

The lesson from this figure is apparent. A tax has a deadweight loss because it induces buyers and sellers to change their behavior. The tax raises the price paid by buyers, so they consume less. At the same time, the tax lowers the price received by sellers, so they produce less. Because of these changes in behavior, the equilibrium quantity in the market shrinks below the optimal quantity. The more responsive buyers and sellers are to changes in the price, the more the equilibrium quantity shrinks. Hence, *the greater the elasticities of supply and demand, the greater the deadweight loss of a tax.*

CASE STUDY

THE DEADWEIGHT LOSS DEBATE

Supply, demand, elasticity, deadweight loss—all this economic theory is enough to make your head spin. But believe it or not, these ideas are at the heart of a profound political question: How big should the government be? The debate hinges on these concepts because the larger the deadweight loss of taxation, the larger the cost of any government program. If taxation entails large deadweight losses, then these losses are a strong argument for a leaner government that does less and taxes less. But if taxes impose small deadweight losses, then government programs are less costly than they otherwise might be, which in turn argues for a more expansive government.

So how big are the deadweight losses of taxation? Economists disagree on the answer to this question. To see the nature of this disagreement, consider the most important tax in the U.S. economy: the tax on labor. The Social Security tax, the Medicare tax, and much of the federal income tax are labor taxes. Many state governments also tax labor earnings through state income taxes. A labor tax places a wedge between the wage that firms pay and the wage that workers receive. For a typical worker, if all forms of labor taxes are added together, the *marginal tax rate* on labor income—the tax on the last dollar of earnings—is about 40 percent.

The size of the labor tax is easy to determine, but calculating the deadweight loss of this tax is less straightforward. Economists disagree about whether this 40 percent labor tax has a small or a large deadweight loss. This disagreement arises because economists hold different views about the elasticity of labor supply.

Economists who argue that labor taxes do not greatly distort market outcomes believe that labor supply is fairly inelastic. Most people, they claim, would work full-time regardless of the wage. If so, the labor supply curve is almost vertical, and a tax on labor has a small deadweight loss. Some evidence suggests that this may be the case for workers who are in their prime working years and who are the main breadwinners of their families.

Economists who argue that labor taxes are highly distortionary believe that labor supply is more elastic. While admitting that some groups of workers may not change the quantity of labor they supply by very much in response to changes in labor taxes, these economists claim that many other groups respond more to incentives. Here are some examples:

- Some workers can adjust the number of hours they work—for instance, by working overtime. The higher the wage, the more hours they choose to work.
- Many families have second earners—often married women with children—with some discretion over whether to do unpaid work at home or paid work in the marketplace. When deciding whether to take a job, these second earners compare the benefits of being at home (including savings on the cost of child care) with the wages they could earn.
- Many of the elderly can choose when to retire, and their decisions are partly based on the wage. Once they are retired, the wage determines their incentive to work part-time.

- Some people consider engaging in illegal economic activity, such as the drug trade, or working at jobs that pay "under the table" to evade taxes. Economists call this the *underground economy*. In deciding whether to work in the underground economy or at a legitimate job, these potential criminals compare what they can earn by breaking the law with the wage they can earn legally.

EPA EUROPEAN PRESSPHOTO AGENCY B.V. / ALAMY

"What's your position on the elasticity of labor supply?"

In each of these cases, the quantity of labor supplied responds to the wage (the price of labor). Thus, these workers' decisions are distorted when their labor earnings are taxed. Labor taxes encourage workers to work fewer hours, second earners to stay at home, the elderly to retire early, and the unscrupulous to enter the underground economy.

The debate over the distortionary effects of labor taxation persists to this day. Indeed, whenever you see two political candidates debating whether the government should provide more services or reduce the tax burden, keep in mind that part of the disagreement may rest on different views about the elasticity of labor supply and the deadweight loss of taxation. ●

QuickQuiz *The demand for beer is more elastic than the demand for milk. Would a tax on beer or a tax on milk have a larger deadweight loss? Why?*

8-3 Deadweight Loss and Tax Revenue as Taxes Vary

Taxes rarely stay the same for long periods of time. Policymakers in local, state, and federal governments are always considering raising one tax or lowering another. Here we consider what happens to the deadweight loss and tax revenue when the size of a tax changes.

Figure 6 shows the effects of a small, medium, and large tax, holding constant the market's supply and demand curves. The deadweight loss—the reduction in total surplus that results when the tax reduces the size of a market below the optimum—equals the area of the triangle between the supply and demand curves. For the small tax in panel (a), the area of the deadweight loss triangle is quite small. But as the size of the tax rises in panels (b) and (c), the deadweight loss grows larger and larger.

Indeed, the deadweight loss of a tax rises even more rapidly than the size of the tax. This occurs because the deadweight loss is the area of a triangle, and the area of a triangle depends on the *square* of its size. If we double the size of a tax, for instance, the base and height of the triangle double, so the deadweight loss rises by a factor of 4. If we triple the size of a tax, the base and height triple, so the deadweight loss rises by a factor of 9.

The government's tax revenue is the size of the tax times the amount of the good sold. As the first three panels of Figure 6 show, tax revenue equals the area of the rectangle between the supply and demand curves. For the small tax in panel (a), tax revenue is small. As the size of the tax increases from panel (a) to panel (b), tax revenue grows. But as the size of the tax increases further from panel (b) to panel (c), tax revenue falls because the higher tax drastically reduces the size of the market. For a very large tax, no revenue would be raised because people would stop buying and selling the good altogether.

The last two panels of Figure 6 summarize these results. In panel (d), we see that as the size of a tax increases, its deadweight loss quickly gets larger. By contrast, panel (e) shows that tax revenue first rises with the size of the tax, but as the tax increases further, the market shrinks so much that tax revenue starts to fall.

FIGURE 6

How Deadweight Loss and Tax Revenue Vary with the Size of a Tax

The deadweight loss is the reduction in total surplus due to the tax. Tax revenue is the amount of the tax multiplied by the amount of the good sold. In panel (a), a small tax has a small deadweight loss and raises a small amount of revenue. In panel (b), a somewhat larger tax has a larger deadweight loss and raises a larger amount of revenue. In panel (c), a very large tax has a very large deadweight loss, but because it has reduced the size of the market so much, the tax raises only a small amount of revenue. Panels (d) and (e) summarize these conclusions. Panel (d) shows that as the size of a tax grows larger, the deadweight loss grows larger. Panel (e) shows that tax revenue first rises and then falls. This relationship is called the Laffer curve.

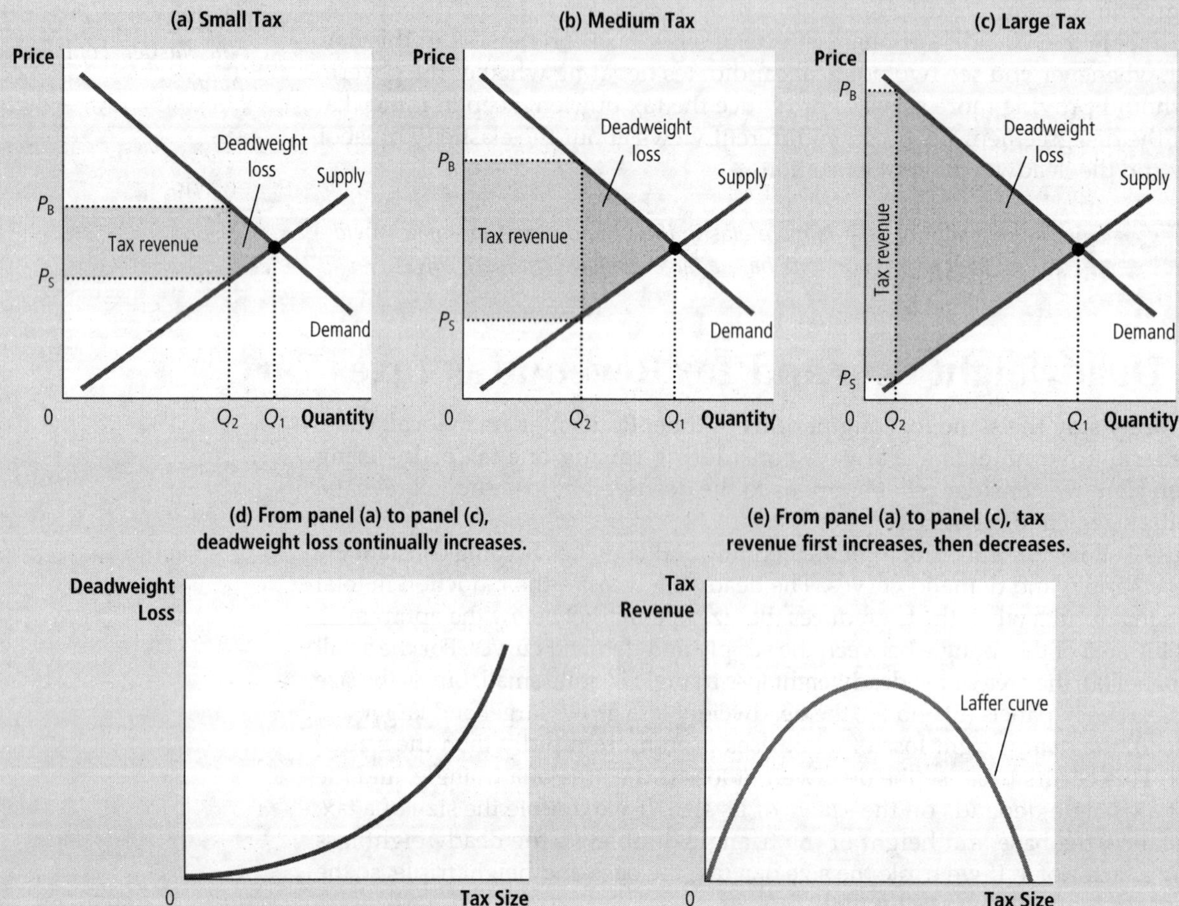

CASE STUDY

THE LAFFER CURVE AND SUPPLY-SIDE ECONOMICS

One day in 1974, economist Arthur Laffer sat in a Washington restaurant with some prominent journalists and politicians. He took out a napkin and drew a figure on it to show how tax rates affect tax revenue. It looked much like panel (e) of our Figure 6. Laffer then suggested that the United States was on the downward-sloping side of this curve. Tax rates were so high, he argued, that reducing them might actually increase tax revenue.

Most economists were skeptical of Laffer's suggestion. They accepted the idea that a cut in tax rates could increase tax revenue as a matter of economic theory, but they doubted whether it would do so in practice. There was scant evidence for Laffer's view that U.S. tax rates had in fact reached such extreme levels.

Nonetheless, the *Laffer curve* (as it became known) captured the imagination of Ronald Reagan. David Stockman, budget director in the first Reagan administration, offers the following story:

> [Reagan] had once been on the Laffer curve himself. "I came into the Big Money making pictures during World War II," he would always say. At that time the wartime income surtax hit 90 percent. "You could only make four pictures and then you were in the top bracket," he would continue. "So we all quit working after four pictures and went off to the country." High tax rates caused less work. Low tax rates caused more. His experience proved it.

When Reagan ran for president in 1980, he made cutting taxes part of his platform. Reagan argued that taxes were so high that they were discouraging hard work and thereby depressing incomes. He argued that lower taxes would give people more incentive to work, which in turn would raise economic well-being. He suggested that incomes could rise by so much that tax revenue might increase, despite the lower tax rates. Because the cut in tax rates was intended to encourage people to increase the quantity of labor they supplied, the views of Laffer and Reagan became known as *supply-side economics*.

Economists continue to debate Laffer's argument. Many believe that subsequent history refuted Laffer's conjecture that lower tax rates would raise tax revenue. Yet because history is open to alternative interpretations, other economists view the events of the 1980s as more favorable to the supply siders. To evaluate Laffer's hypothesis definitively, we would need to rerun history without the Reagan tax cuts and see if tax revenues would have been higher or lower. Unfortunately, that experiment is impossible.

Some economists take an intermediate position on this issue. They believe that while an overall cut in tax rates normally reduces revenue, some taxpayers may occasionally find themselves on the wrong side of the Laffer curve. Other things being equal, a tax cut is more likely to raise tax revenue if the cut applies to those taxpayers facing the highest tax rates. In addition, Laffer's argument may be more compelling for countries with much higher tax rates than the United States. In Sweden in the early 1980s, for instance, the typical worker faced a marginal tax rate of about 80 percent. Such a high tax rate provides a substantial disincentive to work. Studies have suggested that Sweden would have indeed raised more tax revenue if it had lowered its tax rates.

Economists disagree about these issues in part because there is no consensus about the size of the relevant elasticities. The more elastic supply and demand are in any market, the more taxes distort behavior, and the more likely it is that a tax cut will increase tax revenue. There is no debate, however, about the general lesson: How much revenue the government gains or loses from a tax change cannot be computed just by looking at tax rates. It also depends on how the tax change affects people's behavior. ●

QuickQuiz *If the government doubles the tax on gasoline, can you be sure that revenue from the gasoline tax will rise? Can you be sure that the deadweight loss from the gasoline tax will rise? Explain.*

ASK THE EXPERTS

The Laffer Curve

"A cut in federal income tax rates in the United States right now would lead to higher national income within five years than without the tax cut."

What do economists say?

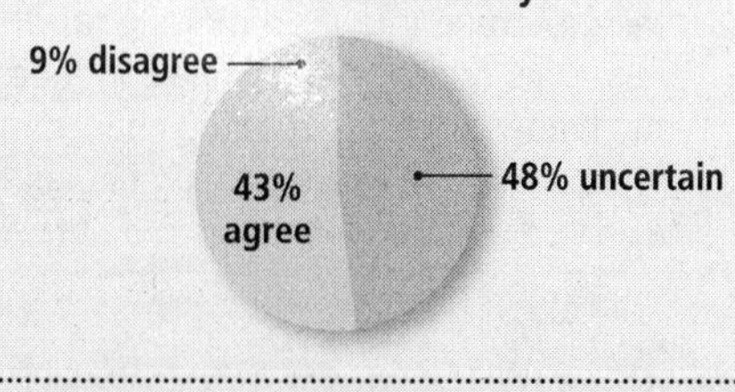

"A cut in federal income tax rates in the United States right now would raise taxable income enough so that the annual total tax revenue would be higher within five years than without the tax cut."

What do economists say?

Source: IGM Economic Experts Panel, June 26, 2012.

8-4 Conclusion

In this chapter, we have used the tools developed in the previous chapter to further our understanding of taxes. One of the *Ten Principles of Economics* discussed in Chapter 1 is that markets are usually a good way to organize economic activity. In Chapter 7, we used the concepts of producer and consumer surplus to make this principle more precise. Here we have seen that when the government imposes taxes on buyers or sellers of a good, society loses some of the benefits of market efficiency. Taxes are costly to market participants not only because taxes transfer resources from those participants to the government but also because they alter incentives and distort market outcomes.

The analysis presented here and in Chapter 6 should give you a good basis for understanding the economic impact of taxes, but this is not the end of the story. Microeconomists study how best to design a tax system, including how to strike the right balance between equality and efficiency. Macroeconomists study how taxes influence the overall economy and how policymakers can use the tax system to stabilize economic activity and to achieve more rapid economic growth. So as you continue your study of economics, don't be surprised when the subject of taxation comes up yet again.

CHAPTER QuickQuiz

1. A tax on a good has a deadweight loss if
   a. the reduction in consumer and producer surplus is greater than the tax revenue.
   b. the tax revenue is greater than the reduction in consumer and producer surplus.
   c. the reduction in consumer surplus is greater than the reduction in producer surplus.
   d. the reduction in producer surplus is greater than the reduction in consumer surplus.
2. Sofia pays Sam $50 to mow her lawn every week. When the government levies a mowing tax of $10 on Sam, he raises his price to $60. Sofia continues to hire him at the higher price. What is the change in producer surplus, change in consumer surplus, and deadweight loss?
   a. $0, $0, $10
   b. $0, −$10, $0
   c. +$10, −$10, $10
   d. +$10, −$10, $0
3. Eggs have a supply curve that is linear and upward-sloping and a demand curve that is linear and downward-sloping. If a 2 cent per egg tax is increased to 3 cents, the deadweight loss of the tax
   a. increases by less than 50 percent and may even decline.
   b. increases by exactly 50 percent.
   c. increases by more than 50 percent.
   d. The answer depends on whether supply or demand is more elastic.
4. Peanut butter has an upward-sloping supply curve and a downward-sloping demand curve. If a 10 cent per pound tax is increased to 15 cents, the government's tax revenue
   a. increases by less than 50 percent and may even decline.
   b. increases by exactly 50 percent.
   c. increases by more than 50 percent.
   d. The answer depends on whether supply or demand is more elastic.
5. The Laffer curve illustrates that, in some circumstances, the government can reduce a tax on a good and increase the
   a. deadweight loss.
   b. government's tax revenue.
   c. equilibrium quantity.
   d. price paid by consumers.
6. If a policymaker wants to raise revenue by taxing goods while minimizing the deadweight losses, he should look for goods with _______ elasticities of demand and _______ elasticities of supply.
   a. small, small
   b. small, large
   c. large, small
   d. large, large

SUMMARY

- A tax on a good reduces the welfare of buyers and sellers of the good, and the reduction in consumer and producer surplus usually exceeds the revenue raised by the government. The fall in total surplus—the sum of consumer surplus, producer surplus, and tax revenue—is called the deadweight loss of the tax.
- Taxes have deadweight losses because they cause buyers to consume less and sellers to produce less, and these changes in behavior shrink the size of the market below the level that maximizes total surplus. Because the elasticities of supply and demand measure how much market participants respond to market conditions, larger elasticities imply larger deadweight losses.
- As a tax grows larger, it distorts incentives more, and its deadweight loss grows larger. Because a tax reduces the size of the market, however, tax revenue does not continually increase. It first rises with the size of a tax, but if the tax gets large enough, tax revenue starts to fall.

KEY CONCEPT

deadweight loss, p. 157

QUESTIONS FOR REVIEW

1. What happens to consumer and producer surplus when the sale of a good is taxed? How does the change in consumer and producer surplus compare to the tax revenue? Explain.
2. Draw a supply-and-demand diagram with a tax on the sale of a good. Show the deadweight loss. Show the tax revenue.
3. How do the elasticities of supply and demand affect the deadweight loss of a tax? Why do they have this effect?
4. Why do experts disagree about whether labor taxes have small or large deadweight losses?
5. What happens to the deadweight loss and tax revenue when a tax is increased?

PROBLEMS AND APPLICATIONS

1. The market for pizza is characterized by a downward-sloping demand curve and an upward-sloping supply curve.
   a. Draw the competitive market equilibrium. Label the price, quantity, consumer surplus, and producer surplus. Is there any deadweight loss? Explain.
   b. Suppose that the government forces each pizzeria to pay a $1 tax on each pizza sold. Illustrate the effect of this tax on the pizza market, being sure to label the consumer surplus, producer surplus, government revenue, and deadweight loss. How does each area compare to the pre-tax case?
   c. If the tax were removed, pizza eaters and sellers would be better off, but the government would lose tax revenue. Suppose that consumers and producers voluntarily transferred some of their gains to the government. Could all parties (including the government) be better off than they were with a tax? Explain using the labeled areas in your graph.
2. Evaluate the following two statements. Do you agree? Why or why not?
   a. "A tax that has no deadweight loss cannot raise any revenue for the government."
   b. "A tax that raises no revenue for the government cannot have any deadweight loss."
3. Consider the market for rubber bands.
   a. If this market has very elastic supply and very inelastic demand, how would the burden of a tax on rubber bands be shared between consumers and producers? Use the tools of consumer surplus and producer surplus in your answer.
   b. If this market has very inelastic supply and very elastic demand, how would the burden of a tax on rubber bands be shared between consumers and producers? Contrast your answer with your answer to part (a).

4. Suppose that the government imposes a tax on heating oil.
   a. Would the deadweight loss from this tax likely be greater in the first year after it is imposed or in the fifth year? Explain.
   b. Would the revenue collected from this tax likely be greater in the first year after it is imposed or in the fifth year? Explain.
5. After economics class one day, your friend suggests that taxing food would be a good way to raise revenue because the demand for food is quite inelastic. In what sense is taxing food a "good" way to raise revenue? In what sense is it not a "good" way to raise revenue?
6. Daniel Patrick Moynihan, the late senator from New York, once introduced a bill that would levy a 10,000 percent tax on certain hollow-tipped bullets.
   a. Do you expect that this tax would raise much revenue? Why or why not?
   b. Even if the tax would raise no revenue, why might Senator Moynihan have proposed it?
7. The government places a tax on the purchase of socks.
   a. Illustrate the effect of this tax on equilibrium price and quantity in the sock market. Identify the following areas both before and after the imposition of the tax: total spending by consumers, total revenue for producers, and government tax revenue.
   b. Does the price received by producers rise or fall? Can you tell whether total receipts for producers rise or fall? Explain.
   c. Does the price paid by consumers rise or fall? Can you tell whether total spending by consumers rises or falls? Explain carefully. (*Hint*: Think about elasticity.) If total consumer spending falls, does consumer surplus rise? Explain.
8. This chapter analyzed the welfare effects of a tax on a good. Now consider the opposite policy. Suppose that the government *subsidizes* a good: For each unit of the good sold, the government pays $2 to the buyer. How does the subsidy affect consumer surplus, producer surplus, tax revenue, and total surplus? Does a subsidy lead to a deadweight loss? Explain.
9. Hotel rooms in Smalltown go for $100, and 1,000 rooms are rented on a typical day.
   a. To raise revenue, the mayor decides to charge hotels a tax of $10 per rented room. After the tax is imposed, the going rate for hotel rooms rises to $108, and the number of rooms rented falls to 900. Calculate the amount of revenue this tax raises for Smalltown and the deadweight loss of the tax. (*Hint*: The area of a triangle is ½ × base × height.)
   b. The mayor now doubles the tax to $20. The price rises to $116, and the number of rooms rented falls to 800. Calculate tax revenue and deadweight loss with this larger tax. Are they double, more than double, or less than double? Explain.
10. Suppose that a market is described by the following supply and demand equations:

$$Q^S = 2P$$

$$Q^D = 300 - P$$

   a. Solve for the equilibrium price and the equilibrium quantity.
   b. Suppose that a tax of T is placed on buyers, so the new demand equation is

$$Q^D = 300 - (P + T)$$

   Solve for the new equilibrium. What happens to the price received by sellers, the price paid by buyers, and the quantity sold?
   c. Tax revenue is $T \times Q$. Use your answer from part (b) to solve for tax revenue as a function of T. Graph this relationship for T between 0 and 300.
   d. The deadweight loss of a tax is the area of the triangle between the supply and demand curves. Recalling that the area of a triangle is ½ × base × height, solve for deadweight loss as a function of T. Graph this relationship for T between 0 and 300. (*Hint*: Looking sideways, the base of the deadweight loss triangle is T, and the height is the difference between the quantity sold with the tax and the quantity sold without the tax.)
   e. The government now levies a tax of $200 per unit on this good. Is this a good policy? Why or why not? Can you propose a better policy?

To find additional study resources, visit cengagebrain.com, and search for "Mankiw."

Application: International Trade

CHAPTER

9

If you check the labels on the clothes you are wearing, you will probably find that some were made in another country. A century ago, the textile and clothing industry was a major part of the U.S. economy, but that is no longer the case. Faced with foreign competitors that can produce quality goods at low cost, many U.S. firms found it increasingly difficult to produce and sell textiles and clothing at a profit. As a result, they laid off their workers and shut down their factories. Today, most of the textiles and clothing that Americans consume are imported.

The story of the textile industry raises important questions for economic policy: How does international trade affect economic well-being? Who gains and who loses from free trade among countries, and how do the gains compare to the losses?

Chapter 3 introduced the study of international trade by applying the principle of comparative advantage. According to this principle, all countries can benefit from trading with one another because trade allows each country to specialize in doing what it does best. But the analysis in Chapter 3 was incomplete. It did not explain how the international marketplace achieves these gains from trade or how the gains are distributed among the various economic participants.

We now return to the study of international trade to tackle these questions. Over the past several chapters, we have developed many tools for analyzing how markets work: supply, demand, equilibrium, consumer surplus, producer surplus, and so on. With these tools, we can learn more about how international trade affects economic well-being.

9-1 The Determinants of Trade

Consider the market for textiles. The textile market is well suited to studying the gains and losses from international trade: Textiles are made in many countries around the world, and there is much world trade in textiles. Moreover, the textile market is one in which policymakers often consider (and sometimes implement) trade restrictions to protect domestic producers from foreign competitors. Here we examine the textile market in the imaginary country of Isoland.

9-1a The Equilibrium without Trade

As our story begins, the Isolandian textile market is isolated from the rest of the world. By government decree, no one in Isoland is allowed to import or export textiles, and the penalty for violating the decree is so large that no one dares try.

Because there is no international trade, the market for textiles in Isoland consists solely of Isolandian buyers and sellers. As Figure 1 shows, the domestic price adjusts to balance the quantity supplied by domestic sellers and the quantity demanded by domestic buyers. The figure shows the consumer and producer surplus in the equilibrium without trade. The sum of consumer and producer surplus measures the total benefits that buyers and sellers receive from participating in the textile market.

FIGURE 1

The Equilibrium without International Trade
When an economy cannot trade in world markets, the price adjusts to balance domestic supply and demand. This figure shows consumer and producer surplus in an equilibrium without international trade for the textile market in the imaginary country of Isoland.

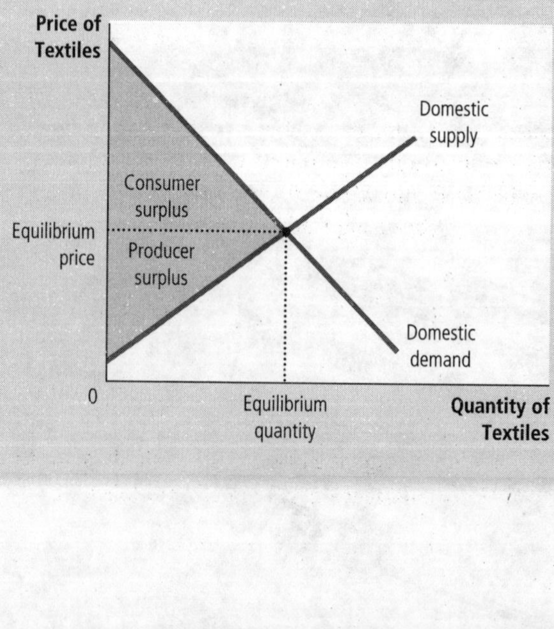

Now suppose that, in a political upset, Isoland elects a new president. The president campaigned on a platform of "change" and promised the voters bold new ideas. Her first act is to assemble a team of economists to evaluate Isolandian trade policy. She asks them to report on three questions:

- If the government allows Isolandians to import and export textiles, what will happen to the price of textiles and the quantity of textiles sold in the domestic textile market?
- Who will gain from free trade in textiles and who will lose, and will the gains exceed the losses?
- Should a tariff (a tax on textile imports) be part of the new trade policy?

After reviewing supply and demand in their favorite textbook (this one, of course), the Isolandian economics team begins its analysis.

9-1b The World Price and Comparative Advantage

The first issue our economists take up is whether Isoland is likely to become a textile importer or a textile exporter. In other words, if free trade is allowed, will Isolandians end up buying or selling textiles in world markets?

To answer this question, the economists compare the current Isolandian price of textiles to the price of textiles in other countries. We call the price prevailing in world markets the **world price**. If the world price of textiles is higher than the domestic price, then Isoland will export textiles once trade is permitted. Isolandian textile producers will be eager to receive the higher prices available abroad and will start selling their textiles to buyers in other countries. Conversely, if the world price of textiles is lower than the domestic price, then Isoland will import textiles. Because foreign sellers offer a better price, Isolandian textile consumers will quickly start buying textiles from other countries.

world price
the price of a good that prevails in the world market for that good

In essence, comparing the world price with the domestic price before trade reveals whether Isoland has a comparative advantage in producing textiles. The domestic price reflects the opportunity cost of textiles: It tells us how much an Isolandian must give up to obtain one unit of textiles. If the domestic price is low, the cost of producing textiles in Isoland is low, suggesting that Isoland has a comparative advantage in producing textiles relative to the rest of the world. If the domestic price is high, then the cost of producing textiles in Isoland is high, suggesting that foreign countries have a comparative advantage in producing textiles.

As we saw in Chapter 3, trade among nations is ultimately based on comparative advantage. That is, trade is beneficial because it allows each nation to specialize in doing what it does best. By comparing the world price with the domestic price before trade, we can determine whether Isoland is better or worse than the rest of the world at producing textiles.

QuickQuiz *The country Autarka does not allow international trade. In Autarka, you can buy a wool suit for 3 ounces of gold. Meanwhile, in neighboring countries, you can buy the same suit for 2 ounces of gold. If Autarka were to allow free trade, would it import or export wool suits? Why?*

9-2 The Winners and Losers from Trade

To analyze the welfare effects of free trade, the Isolandian economists begin with the assumption that Isoland is a small economy compared to the rest of the world. This small-economy assumption means that Isoland's actions have little effect on world markets. Specifically, any change in Isoland's trade policy will not affect the world price of textiles. The Isolandians are said to be *price takers* in the world economy. That is, they take the world price of textiles as given. Isoland can be an exporting country by selling textiles at this price or an importing country by buying textiles at this price.

The small-economy assumption is not necessary to analyze the gains and losses from international trade. But the Isolandian economists know from experience (and from reading Chapter 2 of this book) that making simplifying assumptions is a key part of building a useful economic model. The assumption that Isoland is a small economy simplifies the analysis, and the basic lessons do not change in the more complicated case of a large economy.

9-2a The Gains and Losses of an Exporting Country

Figure 2 shows the Isolandian textile market when the domestic equilibrium price before trade is below the world price. Once trade is allowed, the domestic price rises to equal the world price. No seller of textiles would accept less than the world price, and no buyer would pay more than the world price.

FIGURE 2

International Trade in an Exporting Country

Once trade is allowed, the domestic price rises to equal the world price. The supply curve shows the quantity of textiles produced domestically, and the demand curve shows the quantity consumed domestically. Exports from Isoland equal the difference between the domestic quantity supplied and the domestic quantity demanded at the world price. Sellers are better off (producer surplus rises from C to B + C + D), and buyers are worse off (consumer surplus falls from A + B to A). Total surplus rises by an amount equal to area D, indicating that trade raises the economic well-being of the country as a whole.

	Before Trade	After Trade	Change
Consumer Surplus	A + B	A	−B
Producer Surplus	C	B + C + D	+ (B + D)
Total Surplus	A + B + C	A + B + C + D	+ D

The area D shows the increase in total surplus and represents the gains from trade.

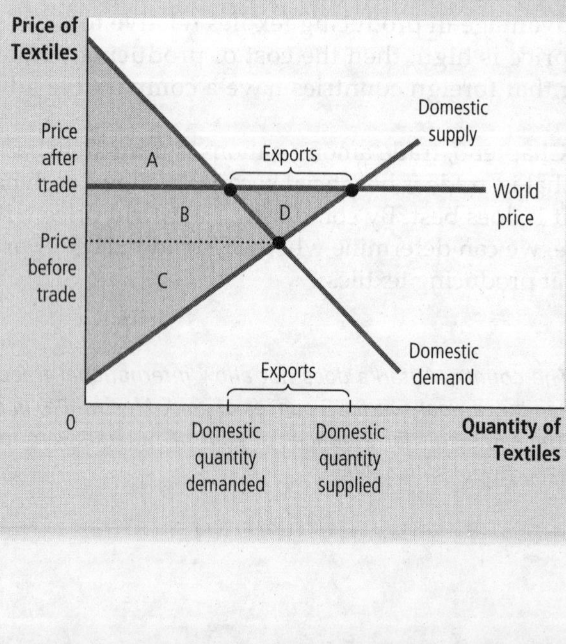

After the domestic price has risen to equal the world price, the domestic quantity supplied differs from the domestic quantity demanded. The supply curve shows the quantity of textiles supplied by Isolandian sellers. The demand curve shows the quantity of textiles demanded by Isolandian buyers. Because the domestic quantity supplied is greater than the domestic quantity demanded, Isoland sells textiles to other countries. Thus, Isoland becomes a textile exporter.

Although domestic quantity supplied and domestic quantity demanded differ, the textile market is still in equilibrium because there is now another participant in the market: the rest of the world. One can view the horizontal line at the world price as representing the rest of the world's demand for textiles. This demand curve is perfectly elastic because Isoland, as a small economy, can sell as many textiles as it wants at the world price.

Consider the gains and losses from opening up trade. Clearly, not everyone benefits. Trade forces the domestic price to rise to the world price. Domestic producers of textiles are better off because they can now sell textiles at a higher price, but domestic consumers of textiles are worse off because they now have to buy textiles at a higher price.

To measure these gains and losses, we look at the changes in consumer and producer surplus. Before trade is allowed, the price of textiles adjusts to balance domestic supply and domestic demand. Consumer surplus, the area between the demand curve and the before-trade price, is area A + B. Producer surplus, the area between the supply curve and the before-trade price, is area C. Total surplus before trade, the sum of consumer and producer surplus, is area A + B + C.

After trade is allowed, the domestic price rises to the world price. Consumer surplus shrinks to area A (the area between the demand curve and the world price). Producer surplus increases to area B + C + D (the area between the supply curve and the world price). Thus, total surplus with trade is area A + B + C + D.

These welfare calculations show who wins and who loses from trade in an exporting country. Sellers benefit because producer surplus increases by the area B + D. Buyers are worse off because consumer surplus decreases by the area B. Because the gains of sellers exceed the losses of buyers by the area D, total surplus in Isoland increases.

This analysis of an exporting country yields two conclusions:

- When a country allows trade and becomes an exporter of a good, domestic producers of the good are better off, and domestic consumers of the good are worse off.
- Trade raises the economic well-being of a nation in the sense that the gains of the winners exceed the losses of the losers.

9-2b The Gains and Losses of an Importing Country

Now suppose that the domestic price before trade is above the world price. Once again, after trade is allowed, the domestic price must equal the world price. As Figure 3 shows, the domestic quantity supplied is less than the domestic quantity demanded. The difference between the domestic quantity demanded and the domestic quantity supplied is bought from other countries, and Isoland becomes a textile importer.

In this case, the horizontal line at the world price represents the supply of the rest of the world. This supply curve is perfectly elastic because Isoland is a small economy and, therefore, can buy as many textiles as it wants at the world price.

FIGURE 3

International Trade in an Importing Country
Once trade is allowed, the domestic price falls to equal the world price. The supply curve shows the amount produced domestically, and the demand curve shows the amount consumed domestically. Imports equal the difference between the domestic quantity demanded and the domestic quantity supplied at the world price. Buyers are better off (consumer surplus rises from A to A + B + D), and sellers are worse off (producer surplus falls from B + C to C). Total surplus rises by an amount equal to area D, indicating that trade raises the economic well-being of the country as a whole.

	Before Trade	After Trade	Change
Consumer Surplus	A	A + B + D	+ (B + D)
Producer Surplus	B + C	C	− B
Total Surplus	A + B + C	A + B + C + D	+ D

The area D shows the increase in total surplus and represents the gains from trade.

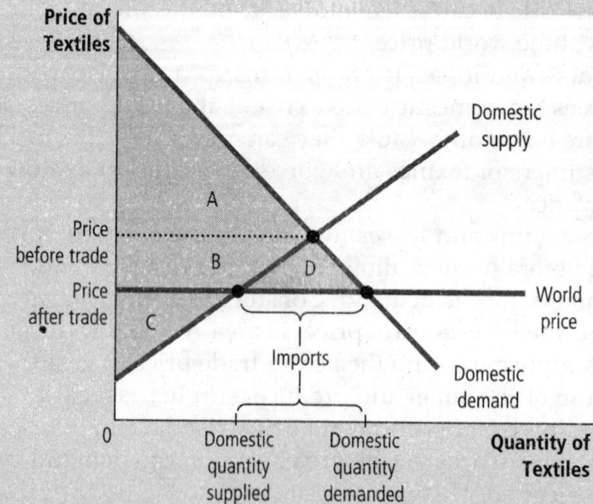

Once again, consider the gains and losses from trade. As in the previous case, not everyone benefits, but here the winners and losers are reversed. When trade forces the domestic price to fall, domestic consumers are better off (they can now buy textiles at a lower price), and domestic producers are worse off (they now have to sell textiles at a lower price). Changes in consumer and producer surplus measure the size of the gains and losses. Before trade, consumer surplus is area A, producer surplus is area B + C, and total surplus is area A + B + C. After trade is allowed, consumer surplus is area A + B + D, producer surplus is area C, and total surplus is area A + B + C + D.

These welfare calculations show who wins and who loses from trade in an importing country. Buyers benefit because consumer surplus increases by the area B + D. Sellers are worse off because producer surplus falls by the area B. The gains of buyers exceed the losses of sellers, and total surplus increases by the area D.

This analysis of an importing country yields two conclusions parallel to those for an exporting country:

- When a country allows trade and becomes an importer of a good, domestic consumers of the good are better off, and domestic producers of the good are worse off.
- Trade raises the economic well-being of a nation in the sense that the gains of the winners exceed the losses of the losers.

Having completed our analysis of trade, we can better understand one of the *Ten Principles of Economics* in Chapter 1: Trade can make everyone better off. If Isoland opens its textile market to international trade, the change creates winners and losers, regardless of whether Isoland ends up exporting or importing textiles. In either case, however, the gains of the winners exceed the losses of the losers, so the winners could compensate the losers and still be better off. In this sense, trade *can* make everyone better off. But *will* trade make everyone better off? Probably not. In practice, compensation for the losers from international trade is rare. Without such compensation, opening an economy to international trade is a policy that expands the size of the economic pie, but it can leave some participants in the economy with a smaller slice.

We can now see why the debate over trade policy is often contentious. Whenever a policy creates winners and losers, the stage is set for a political battle. Nations sometimes fail to enjoy the gains from trade because the losers from free trade are better organized than the winners. The losers may turn their cohesiveness into political clout and lobby for trade restrictions such as tariffs or import quotas.

9-2c Effects of a Tariff

tariff
a tax on goods produced abroad and sold domestically

The Isolandian economists next consider the effects of a **tariff**—a tax on imported goods. The economists quickly realize that a tariff on textiles will have no effect if Isoland becomes a textile exporter. If no one in Isoland is interested in importing textiles, a tax on textile imports is irrelevant. The tariff matters only if Isoland becomes a textile importer. Concentrating their attention on this case, the economists compare welfare with and without the tariff.

Figure 4 shows the Isolandian market for textiles. Under free trade, the domestic price equals the world price. A tariff raises the price of imported textiles above the world price by the amount of the tariff. Domestic suppliers of textiles, who compete with suppliers of imported textiles, can now sell their textiles for the world price plus the amount of the tariff. Thus, the price of textiles—both imported and domestic—rises by the amount of the tariff and is, therefore, closer to the price that would prevail without trade.

The change in price affects the behavior of domestic buyers and sellers. Because the tariff raises the price of textiles, it reduces the domestic quantity demanded from Q_1^D to Q_2^D and raises the domestic quantity supplied from Q_1^S to Q_2^S. *Thus, the tariff reduces the quantity of imports and moves the domestic market closer to its equilibrium without trade.*

Now consider the gains and losses from the tariff. Because the tariff raises the domestic price, domestic sellers are better off, and domestic buyers are worse off. In addition, the government raises revenue. To measure these gains and losses, we look at the changes in consumer surplus, producer surplus, and government revenue. These changes are summarized in the table in Figure 4.

Before the tariff, the domestic price equals the world price. Consumer surplus, the area between the demand curve and the world price, is area A + B + C + D + E + F. Producer surplus, the area between the supply curve and the world price, is area G. Government revenue equals zero. Total surplus, the sum of consumer surplus, producer surplus, and government revenue, is area A + B + C + D + E + F + G.

Once the government imposes a tariff, the domestic price exceeds the world price by the amount of the tariff. Consumer surplus is now area A + B. Producer surplus is area C + G. Government revenue, which is the size of the tariff multiplied by the quantity of after-tariff imports, is the area E. Thus, total surplus with the tariff is area A + B + C + E + G.

FIGURE 4

The Effects of a Tariff

A tariff, a tax on imports, reduces the quantity of imports and moves a market closer to the equilibrium that would exist without trade. Total surplus falls by an amount equal to area D + F. These two triangles represent the deadweight loss from the tariff.

	Before Tariff	After Tariff	Change
Consumer Surplus	A + B + C + D + E + F	A + B	−(C + D + E + F)
Producer Surplus	G	C + G	+ C
Government Revenue	None	E	+ E
Total Surplus	A + B + C + D + E + F + G	A + B + C + E + G	−(D + F)

The area D + F shows the fall in total surplus and represents the deadweight loss of the tariff.

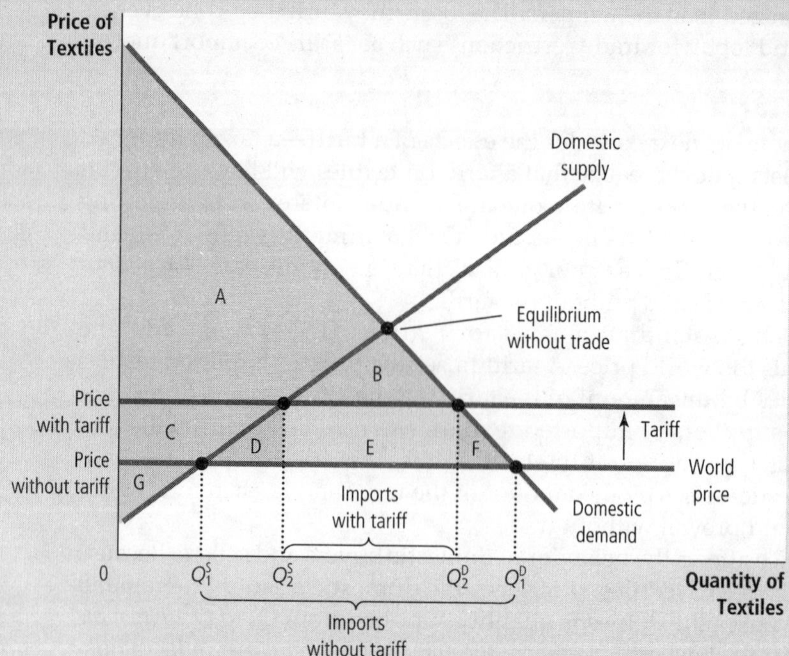

To determine the total welfare effects of the tariff, we add the change in consumer surplus (which is negative), the change in producer surplus (positive), and the change in government revenue (positive). We find that total surplus in the market decreases by the area D + F. This fall in total surplus is called the *deadweight loss* of the tariff.

A tariff causes a deadweight loss because a tariff is a type of tax. Like most taxes, it distorts incentives and pushes the allocation of scarce resources away from the optimum. In this case, we can identify two effects. First, when the tariff raises the domestic price of textiles above the world price, it encourages domestic producers to increase production from Q_1^S to Q_2^S. Even though the cost of making these incremental units exceeds the cost of buying them at the world price, the tariff makes it profitable for domestic producers to manufacture them nonetheless. Second, when the tariff raises the price that domestic textile consumers have

FYI

Import Quotas: Another Way to Restrict Trade

Beyond tariffs, another way that nations sometimes restrict international trade is by putting limits on how much of a good can be imported. In this book, we will not analyze such a policy, other than to point out the conclusion: Import quotas are much like tariffs. Both tariffs and import quotas reduce the quantity of imports, raise the domestic price of the good, decrease the welfare of domestic consumers, increase the welfare of domestic producers, and cause deadweight losses.

There is only one difference between these two types of trade restriction: A tariff raises revenue for the government, whereas an import quota creates surplus for those who obtain the licenses to import. The profit for the holder of an import license is the difference between the domestic price (at which she sells the imported good) and the world price (at which she buys it).

Tariffs and import quotas are even more similar if the government charges a fee for the import licenses. Suppose the government sets the license fee equal to the difference between the domestic price and the world price. In this case, the entire profit of license holders is paid to the government in license fees, and the import quota works exactly like a tariff. Consumer surplus, producer surplus, and government revenue are precisely the same under the two policies.

In practice, however, countries that restrict trade with import quotas rarely do so by selling the import licenses. For example, the U.S. government has at times pressured Japan to "voluntarily" limit the sale of Japanese cars in the United States. In this case, the Japanese government allocates the import licenses to Japanese firms, and the surplus from these licenses accrues to those firms. From the standpoint of U.S. welfare, this kind of import quota is worse than a U.S. tariff on imported cars. Both a tariff and an import quota raise prices, restrict trade, and cause deadweight losses, but at least the tariff produces revenue for the U.S. government rather than profit for foreign producers. ■

to pay, it encourages them to reduce their consumption of textiles from Q_1^D to Q_2^D. Even though domestic consumers value these incremental units at more than the world price, the tariff induces them to cut back their purchases. Area D represents the deadweight loss from the overproduction of textiles, and area F represents the deadweight loss from the underconsumption of textiles. The total deadweight loss of the tariff is the sum of these two triangles.

9-2d The Lessons for Trade Policy

The team of Isolandian economists can now write to the new president:

Dear Madam President,

You asked us three questions about opening up trade. After much hard work, we have the answers.

Question: If the government allows Isolandians to import and export textiles, what will happen to the price of textiles and the quantity of textiles sold in the domestic textile market?

Answer: Once trade is allowed, the Isolandian price of textiles will be driven to equal the price prevailing around the world.

If the world price is now higher than the Isolandian price, our price will rise. The higher price will reduce the amount of textiles Isolandians consume and raise the amount of textiles that Isolandians produce. Isoland will, therefore, become a textile exporter. This occurs because, in this case, Isoland has a comparative advantage in producing textiles.

Conversely, if the world price is now lower than the Isolandian price, our price will fall. The lower price will raise the amount of textiles that Isolandians consume and lower the amount of textiles that Isolandians produce. Isoland will, therefore, become a textile importer. This occurs because, in this case, other countries have a comparative advantage in producing textiles.

Question: Who will gain from free trade in textiles and who will lose, and will the gains exceed the losses?

Answer: The answer depends on whether the price rises or falls when trade is allowed. If the price rises, producers of textiles gain, and consumers of textiles lose. If the price falls, consumers gain, and producers lose. In both cases, the gains are larger than the losses. Thus, free trade raises the total welfare of Isolandians.

Question: Should a tariff be part of the new trade policy?

Answer: A tariff has an impact only if Isoland becomes a textile importer. In this case, a tariff moves the economy closer to the no-trade equilibrium and, like most taxes, causes deadweight losses. A tariff improves the welfare of domestic producers and raises revenue for the government, but these gains are more than offset by the losses suffered by consumers. The best policy, from the standpoint of economic efficiency, would be to allow trade without a tariff.

We hope you find these answers helpful as you decide on your new policy.

Your faithful servants,
Isolandian economics team

9-2e Other Benefits of International Trade

The conclusions of the Isolandian economics team are based on the standard analysis of international trade. Their analysis uses the most fundamental tools in the economist's toolbox: supply, demand, and producer and consumer surplus. It shows that there are winners and losers when a nation opens itself up to trade, but the gains of the winners exceed the losses of the losers.

The case for free trade can be made even stronger, however, because there are several other economic benefits of trade beyond those emphasized in the standard analysis. In a nutshell, here are some of these other benefits:

- **Increased variety of goods.** Goods produced in different countries are not exactly the same. German beer, for instance, is not the same as American beer. Free trade gives consumers in all countries greater variety to choose from.
- **Lower costs through economies of scale.** Some goods can be produced at low cost only if they are produced in large quantities—a phenomenon called *economies of scale*. A firm in a small country cannot take full advantage of economies of scale if it can sell only in a small domestic market. Free trade gives firms access to larger world markets and allows them to realize economies of scale more fully.
- **Increased competition.** A company shielded from foreign competitors is more likely to have market power, which in turn gives it the ability to raise prices above competitive levels. This is a type of market failure. Opening up trade fosters competition and gives the invisible hand a better chance to work its magic.

- **Enhanced flow of ideas.** The transfer of technological advances around the world is often thought to be linked to the trading of the goods that embody those advances. The best way for a poor agricultural nation to learn about the computer revolution, for instance, is to buy some computers from abroad rather than trying to make them domestically.

Thus, free international trade increases variety for consumers, allows firms to take advantage of economies of scale, makes markets more competitive, and facilitates the spread of technology. If the Isolandian economists also took these effects into account, their advice to the president would be even more forceful.

QuickQuiz *Draw a supply-and-demand diagram for wool suits in the country of Autarka. When trade is allowed, the price of a suit falls from 3 to 2 ounces of gold. In your diagram, show the change in consumer surplus, the change in producer surplus, and the change in total surplus. How would a tariff on suit imports alter these effects?*

9-3 The Arguments for Restricting Trade

The letter from the economics team starts to persuade the new president of Isoland to consider allowing trade in textiles. She notes that the domestic price is now high compared to the world price. Free trade would, therefore, cause the price of textiles to fall and hurt domestic textile producers. Before implementing the new policy, she asks Isolandian textile companies to comment on the economists' advice.

Not surprisingly, the textile companies oppose free trade in textiles. They believe that the government should protect the domestic textile industry from foreign competition. Let's consider some of the arguments they might give to support their position and how the economics team would respond.

9-3a The Jobs Argument

Opponents of free trade often argue that trade with other countries destroys domestic jobs. In our example, free trade in textiles would cause the price of textiles to fall, reducing the quantity of textiles produced in Isoland and thus

"You like protectionism as a 'working man.' How about as a consumer?"

reducing employment in the Isolandian textile industry. Some Isolandian textile workers would lose their jobs.

Yet free trade creates jobs at the same time that it destroys them. When Isolandians buy textiles from other countries, those countries obtain the resources to buy other goods from Isoland. Isolandian workers would move from the textile industry to those industries in which Isoland has a comparative advantage. The transition may impose hardship on some workers in the short run, but it allows Isolandians as a whole to enjoy a higher standard of living.

Opponents of trade are often skeptical that trade creates jobs. They might respond that *everything* can be produced more cheaply abroad. Under free trade, they might argue, Isolandians could not be profitably employed in any industry. As Chapter 3 explains, however, the gains from trade are based on comparative advantage, not absolute advantage. Even if one country is better than another country at producing everything, each country can still gain from trading with the other. Workers in each country will eventually find jobs in an industry in which that country has a comparative advantage.

9-3b The National-Security Argument

When an industry is threatened with competition from other countries, opponents of free trade often argue that the industry is vital to national security. For example, if Isoland were considering free trade in steel, domestic steel companies might point out that steel is used to make guns and tanks. Free trade would allow Isoland to become dependent on foreign countries to supply steel. If a war later broke out and the foreign supply was interrupted, Isoland might be unable to produce enough steel and weapons to defend itself.

Economists acknowledge that protecting key industries may be appropriate when there are legitimate concerns over national security. Yet they fear that this argument may be used too quickly by producers eager to gain at consumers' expense.

One should be wary of the national-security argument when it is made by representatives of industry rather than the defense establishment. Companies have an incentive to exaggerate their role in national defense to obtain protection from foreign competition. A nation's generals may see things very differently. Indeed, when the military is a consumer of an industry's output, it would benefit from imports. Cheaper steel in Isoland, for example, would allow the Isolandian military to accumulate a stockpile of weapons at lower cost.

9-3c The Infant-Industry Argument

New industries sometimes argue for temporary trade restrictions to help them get started. After a period of protection, the argument goes, these industries will mature and be able to compete with foreign firms. Similarly, older industries sometimes argue that they need temporary protection to help them adjust to new conditions.

Economists are often skeptical about such claims, largely because the infant-industry argument is difficult to implement in practice. To apply protection successfully, the government would need to decide which industries will eventually be profitable and decide whether the benefits of establishing these industries exceed the costs of this protection to consumers. Yet "picking winners" is extraordinarily difficult. It is made even more difficult by the political process, which often awards protection to those industries that are politically powerful. And once a powerful industry is protected from foreign competition, the "temporary" policy is sometimes hard to remove.

In addition, many economists are skeptical about the infant-industry argument in principle. Suppose, for instance, that an industry is young and unable to compete profitably against foreign rivals, but there is reason to believe that the industry can be profitable in the long run. In this case, firm owners should be willing to incur temporary losses to obtain the eventual profits. Protection is not necessary for an infant industry to grow. History shows that start-up firms often incur temporary losses and succeed in the long run, even without protection from competition.

9-3d The Unfair-Competition Argument

A common argument is that free trade is desirable only if all countries play by the same rules. If firms in different countries are subject to different laws and regulations, then it is unfair (the argument goes) to expect the firms to compete in the international marketplace. For instance, suppose that the government of Neighborland subsidizes its textile industry by giving textile companies large tax breaks. The Isolandian textile industry might argue that it should be protected from this foreign competition because Neighborland is not competing fairly.

Would it, in fact, hurt Isoland to buy textiles from another country at a subsidized price? Certainly, Isolandian textile producers would suffer, but Isolandian textile consumers would benefit from the low price. The case for free trade is the same as before: The gains of the consumers from buying at the low price would exceed the losses of the producers. Neighborland's subsidy to its textile industry may be a bad policy, but it is the taxpayers of Neighborland who bear the burden. Isoland can benefit from the opportunity to buy textiles at a subsidized price. Rather than objecting to the foreign subsidies, perhaps Isoland should send Neighborland a thank-you note.

9-3e The Protection-as-a-Bargaining-Chip Argument

Another argument for trade restrictions concerns the strategy of bargaining. Many policymakers claim to support free trade but, at the same time, argue that trade restrictions can be useful when we bargain with our trading partners. They claim that the threat of a trade restriction can help remove a trade restriction already imposed by a foreign government. For example, Isoland might threaten to impose a tariff on textiles unless Neighborland removes its tariff on wheat. If Neighborland responds to this threat by removing its tariff, the result can be freer trade.

The problem with this bargaining strategy is that the threat may not work. If it doesn't work, the country faces a choice between two bad options. It can carry out its threat and implement the trade restriction, which would reduce its own economic welfare. Or it can back down from its threat, which would cause it to lose prestige in international affairs. Faced with this choice, the country would probably wish that it had never made the threat in the first place.

CASE STUDY

TRADE AGREEMENTS AND THE WORLD TRADE ORGANIZATION

A country can take one of two approaches to achieving free trade. It can take a *unilateral* approach and remove its trade restrictions on its own. This is the approach that Great Britain took in the 19th century and that Chile and South Korea have taken in recent years. Alternatively, a country can take a *multilateral* approach and reduce its trade restrictions while other countries do the same. In other words, it can bargain with its trading partners in an attempt to reduce trade restrictions around the world.

One important example of the multilateral approach is the North American Free Trade Agreement (NAFTA), which in 1993 lowered trade barriers among the United States, Mexico, and Canada. Another is the General Agreement on Tariffs and Trade (GATT), which is a continuing series of negotiations among many of the world's countries with the goal of promoting free trade. The United States helped to found GATT after World War II in response to the high tariffs imposed during the Great Depression of the 1930s. Many economists believe that the high tariffs contributed to the worldwide economic hardship of that period. GATT has successfully reduced the average tariff among member countries from about 40 percent after World War II to about 5 percent today.

The rules established under GATT are now enforced by an international institution called the World Trade Organization (WTO). The WTO was established in 1995 and has its headquarters in Geneva, Switzerland. As of 2015, 162 countries have joined the organization, accounting for more than 97 percent of world trade. The functions of the WTO are to administer trade agreements, provide a forum for negotiations, and handle disputes among member countries.

What are the pros and cons of the multilateral approach to free trade? One advantage is that the multilateral approach has the potential to result in freer trade than a unilateral approach because it can reduce trade restrictions abroad as well as at home. If international negotiations fail, however, the result could be more restricted trade than under a unilateral approach.

In addition, the multilateral approach may have a political advantage. In most markets, producers are fewer and better organized than consumers—and thus wield greater political influence. Reducing the Isolandian tariff on textiles, for example, may be politically difficult if considered by itself. The textile companies would oppose free trade, and the buyers of textiles who would benefit are so numerous that organizing their support would be difficult. Yet suppose that Neighborland promises to reduce its tariff on wheat at the same time that Isoland reduces its tariff on textiles. In this case, the Isolandian wheat farmers, who are also politically powerful, would back the agreement. Thus, the multilateral approach to free trade can sometimes win political support when a unilateral approach cannot. ●

ASK THE EXPERTS

Trade Deals

"Past major trade deals have benefited most Americans."

What do economists say?

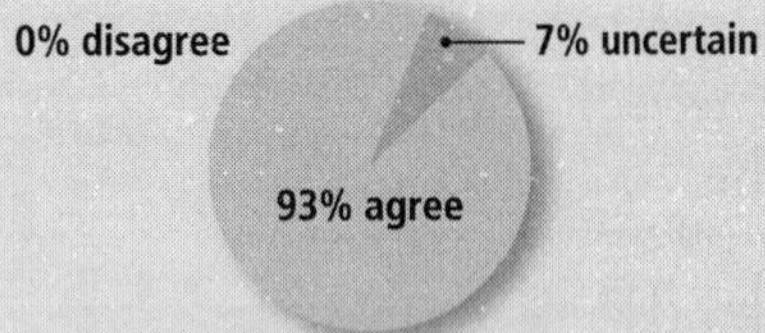

"Refusing to liberalize trade unless partner countries adopt new labor or environmental rules is a bad policy, because even if the new standards would reduce distortions on some dimensions, such a policy involves threatening to maintain large distortions in the form of restricted trade."

What do economists say?

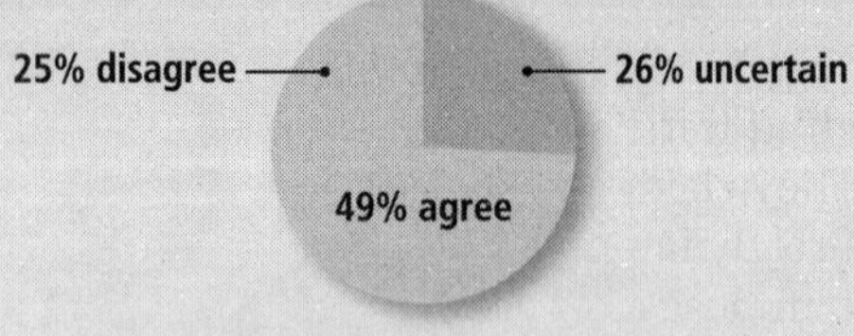

Source: IGM Economic Experts Panel, November 11, 2014 and March 27, 2013.

QuickQuiz *The textile industry of Autarka advocates a ban on the import of wool suits. Describe five arguments its lobbyists might make. Give a response to each of these arguments.*

9-4 Conclusion

Economists and the public often disagree about free trade. In 2015, NBC News and *The Wall Street Journal* asked the American public, "In general, do you think that free trade between the United States and foreign countries has helped the United States, has hurt the United States, or has not made much of a difference either way?" Only 29 percent of those polled said free international trade helped, whereas 34 percent thought it hurt. (The rest thought it made no difference or were unsure.) By contrast, economists overwhelmingly support free international trade. They view free trade as a way of allocating production efficiently and raising living standards both at home and abroad.

Economists view the United States as an ongoing experiment that confirms the virtues of free trade. Throughout its history, the United States has allowed unrestricted trade among the states, and the country as a whole has benefited from the specialization that trade allows. Florida grows oranges, Alaska pumps oil, California makes wine, and so on. Americans would not enjoy the high standard of living they do today if people could consume only those goods and services produced in their own states. The world could similarly benefit from free trade among countries.

To better understand economists' view of trade, let's continue our parable. Suppose that the president of Isoland, after reading the latest poll results, ignores the advice of her economics team and decides not to allow free trade in textiles. The country remains in the equilibrium without international trade.

Then, one day, some Isolandian inventor discovers a new way to make textiles at very low cost. The process is quite mysterious, however, and the inventor insists on keeping it a secret. What is odd is that the inventor doesn't need traditional inputs such as cotton or wool. The only material input he needs is wheat. And even more oddly, to manufacture textiles from wheat, he hardly needs any labor input at all.

The inventor is hailed as a genius. Because everyone buys clothing, the lower cost of textiles allows all Isolandians to enjoy a higher standard of living. Workers who had previously produced textiles experience some hardship when their factories close, but they eventually find work in other industries. Some become farmers and grow the wheat that the inventor turns into textiles. Others enter new industries that emerge as a result of higher Isolandian living standards. Everyone understands that the displacement of workers in outmoded industries is an inevitable part of technological progress and economic growth.

After several years, a newspaper reporter decides to investigate this mysterious new textiles process. She sneaks into the inventor's factory and learns that the inventor is a fraud. The inventor has not been making textiles at all. Instead, he has been smuggling wheat abroad in exchange for textiles from other countries. The only thing that the inventor had discovered was the gains from international trade.

When the truth is revealed, the government shuts down the inventor's operation. The price of textiles rises, and workers return to jobs in textile factories. Living standards in Isoland fall back to their former levels. The inventor is jailed and held up to public ridicule. After all, he was no inventor. He was just an economist.

CHAPTER QuickQuiz

1. If a nation that does not allow international trade in steel has a domestic price of steel lower than the world price, then
   a. the nation has a comparative advantage in producing steel and would become a steel exporter if it opened up trade.
   b. the nation has a comparative advantage in producing steel and would become a steel importer if it opened up trade.
   c. the nation does not have a comparative advantage in producing steel and would become a steel exporter if it opened up trade.
   d. the nation does not have a comparative advantage in producing steel and would become a steel importer if it opened up trade.

2. When the nation of Ectenia opens itself to world trade in coffee beans, the domestic price of coffee beans falls. Which of the following describes the situation?
   a. Domestic production of coffee rises, and Ectenia becomes a coffee importer.
   b. Domestic production of coffee rises, and Ectenia becomes a coffee exporter.
   c. Domestic production of coffee falls, and Ectenia becomes a coffee importer.
   d. Domestic production of coffee falls, and Ectenia becomes a coffee exporter.
3. When a nation opens itself to trade in a good and becomes an importer,
   a. producer surplus decreases, but consumer surplus and total surplus both increase.
   b. producer surplus decreases, consumer surplus increases, and so the impact on total surplus is ambiguous.
   c. producer surplus and total surplus increase, but consumer surplus decreases.
   d. producer surplus, consumer surplus, and total surplus all increase.
4. If a nation that imports a good imposes a tariff, it will increase
   a. the domestic quantity demanded.
   b. the domestic quantity supplied.
   c. the quantity imported from abroad.
   d. all of the above.
5. Which of the following trade policies would benefit producers, hurt consumers, and increase the amount of trade?
   a. the increase of a tariff in an importing country
   b. the reduction of a tariff in an importing country
   c. starting to allow trade when the world price is greater than the domestic price
   d. starting to allow trade when the world price is less than the domestic price
6. The main difference between imposing a tariff and handing out licenses under an import quota is that a tariff increases
   a. consumer surplus.
   b. producer surplus.
   c. international trade.
   d. government revenue.

SUMMARY

- The effects of free trade can be determined by comparing the domestic price before trade with the world price. A low domestic price indicates that the country has a comparative advantage in producing the good and that the country will become an exporter. A high domestic price indicates that the rest of the world has a comparative advantage in producing the good and that the country will become an importer.
- When a country allows trade and becomes an exporter of a good, producers of the good are better off, and consumers of the good are worse off. When a country allows trade and becomes an importer of a good, consumers are better off, and producers are worse off. In both cases, the gains from trade exceed the losses.
- A tariff—a tax on imports—moves a market closer to the equilibrium that would exist without trade and, therefore, reduces the gains from trade. Although domestic producers are better off and the government raises revenue, the losses to consumers exceed these gains.
- There are various arguments for restricting trade: protecting jobs, defending national security, helping infant industries, preventing unfair competition, and responding to foreign trade restrictions. Although some of these arguments have merit in some cases, most economists believe that free trade is usually the better policy.

KEY CONCEPTS

world price, p. 169

tariff, p. 173

QUESTIONS FOR REVIEW

1. What does the domestic price that prevails without international trade tell us about a nation's comparative advantage?
2. When does a country become an exporter of a good? An importer?

3. Draw the supply-and-demand diagram for an importing country. Identify consumer surplus and producer surplus before trade is allowed. Identify consumer surplus and producer surplus with free trade. What is the change in total surplus?
4. Describe what a tariff is and its economic effects.
5. List five arguments often given to support trade restrictions. How do economists respond to these arguments?
6. What is the difference between the unilateral and multilateral approaches to achieving free trade? Give an example of each.

PROBLEMS AND APPLICATIONS

1. The world price of wine is below the price that would prevail in Canada in the absence of trade.
   a. Assuming that Canadian imports of wine are a small part of total world wine production, draw a graph for the Canadian market for wine under free trade. Identify consumer surplus, producer surplus, and total surplus in an appropriate table.
   b. Now suppose that an unusual shift of the Gulf Stream leads to an unseasonably cold summer in Europe, destroying much of the grape harvest there. What effect does this shock have on the world price of wine? Using your graph and table from part (a), show the effect on consumer surplus, producer surplus, and total surplus in Canada. Who are the winners and losers? Is Canada as a whole better or worse off?
2. Suppose that Congress imposes a tariff on imported automobiles to protect the U.S. auto industry from foreign competition. Assuming that the United States is a price taker in the world auto market, show the following on a diagram: the change in the quantity of imports, the loss to U.S. consumers, the gain to U.S. manufacturers, government revenue, and the deadweight loss associated with the tariff. The loss to consumers can be decomposed into three pieces: a gain to domestic producers, revenue for the government, and a deadweight loss. Use your diagram to identify these three pieces.
3. When China's clothing industry expands, the increase in world supply lowers the world price of clothing.
   a. Draw an appropriate diagram to analyze how this change in price affects consumer surplus, producer surplus, and total surplus in a nation that imports clothing, such as the United States.
   b. Now draw an appropriate diagram to show how this change in price affects consumer surplus, producer surplus, and total surplus in a nation that exports clothing, such as the Dominican Republic.
   c. Compare your answers to parts (a) and (b). What are the similarities and what are the differences? Which country should be concerned about the expansion of the Chinese textile industry? Which country should be applauding it? Explain.
4. Consider the arguments for restricting trade.
   a. Imagine that you are a lobbyist for timber, an established industry suffering from low-priced foreign competition, and you are trying to get Congress to pass trade restrictions. Which two or three of the five arguments discussed in the chapter do you think would be most persuasive to the average member of Congress? Explain your reasoning.
   b. Now assume you are an astute student of economics (not a hard assumption, we hope). Although all the arguments for restricting trade have their shortcomings, name the two or three arguments that seem to make the most economic sense to you. For each, describe the economic rationale for and against these arguments for trade restrictions.
5. The nation of Textilia does not allow imports of clothing. In its equilibrium without trade, a T-shirt costs $20, and the equilibrium quantity is 3 million T-shirts. One day, after reading Adam Smith's *The Wealth of Nations* while on vacation, the president decides to open the Textilian market to international trade. The market price of a T-shirt falls to the world price of $16. The number of T-shirts consumed in Textilia rises to 4 million, while the number of T-shirts produced declines to 1 million.
   a. Illustrate the situation just described in a graph. Your graph should show all the numbers.
   b. Calculate the change in consumer surplus, producer surplus, and total surplus that results from opening up trade. (*Hint*: Recall that the area of a triangle is ½ × base × height.)
6. China is a major producer of grains, such as wheat, corn, and rice. Some years ago, the Chinese government, concerned that grain exports were driving up food prices for domestic consumers, imposed a tax on grain exports.
   a. Draw the graph that describes the market for grain in an exporting country. Use this graph as the starting point to answer the following questions.
   b. How does an export tax affect domestic grain prices?

c. How does it affect the welfare of domestic consumers, the welfare of domestic producers, and government revenue?
d. What happens to total welfare in China, as measured by the sum of consumer surplus, producer surplus, and tax revenue?

7. Consider a country that imports a good from abroad. For each of following statements, state whether it is true or false. Explain your answer.
   a. "The greater the elasticity of demand, the greater the gains from trade."
   b. "If demand is perfectly inelastic, there are no gains from trade."
   c. "If demand is perfectly inelastic, consumers do not benefit from trade."

8. Having rejected a tariff on textiles (a tax on imports), the president of Isoland is now considering the same-sized tax on textile consumption (including both imported and domestically produced textiles).
   a. Using Figure 4, identify the quantity consumed and the quantity produced in Isoland under a textile consumption tax.
   b. Construct a table similar to that in Figure 4 for the textile consumption tax.
   c. Which raises more revenue for the government—the consumption tax or the tariff? Which has a smaller deadweight loss? Explain.

9. Assume the United States is an importer of televisions and there are no trade restrictions. U.S. consumers buy 1 million televisions per year, of which 400,000 are produced domestically and 600,000 are imported.
   a. Suppose that a technological advance among Japanese television manufacturers causes the world price of televisions to fall by $100. Draw a graph to show how this change affects the welfare of U.S. consumers and U.S. producers and how it affects total surplus in the United States.
   b. After the fall in price, consumers buy 1.2 million televisions, of which 200,000 are produced domestically and 1 million are imported. Calculate the change in consumer surplus, producer surplus, and total surplus from the price reduction.
   c. If the government responded by putting a $100 tariff on imported televisions, what would this do? Calculate the revenue that would be raised and the deadweight loss. Would it be a good policy from the standpoint of U.S. welfare? Who might support the policy?
   d. Suppose that the fall in price is attributable not to technological advance but to a $100 per television subsidy from the Japanese government to Japanese industry. How would this affect your analysis?

10. Consider a small country that exports steel. Suppose that a "pro-trade" government decides to subsidize the export of steel by paying a certain amount for each ton sold abroad. How does this export subsidy affect the domestic price of steel, the quantity of steel produced, the quantity of steel consumed, and the quantity of steel exported? How does it affect consumer surplus, producer surplus, government revenue, and total surplus? Is it a good policy from the standpoint of economic efficiency? (*Hint*: The analysis of an export subsidy is similar to the analysis of a tariff.)

To find additional study resources, visit cengagebrain.com, and search for "Mankiw."

PART IV
The Economics of the Public Sector

CHAPTER 10

Externalities

Firms that make and sell paper also create, as a by-product of the manufacturing process, a chemical called dioxin. Scientists believe that once dioxin enters the environment, it raises the population's risk of cancer, birth defects, and other health problems.

Is the production and release of dioxin a problem for society? In Chapters 4 through 9, we examined how markets allocate scarce resources with the forces of supply and demand, and we saw that the equilibrium of supply and demand is typically an efficient allocation of resources. To use Adam Smith's famous

metaphor, the "invisible hand" of the marketplace leads self-interested buyers and sellers in a market to maximize the total benefit that society derives from that market. This insight is the basis for one of the *Ten Principles of Economics* in Chapter 1: Markets are usually a good way to organize economic activity. Should we conclude, therefore, that the invisible hand prevents firms in the paper market from emitting too much dioxin?

Markets do many things well, but they do not do everything well. In this chapter, we begin our study of another of the *Ten Principles of Economics*: Government action can sometimes improve upon market outcomes. We examine why markets sometimes fail to allocate resources efficiently, how government policies can potentially improve the market's allocation, and what kinds of policies are likely to work best.

externality
the uncompensated impact of one person's actions on the well-being of a bystander

The market failures examined in this chapter fall under a general category called *externalities*. An **externality** arises when a person engages in an activity that influences the well-being of a bystander but neither pays nor receives compensation for that effect. If the impact on the bystander is adverse, it is called a *negative externality*. If it is beneficial, it is called a *positive externality*. In the presence of externalities, society's interest in a market outcome extends beyond the well-being of buyers and sellers who participate in the market to include the well-being of bystanders who are affected indirectly. Because buyers and sellers neglect the external effects of their actions when deciding how much to demand or supply, the market equilibrium is not efficient when there are externalities. That is, the equilibrium fails to maximize the total benefit to society as a whole. The release of dioxin into the environment, for instance, is a negative externality. Self-interested paper firms will not consider the full cost of the pollution they create in their production process, and consumers of paper will not consider the full cost of the pollution they contribute to as a result of their purchasing decisions. Therefore, the firms will emit too much pollution unless the government prevents or discourages them from doing so.

Externalities come in many varieties, as do the policy responses that try to deal with the market failure. Here are some examples:

- The exhaust from automobiles is a negative externality because it creates smog that other people have to breathe. Because drivers may ignore this externality when deciding what cars to buy and how much to use them, they tend to pollute too much. The federal government addresses this problem by setting emission standards for cars. It also taxes gasoline to reduce the amount that people drive.
- Restored historic buildings convey a positive externality because people who walk or ride by them can enjoy the beauty and sense of history that these buildings provide. Building owners do not get the full benefit of restoration and, therefore, tend to tear down older buildings too quickly. Many local governments respond to this problem by regulating the destruction of historic buildings and by providing tax breaks to owners who restore them.
- Barking dogs create a negative externality because neighbors are disturbed by the noise. Dog owners do not bear the full cost of the noise and, therefore, tend to take too few precautions to prevent their dogs from barking. Local governments address this problem by making it illegal to "disturb the peace."
- Research into new technologies provides a positive externality because it creates knowledge that other people can use. If individual inventors, firms, and

universities cannot capture the benefits of their inventions, they will devote too few resources to research. The federal government addresses this problem partially through the patent system, which gives inventors exclusive use of their inventions for a limited time.

In each of these cases, some decision maker fails to take into account the external effects of his behavior. The government responds by trying to influence this behavior to protect the interests of bystanders.

10-1 Externalities and Market Inefficiency

In this section, we use the tools of welfare economics developed in Chapter 7 to examine how externalities affect economic well-being. The analysis shows precisely why externalities cause markets to allocate resources inefficiently. Later in the chapter, we examine various ways private individuals and public policymakers can remedy this type of market failure.

10-1a Welfare Economics: A Recap

We begin by recalling the key lessons of welfare economics from Chapter 7. To make our analysis concrete, we consider a specific market—the market for aluminum. Figure 1 shows the supply and demand curves in the market for aluminum.

Recall from Chapter 7 that the supply and demand curves contain important information about costs and benefits. The demand curve for aluminum reflects the value of aluminum to consumers, as measured by the prices they are willing to pay. At any given quantity, the height of the demand curve shows the willingness to pay of the marginal buyer. In other words, it shows the value to the consumer of the last unit of aluminum bought. Similarly, the supply curve reflects the costs of producing aluminum. At any given quantity, the height of the supply curve shows the cost to the marginal seller. In other words, it shows the cost to the producer of the last unit of aluminum sold.

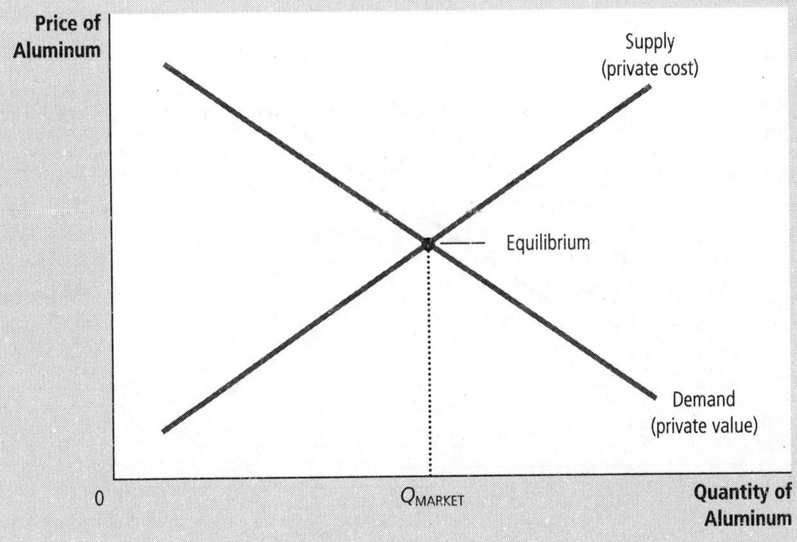

FIGURE 1

The Market for Aluminum
The demand curve reflects the value to buyers, and the supply curve reflects the costs of sellers. The equilibrium quantity, Q_{MARKET}, maximizes the total value to buyers minus the total costs of sellers. In the absence of externalities, therefore, the market equilibrium is efficient.

In the absence of government intervention, the price adjusts to balance the supply and demand for aluminum. The quantity produced and consumed in the market equilibrium, shown as Q_{MARKET} in Figure 1, is efficient in the sense that it maximizes the sum of producer and consumer surplus. That is, the market allocates resources in a way that maximizes the total value to the consumers who buy and use aluminum minus the total costs to the producers who make and sell aluminum.

10-1b Negative Externalities

Now let's suppose that aluminum factories emit pollution: For each unit of aluminum produced, a certain amount of smoke enters the atmosphere. Because this smoke creates a health risk for those who breathe the air, it is a negative externality. How does this externality affect the efficiency of the market outcome?

"All I can say is that if being a leading manufacturer means being a leading polluter, so be it."

Because of the externality, the cost to *society* of producing aluminum is larger than the cost to the aluminum producers. For each unit of aluminum produced, the *social cost* includes the private costs of the aluminum producers plus the costs to those bystanders affected adversely by the pollution. Figure 2 shows the social cost of producing aluminum. The social-cost curve is above the supply curve because it takes into account the external costs imposed on society by aluminum production. The difference between these two curves reflects the cost of the pollution emitted.

What quantity of aluminum should be produced? To answer this question, we once again consider what a benevolent social planner would do. The planner wants to maximize the total surplus derived from the market—the value to consumers of aluminum minus the cost of producing aluminum. The planner understands, however, that the cost of producing aluminum includes the external costs of the pollution.

FIGURE 2

Pollution and the Social Optimum

In the presence of a negative externality, such as pollution, the social cost of the good exceeds the private cost. The optimal quantity, $Q_{OPTIMUM}$, is therefore smaller than the equilibrium quantity, Q_{MARKET}.

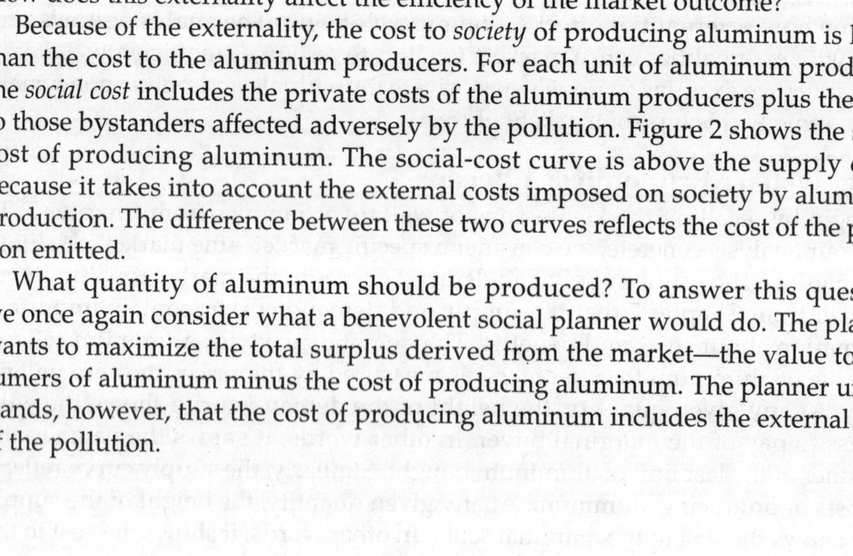

The planner would choose the level of aluminum production at which the demand curve crosses the social-cost curve. This intersection determines the optimal amount of aluminum from the standpoint of society as a whole. Below this level of production, the value of the aluminum to consumers (as measured by the height of the demand curve) exceeds the social cost of producing it (as measured by the height of the social-cost curve). Above this level of production, the social cost of producing additional aluminum exceeds the value to consumers.

Note that the equilibrium quantity of aluminum, Q_{MARKET}, is larger than the socially optimal quantity, $Q_{OPTIMUM}$. This inefficiency occurs because the market equilibrium reflects only the private costs of production. In the market equilibrium, the marginal consumer values aluminum at less than the social cost of producing it. That is, at Q_{MARKET}, the demand curve lies below the social-cost curve. Thus, reducing aluminum production and consumption below the market equilibrium level raises total economic well-being.

How can the social planner achieve the optimal outcome? One way would be to tax aluminum producers for each ton of aluminum sold. The tax would shift the supply curve for aluminum upward by the size of the tax. If the tax accurately reflected the external cost of pollutants released into the atmosphere, the new supply curve would coincide with the social-cost curve. In the new market equilibrium, aluminum producers would produce the socially optimal quantity of aluminum.

The use of such a tax is called **internalizing the externality** because it gives buyers and sellers in the market an incentive to take into account the external effects of their actions. Aluminum producers would, in essence, take the costs of pollution into account when deciding how much aluminum to supply because the tax would make them pay for these external costs. And, because the market price would reflect the tax on producers, consumers of aluminum would have an incentive to buy a smaller quantity. The policy is based on one of the *Ten Principles of Economics*: People respond to incentives. Later in this chapter, we consider in more detail how policymakers can deal with externalities.

internalizing the externality
altering incentives so that people take into account the external effects of their actions

10-1c Positive Externalities

Although some activities impose costs on third parties, others yield benefits. Consider education, for example. To a large extent, the benefit of education is private: The consumer of education becomes a more productive worker and thus reaps much of the benefit in the form of higher wages. Beyond these private benefits, however, education also yields positive externalities. One externality is that a more educated population leads to more informed voters, which means better government for everyone. Another externality is that a more educated population tends to result in lower crime rates. A third externality is that a more educated population may encourage the development and dissemination of technological advances, leading to higher productivity and wages for everyone. Because of these three positive externalities, a person may prefer to have neighbors who are well educated.

The analysis of positive externalities is similar to the analysis of negative externalities. As Figure 3 shows, the demand curve does not reflect the value to society of the good. Because the social value is greater than the private value, the social-value curve lies above the demand curve. The optimal quantity is found where the social-value curve and the supply curve intersect. Hence, the socially optimal quantity is greater than the quantity that the private market would naturally reach on its own.

FIGURE 3

Education and the Social Optimum
In the presence of a positive externality, the social value of the good exceeds the private value. The optimal quantity, $Q_{OPTIMUM}$, is therefore larger than the equilibrium quantity, Q_{MARKET}.

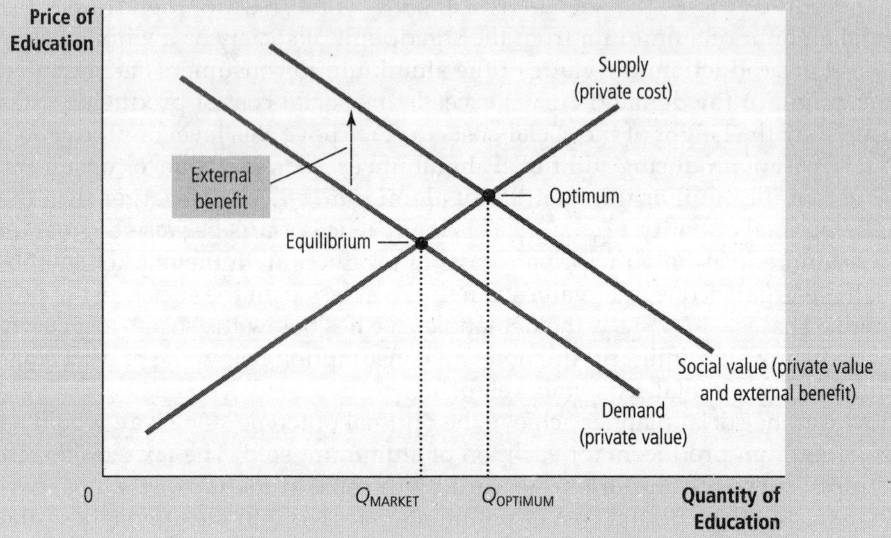

Once again, the government can correct the market failure by inducing market participants to internalize the externality. The appropriate response in the case of positive externalities is exactly the opposite to the case of negative externalities. To move the market equilibrium closer to the social optimum, a positive externality requires a subsidy. In fact, that is exactly the policy the government follows: Education is heavily subsidized through public schools and government scholarships.

To summarize: *Negative externalities lead markets to produce a larger quantity than is socially desirable. Positive externalities lead markets to produce a smaller quantity than is socially desirable. To remedy the problem, the government can internalize the externality by taxing goods that have negative externalities and subsidizing goods that have positive externalities.*

CASE STUDY

TECHNOLOGY SPILLOVERS, INDUSTRIAL POLICY, AND PATENT PROTECTION

A potentially important type of positive externality is called a *technology spillover*—the impact of one firm's research and production efforts on other firms' access to technological advance. For example, consider the market for industrial robots. Robots are at the frontier of a rapidly changing technology. Whenever a firm builds a robot, there is some chance that the firm will discover a new and better design. This new design may benefit not only this firm but also society as a whole because the design will enter society's pool of technological knowledge. That is, the new design may have positive externalities for other producers in the economy.

In this case, the government can internalize the externality by subsidizing the production of robots. If the government paid firms a subsidy for each robot produced, the supply curve would shift down by the amount of the subsidy, and this shift would increase the equilibrium quantity of robots. To ensure that the market equilibrium equals the social optimum, the subsidy should equal the value of the technology spillover.

How large are technology spillovers, and what do they imply for public policy? This is an important question because technological progress is the key to raising living standards over time. Yet it is also a difficult question about which economists often disagree.

Some economists believe that technology spillovers are pervasive and that the government should encourage those industries that yield the largest spillovers. For instance, these economists argue that if making computer chips yields greater spillovers than making potato chips, the government should encourage the production of computer chips relative to the production of potato chips. The U.S. tax code does this in a limited way by offering special tax breaks for expenditures on research and development. Some nations go further by subsidizing specific industries that supposedly yield large technology spillovers. Government intervention that aims to promote technology-enhancing industries is sometimes called *industrial policy*.

Other economists are skeptical about industrial policy. Even if technology spillovers are common, pursuing an industrial policy requires the government to gauge the size of the spillovers from different markets. This measurement problem is difficult at best. Without accurate measurements, the political system may end up subsidizing industries with the most political clout rather than those that yield the largest positive externalities.

Another way to deal with technology spillovers is patent protection. The patent laws protect the rights of inventors by giving them exclusive use of their inventions for a period of time. When a firm makes a technological breakthrough, it can patent the idea and capture much of the economic benefit for itself. The patent internalizes the externality by giving the firm a *property right* over its invention. If other firms want to use the new technology, they have to obtain permission from the inventing firm and pay it a royalty. Thus, the patent system gives firms a greater incentive to engage in research and other activities that advance technology. ●

QuickQuiz *Give an example of a negative externality and a positive externality. Explain why market outcomes are inefficient in the presence of these externalities.*

10-2 Public Policies toward Externalities

We have discussed why externalities lead markets to allocate resources inefficiently but have mentioned only briefly how this inefficiency can be remedied. In practice, both public policymakers and private individuals respond to externalities in various ways. All of the remedies share the goal of moving the allocation of resources closer to the social optimum.

This section considers governmental solutions. As a general matter, the government can respond to externalities in one of two ways. *Command-and-control policies* regulate behavior directly. *Market-based policies* provide incentives so that private decision makers will choose to solve the problem on their own.

10-2a Command-and-Control Policies: Regulation

The government can remedy an externality by either requiring or forbidding certain behaviors. For example, it is a crime to dump poisonous chemicals into the water supply. In this case, the external costs to society far exceed the benefits to the polluter. The government therefore institutes a command-and-control policy that prohibits this act altogether.

ASK THE EXPERTS

Vaccines

"Declining to be vaccinated against contagious diseases such as measles imposes costs on other people, which is a negative externality."

What do economists say?

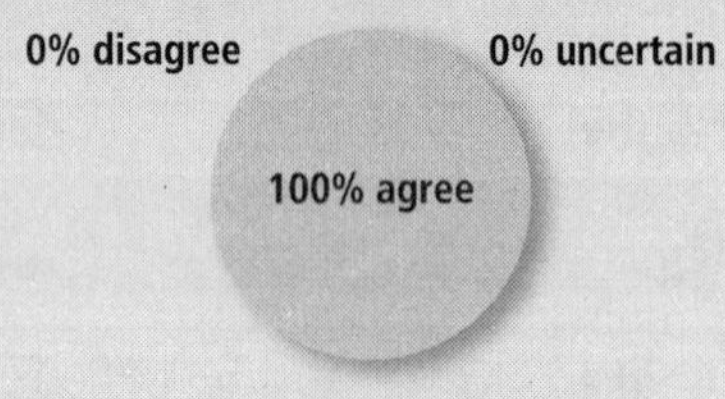

"Considering the costs of restricting free choice, and the share of people in the US who choose not to vaccinate their children for measles, the social benefit of mandating measles vaccines for all Americans (except those with compelling medical reasons) would exceed the social cost."

What do economists say?

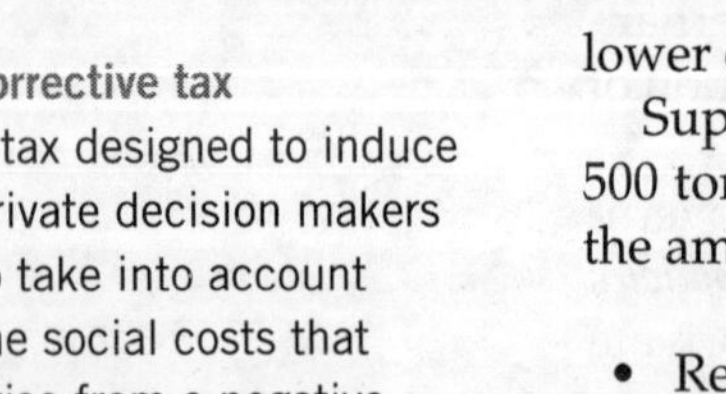

Source: IGM Economic Experts Panel, March 10, 2015.

In most cases of pollution, however, the situation is not this simple. Despite the stated goals of some environmentalists, it would be impossible to prohibit all polluting activity. For example, virtually all forms of transportation—even the horse—produce some undesirable polluting by-products. But it would not be sensible for the government to ban all transportation. As a result, instead of trying to eradicate pollution entirely, society has to weigh the costs and benefits to decide the kinds and quantities of pollution it will allow. In the United States, the Environmental Protection Agency (EPA) is the government agency tasked with developing and enforcing regulations aimed at protecting the environment.

Environmental regulations can take many forms. Sometimes the EPA dictates a maximum level of pollution that a factory may emit. Other times the EPA requires that firms adopt a particular technology to reduce emissions. In all cases, to design good rules, the government regulators need to know the details about specific industries and about the alternative technologies that those industries could adopt. This information is often difficult for government regulators to obtain.

10-2b Market-Based Policy 1: Corrective Taxes and Subsidies

Instead of regulating behavior in response to an externality, the government can use market-based policies to align private incentives with social efficiency. For instance, as we saw earlier, the government can internalize the externality by taxing activities that have negative externalities and subsidizing activities that have positive externalities. Taxes enacted to deal with the effects of negative externalities are called **corrective taxes**. They are also called *Pigovian taxes* after economist Arthur Pigou (1877–1959), an early advocate of their use. An ideal corrective tax would equal the external cost from an activity with negative externalities, and an ideal corrective subsidy would equal the external benefit from an activity with positive externalities.

Economists usually prefer corrective taxes to regulations as a way to deal with pollution because they can reduce pollution at a lower cost to society. To see why, let us consider an example.

corrective tax
a tax designed to induce private decision makers to take into account the social costs that arise from a negative externality

Suppose that two factories—a paper mill and a steel mill—are each dumping 500 tons of glop into a river every year. The EPA decides that it wants to reduce the amount of pollution. It considers two solutions:

- Regulation: The EPA could tell each factory to reduce its pollution to 300 tons of glop per year.
- Corrective tax: The EPA could levy a tax on each factory of $50,000 for each ton of glop it emits.

The regulation would dictate a level of pollution, whereas the tax would give factory owners an economic incentive to reduce pollution. Which solution do you think is better?

Most economists prefer the tax. To explain this preference, they would first point out that a tax is just as effective as regulation in reducing the overall level of pollution. The EPA can achieve whatever level of pollution it wants by setting the tax at the appropriate level. The higher the tax, the larger the reduction in pollution. If the tax is high enough, the factories will close down altogether, reducing pollution to zero.

Although regulation and corrective taxes are both capable of reducing pollution, the tax accomplishes this goal more efficiently. The regulation requires each factory to reduce pollution by the same amount. An equal reduction, however, is not necessarily the least expensive way to clean up the water. It is possible that the paper mill can reduce pollution at lower cost than the steel mill. If so, the paper mill would respond to the tax by reducing pollution substantially to avoid the tax, whereas the steel mill would respond by reducing pollution less and paying the tax.

Arthur Pigou

In essence, the corrective tax places a price on the right to pollute. Just as markets allocate goods to those buyers who value them most highly, a corrective tax allocates pollution to those factories that face the highest cost of reducing it. Thus, the EPA can achieve any level of pollution at the lowest total cost by using a tax.

Economists also argue that corrective taxes are better for the environment. Under the command-and-control policy of regulation, the factories have no reason to reduce emission further once they have reached the target of 300 tons of glop. By contrast, the tax gives the factories an incentive to develop cleaner technologies because a cleaner technology would reduce the amount of tax the factory has to pay.

Corrective taxes are unlike most other taxes. As we discussed in Chapter 8, most taxes distort incentives and move the allocation of resources away from the social optimum. The reduction in economic well-being—that is, in consumer and producer surplus—exceeds the amount of revenue the government raises, resulting in a deadweight loss. By contrast, when externalities are present, society also cares about the well-being of the affected bystanders. Corrective taxes alter incentives that market participants face to account for the presence of externalities and thereby move the allocation of resources closer to the social optimum. Thus, while corrective taxes raise revenue for the government, they also enhance economic efficiency.

CASE STUDY

WHY IS GASOLINE TAXED SO HEAVILY?

In many nations, gasoline is among the most heavily taxed goods. The gas tax can be viewed as a corrective tax aimed at addressing three negative externalities associated with driving:

- *Congestion:* If you have ever been stuck in bumper-to-bumper traffic, you have probably wished that there were fewer cars on the road. A gasoline tax keeps congestion down by encouraging people to take public transportation, carpool more often, and live closer to work.
- *Accidents:* Whenever people buy large cars or sport utility vehicles, they may make themselves safer but they certainly put their neighbors at risk. According to the National Highway Traffic Safety Administration, a person driving a typical car is five times as likely to die if hit by a sport utility vehicle than if hit by another car. The gas tax is an indirect way of making

people pay when their large, gas-guzzling vehicles impose risk on others. It would induce them to take this risk into account when choosing what vehicle to purchase.

- *Pollution:* Cars cause smog. Moreover, the burning of fossil fuels such as gasoline is widely believed to be the primary cause of global warming. Experts disagree about how dangerous this threat is, but there is no doubt that the gas tax reduces the threat by discouraging the use of gasoline.

So the gas tax, rather than causing deadweight losses like most taxes, actually makes the economy work better. It means less traffic congestion, safer roads, and a cleaner environment.

How high should the tax on gasoline be? Most European countries impose gasoline taxes that are much higher than those in the United States. Many observers have suggested that the United States should also tax gasoline more heavily. A 2007 study published in the *Journal of Economic Literature* summarized the research on the size of the various externalities associated with driving. It concluded that the optimal corrective tax on gasoline was $2.28 per gallon in 2005 dollars; after adjusting for inflation, that amount is equivalent to about $2.78 per gallon in 2015 dollars. By contrast, the actual tax in the United States in 2015 was only about 50 cents per gallon.

The tax revenue from a gasoline tax could be used to lower taxes that distort incentives and cause deadweight losses, such as income taxes. In addition, some of the burdensome government regulations that require automakers to produce more fuel-efficient cars would prove unnecessary. This idea, however, has never been politically popular. ●

10-2c Market-Based Policy 2: Tradable Pollution Permits

Returning to our example of the paper mill and the steel mill, let us suppose that, despite the advice of its economists, the EPA adopts the regulation and requires each factory to reduce its pollution to 300 tons of glop per year. Then one day, after the regulation is in place and both mills have complied, the two firms go to the EPA with a proposal. The steel mill wants to increase its emission of glop from 300 to 400 tons. The paper mill has agreed to reduce its emission from 300 to 200 tons if the steel mill pays it $5 million. The total emission of glop would remain at 600 tons. Should the EPA allow the two factories to make this deal?

ASK THE EXPERTS

Carbon Taxes

"The Brookings Institution recently described a U.S. carbon tax of $20 per ton, increasing at 4 percent per year, which would raise an estimated $150 billion per year in federal revenues over the next decade. Given the negative externalities created by carbon dioxide emissions, a federal carbon tax at this rate would involve fewer harmful net distortions to the U.S. economy than a tax increase that generated the same revenue by raising marginal tax rates on labor income across the board."

What do economists say?

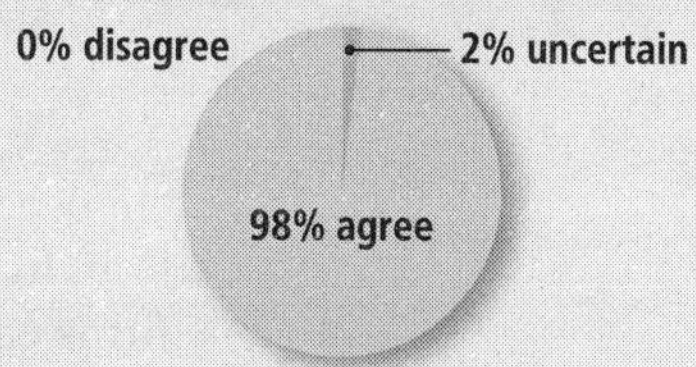

"A tax on the carbon content of fuels would be a less expensive way to reduce carbon-dioxide emissions than would a collection of policies such as 'corporate average fuel economy' requirements for automobiles."

What do economists say?

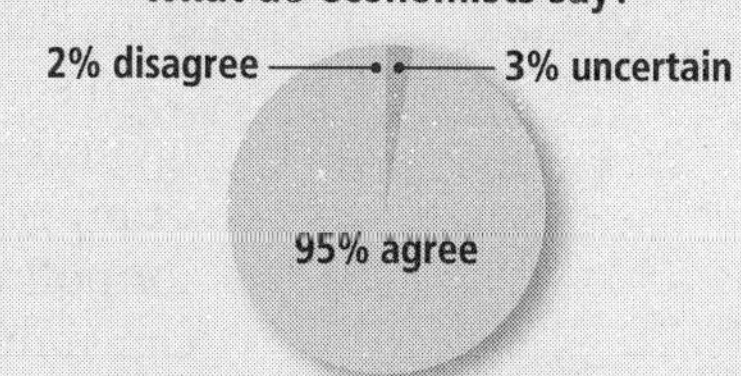

From the standpoint of economic efficiency, allowing the deal is good policy. The deal must make the owners of the two factories better off because they are voluntarily agreeing to it. Moreover, the deal does not have any external effects because the total amount of pollution stays the same. Thus, social welfare is enhanced by allowing the paper mill to sell its pollution rights to the steel mill.

The same logic applies to any voluntary transfer of the right to pollute from one firm to another. If the EPA allows firms to make these deals, it will, in essence, create a new scarce resource: pollution permits. A market to trade these permits will eventually develop, and that market will be governed by the forces of supply and demand. The invisible hand will ensure that this new market allocates the right to pollute efficiently. That is, the permits will end up in the hands of those firms that value them most highly, as judged by their willingness to pay. A firm's willingness to pay for the right to pollute, in turn, will depend on its cost of reducing pollution: The more costly it is for a firm to cut back on pollution, the more it will be willing to pay for a permit.

An advantage of allowing a market for pollution permits is that the initial allocation of pollution permits among firms does not matter from the standpoint of economic efficiency. Those firms that can reduce pollution at a low cost will sell whatever permits they get, while firms that can reduce pollution only at a high cost will buy whatever permits they need. As long as there is a free market for the pollution rights, the final allocation will be efficient regardless of the initial allocation.

Reducing pollution using pollution permits may seem very different from using corrective taxes, but the two policies have much in common. In both cases, firms pay for their pollution. With corrective taxes, polluting firms must pay a tax to the government. With pollution permits, polluting firms must pay to buy the permits. (Even firms that already own permits must pay to pollute: The opportunity cost of polluting is what they could have received by selling their permits on the open market.) Both corrective taxes and pollution permits internalize the externality of pollution by making it costly for firms to pollute.

The similarity of the two policies can be seen by considering the market for pollution. Both panels in Figure 4 show the demand curve for the right to pollute. This curve shows that the lower the price of polluting, the more firms will

In panel (a), the EPA sets a price on pollution by levying a corrective tax, and the demand curve determines the quantity of pollution. In panel (b), the EPA limits the quantity of pollution by limiting the number of pollution permits, and the demand curve determines the price of pollution. The price and quantity of pollution are the same in the two cases.

FIGURE 4

The Equivalence of Corrective Taxes and Pollution Permits

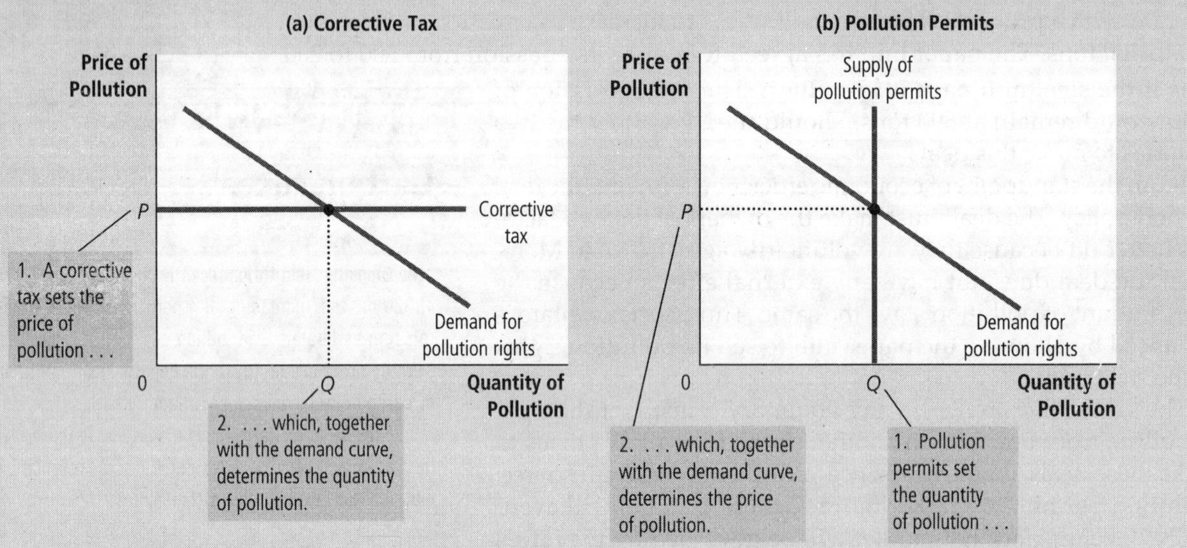

choose to pollute. In panel (a), the EPA uses a corrective tax to set a price for pollution. In this case, the supply curve for pollution rights is perfectly elastic (because firms can pollute as much as they want by paying the tax), and the position of the demand curve determines the quantity of pollution. In panel (b), the EPA sets a quantity of pollution by issuing pollution permits. In this case, the supply curve for pollution rights is perfectly inelastic (because the quantity of pollution is fixed by the number of permits), and the position of the demand curve determines the price of pollution. Hence, the EPA can achieve any point on a given demand curve either by setting a price with a corrective tax or by setting a quantity with pollution permits.

In some circumstances, however, selling pollution permits may be better than levying a corrective tax. Suppose the EPA wants no more than 600 tons of glop dumped into the river. But because the EPA does not know the demand curve for pollution, it is not sure what size tax would achieve that goal. In this case, it can simply auction off 600 pollution permits. The auction price would yield the appropriate size of the corrective tax.

The idea of the government auctioning off the right to pollute may at first sound like a creature of some economist's imagination. And in fact, that is how the idea began. But increasingly, the EPA has used this system as a way to control pollution. A notable success story has been the case of sulfur dioxide (SO_2), a leading cause of acid rain. In 1990, amendments to the Clean Air Act required power plants to reduce SO_2 emissions substantially. At the same time, the amendments set up a system that allowed plants to trade their SO_2 allowances. Initially, both industry representatives and environmentalists were skeptical of the proposal, but over time the system reduced pollution with minimal disruption. Pollution permits, like corrective taxes, are now widely viewed as a cost-effective way to keep the environment clean.

10-2d Objections to the Economic Analysis of Pollution

"We cannot give anyone the option of polluting for a fee." This comment from the late Senator Edmund Muskie reflects the view of some environmentalists. Clean air and clean water, they argue, are fundamental human rights that should not be debased by considering them in economic terms. How can you put a price on clean air and clean water? The environment is so important, they claim, that we should protect it as much as possible, regardless of the cost.

Economists have little sympathy for this type of argument. To economists, good environmental policy begins by acknowledging the first of the *Ten Principles of Economics* in Chapter 1: People face trade-offs. Certainly, clean air and clean water have value. But their value must be compared to their opportunity cost—that is, to what one must give up to obtain them. Eliminating all pollution is impossible. Trying to eliminate all pollution would reverse many of the technological advances that allow us to enjoy a high standard of living. Few people would be willing to accept poor nutrition, inadequate medical care, or shoddy housing to make the environment as clean as possible.

Economists argue that some environmental activists hurt their own cause by not thinking in economic terms. A clean environment can be viewed as simply another good. Like all normal goods, it has a positive income elasticity: Rich countries can afford a cleaner environment than poor ones and, therefore, usually have more rigorous environmental protection. In addition, like most other goods, clean air and clean water obey the law of demand: The lower the price of environmental protection, the more the public will want. The economic approach of using pollution permits and corrective taxes reduces the cost of environmental protection and should, therefore, increase the public's demand for a clean environment.

QuickQuiz *A glue factory and a steel mill emit smoke containing a chemical that is harmful if inhaled in large amounts. Describe three ways the town government might respond to this externality. What are the pros and cons of each solution?*

10-3 Private Solutions to Externalities

Although externalities tend to cause markets to be inefficient, government action is not always needed to solve the problem. In some circumstances, people can develop private solutions.

10-3a The Types of Private Solutions

Sometimes the problem of externalities is solved with moral codes and social sanctions. Consider, for instance, why most people do not litter. Although there are laws against littering, these laws are not rigorously enforced. Most people choose not to litter just because it is the wrong thing to do. The Golden Rule taught to most children says, "Do unto others as you would have them do unto you." This moral injunction tells us to take account of how our actions affect other people. In economic terms, it tells us to internalize externalities.

Another private solution to externalities involves charities. For example, the Sierra Club, whose goal is to protect the environment, is a nonprofit organization funded with private donations. As another example, colleges and universities receive gifts from alumni, corporations, and foundations in part because education has positive externalities for society. The government encourages this private solution to externalities through the tax system by allowing an income tax deduction for charitable donations.

The private market can often solve the problem of externalities by relying on the self-interest of the relevant parties. Sometimes the solution takes the form of integrating different types of businesses. For example, consider an apple grower and a beekeeper who are located next to each other. Each business confers a positive externality on the other: By pollinating the flowers on the trees, the bees help the orchard produce apples, while the bees use the nectar they get from the apple trees to produce honey. Nonetheless, when the apple grower is deciding how many trees to plant and the beekeeper is deciding how many bees to keep, they neglect the positive externality. As a result, the apple grower plants too few trees and the beekeeper keeps too few bees. These externalities could be internalized if the beekeeper bought the apple orchard or if the apple grower bought the beehives: Both activities would then take place within the same firm, and this single firm could choose the optimal number of trees and bees. Internalizing externalities is one reason that some firms are involved in multiple types of businesses.

Another way for the private market to deal with external effects is for the interested parties to enter into a contract. In the foregoing example, a contract between the apple grower and the beekeeper can solve the problem of too few trees and too few bees. The contract can specify the number of trees, the number of bees, and perhaps a payment from one party to the other. By setting the right number of trees and bees, the contract can solve the inefficiency that normally arises from these externalities and make both parties better off.

10-3b The Coase Theorem

Coase theorem
the proposition that if private parties can bargain without cost over the allocation of resources, they can solve the problem of externalities on their own

How effective is the private market in dealing with externalities? A famous result, called the **Coase theorem** after economist Ronald Coase, suggests that it can be very effective in some circumstances. According to the Coase theorem, if private parties can bargain over the allocation of resources at no cost, then the private market will always solve the problem of externalities and allocate resources efficiently.

To see how the Coase theorem works, consider an example. Suppose that Dick owns a dog named Spot. Spot barks and disturbs Jane, Dick's neighbor. Dick gets a benefit from owning the dog, but the dog confers a negative externality on Jane. Should Dick be forced to send Spot to the pound, or should Jane have to suffer sleepless nights because of Spot's barking?

Consider first what outcome is socially efficient. A social planner, considering the two alternatives, would compare the benefit that Dick gets from the dog to the cost that Jane bears from the barking. If the benefit exceeds the cost, it is efficient for Dick to keep the dog and for Jane to live with the barking. Yet if the cost exceeds the benefit, then Dick should get rid of the dog.

According to the Coase theorem, the private market will reach the efficient outcome on its own. How? Jane can simply offer to pay Dick to get rid of the dog. Dick will accept the deal if the amount of money Jane offers is greater than the benefit of keeping the dog.

By bargaining over the price, Dick and Jane can always reach the efficient outcome. For instance, suppose that Dick gets a $500 benefit from the dog and Jane bears an $800 cost from the barking. In this case, Jane can offer Dick $600 to get rid of the dog, and Dick will gladly accept. Both parties are better off than they were before, and the efficient outcome is reached.

It is possible, of course, that Jane would not be willing to offer any price that Dick would accept. For instance, suppose that Dick gets a $1,000 benefit from the dog and Jane bears an $800 cost from the barking. In this case, Dick would turn down any offer below $1,000, while Jane would not offer any amount above $800. Therefore, Dick ends up keeping the dog. Given these costs and benefits, however, this outcome is efficient.

So far, we have assumed that Dick has the legal right to keep a barking dog. In other words, we have assumed that Dick can keep Spot unless Jane pays him enough to induce him to give up the dog voluntarily. But how different would the outcome be if Jane had the legal right to peace and quiet?

According to the Coase theorem, the initial distribution of rights does not matter for the market's ability to reach the efficient outcome. For instance, suppose that Jane can legally compel Dick to get rid of the dog. Having this right works to Jane's advantage, but it probably will not change the outcome. In this case, Dick can offer to pay Jane to allow him to keep the dog. If the benefit of the dog to Dick exceeds the cost of the barking to Jane, then Dick and Jane will strike a bargain in which Dick keeps the dog.

Although Dick and Jane can reach the efficient outcome regardless of how rights are initially distributed, the distribution of rights is not irrelevant: It determines the distribution of economic well-being. Whether Dick has the right to a barking dog or Jane the right to peace and quiet determines who pays whom in the final bargain. But in either case, the two parties can bargain with each other and solve the externality problem. Dick will end up keeping the dog only if his benefit exceeds Jane's cost.

To sum up: *The Coase theorem says that private economic actors can potentially solve the problem of externalities among themselves. Whatever the initial distribution of rights, the interested parties can reach a bargain in which everyone is better off and the outcome is efficient.*

10-3c Why Private Solutions Do Not Always Work

Despite the appealing logic of the Coase theorem, private individuals on their own often fail to resolve the problems caused by externalities. The Coase theorem applies only when the interested parties have no trouble reaching and enforcing an agreement. In the real world, however, bargaining does not always work, even when a mutually beneficial agreement is possible.

Sometimes the interested parties fail to solve an externality problem because of **transaction costs**, the costs that parties incur in the process of agreeing to and following through on a bargain. In our example, imagine that Dick and Jane speak different languages so that, to reach an agreement, they need to hire a translator. If the benefit of solving the barking problem is less than the cost of the translator, Dick and Jane might choose to leave the problem unsolved. In more realistic examples, the transaction costs are the expenses not of translators but of lawyers required to draft and enforce contracts.

transaction costs
the costs that parties incur during the process of agreeing to and following through on a bargain

At other times, bargaining simply breaks down. The recurrence of wars and labor strikes shows that reaching agreement can be difficult and that failing to reach agreement can be costly. The problem is often that each party tries to hold out for a better deal. For example, suppose that Dick gets a $500 benefit from having the dog and Jane bears an $800 cost from the barking. Although it is efficient for Jane to pay Dick to find another home for the dog, there are many prices that could lead to this outcome. Dick might demand $750, and Jane might offer only $550. As they haggle over the price, the inefficient outcome with the barking dog persists.

Reaching an efficient bargain is especially difficult when the number of interested parties is large, because coordinating everyone is costly. For example, consider a factory that pollutes the water of a nearby lake. The pollution confers a negative externality on the local fishermen. According to the Coase theorem, if the pollution is inefficient, then the factory and the fishermen could reach a bargain in which the fishermen pay the factory not to pollute. If there are many fishermen, however, trying to coordinate them all to bargain with the factory may be almost impossible.

When private bargaining does not work, the government can sometimes play a role. The government is an institution designed for collective action. In this example, the government can act on behalf of the fishermen, even when it is impractical for the fishermen to act for themselves.

QuickQuiz *Give an example of a private solution to an externality. • What is the Coase theorem? • Why are private economic participants sometimes unable to solve the problems caused by an externality?*

10-4 Conclusion

The invisible hand is powerful but not omnipotent. A market's equilibrium maximizes the sum of producer and consumer surplus. When the buyers and sellers in the market are the only interested parties, this outcome is efficient from the standpoint of society as a whole. But when there are external effects, such as pollution, evaluating a market outcome requires taking into account the well-being of third parties as well. In this case, the invisible hand of the marketplace may fail to allocate resources efficiently.

In some cases, people can solve the problem of externalities on their own. The Coase theorem suggests that the interested parties can bargain among themselves and agree on an efficient solution. Sometimes, however, an efficient outcome cannot be reached, perhaps because the large number of interested parties makes bargaining difficult.

When people cannot solve the problem of externalities privately, the government often steps in. Yet even with government intervention, society should not abandon market forces entirely. Rather, the government can address the problem by requiring decision makers to bear the full costs of their actions. Pollution permits and corrective taxes on emissions, for instance, are designed to internalize the externality of pollution. These are increasingly the policies of choice for those interested in protecting the environment. Market forces, properly redirected, are often the best remedy for market failure.

CHAPTER Quick**Quiz**

1. Which of the following is an example of a positive externality?
   a. Dev mows Hillary's lawn and is paid $100 for performing the service.
   b. While mowing the lawn, Dev's lawnmower spews out smoke that Hillary's neighbor Kristen has to breathe.
   c. Hillary's newly cut lawn makes her neighborhood more attractive.
   d. Hillary's neighbors pay her if she promises to get her lawn cut on a regular basis.
2. If the production of a good yields a negative externality, then the social-cost curve lies _______ the supply curve, and the socially optimal quantity is _______ than the equilibrium quantity.
   a. above, greater
   b. above, less

c. below, greater
d. below, less

3. When the government levies a tax on a good equal to the external cost associated with the good's production, it ________ the price paid by consumers and makes the market outcome ________ efficient.
   a. increases, more
   b. increases, less
   c. decreases, more
   d. decreases, less

4. Which of the following statements about corrective taxes is generally NOT true?
   a. Economists prefer them to command-and-control regulation.
   b. They raise government revenue.
   c. They cause deadweight losses.
   d. They reduce the quantity sold in a market.

5. The government auctions off 500 units of pollution rights. They sell for $50 per unit, raising total revenue of $25,000. This policy is equivalent to a corrective tax of _____ per unit of pollution.
   a. $10
   b. $50
   c. $450
   d. $500

6. The Coase theorem does NOT apply if
   a. there is a significant externality between two parties.
   b. the court system vigorously enforces all contracts.
   c. transaction costs make negotiating difficult.
   d. both parties understand the externality fully.

SUMMARY

- When a transaction between a buyer and seller directly affects a third party, the effect is called an externality. If an activity yields negative externalities, such as pollution, the socially optimal quantity in a market is less than the equilibrium quantity. If an activity yields positive externalities, such as technology spillovers, the socially optimal quantity is greater than the equilibrium quantity.
- Governments pursue various policies to remedy the inefficiencies caused by externalities. Sometimes the government prevents socially inefficient activity by regulating behavior. Other times it internalizes an externality using corrective taxes. Another public policy is to issue permits. For example, the government could protect the environment by issuing a limited number of pollution permits. The result of this policy is similar to imposing corrective taxes on polluters.
- Those affected by externalities can sometimes solve the problem privately. For instance, when one business imposes an externality on another business, the two businesses can internalize the externality by merging. Alternatively, the interested parties can solve the problem by negotiating a contract. According to the Coase theorem, if people can bargain without cost, then they can always reach an agreement in which resources are allocated efficiently. In many cases, however, reaching a bargain among the many interested parties is difficult, so the Coase theorem does not apply.

KEY CONCEPTS

externality, p. 190
internalizing the externality, p. 193
corrective tax, p. 196
Coase theorem, p. 203
transaction costs, p. 204

QUESTIONS FOR REVIEW

1. Give an example of a negative externality and an example of a positive externality.
2. Draw a supply-and-demand diagram to explain the effect of a negative externality that occurs as a result of a firm's production process.
3. In what way does the patent system help society solve an externality problem?
4. What are corrective taxes? Why do economists prefer them to regulations as a way to protect the environment from pollution?

5. List some of the ways that the problems caused by externalities can be solved without government intervention.
6. Imagine that you are a nonsmoker sharing a room with a smoker. According to the Coase theorem, what determines whether your roommate smokes in the room? Is this outcome efficient? How do you and your roommate reach this solution?

PROBLEMS AND APPLICATIONS

1. Consider two ways to protect your car from theft. The Club (a steering wheel lock) makes it difficult for a car thief to take your car. Lojack (a tracking system) makes it easier for the police to catch the car thief who has stolen it. Which of these methods conveys a negative externality on other car owners? Which conveys a positive externality? Do you think there are any policy implications of your analysis?
2. Consider the market for fire extinguishers.
   a. Why might fire extinguishers exhibit positive externalities?
   b. Draw a graph of the market for fire extinguishers, labeling the demand curve, the social-value curve, the supply curve, and the social-cost curve.
   c. Indicate the market equilibrium level of output and the efficient level of output. Give an intuitive explanation for why these quantities differ.
   d. If the external benefit is $10 per extinguisher, describe a government policy that would yield the efficient outcome.
3. Greater consumption of alcohol leads to more motor vehicle accidents and, thus, imposes costs on people who do not drink and drive.
   a. Illustrate the market for alcohol, labeling the demand curve, the social-value curve, the supply curve, the social-cost curve, the market equilibrium level of output, and the efficient level of output.
   b. On your graph, shade the area corresponding to the deadweight loss of the market equilibrium. (*Hint*: The deadweight loss occurs because some units of alcohol are consumed for which the social cost exceeds the social value.) Explain.
4. Many observers believe that the levels of pollution in our society are too high.
   a. If society wishes to reduce overall pollution by a certain amount, why is it efficient to have different amounts of reduction at different firms?
   b. Command-and-control approaches often rely on uniform reductions among firms. Why are these approaches generally unable to target the firms that should undertake bigger reductions?
   c. Economists argue that appropriate corrective taxes or tradable pollution rights will result in efficient pollution reduction. How do these approaches target the firms that should undertake bigger reductions?
5. The many identical residents of Whoville love drinking Zlurp. Each resident has the following willingness to pay for the tasty refreshment:

First bottle	$5
Second bottle	4
Third bottle	3
Fourth bottle	2
Fifth bottle	1
Further bottles	0

   a. The cost of producing Zlurp is $1.50, and the competitive suppliers sell it at this price. (The supply curve is horizontal.) How many bottles will each Whovillian consume? What is each person's consumer surplus?
   b. Producing Zlurp creates pollution. Each bottle has an external cost of $1. Taking this additional cost into account, what is total surplus per person in the allocation you described in part (a)?
   c. Cindy Lou Who, one of the residents of Whoville, decides on her own to reduce her consumption of Zlurp by one bottle. What happens to Cindy's welfare (her consumer surplus minus the cost of pollution she experiences)? How does Cindy's decision affect total surplus in Whoville?
   d. Mayor Grinch imposes a $1 tax on Zlurp. What is consumption per person now? Calculate consumer surplus, the external cost, government revenue, and total surplus per person.
   e. Based on your calculations, would you support the mayor's policy? Why or why not?
6. Bruno loves playing rock 'n' roll music at high volume. Placido loves opera and hates rock 'n' roll. Unfortunately, they are next-door neighbors in an apartment building with paper-thin walls.
   a. What is the externality here?
   b. What command-and-control policy might the landlord impose? Could such a policy lead to an inefficient outcome?
   c. Suppose the landlord lets the tenants do whatever they want. According to the Coase theorem,

how might Bruno and Placido reach an efficient outcome on their own? What might prevent them from reaching an efficient outcome?

7. Figure 4 shows that for any given demand curve for the right to pollute, the government can achieve the same outcome either by setting a price with a corrective tax or by setting a quantity with pollution permits. Suppose there is a sharp improvement in the technology for controlling pollution.
   a. Using graphs similar to those in Figure 4, illustrate the effect of this development on the demand for pollution rights.
   b. What is the effect on the price and quantity of pollution under each regulatory system? Explain.

8. Suppose that the government decides to issue tradable permits for a certain form of pollution.
   a. Does it matter for economic efficiency whether the government distributes or auctions the permits? Why or why not?
   b. If the government chooses to distribute the permits, does the allocation of permits among firms matter for efficiency? Explain.

9. There are three industrial firms in Happy Valley.

Firm	Initial Pollution Level	Cost of Reducing Pollution by 1 Unit
A	30 units	\$20
B	40 units	\$30
C	20 units	\$10

The government wants to reduce pollution to 60 units, so it gives each firm 20 tradable pollution permits.
   a. Who sells permits and how many do they sell? Who buys permits and how many do they buy? Briefly explain why the sellers and buyers are each willing to do so. What is the total cost of pollution reduction in this situation?
   b. How much higher would the costs of pollution reduction be if the permits could not be traded?

To find additional study resources, visit cengagebrain.com, and search for "Mankiw."

Public Goods and Common Resources

CHAPTER

11

An old song lyric maintains that "the best things in life are free." A moment's thought reveals a long list of goods that the songwriter could have had in mind. Nature provides some of them, such as rivers, mountains, beaches, lakes, and oceans. The government provides others, such as playgrounds, parks, and parades. In each case, people often do not pay a fee when they choose to enjoy the benefit of the good.

Goods without prices provide a special challenge for economic analysis. Most goods in our economy are allocated through markets, in which buyers pay for what they receive and sellers are paid for what they provide. For these goods,

prices are the signals that guide the decisions of buyers and sellers, and these decisions lead to an efficient allocation of resources. When goods are available free of charge, however, the market forces that normally allocate resources in our economy are absent.

In this chapter, we examine the problems that arise for the allocation of resources when there are goods without market prices. Our analysis will shed light on one of the *Ten Principles of Economics* in Chapter 1: Governments can sometimes improve market outcomes. When a good does not have a price attached to it, private markets cannot ensure that the good is produced and consumed in the proper amounts. In such cases, government policy can potentially remedy the market failure and increase economic well-being.

11-1 The Different Kinds of Goods

How well do markets work in providing the goods that people want? The answer to this question depends on the good being considered. As we discussed in Chapter 7, a market can provide the efficient number of ice-cream cones: The price of ice-cream cones adjusts to balance supply and demand, and this equilibrium maximizes the sum of producer and consumer surplus. Yet as we discussed in Chapter 10, the market cannot be counted on to prevent aluminum manufacturers from polluting the air we breathe: Buyers and sellers in a market typically do not take into account the external effects of their decisions. Thus, markets work well if the good is ice cream, but they don't if the good is clean air.

When thinking about the various goods in the economy, it is useful to group them according to two characteristics:

excludability
the property of a good whereby a person can be prevented from using it

rivalry in consumption
the property of a good whereby one person's use diminishes other people's use

- Is the good **excludable**? That is, can people be prevented from using the good?
- Is the good **rival in consumption**? That is, does one person's use of the good reduce another person's ability to use it?

Using these two characteristics, Figure 1 divides goods into four categories:

private goods
goods that are both excludable and rival in consumption

public goods
goods that are neither excludable nor rival in consumption

1. **Private goods** are both excludable and rival in consumption. Consider an ice-cream cone, for example. An ice-cream cone is excludable because it is possible to prevent someone from eating one—you just don't give it to her. An ice-cream cone is rival in consumption because if one person eats an ice-cream cone, another person cannot eat the same cone. Most goods in the economy are private goods like ice-cream cones: You don't get one unless you pay for it, and once you have it, you are the only person who benefits. When we analyzed supply and demand in Chapters 4, 5, and 6 and the efficiency of markets in Chapters 7, 8, and 9, we implicitly assumed that goods were both excludable and rival in consumption.
2. **Public goods** are neither excludable nor rival in consumption. That is, people cannot be prevented from using a public good, and one person's use of a public good does not reduce another person's ability to use it. For example, a tornado siren in a small town is a public good. Once the siren sounds, it is impossible to prevent any single person from hearing it (so it is not excludable). Moreover, when one person gets the benefit of the warning, she does not reduce the benefit to anyone else (so it is not rival in consumption).

		Rival in consumption? Yes	No
Excludable?	**Yes**	Private Goods • Ice-cream cones • Clothing • Congested toll roads	Club Goods • Fire protection • Cable TV • Uncongested toll roads
	No	Common Resources • Fish in the ocean • The environment • Congested nontoll roads	Public Goods • Tornado siren • National defense • Uncongested nontoll roads

FIGURE 1

Four Types of Goods
Goods can be grouped into four categories according to two characteristics: (1) A good is *excludable* if people can be prevented from using it. (2) A good is *rival in consumption* if one person's use of the good diminishes other people's use of it. This diagram gives examples of goods in each category.

3. **Common resources** are rival in consumption but not excludable. For example, fish in the ocean are rival in consumption: When one person catches fish, there are fewer fish for the next person to catch. But these fish are not an excludable good because it is difficult to stop fishermen from taking fish out of a vast ocean.

common resources
goods that are rival in consumption but not excludable

4. **Club goods** are excludable but not rival in consumption. For instance, consider fire protection in a small town. It is easy to exclude someone from using this good: The fire department can just let her house burn down. But fire protection is not rival in consumption: Once a town has paid for the fire department, the additional cost of protecting one more house is small. (We discuss club goods again in Chapter 15, where we see that they are one type of a *natural monopoly*.)

club goods
goods that are excludable but not rival in consumption

Although Figure 1 offers a clean separation of goods into four categories, the boundaries between the categories are sometimes fuzzy. Whether goods are excludable or rival in consumption is often a matter of degree. Fish in an ocean may not be excludable because monitoring fishing is so difficult, but a large enough coast guard could make fish at least partly excludable. Similarly, although fish are generally rival in consumption, this would be less true if the population of fishermen were small relative to the population of fish. (Think of North American fishing waters before the arrival of European settlers.) For purposes of our analysis, however, it will be helpful to group goods into these four categories.

In this chapter, we examine goods that are not excludable: public goods and common resources. Because people cannot be prevented from using these goods, they are available to everyone free of charge. The study of public goods and common resources is closely related to the study of externalities. For both of these types of goods, externalities arise because something of value has no price attached to it. If one person were to provide a public good, such as a tornado siren, other people would be better off. They would receive a benefit without paying for it—a positive externality. Similarly, when one person uses a common resource such as the fish in the ocean, other people are worse off because there are fewer fish to catch. They suffer a loss but are not compensated for it—a negative externality. Because of these external effects, private decisions about consumption and production can lead to an inefficient allocation of resources, and government intervention can potentially raise economic well-being.

QuickQuiz *Define* public goods *and* common resources *and give an example of each.*

11-2 Public Goods

To understand how public goods differ from other goods and why they present problems for society, let's consider an example: a fireworks display. This good is not excludable because it is impossible to prevent someone from seeing fireworks, and it is not rival in consumption because one person's enjoyment of fireworks does not reduce anyone else's enjoyment of them.

11-2a The Free-Rider Problem

The citizens of Smalltown, U.S.A., like seeing fireworks on the Fourth of July. Each of the town's 500 residents places a $10 value on the experience for a total benefit of $5,000. The cost of putting on a fireworks display is $1,000. Because the $5,000 benefit exceeds the $1,000 cost, it is efficient for Smalltown to have a fireworks display on the Fourth of July.

Would the private market produce the efficient outcome? Probably not. Imagine that Ella, a Smalltown entrepreneur, decided to put on a fireworks display. Ella would surely have trouble selling tickets to the event because her potential customers would quickly figure out that they could see the fireworks even without a ticket. Because fireworks are not excludable, people have an incentive to be free riders. A **free rider** is a person who receives the benefit of a good but does not pay for it. Because people would have an incentive to be free riders rather than ticket buyers, the market would fail to provide the efficient outcome.

free rider
a person who receives the benefit of a good but avoids paying for it

One way to view this market failure is that it arises because of an externality. If Ella puts on the fireworks display, she confers an external benefit on those who see the display without paying for it. When deciding whether to put on the display, however, Ella does not take the external benefits into account. Even though the fireworks display is socially desirable, it is not profitable. As a result, Ella makes the privately rational but socially inefficient decision not to put on the display.

Although the private market fails to supply the fireworks display demanded by Smalltown residents, the solution to Smalltown's problem is obvious: The local government can sponsor a Fourth of July celebration. The town council can raise everyone's taxes by $2 and use the revenue to hire Ella to produce the fireworks. Everyone in Smalltown is better off by $8—the $10 at which residents value the fireworks minus the $2 tax bill. Ella can help Smalltown reach the efficient outcome as a public employee even though she could not do so as a private entrepreneur.

The story of Smalltown is simplified but realistic. In fact, many local governments in the United States pay for fireworks on the Fourth of July. Moreover, the story shows a general lesson about public goods: Because public goods are not excludable, the free-rider problem prevents the private market from supplying them. The government, however, can remedy the problem. If the government decides that the total benefits of a public good exceed its costs, it can provide the public good, pay for it with tax revenue, and potentially make everyone better off.

11-2b Some Important Public Goods

There are many examples of public goods. Here we consider three of the most important.

National Defense The defense of a country from foreign aggressors is a classic example of a public good. Once the country is defended, it is impossible to prevent any single person from enjoying the benefit of this defense. And when one person enjoys the benefit of national defense, she does not reduce the benefit to anyone else. Thus, national defense is neither excludable nor rival in consumption.

National defense is also one of the most expensive public goods. In 2014, the U.S. federal government spent a total of $748 billion on national defense, more than $2,346 per person. People disagree about whether this amount is too small or too large, but almost no one doubts that some government spending for national defense is necessary. Even economists who advocate small government agree that national defense is a public good the government should provide.

"I like the concept if we can do it with no new taxes."

Basic Research Knowledge is created through research. In evaluating the appropriate public policy toward knowledge creation, it is important to distinguish general knowledge from specific technological knowledge. Specific technological knowledge, such as the invention of a longer-lasting battery, a smaller microchip, or a better digital music player, can be patented. The patent gives the inventor the exclusive right to the knowledge she has created for a period of time. Anyone else who wants to use the patented information must pay the inventor for the right to do so. In other words, the patent makes the knowledge created by the inventor excludable.

By contrast, general knowledge is a public good. For example, a mathematician cannot patent a theorem. Once a theorem is proven, the knowledge is not excludable: The theorem enters society's general pool of knowledge that anyone can use without charge. The theorem is also not rival in consumption: One person's use of the theorem does not prevent any other person from using the theorem.

Profit-seeking firms spend a lot on research trying to develop new products that they can patent and sell, but they do not spend much on basic research. Their incentive, instead, is to free ride on the general knowledge created by others. As a result, in the absence of any public policy, society would devote too few resources to creating new knowledge.

The government tries to provide the public good of general knowledge in various ways. Government agencies, such as the National Institutes of Health and the National Science Foundation, subsidize basic research in medicine, mathematics, physics, chemistry, biology, and even economics. Some people justify government funding of the space program on the grounds that it adds to society's pool of knowledge. Determining the appropriate level of government support for these endeavors is difficult because the benefits are hard to measure. Moreover, the members of Congress who appropriate funds for research usually have little expertise in science and, therefore, are not in the best position to judge what lines of research will produce the largest benefits. So, while basic research is surely a public good, we should not be surprised if the public sector fails to pay for the right amount and the right kinds.

Fighting Poverty Many government programs are aimed at helping the poor. The welfare system (officially called TANF, Temporary Assistance for Needy Families) provides a small income for some poor families. Food stamps (officially called SNAP, Supplemental Nutrition Assistance Program) subsidize the purchase of food for those with low incomes. And various government housing programs make shelter more affordable. These antipoverty programs are financed by taxes paid by families that are financially more successful.

Economists disagree among themselves about what role the government should play in fighting poverty. We discuss this debate more fully in Chapter 20, but here we note one important argument: Advocates of antipoverty programs claim that fighting poverty is a public good. Even if everyone prefers living in a society without poverty, fighting poverty is not a "good" that private actions will adequately provide.

To see why, suppose someone tried to organize a group of wealthy individuals to try to eliminate poverty. They would be providing a public good. This good would not be rival in consumption: One person's enjoyment of living in a society without poverty would not reduce anyone else's enjoyment of it. The good would not be excludable: Once poverty is eliminated, no one can be prevented from taking pleasure in this fact. As a result, there would be a tendency for people to free ride on the generosity of others, enjoying the benefits of poverty elimination without contributing to the cause.

Because of the free-rider problem, eliminating poverty through private charity will probably not work. Yet government action can solve this problem. Taxing the wealthy to raise the living standards of the poor can potentially make everyone better off. The poor are better off because they now enjoy a higher standard of living, and those paying the taxes are better off because they enjoy living in a society with less poverty.

CASE STUDY

ARE LIGHTHOUSES PUBLIC GOODS?

Some goods can switch between being public goods and being private goods depending on the circumstances. For example, a fireworks display is a public good if performed in a town with many residents. Yet if performed at a private amusement park, such as Walt Disney World, a fireworks display is more like a private good because visitors to the park pay for admission.

Another example is a lighthouse. Economists have long used lighthouses as an example of a public good. Lighthouses mark specific locations along the coast so that passing ships can avoid treacherous waters. The benefit that the lighthouse provides to the ship captain is neither excludable nor rival in consumption, so each captain has an incentive to free ride by using the lighthouse to navigate without paying for the service. Because of this free-rider problem, private markets usually fail to provide the lighthouses that ship captains need. As a result, most lighthouses today are operated by the government.

KEVIN BRINE/SHUTTERSTOCK.COM

What kind of good is this?

In some cases, however, lighthouses have been closer to private goods. On the coast of England in the 19th century, for example, some lighthouses were privately owned and operated. Instead of trying to charge ship captains for the service, however, the owner of the lighthouse charged the owner of the nearby port. If the port owner did not pay, the lighthouse owner turned off the light, and ships avoided that port.

In deciding whether something is a public good, one must determine who the beneficiaries are and whether these beneficiaries can be excluded from using the good. A free-rider problem arises when the number of beneficiaries is large and exclusion of any one of them is impossible. If a lighthouse benefits many ship captains, it is a public good. If it primarily benefits a single port owner, it is more like a private good. ●

11-2c The Difficult Job of Cost–Benefit Analysis

So far we have seen that the government provides public goods because the private market on its own will not produce an efficient quantity. Yet deciding that the government must play a role is only the first step. The government must then determine what kinds of public goods to provide and in what quantities.

Suppose that the government is considering a public project, such as building a new highway. To judge whether to build the highway, it must compare the total benefits for all those who would use it to the costs of building and maintaining it. To make this decision, the government might hire a team of economists and engineers to conduct a study, called a **cost–benefit analysis**, to estimate the total costs and benefits of the project to society as a whole.

cost–benefit analysis
a study that compares the costs and benefits to society of providing a public good

Cost–benefit analysts have a tough job. Because the highway will be available to everyone free of charge, there is no price with which to judge the value of the highway. Simply asking people how much they would value the highway is not reliable: Quantifying benefits is difficult using the results from a questionnaire, and respondents have little incentive to tell the truth. Those who would use the highway have an incentive to exaggerate the benefit they receive to get the highway built. Those who would be harmed by the highway have an incentive to exaggerate the costs to them to prevent the highway from being built.

The efficient provision of public goods is, therefore, intrinsically more difficult than the efficient provision of private goods. When buyers of a private good enter a market, they reveal the value they place on it through the prices they are willing to pay. At the same time, sellers reveal their costs with the prices they are willing to accept. The equilibrium is an efficient allocation of resources because it reflects all this information. By contrast, cost–benefit analysts do not have any price signals to observe when evaluating whether the government should provide a public good and how much to provide. Their findings on the costs and benefits of public projects are rough approximations at best.

CASE STUDY

HOW MUCH IS A LIFE WORTH?

Imagine that you have been elected to serve as a member of your local town council. The town engineer comes to you with a proposal: The town can spend $10,000 to install and operate a traffic light at a town intersection that now has only a stop sign. The benefit of the traffic light is increased safety. The engineer estimates, based on data from similar intersections, that the traffic light would reduce the risk of a fatal traffic accident over the lifetime of the traffic light from 1.6 to 1.1 percent. Should you spend the money for the new light?

To answer this question, you turn to cost–benefit analysis. But you quickly run into an obstacle: The costs and benefits must be measured in the same units if you are to compare them meaningfully. The cost is measured in dollars, but the benefit—the possibility of saving a person's life—is not directly monetary. To make your decision, you have to put a dollar value on a human life.

At first, you may be tempted to conclude that a human life is priceless. After all, there is probably no amount of money that you could be paid to voluntarily give up your life or that of a loved one. This suggests that a human life has an infinite dollar value.

For the purposes of cost–benefit analysis, however, this answer leads to nonsensical results. If we truly placed an infinite value on human life, we should place traffic lights on every street corner, and we should all drive large cars loaded with the latest safety features. Yet traffic lights are not at every corner, and people sometimes choose to pay less for smaller cars without safety options such as side-impact air bags or antilock brakes. In both our public and private decisions, we are at times willing to risk our lives to save some money.

Once we have accepted the idea that a person's life has an implicit dollar value, how can we determine what that value is? One approach, sometimes used by courts to award damages in wrongful-death suits, is to look at the total amount of money a person would have earned if she had lived. Economists are often critical of this approach because it ignores other opportunity costs of losing one's life. It thus has the bizarre implication that the life of a retired or disabled person has no value.

A better way to value human life is to look at the risks that people are voluntarily willing to take and how much they must be paid for taking them. For example, mortality risk varies across jobs. Construction workers in high-rise buildings face greater risk of death on the job than office workers do. By comparing wages in risky and less risky occupations, controlling for education, experience, and other determinants of wages, economists can get some sense about what value people put on their own lives. Studies using this approach conclude that the value of a human life is about $10 million.

We can now return to our original example and respond to the town engineer. The traffic light reduces the risk of fatality by 0.5 percentage points. Thus, the expected benefit from installing the traffic light is 0.005 × $10 million, or $50,000. This estimate of the benefit exceeds the cost of $10,000, so you should approve the project. ●

QuickQuiz *What is the free-rider problem? Why does the free-rider problem induce the government to provide public goods? • How should the government decide whether to provide a public good?*

11-3 Common Resources

Common resources, like public goods, are not excludable: They are available free of charge to anyone who wants to use them. Common resources are, however, rival in consumption: One person's use of the common resource reduces other people's ability to use it. Thus, common resources give rise to a new problem: Once the good is provided, policymakers need to be concerned about how much it is used. This problem is best understood from the classic parable called the **Tragedy of the Commons**.

Tragedy of the Commons a parable that illustrates why common resources are used more than is desirable from the standpoint of society as a whole

11-3a The Tragedy of the Commons

Consider life in a small medieval town. Of the many economic activities that take place in the town, one of the most important is raising sheep. Many of the town's families own flocks of sheep and support themselves by selling the sheep's wool, which is used to make clothing.

As our story begins, the sheep spend much of their time grazing on the land surrounding the town, called the Town Common. No family owns the land. Instead, the town residents own the land collectively, and all the residents are allowed to graze their sheep on it. Collective ownership works well because land is plentiful. As long as everyone can get all the good grazing land they want, the Town Common is not rival in consumption, and allowing residents' sheep to graze for free causes no problems. Everyone in the town is happy.

As the years pass, the population of the town grows, and so does the number of sheep grazing on the Town Common. With a growing number of sheep and a fixed amount of land, the land starts to lose its ability to replenish itself. Eventually, the land is grazed so heavily that it becomes barren. With no grass left on the Town Common, raising sheep is impossible, and the town's once prosperous wool industry disappears. Many families lose their source of livelihood.

What causes the tragedy? Why do the shepherds allow the sheep population to grow so large that it destroys the Town Common? The reason is that social and private incentives differ. Avoiding the destruction of the grazing land depends on the collective action of the shepherds. If the shepherds acted together, they could reduce the sheep population to a size that the Town Common can support. Yet no single family has an incentive to reduce the size of its own flock because each flock represents only a small part of the problem.

In essence, the Tragedy of the Commons arises because of an externality. When one family's flock grazes on the common land, it reduces the quality of the land available for other families. Because people neglect this negative externality when deciding how many sheep to own, the result is an excessive number of sheep.

If the tragedy had been foreseen, the town could have solved the problem in various ways. It could have regulated the number of sheep in each family's flock, internalized the externality by taxing sheep, or auctioned off a limited number of sheep-grazing permits. That is, the medieval town could have dealt with the problem of overgrazing in the way that modern society deals with the problem of pollution.

In the case of land, however, there is a simpler solution. The town can divide the land among town families. Each family can enclose its parcel of land with a fence and then protect it from excessive grazing. In this way, the land becomes a private good rather than a common resource. This outcome in fact occurred during the enclosure movement in England during the 17th century.

The Tragedy of the Commons is a story with a general lesson: When one person uses a common resource, she diminishes other people's enjoyment of it. Because of this negative externality, common resources tend to be used excessively. The government can solve the problem by using regulation or taxes to reduce consumption of the common resource. Alternatively, the government can sometimes turn the common resource into a private good.

This lesson has been known for thousands of years. The ancient Greek philosopher Aristotle pointed out the problem with common resources: "What is common to many is taken least care of, for all men have greater regard for what is their own than for what they possess in common with others."

ASK THE EXPERTS

Congestion Pricing

"In general, using more congestion charges in crowded transportation networks — such as higher tolls during peak travel times in cities, and peak fees for airplane takeoff and landing slots — and using the proceeds to lower other taxes would make citizens on average better off."

What do economists say?

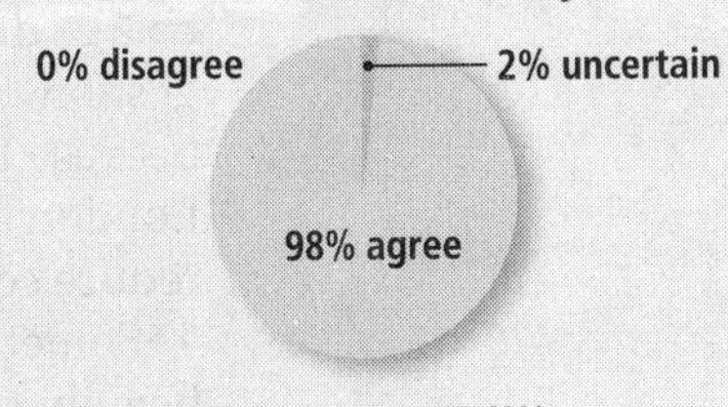

Source: IGM Economic Experts Panel, January 11, 2012.

11-3b Some Important Common Resources

There are many examples of common resources. In almost all cases, the same problem arises as in the Tragedy of the Commons: Private decision makers use the common resource too much. As a result, governments often regulate behavior or impose fees to mitigate the problem of overuse.

Clean Air and Water As we discussed in Chapter 10, markets do not adequately protect the environment. Pollution is a negative externality that can be remedied with regulations or with corrective taxes on polluting activities. One can view this market failure as an example of a common-resource problem. Clean air and clean water are common resources like open grazing land, and excessive pollution is like excessive grazing. Environmental degradation is a modern Tragedy of the Commons.

Congested Roads Roads can be either public goods or common resources. If a road is not congested, then one person's use does not affect anyone else. In this case, use is not rival in

IN THE NEWS

The Case for Toll Roads

Many economists think drivers should be charged more for using roads. Here is why.

Why You'll Love Paying for Roads That Used to Be Free

By Eric A. Morris

To end the scourge of traffic congestion, Julius Caesar banned most carts from the streets of Rome during daylight hours. It didn't work—traffic jams just shifted to dusk. Two thousand years later, we have put a man on the moon and developed garments infinitely more practical than the toga, but we seem little nearer to solving the congestion problem.

If you live in a city, particularly a large one, you probably need little convincing that traffic congestion is frustrating and wasteful. According to the Texas Transportation Institute, the average American urban traveler lost 38 hours, nearly one full work week, to congestion in 2005. And congestion is getting worse, not better; urban travelers in 1982 were delayed only 14 hours that year.

Americans want action, but unfortunately there aren't too many great ideas about what that action might be. As Anthony Downs's excellent book *Still Stuck in Traffic: Coping With Peak-Hour Traffic Congestion* chronicles, most of the proposed solutions are too difficult to implement, won't work, or both.

Fortunately, there is one remedy which is both doable and largely guaranteed to succeed. In the space of a year or two we could have you zipping along the 405 or the LIE at the height of rush hour at a comfortable 55 miles per hour.

There's just one small problem with this silver bullet for congestion: many people seem to prefer the werewolf. Despite its merits, this policy, which is known as "congestion pricing," "value pricing," or "variable tolling," is not an easy political sell.

For decades, economists and other transportation thinkers have advocated imposing tolls that vary with congestion levels on roadways. Simply put, the more congestion, the higher the toll, until the congestion goes away.

To many people, this sounds like a scheme by mustache-twirling bureaucrats and their academic apologists to fleece drivers out of their hard-earned cash. Why should drivers have to pay to use roads their tax dollars have already paid for? Won't the remaining free roads be swamped as drivers are forced off the tolled roads? Won't the working-class and poor be the victims here, as the tolled routes turn into "Lexus lanes"?

And besides, adopting this policy would mean listening to economists, and who wants to do that?

There's a real problem with this logic, which is that, on its own terms, it makes perfect sense (except for the listening to economists part). Opponents of tolls are certainly not stupid, and their arguments deserve serious consideration. But in the end, their concerns are largely overblown, and the benefits of tolling swamp the potential costs.

Unfortunately, it can be hard to convey this because the theory behind tolling is somewhat complex and counterintuitive. This is too bad, because variable tolling is an excellent public policy. Here's why: the basic economic theory is that when you give out something valuable—in this case, road space—for less than its true value, shortages result.

Ultimately, there's no free lunch; instead of paying with money, you pay with the effort

consumption, and the road is a public good. Yet if a road is congested, then use of that road yields a negative externality. When one person drives on the road, it becomes more crowded, and other people must drive more slowly. In this case, the road is a common resource.

One way for the government to address the problem of road congestion is to charge drivers a toll. A toll is, in essence, a corrective tax on the externality of congestion. Sometimes, as in the case of local roads, tolls are not a practical solution because the cost of collecting them is too high. But several major cities, including London and Stockholm, have found increasing tolls to be a very effective way to reduce congestion.

Sometimes congestion is a problem only at certain times of day. If a bridge is heavily traveled only during rush hour, for instance, the congestion externality is largest during this time. The efficient way to deal with these externalities is and time needed to acquire the good. Think of Soviet shoppers spending their lives in endless queues to purchase artificially low-priced but exceedingly scarce goods. Then think of Americans who can fulfill nearly any consumerist fantasy quickly but at a monetary cost. Free but congested roads have left us shivering on the streets of Moscow.

To consider it another way, delay is an externality imposed by drivers on their peers. By driving onto a busy road and contributing to congestion, drivers slow the speeds of others—but they never have to pay for it, at least not directly. In the end, of course, everybody pays, because as we impose congestion on others, others impose it on us. This degenerates into a game that nobody can win.

Markets work best when externalities are internalized: i.e., you pay for the hassle you inflict on others. . . . Using tolls to help internalize the congestion externality would somewhat reduce the number of trips made on the most congested roads at the peak usage periods; some trips would be moved to less congested times and routes, and others would be foregone entirely. This way we would cut down on the congestion costs we impose on each other.

Granted, tolls cannot fully cope with accidents and other incidents, which are major causes of delay. But pricing can largely eliminate chronic, recurring congestion. No matter how high the demand for a road, there is a level of toll that will keep it flowing freely.

To make tolling truly effective, the price must be right. Too high a price drives away too many cars and the road does not function at its capacity. Too low a price and congestion isn't licked.

The best solution is to vary the tolls in real time based on an analysis of current traffic conditions. Pilot toll projects on roads (like the I-394 in Minnesota and the I-15 in Southern California) use sensors embedded in the pavement to monitor the number and speeds of vehicles on the facility.

A simple computer program then determines the number of cars that should be allowed in. The computer then calculates the level of toll that will attract that number of cars—and no more. Prices are then updated every few minutes on electronic message signs. Hi-tech transponders and antenna arrays make waiting at toll booths a thing of the past.

The bottom line is that speeds are kept high (over 45 m.p.h.) so that throughput is higher than when vehicles are allowed to crowd all at once onto roadways at rush hour, slowing traffic to a crawl.

To maximize efficiency, economists would like to price all travel, starting with the freeways. But given that elected officials have no burning desire to lose their jobs, a more realistic option, for now, is to toll just some freeway lanes that are either new capacity or underused carpool lanes. The other lanes would be left free—and congested. Drivers will then have a choice: wait or pay. Granted, neither is ideal. But right now drivers have no choice at all.

What's the bottom line here? The state of Washington recently opened congestion-priced lanes on its State Route 167. The peak toll in the first month of operation (reached on the evening of Wednesday, May 21) was $5.75. I know, I know, you would never pay such an exorbitant amount when America has taught you that free roads are your birthright. But that money bought Washington drivers a 27-minute time savings. Is a half hour of your time worth $6?

I think I already know the answer, and it is "it depends." Most people's value of time varies widely depending on their activities on any given day. Late for picking the kids up from daycare? Paying $6 to save a half hour is an incredible bargain. Have to clean the house? The longer your trip home takes, the better. Tolling will introduce a new level of flexibility and freedom into your life, giving you the power to tailor your travel costs to fit your schedule. ■

Source: Freakonomics blog, January 6, 2009.

to charge higher tolls during rush hour. This toll would provide an incentive for drivers to alter their schedules, reducing traffic when congestion is greatest.

Another policy that responds to the problem of road congestion (discussed in the previous chapter) is the tax on gasoline. A higher gasoline tax increases the price of gasoline, reduces the amount that people drive, and reduces road congestion. The gasoline tax is an imperfect solution to congestion, however, because it affects other decisions besides the amount of driving on congested roads. In particular, the tax also discourages driving on uncongested roads, even though there is no congestion externality for these roads.

Fish, Whales, and Other Wildlife Many species of animals are common resources. Fish and whales, for instance, have commercial value, and anyone can go to the ocean and catch whatever is available. Each person has little incentive to maintain the species for the next year. Just as excessive grazing can destroy the Town Common, excessive fishing and whaling can destroy commercially valuable marine populations.

Oceans remain one of the least regulated common resources. Two problems prevent an easy solution. First, many countries have access to the oceans, so any solution would require international cooperation among countries that hold different values. Second, because the oceans are so vast, enforcing any agreement is difficult. As a result, fishing rights have been a frequent source of international tension among normally friendly countries.

Within the United States, various laws aim to manage the use of fish and other wildlife. For example, the government charges for fishing and hunting licenses, and it restricts the lengths of the fishing and hunting seasons. Fishermen are often required to throw back small fish, and hunters can kill only a limited number of animals. All these laws reduce the use of a common resource and help maintain animal populations.

CASE STUDY

WHY THE COW IS NOT EXTINCT

Throughout history, many species of animals have been threatened with extinction. When Europeans first arrived in North America, more than 60 million buffalo roamed the continent. Unfortunately, however, hunting the buffalo was so popular during the 19th century that by 1900 the animal's population had fallen to about 400 before the government stepped in to protect the species. In some African countries today, elephants face a similar challenge, as poachers kill them for the ivory in their tusks.

Yet not all animals with commercial value face this threat. The cow, for example, is a valuable source of food, but no one worries that the cow will soon be extinct. Indeed, the great demand for beef seems to ensure that the species will continue to thrive.

VICENTE BARCELO VARONA/SHUTTERSTOCK.COM

"Will the market protect me?"

Why does the commercial value of ivory threaten the elephant, while the commercial value of beef protects the cow? The reason is that elephants are a common resource, whereas cows are a private good. Elephants roam freely without any owners. Each poacher has a strong incentive to kill as many elephants as she can find. Because poachers are numerous, each poacher has only a slight incentive to preserve the elephant population. By contrast, cattle live on ranches that are privately owned. Each rancher makes a great effort to maintain the cattle population on her ranch because she reaps the benefit.

Governments have tried to solve the elephant's problem in two ways. Some countries, such as Kenya, Tanzania, and Uganda, have made it illegal to kill elephants and sell their ivory. Yet these laws have been hard to enforce, and the battle between the authorities and the poachers has become increasingly violent. Meanwhile, elephant populations have continued to dwindle. By contrast, other countries, such as Botswana, Malawi, Namibia, and Zimbabwe, have made elephants a private good by allowing people to kill elephants, but only those on their own property. Landowners now have an incentive to preserve the species on their own land, and as a result, elephant populations have started to rise. With private ownership and the profit motive now on its side, the African elephant might someday be as safe from extinction as the cow. ●

QuickQuiz *Why do governments try to limit the use of common resources?*

11-4 Conclusion: The Importance of Property Rights

In this and the previous chapter, we have seen there are some "goods" that the market does not provide adequately. Markets do not ensure that the air we breathe is clean or that our country is defended from foreign aggressors. Instead, societies rely on the government to protect the environment and to provide for the national defense.

The problems we considered in these chapters arise in many different markets, but they share a common theme. In all cases, the market fails to allocate resources efficiently because *property rights* are not well established. That is, some item of value does not have an owner with the legal authority to control it. For example, although no one doubts that the "good" of clean air or national defense is valuable, no one has the right to attach a price to it and profit from its use. A factory pollutes too much because no one charges the factory for the pollution it emits. The market does not provide for national defense because no one can charge those who are defended for the benefit they receive.

When the absence of property rights causes a market failure, the government can potentially solve the problem. Sometimes, as in the sale of pollution permits, the solution is for the government to help define property rights and thereby unleash market forces. Other times, as in restricted hunting seasons, the solution is for the government to regulate private behavior. Still other times, as in the provision of national defense, the solution is for the government to use tax revenue to supply a good that the market fails to supply. In each of these cases, if the policy is well planned and well run, it can make the allocation of resources more efficient and thus raise economic well-being.

CHAPTER QuickQuiz

1. Which categories of goods are excludable?
   a. private goods and club goods
   b. private goods and common resources
   c. public goods and club goods
   d. public goods and common resources
2. Which categories of goods are rival in consumption?
   a. private goods and club goods
   b. private goods and common resources
   c. public goods and club goods
   d. public goods and common resources
3. Which of the following is an example of a public good?
   a. residential housing
   b. national defense
   c. restaurant meals
   d. fish in the ocean
4. Which of the following is an example of a common resource?
   a. residential housing
   b. national defense
   c. restaurant meals
   d. fish in the ocean
5. Public goods are
   a. efficiently provided by market forces.
   b. underprovided in the absence of government.
   c. overused in the absence of government.
   d. a type of natural monopoly.
6. Common resources are
   a. efficiently provided by market forces.
   b. underprovided in the absence of government.
   c. overused in the absence of government.
   d. a type of natural monopoly.

SUMMARY

- Goods differ in whether they are excludable and whether they are rival in consumption. A good is excludable if it is possible to prevent someone from using it. A good is rival in consumption if one person's use of the good reduces others' ability to use the same unit of the good. Markets work best for private goods, which are both excludable and rival in consumption. Markets do not work as well for other types of goods.
- Public goods are neither rival in consumption nor excludable. Examples of public goods include fireworks displays, national defense, and the discovery of fundamental knowledge. Because people are not charged for their use of the public good, they have an incentive to free ride, making private provision of the good untenable. Therefore, governments provide public goods, basing their decision about the quantity of each good on cost–benefit analysis.
- Common resources are rival in consumption but not excludable. Examples include common grazing land, clean air, and congested roads. Because people are not charged for their use of common resources, they tend to use them excessively. Therefore, governments use various methods, such as regulations and corrective taxes, to limit the use of common resources.

KEY CONCEPTS

excludability, p. 212
rivalry in consumption, p. 212
private goods, p. 212
public goods, p. 212
common resources, p. 213
club goods, p. 213
free rider, p. 214
cost–benefit analysis, p. 217
Tragedy of the Commons, p. 218

QUESTIONS FOR REVIEW

1. Explain what is meant by a good being "excludable." Explain what is meant by a good being "rival in consumption." Is a slice of pizza excludable? Is it rival in consumption?
2. Define and give an example of a public good. Can the private market provide this good on its own? Explain.
3. What is cost–benefit analysis of public goods? Why is it important? Why is it hard?
4. Define and give an example of a common resource. Without government intervention, will people use this good too much or too little? Why?

PROBLEMS AND APPLICATIONS

1. Think about the goods and services provided by your local government.
   a. Using the classification in Figure 1, explain which category each of the following goods falls into:
      - police protection
      - snow plowing
      - education
      - rural roads
      - city streets

   b. Why do you think the government provides items that are not public goods?
2. Both public goods and common resources involve externalities.
   a. Are the externalities associated with public goods generally positive or negative? Use examples in your answer. Is the free-market quantity of public goods generally greater or less than the efficient quantity?
   b. Are the externalities associated with common resources generally positive or negative? Use examples in your answer. Is the free-market use of common resources generally greater or less than the efficient use?
3. Fredo loves watching *Downton Abbey* on his local public TV station, but he never sends any money to support the station during its fund-raising drives.
   a. What name do economists have for people like Fredo?
   b. How can the government solve the problem caused by people like Fredo?
   c. Can you think of ways the private market can solve this problem? How does the existence of cable TV alter the situation?

4. Wireless, high-speed Internet is provided for free in the airport of the city of Communityville.
   a. At first, only a few people use the service. What type of a good is this and why?
   b. Eventually, as more people find out about the service and start using it, the speed of the connection begins to fall. Now what type of a good is the wireless Internet service?
   c. What problem might result and why? What is one possible way to correct this problem?

5. Four roommates are planning to spend the weekend in their dorm room watching old movies, and they are debating how many to watch. Here is their willingness to pay for each film:

	Steven	Peter	James	Christopher
First film	$7	$5	$3	$2
Second film	6	4	2	1
Third film	5	3	1	0
Fourth film	4	2	0	0
Fifth film	3	1	0	0

   a. Within the dorm room, is the showing of a movie a public good? Why or why not?
   b. If it costs $8 to rent a movie, how many movies should the roommates rent to maximize total surplus?
   c. If they choose the optimal number from part (b) and then split the cost of renting the movies equally, how much surplus does each person obtain from watching the movies?
   d. Is there any way to split the cost to ensure that everyone benefits? What practical problems does this solution raise?
   e. Suppose they agree in advance to choose the efficient number and to split the cost of the movies equally. When Steven is asked his willingness to pay, will he have an incentive to tell the truth? If so, why? If not, what will he be tempted to say?
   f. What does this example teach you about the optimal provision of public goods?

6. Some economists argue that private firms will not undertake the efficient amount of basic scientific research.
   a. Explain why this might be so. In your answer, classify basic research in one of the categories shown in Figure 1.
   b. What sort of policy has the United States adopted in response to this problem?
   c. It is often argued that this policy increases the technological capability of American producers relative to that of foreign firms. Is this argument consistent with your classification of basic research in part (a)? (*Hint*: Can excludability apply to some potential beneficiaries of a public good and not others?)

7. Two towns, each with three members, are deciding whether to put on a fireworks display to celebrate the New Year. Fireworks cost $360. In each town, some people enjoy fireworks more than others.
   a. In the town of Bayport, each of the residents values the public good as follows:

Frank	$50
Joe	$100
Callie	$300

   Would fireworks pass a cost–benefit analysis? Explain.
   b. The mayor of Bayport proposes to decide by majority rule and, if the fireworks referendum passes, to split the cost equally among all residents. Who would vote in favor, and who would vote against? Would the vote yield the same answer as the cost–benefit analysis?
   c. In the town of River Heights, each of the residents values the public good as follows:

Nancy	$20
Bess	$140
Ned	$160

   Would fireworks pass a cost–benefit analysis? Explain.
   d. The mayor of River Heights also proposes to decide by majority rule and, if the fireworks referendum passes, to split the cost equally among all residents. Who would vote in favor, and who would vote against? Would the vote yield the same answer as the cost–benefit analysis?
   e. What do you think these examples say about the optimal provision of public goods?

8. There is often litter along highways but rarely in people's yards. Provide an economic explanation for this fact.

9. Many transportation systems, such as the Washington, D.C., Metro (subway), charge higher fares during rush hours than during the rest of the day. Why might they do this?

10. High-income people are willing to pay more than lower-income people to avoid the risk of death. For example, they are more likely to pay for safety features on cars. Do you think cost–benefit analysts should take this fact into account when evaluating public projects? Consider, for instance, a rich town and a poor town, both of which are considering the installation of a traffic light. Should the rich town use a higher dollar value for a human life in making this decision? Why or why not?

To find additional study resources, visit cengagebrain.com, and search for "Mankiw."

The Design of the Tax System

CHAPTER 12

Al "Scarface" Capone, the notorious 1920s gangster and crime boss, was never convicted for his many violent crimes. Yet, eventually, he did go to jail—for tax evasion. He had neglected to heed Ben Franklin's observation that "in this world nothing is certain but death and taxes."

When Franklin made this claim in 1789, the average American paid less than 5 percent of his income in taxes, and that remained true for the next hundred years. Over the course of the 20th century, however, taxes became ever more important in the life of the typical U.S. citizen. Today, all taxes taken together—including personal income taxes, corporate income taxes, payroll taxes, sales taxes, and property taxes—use up more than a quarter of the average American's income. In many European countries, the tax bite is even larger.

Taxes are inevitable because citizens expect their governments to provide them with various goods and services. One of the *Ten Principles of Economics* from Chapter 1 is that markets are usually a good way to organize economic activity. But market economies rely on property rights and the rule of law, and so the government provides police and courts. Another of the *Ten Principles of Economics* is that the government can sometimes improve market outcomes. When the government remedies an externality (such as air pollution), provides a public good (such as national defense), or regulates the use of a common resource (such as fish in a public lake), it can raise economic well-being. But these activities can be costly. For the government to perform these and its many other functions, it needs to raise revenue through taxation.

We began our study of taxation in earlier chapters, where we saw how a tax on a good affects the supply and demand for that good. In Chapter 6, we saw that a tax reduces the quantity sold in a market, and we examined how the burden of a tax is shared by buyers and sellers depending on the elasticities of supply and demand. In Chapter 8, we examined how taxes affect economic well-being. We learned that taxes can cause *deadweight losses*: The reduction in consumer and producer surplus resulting from a tax exceeds the revenue raised by the government.

In this chapter, we build on these lessons to discuss the design of a tax system. We begin with some basic facts about how the U.S. government raises money. We then discuss the fundamental principles of taxation. Most people agree that taxes should impose as small a cost on society as possible and that the burden of taxes should be distributed fairly. That is, the tax system should be both *efficient* and *equitable*. As we will see, however, stating these goals is easier than achieving them.

12-1 An Overview of U.S. Taxation

How much of the nation's income does the government collect as taxes? Figure 1 shows government revenue, including federal, state, and local, as a percentage of total income for the U.S. economy. It shows that the role of government has grown substantially over the past century. In 1902, the government collected only 7 percent of total income; in recent years, government has collected almost 30 percent. In other words, as the economy's income has grown, the government's revenue from taxation has grown even more.

Figure 2 compares the tax burden for several major countries, as measured by the government's tax revenue as a percentage of the nation's total income. The United States has a low tax burden compared to most other advanced economies. Many European nations have much higher taxes, which finance a more generous social safety net, including more substantial income support for the poor and unemployed.

12-1a Taxes Collected by the Federal Government

The U.S. federal government collects about two-thirds of the taxes in our economy. Table 1 shows the receipts of the federal government in 2014. Total receipts that year were $3.3 trillion, a number so large that it is hard to comprehend. To bring this astronomical number down to earth, we can divide it by the size of the U.S. population, which was about 319 million in 2014. We then find that the average American paid $10,235 to the federal government.

This figure shows revenue of the federal government and of state and local governments as a percentage of gross domestic product (GDP), which measures total income in the economy. It shows that the government plays a large role in the U.S. economy and that its role has grown over time.

Source: *Historical Statistics of the United States*; Bureau of Economic Analysis; and author's calculations.

FIGURE 1

Government Revenue as a Percentage of GDP: Changes over Time

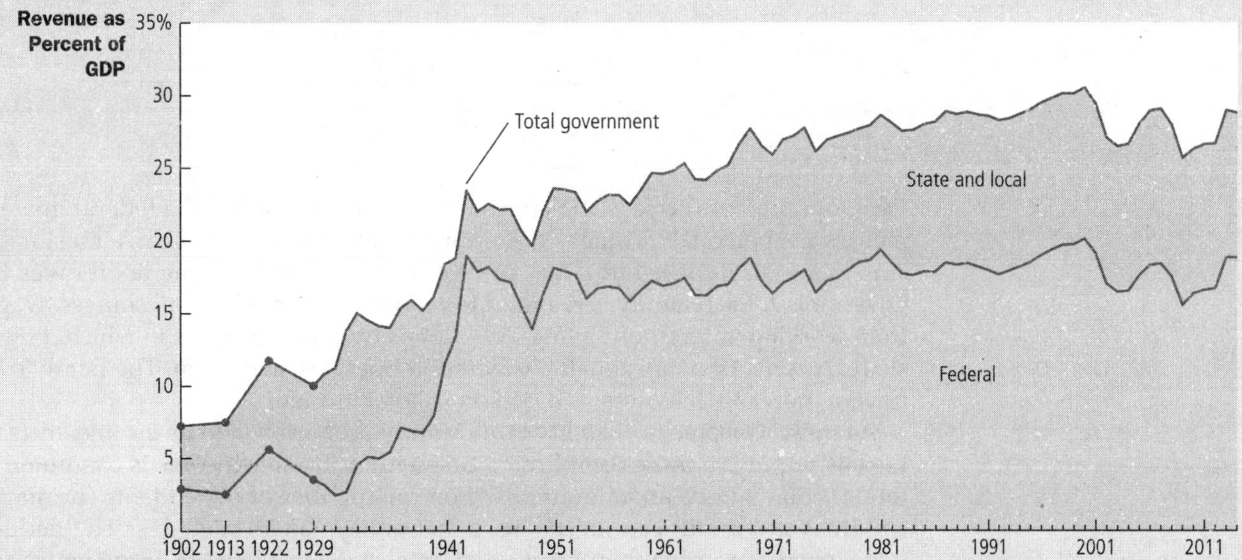

The percentage of income that governments take in taxes varies substantially from country to country.

Source: OECD. Data are for 2013.

FIGURE 2

Government Revenue as a Percentage of GDP: International Comparisons

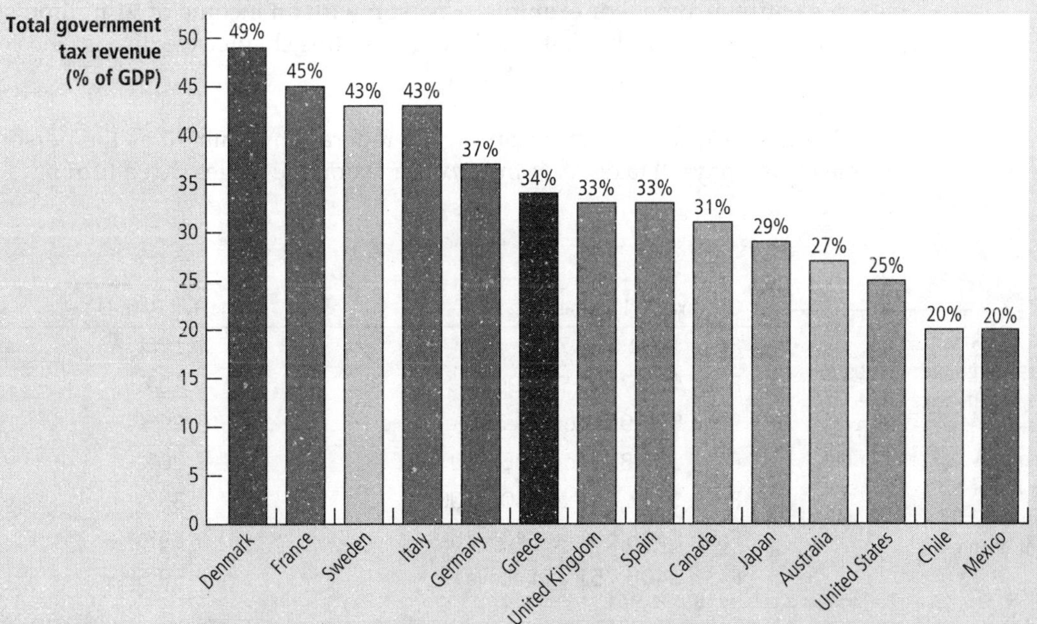

TABLE 1

Receipts of the Federal Government: 2014

Source: Bureau of Economic Analysis. Columns may not sum to total due to rounding.

Tax	Amount (billions)	Amount per Person	Percent of Receipts
Personal income taxes	$1,397	$4,379	43%
Social insurance taxes	1145	3,589	35
Corporate income taxes	418	1,310	13
Other	305	956	9
Total	$3,265	$10,235	100%

Personal Income Taxes The largest source of revenue for the federal government is the personal income tax. As April 15 approaches each year, almost every American family fills out a tax form to determine the income tax it owes the government. Each family is required to report its income from all sources: wages from working, interest on savings, dividends from corporations in which it owns shares, profits from any small businesses it operates, and so on. The family's *tax liability* (how much it owes) is based on its total income.

A family's income tax liability is not simply proportional to its income. Instead, the law requires a more complicated calculation. Taxable income is computed as total income minus an amount based on the number of dependents (primarily children) and minus certain expenses that policymakers have deemed "deductible" (such as mortgage interest payments, state and local tax payments, and charitable giving). Then the tax liability is calculated from taxable income using a schedule like the one shown in Table 2.

This table presents the *marginal tax rate*—the tax rate applied to each additional dollar of income. Because the marginal tax rate rises as income rises, higher-income families pay a larger percentage of their income in taxes. Note that each tax rate in the table applies only to income within the associated range, not to a person's entire income. For example, a person with an income of $1 million still pays only 10 percent of the first $9,075. (Later in this chapter we discuss the concept of the marginal tax rate more fully.)

Payroll Taxes Almost as important to the federal government as the personal income tax are payroll taxes. A *payroll tax* is a tax on the wages that a firm pays its

TABLE 2

The Federal Income Tax Rates: 2014

This table shows the marginal tax rates for an unmarried taxpayer. The taxes owed by a taxpayer depend on all the marginal tax rates up to his income level. For example, a taxpayer with income of $25,000 pays 10 percent of the first $9,075 of income, and then 15 percent of the rest.

On Taxable Income . . .	The Tax Rate Is . . .
From $0 to $9,075	10%
From $9,076 to $36,900	15%
From $36,901 to $89,350	25%
From $89,351 to $186,350	28%
From $186,351 to $405,100	33%
From $405,101 to $406,750	35%
From $406,751 and above	39.6%

workers. Table 1 calls this revenue *social insurance taxes* because the revenue from these taxes is mostly earmarked to pay for Social Security and Medicare. Social Security is an income-support program designed primarily to maintain the living standards of the elderly. Medicare is the government health program for the elderly. In 2014, the total payroll tax was 15.3 percent for annual earnings up to $117,000 and 2.9 percent of earnings above $117,000, together with an additional 0.9 percent for taxpayers with high income (above $200,000 if single, $250,000 if married). For many middle-income households, the payroll tax is the largest tax they pay.

Corporate Income Taxes Next in magnitude, but much smaller than either personal income taxes or social insurance taxes, is the corporate income tax. A *corporation* is a business set up to have its own legal existence, distinct and separate from its owners. The government taxes each corporation based on its profit—the amount the corporation receives for the goods or services it sells minus the costs of producing those goods or services. Notice that corporate profits are, in essence, taxed twice. They are taxed once by the corporate income tax when the corporation earns the profits, and they are taxed again by the personal income tax when the corporation uses its profits to pay dividends to its shareholders. In part to compensate for this double taxation, policymakers have decided to tax dividend income at lower rates than other types of income: In 2014, the top marginal tax rate on dividend income was only 20 percent (plus a 3.8 percent Medicare tax), compared with the top marginal tax rate on ordinary income of 39.6 percent (plus the same 3.8 percent).

Other Taxes The last category, labeled "other" in Table 1, makes up 9 percent of receipts. This category includes *excise taxes*, which are taxes on specific goods like gasoline, cigarettes, and alcoholic beverages. It also includes various small items, such as estate taxes and customs duties.

12-1b Taxes Collected by State and Local Governments

State and local governments collect about a third of all taxes paid. Table 3 shows the receipts of U.S. state and local governments. Total receipts for 2014 were $2,225 billion, or $6,975 per person. The table also shows how this total is broken down into different kinds of taxes.

The two most important taxes for state and local governments are sales taxes and property taxes. Sales taxes are levied as a percentage of the total amount spent

TABLE 3

Receipts of State and Local Governments: 2014

Tax	Amount (billions)	Amount per Person	Percent of Receipts
Sales taxes	$525	$1,646	24%
Property taxes	456	1,429	20
Personal income taxes	383	1,201	17
Corporate income taxes	58	182	3
Federal government	495	1,552	22
Other	308	966	14
Total	$2,225	$6,975	100%

Source: Bureau of Economic Analysis. Columns may not sum to total due to rounding.

at retail stores. Every time a customer buys something, he pays the storekeeper an extra amount that the storekeeper remits to the government. (Some states exclude certain items that are considered necessities, such as food and clothing.) Property taxes are levied on property owners as a percentage of the estimated value of land and structures. Together, these two taxes make up more than 40 percent of all receipts of state and local governments.

State and local governments also levy individual and corporate income taxes. In many cases, state and local income taxes are similar to federal income taxes. In other cases, they are quite different. For example, some states tax income from wages less heavily than income earned in the form of interest and dividends. Some states do not tax income at all.

State and local governments also receive substantial funds from the federal government. To some extent, the federal government's policy of sharing its revenue with state governments redistributes funds from high-income states (which pay more taxes) to low-income states (which receive more benefits). Often, these funds are tied to specific programs that the federal government wants to subsidize. For example, Medicaid provides healthcare for the poor; this program is managed by the states but much of the funding comes from the federal government.

Finally, state and local governments receive receipts from various sources included in the "other" category in Table 3. These include fees for fishing and hunting licenses, tolls from roads and bridges, and fares for public buses and subways.

QuickQuiz *What are the two most important sources of tax revenue for the federal government? • What are the two most important sources of tax revenue for state and local governments?*

12-2 Taxes and Efficiency

Now that we have seen how various levels of the U.S. government raise money in practice, let's consider how one might design a good tax system in principle. The primary aim of a tax system is to raise revenue for the government, but there are many ways to raise any given amount of money. When choosing among the many alternative taxes, policymakers have two objectives: efficiency and equity.

One tax system is more efficient than another if it raises the same amount of revenue at a smaller cost to taxpayers. What are the costs of taxes to taxpayers? The most obvious cost is the tax payment itself. This transfer of money from the taxpayer to the government is an inevitable feature of any tax system. Yet taxes also impose two other costs, which well-designed tax policy tries to avoid or, at least, minimize:

- The deadweight losses that result when taxes distort the decisions people make;
- The administrative burdens that taxpayers bear as they comply with the tax laws.

An efficient tax system is one that imposes small deadweight losses and small administrative burdens.

12-2a Deadweight Losses

One of the *Ten Principles of Economics* is that people respond to incentives, and this includes incentives provided by the tax system. If the government taxes ice cream, people eat less ice cream and more frozen yogurt. If the government taxes housing, people live in smaller houses and spend more of their income on other things. If the government taxes labor earnings, people work less and enjoy more leisure.

Because taxes distort incentives, they entail deadweight losses. As we first discussed in Chapter 8, the deadweight loss of a tax is the reduction in economic well-being of taxpayers in excess of the amount of revenue raised by the government. The deadweight loss is the inefficiency that a tax creates as people allocate resources according to the tax incentive rather than the true costs and benefits of the goods and services that they buy and sell.

To recall how taxes cause deadweight losses, consider an example. Suppose that Jake places an $8 value on a pizza and Jane places a $6 value on it. If there is no tax on pizza, the price of pizza will reflect the cost of making it. Let's suppose that the price of pizza is $5, so both Jake and Jane choose to buy one. Both consumers get some surplus of value over the amount paid. Jake gets consumer surplus of $3, and Jane gets consumer surplus of $1. Total surplus is $4.

Now suppose that the government levies a $2 tax on pizza and the price of pizza rises to $7. (This occurs if supply is perfectly elastic.) Jake still buys a pizza, but now he has consumer surplus of only $1. Jane now decides not to buy a pizza because its price is higher than its value to her. The government collects tax revenue of $2 on Jake's pizza. Total consumer surplus has fallen by $3 (from $4 to $1). Because total surplus has fallen by more than the tax revenue, the tax has a deadweight loss. In this case, the deadweight loss is $1.

Notice that the deadweight loss comes not from Jake, the person who pays the tax, but from Jane, the person who doesn't. The reduction of $2 in Jake's surplus exactly offsets the amount of revenue the government collects. The deadweight loss arises because the tax causes Jane to alter her behavior. When the tax raises the price of pizza, Jane is worse off, and yet there is no offsetting revenue to the government. This reduction in Jane's welfare is the deadweight loss of the tax.

BERRY'S WORLD REPRINTED BY PERMISSION OF UNITED FEATURE SYNDICATE, INC.

"I was gonna fix the place up, but if I did, the city would just raise my taxes!"

CASE STUDY

SHOULD INCOME OR CONSUMPTION BE TAXED?

When taxes cause people to change their behavior—such as inducing Jane to buy less pizza—the taxes cause deadweight losses and make the allocation of resources less efficient. As we have already seen, much government revenue comes from the personal income tax. In a case study in Chapter 8, we discussed how this tax discourages people from working as hard as they otherwise might. Another inefficiency caused by this tax is that it discourages people from saving.

Consider a 25-year-old deciding whether to save $1,000. If he puts this money in a savings account that earns 8 percent and leaves it there, he will have $21,720 when he retires at age 65. Yet if the government taxes one-fourth of his interest income each year, the effective interest rate is only 6 percent. After 40 years of earning 6 percent, the $1,000 grows to only $10,290, less than half of what it would have been without taxation. Thus, because interest income is taxed, saving is much less attractive.

Some economists advocate eliminating the current tax system's disincentive toward saving by changing the basis of taxation. Rather than taxing the amount of income that people earn, the government could tax the amount that people spend. Under this proposal, all income that is saved would not be taxed until the saving is later spent. This alternative system, called a *consumption tax*, would not distort people's saving decisions.

Various provisions of current law already make the tax system a bit like a consumption tax. Taxpayers can put a limited amount of their income into special savings accounts, such as Individual Retirement Accounts and 401(k) plans, and this income and the accumulated interest it earns escape taxation until the money is withdrawn at retirement. For people who do most of their saving through these retirement accounts, their tax bill is, in effect, based on their consumption rather than their income.

European countries tend to rely more on consumption taxes than does the United States. Most of them raise a significant amount of government revenue through a value-added tax, or a VAT. A VAT is like the retail sales tax that many U.S. states use. But rather than collecting all of the tax at the retail level when the consumer buys the final good, the government collects the tax in stages as the good is being produced (that is, as value is added by firms along the chain of production).

Various U.S. policymakers have proposed that the tax code move further in the direction of taxing consumption rather than income. In 2005, economist Alan Greenspan, then Chairman of the Federal Reserve, offered this advice to a presidential commission on tax reform: "As you know, many economists believe that a consumption tax would be best from the perspective of promoting economic growth—particularly if one were designing a tax system from scratch—because a consumption tax is likely to encourage saving and capital formation. However, getting from the current tax system to a consumption tax raises a challenging set of transition issues." ●

12-2b Administrative Burden

If you ask the typical person on April 15 for an opinion about the tax system, you might get an earful (perhaps peppered with expletives) about the headache of filling out tax forms. The administrative burden of any tax system is part of the inefficiency it creates. This burden includes not only the time spent in early April filling out forms but also the time spent throughout the year keeping records for tax purposes and the resources the government uses to enforce the tax laws.

Many taxpayers—especially those in higher tax brackets—hire tax lawyers and accountants to help them with their taxes. These experts in the complex tax laws fill out tax forms for their clients and help them arrange their affairs in a way that reduces the amount of taxes owed. This behavior is legal tax avoidance, which is different from illegal tax evasion.

Critics of our tax system say that these advisers help their clients avoid taxes by abusing some of the detailed provisions of the tax code, often dubbed "loopholes." In some cases, loopholes are congressional mistakes: They arise from ambiguities or omissions in the tax laws. More often, they arise because Congress has chosen to give special treatment to specific types of behavior. For example, the U.S. federal tax code gives preferential treatment to investors in municipal bonds because Congress wanted to make it easier for state and local governments to borrow money To some extent, this provision benefits states and localities, and to some extent, it benefits high-income taxpayers. Most loopholes are well known by those in Congress who make tax policy, but what looks like a loophole to one taxpayer may look like a justifiable tax deduction to another.

The resources devoted to complying with the tax laws are a type of deadweight loss. The government gets only the amount of taxes paid. By contrast, the taxpayer loses not only this amount but also the time and money spent documenting, computing, and avoiding taxes.

The administrative burden of the tax system could be reduced by simplifying the tax laws. Yet simplification is often politically difficult. Most people are ready to simplify the tax code by eliminating the loopholes that benefit others, but few are eager to give up the loopholes that they benefit from themselves. In the end, the complexity of the tax law results from the political process as various taxpayers with their own special interests lobby for their causes.

12-2c Marginal Tax Rates versus Average Tax Rates

When discussing the efficiency and equity of income taxes, economists distinguish between two notions of the tax rate: the average and the marginal. The **average tax rate** is total taxes paid divided by total income. The **marginal tax rate** is the amount by which taxes increase from an additional dollar of income.

average tax rate
total taxes paid divided by total income

marginal tax rate
the amount by which taxes increase from an additional dollar of income

For example, suppose that the government taxes 20 percent of the first $50,000 of income and 50 percent of all income above $50,000. Under this tax, a person who makes $60,000 pays a tax of $15,000: 20 percent of the first $50,000 ($0.20 \times \$50{,}000 = \$10{,}000$) plus 50 percent of the remaining $10,000 ($0.50 \times \$10{,}000 = \$5{,}000$). For this person, the average tax rate is $15,000 / $60,000, or 25 percent. But the marginal tax rate is 50 percent. If the taxpayer earned an additional dollar of income, that dollar would be subject to the 50 percent tax rate, so the amount the taxpayer would owe to the government would rise by $0.50.

The marginal and average tax rates each contain a useful piece of information. If we are trying to gauge the sacrifice made by a taxpayer, the average tax rate is more appropriate because it measures the fraction of income paid in taxes. By contrast, if we are trying to gauge how the tax system distorts incentives, the marginal tax rate is more meaningful. One of the *Ten Principles of Economics* in Chapter 1 is that rational people think at the margin. A corollary to this principle is that the marginal tax rate measures how much the tax system discourages people from working. If you are thinking of working an extra few hours, the marginal tax rate determines how much the government takes of your additional earnings. It is the marginal tax rate, therefore, that determines the deadweight loss of an income tax.

12-2d Lump-Sum Taxes

Suppose the government imposes a tax of $4,000 on everyone. That is, everyone owes the same amount, regardless of earnings or any actions that a person might take. Such a tax is called a **lump-sum tax.**

lump-sum tax
a tax that is the same amount for every person

A lump-sum tax shows clearly the difference between average and marginal tax rates. For a taxpayer with income of $20,000, the average tax rate of a $4,000 lump-sum tax is 20 percent; for a taxpayer with income of $40,000, the average tax rate is 10 percent. For both taxpayers, the marginal tax rate is zero because no tax is owed on an additional dollar of income.

A lump-sum tax is the most efficient tax possible. Because a person's decisions do not alter the amount owed, the tax does not distort incentives and, therefore, does not cause deadweight losses. Because everyone can easily compute the amount owed and because there is no benefit to hiring tax lawyers and accountants, the lump-sum tax imposes a minimal administrative burden on taxpayers.

If lump-sum taxes are so efficient, why do we rarely observe them in the real world? The reason is that efficiency is only one goal of the tax system. A lump-sum tax would take the same amount from the poor and the rich, an outcome most people would view as unfair. To understand the tax systems that we observe, we must therefore consider the other major goal of tax policy: equity.

QuickQuiz *What is meant by the efficiency of a tax system? • What can make a tax system inefficient?*

12-3 Taxes and Equity

Ever since American colonists dumped imported tea into Boston harbor to protest high British taxes, tax policy has generated some of the most heated debates in American politics. The heat is rarely fueled by questions of efficiency. Instead, it arises from disagreements over how the tax burden should be distributed. Senator Russell Long once mimicked the public debate with this ditty:

Don't tax you.
Don't tax me.
Tax that fella behind the tree.

Of course, if we rely on the government to provide some of the goods and services we want, then someone must pay taxes to fund those goods and services. In this section, we consider the equity of a tax system. How should the burden of taxes be divided among the population? How do we evaluate whether a tax system is fair? Everyone agrees that the tax system should be equitable, but there is much disagreement about how to judge the equity of a tax system.

12-3a The Benefits Principle

benefits principle the idea that people should pay taxes based on the benefits they receive from government services

One principle of taxation, called the **benefits principle**, states that people should pay taxes based on the benefits they receive from government services. This principle tries to make public goods similar to private goods. It seems fair that a person who often goes to the movies pays more in total for movie tickets than a person who rarely goes. Similarly, a person who gets great benefit from a public good should pay more for it than a person who gets little benefit.

The gasoline tax, for instance, is sometimes justified using the benefits principle. In some states, revenues from the gasoline tax are used to build and maintain roads. Because those who buy gasoline are the same people who use the roads, the gasoline tax might be viewed as a fair way to pay for this government service.

The benefits principle can also be used to argue that wealthy citizens should pay higher taxes than poorer ones. Why? Simply because the wealthy benefit more from public services. Consider, for example, the benefits of police protection from theft. Citizens with much to protect benefit more from police than do those with less to protect. Therefore, according to the benefits principle, the wealthy should contribute more than the poor to the cost of maintaining the police force.

The same argument can be used for many other public services, such as fire protection, national defense, and the court system.

It is even possible to use the benefits principle to argue for antipoverty programs funded by taxes on the wealthy. As we discussed in Chapter 11, people may prefer living in a society without poverty, suggesting that antipoverty programs are a public good. If the wealthy place a greater dollar value on this public good than members of the middle class do, perhaps just because the wealthy have more to spend, then according to the benefits principle, they should be taxed more heavily to pay for these programs.

12-3b The Ability-to-Pay Principle

Another way to evaluate the equity of a tax system is called the **ability-to-pay principle**, which states that taxes should be levied on a person according to how well that person can shoulder the burden. This principle is sometimes justified by the claim that all citizens should make an "equal sacrifice" to support the government. The magnitude of a person's sacrifice, however, depends not only on the size of his tax payment but also on his income and other circumstances: A $1,000 tax paid by a poor person may require a larger sacrifice than a $10,000 tax paid by a rich one.

The ability-to-pay principle leads to two corollary notions of equity: vertical equity and horizontal equity. **Vertical equity** states that taxpayers with a greater ability to pay should contribute a larger amount. **Horizontal equity** states that taxpayers with similar abilities to pay should contribute the same amount. These notions of equity are widely accepted, but applying them to evaluate a tax system is rarely straightforward.

ability-to-pay principle
the idea that taxes should be levied on a person according to how well that person can shoulder the burden

vertical equity
the idea that taxpayers with a greater ability to pay taxes should pay larger amounts

horizontal equity
the idea that taxpayers with similar abilities to pay taxes should pay the same amount

proportional tax
a tax for which high-income and low-income taxpayers pay the same fraction of income

regressive tax
a tax for which high-income taxpayers pay a smaller fraction of their income than do low-income taxpayers

progressive tax
a tax for which high-income taxpayers pay a larger fraction of their income than do low-income taxpayers

Vertical Equity If taxes are based on ability to pay, then richer taxpayers should pay more than poorer taxpayers. But how much more should the rich pay? The debate over tax policy often focuses on this question.

Consider the three tax systems in Table 4. In each case, taxpayers with higher incomes pay more. Yet the systems differ in how quickly taxes rise with income. The first system is called **proportional** because all taxpayers pay the same fraction of income. The second system is called **regressive** because high-income taxpayers pay a smaller fraction of their income, even though they pay a larger amount. The third system is called **progressive** because high-income taxpayers pay a larger fraction of their income.

Which of these three tax systems is most fair? There is no obvious answer, and economic theory does not offer any help in trying to find one. Equity, like beauty, is in the eye of the beholder.

TABLE 4
Three Tax Systems

	Proportional Tax		Regressive Tax		Progressive Tax	
Income	Amount of Tax	Percent of Income	Amount of Tax	Percent of Income	Amount of Tax	Percent of Income
$50,000	$12,500	25%	$15,000	30%	$10,000	20%
100,000	25,000	25	25,000	25	25,000	25
200,000	50,000	25	40,000	20	60,000	30

CASE STUDY

HOW THE TAX BURDEN IS DISTRIBUTED

The debate over tax policy often concerns whether the wealthy pay their fair share. There is no objective way to make this judgment. In evaluating the issue for yourself, however, it is useful to know how much families with different incomes pay under the current tax system.

Table 5 presents some data on how federal taxes are distributed among income classes. These figures are for 2011, the most recent year available as this book was going to press, and were tabulated by the Congressional Budget Office (CBO). They include all federal taxes—personal income taxes, payroll taxes, corporate income taxes, and excise taxes—but not state and local taxes. When calculating a household's tax burden, the CBO allocates corporate income taxes to the owners of capital and payroll taxes to workers.

To construct the table, households are ranked according to their income and placed into five groups of equal size, called *quintiles*. The table also presents data on the richest 1 percent of Americans. The second column of the table shows the average income of each group. Income includes both market income (income that households have earned from their work and savings) and transfer payments from government programs, such as Social Security and welfare. The poorest one-fifth of households had average income of $24,600, and the richest one-fifth had average income of $245,700. The richest 1 percent had average income of over $1.4 million.

The third column of the table shows total taxes as a percentage of income. As you can see, the U.S. federal tax system is progressive. The poorest fifth of households paid 1.9 percent of their incomes in taxes, and the richest fifth paid 23.4 percent. The top 1 percent paid 29.0 percent of their incomes.

The fourth and fifth columns compare the distribution of income with the distribution of taxes. The poorest quintile earned 5.3 percent of all income and paid 0.6 percent of all taxes. The richest quintile earned 51.9 percent of all income and paid 68.7 percent of all taxes. The richest 1 percent (which, remember, is 1/20 the size of each quintile) earned 14.6 percent of all income and paid 24.0 percent of all taxes.

These numbers on taxes paid are a good starting point for understanding how the burden of government is distributed, but they give an incomplete picture. Money flows not only from households to the government in the form of taxes but also from the government back to households in the form of transfer payments. In some ways, transfer payments are the opposite of taxes. Including transfers as negative taxes substantially changes the distribution of the tax burden.

TABLE 5

The Burden of Federal Taxes

Source: Congressional Budget Office. Figures are for 2011.

Quintile	Average Income	Taxes as a Percentage of Income	Percentage of All Income	Percentage of All Taxes
Lowest	$24,600	1.9%	5.3%	0.6%
Second	45,300	7.0	9.6	3.8
Middle	66,400	11.2	14.1	8.9
Fourth	97,500	15.2	20.4	17.6
Highest	245,700	23.4	51.9	68.7
Top 1%	1,453,100	29.0	14.6	24.0

The richest quintile of households still pays about one-quarter of its income to the government, even after transfers are subtracted, and the top 1 percent still pays almost 30 percent. By contrast, the average tax rate for the poorest quintile becomes a sizeable negative number. That is, typical households in the bottom of the income distribution receive substantially more in transfers than they pay in taxes. The lesson is clear: To understand fully the progressivity of government policies, one must take into account both what people pay and what they receive.

Finally, it is worth noting that the numbers in Table 5 are a bit out of date. In late 2012, the U.S. Congress passed and President Obama signed a tax bill that increased taxes significantly from those that prevailed previously, particularly for taxpayers at the top of the income distribution. As a result, the tax system in place for 2013 and beyond is more progressive than the one shown in the table. The Congressional Budget Office projects that for the top 1 percent, taxes as a percentage of income increased from 29.0 to 33.3 percent. ●

Horizontal Equity If taxes are based on ability to pay, then similar taxpayers should pay similar amounts of taxes. But what determines if two taxpayers are similar? Families differ in many ways. To evaluate whether a tax code is horizontally equitable, one must determine which differences are relevant for a family's ability to pay and which differences are not.

Suppose the Smith and Jones families each have income of $100,000. The Smiths have no children, but Mr. Smith has an illness that results in medical expenses of $40,000. The Joneses are in good health, but they have four children. Two of the Jones children are in college, generating tuition bills of $60,000. Would it be fair for these two families to pay the same tax because they have the same income? Would it be fair to give the Smiths a tax break to help them offset their high medical expenses? Would it be fair to give the Joneses a tax break to help them with their tuition expenses?

There are no easy answers to these questions. In practice, the U.S. tax code is filled with special provisions that alter a family's tax obligations based on its specific circumstances.

12-3c Tax Incidence and Tax Equity

Tax incidence—the study of who bears the burden of taxes—is central to evaluating tax equity. As we first saw in Chapter 6, the person who bears the burden of a tax is not always the person who gets the tax bill from the government. Because taxes alter supply and demand, they alter equilibrium prices. As a result, they affect people beyond those who, according to statute, actually pay the tax. When evaluating the vertical and horizontal equity of any tax, it is important to take these indirect effects into account.

Many discussions of tax equity ignore the indirect effects of taxes and are based on what economists mockingly call the *flypaper theory* of tax incidence. According to this theory, the burden of a tax, like a fly on flypaper, sticks wherever it first lands. This assumption, however, is rarely valid.

For example, a person not trained in economics might argue that a tax on expensive fur coats is vertically equitable because most buyers of furs are wealthy. Yet if these buyers can easily substitute other luxuries for furs, then a tax on furs might only reduce the sale of furs. In the end, the burden of the tax will fall more on those who make and sell furs than on those who buy them. Because most workers who make furs are not wealthy, the equity of a fur tax could be quite different from what the flypaper theory indicates.

CASE STUDY

WHO PAYS THE CORPORATE INCOME TAX?

The corporate income tax provides a good example of the importance of tax incidence for tax policy. The corporate tax is popular among voters. After all, corporations are not people. Voters are always eager to get a tax cut and let some impersonal corporation pick up the tab.

BILL PUGLIANO/GETTY IMAGES

This worker pays part of the corporate income tax.

But before deciding that the corporate income tax is a good way for the government to raise revenue, we should consider who bears the burden of the corporate tax. This is a difficult question on which economists disagree, but one thing is certain: *People pay all taxes*. When the government levies a tax on a corporation, the corporation is more like a tax collector than a taxpayer. The burden of the tax ultimately falls on people—the owners, customers, or workers of the corporation.

Many economists believe that workers and customers bear much of the burden of the corporate income tax. To see why, consider an example. Suppose that the U.S. government decides to raise the tax on the income earned by car companies. At first, this tax hurts the owners of the car companies, who receive less profit. But over time, these owners will respond to the tax. Because producing cars is less profitable, they invest less in building new car factories. Instead, they invest their wealth in other ways—for example, by buying larger houses or by building factories in other industries or other countries. With fewer car factories, the supply of cars declines, as does the demand for autoworkers. Thus, a tax on corporations making cars causes the price of cars to rise and the wages of autoworkers to fall.

The corporate income tax shows how dangerous the flypaper theory of tax incidence can be. The corporate income tax is popular in part because it *appears* to be paid by rich corporations. Yet those who bear the ultimate burden of the tax—the customers and workers of corporations—are often not rich. If the true incidence of the corporate tax were more widely known, this tax might be less popular among voters. ●

QuickQuiz *Explain the benefits principle and the ability-to-pay principle. • What are vertical equity and horizontal equity? • Why is studying tax incidence important for determining the equity of a tax system?*

12-4 Conclusion: The Trade-off between Equity and Efficiency

Almost everyone agrees that equity and efficiency are the two most important goals of a tax system. But these two goals often conflict, especially when equity is judged by the progressivity of the tax system. People often disagree about tax policy because they attach different weights to these goals.

The recent history of tax policy shows how political leaders differ in their views on equity and efficiency. When Ronald Reagan was elected president in 1980, the marginal tax rate on the earnings of the richest Americans was 50 percent. On interest income, the marginal tax rate was 70 percent. Reagan argued that such high tax rates greatly distorted economic incentives to work and save. In other words, he claimed that these high tax rates cost too much in terms of economic efficiency. Tax reform was, therefore, a high priority of his administration. Reagan signed into law large cuts in tax rates in 1981 and then again in 1986. When Reagan left office in 1989, the richest Americans faced a marginal tax rate of only 28 percent.

The pendulum of political debate swings both ways. When Bill Clinton ran for president in 1992, he argued that the rich were not paying their fair share of taxes. In other words, the low tax rates on the rich violated his view of vertical equity. In 1993, President Clinton signed into law a bill that raised the tax rates on the richest Americans to about 40 percent. When George W. Bush ran for president, he reprised many of Reagan's themes, and as president he reversed part of the Clinton tax increase, reducing the highest tax rate to 35 percent. Barack Obama pledged during the 2008 presidential campaign that he would raise taxes on high-income households, and starting in 2013 the top marginal tax rate was back at about 40 percent.

Economics alone cannot determine the best way to balance the goals of efficiency and equity. This issue involves political philosophy as well as economics. But economists have an important role in this debate: They can shed light on the trade-offs that society inevitably faces when designing the tax system and can help us avoid policies that sacrifice efficiency without any benefit in terms of equity.

CHAPTER QuickQuiz

1. The two largest sources of tax revenue for the U.S. federal government are
   a. personal and corporate income taxes.
   b. personal income taxes and payroll taxes for social insurance.
   c. corporate income taxes and payroll taxes for social insurance.
   d. payroll taxes for social insurance and property taxes.
2. Aiden gives piano lessons. He has an opportunity cost of $50 per lesson and charges $60. He has two students: Brandon, who has a willingness to pay of $70, and Chloe, who has a willingness to pay of $90. When the government puts a $20 tax on piano lessons and Aiden raises his price to $80, the deadweight loss is _____ and the tax revenue is _____.
   a. $10, $20
   b. $10, $40
   c. $20, $20
   d. $20, $40
3. If the tax code exempts the first $20,000 of income from taxation and then taxes 25 percent of all income above that level, then a person who earns $50,000 has an average tax rate of _____ percent and a marginal tax rate of _____ percent.
   a. 15, 25
   b. 25, 15
   c. 25, 30
   d. 30, 25
4. A toll is a tax on citizens who use toll roads. This policy can be viewed as an application of
   a. the benefits principle.
   b. horizontal equity.
   c. vertical equity.
   d. tax progressivity.
5. In the United States, taxpayers in the top 1 percent of the income distribution pay about _____ percent of their income in federal taxes.
   a. 5
   b. 10
   c. 20
   d. 30
6. If the corporate income tax induces businesses to reduce their capital investment, then
   a. the tax does not have any deadweight loss.
   b. corporate shareholders benefit from the tax.
   c. workers bear some of the burden of the tax.
   d. the tax achieves the goal of vertical equity.

SUMMARY

- The U.S. government raises revenue using various taxes. The most important taxes for the federal government are personal income taxes and payroll taxes for social insurance. The most important taxes for state and local governments are sales taxes and property taxes.
- The efficiency of a tax system refers to the costs it imposes on taxpayers. There are two costs of taxes beyond the transfer of resources from the taxpayer to the government. The first is the deadweight loss that arises as taxes alter incentives and distort the allocation of resources. The second is the administrative burden of complying with the tax laws.
- The equity of a tax system concerns whether the tax burden is distributed fairly among the population. According to the benefits principle, it is fair for people to pay taxes based on the benefits they receive from the government. According to the ability-to-pay principle, it is fair for people to pay taxes based on their capability to handle the financial burden. When evaluating the equity of a tax system, it is important to remember a lesson from the study of tax incidence: The distribution of tax burdens is not the same as the distribution of tax bills.
- When considering changes in the tax laws, policymakers often face a trade-off between efficiency and equity. Much of the debate over tax policy arises because people give different weights to these two goals.

KEY CONCEPTS

average tax rate, p. 235
marginal tax rate, p. 235
lump-sum tax, p. 235
benefits principle, p. 236
ability-to-pay principle, p. 237
vertical equity, p. 237
horizontal equity, p. 237
proportional tax, p. 237
regressive tax, p. 237
progressive tax, p. 237

QUESTIONS FOR REVIEW

1. Over the past century, has the government's tax revenue grown more or less slowly than the rest of the economy?
2. Explain how corporate profits are taxed twice.
3. Why is the burden of a tax to taxpayers greater than the revenue received by the government?
4. Why do some economists advocate taxing consumption rather than income?
5. What is the marginal tax rate on a lump-sum tax? How is this related to the efficiency of the tax?
6. Give two arguments why wealthy taxpayers should pay more taxes than poor taxpayers.
7. What is the concept of horizontal equity and why is it hard to apply?

PROBLEMS AND APPLICATIONS

1. The information in many of the tables in this chapter can be found in the *Economic Report of the President*, which appears annually. Using a recent issue of the report at your library or on the Internet, answer the following questions and provide some numbers to support your answers. (*Hint*: The website of the Government Printing Office is http://www.gpo.gov.)
   a. Figure 1 shows that government revenue as a percentage of total income has increased over time. Is this increase primarily attributable to changes in federal government revenue or in state and local government revenue?
   b. Looking at the combined revenue of the federal government and state and local governments, how has the composition of total revenue changed over time? Are personal income taxes more or less important? Social insurance taxes? Corporate profits taxes?
2. Suppose you are a typical person in the U.S. economy. You pay 4 percent of your income in a state income tax and 15.3 percent of your labor earnings in federal payroll taxes (employer and employee shares combined). You also pay federal income taxes as in Table 2. How much tax of each type do you pay if you earn $30,000 a year? Taking all taxes into account, what are your average and marginal tax rates? What happens to your tax bill and to your average and marginal tax rates if your income rises to $60,000?
3. Some states exclude necessities, such as food and clothing, from their sales tax. Other states do not. Discuss the merits of this exclusion. Consider both efficiency and equity.
4. When someone owns an asset (such as a share of stock) that rises in value, he has an "accrued" capital gain. If he sells the asset, he "realizes" the gains that have previously accrued. Under the U.S. income tax system, realized capital gains are taxed, but accrued gains are not.
   a. Explain how individuals' behavior is affected by this rule.
   b. Some economists believe that cuts in capital gains tax rates, especially temporary ones, can raise tax revenue. How might this be so?
   c. Do you think it is a good rule to tax realized but not accrued capital gains? Why or why not?
5. Suppose that your state raises its sales tax from 5 percent to 6 percent. The state revenue commissioner forecasts a 20 percent increase in sales tax revenue. Is this plausible? Explain.
6. The Tax Reform Act of 1986 eliminated the deductibility of interest payments on consumer debt (mostly credit cards and auto loans) but maintained the deductibility of interest payments on mortgages and home equity loans. What do you think happened to the relative amounts of borrowing through consumer debt and home equity debt?
7. Categorize each of the following funding schemes as examples of the benefits principle or the ability-to-pay principle.
   a. Visitors to many national parks pay an entrance fee.
   b. Local property taxes support elementary and secondary schools.
   c. An airport trust fund collects a tax on each plane ticket sold and uses the money to improve airports and the air traffic control system.

To find additional study resources, visit cengagebrain.com, and search for "Mankiw."

PART V

Firm Behavior and the Organization of Industry

CHAPTER

13

The Costs of Production

The economy is made up of thousands of firms that produce the goods and services you enjoy every day: General Motors produces automobiles, General Electric produces lightbulbs, and General Mills produces breakfast cereals. Some firms, such as these three, are large; they employ thousands of workers and have thousands of stockholders who share the firms' profits. Other firms, such as the local barbershop or café, are small; they employ only a few workers and are owned by a single person or family.

In previous chapters, we used the supply curve to summarize firms' production decisions. According to the law of supply, firms are willing to produce

and sell a greater quantity of a good when the price of the good is higher. This response leads to a supply curve that slopes upward. For analyzing many questions, the law of supply is all you need to know about firm behavior.

In this chapter and the ones that follow, we examine firm behavior in more detail. This topic will give you a better understanding of the decisions behind the supply curve. In addition, it will introduce you to a part of economics called *industrial organization*—the study of how firms' decisions about prices and quantities depend on the market conditions they face. The town in which you live, for instance, may have several pizzerias but only one cable television company. This raises a key question: How does the number of firms affect the prices in a market and the efficiency of the market outcome? The field of industrial organization addresses exactly this question.

Before turning to these issues, we need to discuss the costs of production. All firms, from Delta Air Lines to your local deli, incur costs while making the goods and services that they sell. As we will see in the coming chapters, a firm's costs are a key determinant of its production and pricing decisions. In this chapter, we define some of the variables that economists use to measure a firm's costs, and we consider the relationships among these variables.

A word of warning: This topic is dry and technical. To be honest, one might even call it boring. But this material provides a crucial foundation for the fascinating topics that follow.

13-1 What Are Costs?

We begin our discussion of costs at Caroline's Cookie Factory. Caroline, the owner of the firm, buys flour, sugar, chocolate chips, and other cookie ingredients. She also buys the mixers and ovens and hires workers to run this equipment. She then sells the cookies to consumers. By examining some of the issues that Caroline faces in her business, we can learn some lessons about costs that apply to all firms in an economy.

13-1a Total Revenue, Total Cost, and Profit

We begin with the firm's objective. To understand the decisions a firm makes, we must understand what it is trying to do. Although it is conceivable that Caroline started her firm because of an altruistic desire to provide the world with cookies or, perhaps, out of love for the cookie business, it is more likely that she started the business to make money. Economists normally assume that the goal of a firm is to maximize profit, and they find that this assumption works well in most cases.

total revenue
the amount a firm receives for the sale of its output

total cost
the market value of the inputs a firm uses in production

profit
total revenue minus total cost

What is a firm's profit? The amount that the firm receives for the sale of its output (cookies) is called **total revenue**. The amount that the firm pays to buy inputs (flour, sugar, workers, ovens, and so forth) is called **total cost**. Caroline gets to keep any revenue that is not needed to cover costs. **Profit** is a firm's total revenue minus its total cost:

$$\text{Profit} = \text{Total revenue} - \text{Total cost}$$

Caroline's objective is to make her firm's profit as large as possible.

To see how a firm goes about maximizing profit, we must consider fully how to measure its total revenue and its total cost. Total revenue is the easy part: It equals the quantity of output the firm produces multiplied by the price at which it sells its output. If Caroline produces 10,000 cookies and sells them at $2 a cookie, her total revenue is $20,000. The measurement of a firm's total cost, however, is more subtle.

13-1b Costs as Opportunity Costs

When measuring costs at Caroline's Cookie Factory or any other firm, it is important to keep in mind one of the *Ten Principles of Economics* from Chapter 1: The cost of something is what you give up to get it. Recall that the *opportunity cost* of an item refers to all the things that must be forgone to acquire that item. When economists speak of a firm's cost of production, they include all the opportunity costs of making its output of goods and services.

While some of a firm's opportunity costs of production are obvious, others are less so. When Caroline pays $1,000 for flour, that $1,000 is an opportunity cost because Caroline can no longer use that $1,000 to buy something else. Similarly, when Caroline hires workers to make the cookies, the wages she pays are part of the firm's costs. Because these opportunity costs require the firm to pay out some money, they are called **explicit costs**. By contrast, some of a firm's opportunity costs, called **implicit costs**, do not require a cash outlay. Imagine that Caroline is skilled with computers and could earn $100 per hour working as a programmer. For every hour that Caroline works at her cookie factory, she gives up $100 in income, and this forgone income is also part of her costs. The total cost of Caroline's business is the sum of her explicit and implicit costs.

explicit costs
input costs that require an outlay of money by the firm

implicit costs
input costs that do not require an outlay of money by the firm

The distinction between explicit and implicit costs highlights an important difference between how economists and accountants analyze a business. Economists are interested in studying how firms make production and pricing decisions. Because these decisions are based on both explicit and implicit costs, economists include both when measuring a firm's costs. By contrast, accountants have the job of keeping track of the money that flows into and out of firms. As a result, they measure the explicit costs but usually ignore the implicit costs.

The difference between the methods of economists and accountants is easy to see in the case of Caroline's Cookie Factory. When Caroline gives up the opportunity to earn money as a computer programmer, her accountant will not count this as a cost of her cookie business. Because no money flows out of the business to pay for this cost, it never shows up on the accountant's financial statements. An economist, however, will count the forgone income as a cost because it will affect the decisions that Caroline makes in her cookie business. For example, if Caroline's wage as a computer programmer rises from $100 to $500 per hour, she might decide that running her cookie business is too costly. She might choose to shut down the factory so she can take a job as a programmer.

13-1c The Cost of Capital as an Opportunity Cost

An important implicit cost of almost every business is the opportunity cost of the financial capital that has been invested in the business. Suppose, for instance, that Caroline used $300,000 of her savings to buy the cookie factory from its previous owner. If Caroline had instead left this money in a savings account that pays an interest rate of 5 percent, she would have earned $15,000 per year. To own her cookie factory, therefore, Caroline has given up $15,000 a year in interest income. This forgone $15,000 is one of the implicit opportunity costs of Caroline's business.

As we have already noted, economists and accountants treat costs differently, and this is especially true in their treatment of the cost of capital. An economist views the $15,000 in interest income that Caroline gives up every year as an implicit cost of her business. Caroline's accountant, however, will not show this $15,000 as a cost because no money flows out of the business to pay for it.

To further explore the difference between the methods of economists and accountants, let's change the example slightly. Suppose now that Caroline did not have the entire $300,000 to buy the factory but, instead, used $100,000 of her own savings and borrowed $200,000 from a bank at an interest rate of 5 percent. Caroline's accountant, who only measures explicit costs, will now count the $10,000 interest paid on the bank loan every year as a cost because this amount of money now flows out of the firm. By contrast, according to an economist, the opportunity cost of owning the business is still $15,000. The opportunity cost equals the interest on the bank loan (an explicit cost of $10,000) plus the forgone interest on savings (an implicit cost of $5,000).

13-1d Economic Profit versus Accounting Profit

Now let's return to the firm's objective: profit. Because economists and accountants measure costs differently, they also measure profit differently. An economist measures a firm's **economic profit** as the firm's total revenue minus all the opportunity costs (explicit and implicit) of producing the goods and services sold. An accountant measures the firm's **accounting profit** as the firm's total revenue minus only the firm's explicit costs.

economic profit
total revenue minus total cost, including both explicit and implicit costs

accounting profit
total revenue minus total explicit cost

Figure 1 summarizes this difference. Notice that because the accountant ignores the implicit costs, accounting profit is usually larger than economic profit. For a business to be profitable from an economist's standpoint, total revenue must exceed all the opportunity costs, both explicit and implicit.

Economic profit is an important concept because it motivates the firms that supply goods and services. As we will see, a firm making positive economic profit will stay in business. It is covering all its opportunity costs and has some revenue left to reward the firm owners. When a firm is making economic losses (that is, when economic profits are negative), the business owners are failing to earn enough revenue to cover all the costs of production. Unless conditions change,

FIGURE 1

Economists versus Accountants
Economists include all opportunity costs when analyzing a firm, whereas accountants measure only explicit costs. Therefore, economic profit is smaller than accounting profit.

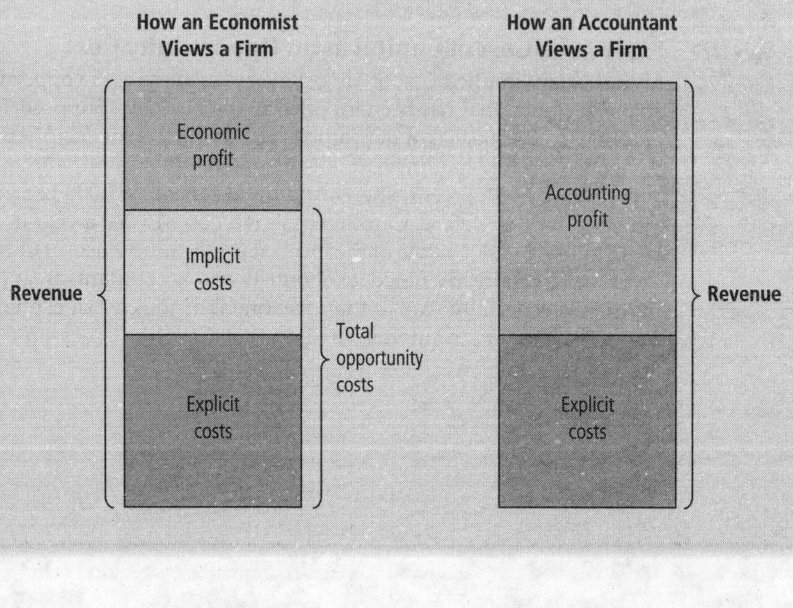

the firm owners will eventually close down the business and exit the industry. To understand business decisions, we need to keep an eye on economic profit.

QuickQuiz *Farmer McDonald gives banjo lessons for $20 an hour. One day, he spends 10 hours planting $100 worth of seeds on his farm. What opportunity cost has he incurred? What cost would his accountant measure? If these seeds yield $200 worth of crops, does McDonald earn an accounting profit? Does he earn an economic profit?*

13-2 Production and Costs

Firms incur costs when they buy inputs to produce the goods and services that they plan to sell. In this section, we examine the link between a firm's production process and its total cost. Once again, we consider Caroline's Cookie Factory.

In the analysis that follows, we make an important simplifying assumption: We assume that the size of Caroline's factory is fixed and that Caroline can vary the quantity of cookies produced only by changing the number of workers she employs. This assumption is realistic in the short run but not in the long run. That is, Caroline cannot build a larger factory overnight, but she could do so over the next year or two. This analysis, therefore, describes the production decisions that Caroline faces in the short run. We examine the relationship between costs and time horizon more fully later in the chapter.

13-2a The Production Function

Table 1 shows how the quantity of cookies produced per hour at Caroline's factory depends on the number of workers. As you can see in columns (1) and (2), if there are no workers in the factory, Caroline produces no cookies.

TABLE 1

A Production Function and Total Cost: Caroline's Cookie Factory

(1) Number of Workers	(2) Output (quantity of cookies produced per hour)	(3) Marginal Product of Labor	(4) Cost of Factory	(5) Cost of Workers	(6) Total Cost of Inputs (cost of factory + cost of workers)
0	0		$30	$0	$30
		50			
1	50		30	10	40
		40			
2	90		30	20	50
		30			
3	120		30	30	60
		20			
4	140		30	40	70
		10			
5	150		30	50	80
		5			
6	155		30	60	90

When there is 1 worker, she produces 50 cookies. When there are 2 workers, she produces 90 cookies and so on. Panel (a) of Figure 2 presents a graph of these two columns of numbers. The number of workers is on the horizontal axis, and the number of cookies produced is on the vertical axis. This relationship between the quantity of inputs (workers) and quantity of output (cookies) is called the **production function**.

production function
the relationship between the quantity of inputs used to make a good and the quantity of output of that good

One of the *Ten Principles of Economics* introduced in Chapter 1 is that rational people think at the margin. As we will see in future chapters, this idea is the key to understanding the decisions a firm makes about how many workers to hire and how much output to produce. To take a step toward understanding these decisions, column (3) in the table gives the marginal product of a worker. The **marginal product** of any input in the production process is the increase in the quantity of output obtained from one additional unit of that input. When the number of workers goes from 1 to 2, cookie production increases from 50 to 90, so the marginal product of the second worker is 40 cookies. And when the number of

marginal product
the increase in output that arises from an additional unit of input

FIGURE 2

Caroline's Production Function and Total-Cost Curve

The production function in panel (a) shows the relationship between the number of workers hired and the quantity of output produced. Here the number of workers hired (on the horizontal axis) is from column (1) in Table 1, and the quantity of output produced (on the vertical axis) is from column (2). The production function gets flatter as the number of workers increases, reflecting diminishing marginal product. The total-cost curve in panel (b) shows the relationship between the quantity of output produced and total cost of production. Here the quantity of output produced (on the horizontal axis) is from column (2) in Table 1, and the total cost (on the vertical axis) is from column (6). The total-cost curve gets steeper as the quantity of output increases because of diminishing marginal product.

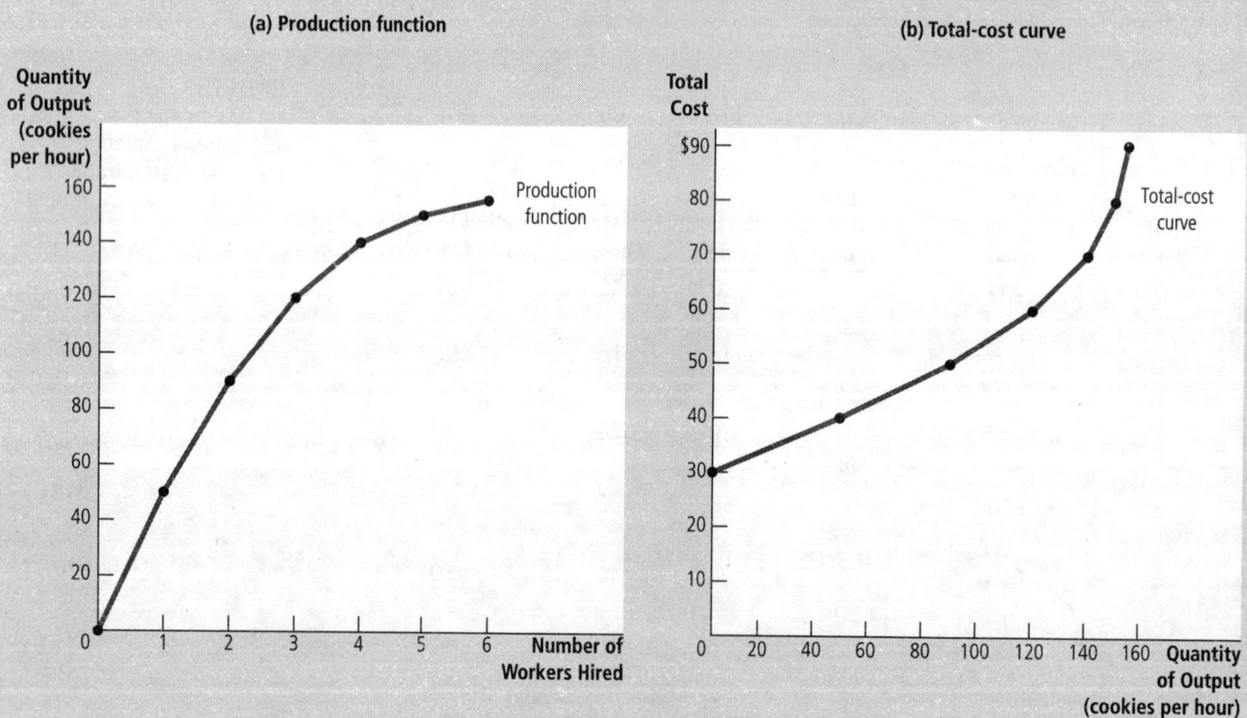

workers goes from 2 to 3, cookie production increases from 90 to 120, so the marginal product of the third worker is 30 cookies. In the table, the marginal product is shown halfway between two rows because it represents the change in output as the number of workers increases from one level to another.

Notice that as the number of workers increases, the marginal product declines. The second worker has a marginal product of 40 cookies, the third worker has a marginal product of 30 cookies, and the fourth worker has a marginal product of 20 cookies. This property is called **diminishing marginal product**. At first, when only a few workers are hired, they have easy access to Caroline's kitchen equipment. As the number of workers increases, additional workers have to share equipment and work in more crowded conditions. Eventually, the kitchen becomes so overcrowded that workers often get in each other's way. Hence, as more workers are hired, each additional worker contributes fewer additional cookies to total production.

diminishing marginal product
the property whereby the marginal product of an input declines as the quantity of the input increases

Diminishing marginal product is also apparent in Figure 2. The production function's slope ("rise over run") tells us the change in Caroline's output of cookies ("rise") for each additional input of labor ("run"). That is, the slope of the production function measures the marginal product. As the number of workers increases, the marginal product declines, and the production function becomes flatter.

13-2b From the Production Function to the Total-Cost Curve

Columns (4), (5), and (6) in Table 1 show Caroline's cost of producing cookies. In this example, the cost of Caroline's factory is \$30 per hour, and the cost of a worker is \$10 per hour. If she hires 1 worker, her total cost is \$40 per hour. If she hires 2 workers, her total cost is \$50 per hour, and so on. With this information, the table now shows how the number of workers Caroline hires is related to the quantity of cookies she produces and to her total cost of production.

Our goal in the next several chapters is to study firms' production and pricing decisions. For this purpose, the most important relationship in Table 1 is between quantity produced [in column (2)] and total cost [in column (6)]. Panel (b) of Figure 2 graphs these two columns of data with quantity produced on the horizontal axis and total cost on the vertical axis. This graph is called the *total-cost curve*.

Now compare the total-cost curve in panel (b) with the production function in panel (a). These two curves are opposite sides of the same coin. The total-cost curve gets steeper as the amount produced rises, whereas the production function gets flatter as production rises. These changes in slope occur for the same reason. High production of cookies means that Caroline's kitchen is crowded with many workers. Because the kitchen is crowded, each additional worker adds less to production, reflecting diminishing marginal product. Therefore, the production function is relatively flat. But now turn this logic around: When the kitchen is crowded, producing an additional cookie requires a lot of additional labor and is thus very costly. Therefore, when the quantity produced is large, the total-cost curve is relatively steep.

QuickQuiz *If Farmer Jones plants no seeds on her farm, she gets no harvest. If she plants 1 bag of seeds, she gets 3 bushels of wheat. If she plants 2 bags, she gets 5 bushels. If she plants 3 bags, she gets 6 bushels. A bag of seeds costs \$100, and seeds are her only cost. Use these data to graph the farmer's production function and total-cost curve. Explain their shapes.*

13-3 The Various Measures of Cost

Our analysis of Caroline's Cookie Factory demonstrated how a firm's total cost reflects its production function. From data on a firm's total cost, we can derive several related measures of cost, which will turn out to be useful when we analyze production and pricing decisions in future chapters. To see how these related measures are derived, we consider the example in Table 2. This table presents cost data on Caroline's neighbor—Conrad's Coffee Shop.

Column (1) in the table shows the number of cups of coffee that Conrad might produce, ranging from 0 to 10 cups per hour. Column (2) shows Conrad's total cost of producing coffee. Figure 3 plots Conrad's total-cost curve. The quantity of coffee [from column (1)] is on the horizontal axis, and total cost [from column (2)] is on the vertical axis. Conrad's total-cost curve has a shape similar to Caroline's. In particular, it becomes steeper as the quantity produced rises, which (as we have discussed) reflects diminishing marginal product.

TABLE 2

The Various Measures of Cost: Conrad's Coffee Shop

(1) Output (cups of coffee per hour)	(2) Total Cost	(3) Fixed Cost	(4) Variable Cost	(5) Average Fixed Cost	(6) Average Variable Cost	(7) Average Total Cost	(8) Marginal Cost
0	$3.00	$3.00	$0.00	—	—	—	
							$0.30
1	3.30	3.00	0.30	$3.00	$0.30	$3.30	
							0.50
2	3.80	3.00	0.80	1.50	0.40	1.90	
							0.70
3	4.50	3.00	1.50	1.00	0.50	1.50	
							0.90
4	5.40	3.00	2.40	0.75	0.60	1.35	
							1.10
5	6.50	3.00	3.50	0.60	0.70	1.30	
							1.30
6	7.80	3.00	4.80	0.50	0.80	1.30	
							1.50
7	9.30	3.00	6.30	0.43	0.90	1.33	
							1.70
8	11.00	3.00	8.00	0.38	1.00	1.38	
							1.90
9	12.90	3.00	9.90	0.33	1.10	1.43	
							2.10
10	15.00	3.00	12.00	0.30	1.20	1.50	

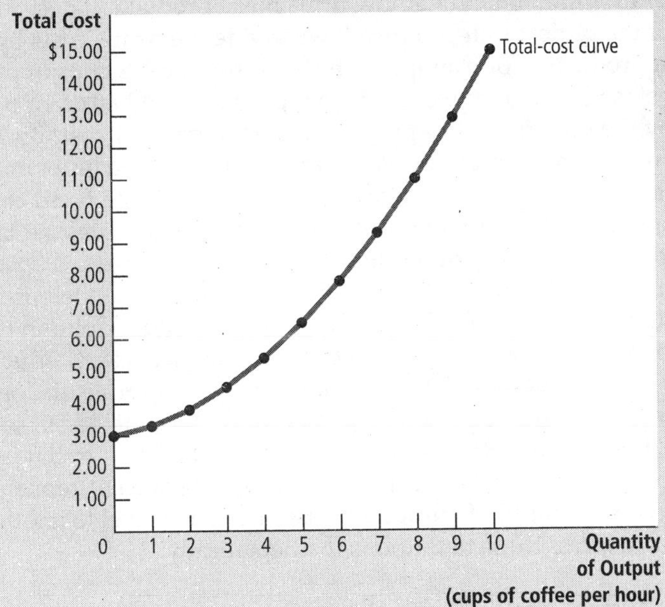

FIGURE 3

Conrad's Total-Cost Curve
Here the quantity of output produced (on the horizontal axis) is from column (1) in Table 2, and the total cost (on the vertical axis) is from column (2). As in Figure 2, the total-cost curve gets steeper as the quantity of output increases because of diminishing marginal product.

13-3a Fixed and Variable Costs

Conrad's total cost can be divided into two types. Some costs, called **fixed costs**, do not vary with the quantity of output produced. They are incurred even if the firm produces nothing at all. Conrad's fixed costs include any rent he pays because this cost is the same regardless of how much coffee he produces. Similarly, if Conrad needs to hire a full-time bookkeeper to pay bills, regardless of the quantity of coffee produced, the bookkeeper's salary is a fixed cost. The third column in Table 2 shows Conrad's fixed cost, which in this example is $3.00.

fixed costs
costs that do not vary with the quantity of output produced

Some of the firm's costs, called **variable costs**, change as the firm alters the quantity of output produced. Conrad's variable costs include the cost of coffee beans, milk, sugar, and paper cups: The more cups of coffee Conrad makes, the more of these items he needs to buy. Similarly, if Conrad has to hire more workers to make more cups of coffee, the salaries of these workers are variable costs. Column (4) in the table shows Conrad's variable cost. The variable cost is 0 if he produces nothing, $0.30 if he produces 1 cup of coffee, $0.80 if he produces 2 cups, and so on.

variable costs
costs that vary with the quantity of output produced

A firm's total cost is the sum of fixed and variable costs. In Table 2, total cost in column (2) equals fixed cost in column (3) plus variable cost in column (4).

13-3b Average and Marginal Cost

As the owner of his firm, Conrad has to decide how much to produce. One issue he will want to consider when making this decision is how the level of production affects his firm's costs. Conrad might ask his production supervisor the following two questions about the cost of producing coffee:

- How much does it cost to make the typical cup of coffee?
- How much does it cost to increase production of coffee by 1 cup?

These two questions might seem to have the same answer, but they do not. Both answers are important for understanding how firms make production decisions.

To find the cost of the typical unit produced, we divide the firm's costs by the quantity of output it produces. For example, if the firm produces 2 cups of coffee per hour, its total cost is $3.80, and the cost of the typical cup is $3.80/2, or $1.90. Total cost divided by the quantity of output is called **average total cost**. Because total cost is the sum of fixed and variable costs, average total cost can be expressed as the sum of average fixed cost and average variable cost. **Average fixed cost** is the fixed cost divided by the quantity of output, and **average variable cost** is the variable cost divided by the quantity of output.

average total cost
total cost divided by the quantity of output

average fixed cost
fixed cost divided by the quantity of output

average variable cost
variable cost divided by the quantity of output

marginal cost
the increase in total cost that arises from an extra unit of production

Average total cost tells us the cost of the typical unit, but it does not tell us how much total cost will change as the firm alters its level of production. Column (8) in Table 2 shows the amount that total cost rises when the firm increases production by 1 unit of output. This number is called **marginal cost**. For example, if Conrad increases production from 2 to 3 cups, total cost rises from $3.80 to $4.50, so the marginal cost of the third cup of coffee is $4.50 minus $3.80, or $0.70. In the table, the marginal cost appears halfway between any two rows because it represents the change in total cost as quantity of output increases from one level to another.

It may be helpful to express these definitions mathematically:

$$\text{Average total cost} = \text{Total cost}/\text{Quantity}$$
$$ATC = TC/Q,$$

and

$$\text{Marginal cost} = \text{Change in total cost}/\text{Change in quantity}$$
$$MC = \Delta TC/\Delta Q$$

Here Δ, the Greek letter delta, represents the change in a variable. These equations show how average total cost and marginal cost are derived from total cost. *Average total cost tells us the cost of a typical unit of output if total cost is divided evenly over all the units produced. Marginal cost tells us the increase in total cost that arises from producing an additional unit of output.* As we will see more fully in the next chapter, business managers like Conrad need to keep in mind the concepts of average total cost and marginal cost when deciding how much of their product to supply to the market.

13-3c Cost Curves and Their Shapes

Just as we found graphs of supply and demand useful when analyzing the behavior of markets in previous chapters, we will find graphs of average and marginal cost useful when analyzing the behavior of firms. Figure 4 graphs Conrad's costs using the data from Table 2. The horizontal axis measures the quantity the firm produces, and the vertical axis measures marginal and average costs. The graph shows four curves: average total cost (*ATC*), average fixed cost (*AFC*), average variable cost (*AVC*), and marginal cost (*MC*).

The cost curves shown here for Conrad's Coffee Shop have some features that are common to the cost curves of many firms in the economy. Let's examine three features in particular: the shape of the marginal-cost curve, the shape of the average-total-cost curve, and the relationship between marginal cost and average total cost.

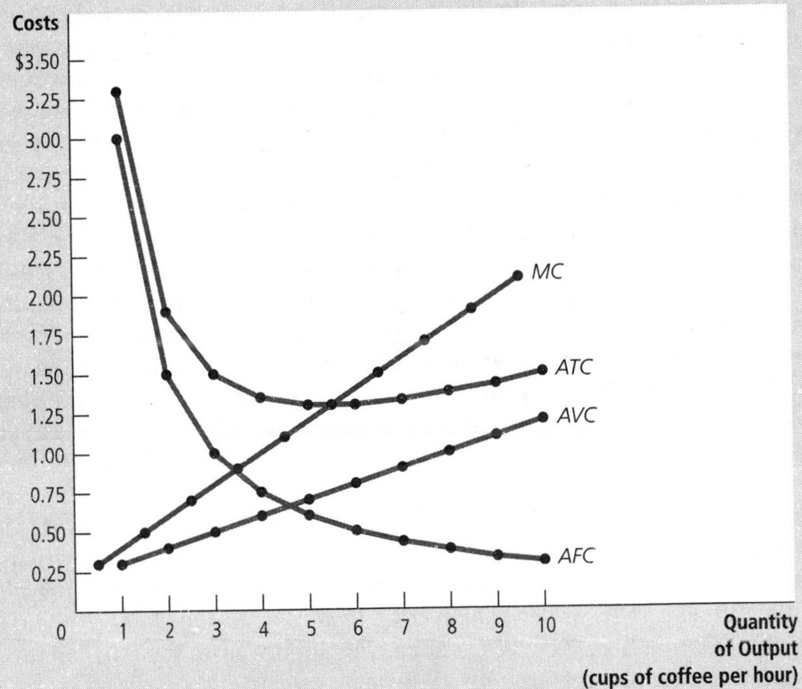

FIGURE 4

Conrad's Average-Cost and Marginal-Cost Curves
This figure shows the average total cost (*ATC*), average fixed cost (*AFC*), average variable cost (*AVC*), and marginal cost (*MC*) for Conrad's Coffee Shop. All of these curves are obtained by graphing the data in Table 2. These cost curves show three common features: (1) Marginal cost rises with the quantity of output. (2) The average-total-cost curve is U-shaped. (3) The marginal-cost curve crosses the average-total-cost curve at the minimum of average total cost.

Rising Marginal Cost Conrad's marginal cost rises as the quantity of output produced increases. This upward slope reflects the property of diminishing marginal product. When Conrad produces a small quantity of coffee, he has few workers, and much of his equipment is not used. Because he can easily put these idle resources to use, the marginal product of an extra worker is large, and the marginal cost of an extra cup of coffee is small. By contrast, when Conrad produces a large quantity of coffee, his shop is crowded with workers, and most of his equipment is fully utilized. Conrad can produce more coffee by adding workers, but these new workers have to work in crowded conditions and may have to wait to use the equipment. Therefore, when the quantity of coffee produced is already high, the marginal product of an extra worker is low, and the marginal cost of an extra cup of coffee is large.

U-Shaped Average Total Cost Conrad's average-total-cost curve is U-shaped, as shown in Figure 4. To understand why, remember that average total cost is the sum of average fixed cost and average variable cost. Average fixed cost always declines as output rises because the fixed cost is getting spread over a larger number of units. Average variable cost usually rises as output increases because of diminishing marginal product.

Average total cost reflects the shapes of both average fixed cost and average variable cost. At very low levels of output, such as 1 or 2 cups per hour, average total cost is very high. Even though average variable cost is low, average fixed cost is high because the fixed cost is spread over only a few units. As output increases, the fixed cost is spread over more units. Average fixed cost declines, rapidly at first and then more slowly. As a result, average total cost also declines until the firm's output reaches 5 cups of coffee per hour, when average total cost is $1.30 per cup. When the firm produces more than 6 cups per hour, however, the increase in average variable cost becomes the dominant force, and average total cost starts rising. The tug of war between average fixed cost and average variable cost generates the U-shape in average total cost.

The bottom of the U-shape occurs at the quantity that minimizes average total cost. This quantity is sometimes called the **efficient scale** of the firm. For Conrad, the efficient scale is 5 or 6 cups of coffee per hour. If he produces more or less than this amount, his average total cost rises above the minimum of $1.30. At lower levels of output, average total cost is higher than $1.30 because the fixed cost is spread over so few units. At higher levels of output, average total cost is higher than $1.30 because the marginal product of inputs has diminished significantly. At the efficient scale, these two forces are balanced to yield the lowest average total cost.

efficient scale
the quantity of output that minimizes average total cost

The Relationship between Marginal Cost and Average Total Cost If you look at Figure 4 (or back at Table 2), you will see something that may be surprising at first. *Whenever marginal cost is less than average total cost, average total cost is falling. Whenever marginal cost is greater than average total cost, average total cost is rising.* This feature of Conrad's cost curves is not a coincidence from the particular numbers used in the example: It is true for all firms.

To see why, consider an analogy. Average total cost is like your cumulative grade point average. Marginal cost is like the grade you get in the next course you take. If your grade in your next course is less than your grade point average, your grade point average will fall. If your grade in your next course is higher than your grade point average, your grade point average will rise. The mathematics of average and marginal costs is exactly the same as the mathematics of average and marginal grades.

This relationship between average total cost and marginal cost has an important corollary: *The marginal-cost curve crosses the average-total-cost curve at its minimum.* Why? At low levels of output, marginal cost is below average total cost, so average total cost is falling. But after the two curves cross, marginal cost rises above average total cost. As a result, average total cost must start to rise at this level of output. Hence, this point of intersection is the minimum of average total cost. As we will see in the next chapter, minimum average total cost plays a key role in the analysis of competitive firms.

13-3d Typical Cost Curves

In the examples we have studied so far, the firms have exhibited diminishing marginal product and, therefore, rising marginal cost at all levels of output. This simplifying assumption was useful because it allowed us to focus on the key features of cost curves that are useful in analyzing firm behavior. Yet actual firms are usually more complicated than this. In many firms, marginal product does not start to fall immediately after the first worker is hired. Depending on the production process, the second or third worker might have a higher marginal product than the first because a team of workers can divide tasks and work more productively than a single worker. Firms exhibiting this pattern would experience increasing marginal product for a while before diminishing marginal product set in.

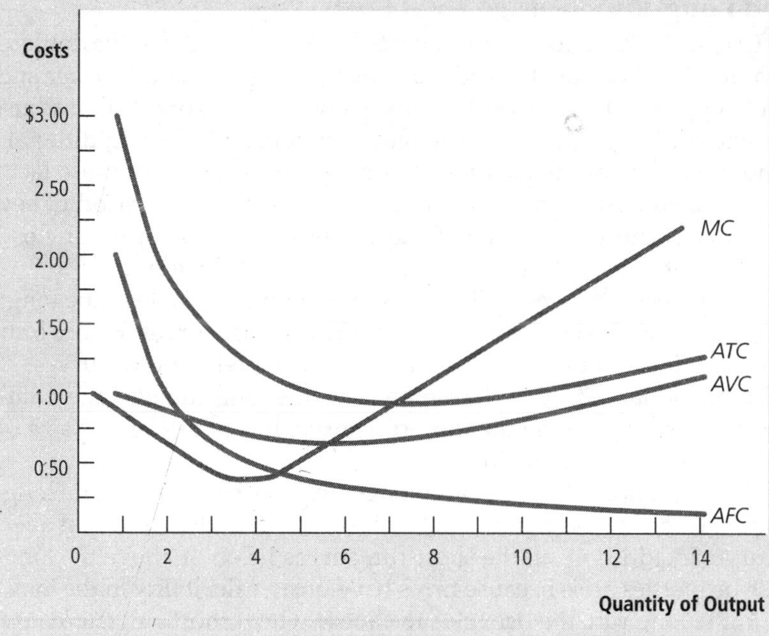

FIGURE 5

Cost Curves for a Typical Firm Many firms experience increasing marginal product before diminishing marginal product. As a result, they have cost curves shaped like those in this figure. Notice that marginal cost and average variable cost fall for a while before starting to rise.

Figure 5 shows the cost curves for such a firm, including average total cost (*ATC*), average fixed cost (*AFC*), average variable cost (*AVC*), and marginal cost (*MC*). At low levels of output, the firm experiences increasing marginal product, and the marginal-cost curve falls. Eventually, the firm starts to experience diminishing marginal product, and the marginal-cost curve starts to rise. This combination of increasing then diminishing marginal product also makes the average-variable-cost curve U-shaped.

Despite these differences from our previous example, the cost curves in Figure 5 share the three properties that are most important to remember:

- Marginal cost eventually rises with the quantity of output.
- The average-total-cost curve is U-shaped.
- The marginal-cost curve crosses the average-total-cost curve at the minimum of average total cost.

QuickQuiz *Suppose Honda's total cost of producing 4 cars is $225,000 and its total cost of producing 5 cars is $250,000. What is the average total cost of producing 5 cars? What is the marginal cost of the fifth car? • Draw the marginal-cost curve and the average-total-cost curve for a typical firm, and explain why these curves cross where they do.*

13-4 Costs in the Short Run and in the Long Run

We noted earlier in this chapter that a firm's costs might depend on the time horizon under consideration. Let's examine more precisely why this might be the case.

13-4a The Relationship between Short-Run and Long-Run Average Total Cost

For many firms, the division of total costs between fixed and variable costs depends on the time horizon. Consider, for instance, a car manufacturer such as Ford Motor Company. Over a period of only a few months, Ford cannot adjust the number or sizes of its car factories. The only way it can produce additional cars is to hire more workers at the factories it already has. The cost of these factories is, therefore, a fixed cost in the short run. By contrast, over a period of several years, Ford can expand the size of its factories, build new factories, or close old ones. Thus, the cost of its factories is a variable cost in the long run.

Because many decisions are fixed in the short run but variable in the long run, a firm's long-run cost curves differ from its short-run cost curves. Figure 6 shows an example. The figure presents three short-run average-total-cost curves—for a small, medium, and large factory. It also presents the long-run average-total-cost curve. As the firm moves along the long-run curve, it is adjusting the size of the factory to the quantity of production.

This graph shows how short-run and long-run costs are related. The long-run average-total-cost curve has a much flatter U-shape than the short-run average-total-cost curve. In addition, all the short-run curves lie on or above the long-run curve. These properties arise because firms have greater flexibility in the long run. In essence, in the long run, the firm gets to choose which short-run curve it wants to use. But in the short run, it has to use whatever short-run curve it has, based on decisions it has made in the past.

The figure shows an example of how a change in production alters costs over different time horizons. When Ford wants to increase production from 1,000 to 1,200 cars per day, it has no choice in the short run but to hire more workers at its existing medium-sized factory. Because of diminishing marginal product, average total cost rises from $10,000 to $12,000 per car. In the long run, however, Ford can expand both the size of the factory and its workforce, and average total cost returns to $10,000.

FIGURE 6

Average Total Cost in the Short and Long Runs
Because fixed costs are variable in the long run, the average-total-cost curve in the short run differs from the average-total-cost curve in the long run.

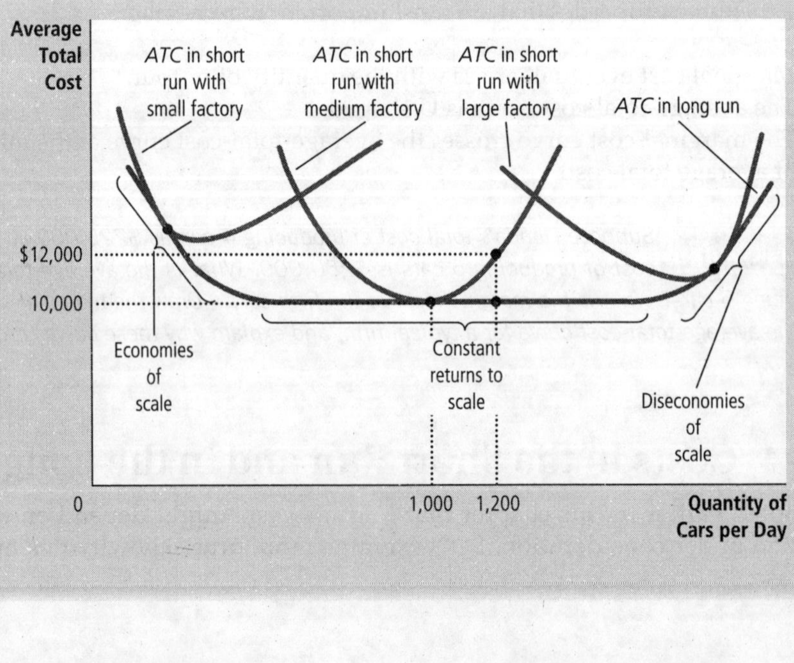

How long does it take a firm to get to the long run? The answer depends on the firm. It can take a year or more for a major manufacturing firm, such as a car company, to build a larger factory. By contrast, a person running a coffee shop can buy another coffee maker within a few days. There is, therefore, no single answer to the question of how long it takes a firm to adjust its production facilities.

13-4b Economies and Diseconomies of Scale

The shape of the long-run average-total-cost curve conveys important information about the production processes that a firm has available for manufacturing a good. In particular, it tells us how costs vary with the scale—that is, the size—of a firm's operations. When long-run average total cost declines as output increases, there are said to be **economies of scale**. When long-run average total cost rises as output increases, there are said to be **diseconomies of scale**. When long-run average total cost does not vary with the level of output, there are said to be **constant returns to scale**. As we can see in Figure 6, Ford has economies of scale at low levels of output, constant returns to scale at intermediate levels of output, and diseconomies of scale at high levels of output.

economies of scale
the property whereby long-run average total cost falls as the quantity of output increases

diseconomies of scale
the property whereby long-run average total cost rises as the quantity of output increases

constant returns to scale
the property whereby long-run average total cost stays the same as the quantity of output changes

What might cause economies or diseconomies of scale? Economies of scale often arise because higher production levels allow *specialization* among workers, which permits each worker to become better at a specific task. For instance, if Ford hires a large number of workers and produces a large number of cars, it can reduce costs using modern assembly-line production. Diseconomies of scale can arise because of *coordination problems* that are inherent in any large organization. The more cars Ford produces, the more stretched the management team becomes, and the less effective the managers become at keeping costs down.

FYI

Lessons from a Pin Factory

"Jack of all trades, master of none." This well-known adage sheds light on the nature of cost curves. A person who tries to do everything usually ends up doing nothing very well. If a firm wants its workers to be as productive as they can be, it is often best to give each worker a limited task that she can master. But this organization of work is possible only if a firm employs many workers and produces a large quantity of output.

In his celebrated book *An Inquiry into the Nature and Causes of the Wealth of Nations*, Adam Smith described a visit he made to a pin factory. Smith was impressed by the specialization among the workers and the resulting economies of scale. He wrote,

> *One man draws out the wire, another straightens it, a third cuts it, a fourth points it, a fifth grinds it at the top for receiving the head; to make the head requires two or three distinct operations; to put it on is a peculiar business; to whiten it is another; it is even a trade by itself to put them into paper.*

Smith reported that because of this specialization, the pin factory produced thousands of pins per worker every day. He conjectured that if the workers had chosen to work separately, rather than as a team of specialists, "they certainly could not each of them make twenty, perhaps not one pin a day." In other words, because of specialization, a large pin factory could achieve higher output per worker and lower average cost per pin than a small pin factory.

The specialization that Smith observed in the pin factory is prevalent in the modern economy. If you want to build a house, for instance, you could try to do all the work yourself. But most people turn to a builder, who in turn hires carpenters, plumbers, electricians, painters, and many other types of workers. These workers focus their training and experience in particular jobs, and as a result, they become better at their jobs than if they were generalists. Indeed, the use of specialization to achieve economies of scale is one reason modern societies are as prosperous as they are. ■

This analysis shows why long-run average-total-cost curves are often U-shaped. At low levels of production, the firm benefits from increased size because it can take advantage of greater specialization. Coordination problems, meanwhile, are not yet acute. By contrast, at high levels of production, the benefits of specialization have already been realized, and coordination problems become more severe as the firm grows larger. Thus, long-run average total cost is falling at low levels of production because of increasing specialization and rising at high levels of production because of growing coordination problems.

QuickQuiz *If Boeing produces 9 jets per month, its long-run total cost is $9.0 million per month. If it produces 10 jets per month, its long-run total cost is $9.5 million per month. Does Boeing exhibit economies or diseconomies of scale?*

13-5 Conclusion

The purpose of this chapter has been to develop some tools to study how firms make production and pricing decisions. You should now understand what economists mean by the term *costs* and how costs vary with the quantity of output a firm produces. To refresh your memory, Table 3 summarizes some of the definitions we have encountered.

By themselves, a firm's cost curves do not tell us what decisions the firm will make. But they are a key component of that decision, as we will see in the next chapter.

TABLE 3

The Many Types of Cost: A Summary

Term	Definition	Mathematical Description
Explicit costs	Costs that require an outlay of money by the firm	
Implicit costs	Costs that do not require an outlay of money by the firm	
Fixed costs	Costs that do not vary with the quantity of output produced	FC
Variable costs	Costs that vary with the quantity of output produced	VC
Total cost	The market value of all the inputs that a firm uses in production	$TC = FC + VC$
Average fixed cost	Fixed cost divided by the quantity of output	$AFC = FC / Q$
Average variable cost	Variable cost divided by the quantity of output	$AVC = VC / Q$
Average total cost	Total cost divided by the quantity of output	$ATC = TC / Q$
Marginal cost	The increase in total cost that arises from an extra unit of production	$MC = \Delta TC / \Delta Q$

CHAPTER QuickQuiz

1. Xavier opens up a lemonade stand for two hours. He spends $10 for ingredients and sells $60 worth of lemonade. In the same two hours, he could have mowed his neighbor's lawn for $40. Xavier has an accounting profit of _____ and an economic profit of _____.
   a. $50, $10
   b. $90, $50
   c. $10, $50
   d. $50, $90
2. Diminishing marginal product explains why, as a firm's output increases,
   a. the production function and total-cost curve both get steeper.
   b. the production function and total-cost curve both get flatter.
   c. the production function gets steeper, while the total-cost curve gets flatter.
   d. the production function gets flatter, while the total-cost curve gets steeper.
3. A firm is producing 1,000 units at a total cost of $5,000. If it were to increase production to 1,001 units, its total cost would rise to $5,008. What does this information tell you about the firm?
   a. Marginal cost is $5, and average variable cost is $8.
   b. Marginal cost is $8, and average variable cost is $5.
   c. Marginal cost is $5, and average total cost is $8.
   d. Marginal cost is $8, and average total cost is $5.
4. A firm is producing 20 units with an average total cost of $25 and a marginal cost of $15. If it were to increase production to 21 units, which of the following must occur?
   a. Marginal cost would decrease.
   b. Marginal cost would increase.
   c. Average total cost would decrease.
   d. Average total cost would increase.
5. The government imposes a $1,000 per year license fee on all pizza restaurants. As a result, which cost curves shift?
   a. average total cost and marginal cost
   b. average total cost and average fixed cost
   c. average variable cost and marginal cost
   d. average variable cost and average fixed cost
6. If a higher level of production allows workers to specialize in particular tasks, a firm will likely exhibit ________ of scale and ________ average total cost.
   a. economies, falling
   b. economies, rising
   c. diseconomies, falling
   d. diseconomies, rising

SUMMARY

- The goal of firms is to maximize profit, which equals total revenue minus total cost.
- When analyzing a firm's behavior, it is important to include all the opportunity costs of production. Some of the opportunity costs, such as the wages a firm pays its workers, are explicit. Other opportunity costs, such as the wages the firm owner gives up by working at the firm rather than taking another job, are implicit. Economic profit takes both explicit and implicit costs into account, whereas accounting profit considers only explicit costs.
- A firm's costs reflect its production process. A typical firm's production function gets flatter as the quantity of an input increases, displaying the property of diminishing marginal product. As a result, a firm's total-cost curve gets steeper as the quantity produced rises.
- A firm's total costs can be divided into fixed costs and variable costs. Fixed costs are costs that do not change when the firm alters the quantity of output produced. Variable costs are costs that change when the firm alters the quantity of output produced.
- From a firm's total cost, two related measures of cost are derived. Average total cost is total cost divided by the quantity of output. Marginal cost is the amount by which total cost rises if output increases by 1 unit.
- When analyzing firm behavior, it is often useful to graph average total cost and marginal cost. For a typical firm, marginal cost rises with the quantity of output. Average total cost first falls as output increases and then rises as output increases further. The marginal-cost curve always crosses the average-total-cost curve at the minimum of average total cost.
- A firm's costs often depend on the time horizon considered. In particular, many costs are fixed in the short run but variable in the long run. As a result, when the firm changes its level of production, average total cost may rise more in the short run than in the long run.

KEY CONCEPTS

total revenue, p. 248
total cost, p. 248
profit, p. 248
explicit costs, p. 249
implicit costs, p. 249
economic profit, p. 250
accounting profit, p. 250
production function, p. 252
marginal product, p. 252
diminishing marginal product, p. 253
fixed costs, p. 255
variable costs, p. 255
average total cost, p. 256
average fixed cost, p. 256
average variable cost, p. 256
marginal cost, p. 256
efficient scale, p. 258
economies of scale, p. 261
diseconomies of scale, p. 261
constant returns to scale, p. 261

QUESTIONS FOR REVIEW

1. What is the relationship between a firm's total revenue, profit, and total cost?
2. Give an example of an opportunity cost that an accountant would not count as a cost. Why would the accountant ignore this cost?
3. What is marginal product, and what does it mean if it is diminishing?
4. Draw a production function that exhibits diminishing marginal product of labor. Draw the associated total-cost curve. (In both cases, be sure to label the axes.) Explain the shapes of the two curves you have drawn.
5. Define *total cost, average total cost,* and *marginal cost.* How are they related?
6. Draw the marginal-cost and average-total-cost curves for a typical firm. Explain why the curves have the shapes that they do and why they intersect where they do.
7. How and why does a firm's average-total-cost curve differ in the short run compared with the long run?
8. Define *economies of scale* and explain why they might arise. Define *diseconomies of scale* and explain why they might arise.

PROBLEMS AND APPLICATIONS

1. This chapter discusses many types of costs: opportunity cost, total cost, fixed cost, variable cost, average total cost, and marginal cost. Fill in the type of cost that best completes each sentence:
   a. What you give up in taking some action is called the ______.
   b. ______ is falling when marginal cost is below it and rising when marginal cost is above it.
   c. A cost that does not depend on the quantity produced is a(n) ______.
   d. In the ice-cream industry in the short run, ______ includes the cost of cream and sugar but not the cost of the factory.
   e. Profits equal total revenue minus ______.
   f. The cost of producing an extra unit of output is the ______.
2. Your aunt is thinking about opening a hardware store. She estimates that it would cost $500,000 per year to rent the location and buy the stock. In addition, she would have to quit her $50,000 per year job as an accountant.
   a. Define *opportunity cost.*
   b. What is your aunt's opportunity cost of running the hardware store for a year? If your aunt thinks she can sell $510,000 worth of merchandise in a year, should she open the store? Explain.
3. A commercial fisherman notices the following relationship between hours spent fishing and the quantity of fish caught:

Hours	Quantity of Fish (in pounds)
0 hours	0 lb.
1	10
2	18
3	24
4	28
5	30

   a. What is the marginal product of each hour spent fishing?

b. Use these data to graph the fisherman's production function. Explain its shape.
c. The fisherman has a fixed cost of $10 (his pole). The opportunity cost of his time is $5 per hour. Graph the fisherman's total-cost curve. Explain its shape.

4. Nimbus, Inc., makes brooms and then sells them door-to-door. Here is the relationship between the number of workers and Nimbus's output during a given day:

Workers	Output	Marginal Product	Total Cost	Average Total Cost	Marginal Cost
0	0		—	—	
		—			—
1	20		—	—	
		—			—
2	50		—	—	
		—			—
3	90		—	—	
		—			—
4	120		—	—	
		—			—
5	140		—	—	
		—			—
6	150		—	—	
		—			—
7	155		—	—	

a. Fill in the column of marginal products. What pattern do you see? How might you explain it?
b. A worker costs $100 a day, and the firm has fixed costs of $200. Use this information to fill in the column for total cost.
c. Fill in the column for average total cost. (Recall that $ATC = TC/Q$.) What pattern do you see?
d. Now fill in the column for marginal cost. (Recall that $MC = \Delta TC/\Delta Q$.) What pattern do you see?
e. Compare the column for marginal product with the column for marginal cost. Explain the relationship.
f. Compare the column for average total cost with the column for marginal cost. Explain the relationship.

5. You are the chief financial officer for a firm that sells digital music players. Your firm has the following average-total-cost schedule:

Quantity	Average Total Cost
600 players	$300
601	301

Your current level of production is 600 devices, all of which have been sold. Someone calls, desperate to buy one of your music players. The caller offers you $550 for it. Should you accept the offer? Why or why not?

6. Consider the following cost information for a pizzeria:

Quantity	Total Cost	Variable Cost
0 dozen pizzas	$300	$ 0
1	350	50
2	390	90
3	420	120
4	450	150
5	490	190
6	540	240

a. What is the pizzeria's fixed cost?
b. Construct a table in which you calculate the marginal cost per dozen pizzas using the information on total cost. Also, calculate the marginal cost per dozen pizzas using the information on variable cost. What is the relationship between these sets of numbers? Explain.

7. Your cousin Vinnie owns a painting company with fixed costs of $200 and the following schedule for variable costs:

Quantity of Houses Painted per Month	1	2	3	4	5	6	7
Variable Costs	$10	$20	$40	$80	$160	$320	$640

Calculate average fixed cost, average variable cost, and average total cost for each quantity. What is the efficient scale of the painting company?

8. The city government is considering two tax proposals:
   - A lump-sum tax of $300 on each producer of hamburgers.
   - A tax of $1 per burger, paid by producers of hamburgers.

a. Which of the following curves—average fixed cost, average variable cost, average total cost, and marginal cost—would shift as a result of the lump-sum tax? Why? Show this in a graph. Label the graph as precisely as possible.
b. Which of these same four curves would shift as a result of the per-burger tax? Why? Show this in a new graph. Label the graph as precisely as possible.

9. Jane's Juice Bar has the following cost schedules:

Quantity	Variable Cost	Total Cost
0 vats of juice	$ 0	$ 30
1	10	40
2	25	55
3	45	75
4	70	100
5	100	130
6	135	165

a. Calculate average variable cost, average total cost, and marginal cost for each quantity.
b. Graph all three curves. What is the relationship between the marginal-cost curve and the average-total-cost curve? Between the marginal-cost curve and the average-variable-cost curve? Explain.

10. Consider the following table of long-run total costs for three different firms:

Quantity	1	2	3	4	5	6	7
Firm A	$60	$70	$80	$90	$100	$110	$120
Firm B	11	24	39	56	75	96	119
Firm C	21	34	49	66	85	106	129

Does each of these firms experience economies of scale or diseconomies of scale?

To find additional study resources, visit cengagebrain.com, and search for "Mankiw."

Firms in Competitive Markets

CHAPTER

14

If your local gas station raised its price for gasoline by 20 percent, it would see a large drop in the amount of gasoline it sold. Its customers would quickly switch to buying their gasoline at other gas stations. By contrast, if your local water company raised the price of water by 20 percent, it would see only a small decrease in the amount of water it sold. People might water their lawns less often and buy more water-efficient showerheads, but they would be hard-pressed to reduce water consumption greatly or to find another supplier. The difference between the gasoline market and the water market is that many firms supply gasoline to the local market, but only one firm supplies water. As you might expect, this difference in market structure shapes the pricing and production decisions of the firms that operate in these markets.

In this chapter, we examine the behavior of competitive firms, such as your local gas station. You may recall that a market is competitive if each buyer and seller is small compared to the size of the market and, therefore, has little ability to influence market prices. By contrast, if a firm can influence the market price of the good it sells, it is said to have *market power*. Later in the book, we examine the behavior of firms with market power, such as your local water company.

Our analysis of competitive firms in this chapter sheds light on the decisions that lie behind the supply curve in a competitive market. Not surprisingly, we find that a market supply curve is tightly linked to firms' costs of production. Less obvious, however, is the question of which among a firm's many types of cost—fixed, variable, average, and marginal—are most relevant for its supply decisions. We see that all these measures of cost play important and interrelated roles.

14-1 What Is a Competitive Market?

Our goal in this chapter is to examine how firms make production decisions in competitive markets. As a background for this analysis, we begin by reviewing what a competitive market is.

14-1a The Meaning of Competition

competitive market
a market with many buyers and sellers trading identical products so that each buyer and seller is a price taker

A **competitive market**, sometimes called a *perfectly competitive market*, has two characteristics:

- There are many buyers and many sellers in the market.
- The goods offered by the various sellers are largely the same.

As a result of these conditions, the actions of any single buyer or seller in the market have a negligible impact on the market price. Each buyer and seller takes the market price as given.

As an example, consider the market for milk. No single consumer of milk can influence the price of milk because each buys a small amount relative to the size of the market. Similarly, each dairy farmer has limited control over the price because many other sellers are offering milk that is essentially identical. Because each seller can sell all he wants at the going price, he has little reason to charge less, and if he charges more, buyers will go elsewhere. Buyers and sellers in competitive markets must accept the price the market determines and, therefore, are said to be *price takers*.

In addition to the previous two conditions for competition, a third condition is sometimes thought to characterize perfectly competitive markets:

- Firms can freely enter or exit the market.

If, for instance, anyone can start a dairy farm, and if any existing dairy farmer can leave the dairy business, then the dairy industry satisfies this condition. Much of the analysis of competitive firms does not require the assumption of free entry and exit because this condition is not necessary for firms to be price takers. Yet, as we see later in this chapter, when there is free entry and exit in a competitive market, it is a powerful force shaping the long-run equilibrium.

14-1b The Revenue of a Competitive Firm

A firm in a competitive market, like most other firms in the economy, tries to maximize profit (total revenue minus total cost). To see how it does this, we first consider the revenue of a competitive firm. To keep matters concrete, let's consider a specific firm: the Vaca Family Dairy Farm.

The Vaca Farm produces a quantity of milk, *Q*, and sells each unit at the market price, *P*. The farm's total revenue is $P \times Q$. For example, if a gallon of milk sells for \$6 and the farm sells 1,000 gallons, its total revenue is \$6,000.

Because the Vaca Farm is small compared to the world market for milk, it takes the price as given by market conditions. This means, in particular, that the price of milk does not depend on the number of gallons that the Vaca Farm produces and sells. If the Vacas double the amount of milk they produce to 2,000 gallons, the price of milk remains the same, and their total revenue doubles to \$12,000. As a result, total revenue is proportional to the amount of output.

Table 1 shows the revenue for the Vaca Family Dairy Farm. Columns (1) and (2) show the amount of output the farm produces and the price at which it sells its output. Column (3) is the farm's total revenue. The table assumes that the price of milk is \$6 a gallon, so total revenue is \$6 times the number of gallons.

Just as the concepts of average and marginal were useful in the preceding chapter when analyzing costs, they are also useful when analyzing revenue. To see what these concepts tell us, consider these two questions:

- How much revenue does the farm receive for the typical gallon of milk?
- How much additional revenue does the farm receive if it increases production of milk by 1 gallon?

Columns (4) and (5) in Table 1 answer these questions.

TABLE 1

Total, Average, and Marginal Revenue for a Competitive Firm

(1) Quantity (*Q*)	(2) Price (*P*)	(3) Total Revenue ($TR = P \times Q$)	(4) Average Revenue ($AR = TR / Q$)	(5) Marginal Revenue ($MR = \Delta TR / \Delta Q$)
1 gallon	\$6	\$6	\$6	
				\$6
2	6	12	6	
				6
3	6	18	6	
				6
4	6	24	6	
				6
5	6	30	6	
				6
6	6	36	6	
				6
7	6	42	6	
				6
8	6	48	6	

average revenue total revenue divided by the quantity sold

Column (4) in the table shows **average revenue**, which is total revenue [from column (3)] divided by the amount of output [from column (1)]. Average revenue tells us how much revenue a firm receives for the typical unit sold. In Table 1, you can see that average revenue equals $6, the price of a gallon of milk. This illustrates a general lesson that applies not only to competitive firms but to other firms as well. Average revenue is total revenue ($P \times Q$) divided by the quantity (Q). *Therefore, for all types of firms, average revenue equals the price of the good.*

marginal revenue the change in total revenue from an additional unit sold

Column (5) shows **marginal revenue**, which is the change in total revenue from the sale of each additional unit of output. In Table 1, marginal revenue equals $6, the price of a gallon of milk. This result illustrates a lesson that applies only to competitive firms. Total revenue is $P \times Q$, and P is fixed for a competitive firm. Therefore, when Q rises by 1 unit, total revenue rises by P dollars. *For competitive firms, marginal revenue equals the price of the good.*

QuickQuiz *When a competitive firm doubles the amount it sells, what happens to the price of its output and its total revenue?*

14-2 Profit Maximization and the Competitive Firm's Supply Curve

The goal of a firm is to maximize profit, which equals total revenue minus total cost. We have just discussed the competitive firm's revenue, and in the preceding chapter, we discussed the firm's costs. We are now ready to examine how a competitive firm maximizes profit and how that decision determines its supply curve.

14-2a A Simple Example of Profit Maximization

Let's begin our analysis of the firm's supply decision with the example in Table 2. Column (1) in the table shows the number of gallons of milk the Vaca Family Dairy Farm produces. Column (2) shows the farm's total revenue, which is $6 times the number of gallons. Column (3) shows the farm's total cost. Total cost includes fixed costs, which are $3 in this example, and variable costs, which depend on the quantity produced.

Column (4) shows the farm's profit, which is computed by subtracting total cost from total revenue. If the farm produces nothing, it has a loss of $3 (its fixed cost). If it produces 1 gallon, it has a profit of $1. If it produces 2 gallons, it has a profit of $4 and so on. Because the Vaca family's goal is to maximize profit, it chooses to produce the quantity of milk that makes profit as large as possible. In this example, profit is maximized when the farm produces either 4 or 5 gallons of milk, for a profit of $7.

There is another way to look at Vaca Farm's decision: The Vacas can find the profit-maximizing quantity by comparing the marginal revenue and marginal cost from each unit produced. Columns (5) and (6) in Table 2 compute marginal revenue and marginal cost from the changes in total revenue and total cost, and column (7) shows the change in profit for each additional gallon produced. The first gallon of milk the farm produces has a marginal revenue of $6 and a marginal cost of $2; hence, producing that gallon increases profit by $4 (from −$3 to $1). The second gallon produced has a marginal revenue of $6 and a marginal cost of $3, so that gallon increases profit by $3 (from $1 to $4). As long as marginal

TABLE 2

Profit Maximization: A Numerical Example

(1) Quantity (Q)	(2) Total Revenue (TR)	(3) Total Cost (TC)	(4) Profit ($TR - TC$)	(5) Marginal Revenue ($MR = \Delta TR / \Delta Q$)	(6) Marginal Cost ($MC = \Delta TR / \Delta Q$)	(7) Change in Profit ($MR - MC$)
0 gallons	$0	$3	−$3			
				$6	$2	$4
1	6	5	1			
				6	3	3
2	12	8	4			
				6	4	2
3	18	12	6			
				6	5	1
4	24	17	7			
				6	6	0
5	30	23	7			
				6	7	−1
6	36	30	6			
				6	8	−2
7	42	38	4			
				6	9	−3
8	48	47	1			

revenue exceeds marginal cost, increasing the quantity produced raises profit. Once the Vaca Farm has reached 5 gallons of milk, however, the situation changes. The sixth gallon would have a marginal revenue of $6 and a marginal cost of $7, so producing it would reduce profit by $1 (from $7 to $6). As a result, the Vacas would not produce beyond 5 gallons.

One of the *Ten Principles of Economics* in Chapter 1 is that rational people think at the margin. We now see how the Vaca Family Dairy Farm can apply this principle. If marginal revenue is greater than marginal cost—as it is at 1, 2, and 3 gallons—the Vacas should increase the production of milk because it will put more money in their pockets (marginal revenue) than it takes out (marginal cost). If marginal revenue is less than marginal cost—as it is at 6, 7, and 8 gallons—the Vacas should decrease production. If the Vacas think at the margin and make incremental adjustments to the level of production, they end up producing the profit-maximizing quantity.

14-2b The Marginal-Cost Curve and the Firm's Supply Decision

To extend this analysis of profit maximization, consider the cost curves in Figure 1. These cost curves have the three features that, as we discussed in the previous chapter, are thought to describe most firms: The marginal-cost curve (*MC*) is upward-sloping. The average-total-cost curve (*ATC*) is U-shaped. And the marginal-cost curve crosses the average-total-cost curve at the minimum of average total cost. The figure also shows a horizontal line at the market price (*P*). The price line is horizontal because a competitive firm is a price taker: The price

FIGURE 1

Profit Maximization for a Competitive Firm

This figure shows the marginal-cost curve (*MC*), the average-total-cost curve (*ATC*), and the average-variable-cost curve (*AVC*). It also shows the market price (*P*), which for a competitive firm equals both marginal revenue (*MR*) and average revenue (*AR*). At the quantity Q_1, marginal revenue MR_1 exceeds marginal cost MC_1, so raising production increases profit. At the quantity Q_2, marginal cost MC_2 is above marginal revenue MR_2, so reducing production increases profit. The profit-maximizing quantity Q_{MAX} is found where the horizontal line representing the price intersects the marginal-cost curve.

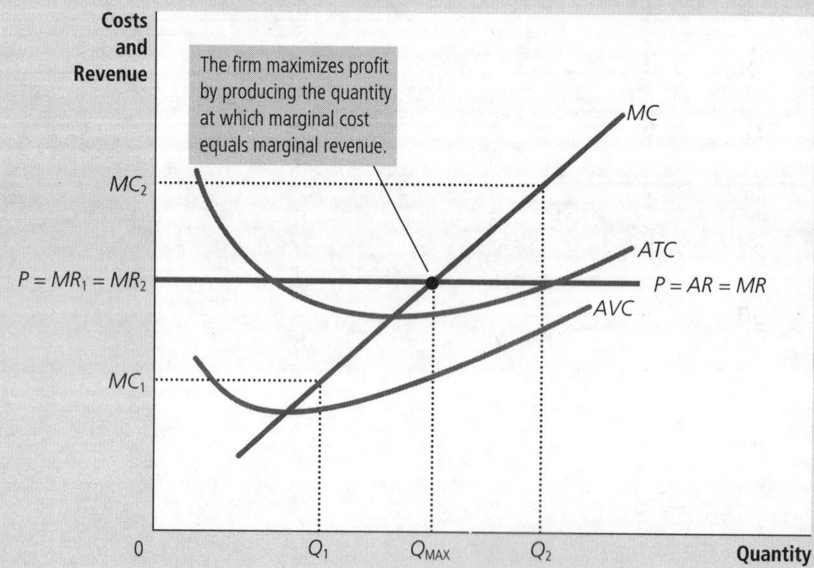

of the firm's output is the same regardless of the quantity that the firm decides to produce. Keep in mind that, for a competitive firm, the price equals both the firm's average revenue (*AR*) and its marginal revenue (*MR*).

We can use Figure 1 to find the quantity of output that maximizes profit. Imagine that the firm is producing at Q_1. At this level of output, the marginal-revenue curve is above the marginal-cost curve, showing that marginal revenue is greater than marginal cost. This means that if the firm were to raise production by 1 unit, the additional revenue (MR_1) would exceed the additional cost (MC_1). Profit, which equals total revenue minus total cost, would increase. Hence, if marginal revenue is greater than marginal cost, as it is at Q_1, the firm can increase profit by increasing production.

A similar argument applies when output is at Q_2. In this case, the marginal-cost curve is above the marginal-revenue curve, showing that marginal cost is greater than marginal revenue. If the firm were to reduce production by 1 unit, the costs saved (MC_2) would exceed the revenue lost (MR_2). Therefore, if marginal revenue is less than marginal cost, as it is at Q_2, the firm can increase profit by reducing production.

Where do these marginal adjustments to production end? Regardless of whether the firm begins with production at a low level (such as Q_1) or at a high level (such as Q_2), the firm will eventually adjust production until the quantity produced reaches Q_{MAX}. This analysis yields three general rules for profit maximization:

- If marginal revenue is greater than marginal cost, the firm should increase its output.
- If marginal cost is greater than marginal revenue, the firm should decrease its output.
- At the profit-maximizing level of output, marginal revenue and marginal cost are exactly equal.

These rules are the key to rational decision making by any profit-maximizing firm. They apply not only to competitive firms but, as we will see in the next chapter, to other types of firms as well.

We can now see how the competitive firm decides what quantity of its good to supply to the market. Because a competitive firm is a price taker, its marginal revenue equals the market price. For any given price, the competitive firm's profit-maximizing quantity of output is found by looking at the intersection of the price with the marginal-cost curve. In Figure 1, that quantity of output is Q_{MAX}.

Suppose that the price prevailing in this market rises, perhaps because of an increase in market demand. Figure 2 shows how a competitive firm responds to the price increase. When the price is P_1, the firm produces quantity Q_1, the quantity that equates marginal cost to the price. When the price rises to P_2, the firm finds that marginal revenue is now higher than marginal cost at the previous level of output, so the firm increases production. The new profit-maximizing quantity is Q_2, at which marginal cost equals the new, higher price. *In essence, because the firm's marginal-cost curve determines the quantity of the good the firm is willing to supply at any price, the marginal-cost curve is also the competitive firm's supply curve.* There are, however, some caveats to this conclusion, which we examine next.

14-2c The Firm's Short-Run Decision to Shut Down

So far, we have been analyzing the question of how much a competitive firm will produce. In certain circumstances, however, the firm will decide to shut down and not produce anything at all.

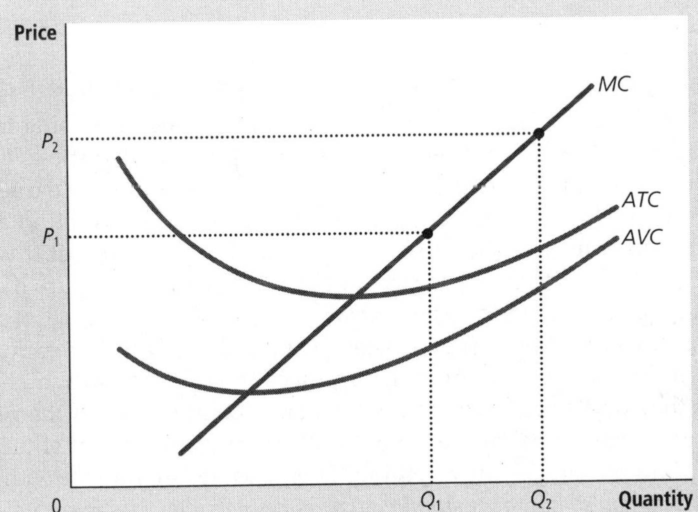

FIGURE 2

Marginal Cost as the Competitive Firm's Supply Curve

An increase in the price from P_1 to P_2 leads to an increase in the firm's profit-maximizing quantity from Q_1 to Q_2. Because the marginal-cost curve shows the quantity supplied by the firm at any given price, it is the firm's supply curve.

Here we need to distinguish between a temporary shutdown of a firm and the permanent exit of a firm from the market. A *shutdown* refers to a short-run decision not to produce anything during a specific period of time because of current market conditions. *Exit* refers to a long-run decision to leave the market. The short-run and long-run decisions differ because most firms cannot avoid their fixed costs in the short run but can do so in the long run. That is, a firm that shuts down temporarily still has to pay its fixed costs, whereas a firm that exits the market does not have to pay any costs at all, fixed or variable.

For example, consider the production decision that a farmer faces. The cost of the land is one of the farmer's fixed costs. If the farmer decides not to produce any crops one season, the land lies fallow, and he cannot recover this cost. When making the short-run decision of whether to shut down for a season, the fixed cost of land is said to be a *sunk cost*. By contrast, if the farmer decides to leave farming altogether, he can sell the land. When making the long-run decision of whether to exit the market, the cost of land is not sunk. (We return to the issue of sunk costs shortly.)

Now let's consider what determines a firm's shutdown decision. If the firm shuts down, it loses all revenue from the sale of its product. At the same time, it saves the variable costs of making its product (but must still pay the fixed costs). Thus, *the firm shuts down if the revenue that it would earn from producing is less than its variable costs of production.*

A bit of mathematics can make this shutdown rule more useful. If TR stands for total revenue and VC stands for variable cost, then the firm's decision can be written as

$$\text{Shut down if } TR < VC.$$

The firm shuts down if total revenue is less than variable cost. By dividing both sides of this inequality by the quantity Q, we can write it as

$$\text{Shut down if } TR/Q < VC/Q.$$

The left side of the inequality, TR/Q, is total revenue $P \times Q$ divided by quantity Q, which is average revenue, most simply expressed as the good's price, P. The right side of the inequality, VC/Q, is average variable cost, AVC. Therefore, the firm's shutdown rule can be restated as

$$\text{Shut down if } P < AVC.$$

That is, a firm chooses to shut down if the price of the good is less than the average variable cost of production. This rule is intuitive: When choosing to produce, the firm compares the price it receives for the typical unit to the average variable cost that it must incur to produce the typical unit. If the price doesn't cover the average variable cost, the firm is better off stopping production altogether. The firm still loses money (because it has to pay fixed costs), but it would lose even more money by staying open. The firm can reopen in the future if conditions change so that price exceeds average variable cost.

We now have a full description of a competitive firm's profit-maximizing strategy. If the firm produces anything, it produces the quantity at which marginal cost equals the good's price, which the firm takes as given. Yet if the price is less than average variable cost at that quantity, the firm is better off shutting down temporarily and not producing anything. These results are illustrated in Figure 3. *The competitive firm's short-run supply curve is the portion of its marginal-cost curve that lies above average variable cost.*

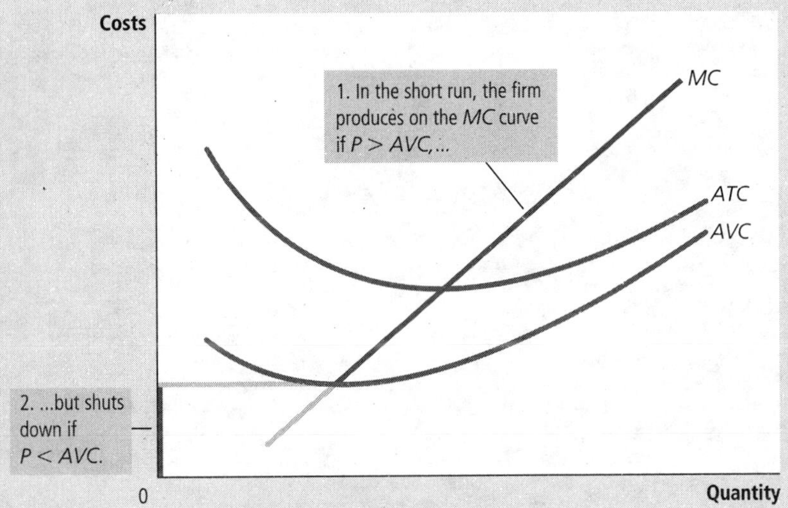

FIGURE 3

The Competitive Firm's Short-Run Supply Curve In the short run, the competitive firm's supply curve is its marginal-cost curve (*MC*) above average variable cost (*AVC*). If the price falls below average variable cost, the firm is better off shutting down temporarily.

14-2d Spilt Milk and Other Sunk Costs

Sometime in your life you may have been told, "Don't cry over spilt milk," or "Let bygones be bygones." These adages hold a deep truth about rational decision making. Economists say that a cost is a **sunk cost** when it has already been committed and cannot be recovered. Because nothing can be done about sunk costs, you should ignore them when making decisions about various aspects of life, including business strategy.

sunk cost
a cost that has already been committed and cannot be recovered

Our analysis of the firm's shutdown decision is one example of the irrelevance of sunk costs. We assume that the firm cannot recover its fixed costs by temporarily stopping production. That is, regardless of the quantity of output supplied (even if it is zero), the firm still has to pay its fixed costs. As a result, the fixed costs are sunk in the short run, and the firm should ignore them when deciding how much to produce. The firm's short-run supply curve is the part of the marginal-cost curve that lies above average variable cost, and the size of the fixed cost does not matter for this supply decision.

The irrelevance of sunk costs is also important when making personal decisions. Imagine, for instance, that you place a $15 value on seeing a newly released movie. You buy a ticket for $10, but before entering the theater, you lose the ticket. Should you buy another ticket? Or should you now go home and refuse to pay a total of $20 to see the movie? The answer is that you should buy another ticket. The benefit of seeing the movie ($15) still exceeds the opportunity cost (the $10 for the second ticket). The $10 you paid for the lost ticket is a sunk cost. As with spilt milk, there is no point in crying about it.

CASE STUDY

NEAR-EMPTY RESTAURANTS AND OFF-SEASON MINIATURE GOLF

Have you ever walked into a restaurant for lunch and found it almost empty? Why, you might have asked, does the restaurant even bother to stay open? It might seem that the revenue from so few customers could not possibly cover the cost of running the restaurant.

In making the decision of whether to open for lunch, a restaurant owner must keep in mind the distinction between fixed and variable costs. Many of

Staying open can be profitable, even with many tables empty.

a restaurant's costs—the rent, kitchen equipment, tables, plates, silverware, and so on—are fixed. Shutting down during lunch would not reduce these costs. In other words, these costs are sunk in the short run. When the owner is deciding whether to serve lunch, only the variable costs—the price of the additional food and the wages of the extra staff—are relevant. The owner shuts down the restaurant at lunchtime only if the revenue from the few lunchtime customers would fail to cover the restaurant's variable costs.

An operator of a miniature-golf course in a summer resort community faces a similar decision. Because revenue varies substantially from season to season, the firm must decide when to open and when to close. Once again, the fixed costs—the costs of buying the land and building the course—are irrelevant in making this short-run decision. The miniature-golf course should be open for business only during those times of year when its revenue exceeds its variable costs. ●

14-2e The Firm's Long-Run Decision to Exit or Enter a Market

A firm's long-run decision to exit a market is similar to its shutdown decision. If the firm exits, it will again lose all revenue from the sale of its product, but now it will save not only its variable costs of production but also its fixed costs. Thus, *the firm exits the market if the revenue it would get from producing is less than its total cost*.

We can again make this rule more useful by writing it mathematically. If TR stands for total revenue and TC stands for total cost, then the firm's exit rule can be written as

$$\text{Exit if } TR < TC.$$

The firm exits if total revenue is less than total cost. By dividing both sides of this inequality by quantity Q, we can write it as

$$\text{Exit if } TR/Q < TC/Q.$$

We can simplify this further by noting that TR/Q is average revenue, which equals the price P, and that TC/Q is average total cost, ATC. Therefore, the firm's exit rule is

$$\text{Exit if } P < ATC.$$

That is, a firm chooses to exit if the price of its good is less than the average total cost of production.

A parallel analysis applies to an entrepreneur who is considering starting a firm. He will enter the market if starting the firm would be profitable, which occurs if the price of the good exceeds the average total cost of production. The entry rule is

$$\text{Enter if } P > ATC.$$

The rule for entry is exactly the opposite of the rule for exit.

We can now describe a competitive firm's long-run profit-maximizing strategy. If the firm produces anything, it chooses the quantity at which marginal cost equals the price of the good. Yet if the price is less than the average total cost at that quantity, the firm chooses to exit (or not enter) the market. These results are illustrated in Figure 4. *The competitive firm's long-run supply curve is the portion of its marginal-cost curve that lies above average total cost.*

14-2f Measuring Profit in Our Graph for the Competitive Firm

As we study exit and entry, it is useful to analyze the firm's profit in more detail. Recall that profit equals total revenue (TR) minus total cost (TC):

$$\text{Profit} = TR - TC.$$

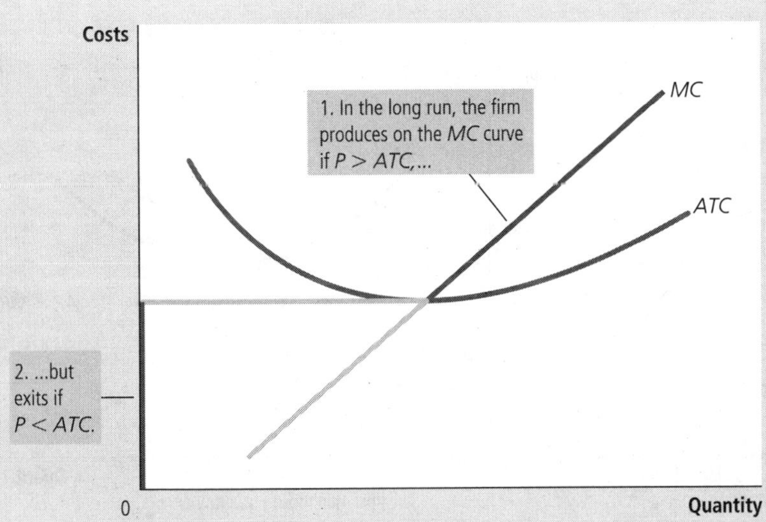

FIGURE 4

The Competitive Firm's Long-Run Supply Curve

In the long run, the competitive firm's supply curve is its marginal-cost curve (MC) above average total cost (ATC). If the price falls below average total cost, the firm is better off exiting the market.

We can rewrite this definition by multiplying and dividing the right side by Q:

$$\text{Profit} = (TR/Q - TC/Q) \times Q.$$

Note that TR/Q is average revenue, which is the price, P, and TC/Q is average total cost, ATC. Therefore,

$$\text{Profit} = (P - ATC) \times Q.$$

This way of expressing the firm's profit allows us to measure profit in our graphs.

Panel (a) of Figure 5 shows a firm earning positive profit. As we have already discussed, the firm maximizes profit by producing the quantity at which price equals marginal cost. Now look at the shaded rectangle. The height of the rectangle is $P - ATC$, the difference between price and average total cost. The width of the rectangle is Q, the quantity produced. Therefore, the area of the rectangle is $(P - ATC) \times Q$, which is the firm's profit.

Similarly, panel (b) of this figure shows a firm with losses (negative profit). In this case, maximizing profit means minimizing losses, a task accomplished once again by producing the quantity at which price equals marginal cost. Now consider the shaded rectangle. The height of the rectangle is $ATC - P$, and the width is Q. The area is $(ATC - P) \times Q$, which is the firm's loss. Because a firm in this situation is not making enough revenue on each unit to cover its average total cost, it would choose to exit the market in the long run.

QuickQuiz *How does a competitive firm determine its profit-maximizing level of output? Explain. • When does a profit-maximizing competitive firm decide to shut down? When does it decide to exit a market?*

FIGURE 5

Profit as the Area between Price and Average Total Cost

The area of the shaded box between price and average total cost represents the firm's profit. The height of this box is price minus average total cost ($P - ATC$), and the width of the box is the quantity of output (Q). In panel (a), price is above average total cost, so the firm has positive profit. In panel (b), price is less than average total cost, so the firm incurs a loss.

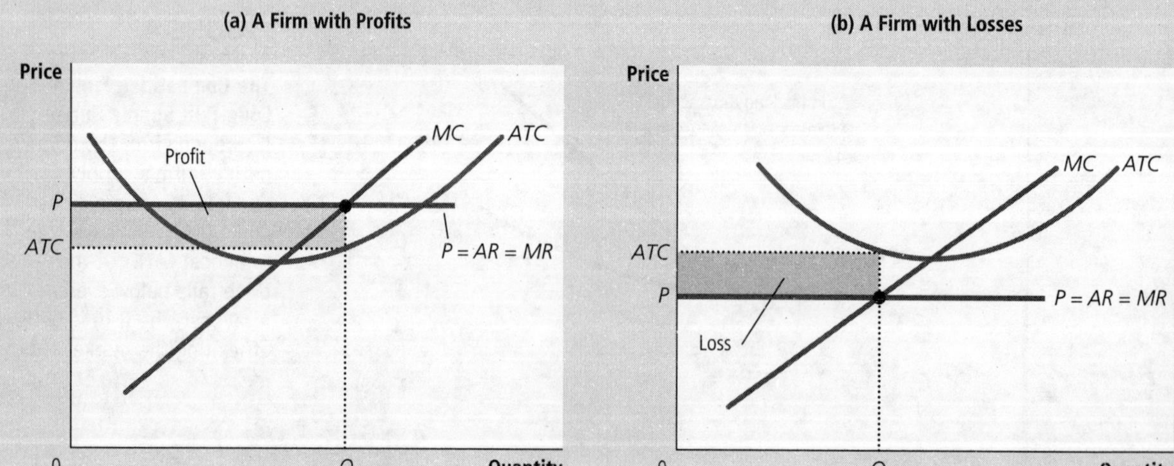

14-3 The Supply Curve in a Competitive Market

Now that we have examined the supply decision of a single firm, we can discuss the supply curve for a market. There are two cases to consider. First, we examine a market with a fixed number of firms. Second, we examine a market in which the number of firms can change as old firms exit the market and new firms enter. Both cases are important, for each applies to a specific time horizon. Over short periods of time, it is often difficult for firms to enter and exit, so the assumption of a fixed number of firms is appropriate. But over long periods of time, the number of firms can adjust to changing market conditions.

14-3a The Short Run: Market Supply with a Fixed Number of Firms

Consider a market with 1,000 identical firms. For any given price, each firm supplies a quantity of output so that its marginal cost equals the price, as shown in panel (a) of Figure 6. That is, as long as price is above average variable cost, each firm's marginal-cost curve is its supply curve. The quantity of output supplied to the market equals the sum of the quantities supplied by each of the 1,000 individual firms. Thus, to derive the market supply curve, we add the quantity supplied by each firm in the market. As panel (b) of Figure 6 shows, because the firms are identical, the quantity supplied to the market is 1,000 times the quantity supplied by each firm.

14-3b The Long Run: Market Supply with Entry and Exit

Now consider what happens if firms are able to enter and exit the market. Let's suppose that everyone has access to the same technology for producing the good

In the short run, the number of firms in the market is fixed. As a result, the market supply curve, shown in panel (b), reflects the individual firms' marginal-cost curves, shown in panel (a). Here, in a market of 1,000 firms, the quantity of output supplied to the market is 1,000 times the quantity supplied by each firm.

FIGURE 6

Short-Run Market Supply

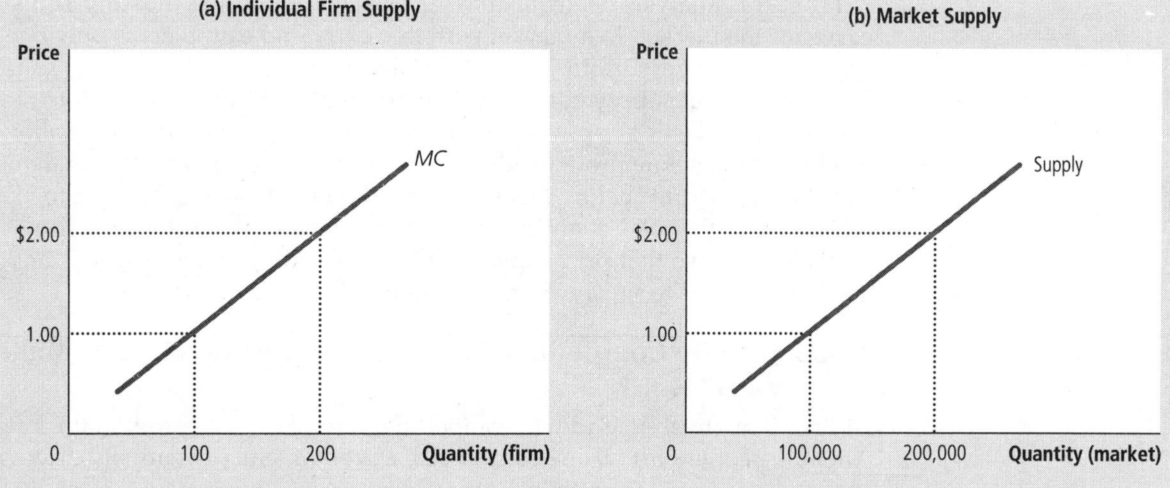

and access to the same markets to buy the inputs for production. Therefore, all current and potential firms have the same cost curves.

Decisions about entry and exit in a market of this type depend on the incentives facing the owners of existing firms and the entrepreneurs who could start new firms. If firms already in the market are profitable, then new firms will have an incentive to enter the market. This entry will expand the number of firms, increase the quantity of the good supplied, and drive down prices and profits. Conversely, if firms in the market are making losses, then some existing firms will exit the market. Their exit will reduce the number of firms, decrease the quantity of the good supplied, and drive up prices and profits. *At the end of this process of entry and exit, firms that remain in the market must be making zero economic profit.*

Recall that we can write a firm's profit as

$$\text{Profit} = (P - ATC) \times Q.$$

This equation shows that an operating firm has zero profit if and only if the price of the good equals the average total cost of producing that good. If price is above average total cost, profit is positive, which encourages new firms to enter. If price is less than average total cost, profit is negative, which encourages some firms to exit. *The process of entry and exit ends only when price and average total cost are driven to equality.*

This analysis has a surprising implication. We noted earlier in the chapter that competitive firms maximize profits by choosing a quantity at which price equals marginal cost. We just noted that free entry and exit force price to equal average total cost. But if price is to equal both marginal cost and average total cost, these two measures of cost must equal each other. Marginal cost and average total cost are equal, however, only when the firm is operating at the minimum of average total cost. Recall from the preceding chapter that the level of production with lowest average total cost is called the firm's *efficient scale*. Therefore, *in the long-run equilibrium of a competitive market with free entry and exit, firms must be operating at their efficient scale.*

Panel (a) of Figure 7 shows a firm in such a long-run equilibrium. In this figure, price P equals marginal cost MC, so the firm is maximizing profit. Price also equals average total cost ATC, so profit is zero. New firms have no incentive to enter the market, and existing firms have no incentive to leave the market.

From this analysis of firm behavior, we can determine the long-run supply curve for the market. In a market with free entry and exit, there is only one price consistent with zero profit—the minimum of average total cost. As a result, the long-run market supply curve must be horizontal at this price, as illustrated by the perfectly elastic supply curve in panel (b) of Figure 7. Any price above this level would generate profit, leading to entry and an increase in the total quantity supplied. Any price below this level would generate losses, leading to exit and a decrease in the total quantity supplied. Eventually, the number of firms in the market adjusts so that price equals the minimum of average total cost, and there are enough firms to satisfy all the demand at this price.

14-3c Why Do Competitive Firms Stay in Business If They Make Zero Profit?

At first, it might seem odd that competitive firms earn zero profit in the long run. After all, people start businesses to make a profit. If entry eventually drives profit to zero, there might seem to be little reason to stay in business.

FIGURE 7

Long-Run Market Supply

In the long run, firms will enter or exit the market until profit is driven to zero. As a result, price equals the minimum of average total cost, as shown in panel (a). The number of firms adjusts to ensure that all demand is satisfied at this price. The long-run market supply curve is horizontal at this price, as shown in panel (b).

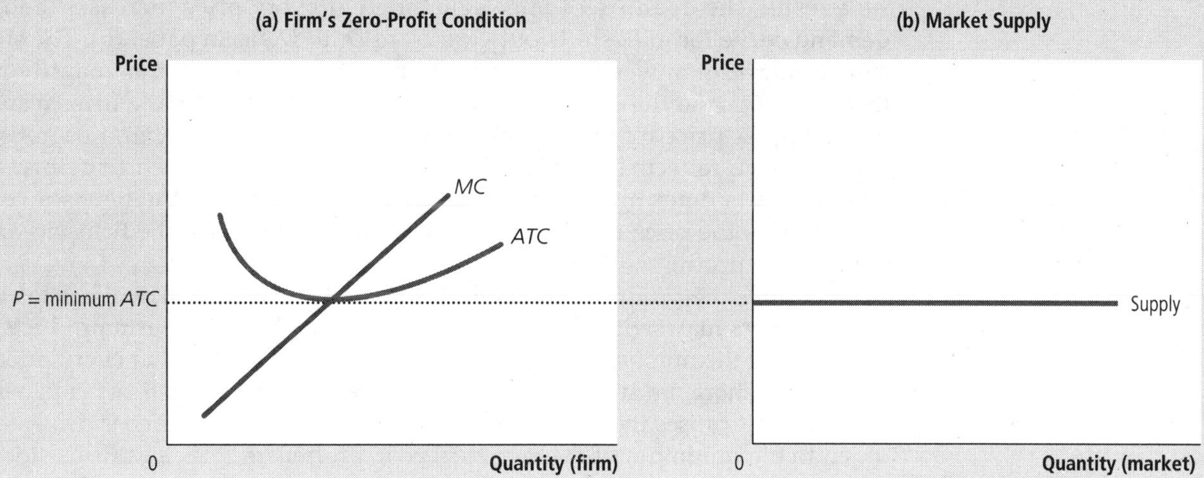

To understand the zero-profit condition more fully, recall that profit equals total revenue minus total cost and that total cost includes all the opportunity costs of the firm. In particular, total cost includes the time and money that the firm owners devote to the business. In the zero-profit equilibrium, the firm's revenue must compensate the owners for these opportunity costs.

Consider an example. Suppose that, to start his farm, a farmer had to invest \$1 million, which otherwise he could have deposited in a bank and earned \$50,000 a year in interest. In addition, he had to give up another job that would have paid him \$30,000 a year. Then the farmer's opportunity cost of farming includes both the interest he could have earned and the forgone wages—a total of \$80,000. Even if his profit is driven to zero, his revenue from farming compensates him for these opportunity costs.

Keep in mind that accountants and economists measure costs differently. As we discussed in the previous chapter, accountants keep track of explicit costs but not implicit costs. That is, they measure costs that require an outflow of money from the firm, but they do not include the opportunity costs of production that do not involve an outflow of money. As a result, in the zero-profit equilibrium, economic profit is zero, but accounting profit is positive. Our farmer's accountant, for instance, would conclude that the farmer earned an accounting profit of \$80,000, which is enough to keep the farmer in business.

"We're a nonprofit organization—we don't intend to be, but we are!"

14-3d A Shift in Demand in the Short Run and Long Run

Now that we have a more complete understanding of how firms make supply decisions, we can better explain how markets respond to changes in demand. Because firms can enter and exit in the long run but not in the short run, the response of a market to a change in demand depends on the time horizon. To see this, let's trace the effects of a shift in demand over time.

Suppose the market for milk begins in a long-run equilibrium. Firms are earning zero profit, so price equals the minimum of average total cost. Panel (a) of Figure 8 shows this situation. The long-run equilibrium is point A, the quantity sold in the market is Q_1, and the price is P_1.

Now suppose scientists discover that milk has miraculous health benefits. As a result, the quantity of milk demanded at every price increases, and the demand curve for milk shifts outward from D_1 to D_2, as in panel (b). The short-run equilibrium moves from point A to point B; as a result, the quantity rises from Q_1 to Q_2, and the price rises from P_1 to P_2. All of the existing firms respond to the higher price by raising the amount they produce. Because each firm's supply curve reflects its marginal-cost curve, how much each firm increases production is determined by the marginal-cost curve. In the new short-run equilibrium, the price of milk exceeds average total cost, so the firms are making positive profit.

Over time, the profit generated in this market encourages new firms to enter. Some farmers may switch to producing milk instead of other farm products, for example. As the number of firms grows, the quantity supplied at every price increases, the short-run supply curve shifts to the right from S_1 to S_2, as in panel (c), and this shift causes the price of milk to fall. Eventually, the price is driven back down to the minimum of average total cost, profits are zero, and firms stop entering. Thus, the market reaches a new long-run equilibrium, point C. The price of milk has returned to P_1, but the quantity produced has risen to Q_3. Each firm is again producing at its efficient scale, but because more firms are in the dairy business, the quantity of milk produced and sold is higher.

14-3e Why the Long-Run Supply Curve Might Slope Upward

So far, we have seen that entry and exit can cause the long-run market supply curve to be perfectly elastic. The essence of our analysis is that there are a large number of potential entrants, each of which faces the same costs. As a result, the long-run market supply curve is horizontal at the minimum of average total cost. When the demand for the good increases, the long-run result is an increase in the number of firms and in the total quantity supplied, without any change in the price.

There are, however, two reasons that the long-run market supply curve might slope upward. The first is that some resources used in production may be available only in limited quantities. For example, consider the market for farm products. Anyone can choose to buy land and start a farm, but the quantity of land is limited. As more people become farmers, the price of farmland is bid up, which raises the costs of all farmers in the market. Thus, an increase in demand for farm products cannot induce an increase in quantity supplied without also inducing a rise in farmers' costs, which in turn means a rise in price. The result is a long-run market supply curve that is upward-sloping, even with free entry into farming.

A second reason for an upward-sloping supply curve is that firms may have different costs. For example, consider the market for painters. Anyone can enter the market for painting services, but not everyone has the same costs. Costs vary in part because some people work faster than others and in part because some people have better alternative uses of their time than others. For any given price, those with lower costs are more likely to enter than those with higher costs. To increase the quantity of painting services supplied, additional entrants must be encouraged to enter the market. Because these new entrants have higher costs,

FIGURE 8

An Increase in Demand in the Short Run and Long Run

The market starts in a long-run equilibrium, shown as point A in panel (a). In this equilibrium, each firm makes zero profit, and the price equals the minimum average total cost. Panel (b) shows what happens in the short run when demand rises from D_1 to D_2. The equilibrium goes from point A to point B, price rises from P_1 to P_2, and the quantity sold in the market rises from Q_1 to Q_2. Because price now exceeds average total cost, each firm now makes a profit, which over time encourages new firms to enter the market. This entry shifts the short-run supply curve to the right from S_1 to S_2, as shown in panel (c). In the new long-run equilibrium, point C, price has returned to P_1 but the quantity sold has increased to Q_3. Profits are again zero, and price is back to the minimum of average total cost, but the market has more firms to satisfy the greater demand.

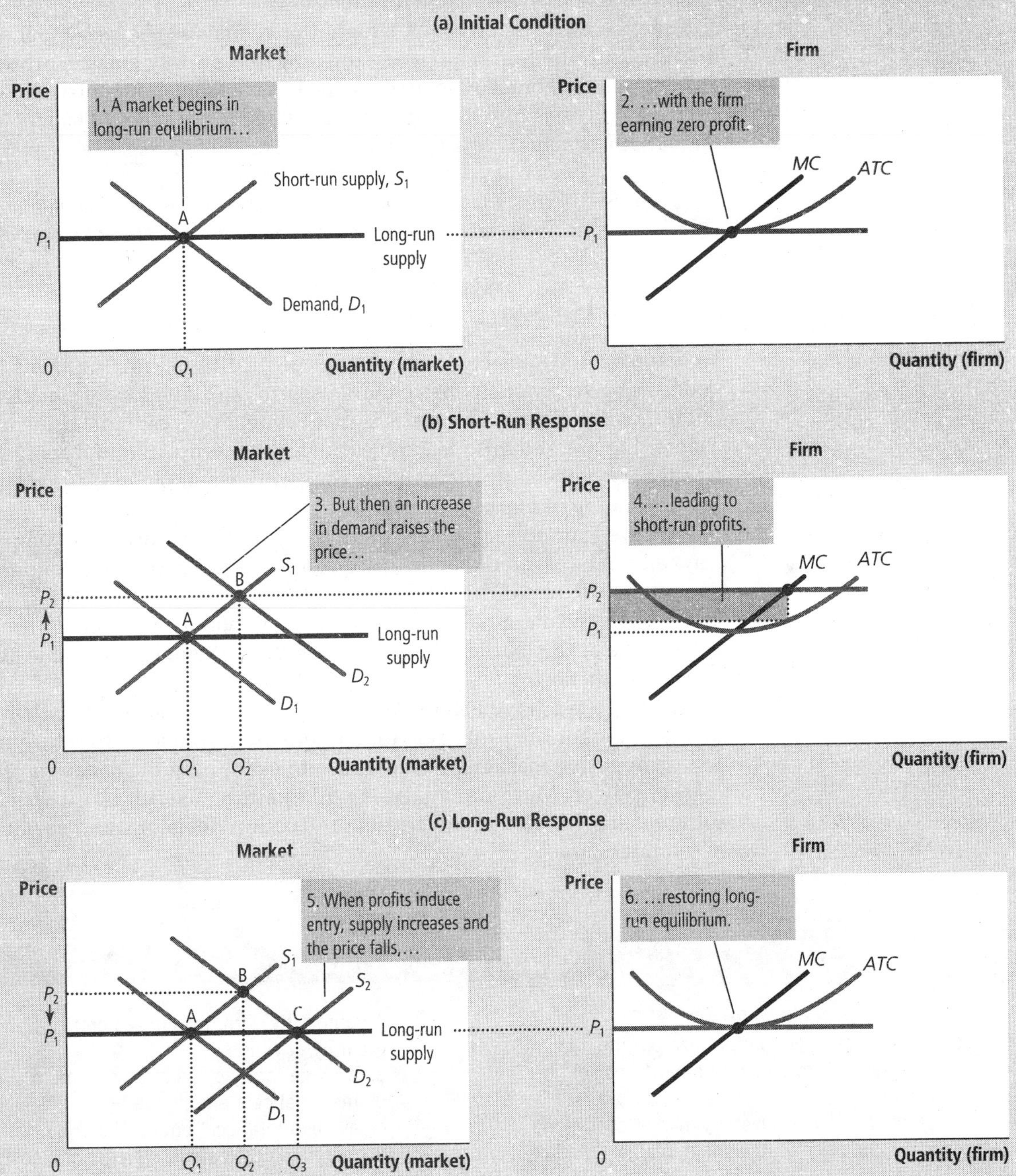

the price must rise to make entry profitable for them. Thus, the long-run market supply curve for painting services slopes upward even with free entry into the market.

Notice that if firms have different costs, some firms earn profit even in the long run. In this case, the price in the market reflects the average total cost of the *marginal firm*—the firm that would exit the market if the price were any lower. This firm earns zero profit, but firms with lower costs earn positive profit. Entry does not eliminate this profit because would-be entrants have higher costs than firms already in the market. Higher-cost firms will enter only if the price rises, making the market profitable for them.

Thus, for these two reasons, a higher price may be necessary to induce a larger quantity supplied, in which case the long-run supply curve is upward-sloping rather than horizontal. Nonetheless, the basic lesson about entry and exit remains true. *Because firms can enter and exit more easily in the long run than in the short run, the long-run supply curve is typically more elastic than the short-run supply curve.*

QuickQuiz *In the long run with free entry and exit, is the price in a market equal to marginal cost, average total cost, both, or neither? Explain with a diagram.*

14-4 Conclusion: Behind the Supply Curve

We have been discussing the behavior of profit-maximizing firms that supply goods in perfectly competitive markets. You may recall from Chapter 1 that one of the *Ten Principles of Economics* is that rational people think at the margin. This chapter has applied this idea to the competitive firm. Marginal analysis has given us a theory of the supply curve in a competitive market and, as a result, a deeper understanding of market outcomes.

We have learned that when you buy a good from a firm in a competitive market, you can be assured that the price you pay is close to the cost of producing that good. In particular, if firms are competitive and profit-maximizing, the price of a good equals the marginal cost of making that good. In addition, if firms can freely enter and exit the market, the price also equals the lowest possible average total cost of production.

Although we have assumed throughout this chapter that firms are price takers, many of the tools developed here are also useful for studying firms in less competitive markets. We now turn to examining the behavior of firms with market power. Marginal analysis will again be useful, but it will have quite different implications for a firm's production decisions and for the nature of market outcomes.

CHAPTER QuickQuiz

1. A perfectly competitive firm
   a. chooses its price to maximize profits.
   b. sets its price to undercut other firms selling similar products.
   c. takes its price as given by market conditions.
   d. picks the price that yields the largest market share.

2. A competitive firm maximizes profit by choosing the quantity at which
   a. average total cost is at its minimum.
   b. marginal cost equals the price.
   c. average total cost equals the price.
   d. marginal cost equals average total cost.

3. A competitive firm's short-run supply curve is its ________ cost curve above its ________ cost curve.
   a. average total, marginal
   b. average variable, marginal
   c. marginal, average total
   d. marginal, average variable
4. If a profit-maximizing, competitive firm is producing a quantity at which marginal cost is between average variable cost and average total cost, it will
   a. keep producing in the short run but exit the market in the long run.
   b. shut down in the short run but return to production in the long run.
   c. shut down in the short run and exit the market in the long run.
   d. keep producing both in the short run and in the long run.
5. In the long-run equilibrium of a competitive market with identical firms, what are the relationships among price *P*, marginal cost *MC*, and average total cost *ATC*?
   a. $P > MC$ and $P > ATC$.
   b. $P > MC$ and $P = ATC$.
   c. $P = MC$ and $P > ATC$.
   d. $P = MC$ and $P = ATC$.
6. Pretzel stands in New York City are a perfectly competitive industry in long-run equilibrium. One day, the city starts imposing a $100 per month tax on each stand. How does this policy affect the number of pretzels consumed in the short run and the long run?
   a. down in the short run, no change in the long run
   b. up in the short run, no change in the long run
   c. no change in the short run, down in the long run
   d. no change in the short run, up in the long run

SUMMARY

- Because a competitive firm is a price taker, its revenue is proportional to the amount of output it produces. The price of the good equals both the firm's average revenue and its marginal revenue.
- To maximize profit, a firm chooses a quantity of output such that marginal revenue equals marginal cost. Because marginal revenue for a competitive firm equals the market price, the firm chooses quantity so that price equals marginal cost. Thus, the firm's marginal-cost curve is its supply curve.
- In the short run when a firm cannot recover its fixed costs, the firm will choose to shut down temporarily if the price of the good is less than average variable cost. In the long run when the firm can recover both fixed and variable costs, it will choose to exit if the price is less than average total cost.
- In a market with free entry and exit, profit is driven to zero in the long run. In this long-run equilibrium, all firms produce at the efficient scale, price equals the minimum of average total cost, and the number of firms adjusts to satisfy the quantity demanded at this price.
- Changes in demand have different effects over different time horizons. In the short run, an increase in demand raises prices and leads to profits, and a decrease in demand lowers prices and leads to losses. But if firms can freely enter and exit the market, then in the long run, the number of firms adjusts to drive the market back to the zero-profit equilibrium.

KEY CONCEPTS

competitive market, p. 268
average revenue, p. 270
marginal revenue, p. 270
sunk cost, p. 275

QUESTIONS FOR REVIEW

1. What are the main characteristics of a competitive market?
2. Explain the difference between a firm's revenue and its profit. Which do firms maximize?
3. Draw the cost curves for a typical firm. Explain how a competitive firm chooses the level of output that maximizes profit. At that level of output, show on your graph the firm's total revenue and total cost.
4. Under what conditions will a firm shut down temporarily? Explain.
5. Under what conditions will a firm exit a market? Explain.

6. Does a competitive firm's price equal its marginal cost in the short run, in the long run, or both? Explain.
7. Does a competitive firm's price equal the minimum of its average total cost in the short run, in the long run, or both? Explain.
8. Are market supply curves typically more elastic in the short run or in the long run? Explain.

PROBLEMS AND APPLICATIONS

1. Many small boats are made of fiberglass and a resin derived from crude oil. Suppose that the price of oil rises.
   a. Using diagrams, show what happens to the cost curves of an individual boat-making firm and to the market supply curve.
   b. What happens to the profits of boat makers in the short run? What happens to the number of boat makers in the long run?
2. Bob's lawn-mowing service is a profit-maximizing, competitive firm. Bob mows lawns for $27 each. His total cost each day is $280, of which $30 is a fixed cost. He mows 10 lawns a day. What can you say about Bob's short-run decision regarding shutdown and his long-run decision regarding exit?
3. Consider total cost and total revenue given in the following table:

Quantity	0	1	2	3	4	5	6	7
Total cost	$8	9	10	11	13	19	27	37
Total revenue	$0	8	16	24	32	40	48	56

   a. Calculate profit for each quantity. How much should the firm produce to maximize profit?
   b. Calculate marginal revenue and marginal cost for each quantity. Graph them. (*Hint*: Put the points between whole numbers. For example, the marginal cost between 2 and 3 should be graphed at 2½.) At what quantity do these curves cross? How does this relate to your answer to part (a)?
   c. Can you tell whether this firm is in a competitive industry? If so, can you tell whether the industry is in a long-run equilibrium?
4. Ball Bearings, Inc., faces costs of production as follows:

Quantity	Total Fixed Cost	Total Variable Cost
0	$100	$0
1	100	50
2	100	70
3	100	90
4	100	140
5	100	200
6	100	360

   a. Calculate the company's average fixed cost, average variable cost, average total cost, and marginal cost at each level of production.
   b. The price of a case of ball bearings is $50. Seeing that he can't make a profit, the chief executive officer (CEO) decides to shut down operations. What is the firm's profit/loss? Was this a wise decision? Explain.
   c. Vaguely remembering his introductory economics course, the chief financial officer tells the CEO it is better to produce 1 case of ball bearings, because marginal revenue equals marginal cost at that quantity. What is the firm's profit/loss at that level of production? Was this the best decision? Explain.
5. Suppose the book-printing industry is competitive and begins in a long-run equilibrium.
   a. Draw a diagram showing the average total cost, marginal cost, marginal revenue, and supply curve of the typical firm in the industry.
   b. Hi-Tech Printing Company invents a new process that sharply reduces the cost of printing books. What happens to Hi-Tech's profits and to the price of books in the short run when Hi-Tech's patent prevents other firms from using the new technology?
   c. What happens in the long run when the patent expires and other firms are free to use the technology?
6. A firm in a competitive market receives $500 in total revenue and has marginal revenue of $10. What is the average revenue, and how many units were sold?
7. A profit-maximizing firm in a competitive market is currently producing 100 units of output. It has average revenue of $10, average total cost of $8, and fixed cost of $200.
   a. What is its profit?
   b. What is its marginal cost?
   c. What is its average variable cost?
   d. Is the efficient scale of the firm more than, less than, or exactly 100 units?

8. The market for fertilizer is perfectly competitive. Firms in the market are producing output but are currently incurring economic losses.
   a. How does the price of fertilizer compare to the average total cost, the average variable cost, and the marginal cost of producing fertilizer?
   b. Draw two graphs, side by side, illustrating the present situation for the typical firm and for the market.
   c. Assuming there is no change in either demand or the firms' cost curves, explain what will happen in the long run to the price of fertilizer, marginal cost, average total cost, the quantity supplied by each firm, and the total quantity supplied to the market.
9. The market for apple pies in the city of Ectenia is competitive and has the following demand schedule:

Price	Quantity Demanded
$1	1,200 pies
2	1,100
3	1,000
4	900
5	800
6	700
7	600
8	500
9	400
10	300
11	200
12	100
13	0

Each producer in the market has fixed costs of $9 and the following marginal cost:

Quantity	Marginal Cost
1 pie	$2
2	4
3	6
4	8
5	10
6	12

   a. Compute each producer's total cost and average total cost for 1 to 6 pies.
   b. The price of a pie is now $11. How many pies are sold? How many pies does each producer make? How many producers are there? How much profit does each producer earn?
   c. Is the situation described in part (b) a long-run equilibrium? Why or why not?
   d. Suppose that in the long run there is free entry and exit. How much profit does each producer earn in the long-run equilibrium? What is the market price? How many pies does each producer make? How many pies are sold in the market? How many pie producers are operating?
10. An industry currently has 100 firms, each of which has fixed cost of $16 and average variable cost as follows:

Quantity	Average Variable Cost
1	$1
2	2
3	3
4	4
5	5
6	6

   a. Compute a firm's marginal cost and average total cost for each quantity from 1 to 6.
   b. The equilibrium price is currently $10. How much does each firm produce? What is the total quantity supplied in the market?
   c. In the long run, firms can enter and exit the market, and all entrants have the same costs as above. As this market makes the transition to its long-run equilibrium, will the price rise or fall? Will the quantity demanded rise or fall? Will the quantity supplied by each firm rise or fall? Explain your answers.
   d. Graph the long-run supply curve for this market, with specific numbers on the axes as relevant.
11. Suppose that each firm in a competitive industry has the following costs:

Total cost: $TC = 50 + ½ q^2$
Marginal cost: $MC = q$

where q is an individual firm's quantity produced. The market demand curve for this product is

Demand: $Q^D = 120 - P$

where P is the price and Q is the total quantity of the good. Currently, there are 9 firms in the market.
   a. What is each firm's fixed cost? What is its variable cost? Give the equation for average total cost.
   b. Graph average-total-cost curve and the marginal-cost curve for q from 5 to 15. At what quantity is average-total-cost curve at its

minimum? What is marginal cost and average total cost at that quantity?

c. Give the equation for each firm's supply curve.

d. Give the equation for the market supply curve for the short run in which the number of firms is fixed.

e. What is the equilibrium price and quantity for this market in the short run?

f. In this equilibrium, how much does each firm produce? Calculate each firm's profit or loss. Is there incentive for firms to enter or exit?

g. In the long run with free entry and exit, what is the equilibrium price and quantity in this market?

h. In this long-run equilibrium, how much does each firm produce? How many firms are in the market?

To find additional study resources, visit cengagebrain.com, and search for "Mankiw."

Monopoly

CHAPTER

15

If you own a personal computer, it probably uses some version of Windows, the operating system sold by the Microsoft Corporation. When Microsoft first designed Windows many years ago, it applied for and received a copyright from the government. The copyright gives Microsoft the exclusive right to make and sell copies of the Windows operating system. If a person wants to buy a copy of Windows, she has little choice but to give Microsoft the approximately $100 that the firm has decided to charge for its product. Microsoft is said to have a *monopoly* in the market for Windows.

Microsoft's business decisions are not well described by the model of firm behavior we developed in the previous chapter. In that chapter,

we analyzed competitive markets, in which many firms offer essentially identical products, so each firm has little influence over the price it receives. By contrast, a monopoly such as Microsoft has no close competitors and, therefore, has the power to influence the market price of its product. Whereas a competitive firm is a *price taker*, a monopoly firm is a *price maker*.

In this chapter, we examine the implications of this market power. We will see that market power alters the relationship between a firm's costs and the price at which it sells its product. A competitive firm takes the price of its output as given by the market and then chooses the quantity it will supply so that price equals marginal cost. By contrast, a monopoly charges a price that exceeds marginal cost. Sure enough, we observe this practice in the case of Microsoft's Windows. The marginal cost of Windows—the extra cost that Microsoft incurs by downloading one more copy of the program onto a CD—is only a few dollars. The market price of Windows is many times its marginal cost.

It is not surprising that monopolies charge high prices for their products. Customers of monopolies might seem to have little choice but to pay whatever the monopoly charges. But if so, why does a copy of Windows not cost $1,000? Or $10,000? The reason is that if Microsoft were to set the price that high, fewer people would buy the product. People would buy fewer computers, switch to other operating systems, or make illegal copies. A monopoly firm can control the price of the good it sells, but because a high price reduces the quantity that its customers buy, the monopoly's profits are not unlimited.

As we examine the production and pricing decisions of monopolies, we also consider the implications of monopoly for society as a whole. Monopoly firms, like competitive firms, aim to maximize profit. But this goal has very different ramifications for competitive and monopoly firms. In competitive markets, self-interested consumers and producers reach an equilibrium that promotes general economic well-being, as if guided by an invisible hand. By contrast, because monopoly firms are unchecked by competition, the outcome in a market with a monopoly is often not in the best interest of society.

One of the *Ten Principles of Economics* in Chapter 1 is that governments can sometimes improve market outcomes. The analysis in this chapter sheds more light on this principle. As we examine the problems that monopolies raise for society, we discuss the various ways in which government policymakers might respond to these problems. The U.S. government, for example, keeps a close eye on Microsoft's business decisions. In 1994, it blocked Microsoft from buying Intuit, a leading seller of personal finance software, on the grounds that combining the two firms would concentrate too much market power. Similarly, in 1998, the U.S. Department of Justice objected when Microsoft started integrating its Internet browser into its Windows operating system, claiming that this addition would extend the firm's market power into new areas. In recent years, regulators in the United States and abroad have shifted their focus to firms with growing market power, such as Google and Samsung, but continue to monitor Microsoft's compliance with the antitrust laws.

15-1 Why Monopolies Arise

monopoly
a firm that is the sole seller of a product without any close substitutes

A firm is a **monopoly** if it is the sole seller of its product and if its product does not have any close substitutes. The fundamental cause of monopoly is *barriers to entry*: A monopoly remains the only seller in its market because other firms cannot enter the market and compete with it. Barriers to entry, in turn, have three main sources:

- *Monopoly resources:* A key resource required for production is owned by a single firm.
- *Government regulation:* The government gives a single firm the exclusive right to produce some good or service.
- *The production process:* A single firm can produce output at a lower cost than can a larger number of firms.

Let's briefly discuss each of these.

THE WALL STREET JOURNAL - PERMISSION, CARTOON FEATURES SYNDICATE

"Rather than a monopoly, we like to consider ourselves 'the only game in town.'"

15-1a Monopoly Resources

The simplest way for a monopoly to arise is for a single firm to own a key resource. For example, consider the market for water in a small town. If dozens of town residents have working wells, the model of competitive markets discussed in the preceding chapter describes the behavior of sellers. Competition among suppliers drives the price of a gallon of water to equal the marginal cost of pumping an extra gallon. But if there is only one well in town and it is impossible to get water from anywhere else, then the owner of the well has a monopoly on water. Not surprisingly, the monopolist has much greater market power than any single firm in a competitive market. In the case of a necessity like water, the monopolist can command quite a high price, even if the marginal cost of pumping an extra gallon is low.

A classic example of market power arising from the ownership of a key resource is DeBeers, the South African diamond company. Founded in 1888 by Cecil Rhodes, an English businessman (and benefactor of the Rhodes scholarship), DeBeers has at times controlled up to 80 percent of the production from the world's diamond mines. Because its market share is less than 100 percent, DeBeers is not exactly a monopoly, but the company has nonetheless exerted substantial influence over the market price of diamonds.

Although exclusive ownership of a key resource is a potential cause of monopoly, in practice monopolies rarely arise for this reason. Economies are large, and resources are owned by many people. The natural scope of many markets is worldwide, because goods are often traded internationally. There are, therefore, few examples of firms that own a resource for which there are no close substitutes.

15-1b Government-Created Monopolies

In many cases, monopolies arise because the government has given one person or firm the exclusive right to sell some good or service. Sometimes the monopoly arises from the sheer political clout of the would-be monopolist. Kings, for example, once granted exclusive business licenses to their friends and allies. At other times, the government grants a monopoly because doing so is viewed to be in the public interest.

The patent and copyright laws are two important examples. When a pharmaceutical company discovers a new drug, it can apply to the government for a patent. If the government deems the drug to be truly original, it approves the patent, which gives the company the exclusive right to manufacture and sell the drug for 20 years. Similarly, when a novelist finishes a book, she can copyright it. The copyright is a government guarantee that no one can print and sell the work without the author's permission. The copyright makes the novelist a monopolist in the sale of her novel.

The effects of patent and copyright laws are easy to see. Because these laws give one producer a monopoly, they lead to higher prices than would occur under competition. But by allowing these monopoly producers to charge higher prices and earn higher profits, the laws also encourage some desirable behavior. Drug companies are allowed to be monopolists in the drugs they discover to encourage research. Authors are allowed to be monopolists in the sale of their books to encourage them to write more and better books.

Thus, the laws governing patents and copyrights have both benefits and costs. The benefits of the patent and copyright laws are the increased incentives for creative activity. These benefits are offset, to some extent, by the costs of monopoly pricing, which we examine later in this chapter.

15-1c Natural Monopolies

natural monopoly
a type of monopoly that arises because a single firm can supply a good or service to an entire market at a lower cost than could two or more firms

An industry is a **natural monopoly** when a single firm can supply a good or service to an entire market at a lower cost than could two or more firms. A natural monopoly arises when there are economies of scale over the relevant range of output. Figure 1 shows the average total costs of a firm with economies of scale. In this case, a single firm can produce any amount of output at the lowest cost. That is, for any given amount of output, a larger number of firms leads to less output per firm and higher average total cost.

An example of a natural monopoly is the distribution of water. To provide water to residents of a town, a firm must build a network of pipes throughout the town. If two or more firms were to compete in the provision of this service, each firm would have to pay the fixed cost of building a network. Thus, the average total cost of water is lowest if a single firm serves the entire market.

We saw other examples of natural monopolies when we discussed public goods and common resources in Chapter 11. We noted that *club goods* are excludable but not rival in consumption. An example is a bridge used so infrequently that it is never congested. The bridge is excludable because a toll collector can prevent someone from using it. The bridge is not rival in consumption because use of the bridge by one person does not diminish the ability of others to use it. Because there is a large fixed cost of building the bridge and a negligible marginal cost of additional users, the average total cost of a trip across the bridge (the total cost divided by the number of trips) falls as the number of trips rises. Hence, the bridge is a natural monopoly.

FIGURE 1

Economies of Scale as a Cause of Monopoly
When a firm's average-total-cost curve continually declines, the firm has what is called a natural monopoly. In this case, when production is divided among more firms, each firm produces less, and average total cost rises. As a result, a single firm can produce any given amount at the lowest cost.

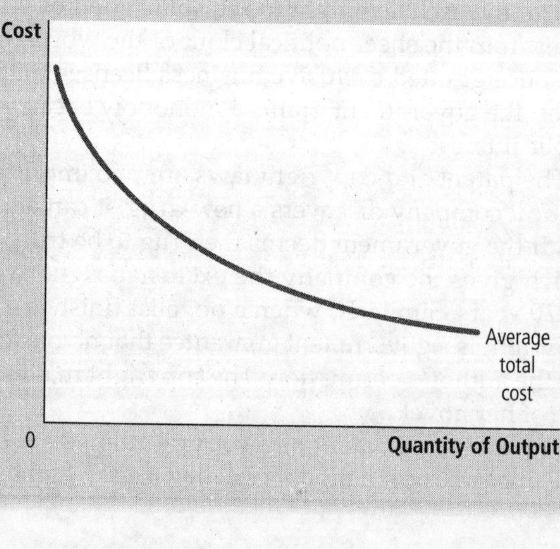

When a firm is a natural monopoly, it is less concerned about new entrants eroding its monopoly power. Normally, a firm has trouble maintaining a monopoly position without ownership of a key resource or protection from the government. The monopolist's profit attracts entrants into the market, and these entrants make the market more competitive. By contrast, entering a market in which another firm has a natural monopoly is unattractive. Would-be entrants know that they cannot achieve the same low costs that the monopolist enjoys because, after entry, each firm would have a smaller piece of the market.

In some cases, the size of the market is one determinant of whether an industry is a natural monopoly. Again, consider a bridge across a river. When the population is small, the bridge may be a natural monopoly. A single bridge can satisfy the entire demand for trips across the river at the lowest cost. Yet as the population grows and the bridge becomes congested, satisfying the entire demand may require two or more bridges across the same river. Thus, as a market expands, a natural monopoly can evolve into a more competitive market.

QuickQuiz *What are the three reasons that a market might have a monopoly? • Give two examples of monopolies and explain the reason for each.*

15-2 How Monopolies Make Production and Pricing Decisions

Now that we know how monopolies arise, we can consider how a monopoly firm decides how much of its product to make and what price to charge for it. The analysis of monopoly behavior in this section is the starting point for evaluating whether monopolies are desirable and what policies the government might pursue in monopoly markets.

15-2a Monopoly versus Competition

The key difference between a competitive firm and a monopoly is the monopoly's ability to influence the price of its output. A competitive firm is small relative to the market in which it operates and, therefore, has no power to influence the price of its output. It takes the price as given by market conditions. By contrast, because a monopoly is the sole producer in its market, it can alter the price of its good by adjusting the quantity it supplies to the market.

One way to view this difference between a competitive firm and a monopoly is to consider the demand curve that each firm faces. When we analyzed profit maximization by competitive firms in the preceding chapter, we drew the market price as a horizontal line. Because a competitive firm can sell as much or as little as it wants at this price, the competitive firm faces a horizontal demand curve, as in panel (a) of Figure 2. In effect, because the competitive firm sells a product with many perfect substitutes (the products of all the other firms in its market), the demand curve that any one firm faces is perfectly elastic.

By contrast, because a monopoly is the sole producer in its market, its demand curve is the market demand curve. Thus, the monopolist's demand curve slopes downward, as in panel (b) of Figure 2. If the monopolist raises the price of its good, consumers buy less of it. Looked at another way, if the monopolist reduces the quantity of output it produces and sells, the price of its output increases.

The market demand curve provides a constraint on a monopoly's ability to profit from its market power. A monopolist would prefer, if it were possible, to

FIGURE 2

Demand Curves for Competitive and Monopoly Firms

Because competitive firms are price takers, they face horizontal demand curves, as in panel (a). Because a monopoly firm is the sole producer in its market, it faces the downward-sloping market demand curve, as in panel (b). As a result, the monopoly has to accept a lower price if it wants to sell more output.

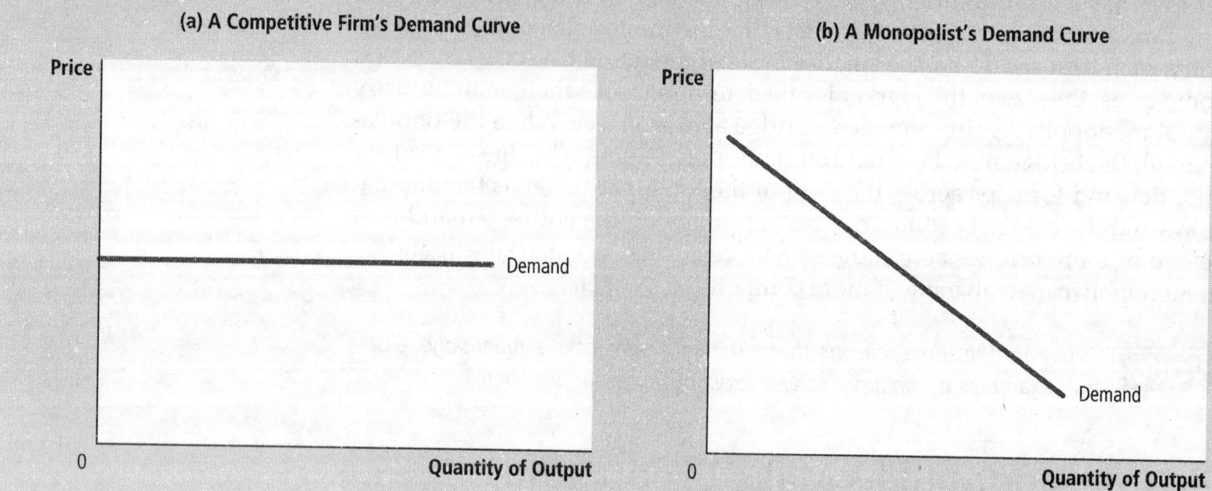

charge a high price and sell a large quantity at that high price. The market demand curve makes that outcome impossible. In particular, the market demand curve describes the combinations of price and quantity that are available to a monopoly firm. By adjusting the quantity produced (or equivalently, the price charged), the monopolist can choose any point on the demand curve, but it cannot choose a point off the demand curve.

What price and quantity of output will the monopolist choose? As with competitive firms, we assume that the monopolist's goal is to maximize profit. Because the firm's profit is total revenue minus total costs, our next task in explaining monopoly behavior is to examine a monopolist's revenue.

15-2b A Monopoly's Revenue

Consider a town with a single producer of water. Table 1 shows how the monopoly's revenue might depend on the amount of water produced.

Columns (1) and (2) show the monopolist's demand schedule. If the monopolist produces 1 gallon of water, it can sell that gallon for $10. If it produces 2 gallons, it must lower the price to $9 to sell both gallons. If it produces 3 gallons, it must lower the price to $8. And so on. If you graphed these two columns of numbers, you would get a typical downward-sloping demand curve.

Column (3) of the table presents the monopolist's *total revenue*. It equals the quantity sold [from column (1)] times the price [from column (2)]. Column (4) computes the firm's *average revenue*, the amount of revenue the firm receives per unit sold. We compute average revenue by taking the number for total revenue in column (3) and dividing it by the quantity of output in column (1). As we discussed in the previous chapter, average revenue always equals the price of the good. This is true for monopolists as well as for competitive firms.

TABLE 1

A Monopoly's Total, Average, and Marginal Revenue

(1) Quantity of Water (Q)	(2) Price (P)	(3) Total Revenue ($TR = P \times Q$)	(4) Average Revenue ($AR = TR / Q$)	(5) Marginal Revenue ($MR = \Delta TR / \Delta Q$)
0 gallons	$11	$ 0	—	
				$10
1	10	10	$10	
				8
2	9	18	9	
				6
3	8	24	8	
				4
4	7	28	7	
				2
5	6	30	6	
				0
6	5	30	5	
				−2
7	4	28	4	
				−4
8	3	24	3	

Column (5) of Table 1 computes the firm's *marginal revenue*, the amount of revenue that the firm receives for each additional unit of output. We compute marginal revenue by taking the change in total revenue when output increases by 1 unit. For example, when the firm is producing 3 gallons of water, it receives total revenue of $24. Raising production to 4 gallons increases total revenue to $28. Thus, marginal revenue from the sale of the fourth gallon is $28 minus $24, or $4.

Table 1 shows a result that is important for understanding monopoly behavior: *A monopolist's marginal revenue is less than the price of its good.* For example, if the firm raises production of water from 3 to 4 gallons, it increases total revenue by only $4, even though it sells each gallon for $7. For a monopoly, marginal revenue is lower than price because a monopoly faces a downward-sloping demand curve. To increase the amount sold, a monopoly firm must lower the price it charges to all customers. Hence, to sell the fourth gallon of water, the monopolist must earn $1 less revenue for each of the first 3 gallons. This $3 loss accounts for the difference between the price of the fourth gallon ($7) and the marginal revenue of that fourth gallon ($4).

Marginal revenue for monopolies is very different from marginal revenue for competitive firms. When a monopoly increases the amount it sells, this action has two effects on total revenue ($P \times Q$):

- *The output effect:* More output is sold, so Q is higher, which tends to increase total revenue.
- *The price effect*: The price falls, so P is lower, which tends to decrease total revenue.

Because a competitive firm can sell all it wants at the market price, there is no price effect. When it increases production by 1 unit, it receives the market price for that unit, and it does not receive any less for the units it was already selling. That is, because the competitive firm is a price taker, its marginal revenue equals the price of its good. By contrast, when a monopoly increases production by 1 unit, it must reduce the price it charges for every unit it sells, and this cut in price reduces revenue on the units it was already selling. As a result, a monopoly's marginal revenue is less than its price.

Figure 3 graphs the demand curve and the marginal-revenue curve for a monopoly firm. (Because the firm's price equals its average revenue, the demand curve is also the average-revenue curve.) These two curves always start at the same point on the vertical axis because the marginal revenue of the first unit sold equals the price of the good. But for the reason we just discussed, the monopolist's marginal revenue on all units after the first is less than the price of the good. Thus, a monopoly's marginal-revenue curve lies below its demand curve.

You can see in Figure 3 (as well as in Table 1) that marginal revenue can even become negative. Marginal revenue is negative when the price effect on revenue is greater than the output effect. In this case, when the firm produces an extra unit of output, the price falls by enough to cause the firm's total revenue to decline, even though the firm is selling more units.

15-2c Profit Maximization

Now that we have considered the revenue of a monopoly firm, we are ready to examine how such a firm maximizes profit. Recall from Chapter 1 that one of the *Ten Principles of Economics* is that rational people think at the margin. This lesson is as true for monopolists as it is for competitive firms. Here we apply the logic of marginal analysis to the monopolist's decision about how much to produce.

Figure 4 graphs the demand curve, the marginal-revenue curve, and the cost curves for a monopoly firm. All these curves should seem familiar: The demand and marginal-revenue curves are like those in Figure 3, and the cost curves are like those we encountered in the last two chapters. These curves contain all the

FIGURE 3

Demand and Marginal-Revenue Curves for a Monopoly

The demand curve shows how the quantity sold affects the price of the good. The marginal-revenue curve shows how the firm's revenue changes when the quantity increases by 1 unit. Because the price on *all* units sold must fall if the monopoly increases production, marginal revenue is less than the price.

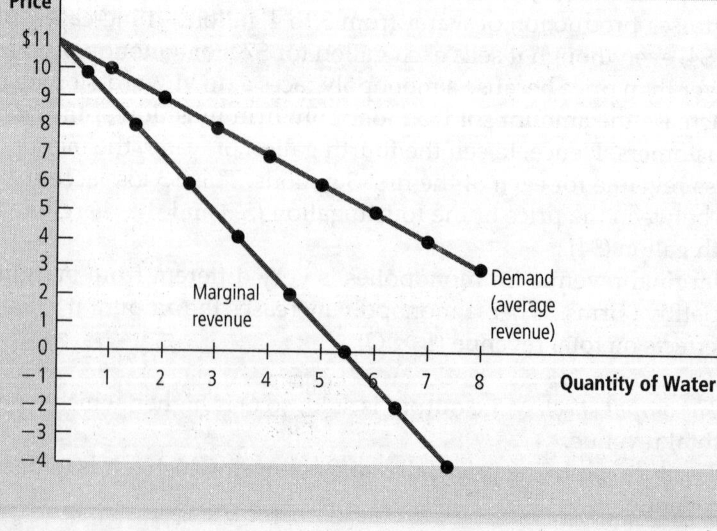

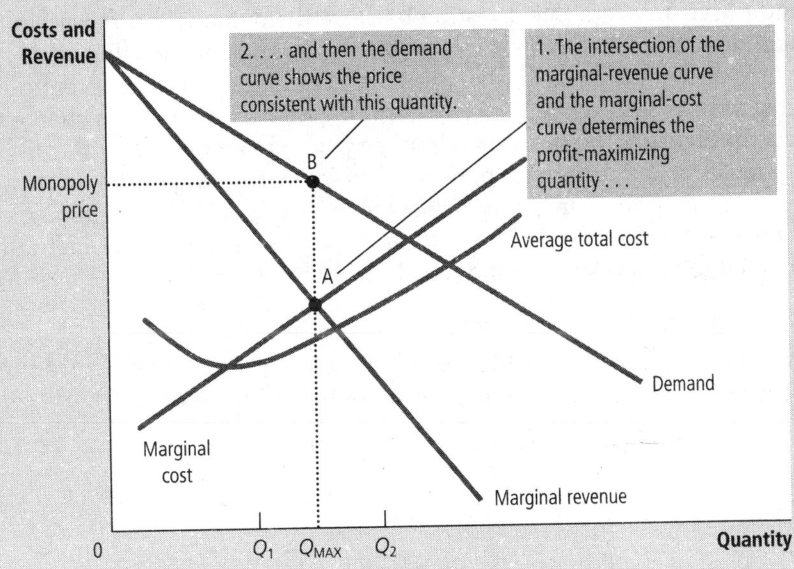

FIGURE 4

Profit Maximization for a Monopoly
A monopoly maximizes profit by choosing the quantity at which marginal revenue equals marginal cost (point A). It then uses the demand curve to find the price that will induce consumers to buy that quantity (point B).

information we need to determine the level of output that a profit-maximizing monopolist will choose.

Suppose, first, that the firm is producing at a low level of output, such as Q_1. In this case, marginal cost is less than marginal revenue. If the firm increased production by 1 unit, the additional revenue would exceed the additional costs, and profit would rise. Thus, when marginal cost is less than marginal revenue, the firm can increase profit by producing more units.

A similar argument applies at high levels of output, such as Q_2. In this case, marginal cost is greater than marginal revenue. If the firm reduced production by 1 unit, the costs saved would exceed the revenue lost. Thus, if marginal cost is greater than marginal revenue, the firm can raise profit by reducing production.

In the end, the firm adjusts its level of production until the quantity reaches Q_{MAX}, at which marginal revenue equals marginal cost. Thus, *the monopolist's profit-maximizing quantity of output is determined by the intersection of the marginal-revenue curve and the marginal-cost curve.* In Figure 4, this intersection occurs at point A.

You might recall from the previous chapter that competitive firms also choose the quantity of output at which marginal revenue equals marginal cost. In following this rule for profit maximization, competitive firms and monopolies are alike. But there is also an important difference between these types of firms: The marginal revenue of a competitive firm equals its price, whereas the marginal revenue of a monopoly is less than its price. That is,

For a competitive firm: $P = MR = MC$.

For a monopoly firm: $P > MR = MC$.

The equality of marginal revenue and marginal cost determines the profit-maximizing quantity for both types of firm. What differs is how the price is related to marginal revenue and marginal cost.

How does the monopoly find the profit-maximizing price for its product? The demand curve answers this question because the demand curve relates the amount that customers are willing to pay to the quantity sold. Thus, after the monopoly firm chooses the quantity of output that equates marginal revenue and marginal cost, it uses the demand curve to find the highest price it can charge for that quantity. In Figure 4, the profit-maximizing price is found at point B.

We can now see a key difference between markets with competitive firms and markets with a monopoly firm: *In competitive markets, price equals marginal cost. In monopolized markets, price exceeds marginal cost.* As we will see in a moment, this finding is crucial to understanding the social cost of monopoly.

15-2d A Monopoly's Profit

How much profit does a monopoly make? To see a monopoly firm's profit in a graph, recall that profit equals total revenue (TR) minus total costs (TC):

$$\text{Profit} = TR - TC.$$

We can rewrite this as

$$\text{Profit} = (TR/Q - TC/Q) \times Q.$$

TR/Q is average revenue, which equals the price, P, and TC/Q is average total cost, ATC. Therefore,

$$\text{Profit} = (P - ATC) \times Q.$$

This equation for profit (which also holds for competitive firms) allows us to measure the monopolist's profit in our graph.

Consider the shaded box in Figure 5. The height of the box (the segment BC) is price minus average total cost, $P - ATC$, which is the profit on the typical unit sold. The width of the box (the segment DC) is the quantity sold, Q_{MAX}. Therefore, the area of this box is the monopoly firm's total profit.

FYI

Why a Monopoly Does Not Have a Supply Curve

You may have noticed that we have analyzed the price in a monopoly market using the market demand curve and the firm's cost curves. We have not made any mention of the market supply curve. By contrast, when we analyzed prices in competitive markets beginning in Chapter 4, the two most important words were always *supply* and *demand.*

What happened to the supply curve? Although monopoly firms make decisions about what quantity to supply, a monopoly does not have a supply curve. A supply curve tells us the quantity that firms choose to supply at any given price. This concept makes sense when we are analyzing competitive firms, which are price takers. But a monopoly firm is a price maker, not a price taker. It is not meaningful to ask what amount such a firm would produce at any given price because it cannot take the price as given. Instead, when the firm chooses the quantity to supply, that decision (along with the demand curve) determines the price.

Indeed, the monopolist's decision about how much to supply is impossible to separate from the demand curve it faces. The shape of the demand curve determines the shape of the marginal-revenue curve, which in turn determines the monopolist's profit-maximizing quantity. In a competitive market, each firm's supply decisions can be analyzed without knowing the demand curve, but that is not true in a monopoly market. Therefore, we never talk about a monopoly's supply curve. ■

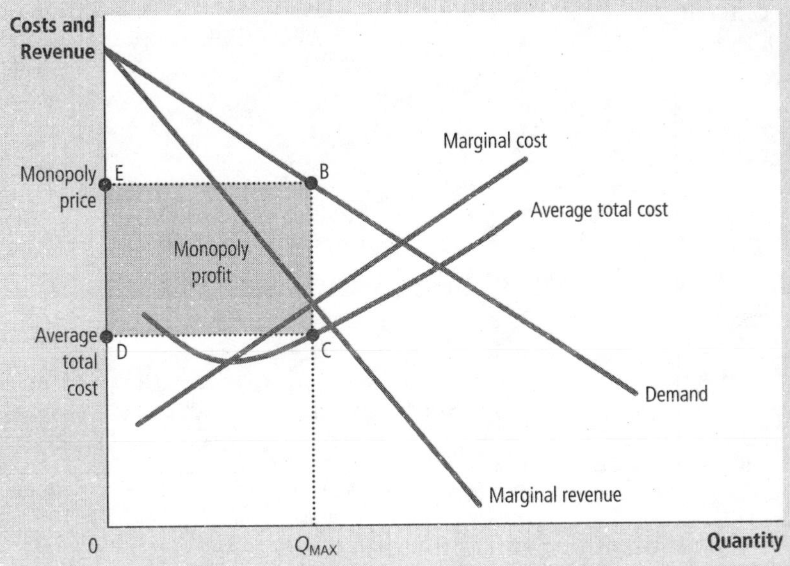

FIGURE 5

The Monopolist's Profit
The area of the box BCDE equals the profit of the monopoly firm. The height of the box (BC) is price minus average total cost, which equals profit per unit sold. The width of the box (DC) is the number of units sold.

CASE STUDY

MONOPOLY DRUGS VERSUS GENERIC DRUGS

According to our analysis, prices are determined differently in monopolized markets and competitive markets. A natural place to test this theory is the market for pharmaceutical drugs because this market takes on both market structures. When a firm discovers a new drug, patent laws give the firm a monopoly on the sale of that drug. But eventually, the firm's patent runs out, and any company can make and sell the drug. At that time, the market switches from being monopolistic to being competitive.

What should happen to the price of a drug when the patent runs out? Figure 6 shows the market for a typical drug. In this figure, the marginal cost of producing the drug is constant. (This is approximately true for many drugs.) During the life of the patent, the monopoly firm maximizes profit by producing the quantity at which marginal revenue equals marginal cost and charging a price well above marginal cost. But when the patent runs out, the profit from making the drug should encourage new firms to enter the market. As the market becomes more competitive, the price should fall to equal marginal cost.

Experience is, in fact, consistent with our theory. When the patent on a drug expires, other companies quickly enter and begin selling generic products that are chemically identical to the former monopolist's brand-name product. Just as our analysis predicts, the price of the competitively produced generic drug is well below the price that the monopolist was charging.

The expiration of a patent, however, does not cause the monopolist to lose all of its market power. Some consumers remain loyal to the brand-name drug, perhaps out of fear that the new generic drugs are not actually the same as the drug they have been using for years. As a result, the former monopolist can continue to charge a price above the price charged by its new competitors.

For example, one of the most widely used antidepressants is the drug fluoxetine, which is taken by millions of Americans. Because the patent on this drug expired in 2001, a consumer today has the choice between the original drug, sold under the

FIGURE 6

The Market for Drugs
When a patent gives a firm a monopoly over the sale of a drug, the firm charges the monopoly price, which is well above the marginal cost of making the drug. When the patent on a drug runs out, new firms enter the market, making it more competitive. As a result, the price falls from the monopoly price to marginal cost.

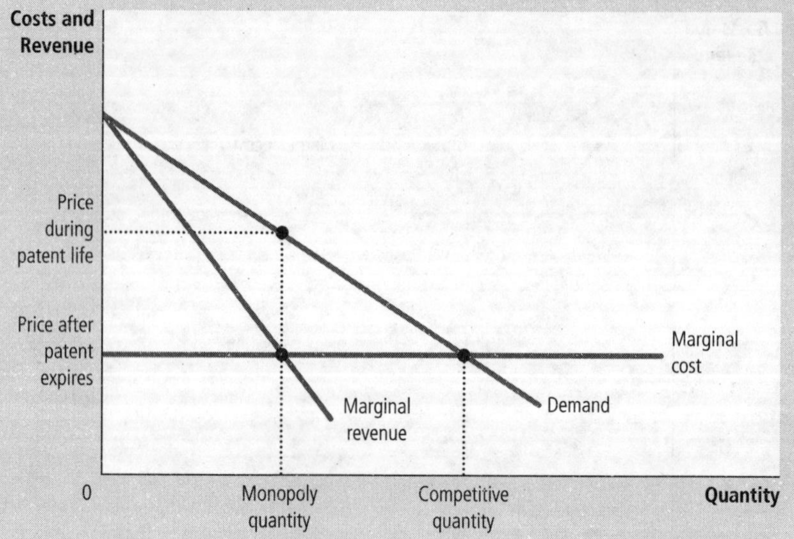

brand name Prozac, and a generic version of the same medicine. Prozac sells for about three times the price of generic fluoxetine. This price differential can persist because some consumers are not convinced that the two pills are perfect substitutes. ●

QuickQuiz *Explain how a monopolist chooses the quantity of output to produce and the price to charge.*

15-3 The Welfare Cost of Monopolies

Is monopoly a good way to organize a market? We have seen that a monopoly, in contrast to a competitive firm, charges a price above marginal cost. From the standpoint of consumers, this high price makes monopoly undesirable. At the same time, however, the monopoly is earning profit from charging this high price. From the standpoint of the owners of the firm, the high price makes monopoly very desirable. Is it possible that the benefits to the firm's owners exceed the costs imposed on consumers, making monopoly desirable from the standpoint of society as a whole?

We can answer this question using the tools of welfare economics. Recall from Chapter 7 that total surplus measures the economic well-being of buyers and sellers in a market. Total surplus is the sum of consumer surplus and producer surplus. Consumer surplus is consumers' willingness to pay for a good minus the amount they actually pay for it. Producer surplus is the amount producers receive for a good minus their costs of producing it. In this case, there is a single producer—the monopolist.

You can probably guess the result of this analysis. In Chapter 7, we concluded that the equilibrium of supply and demand in a competitive market is not only a natural outcome but also a desirable one. The invisible hand of the market leads to an allocation of resources that makes total surplus as large as it can be. Because a monopoly leads to an allocation of resources different from that in a competitive market, the outcome must, in some way, fail to maximize total economic well-being.

15-3a The Deadweight Loss

We begin by considering what the monopoly firm would do if it were run by a benevolent social planner. The social planner cares not only about the profit earned by the firm's owners but also about the benefits received by the firm's consumers. The planner tries to maximize total surplus, which equals producer surplus (profit) plus consumer surplus. Keep in mind that total surplus equals the value of the good to consumers minus the costs of making the good incurred by the monopoly producer.

Figure 7 analyzes how a benevolent social planner would choose the monopoly's level of output. The demand curve reflects the value of the good to consumers, as measured by their willingness to pay for it. The marginal-cost curve reflects the costs of the monopolist. Thus, *the socially efficient quantity is found where the demand curve and the marginal-cost curve intersect.* Below this quantity, the value of an extra unit to consumers exceeds the cost of providing it, so increasing output would raise total surplus. Above this quantity, the cost of producing an extra unit exceeds the value of that unit to consumers, so decreasing output would raise total surplus. At the optimal quantity, the value of an extra unit to consumers exactly equals the marginal cost of production.

If the social planner were running the monopoly, the firm could achieve this efficient outcome by charging the price found at the intersection of the demand and marginal-cost curves. Thus, like a competitive firm and unlike a profit-maximizing monopoly, a social planner would charge a price equal to marginal cost. Because this price would give consumers an accurate signal about the cost of producing the good, consumers would buy the efficient quantity.

We can evaluate the welfare effects of monopoly by comparing the level of output that the monopolist chooses to the level of output that a social planner would

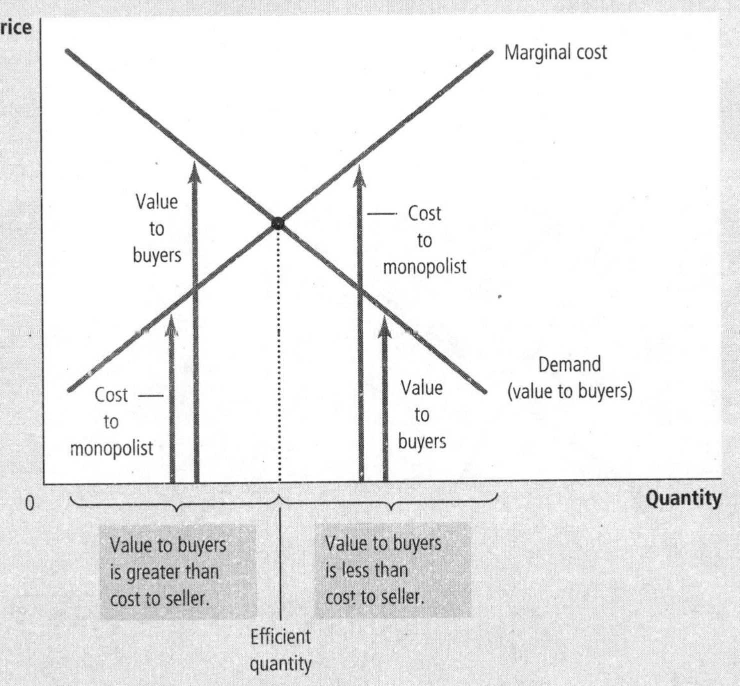

FIGURE 7

The Efficient Level of Output

A benevolent social planner maximizes total surplus in the market by choosing the level of output where the demand curve and marginal-cost curve intersect. Below this level, the value of the good to the marginal buyer (as reflected in the demand curve) exceeds the marginal cost of making the good. Above this level, the value to the marginal buyer is less than marginal cost.

choose. As we have seen, the monopolist chooses to produce and sell the quantity of output at which the marginal-revenue and marginal-cost curves intersect; the social planner would choose the quantity at which the demand and marginal-cost curves intersect. Figure 8 shows the comparison. *The monopolist produces less than the socially efficient quantity of output.*

We can also view the inefficiency of monopoly in terms of the monopolist's price. Because the market demand curve describes a negative relationship between the price and quantity of the good, a quantity that is inefficiently low is equivalent to a price that is inefficiently high. When a monopolist charges a price above marginal cost, some potential consumers value the good at more than its marginal cost but less than the monopolist's price. These consumers do not buy the good. Because the value these consumers place on the good is greater than the cost of providing it to them, this result is inefficient. Thus, monopoly pricing prevents some mutually beneficial trades from taking place.

The inefficiency of monopoly can be measured with a deadweight loss triangle, as illustrated in Figure 8. Because the demand curve reflects the value to consumers and the marginal-cost curve reflects the costs to the monopoly producer, the area of the deadweight loss triangle between the demand curve and the marginal-cost curve equals the total surplus lost because of monopoly pricing. It represents the reduction in economic well-being that results from the monopoly's use of its market power.

The deadweight loss caused by a monopoly is similar to the deadweight loss caused by a tax. Indeed, a monopolist is like a private tax collector. As we saw in Chapter 8, a tax on a good places a wedge between consumers' willingness to pay (as reflected by the demand curve) and producers' costs (as reflected by the supply curve). Because a monopoly exerts its market power by charging a price above marginal cost, it creates a similar wedge. In both cases, the wedge causes the quantity sold to fall short of the social optimum. The difference between the two cases is that the government gets the revenue from a tax, whereas a private firm gets the monopoly profit.

FIGURE 8

The Inefficiency of Monopoly
Because a monopoly charges a price above marginal cost, not all consumers who value the good at more than its cost buy it. Thus, the quantity produced and sold by a monopoly is below the socially efficient level. The deadweight loss is represented by the area of the triangle between the demand curve (which reflects the value of the good to consumers) and the marginal-cost curve (which reflects the costs of the monopoly producer).

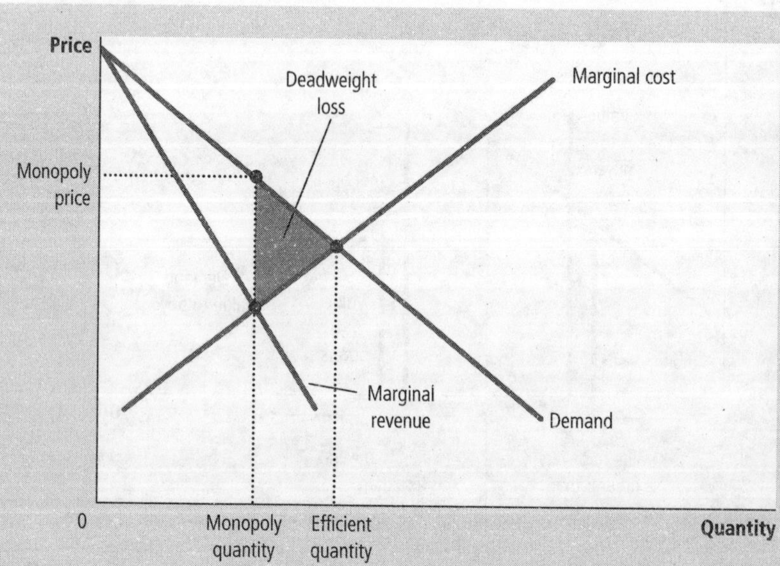

15-3b The Monopoly's Profit: A Social Cost?

It is tempting to decry monopolies for "profiteering" at the expense of the public. And indeed, a monopoly firm does earn a profit by virtue of its market power. According to the economic analysis of monopoly, however, the firm's profit is not in itself necessarily a problem for society.

Welfare in a monopolized market, as in all markets, includes the welfare of both consumers and producers. Whenever a consumer pays an extra dollar to a producer because of a monopoly price, the consumer is worse off by a dollar and the producer is better off by the same amount. This transfer from the consumers of the good to the owners of the monopoly does not affect the market's total surplus—the sum of consumer and producer surplus. In other words, the monopoly profit itself represents not a reduction in the size of the economic pie but merely a bigger slice for producers and a smaller slice for consumers. Unless consumers are for some reason more deserving than producers—a normative judgment about equity that goes beyond the realm of economic efficiency—the monopoly profit is not a social problem.

The problem in a monopolized market arises because the firm produces and sells a quantity of output below the level that maximizes total surplus. The deadweight loss measures how much the economic pie shrinks as a result. This inefficiency is connected to the monopoly's high price: Consumers buy fewer units when the firm raises its price above marginal cost. But keep in mind that the profit earned on the units that continue to be sold is not the problem. The problem stems from the inefficiently low quantity of output. Put differently, if the high monopoly price did not discourage some consumers from buying the good, it would raise producer surplus by exactly the amount it reduced consumer surplus, leaving total surplus the same as that achieved by a benevolent social planner.

There is, however, a possible exception to this conclusion. Suppose that a monopoly firm has to incur additional costs to maintain its monopoly position. For example, a firm with a government-created monopoly might need to hire lobbyists to convince lawmakers to continue its monopoly. In this case, the monopoly may use up some of its monopoly profits paying for these additional costs. If so, the social loss from monopoly includes both these costs and the deadweight loss resulting from reduced output.

QuickQuiz *How does a monopolist's quantity of output compare to the quantity of output that maximizes total surplus? How does this difference relate to the deadweight loss?*

15-4 Price Discrimination

So far, we have been assuming that the monopoly firm charges the same price to all customers. Yet in many cases, firms sell the same good to different customers for different prices, even though the costs of producing for the two customers are the same. This practice is called **price discrimination**.

price discrimination the business practice of selling the same good at different prices to different customers

Before discussing the behavior of a price-discriminating monopolist, we should note that price discrimination is not possible when a good is sold in a competitive market. In a competitive market, many firms are selling the same good at the market price. No firm is willing to charge a lower price to any customer because the firm can sell all it wants at the market price. And if any firm tried to charge a higher price to a customer, that customer would buy from another firm. For a firm to price discriminate, it must have some market power.

15-4a A Parable about Pricing

To understand why a monopolist would price discriminate, let's consider an example. Imagine that you are the president of Readalot Publishing Company. Readalot's best-selling author has just written a new novel. To keep things simple, let's imagine that you pay the author a flat $2 million for the exclusive rights to publish the book. Let's also assume that the cost of printing the book is zero (as it would be, for example, for an e-book). Readalot's profit, therefore, is the revenue from selling the book minus the $2 million it has paid to the author. Given these assumptions, how would you, as Readalot's president, decide the book's price?

Your first step is to estimate the demand for the book. Readalot's marketing department tells you that the book will attract two types of readers. The book will appeal to the author's 100,000 die-hard fans who are willing to pay as much as $30. In addition, it will appeal to about 400,000 less enthusiastic readers who will pay up to $5.

If Readalot charges a single price to all customers, what price maximizes profit? There are two natural prices to consider: $30 is the highest price Readalot can charge and still get the 100,000 die-hard fans, and $5 is the highest price it can charge and still get the entire market of 500,000 potential readers. Solving Readalot's problem is a matter of simple arithmetic. At a price of $30, Readalot sells 100,000 copies, has revenue of $3 million, and makes profit of $1 million. At a price of $5, it sells 500,000 copies, has revenue of $2.5 million, and makes profit of $500,000. Thus, Readalot maximizes profit by charging $30 and forgoing the opportunity to sell to the 400,000 less enthusiastic readers.

Notice that Readalot's decision causes a deadweight loss. There are 400,000 readers willing to pay $5 for the book, and the marginal cost of providing it to them is zero. Thus, $2 million of total surplus is lost when Readalot charges the higher price. This deadweight loss is the inefficiency that arises whenever a monopolist charges a price above marginal cost.

Now suppose that Readalot's marketing department makes a discovery: These two groups of readers are in separate markets. The die-hard fans live in Australia, and the other readers live in the United States. Moreover, it is hard for readers in one country to buy books in the other.

In response to this discovery, Readalot can change its marketing strategy and increase profits. To the 100,000 Australian readers, it can charge $30 for the book. To the 400,000 American readers, it can charge $5 for the book. In this case, revenue is $3 million in Australia and $2 million in the United States, for a total of $5 million. Profit is then $3 million, which is substantially greater than the $1 million the company could earn charging the same $30 price to all customers. Not surprisingly, Readalot chooses to follow this strategy of price discrimination.

The story of Readalot Publishing is hypothetical, but it describes the business practice of many publishing companies. Consider the price differential between hardcover books and paperbacks. When a publisher has a new novel, it initially releases an expensive hardcover edition and later releases a cheaper paperback edition. The difference in price between these two editions far exceeds the difference in printing costs. The publisher is price discriminating by selling the hardcover to die-hard fans and the paperback to less enthusiastic readers, thereby increasing its profit.

15-4b The Moral of the Story

Like any parable, the story of Readalot Publishing is stylized. Yet also like any parable, it teaches some general lessons. In this case, three lessons can be learned about price discrimination.

The first and most obvious lesson is that price discrimination is a rational strategy for a profit-maximizing monopolist. That is, by charging different prices to different customers, a monopolist can increase its profit. In essence, a price-discriminating monopolist charges each customer a price closer to her willingness to pay than is possible with a single price.

The second lesson is that price discrimination requires the ability to separate customers according to their willingness to pay. In our example, customers were separated geographically. But sometimes monopolists choose other differences, such as age or income, to distinguish among customers.

A corollary to this second lesson is that certain market forces can prevent firms from price discriminating. In particular, one such force is *arbitrage*, the process of buying a good in one market at a low price and selling it in another market at a higher price to profit from the price difference. In our example, if Australian bookstores could buy the book in the United States and resell it to Australian readers, the arbitrage would prevent Readalot from price discriminating, because no Australian would buy the book at the higher price.

The third lesson from our parable is the most surprising: Price discrimination can raise economic welfare. Recall that a deadweight loss arises when Readalot charges a single $30 price because the 400,000 less enthusiastic readers do not end up with the book, even though they value it at more than its marginal cost of production. By contrast, when Readalot price discriminates, all readers get the book and the outcome is efficient. Thus, price discrimination can eliminate the inefficiency inherent in monopoly pricing.

Note that in this example the increase in welfare from price discrimination shows up as higher producer surplus rather than higher consumer surplus. Consumers are no better off for having bought the book: The price they pay exactly equals the value they place on the book, so they receive no consumer surplus. The entire increase in total surplus from price discrimination accrues to Readalot Publishing in the form of higher profit.

15-4c The Analytics of Price Discrimination

Let's consider a bit more formally how price discrimination affects economic welfare. We begin by assuming that the monopolist can price discriminate perfectly. *Perfect price discrimination* describes a situation in which the monopolist knows exactly each customer's willingness to pay and can charge each customer a different price. In this case, the monopolist charges each customer exactly her willingness to pay, and the monopolist gets the entire surplus in every transaction.

Figure 9 illustrates producer and consumer surplus with and without price discrimination. To keep things simple, this figure is drawn assuming constant per unit costs—that is, marginal cost and average total cost are constant and equal. Without price discrimination, the firm charges a single price above marginal cost, as shown in panel (a). Because some potential customers who value the good at more than marginal cost do not buy it at this high price, the monopoly causes a deadweight loss. Yet when a firm can perfectly price discriminate, as shown in panel (b), each customer who values the good at more than marginal cost buys the good and is charged her willingness to pay. All mutually beneficial trades take

FIGURE 9

Welfare with and without Price Discrimination

Panel (a) shows a monopoly that charges the same price to all customers. Total surplus in this market equals the sum of profit (producer surplus) and consumer surplus. Panel (b) shows a monopoly that can perfectly price discriminate. Because consumer surplus equals zero, total surplus now equals the firm's profit. Comparing these two panels, you can see that perfect price discrimination raises profit, raises total surplus, and lowers consumer surplus.

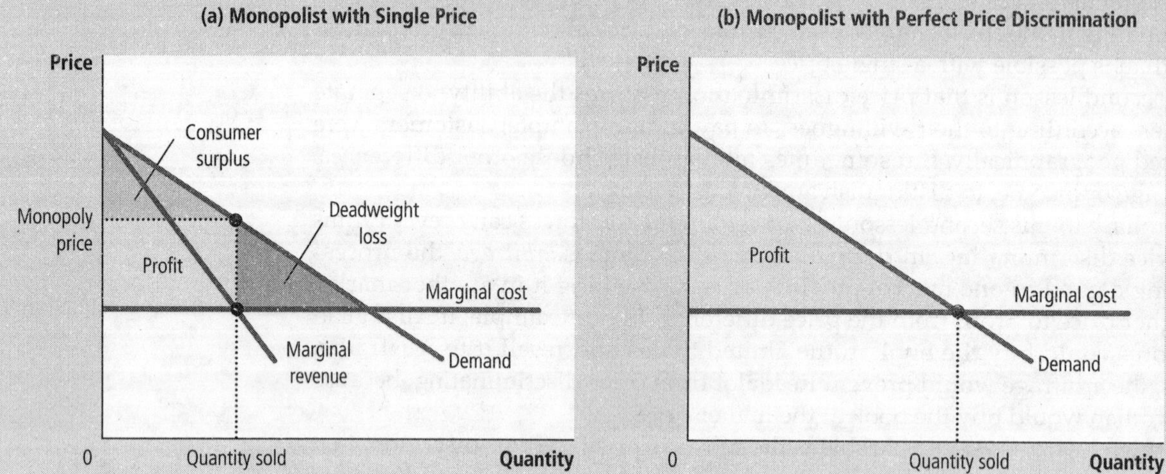

place, no deadweight loss occurs, and the entire surplus derived from the market goes to the monopoly producer in the form of profit.

In reality, of course, price discrimination is not perfect. Customers do not walk into stores with signs displaying their willingness to pay. Instead, firms price discriminate by dividing customers into groups: young versus old, weekday versus weekend shoppers, Americans versus Australians, and so on. Unlike those in our parable of Readalot Publishing, customers within each group differ in their willingness to pay for the product, making perfect price discrimination impossible.

How does this imperfect price discrimination affect welfare? The analysis of these pricing schemes is complicated, and it turns out that there is no general answer to this question. Compared with the single-price monopoly outcome, imperfect price discrimination can raise, lower, or leave unchanged the total surplus in a market. The only certain conclusion is that price discrimination raises the monopoly's profit; otherwise, the firm would choose to charge all customers the same price.

15-4d Examples of Price Discrimination

Firms in our economy use various business strategies aimed at charging different prices to different customers. Now that we understand the economics of price discrimination, let's consider some examples.

Movie Tickets Many movie theaters charge a lower price for children and senior citizens than for other patrons. This fact is hard to explain in a competitive market. In a competitive market, price equals marginal cost, and the marginal cost of providing a seat for a child or senior citizen is the same as the marginal cost of providing a seat for anyone else. Yet the differential pricing is easily explained if movie theaters have some local monopoly power and if children and senior citizens have a lower willingness to pay for a ticket. In this case, movie theaters raise their profit by price discriminating.

Airline Prices Seats on airplanes are sold at many different prices. Most airlines charge a lower price for a round-trip ticket between two cities if the traveler stays over a Saturday night. At first, this seems odd. Why should it matter to the airline whether a passenger stays over a Saturday night? The reason is that this rule provides a way to separate business travelers and leisure travelers. A passenger on a business trip has a high willingness to pay and, most likely, does not want to stay over a Saturday night. By contrast, a passenger traveling for personal reasons has a lower willingness to pay and is more likely to be willing to stay over a Saturday night. Thus, the airlines can successfully price discriminate by charging a lower price for passengers who stay over a Saturday night.

"Would it bother you to hear how little I paid for this flight?"

Discount Coupons Many companies offer discount coupons to the public in newspapers, magazines, or online. A buyer simply has to clip the coupon to get $0.50 off her next purchase. Why do companies offer these coupons? Why don't they just cut the price of the product by $0.50?

The answer is that coupons allow companies to price discriminate. Companies know that not all customers are willing to spend time clipping coupons. Moreover, the willingness to clip coupons is related to the customer's willingness to pay for the good. A rich and busy executive is unlikely to spend her time clipping discount coupons out of the newspaper, and she is probably willing to pay a higher price for many goods. A person who is unemployed is more likely to clip coupons and to have a lower willingness to pay. Thus, by charging a lower price only to those customers who clip coupons, firms can successfully price discriminate.

Financial Aid Many colleges and universities give financial aid to needy students. One can view this policy as a type of price discrimination. Wealthy students have greater financial resources and, therefore, a higher willingness to pay than needy students. By charging high tuition and selectively offering financial aid, schools in effect charge prices to customers based on the value they place on going to that school. This behavior is similar to that of any price-discriminating monopolist.

Quantity Discounts So far in our examples of price discrimination, the monopolist charges different prices to different customers. Sometimes, however, monopolists price discriminate by charging different prices to the same customer for different units that the customer buys. For example, many firms offer lower prices to customers who buy large quantities. A bakery might charge $0.50 for each donut but $5 for a dozen. This is a form of price discrimination because the customer pays a higher price for the first unit she buys than for the twelfth. Quantity discounts are often a successful way of price discriminating because a customer's willingness to pay for an additional unit declines as she buys more units.

QuickQuiz *Give two examples of price discrimination. • Explain how perfect price discrimination affects consumer surplus, producer surplus, and total surplus.*

IN THE NEWS

Price Discrimination in Higher Education

Colleges and universities are increasingly charging different prices to different students, which makes data on the cost of education harder to interpret.

Misconceptions 101: Why College Costs Aren't Soaring

By Evan Soltas

Conventional wisdom suggests that U.S. colleges and universities have become sharply more expensive in recent years.

"When kids do graduate, the most daunting challenge can be the cost of college," President Barack Obama said in his 2012 State of the Union address. "We can't just keep subsidizing skyrocketing tuition; we'll run out of money."

At first, the view that the cost of college is rising appears to have data on its side. Published tuition prices and fees at colleges have risen three times faster than the rate of Consumer Price Index inflation since 1978, according to the Bureau of Labor Statistics....

Real tuition and fees have increased, to be sure, but hardly as significantly as the media often report or the data suggest at face value. The inflation-adjusted net price of college has risen only modestly over the last two decades, according to data from the College Board's Annual Survey of Colleges.

What has happened is a shift toward price discrimination—offering multiple prices for the same product. Universities have offset the increase in sticker price for most families through an expansion of grant-based financial aid and scholarships. That has caused the BLS measure to rise without increasing the net cost.

Wealthier families now pay more than ever to send their children to college. But for much of the middle class, the real net cost of college has not changed significantly; for much of the poor, the expansion of aid has increased the accessibility and affordability of a college education....

MICHAELJUNG/SHUTTERSTOCK

The nation's most selective institutions are leading the trend toward income-based price discrimination. For example, at Harvard University, the majority of students receive financial aid: In 2012, one year of undergraduate education had a sticker price of $54,496 and came with an average grant of roughly $41,000.

In other words, the cost burden of college has become significantly more progressive since the 1990s. Students from wealthier families not only now pay more for their own educations but also have come to heavily subsidize the costs of the less fortunate. ■

Source: Bloomberg.com, November 27, 2012.

15-5 Public Policy toward Monopolies

We have seen that monopolies, in contrast to competitive markets, fail to allocate resources efficiently. Monopolies produce less than the socially desirable quantity of output and charge prices above marginal cost. Policymakers in the government can respond to the problem of monopoly in one of four ways:

- By trying to make monopolized industries more competitive
- By regulating the behavior of the monopolies
- By turning some private monopolies into public enterprises
- By doing nothing at all

15-5a Increasing Competition with Antitrust Laws

If Coca-Cola and PepsiCo wanted to merge, the deal would be closely examined by the federal government before it went into effect. The lawyers and economists in the Department of Justice might well decide that a merger between these two large soft-drink companies would make the U.S. soft-drink market substantially less competitive and, as a result, would reduce the economic well-being of the country as a whole. If so, the Department of Justice would challenge the merger in court, and if the judge agreed, the two companies would not be allowed to merge. It is precisely this kind of challenge that prevented software giant Microsoft from buying Intuit in 1994. Similarly, in 2011, the government blocked the phone giant AT&T from buying its competitor T-Mobile.

The government derives this power over private industry from the antitrust laws, a collection of statutes aimed at curbing monopoly power. The first and most important of these laws was the Sherman Antitrust Act, which Congress passed in 1890 to reduce the market power of the large and powerful "trusts" that were viewed as dominating the economy at the time. The Clayton Antitrust Act, passed in 1914, strengthened the government's powers and authorized private lawsuits. As the U.S. Supreme Court once put it, the antitrust laws are "a comprehensive charter of economic liberty aimed at preserving free and unfettered competition as the rule of trade."

SCIENCECARTOONSPLUS.COM

"But if we do merge with Amalgamated, we'll have enough resources to fight the antitrust violation caused by the merger."

The antitrust laws give the government various ways to promote competition. They allow the government to prevent mergers, such as the merger between AT&T and T-Mobile. At times, they allow the government to break up a large company into a group of smaller ones. Finally, the antitrust laws prevent companies from coordinating their activities in ways that make markets less competitive.

Antitrust laws have costs as well as benefits. Sometimes companies merge not to reduce competition but to lower costs through more efficient joint production. These benefits from mergers are sometimes called *synergies*. For example, many U.S. banks have merged in recent years and, by combining operations, have been able to reduce administrative staff. The airline industry has experienced a similar consolidation. If antitrust laws are to raise social welfare, the government must be able to determine which mergers are desirable and which are not. That is, it must be able to measure and compare the social benefit from synergies with the social costs of reduced competition. Critics of the antitrust laws are skeptical that the government can perform the necessary cost–benefit analysis with sufficient accuracy. In the end, the application of antitrust laws is often controversial, even among the experts.

15-5b Regulation

Another way the government deals with the problem of monopoly is by regulating the behavior of monopolists. This solution is common in the case of natural monopolies, such as water and electric companies. These companies are not allowed to charge any price they want. Instead, government agencies regulate their prices.

What price should the government set for a natural monopoly? This question is not as easy as it might at first appear. One might conclude that the price should equal the monopolist's marginal cost. If price equals marginal cost, customers will buy the quantity of the monopolist's output that maximizes total surplus and the allocation of resources will be efficient.

There are, however, two practical problems with marginal-cost pricing as a regulatory system. The first arises from the logic of cost curves. By definition, natural monopolies have

ASK THE EXPERTS

Airline Mergers

"If regulators had not approved mergers in the past decade between major networked airlines, travelers would be better off today."

What do economists say?

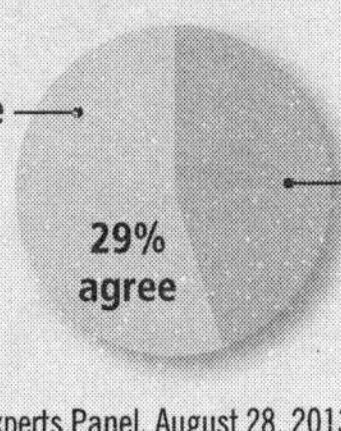

Source: IGM Economic Experts Panel, August 28, 2013.

declining average total cost. As we first discussed in Chapter 13, when average total cost is declining, marginal cost is less than average total cost. This situation is illustrated in Figure 10, which shows a firm with a large fixed cost and then constant marginal cost thereafter. If regulators were to set price equal to marginal cost, that price would be less than the firm's average total cost and the firm would lose money. Instead of charging such a low price, the monopoly firm would just exit the industry.

Regulators can respond to this problem in various ways, none of which is perfect. One way is to subsidize the monopolist. In essence, the government picks up the losses inherent in marginal-cost pricing. Yet to pay for the subsidy, the government needs to raise money through taxation, which involves its own deadweight losses. Alternatively, the regulators can allow the monopolist to charge a price higher than marginal cost. If the regulated price equals average total cost, the monopolist earns exactly zero economic profit. Yet average-cost pricing leads to deadweight losses because the monopolist's price no longer reflects the marginal cost of producing the good. In essence, average-cost pricing is like a tax on the good the monopolist is selling.

The second problem with marginal-cost pricing as a regulatory system (and with average-cost pricing as well) is that it gives the monopolist no incentive to reduce costs. Each firm in a competitive market tries to reduce its costs because lower costs mean higher profits. But if a regulated monopolist knows that regulators will reduce prices whenever costs fall, the monopolist will not benefit from lower costs. In practice, regulators deal with this problem by allowing monopolists to keep some of the benefits from lower costs in the form of higher profit, a practice that requires some departure from marginal-cost pricing.

15-5c Public Ownership

The third policy used by the government to deal with monopoly is public ownership. That is, rather than regulating a natural monopoly that is run by a private firm, the government can run the monopoly itself. This solution is common in many European countries, where the government owns and operates utilities

FIGURE 10

Marginal-Cost Pricing for a Natural Monopoly

Because a natural monopoly has declining average total cost, marginal cost is less than average total cost. Therefore, if regulators require a natural monopoly to charge a price equal to marginal cost, price will be below average total cost, and the monopoly will lose money.

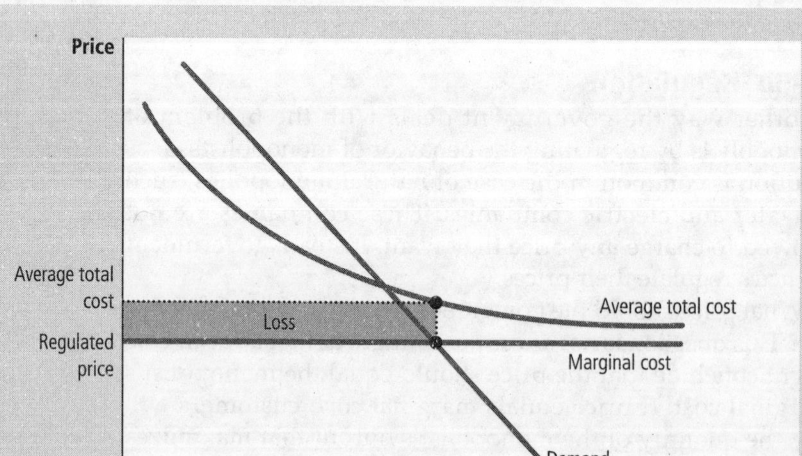

such as telephone, water, and electric companies. In the United States, the government runs the Postal Service. The delivery of ordinary first-class mail is often thought to be a natural monopoly.

Economists usually prefer private to public ownership of natural monopolies. The key issue is how the ownership of the firm affects the costs of production. Private owners have an incentive to minimize costs as long as they reap part of the benefit in the form of higher profit. If the firm's managers are doing a bad job of keeping costs down, the firm's owners will fire them. By contrast, if the government bureaucrats who run a monopoly do a bad job, the losers are the customers and taxpayers, whose only recourse is the political system. The bureaucrats may become a special-interest group and attempt to block cost-reducing reforms. Put simply, as a way of ensuring that firms are well run, the voting booth is less reliable than the profit motive.

15-5d Doing Nothing

Each of the foregoing policies aimed at reducing the problem of monopoly has drawbacks. As a result, some economists argue that it is often best for the government not to try to remedy the inefficiencies of monopoly pricing. Here is the assessment of economist George Stigler, who won the Nobel Prize for his work in industrial organization:

> A famous theorem in economics states that a competitive enterprise economy will produce the largest possible income from a given stock of resources. No real economy meets the exact conditions of the theorem, and all real economies will fall short of the ideal economy—a difference called "market failure." In my view, however, the degree of "market failure" for the American economy is much smaller than the "political failure" arising from the imperfections of economic policies found in real political systems.

As this quotation makes clear, determining the proper role of the government in the economy requires judgments about politics as well as economics.

QuickQuiz *Describe the ways policymakers can respond to the inefficiencies caused by monopolies. List a potential problem with each of these policy responses.*

15-6 Conclusion: The Prevalence of Monopolies

This chapter has discussed the behavior of firms that have control over the prices they charge. We have seen that these firms behave very differently from the competitive firms studied in the previous chapter. Table 2 summarizes some of the key similarities and differences between competitive and monopoly markets.

From the standpoint of public policy, a crucial result is that a monopolist produces less than the socially efficient quantity and charges a price above marginal cost. As a result, a monopoly causes deadweight losses. In some cases, these inefficiencies can be mitigated through price discrimination by the monopolist. But other times, they call for policymakers to take an active role.

How prevalent are the problems of monopoly? There are two answers to this question.

In one sense, monopolies are common. Most firms have some control over the prices they charge. They are not forced to charge the market price for their goods

TABLE 2

Competition versus Monopoly: A Summary Comparison

	Competition	Monopoly
Similarities		
Goal of firms	Maximize profits	Maximize profits
Rule for maximizing	$MR = MC$	$MR = MC$
Can earn economic profits in the short run?	Yes	Yes
Differences		
Number of firms	Many	One
Marginal revenue	$MR = P$	$MR < P$
Price	$P = MC$	$P > MC$
Produces welfare-maximizing level of output?	Yes	No
Entry in the long run?	Yes	No
Can earn economic profits in the long run?	No	Yes
Price discrimination possible?	No	Yes

because their goods are not exactly the same as those offered by other firms. A Ford Taurus is not the same as a Toyota Camry. Ben and Jerry's ice cream is not the same as Breyer's. Each of these goods has a downward-sloping demand curve, which gives each producer some degree of monopoly power.

Yet firms with substantial monopoly power are rare. Few goods are truly unique. Most have substitutes that, even if not exactly the same, are similar. Ben and Jerry can raise the price of their ice cream a little without losing all their sales, but if they raise it a lot, sales will fall substantially as their customers switch to other brands.

In the end, monopoly power is a matter of degree. It is true that many firms have some monopoly power. It is also true that their monopoly power is usually limited. In such a situation, we will not go far wrong assuming that firms operate in competitive markets, even if that is not precisely the case.

CHAPTER QuickQuiz

1. A firm is a natural monopoly if it exhibits the following as its output increases:
   a. decreasing marginal revenue.
   b. increasing marginal cost.
   c. decreasing average revenue.
   d. decreasing average total cost.

2. For a profit-maximizing monopoly that charges the same price to all consumers, what is the relationship between price P, marginal revenue MR, and marginal cost MC?
   a. $P = MR$ and $MR = MC$.
   b. $P > MR$ and $MR = MC$.
   c. $P = MR$ and $MR > MC$
   d. $P > MR$ and $MR > MC$.

3. If a monopoly's fixed costs increase, its price will _____ and its profit will _____.
   a. increase, decrease
   b. decrease, increase
   c. increase, stay the same
   d. stay the same, decrease
4. Compared to the social optimum, a monopoly firm chooses
   a. a quantity that is too low and a price that is too high.
   b. a quantity that is too high and a price that is too low.
   c. a quantity and a price that are both too high.
   d. a quantity and a price that are both too low.
5. The deadweight loss from monopoly arises because
   a. the monopoly firm makes higher profits than a competitive firm would.
   b. some potential consumers who forgo buying the good value it more than its marginal cost.
   c. consumers who buy the good have to pay more than marginal cost, reducing their consumer surplus.
   d. the monopoly firm chooses a quantity that fails to equate price and average revenue.
6. When a monopolist switches from charging a single price to practicing perfect price discrimination, it reduces
   a. the quantity produced.
   b. the firm's profit.
   c. consumer surplus.
   d. total surplus.

SUMMARY

- A monopoly is a firm that is the sole seller in its market. A monopoly arises when a single firm owns a key resource, when the government gives a firm the exclusive right to produce a good, or when a single firm can supply the entire market at a lower cost than many firms could.
- Because a monopoly is the sole producer in its market, it faces a downward-sloping demand curve for its product. When a monopoly increases production by 1 unit, it causes the price of its good to fall, which reduces the amount of revenue earned on all units produced. As a result, a monopoly's marginal revenue is always below the price of its good.
- Like a competitive firm, a monopoly firm maximizes profit by producing the quantity at which marginal revenue equals marginal cost. The monopoly then sets the price at which that quantity is demanded. Unlike a competitive firm, a monopoly firm's price exceeds its marginal revenue, so its price exceeds marginal cost.
- A monopolist's profit-maximizing level of output is below the level that maximizes the sum of consumer and producer surplus. That is, when the monopoly charges a price above marginal cost, some consumers who value the good more than its cost of production do not buy it. As a result, monopoly causes deadweight losses similar to those caused by taxes.
- A monopolist can often increase profits by charging different prices for the same good based on a buyer's willingness to pay. This practice of price discrimination can raise economic welfare by getting the good to some consumers who would otherwise not buy it. In the extreme case of perfect price discrimination, the deadweight loss of monopoly is completely eliminated and the entire surplus in the market goes to the monopoly producer. More generally, when price discrimination is imperfect, it can either raise or lower welfare compared to the outcome with a single monopoly price.
- Policymakers can respond to the inefficiency of monopoly behavior in four ways. They can use the antitrust laws to try to make the industry more competitive. They can regulate the prices that the monopoly charges. They can turn the monopolist into a government-run enterprise. Or, if the market failure is deemed small compared to the inevitable imperfections of policies, they can do nothing at all.

KEY CONCEPTS

monopoly, p. 290   natural monopoly, p. 292   price discrimination, p. 303

QUESTIONS FOR REVIEW

1. Give an example of a government-created monopoly. Is creating this monopoly necessarily bad public policy? Explain.
2. Define *natural monopoly*. What does the size of a market have to do with whether an industry is a natural monopoly?
3. Why is a monopolist's marginal revenue less than the price of its good? Can marginal revenue ever be negative? Explain.
4. Draw the demand, marginal-revenue, average-total-cost, and marginal-cost curves for a monopolist. Show the profit-maximizing level of output, the profit-maximizing price, and the amount of profit.
5. In your diagram from the previous question, show the level of output that maximizes total surplus. Show the deadweight loss from the monopoly. Explain your answer.
6. Give two examples of price discrimination. In each case, explain why the monopolist chooses to follow this business strategy.
7. What gives the government the power to regulate mergers between firms? Give a good reason and a bad reason (from the perspective of society's welfare) that two firms might want to merge.
8. Describe the two problems that arise when regulators tell a natural monopoly that it must set a price equal to marginal cost.

PROBLEMS AND APPLICATIONS

1. A publisher faces the following demand schedule for the next novel from one of its popular authors:

Price	Quantity Demanded
$100	0 novels
90	100,000
80	200,000
70	300,000
60	400,000
50	500,000
40	600,000
30	700,000
20	800,000
10	900,000
0	1,000,000

The author is paid $2 million to write the book, and the marginal cost of publishing the book is a constant $10 per book.

a. Compute total revenue, total cost, and profit at each quantity. What quantity would a profit-maximizing publisher choose? What price would it charge?
b. Compute marginal revenue. (Recall that $MR = \Delta TR/\Delta Q$.) How does marginal revenue compare to the price? Explain.
c. Graph the marginal-revenue, marginal-cost, and demand curves. At what quantity do the marginal-revenue and marginal-cost curves cross? What does this signify?
d. In your graph, shade in the deadweight loss. Explain in words what this means.
e. If the author were paid $3 million instead of $2 million to write the book, how would this affect the publisher's decision regarding what price to charge? Explain.
f. Suppose the publisher was not profit-maximizing but was concerned with maximizing economic efficiency. What price would it charge for the book? How much profit would it make at this price?

2. A small town is served by many competing supermarkets, which have the same constant marginal cost.
a. Using a diagram of the market for groceries, show the consumer surplus, producer surplus, and total surplus.
b. Now suppose that the independent supermarkets combine into one chain. Using a new diagram, show the new consumer surplus, producer surplus, and total surplus. Relative to the competitive market, what is the transfer from consumers to producers? What is the deadweight loss?

3. Johnny Rockabilly has just finished recording his latest CD. His record company's marketing department determines that the demand for the CD is as follows:

Price	Number of CDs
$24	10,000
22	20,000
20	30,000
18	40,000
16	50,000
14	60,000

The company can produce the CD with no fixed cost and a variable cost of $5 per CD.

a. Find total revenue for quantity equal to 10,000, 20,000, and so on. What is the marginal revenue for each 10,000 increase in the quantity sold?
b. What quantity of CDs would maximize profit? What would the price be? What would the profit be?
c. If you were Johnny's agent, what recording fee would you advise Johnny to demand from the record company? Why?

4. A company is considering building a bridge across a river. The bridge would cost $2 million to build and nothing to maintain. The following table shows the company's anticipated demand over the lifetime of the bridge:

Price per Crossing	Number of Crossings, in Thousands
$8	0
7	100
6	200
5	300
4	400
3	500
2	600
1	700
0	800

a. If the company were to build the bridge, what would be its profit-maximizing price? Would that be the efficient level of output? Why or why not?
b. If the company is interested in maximizing profit, should it build the bridge? What would be its profit or loss?
c. If the government were to build the bridge, what price should it charge?
d. Should the government build the bridge? Explain.

5. Consider the relationship between monopoly pricing and price elasticity of demand.
a. Explain why a monopolist will never produce a quantity at which the demand curve is inelastic. (*Hint:* If demand is inelastic and the firm raises its price, what happens to total revenue and total costs?)
b. Draw a diagram for a monopolist, precisely labeling the portion of the demand curve that is inelastic. (*Hint:* The answer is related to the marginal-revenue curve.)
c. On your diagram, show the quantity and price that maximize total revenue.

6. You live in a town with 300 adults and 200 children, and you are thinking about putting on a play to entertain your neighbors and make some money. A play has a fixed cost of $2,000, but selling an extra ticket has zero marginal cost. Here are the demand schedules for your two types of customer:

Price	Adults	Children
$10	0	0
9	100	0
8	200	0
7	300	0
6	300	0
5	300	100
4	300	200
3	300	200
2	300	200
1	300	200
0	300	200

a. To maximize profit, what price would you charge for an adult ticket? For a child's ticket? How much profit do you make?
b. The city council passes a law prohibiting you from charging different prices to different customers. What price do you set for a ticket now? How much profit do you make?
c. Who is worse off because of the law prohibiting price discrimination? Who is better off? (If you can, quantify the changes in welfare.)
d. If the fixed cost of the play were $2,500 rather than $2,000, how would your answers to parts (a), (b), and (c) change?

7. The residents of the town Ectenia all love economics, and the mayor proposes building an economics museum. The museum has a fixed cost of $2,400,000 and no variable costs. There are 100,000 town residents, and each has the same demand for museum visits: $Q^D = 10 - P$, where P is the price of admission.
   a. Graph the museum's average-total-cost curve and its marginal-cost curve. What kind of market would describe the museum?
   b. The mayor proposes financing the museum with a lump-sum tax of $24 and then opening the museum to the public for free. How many times would each person visit? Calculate the benefit each person would get from the museum, measured as consumer surplus minus the new tax.
   c. The mayor's anti-tax opponent says the museum should finance itself by charging an admission fee. What is the lowest price the museum can charge without incurring losses? (*Hint*: Find the number of visits and museum profits for prices of $2, $3, $4, and $5.)
   d. For the break-even price you found in part (c), calculate each resident's consumer surplus. Compared with the mayor's plan, who is better off with this admission fee, and who is worse off? Explain.
   e. What real-world considerations absent in the problem above might provide reasons to favor an admission fee?

8. Henry Potter owns the only well in town that produces clean drinking water. He faces the following demand, marginal revenue, and marginal cost curves:

$$\text{Demand: } P = 70 - Q$$
$$\text{Marginal Revenue: } MR = 70 - 2Q$$
$$\text{Marginal Cost: } MC = 10 + Q$$

   a. Graph these three curves. Assuming that Mr. Potter maximizes profit, what quantity does he produce? What price does he charge? Show these results on your graph.
   b. Mayor George Bailey, concerned about water consumers, is considering a price ceiling that is 10 percent below the monopoly price derived in part (a). What quantity would be demanded at this new price? Would the profit-maximizing Mr. Potter produce that amount? Explain. (*Hint*: Think about marginal cost.)
   c. George's Uncle Billy says that a price ceiling is a bad idea because price ceilings cause shortages. Is he right in this case? What size shortage would the price ceiling create? Explain.
   d. George's friend Clarence, who is even more concerned about consumers, suggests a price ceiling 50 percent below the monopoly price. What quantity would be demanded at this price? How much would Mr. Potter produce? In this case, is Uncle Billy right? What size shortage would the price ceiling create?

9. Only one firm produces and sells soccer balls in the country of Wiknam, and as the story begins, international trade in soccer balls is prohibited. The following equations describe the monopolist's demand, marginal revenue, total cost, and marginal cost:

$$\text{Demand: } P = 10 - Q$$
$$\text{Marginal Revenue: } MR = 10 - 2Q$$
$$\text{Total Cost: } TC = 3 + Q + 0.5\,Q^2$$
$$\text{Marginal Cost: } MC = 1 + Q,$$

where Q is quantity and P is the price measured in Wiknamian dollars.
   a. How many soccer balls does the monopolist produce? At what price are they sold? What is the monopolist's profit?
   b. One day, the King of Wiknam decrees that henceforth there will be free trade—either imports or exports—of soccer balls at the world price of $6. The firm is now a price taker in a competitive market. What happens to domestic production of soccer balls? To domestic consumption? Does Wiknam export or import soccer balls?
   c. In our analysis of international trade in Chapter 9, a country becomes an exporter when the price without trade is below the world price and an importer when the price without trade is above the world price. Does that conclusion hold in your answers to parts (a) and (b)? Explain.
   d. Suppose that the world price was not $6 but, instead, happened to be exactly the same as the domestic price without trade as determined in part (a). Would allowing trade have changed anything in the Wiknamian economy? Explain. How does the result here compare with the analysis in Chapter 9?

10. Based on market research, a film production company in Ectenia obtains the following information about the demand and production costs of its new DVD:

$$\text{Demand: } P = 1{,}000 - 10Q$$
$$\text{Total Revenue: } TR = 1{,}000Q - 10Q^2$$
$$\text{Marginal Revenue: } MR = 1{,}000 - 20Q$$
$$\text{Marginal Cost: } MC = 100 + 10Q,$$

where Q indicates the number of copies sold and P is the price in Ectenian dollars.

a. Find the price and quantity that maximize the company's profit.
b. Find the price and quantity that would maximize social welfare.
c. Calculate the deadweight loss from monopoly.
d. Suppose, in addition to the costs above, the director of the film has to be paid. The company is considering four options:
   i. a flat fee of 2,000 Ectenian dollars.
   ii. 50 percent of the profits.
   iii. 150 Ectenian dollars per unit sold.
   iv. 50 percent of the revenue.

For each option, calculate the profit-maximizing price and quantity. Which, if any, of these compensation schemes would alter the deadweight loss from monopoly? Explain.

11. Larry, Curly, and Moe run the only saloon in town. Larry wants to sell as many drinks as possible without losing money. Curly wants the saloon to bring in as much revenue as possible. Moe wants to make the largest possible profits. Using a single diagram of the saloon's demand curve and its cost curves, show the price and quantity combinations favored by each of the three partners. Explain. (*Hint*: Only one of these partners will want to set marginal revenue equal to marginal cost.)

12. Many schemes for price discrimination involve some cost. For example, discount coupons take up the time and resources of both the buyer and the seller. This question considers the implications of costly price discrimination. To keep things simple, let's assume that our monopolist's production costs are simply proportional to output so that average total cost and marginal cost are constant and equal to each other.

a. Draw the cost, demand, and marginal-revenue curves for the monopolist. Show the price the monopolist would charge without price discrimination.
b. In your diagram, mark the area equal to the monopolist's profit and call it X. Mark the area equal to consumer surplus and call it Y. Mark the area equal to the deadweight loss and call it Z.
c. Now suppose that the monopolist can perfectly price discriminate. What is the monopolist's profit? (Give your answer in terms of X, Y, and Z.)
d. What is the change in the monopolist's profit from price discrimination? What is the change in total surplus from price discrimination? Which change is larger? Explain. (Give your answer in terms of X, Y, and Z.)
e. Now suppose that there is some cost associated with price discrimination. To model this cost, let's assume that the monopolist has to pay a fixed cost C to price discriminate. How would a monopolist make the decision whether to pay this fixed cost? (Give your answer in terms of X, Y, Z, and C.)
f. How would a benevolent social planner, who cares about total surplus, decide whether the monopolist should price discriminate? (Give your answer in terms of X, Y, Z, and C.)
g. Compare your answers to parts (e) and (f). How does the monopolist's incentive to price discriminate differ from the social planner's? Is it possible that the monopolist will price discriminate even though doing so is not socially desirable?

To find additional study resources, visit cengagebrain.com, and search for "Mankiw."

CHAPTER

16

Monopolistic Competition

You walk into a bookstore to buy a book to read during your next vacation. On the store's shelves you find a Patricia Cornwell mystery, a Stephen King thriller, a Nathaniel Philbrick history, a Suzanne Collins dystopian survival romance, and many other choices. When you pick out a book and buy it, what kind of market are you participating in?

On the one hand, the market for books seems competitive. As you look over the shelves at your bookstore, you find many authors and many publishers vying for your attention. A buyer in this market has thousands of competing products from which to choose. And because anyone can enter the industry by writing and publishing a book, the book business is not very profitable. For every highly paid novelist, there are hundreds of struggling ones.

On the other hand, the market for books seems monopolistic. Because each book is unique, publishers have some latitude in choosing what price to charge. The sellers in this market are price makers rather than price takers. And indeed, the price of books greatly exceeds marginal cost. The price of a typical hardcover novel, for instance, is about $25, whereas the cost of printing one additional copy of the novel is less than $5.

The market for novels fits neither the competitive nor the monopoly model. Instead, it is best described by the model of *monopolistic competition*, the subject of this chapter. The term "monopolistic competition" might at first seem to be an oxymoron, like "jumbo shrimp." But as we will see, monopolistically competitive industries are monopolistic in some ways and competitive in others. The model describes not only the publishing industry but also the market for many other goods and services.

16-1 Between Monopoly and Perfect Competition

The previous two chapters analyzed markets with many competitive firms and markets with a single monopoly firm. In Chapter 14, we saw that the price in a perfectly competitive market always equals the marginal cost of production. We also saw that, in the long run, entry and exit drive economic profit to zero, so the price also equals average total cost. In Chapter 15, we saw how monopoly firms can use their market power to keep prices above marginal cost, leading to a positive economic profit for the firm and a deadweight loss for society. Competition and monopoly are extreme forms of market structure. Competition occurs when there are many firms in a market offering essentially identical products; monopoly occurs when there is only one firm in a market.

Although the cases of perfect competition and monopoly illustrate some important ideas about how markets work, most markets in the economy include elements of both these cases and, therefore, are not completely described by either of them. The typical firm in the economy faces competition, but the competition is not so rigorous that it makes the firm a price taker like the firms analyzed in Chapter 14. The typical firm also has some degree of market power, but its market power is not so great that the firm can be described exactly by the monopoly model presented in Chapter 15. In other words, many industries fall somewhere between the polar cases of perfect competition and monopoly. Economists call this situation *imperfect competition*.

oligopoly
a market structure in which only a few sellers offer similar or identical products

One type of imperfectly competitive market is an **oligopoly**, a market with only a few sellers, each offering a product that is similar or identical to the products offered by other sellers in the market. Economists measure a market's domination by a small number of firms with a statistic called the *concentration ratio*, which is the percentage of total output in the market supplied by the four largest firms. In the U.S. economy, most industries have a four-firm concentration ratio under 50 percent, but in some industries, the biggest firms play a more dominant role. Highly concentrated industries include the market for major household appliances (which has a concentration ratio of 90 percent), tires (91 percent), light bulbs (92 percent), soda (94 percent), and wireless telecommunications (95 percent). These industries are best described as oligopolies. In the next chapter we see that the small number of firms in oligopolies makes strategic interactions among them a key part of the analysis. That is, in choosing how much to produce and what price to charge, each firm in an oligopoly is concerned not only with what its competitors are doing but also with how its competitors would react to what it might do.

A second type of imperfectly competitive market is called **monopolistic competition**. This describes a market structure in which there are many firms selling products that are similar but not identical. In a monopolistically competitive market, each firm has a monopoly over the product it makes, but many other firms make similar products that compete for the same customers.

monopolistic competition
a market structure in which many firms sell products that are similar but not identical

To be more precise, monopolistic competition describes a market with the following attributes:

- *Many sellers:* There are many firms competing for the same group of customers.
- *Product differentiation:* Each firm produces a product that is at least slightly different from those of other firms. Thus, rather than being a price taker, each firm faces a downward-sloping demand curve.
- *Free entry and exit:* Firms can enter or exit the market without restriction. Thus, the number of firms in the market adjusts until economic profits are driven to zero.

A moment's thought reveals a long list of markets with these attributes: books, computer games, restaurants, piano lessons, cookies, clothing, and so on.

Monopolistic competition, like oligopoly, is a market structure that lies between the extreme cases of perfect competition and monopoly. But oligopoly and monopolistic competition are quite different. Oligopoly departs from the perfectly competitive ideal of Chapter 14 because there are only a few sellers in the market. The small number of sellers makes rigorous competition less likely and strategic interactions among them vitally important. By contrast, a monopolistically competitive market has many sellers, each of which is small compared to the market. It departs from the perfectly competitive ideal because each of the sellers offers a somewhat different product.

Figure 1 summarizes the four types of market structure. The first question to ask about any market is how many firms there are. If there is only one firm, the

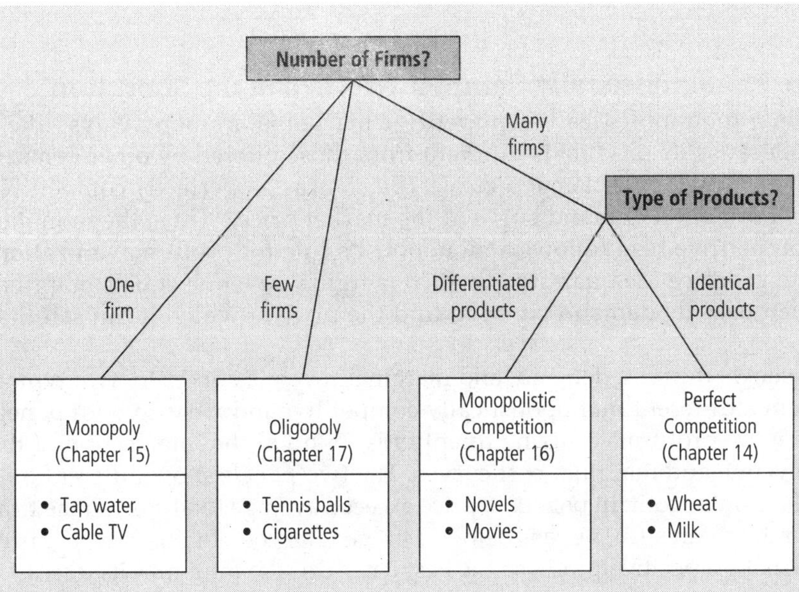

FIGURE 1

The Four Types of Market Structure
Economists who study industrial organization divide markets into four types: monopoly, oligopoly, monopolistic competition, and perfect competition.

market is a monopoly. If there are only a few firms, the market is an oligopoly. If there are many firms, we need to ask another question: Do the firms sell identical or differentiated products? If the many firms sell identical products, the market is perfectly competitive. But if the many firms sell differentiated products, the market is monopolistically competitive.

Because reality is never as clear-cut as theory, at times you may find it hard to decide what structure best describes a market. There is, for instance, no magic number that separates "few" from "many" when counting the number of firms. (Do the approximately dozen companies that now sell cars in the United States make this market an oligopoly, or is the market more competitive? The answer is open to debate.) Similarly, there is no sure way to determine when products are differentiated and when they are identical. (Are different brands of milk really the same? Again, the answer is debatable.) When analyzing actual markets, economists have to keep in mind the lessons learned from studying all types of market structure and then apply each lesson as it seems appropriate.

Now that we understand how economists define the various types of market structure, we can continue our analysis of each of them. In this chapter we examine monopolistic competition. In the next chapter we analyze oligopoly.

QuickQuiz *Define* oligopoly *and* monopolistic competition *and give an example of each.*

16-2 Competition with Differentiated Products

To understand monopolistically competitive markets, we first consider the decisions facing an individual firm. We then examine what happens in the long run as firms enter and exit the industry. Next, we compare the equilibrium under monopolistic competition to the equilibrium under perfect competition that we examined in Chapter 14. Finally, we consider whether the outcome in a monopolistically competitive market is desirable from the standpoint of society as a whole.

16-2a The Monopolistically Competitive Firm in the Short Run

Each firm in a monopolistically competitive market is, in many ways, like a monopoly. Because its product is different from those offered by other firms, it faces a downward-sloping demand curve. (By contrast, a perfectly competitive firm faces a horizontal demand curve at the market price.) Thus, the monopolistically competitive firm follows a monopolist's rule for profit maximization: It chooses to produce the quantity at which marginal revenue equals marginal cost and then uses its demand curve to find the price at which it can sell that quantity.

Figure 2 shows the cost, demand, and marginal-revenue curves for two typical firms, each in a different monopolistically competitive industry. In both panels of the figure, the profit-maximizing quantity is found at the intersection of the marginal-revenue and marginal-cost curves. The two panels show different outcomes for the firm's profit. In panel (a), price exceeds average total cost, so the firm makes a profit. In panel (b), price is below average total cost. In this case, the firm is unable to make a positive profit, so the best it can do is to minimize its losses.

FIGURE 2

Monopolistic Competitors in the Short Run

Monopolistic competitors, like monopolists, maximize profit by producing the quantity at which marginal revenue equals marginal cost. The firm in panel (a) makes a profit because, at this quantity, price is greater than average total cost. The firm in panel (b) makes losses because, at this quantity, price is less than average total cost.

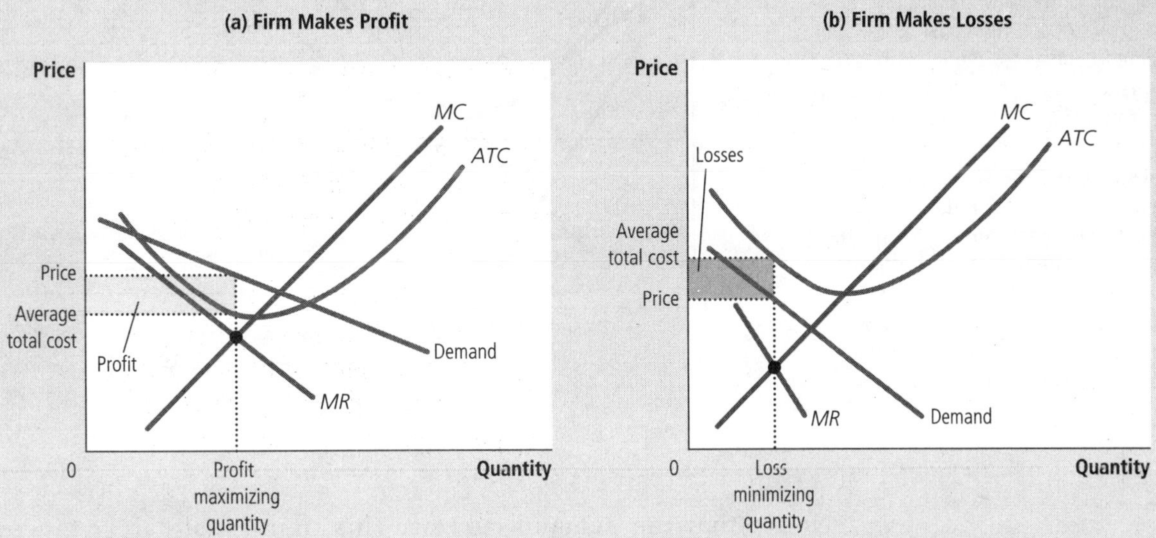

All this should seem familiar. A monopolistically competitive firm chooses its quantity and price just as a monopoly does. In the short run, these two types of market structure are similar.

16-2b The Long-Run Equilibrium

The situations depicted in Figure 2 do not last long. When firms are making profits, as in panel (a), new firms have an incentive to enter the market. This entry increases the number of products from which customers can choose and, therefore, reduces the demand faced by each firm already in the market. In other words, profit encourages entry, and entry shifts the demand curves faced by the incumbent firms to the left. As the demand for incumbent firms' products falls, these firms experience declining profit.

Conversely, when firms are making losses, as in panel (b), firms in the market have an incentive to exit. As firms exit, customers have fewer products from which to choose. This decrease in the number of firms expands the demand faced by those firms that stay in the market. In other words, losses encourage exit, and exit shifts the demand curves of the remaining firms to the right. As the demand for the remaining firms' products rises, these firms experience rising profits (that is, declining losses).

This process of entry and exit continues until the firms in the market are making exactly zero economic profit. Figure 3 depicts the long-run equilibrium. Once the market reaches this equilibrium, new firms have no incentive to enter, and existing firms have no incentive to exit.

FIGURE 3

A Monopolistic Competitor in the Long Run
In a monopolistically competitive market, if firms are making profits, new firms enter, causing the demand curves for the incumbent firms to shift to the left. Similarly, if firms are making losses, some of the firms in the market exit, causing the demand curves of the remaining firms to shift to the right. Because of these shifts in demand, monopolistically competitive firms eventually find themselves in the long-run equilibrium shown here. In this long-run equilibrium, price equals average total cost, and each firm earns zero profit.

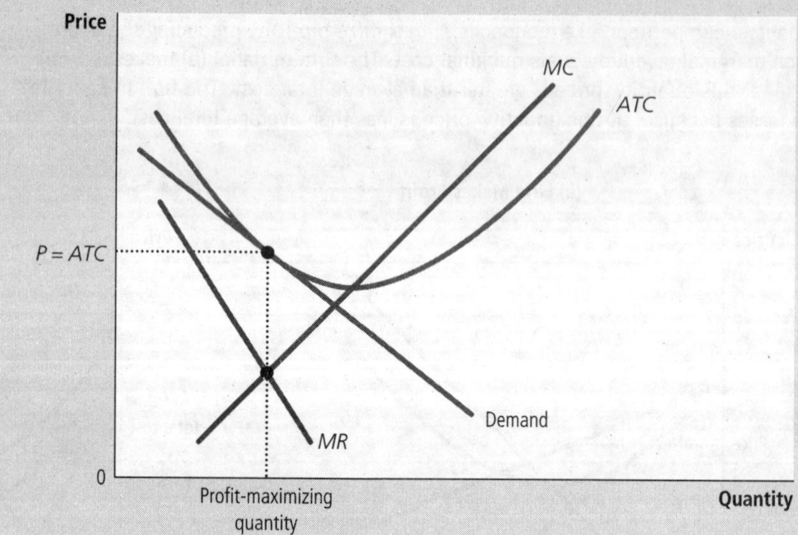

Notice that the demand curve in this figure just barely touches the average-total-cost curve. Mathematically, we say the two curves are *tangent* to each other. These two curves must be tangent once entry and exit have driven profit to zero. Because profit per unit sold is the difference between price (found on the demand curve) and average total cost, the maximum profit is zero only if these two curves touch each other without crossing. Also note that this point of tangency occurs at the same quantity where marginal revenue equals marginal cost. That these two points line up is not a coincidence: It is required because this particular quantity maximizes profit and the maximum profit is exactly zero in the long run.

To sum up, two characteristics describe the long-run equilibrium in a monopolistically competitive market:

- As in a monopoly market, price exceeds marginal cost ($P > MC$). This conclusion arises because profit maximization requires marginal revenue to equal marginal cost ($MR = MC$) and because the downward-sloping demand curve makes marginal revenue less than the price ($MR < P$).
- As in a competitive market, price equals average total cost ($P = ATC$). This conclusion arises because free entry and exit drive economic profit to zero.

The second characteristic shows how monopolistic competition differs from monopoly. Because a monopoly is the sole seller of a product without close substitutes, it can earn positive economic profit, even in the long run. By contrast, because there is free entry into a monopolistically competitive market, the economic profit of a firm in this type of market is driven to zero.

16-2c Monopolistic versus Perfect Competition

Figure 4 compares the long-run equilibrium under monopolistic competition to the long-run equilibrium under perfect competition. (Chapter 14 discussed the

"GIVEN THE DOWNWARD SLOPE OF OUR DEMAND CURVE, AND THE EASE WITH WHICH OTHER FIRMS CAN ENTER THE INDUSTRY, WE CAN STRENGTHEN OUR PROFIT POSITION ONLY BY EQUATING MARGINAL COST AND MARGINAL REVENUE. ORDER MORE JELLY BEANS."

equilibrium with perfect competition.) There are two noteworthy differences between monopolistic and perfect competition: excess capacity and the markup.

Excess Capacity As we have just seen, the process of entry and exit drives each firm in a monopolistically competitive market to a point of tangency between its demand and average-total-cost curves. Panel (a) of Figure 4 shows that the quantity of output at this point is smaller than the quantity that minimizes average total cost. Thus, under monopolistic competition, firms produce on the downward-sloping portion of their average-total-cost curves. In this way, monopolistic competition contrasts starkly with perfect competition. As panel (b) of Figure 4 shows, free entry in competitive markets drives firms to produce at the minimum of average total cost.

The quantity that minimizes average total cost is called the *efficient scale* of the firm. In the long run, perfectly competitive firms produce at the efficient scale, whereas monopolistically competitive firms produce below this level. Firms are said to have *excess capacity* under monopolistic competition. In other words, a monopolistically competitive firm, unlike a perfectly competitive firm, could increase the quantity it produces and lower the average total cost of production. The firm forgoes this opportunity because it would need to cut its price to sell the additional output. It is more profitable for a monopolistic competitor to continue operating with excess capacity.

FIGURE 4

Monopolistic versus Perfect Competition

Panel (a) shows the long-run equilibrium in a monopolistically competitive market, and panel (b) shows the long-run equilibrium in a perfectly competitive market. Two differences are notable. (1) The perfectly competitive firm produces at the efficient scale, where average total cost is minimized. By contrast, the monopolistically competitive firm produces at less than the efficient scale. (2) Price equals marginal cost under perfect competition, but price is above marginal cost under monopolistic competition.

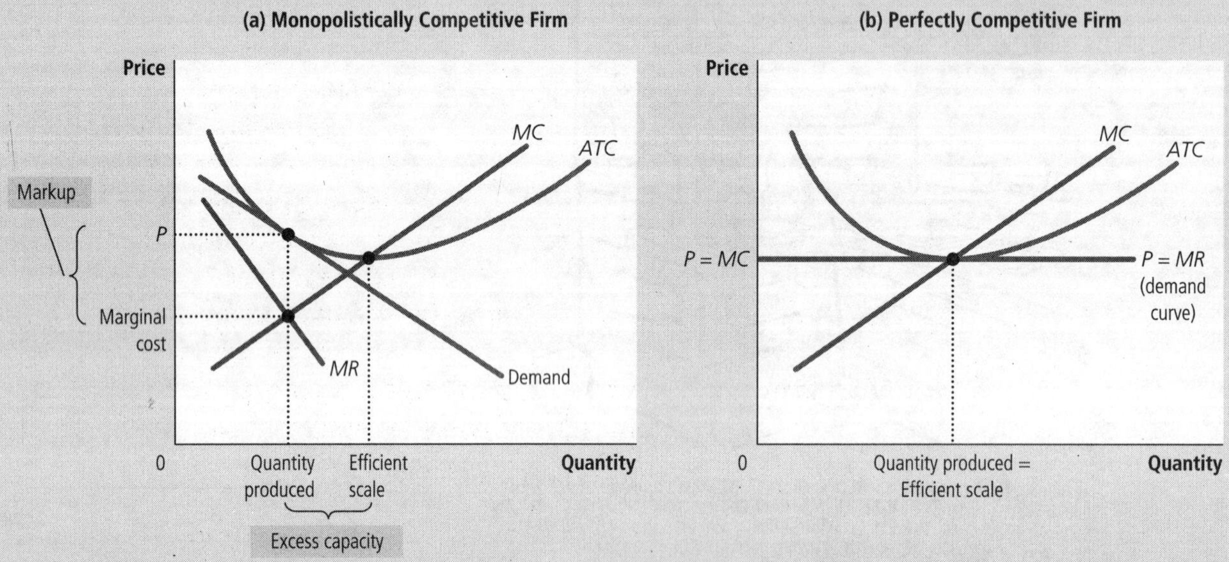

Markup over Marginal Cost A second difference between perfect competition and monopolistic competition is the relationship between price and marginal cost. For a perfectly competitive firm, such as the one shown in panel (b) of Figure 4, price equals marginal cost. For a monopolistically competitive firm, such as the one shown in panel (a), price exceeds marginal cost because the firm always has some market power.

How is this markup over marginal cost consistent with free entry and zero profit? The zero-profit condition ensures only that price equals average total cost. It does *not* ensure that price equals marginal cost. Indeed, in the long-run equilibrium, monopolistically competitive firms operate on the declining portion of their average-total-cost curves, so marginal cost is below average total cost. Thus, for price to equal average total cost, price must be above marginal cost.

In this relationship between price and marginal cost, we see a key behavioral difference between perfect competitors and monopolistic competitors. Imagine that you were to ask a firm the following question: "Would you like to see another customer come through your door ready to buy from you at your current price?" A perfectly competitive firm would answer that it didn't care. Because price exactly equals marginal cost, the profit from an extra unit sold is zero. By contrast, a monopolistically competitive firm is always eager to get another customer. Because its price exceeds marginal cost, an extra unit sold at the posted price means more profit.

According to an old quip, monopolistically competitive markets are those in which sellers send Christmas cards to the buyers. Trying to attract more customers makes sense only if price exceeds marginal cost.

16-2d Monopolistic Competition and the Welfare of Society

Is the outcome in a monopolistically competitive market desirable from the standpoint of society as a whole? Can policymakers improve on the market outcome? In previous chapters we evaluated markets from the standpoint of efficiency by asking whether society is getting the most it can out of its scarce resources. We learned that competitive markets lead to efficient outcomes, unless there are externalities, whereas monopoly markets lead to deadweight losses. Monopolistically competitive markets are more complex than either of these polar cases, so evaluating welfare in these markets is a more subtle exercise.

One source of inefficiency in monopolistically competitive markets is the markup of price over marginal cost. Because of the markup, some consumers who value the good at more than the marginal cost of production (but less than the price) will be deterred from buying it. Thus, a monopolistically competitive market has the normal deadweight loss of monopoly pricing.

This outcome is undesirable compared with the efficient quantity that arises when price equals marginal cost, but policymakers don't have an easy way to fix the problem. To enforce marginal-cost pricing, they would need to regulate all firms that produce differentiated products. Because such products are so common in the economy, the administrative burden of such regulation would be overwhelming.

Moreover, regulating monopolistic competitors entails all the problems of regulating natural monopolies. In particular, because monopolistic competitors are making zero profits already, requiring them to lower their prices to equal marginal cost would cause them to make losses. To keep these firms in business, the government would need to help them cover these losses. Rather than raise taxes to pay for these subsidies, policymakers often decide it is better to live with the inefficiency of monopolistic pricing.

Another source of inefficiency under monopolistic competition is that the number of firms in the market may not be "ideal." That is, there may be too much or too little entry. One way to think about this problem is in terms of the externalities associated with entry. Whenever a new firm considers entering the market with a new product, it takes into account only the profit it would make. Yet its entry would also have the following two effects that are external to the firm:

- *The product-variety externality:* Because consumers get some consumer surplus from the introduction of a new product, the entry of a new firm conveys a positive externality on consumers.
- *The business-stealing externality:* Because other firms lose customers and profits when faced with a new competitor, the entry of a new firm imposes a negative externality on existing firms.

Thus, in a monopolistically competitive market, the entry of new firms entails both positive and negative externalities. Depending on which externality is larger, a monopolistically competitive market could have either too few or too many products.

Both of these externalities are closely related to the conditions for monopolistic competition. The product-variety externality arises because new firms offer products that differ from those of the existing firms. The business-stealing externality arises because firms post a price above marginal cost and, therefore, are always eager to sell additional units. Conversely, because perfectly competitive firms produce identical goods and charge a price equal to marginal cost, neither of these externalities exists under perfect competition.

In the end, we can conclude only that monopolistically competitive markets do not have all the desirable welfare properties of perfectly competitive markets. That is, the invisible hand does not ensure that total surplus is maximized under monopolistic competition. Yet because the inefficiencies are subtle, hard to measure, and hard to fix, there is no easy way for public policy to improve the market outcome.

QuickQuiz *List the three key attributes of monopolistic competition. • Draw and explain a diagram to show the long-run equilibrium in a monopolistically competitive market. How does this equilibrium differ from that in a perfectly competitive market?*

16-3 Advertising

It is nearly impossible to go through a typical day in a modern economy without being bombarded with advertising. Whether you are surfing the Internet, posting on Facebook, reading a magazine, watching television, or driving down the highway, some firm will try to convince you to buy its product. Such behavior is a natural feature of monopolistic competition (as well as some oligopolistic industries). When firms sell differentiated products and charge prices above marginal cost, each firm has an incentive to advertise to attract more buyers to its particular product.

The amount of advertising varies substantially across products. Firms that sell highly differentiated consumer goods, such as over-the-counter drugs, perfumes, soft drinks, razor blades, breakfast cereals, and dog food, typically spend between 10 and 20 percent of their revenue on advertising. Firms that sell industrial products, such as drill presses and communications satellites, typically spend very little on advertising. And firms that sell homogeneous products, such as wheat, salt, sugar, and crude oil, spend nothing at all.

For the economy as a whole, about 2 percent of total firm revenue is spent on advertising. This spending takes many forms, including ads on web sites, social media, television, radio, and billboards and in newspapers, magazines, and direct mail.

16-3a The Debate over Advertising

Is society wasting the resources it devotes to advertising? Or does advertising serve a valuable purpose? Assessing the social value of advertising is difficult and often generates heated argument among economists. Let's consider both sides of the debate.

The Critique of Advertising Critics of advertising argue that firms advertise to manipulate people's tastes. Much advertising is psychological rather than informational. Consider, for example, the typical television commercial for some brand of soft drink. The commercial most likely does not tell the viewer about the product's price or quality. Instead, it might show a group of happy people at a party on a beach on a beautiful sunny day. In their hands are cans of the soft drink. The goal of the commercial is to convey a subconscious (if not subtle) message: "You too can have many friends and be happy, if you drink our product." Critics of advertising argue that such a commercial creates a desire that otherwise might not exist.

Critics also argue that advertising impedes competition. Advertising often tries to convince consumers that products are more different than they truly are. By increasing the perception of product differentiation and fostering brand loyalty, advertising makes buyers less concerned with price differences among similar goods, thereby making the demand for a particular brand less elastic. When a firm faces a less elastic demand curve, it can increase its profits by charging a larger markup over marginal cost.

The Defense of Advertising Defenders of advertising argue that firms use advertising to provide information to customers. Advertising conveys the prices of the goods offered for sale, the existence of new products, and the locations of retail outlets. This information allows customers to make better choices about what to buy and, thus, enhances the ability of markets to allocate resources efficiently.

Defenders also argue that advertising fosters competition. Because advertising allows customers to be more fully informed about all the firms in the market, customers can more easily take advantage of price differences. Thus, each firm has less market power. In addition, advertising allows new firms to enter more easily because it gives entrants a means to attract customers from existing firms.

Over time, policymakers have come to accept the view that advertising can make markets more competitive. One important example is the regulation of advertising for certain professions, such as lawyers, doctors, and pharmacists. In the past, these groups succeeded in getting state governments to prohibit advertising in their fields on the grounds that advertising was "unprofessional." In recent years, however, the courts have concluded that the primary effect of these restrictions on advertising was to curtail competition. They have, therefore, overturned many of the laws that prohibit advertising by members of these professions.

CASE STUDY

ADVERTISING AND THE PRICE OF EYEGLASSES

What effect does advertising have on the price of a good? On the one hand, advertising might make consumers view products as being more different than they otherwise would. If so, it would make markets less competitive and firms' demand curves less elastic, and this would lead firms to charge higher prices. On the other hand, advertising might make it easier for consumers to find the firms offering the best prices. In this case, it would make markets more competitive and firms' demand curves more elastic, which would lead to lower prices.

In an article published in *The Journal of Law and Economics* in 1972, economist Lee Benham tested these two views of advertising. In the United States during the 1960s, the various state governments had vastly different rules about advertising by optometrists. Some states allowed advertising for eyeglasses and eye examinations. Many states, however, prohibited it. For example, the Florida law read as follows:

> It is unlawful for any person, firm, or corporation to . . . advertise either directly or indirectly by any means whatsoever any definite or indefinite price or credit terms on prescriptive or corrective lens, frames, complete prescriptive or corrective glasses, or any optometric service. . . . This section is passed in the interest of public health, safety, and welfare, and its provisions shall be liberally construed to carry out its objects and purposes.

Professional optometrists enthusiastically endorsed these restrictions on advertising.

Benham used the differences in state law as a natural experiment to test the two views of advertising. The results were striking. In those states that prohibited advertising, the average price paid for a pair of eyeglasses was $33, or $256 in 2015 dollars. In states that did not restrict advertising, the average price was $26, or $202 in 2015 dollars. Thus, advertising reduced average prices by more than 20 percent. In the market for eyeglasses, and probably in many other markets as well, advertising fosters competition and leads to lower prices for consumers. ●

16-3b Advertising as a Signal of Quality

Many types of advertising contain little apparent information about the product being advertised. Consider a firm introducing a new breakfast cereal. The firm might saturate the airwaves with advertisements showing some actor eating the cereal and exclaiming how wonderful it tastes. How much information does the advertisement really provide?

The answer is more than you might think. Defenders of advertising argue that even advertising that appears to contain little hard information may in fact tell consumers something about product quality. The willingness of the firm to spend a large amount of money on advertising can itself be a *signal* to consumers about the quality of the product being offered.

Consider the problem facing two firms—General Mills and Kellogg. Each company has just come up with a recipe for a new cereal, which it would sell for $3 a box. To keep things simple, let's assume that the marginal cost of making cereal is zero, so the $3 is all profit. Each company knows that if it spends $10 million on advertising, it will get 1 million consumers to try its new cereal. And each company knows that if consumers like the cereal, they will buy it not once but many times.

First consider General Mills' decision. Based on market research, General Mills knows that its cereal tastes like shredded newspaper with sugar on top. Advertising would sell one box to each of the 1 million consumers, but consumers would quickly learn that the cereal is not very good and stop buying it. General Mills decides it is not worth spending $10 million on advertising to get only $3 million in sales. So it does not bother to advertise. It sends its cooks back to the test kitchen to come up with a better recipe.

Kellogg, on the other hand, knows that its cereal is great. Each person who tries it will buy a box a month for the next year. Thus, the $10 million in advertising will bring in $36 million in sales. Advertising is profitable here because Kellogg has a good product that consumers will buy repeatedly. Thus, Kellogg chooses to advertise.

Now that we have considered the behavior of the two firms, let's consider the behavior of consumers. We began by asserting that consumers are inclined to try a new cereal that they see advertised. But is this behavior rational? Should a consumer try a new cereal just because the seller has chosen to advertise it?

In fact, it may be completely rational for consumers to try new products that they see advertised. In our story, consumers decide to try Kellogg's new cereal because Kellogg advertises. Kellogg chooses to advertise because it knows that its cereal is quite good, while General Mills chooses not to advertise because it knows that its cereal is not good at all. By its willingness to spend money on advertising, Kellogg signals to consumers the quality of its cereal. Each consumer thinks, quite sensibly, "Boy, if the Kellogg Company is willing to spend so much money advertising this new cereal, it must be really good."

What is most surprising about this theory of advertising is that the content of the advertisement is irrelevant. Kellogg signals the quality of its product by its willingness to spend money on advertising. What the advertisements say is not as important as the fact that consumers know ads are expensive. By contrast, cheap advertising cannot be effective at signaling quality to consumers. In our example, if an advertising campaign cost less than $3 million, both General Mills and Kellogg would use it to market their new cereals. Because both good and bad cereals would be advertised, consumers could not infer the quality of a new cereal from the fact that it is advertised. Over time, consumers would learn to ignore such cheap advertising.

This theory can explain why firms pay famous actors large amounts of money to make advertisements that, on the surface, appear to convey no information at all. The information is not in the advertisement's content but simply in its existence and expense.

16-3c Brand Names

Advertising is closely related to the existence of brand names. In many markets, there are two types of firms. Some firms sell products with widely recognized brand names, while other firms sell generic substitutes. For example, in a typical drugstore, you can find Bayer aspirin on the shelf next to generic aspirin. In a typical grocery store, you can find Pepsi next to less familiar colas. Most often, the firm with the brand name spends more on advertising and charges a higher price for its product.

Just as there is disagreement about the economics of advertising, there is disagreement about the economics of brand names. Let's consider both sides of the debate.

Critics argue that brand names cause consumers to perceive differences that do not really exist. In many cases, the generic good is almost indistinguishable from the brand-name good. Consumers' willingness to pay more for the brand-name good, these critics assert, is a form of irrationality fostered by advertising. Economist Edward Chamberlin, one of the early developers of the theory of monopolistic competition, concluded from this argument that brand names were bad for the economy. He proposed that the government discourage their use by refusing to enforce the exclusive trademarks that companies use to identify their products.

More recently, economists have defended brand names as a useful way for consumers to ensure that the goods they buy are of high quality. There are two related arguments. First, brand names provide consumers with *information* about quality when quality cannot be easily judged in advance of purchase. Second, brand names give firms an *incentive* to maintain high quality because firms have a financial stake in maintaining the reputation of their brand names.

To see how these arguments work in practice, consider a famous brand name: McDonald's. Imagine that you are driving through an unfamiliar town and want to stop for lunch. You see a McDonald's and a local restaurant next to it. Which do you choose? The local restaurant may offer better food at lower prices, but you have no way of knowing that. By contrast, McDonald's offers a consistent product across many cities. Its brand name is useful to you as a way of judging the quality of what you are about to buy.

The McDonald's brand name also ensures that the company has an incentive to maintain quality. For example, if some customers were to become ill from spoiled food sold at a McDonald's, the news would be disastrous for the company. McDonald's would lose much of the valuable reputation that it has built up with years of expensive advertising. As a result, it would lose sales and profit not only in the outlet that sold the bad food but also in many other McDonald's outlets throughout the country. By contrast, if some customers were to become ill from bad food at a local restaurant, that restaurant might have to close down, but the lost profits would be much smaller. Hence, McDonald's has a greater incentive to ensure that its food is safe.

The debate over brand names thus centers on the question of whether consumers are rational in preferring brand names to generic substitutes. Critics argue that brand names are the result of an irrational consumer response to advertising. Defenders argue that consumers have good reason to pay more for brand-name products because they can be more confident in the quality of these products.

QuickQuiz *How might advertising make markets less competitive? How might it make markets more competitive? • Give the arguments for and against brand names.*

16-4 Conclusion

Monopolistic competition is true to its name: It is a hybrid of monopoly and competition. Like a monopoly, each monopolistic competitor faces a downward-sloping demand curve and, as a result, charges a price above marginal cost. As in a perfectly competitive market, there are many firms, and entry and exit drive the profit of each monopolistic competitor toward zero in the long run. Table 1 summarizes these lessons.

TABLE 1

Monopolistic Competition: Between Perfect Competition and Monopoly

	Market Structure		
	Perfect Competition	**Monopolistic Competition**	**Monopoly**
Features that all three market structures share			
Goal of firms	Maximize profits	Maximize profits	Maximize profits
Rule for maximizing profit	$MR = MC$	$MR = MC$	$MR = MC$
Can earn economic profits in the short run?	Yes	Yes	Yes
Features that monopolistic competition shares with monopoly			
Price taker?	Yes	No	No
Price	$P = MC$	$P > MC$	$P > MC$
Produces welfare-maximizing level of output?	Yes	No	No
Features that monopolistic competition shares with perfect competition			
Number of firms	Many	Many	One
Entry in the long run?	Yes	Yes	No
Can earn economic profits in the long run?	No	No	Yes

Because monopolistically competitive firms produce differentiated products, each firm advertises to attract customers to its own brand. To some extent, advertising manipulates consumers' tastes, promotes irrational brand loyalty, and impedes competition. To a larger extent, advertising provides information, establishes brand names of reliable quality, and fosters competition.

The theory of monopolistic competition seems to describe many markets in the economy. It is somewhat disappointing, therefore, that the theory does not yield simple and compelling advice for public policy. From the standpoint of the economic theorist, the allocation of resources in monopolistically competitive markets is not perfect. Yet from the standpoint of a practical policymaker, there may be little that can be done to improve it.

CHAPTER QuickQuiz

1. Which of the following conditions does NOT describe a firm in a monopolistically competitive market?
   a. It sells a product different from its competitors.
   b. It takes its price as given by market conditions.
   c. It maximizes profit both in the short run and in the long run.
   d. It has the freedom to enter or exit in the long run.
2. Which of the following markets best fits the definition of monopolistic competition?
   a. wheat
   b. tap water
   c. crude oil
   d. haircuts
3. A monopolistically competitive firm will increase its production if
   a. marginal revenue is greater than marginal cost.
   b. marginal revenue is greater than average total cost.
   c. price is greater than marginal cost.
   d. price is greater than average total cost.
4. New firms will enter a monopolistically competitive market if
   a. marginal revenue is greater than marginal cost.
   b. marginal revenue is greater than average total cost.
   c. price is greater than marginal cost.
   d. price is greater than average total cost.
5. What is true of a monopolistically competitive market in long-run equilibrium?
   a. Price is greater than marginal cost.
   b. Price is equal to marginal revenue.
   c. Firms make positive economic profits.
   d. Firms produce at the minimum of average total cost.
6. If advertising makes consumers more loyal to particular brands, it could ________ the elasticity of demand and ________ the markup of price over marginal cost.
   a. increase, increase
   b. increase, decrease
   c. decrease, increase
   d. decrease, decrease

SUMMARY

- A monopolistically competitive market is characterized by three attributes: many firms, differentiated products, and free entry and exit.
- The long-run equilibrium in a monopolistically competitive market differs from that in a perfectly competitive market in two related ways. First, each firm in a monopolistically competitive market has excess capacity. That is, it chooses a quantity that puts it on the downward-sloping portion of the average-total-cost curve. Second, each firm charges a price above marginal cost.
- Monopolistic competition does not have all the desirable properties of perfect competition. There is the standard deadweight loss of monopoly caused by the markup of price over marginal cost. In addition, the number of firms (and thus the variety of products) can be too large or too small. In practice, the ability of policymakers to correct these inefficiencies is limited.
- The product differentiation inherent in monopolistic competition leads to the use of advertising and brand names. Critics of advertising and brand names argue that firms use them to manipulate consumers' tastes and to reduce competition. Defenders of advertising and brand names argue that firms use them to inform consumers and to compete more vigorously on price and product quality.

KEY CONCEPTS

oligopoly, p. 320

monopolistic competition, p. 321

QUESTIONS FOR REVIEW

1. Describe the three attributes of monopolistic competition. How is monopolistic competition like monopoly? How is it like perfect competition?
2. Draw a diagram depicting a firm that is making a profit in a monopolistically competitive market. Now show what happens to this firm as new firms enter the industry.
3. Draw a diagram of the long-run equilibrium in a monopolistically competitive market. How is price related to average total cost? How is price related to marginal cost?
4. Does a monopolistic competitor produce too much or too little output compared to the most efficient level? What practical considerations make it difficult for policymakers to solve this problem?
5. How might advertising reduce economic well-being? How might advertising increase economic well-being?
6. How might advertising with no apparent informational content in fact convey information to consumers?
7. Explain two benefits that might arise from the existence of brand names.

PROBLEMS AND APPLICATIONS

1. Among monopoly, oligopoly, monopolistic competition, and perfect competition, how would you classify the markets for each of the following drinks?
   a. tap water
   b. bottled water
   c. cola
   d. beer
2. Classify the following markets as perfectly competitive, monopolistic, or monopolistically competitive, and explain your answers.
   a. wooden no. 2 pencils
   b. copper
   c. local electricity service
   d. peanut butter
   e. lipstick
3. For each of the following characteristics, say whether it describes a perfectly competitive firm, a monopolistically competitive firm, both, or neither.
   a. sells a product differentiated from that of its competitors
   b. has marginal revenue less than price
   c. earns economic profit in the long run
   d. produces at the minimum of average total cost in the long run
   e. equates marginal revenue and marginal cost
   f. charges a price above marginal cost
4. For each of the following characteristics, say whether it describes a monopoly firm, a monopolistically competitive firm, both, or neither.
   a. faces a downward-sloping demand curve
   b. has marginal revenue less than price
   c. faces the entry of new firms selling similar products
   d. earns economic profit in the long run
   e. equates marginal revenue and marginal cost
   f. produces the socially efficient quantity of output
5. You are hired as a consultant to a monopolistically competitive firm. The firm reports the following information about its price, marginal cost, and average total cost. Can the firm possibly be maximizing profit? If not, what should it do to increase profit? If the firm is maximizing profit, is the market in a long-run equilibrium? If not, what will happen to restore long-run equilibrium?
   a. $P < MC$, $P > ATC$
   b. $P > MC$, $P < ATC$
   c. $P = MC$, $P > ATC$
   d. $P > MC$, $P = ATC$

6. Sparkle is one of the many firms in the market for toothpaste, which is in long-run equilibrium.
   a. Draw a diagram showing Sparkle's demand curve, marginal-revenue curve, average-total-cost curve, and marginal-cost curve. Label Sparkle's profit-maximizing output and price.
   b. What is Sparkle's profit? Explain.
   c. On your diagram, show the consumer surplus derived from the purchase of Sparkle toothpaste. Also show the deadweight loss relative to the efficient level of output.
   d. If the government forced Sparkle to produce the efficient level of output, what would happen to the firm? What would happen to Sparkle's customers?

7. Consider a monopolistically competitive market with N firms. Each firm's business opportunities are described by the following equations:

$$\text{Demand: } Q = 100/N - P$$
$$\text{Marginal Revenue: } MR = 100/N - 2Q$$
$$\text{Total Cost: } TC = 50 + Q^2$$
$$\text{Marginal Cost: } MC = 2Q$$

   a. How does N, the number of firms in the market, affect each firm's demand curve? Why?
   b. How many units does each firm produce? (The answers to this and the next two questions depend on N.)
   c. What price does each firm charge?
   d. How much profit does each firm make?
   e. In the long run, how many firms will exist in this market?

8. The market for peanut butter in Nutville is monopolistically competitive and in long-run equilibrium. One day, consumer advocate Skippy Jif discovers that all brands of peanut butter in Nutville are identical. Thereafter, the market becomes perfectly competitive and again reaches its long-run equilibrium. Using an appropriate diagram, explain whether each of the following variables increases, decreases, or stays the same for a typical firm in the market.
   a. price
   b. quantity
   c. average total cost
   d. marginal cost
   e. profit

9. For each of the following pairs of firms, explain which firm would be more likely to engage in advertising.
   a. a family-owned farm or a family-owned restaurant
   b. a manufacturer of forklifts or a manufacturer of cars
   c. a company that invented a very comfortable razor or a company that invented a less comfortable razor

10. Sleek Sneakers Co. is one of many firms in the market for shoes.
    a. Assume that Sleek is currently earning short-run economic profit. On a correctly labeled diagram, show Sleek's profit-maximizing output and price, as well as the area representing profit.
    b. What happens to Sleek's price, output, and profit in the long run? Explain this change in words, and show it on a new diagram.
    c. Suppose that over time consumers become more focused on stylistic differences among shoe brands. How would this change in attitudes affect each firm's price elasticity of demand? In the long run, how will this change in demand affect Sleek's price, output, and profit?
    d. At the profit-maximizing price you identified in part (c), is Sleek's demand curve elastic or inelastic? Explain.

To find additional study resources, visit cengagebrain.com, and search for "Mankiw."

CHAPTER 17

Oligopoly

If you play tennis, you have probably used balls from one of four producers: Penn, Wilson, Prince, or Dunlop Slazenger (two brands from the same company). These four firms make almost all the tennis balls sold in the United States. Together they determine the quantity of tennis balls produced and, given the market demand curve, the price at which tennis balls are sold.

The market for tennis balls is an example of an **oligopoly**. The essence of an oligopolistic market is that there are only a few sellers. As a result, the actions of any one seller in the market can have a large impact on the profits of all the other sellers. Oligopolistic firms are interdependent in a way that competitive firms are not. Our goal in this chapter is to see how this interdependence shapes the firms' behavior and what problems it raises for public policy.

oligopoly
a market structure in which only a few sellers offer similar or identical products

game theory
the study of how people behave in strategic situations

The analysis of oligopoly offers an opportunity to introduce **game theory**, the study of how people behave in strategic situations. By "strategic" we mean a situation in which a person, when choosing among alternative courses of action, must consider how others might respond to the action she takes. Strategic thinking is crucial not only in checkers, chess, and tic-tac-toe but also in many business decisions. Because oligopolistic markets have only a small number of firms, each firm must act strategically. Each firm knows that its profit depends on both how much it produces and how much the other firms produce. In making its production decision, each firm in an oligopoly should consider how its decision might affect the production decisions of the other firms in the market.

Game theory is not necessary for understanding competitive or monopoly markets. In a market that is either perfectly competitive or monopolistically competitive, each firm is so small compared to the market that strategic interactions with other firms are not important. In a monopolized market, strategic interactions are absent because the market has only one firm. But, as we will see, game theory is useful for understanding oligopolies and many other situations in which a small number of players interact with one another. Game theory helps explain the strategies that people choose, whether they are playing tennis or selling tennis balls.

17-1 Markets with Only a Few Sellers

Because an oligopolistic market has only a small group of sellers, a key feature of oligopoly is the tension between cooperation and self-interest. The oligopolists are best off when they cooperate and act like a monopolist—producing a small quantity of output and charging a price above marginal cost. Yet because each oligopolist cares only about its own profit, there are powerful incentives at work that hinder a group of firms from maintaining the cooperative outcome.

17-1a A Duopoly Example

To understand the behavior of oligopolies, let's consider an oligopoly with only two members, called a *duopoly*. Duopoly is the simplest type of oligopoly. Oligopolies with three or more members face the same problems as duopolies, so we do not lose much by starting with the simpler case.

Imagine a town in which only two residents, Jack and Jill, own wells that produce water safe for drinking. Each Saturday, Jack and Jill decide how many gallons of water to pump, bring the water to town, and sell it for whatever price the market will bear. To keep things simple, suppose that Jack and Jill can pump as much water as they want without cost. That is, the marginal cost of water equals zero.

Table 1 shows the town's demand schedule for water. The first column shows the total quantity demanded, and the second column shows the price. If the two well owners sell a total of 10 gallons of water, water goes for $110 a gallon. If they sell a total of 20 gallons, the price falls to $100 a gallon. And so on. If you graphed these two columns of numbers, you would get a standard downward-sloping demand curve.

The last column in Table 1 shows total revenue from the sale of water. It equals the quantity sold times the price. Because there is no cost to pumping water, the total revenue of the two producers equals their total profit.

Let's now consider how the organization of the town's water industry affects the price of water and the quantity sold.

TABLE 1

The Demand Schedule for Water

Quantity	Price	Total Revenue (and total profit)
0 gallons	$120	$ 0
10	110	1,100
20	100	2,000
30	90	2,700
40	80	3,200
50	70	3,500
60	60	3,600
70	50	3,500
80	40	3,200
90	30	2,700
100	20	2,000
110	10	1,100
120	0	0

17-1b Competition, Monopolies, and Cartels

Before considering the price and quantity of water that results from the duopoly of Jack and Jill, let's discuss briefly what the outcome would be if the water market were either perfectly competitive or monopolistic. These two polar cases are natural benchmarks.

If the market for water were perfectly competitive, the production decisions of each firm would drive price to equal marginal cost. Because we have assumed that the marginal cost of pumping additional water is zero, the equilibrium price of water under perfect competition would be zero as well. The equilibrium quantity would be 120 gallons. The price of water would reflect the cost of producing it, and the efficient quantity of water would be produced and consumed.

Now consider how a monopoly would behave. Table 1 shows that total profit is maximized at a quantity of 60 gallons and a price of $60 a gallon. A profit-maximizing monopolist, therefore, would produce this quantity and charge this price. As is standard for monopolies, price would exceed marginal cost. The result would be inefficient, because the quantity of water produced and consumed would fall short of the socially efficient level of 120 gallons.

What outcome should we expect from our duopolists? One possibility is that Jack and Jill get together and agree on the quantity of water to produce and the price to charge for it. Such an agreement among firms over production and price is called **collusion**, and the group of firms acting in unison is called a **cartel**. Once a cartel is formed, the market is in effect served by a monopoly and we can apply our analysis from Chapter 15. That is, if Jack and Jill collude, they will agree on the monopoly outcome because that outcome maximizes their total profit. Our two producers produce a total of 60 gallons, which sell at a price of $60 a gallon. Once again, price exceeds marginal cost, and the outcome is socially inefficient.

collusion
an agreement among firms in a market about quantities to produce or prices to charge

cartel
a group of firms acting in unison

A cartel must agree not only on the total level of production but also on the amount produced by each member. In our case, Jack and Jill must agree on how to split the monopoly production of 60 gallons. Each member of the cartel will want a larger share of the market because a larger market share means larger profit. If Jack and Jill agree to split the market equally, each produces 30 gallons, the price is $60 a gallon, and each earns a profit of $1,800.

17-1c The Equilibrium for an Oligopoly

Oligopolists would like to form cartels and earn monopoly profits, but that is often impossible. Squabbling among cartel members over how to divide the profit in the market can make agreement among members difficult. In addition, antitrust laws prohibit explicit agreements among oligopolists as a matter of public policy. Even talking about pricing and production restrictions with competitors can be a criminal offense. Let's therefore consider what happens if Jack and Jill decide separately how much water to produce.

At first, one might expect Jack and Jill to reach the monopoly outcome on their own, because this outcome maximizes their joint profit. In the absence of a binding agreement, however, the monopoly outcome is unlikely. To see why, imagine that Jack expects Jill to produce only 30 gallons (half of the monopoly quantity). Jack would reason as follows:

"I could produce 30 gallons as well. In this case, a total of 60 gallons of water would be sold at a price of $60 a gallon. My profit would be $1,800 (30 gallons × $60 a gallon). Alternatively, I could produce 40 gallons. In this case, a total of 70 gallons of water would be sold at a price of $50 a gallon. My profit would be $2,000 (40 gallons × $50 a gallon). Even though total profit in the market would fall, my profit would be higher, because I would have a larger share of the market."

Of course, Jill might reason the same way. If so, Jack and Jill would each bring 40 gallons to town. Total sales would be 80 gallons, and the price would fall to $40. Thus, if the duopolists individually pursue their own self-interest when deciding how much to produce, they produce a total quantity greater than the monopoly quantity, charge a price lower than the monopoly price, and earn total profit less than the monopoly profit.

Although the logic of self-interest increases the duopoly's output above the monopoly level, it does not push the duopolists all the way to the competitive allocation. Consider what happens when each duopolist produces 40 gallons. The price is $40, and each duopolist makes a profit of $1,600. In this case, Jack's self-interested logic leads to a different conclusion:

"Right now, my profit is $1,600. Suppose I increase my production to 50 gallons. In this case, a total of 90 gallons of water would be sold, and the price would be $30 a gallon. Then my profit would be only $1,500. Rather than increasing production and driving down the price, I am better off keeping my production at 40 gallons."

The outcome in which Jack and Jill each produce 40 gallons looks like some sort of equilibrium. In fact, this outcome is called a Nash equilibrium. (It is named after Nobel Prize-winning mathematician and economic theorist John Nash, whose life was portrayed in the book and movie *A Beautiful Mind*.) A **Nash equilibrium** is a situation in which economic actors interacting with one another each choose their best strategy given the strategies that the others have chosen. In this case, given that Jill is producing 40 gallons, the best strategy for Jack is also to produce 40 gallons. Similarly, given that Jack is producing 40 gallons, the best strategy for Jill is also to produce 40 gallons. Once they reach this Nash equilibrium, neither Jack nor Jill has an incentive to make a different decision.

Nash equilibrium
a situation in which economic actors interacting with one another each choose their best strategy given the strategies that all the other actors have chosen

This example illustrates the tension between cooperation and self-interest. Oligopolists would be better off cooperating and reaching the monopoly outcome. Yet because they each pursue their own self-interest, they do not end up reaching the monopoly outcome and, thus, fail to maximize their joint profit. Each oligopolist is tempted to raise production and capture a larger share of the market. As each of them tries to do this, total production rises, and the price falls.

At the same time, self-interest does not drive the market all the way to the competitive outcome. Like monopolists, oligopolists are aware that increasing the amount they produce reduces the price of their product, which in turn affects profits. Therefore, they stop short of following the competitive firm's rule of producing up to the point where price equals marginal cost.

In summary, *when firms in an oligopoly individually choose production to maximize profit, they produce a quantity of output greater than the level produced by monopoly and less than the level produced by perfect competition. The oligopoly price is less than the monopoly price but greater than the competitive price (which equals marginal cost).*

ASK THE EXPERTS

Nash Equilibrium

"Behavior in many complex and seemingly intractable strategic settings can be understood more clearly by working out what each party in the game will choose to do if they realize that the other parties will be solving the same problem. This insight has helped us understand behavior as diverse as military conflicts, price setting by competing firms and penalty kicking in soccer."

What do economists say?

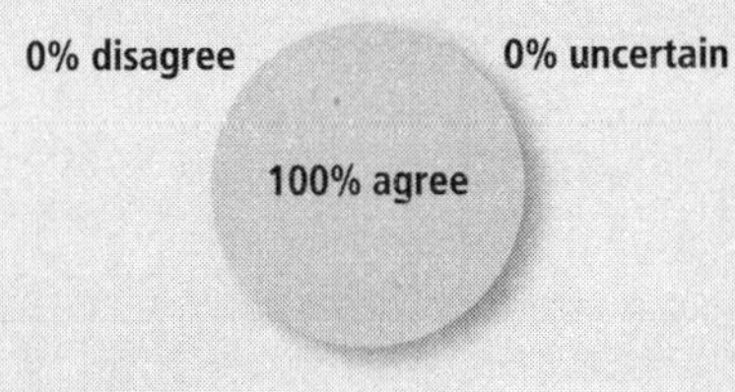

Source: IGM Economic Experts Panel, June 2, 2015.

17-1d How the Size of an Oligopoly Affects the Market Outcome

We can use the insights from this analysis of duopoly to discuss how the size of an oligopoly is likely to affect the outcome in a market. Suppose, for instance, that John and Joan suddenly discover water sources on their property and join Jack and Jill in the water oligopoly. The demand schedule in Table 1 remains the same, but now more producers are available to satisfy this demand. How would an increase in the number of sellers from two to four affect the price and quantity of water in the town?

If the sellers of water could form a cartel, they would once again try to maximize total profit by producing the monopoly quantity and charging the monopoly price. Just as when there were only two sellers, the members of the cartel would need to agree on production levels for each member and find some way to enforce the agreement. As the cartel grows larger, however, this outcome is less likely. Reaching and enforcing an agreement becomes more difficult as the size of the group increases.

If the oligopolists do not form a cartel—perhaps because the antitrust laws prohibit it—they must each decide on their own how much water to produce. To see how the increase in the number of sellers affects the outcome, consider the decision facing each seller. At any time, each well owner has the option to raise production by one gallon. In making this decision, the well owner weighs the following two effects:

- *The output effect:* Because price is above marginal cost, selling one more gallon of water at the going price will raise profit.
- *The price effect:* Raising production will increase the total amount sold, which will lower the price of water and lower the profit on all the other gallons sold.

If the output effect is larger than the price effect, the well owner will increase production. If the price effect is larger than the output effect, the owner will not raise production. (In fact, in this case, it is profitable to reduce production.) Each oligopolist continues to increase production until these two marginal effects exactly balance, taking the other firms' production as given.

Now consider how the number of firms in the industry affects the marginal analysis of each oligopolist. The larger the number of sellers, the less each seller is concerned about her own impact on the market price. That is, as the oligopoly grows in size, the magnitude of the price effect falls. When the oligopoly grows very large, the price effect disappears altogether. In this extreme case, the production decision of an individual firm no longer affects the market price. Each firm takes the market price as given when deciding how much to produce and, therefore increases production as long as price is above marginal cost.

We can now see that a large oligopoly is essentially a group of competitive firms. A competitive firm considers only the output effect when deciding how much to produce: Because a competitive firm is a price taker, the price effect is absent. Thus, *as the number of sellers in an oligopoly grows larger, an oligopolistic market looks more and more like a competitive market. The price approaches marginal cost, and the quantity produced approaches the socially efficient level.*

This analysis of oligopoly offers a new perspective on the effects of international trade. Imagine that Toyota and Honda are the only automakers in Japan, Volkswagen and BMW are the only automakers in Germany, and Ford and General Motors are the only automakers in the United States. If these nations prohibited international trade in autos, each would have an auto oligopoly with only two members, and the market outcome would likely depart substantially from the competitive ideal. With international trade, however, the car market is a world market, and the oligopoly in this example has six members. Allowing free trade increases the number of producers from which each consumer can choose, and this increased competition keeps prices closer to marginal cost. Thus, the theory of oligopoly provides another reason, in addition to the theory of comparative advantage discussed in Chapter 3, why countries can benefit from free trade.

QuickQuiz *If the members of an oligopoly could agree on a total quantity to produce, what quantity would they choose? • If the oligopolists do not act together but instead make production decisions individually, do they produce a total quantity more or less than in your answer to the previous question? Why?*

17-2 The Economics of Cooperation

As we have seen, oligopolies would like to reach the monopoly outcome. Doing so, however, requires cooperation, which at times is difficult to establish and maintain. In this section we look more closely at the problems that arise when cooperation among actors is desirable but difficult. To analyze the economics of cooperation, we need to learn a little about game theory.

prisoners' dilemma
a particular "game" between two captured prisoners that illustrates why cooperation is difficult to maintain even when it is mutually beneficial

In particular, we focus on a "game" called the **prisoners' dilemma**, which provides insight into why cooperation is difficult. Many times in life, people fail to cooperate with one another even when cooperation would make them all better off. An oligopoly is just one example. The story of the prisoners' dilemma contains a general lesson that applies to any group trying to maintain cooperation among its members.

17-2a The Prisoners' Dilemma

The prisoners' dilemma is a story about two criminals who have been captured by the police. Let's call them Bonnie and Clyde. The police have enough evidence to convict Bonnie and Clyde of the minor crime of carrying an unregistered gun, so that each would spend a year in jail. The police also suspect that the two criminals have committed a bank robbery together, but they lack hard evidence to convict them of this major crime. The police question Bonnie and Clyde in separate rooms and offer each of them the following deal:

"Right now, we can lock you up for 1 year. If you confess to the bank robbery and implicate your partner, however, we'll give you immunity and you can go free. Your partner will get 20 years in jail. But if you both confess to the crime, we won't need your testimony and we can avoid the cost of a trial, so you will each get an intermediate sentence of 8 years."

If Bonnie and Clyde, heartless bank robbers that they are, care only about their own individual sentences, what would you expect them to do? Figure 1 shows their choices. Each prisoner has two strategies: confess or remain silent. The sentence each prisoner gets depends on the strategy he or she chooses and the strategy chosen by his or her partner in crime.

Consider first Bonnie's decision. She reasons as follows: "I don't know what Clyde is going to do. If he remains silent, my best strategy is to confess, because then I'll go free rather than spending a year in jail. If he confesses, my best strategy is still to confess, because then I'll spend 8 years in jail rather than 20. So, regardless of what Clyde does, I am better off confessing."

In the language of game theory, a strategy is called a **dominant strategy** if it is the best strategy for a player to follow regardless of the strategies pursued by other players. In this case, confessing is a dominant strategy for Bonnie. She spends less time in jail if she confesses, regardless of whether Clyde confesses or remains silent.

dominant strategy
a strategy that is best for a player in a game regardless of the strategies chosen by the other players

Now consider Clyde's decision. He faces the same choices as Bonnie, and he reasons in much the same way. Regardless of what Bonnie does, Clyde can reduce his jail time by confessing. In other words, confessing is also a dominant strategy for Clyde.

Clyde's Decision \ Bonnie's Decision	Confess	Remain Silent
Confess	Bonnie gets 8 years Clyde gets 8 years	Bonnie gets 20 years Clyde goes free
Remain Silent	Bonnie goes free Clyde gets 20 years	Bonnie gets 1 year Clyde gets 1 year

FIGURE 1

The Prisoners' Dilemma
In this game between two criminals suspected of committing a crime, the sentence that each receives depends both on his or her decision whether to confess or remain silent and on the decision made by the other.

In the end, both Bonnie and Clyde confess, and both spend 8 years in jail. This outcome is a Nash equilibrium: Each criminal is choosing the best strategy available, given the strategy the other is following. Yet, from their standpoint, the outcome is terrible. If they had *both* remained silent, both of them would have been better off, spending only 1 year in jail on the gun charge. Because each pursues his or her own interests, the two prisoners together reach an outcome that is worse for each of them.

You might have thought that Bonnie and Clyde would have foreseen this situation and planned ahead. But even with advanced planning, they would still run into problems. Imagine that, before the police captured Bonnie and Clyde, the two criminals had made a pact not to confess. Clearly, this agreement would make them both better off *if* they both lived up to it, because they would each spend only 1 year in jail. But would the two criminals in fact remain silent, simply because they had agreed to? Once they are being questioned separately, the logic of self-interest takes over and leads them to confess. Cooperation between the two prisoners is difficult to maintain, because cooperation is individually irrational.

17-2b Oligopolies as a Prisoners' Dilemma

What does the prisoners' dilemma have to do with markets and imperfect competition? It turns out that the game oligopolists play in trying to reach the monopoly outcome is similar to the game that the two prisoners play in the prisoners' dilemma.

Consider again the choices facing Jack and Jill. After prolonged negotiation, the two suppliers of water agree to keep production at 30 gallons so that the price will be kept high and together they will earn the maximum profit. After they agree on production levels, however, each of them must decide whether to cooperate and live up to this agreement or to ignore it and produce at a higher level. Figure 2 shows how the profits of the two producers depend on the strategies they choose.

Suppose you are Jack. You might reason as follows: "I could keep production at 30 gallons as we agreed, or I could raise my production and sell 40 gallons. If Jill lives up to the agreement and keeps her production at 30 gallons, then I earn

FIGURE 2

Jack and Jill's Oligopoly Game

In this game between Jack and Jill, the profit that each earns from selling water depends on both the quantity he or she chooses to sell and the quantity the other chooses to sell.

Jill's Decision	Jack's Decision: High Production: 40 Gallons	Jack's Decision: Low Production: 30 Gallons
High Production: 40 Gallons	Jack gets $1,600 profit; Jill gets $1,600 profit	Jack gets $1,500 profit; Jill gets $2,000 profit
Low Production: 30 Gallons	Jack gets $2,000 profit; Jill gets $1,500 profit	Jack gets $1,800 profit; Jill gets $1,800 profit

a profit of $2,000 by selling 40 gallons and $1,800 by selling 30 gallons. In this case, I am better off with the higher-level production. If Jill fails to live up to the agreement and produces 40 gallons, then I earn $1,600 by selling 40 gallons and $1,500 by selling 30 gallons. Once again, I am better off with higher production. So, regardless of what Jill chooses to do, I am better off reneging on our agreement and producing at the higher level."

Producing 40 gallons is a dominant strategy for Jack. Of course, Jill reasons in exactly the same way, and so both produce at the higher level of 40 gallons. The result is the inferior outcome (from Jack and Jill's standpoint) with low profits for each of the two producers.

This example illustrates why oligopolies have trouble maintaining monopoly profits. The monopoly outcome is jointly rational, but each oligopolist has an incentive to cheat. Just as self-interest drives the prisoners in the prisoners' dilemma to confess, self-interest makes it difficult for the oligopolists to maintain the cooperative outcome with low production, high prices, and monopoly profits.

CASE STUDY

OPEC AND THE WORLD OIL MARKET

Our story about the town's market for water is fictional, but if we change water to crude oil, and Jack and Jill to Iran and Iraq, the story is close to being true. Much of the world's oil is produced by a few countries, mostly in the Middle East. These countries together make up an oligopoly. Their decisions about how much oil to pump are much the same as Jack and Jill's decisions about how much water to pump.

The countries that produce most of the world's oil have formed a cartel, called the Organization of the Petroleum Exporting Countries (OPEC). As originally formed in 1960, OPEC included Iran, Iraq, Kuwait, Saudi Arabia, and Venezuela. By 1973, eight other nations had joined: Qatar, Indonesia, Libya, the United Arab Emirates, Algeria, Nigeria, Ecuador, and Gabon. These countries control about three-fourths of the world's oil reserves. Like any cartel, OPEC tries to raise the price of its product through a coordinated reduction in quantity produced. OPEC tries to set production levels for each of the member countries.

The problem that OPEC faces is much the same as the problem that Jack and Jill face in our story. The OPEC countries would like to maintain a high price for oil. But each member of the cartel is tempted to increase its production to get a larger share of the total profit. OPEC members frequently agree to reduce production but then cheat on their agreements.

OPEC was most successful at maintaining cooperation and high prices in the period from 1973 to 1985. The price of crude oil rose from $3 a barrel in 1972 to $11 in 1974 and then to $35 in 1981. But in the mid-1980s, member countries began arguing about production levels, and OPEC became ineffective at maintaining cooperation. By 1986 the price of crude oil had fallen back to $13 a barrel.

In recent years, the members of OPEC have continued to meet regularly, but they have been less successful at reaching and enforcing agreements. As a result, fluctuations in oil prices have been driven more by the natural forces of supply and demand than by the cartel's artificial restrictions on production. While this lack of cooperation among OPEC nations has reduced the profits of the oil-producing nations below what they might have been, it has benefited consumers around the world. ●

17-2c Other Examples of the Prisoners' Dilemma

We have seen how the prisoners' dilemma can be used to understand the problem facing oligopolies. The same logic applies to many other situations as well. Here we consider two examples in which self-interest prevents cooperation and leads to an inferior outcome for the parties involved.

Arms Races In the decades after World War II, the world's two superpowers—the United States and the Soviet Union—were engaged in a prolonged competition over military power. This topic motivated some of the early work on game theory. The game theorists pointed out that an arms race is much like the prisoners' dilemma.

To see why, consider the decisions of the United States and the Soviet Union about whether to build new weapons or to disarm. Each country prefers to have more arms than the other because a larger arsenal would give it more influence in world affairs. But each country also prefers to live in a world safe from the other country's weapons.

Figure 3 shows the deadly game. If the Soviet Union chooses to arm, the United States is better off doing the same to prevent the loss of power. If the Soviet Union chooses to disarm, the United States is better off arming because doing so would make it more powerful. For each country, arming is a dominant strategy. Thus, each country chooses to continue the arms race, resulting in the inferior outcome with both countries at risk.

Throughout the Cold War era from about 1945 to 1991, the United States and the Soviet Union attempted to solve this problem through negotiation and agreements over arms control. The problems that the two countries faced were similar to those that oligopolists encounter in trying to maintain a cartel. Just as oligopolists argue over production levels, the United States and the Soviet Union argued over the amount of arms that each country would be allowed. And just as cartels have trouble enforcing production levels, the United States and the Soviet Union each feared that the other country would cheat on any agreement. In both arms races and oligopolies, the relentless logic of self-interest drives the participants toward the noncooperative outcome, which is worse for both parties.

FIGURE 3

An Arms-Race Game

In this game between two countries, the safety and power of each country depend on both its decision whether to arm and the decision made by the other country.

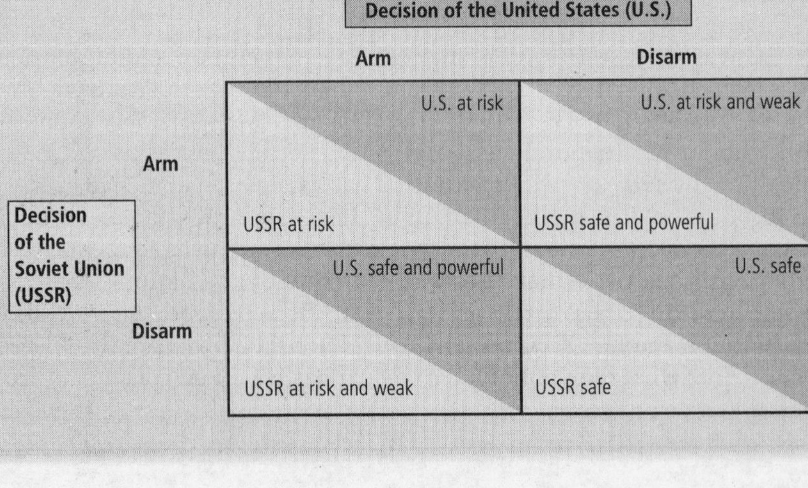

Common Resources In Chapter 11 we saw that people tend to overuse common resources. One can view this problem as an example of the prisoners' dilemma.

Imagine that two oil companies—Exxon and Texaco—own adjacent oil fields. Under the fields is a common pool of oil worth $12 million. Drilling a well to recover the oil costs $1 million. If each company drills one well, each will get half of the oil and earn a $5 million profit ($6 million in revenue minus $1 million in costs).

Because the pool of oil is a common resource, the companies will not use it efficiently. Suppose that either company could drill a second well. If one company has two of the three wells, that company gets two-thirds of the oil, which yields a profit of $6 million. The other company gets one-third of the oil, for a profit of $3 million. Yet if each company drills a second well, the two companies again split the oil. In this case, each bears the cost of a second well, so profit is only $4 million for each company.

Figure 4 shows the game. Drilling two wells is a dominant strategy for each company. Once again, the self-interest of the two players leads them to an inferior outcome.

17-2d The Prisoners' Dilemma and the Welfare of Society

The prisoners' dilemma describes many of life's situations, and it shows that cooperation can be difficult to maintain, even when cooperation would make both players in the game better off. Clearly, this lack of cooperation is a problem for those involved in these situations. But is lack of cooperation a problem from the standpoint of society as a whole? The answer depends on the circumstances.

In some cases, the noncooperative equilibrium is bad for society as well as the players. In the arms-race game in Figure 3, both the United States and the Soviet Union end up at risk. In the common-resources game in Figure 4, the extra wells dug by Texaco and Exxon are pure waste. In both cases, society would be better off if the two players could reach the cooperative outcome.

By contrast, in the case of oligopolists trying to maintain monopoly profits, lack of cooperation is desirable from the standpoint of society as a whole. The monopoly outcome is good for the oligopolists, but it is bad for the consumers

Texaco's Decision \ Exxon's Decision	Drill Two Wells	Drill One Well
Drill Two Wells	Exxon gets $4 million profit; Texaco gets $4 million profit	Exxon gets $3 million profit; Texaco gets $6 million profit
Drill One Well	Exxon gets $6 million profit; Texaco gets $3 million profit	Exxon gets $5 million profit; Texaco gets $5 million profit

FIGURE 4

A Common-Resources Game

In this game between firms pumping oil from a common pool, the profit that each earns depends on both the number of wells it drills and the number of wells drilled by the other firm.

of the product. As we first saw in Chapter 7, the competitive outcome is best for society because it maximizes total surplus. When oligopolists fail to cooperate, the quantity they produce is closer to this optimal level. Put differently, the invisible hand guides markets to allocate resources efficiently only when markets are competitive, and markets are competitive only when firms in the market fail to cooperate with one another.

Similarly, consider the case of the police questioning two suspects. Lack of cooperation between the suspects is desirable, for it allows the police to convict more criminals. The prisoners' dilemma is a dilemma for the prisoners, but it can be a boon to everyone else.

17-2e Why People Sometimes Cooperate

The prisoners' dilemma shows that cooperation is difficult. But is it impossible? Not all prisoners, when questioned by the police, decide to turn in their partners in crime. Cartels sometimes manage to maintain collusive arrangements, despite the incentive for individual members to defect. Very often, players can solve the prisoners' dilemma because they play the game not once but many times.

To see why cooperation is easier to enforce in repeated games, let's return to our duopolists, Jack and Jill, whose choices were given in Figure 2. Jack and Jill would like to agree to maintain the monopoly outcome in which each produces 30 gallons. Yet, if Jack and Jill are to play this game only once, neither has any incentive to live up to this agreement. Self-interest drives each of them to renege and choose the dominant strategy of 40 gallons.

Now suppose that Jack and Jill know that they will play the same game every week. When they make their initial agreement to keep production low, they can also specify what happens if one party reneges. They might agree, for instance, that once one of them reneges and produces 40 gallons, both of them will produce 40 gallons forever after. This penalty is easy to enforce, for if one party is producing at a high level, the other has every reason to do the same.

The threat of this penalty may be all that is needed to maintain cooperation. Each person knows that defecting would raise his or her profit from $1,800 to $2,000. But this benefit would last for only one week. Thereafter, profit would fall to $1,600 and stay there. As long as the players care enough about future profits, they will choose to forgo the one-time gain from defection. Thus, in a game of repeated prisoners' dilemma, the two players may well be able to reach the cooperative outcome.

CASE STUDY

THE PRISONERS' DILEMMA TOURNAMENT

Imagine that you are playing a game of prisoners' dilemma with a person being "questioned" in a separate room. Moreover, imagine that you are going to play not once but many times. Your score at the end of the game is the total number of years in jail. You would like to make this score as small as possible. What strategy would you play? Would you begin by confessing or remaining silent? How would the other player's actions affect your subsequent decisions about confessing?

Repeated prisoners' dilemma is a complicated game. To encourage cooperation, players must penalize each other for not cooperating. Yet the strategy described earlier for Jack and Jill's water cartel—defect forever as soon as the other player defects—is not very forgiving. In a game repeated many times, a strategy that allows players to return to the cooperative outcome after a period of noncooperation may be preferable.

To see what strategies work best, political scientist Robert Axelrod held a tournament. People entered by submitting computer programs designed to play repeated prisoners' dilemma. Each program then played the game against all the other programs. The "winner" was the program that received the fewest total years in jail.

The winning program turned out to be a simple strategy called *tit-for-tat*. According to tit-for-tat, a player should start by cooperating and then do whatever the other player did last time. Thus, a tit-for-tat player cooperates until the other player defects; then she defects until the other player cooperates again. In other words, this strategy starts out friendly, penalizes unfriendly players, and forgives them if warranted. To Axelrod's surprise, this simple strategy did better than all the more complicated strategies that people had sent in.

The tit-for-tat strategy has a long history. It is essentially the biblical strategy of "an eye for an eye, a tooth for a tooth." The prisoners' dilemma tournament suggests that this may be a good rule of thumb for playing some of the games of life. ●

QuickQuiz *Tell the story of the prisoners' dilemma. Write down a table showing the prisoners' choices and explain which outcome is likely. • What does the prisoners' dilemma teach us about oligopolies?*

17-3 Public Policy toward Oligopolies

One of the Ten *Principles of Economics* in Chapter 1 is that governments can sometimes improve market outcomes. This principle applies directly to oligopolistic markets. As we have seen, cooperation among oligopolists is undesirable from the standpoint of society as a whole because it leads to production that is too low and prices that are too high. To move the allocation of resources closer to the social optimum, policymakers should try to induce firms in an oligopoly to compete rather than cooperate. Let's consider how policymakers do this and then examine the controversies that arise in this area of public policy.

17-3a Restraint of Trade and the Antitrust Laws

One way that policy discourages cooperation is through the common law. Normally, freedom of contract is an essential part of a market economy. Businesses and households use contracts to arrange mutually advantageous trades. In doing this, they rely on the court system to enforce contracts. Yet, for many centuries, judges in England and the United States have deemed agreements among competitors to reduce quantities and raise prices to be contrary to the public good. They have therefore refused to enforce such agreements.

The Sherman Antitrust Act of 1890 codified and reinforced this policy:

> Every contract, combination in the form of trust or otherwise, or conspiracy, in restraint of trade or commerce among the several States, or with foreign nations, is declared to be illegal. . . . Every person who shall monopolize, or attempt to monopolize, or combine or conspire with any person or persons to monopolize any part of the trade or commerce among the several States, or with foreign nations, shall be deemed guilty of a misdemeanor, and on conviction thereof, shall be punished by fine not exceeding fifty thousand dollars, or by imprisonment not exceeding one year, or by both said punishments, in the discretion of the court.

The Sherman Act elevated agreements among oligopolists from unenforceable contracts to criminal conspiracies.

The Clayton Act of 1914 further strengthened the antitrust laws. According to this law, if a person could prove that she was damaged by an illegal arrangement to restrain trade, that person could sue and recover three times the damages she sustained. The purpose of this unusual rule of triple damages is to encourage private lawsuits against conspiring oligopolists.

Today, both the U.S. Justice Department and private parties have the authority to bring legal suits to enforce the antitrust laws. As we discussed in Chapter 15, these laws are used to prevent mergers that would lead to excessive market power in any single firm. In addition, these laws are used to prevent oligopolists from acting together in ways that would make their markets less competitive.

CASE STUDY

AN ILLEGAL PHONE CALL

Firms in oligopolies have a strong incentive to collude in order to reduce production, raise prices, and increase profits. The great 18th-century economist Adam Smith was well aware of this potential market failure. In *The Wealth of Nations* he wrote, "People of the same trade seldom meet together, but the conversation ends in a conspiracy against the public, or in some diversion to raise prices."

To see a modern example of Smith's observation, consider the following excerpt of a phone conversation between two airline executives in the early 1980s. The call was reported in the *New York Times* on February 24, 1983. Robert Crandall was president of American Airlines, and Howard Putnam was president of Braniff Airways, a major airline at the time.

CRANDALL: I think it's dumb as hell . . . to sit here and pound the @#$% out of each other and neither one of us making a #$%& dime.

PUTNAM: Do you have a suggestion for me?

CRANDALL: Yes, I have a suggestion for you. Raise your $%*& fares 20 percent. I'll raise mine the next morning.

PUTNAM: Robert, we . . .

CRANDALL: You'll make more money, and I will, too.

PUTNAM: We can't talk about pricing!

CRANDALL: Oh @#$%, Howard. We can talk about any &*#@ thing we want to talk about.

Putnam was right: The Sherman Antitrust Act prohibits competing executives from even talking about fixing prices. When Putnam gave a tape of this conversation to the Justice Department, the Justice Department filed suit against Crandall.

Two years later, Crandall and the Justice Department reached a settlement in which Crandall agreed to various restrictions on his business activities, including his contacts with officials at other airlines. The Justice Department said that the terms of settlement would "protect competition in the airline industry, by preventing American and Crandall from any further attempts to monopolize passenger airline service on any route through discussions with competitors about the prices of airline services." ●

17-3b Controversies over Antitrust Policy

Over time, much controversy has centered on what kinds of behavior the antitrust laws should prohibit. Most commentators agree that price-fixing agreements among competing firms should be illegal. Yet the antitrust laws have been used to condemn some business practices whose effects are not obvious. Here we consider three examples.

Resale Price Maintenance One example of a controversial business practice is *resale price maintenance*. Imagine that Superduper Electronics sells Blu-ray disc players to retail stores for $50. If Superduper requires the retailers to charge customers $75, it is said to engage in resale price maintenance. Any retailer that charged less than $75 would violate its contract with Superduper.

At first, resale price maintenance might seem anticompetitive and, therefore, detrimental to society. Like an agreement among members of a cartel, it prevents the retailers from competing on price. For this reason, the courts have at times viewed resale price maintenance as a violation of the antitrust laws.

Yet some economists defend resale price maintenance on two grounds. First, they deny that it is aimed at reducing competition. If Superduper Electronics wanted to exert its market power, it would do so by raising the wholesale price rather than controlling the resale price. Moreover, Superduper has no incentive to discourage competition among its retailers. Indeed, because a cartel of retailers sells less than a group of competitive retailers, Superduper would be worse off if its retailers were a cartel.

Second, economists believe that resale price maintenance has a legitimate goal. Superduper may want its retailers to provide customers a pleasant showroom and a knowledgeable sales force. Yet, without resale price maintenance, some customers would take advantage of one store's service to learn about the Blu-ray player's special features and then buy the item at a discount retailer that does not provide this service. Good customer service can be viewed as a public good among the retailers that sell Superduper products. As we discussed in Chapter 11, when one person provides a public good, others are able to enjoy it without paying for it. In this case, discount retailers would free ride on the service provided by other retailers, leading to less service than is desirable. Resale price maintenance is one way for Superduper to solve this free-rider problem.

The example of resale price maintenance illustrates an important principle: *Business practices that appear to reduce competition may in fact have legitimate purposes.* This principle makes the application of the antitrust laws all the more difficult. The economists, lawyers, and judges in charge of enforcing these laws must determine what kinds of behavior public policy should prohibit as impeding competition and reducing economic well-being. Often that job is not easy.

Predatory Pricing Firms with market power normally use that power to raise prices above the competitive level. But should policymakers ever be concerned that firms with market power might charge prices that are too low? This question is at the heart of a second debate over antitrust policy.

Imagine that a large airline, call it Coyote Air, has a monopoly on some route. Then Roadrunner Express enters and takes 20 percent of the market, leaving Coyote with 80 percent. In response to this competition, Coyote starts slashing its fares. Some antitrust analysts argue that Coyote's move could be anticompetitive: The price cuts may be intended to drive Roadrunner out of the market so Coyote can recapture its monopoly and raise prices again. Such behavior is called *predatory pricing*.

Although predatory pricing is a common claim in antitrust suits, some economists are skeptical of this argument and believe that predatory pricing is rarely, if ever, a profitable business strategy. Why? For a price war to drive out a rival, prices have to be driven below cost. Yet if Coyote starts selling cheap tickets at a loss, it had better be ready to fly more planes, because low fares will attract more customers. Roadrunner, meanwhile, can respond to Coyote's predatory move by cutting back on flights. As a result, Coyote ends up bearing more than 80 percent of the losses, putting Roadrunner in a good position to survive the price war. As in the old Roadrunner–Coyote cartoons, the predator suffers more than the prey.

Economists continue to debate whether predatory pricing should be a concern for antitrust policymakers. Various questions remain unresolved. Is predatory pricing ever a profitable business strategy? If so, when? Are the courts capable of telling which price cuts are competitive and thus good for consumers and which are predatory? There are no simple answers.

Tying A third example of a controversial business practice is tying. Suppose that Makemoney Movies produces two new films—*The Avengers* and *Hamlet*. If Makemoney offers theaters the two films together at a single price, rather than separately, the studio is said to be tying its two products.

When the practice of tying movies was challenged, the Supreme Court banned it. The court reasoned as follows: Imagine that *The Avengers* is a blockbuster and *Hamlet* is an unprofitable art film. Then the studio could use the high demand for *The Avengers* to force theaters to buy *Hamlet*. It seemed that the studio could use tying as a mechanism for expanding its market power.

Many economists are skeptical of this argument. Imagine that theaters are willing to pay \$20,000 for *The Avengers* and nothing for *Hamlet*. Then the most that a theater would pay for the two movies together is \$20,000—the same as it would pay for *The Avengers* by itself. Forcing the theater to accept a worthless movie as part of the deal does not increase the theater's willingness to pay. Makemoney cannot increase its market power simply by bundling the two movies together.

Why, then, does tying exist? One possibility is that it is a form of price discrimination. Suppose there are two theaters. City Theater is willing to pay \$15,000 for *The Avengers* and \$5,000 for *Hamlet*. Country Theater is just the opposite: It is willing to pay \$5,000 for *The Avengers* and \$15,000 for *Hamlet*. If Makemoney charges separate prices for the two films, its best strategy is to charge \$15,000 for each film, and each theater chooses to show only one film. Yet if Makemoney offers the two movies as a bundle, it can charge each theater \$20,000 for the movies. Thus, if different theaters value the films differently, tying may allow the studio to increase profit by charging a combined price closer to the buyers' total willingness to pay.

Tying remains a controversial business practice. The Supreme Court's argument that tying allows a firm to extend its market power to other goods is not well founded, at least in its simplest form. Yet economists have proposed more elaborate theories for how tying can impede competition. Given our current economic knowledge, it is unclear whether tying has adverse effects for society as a whole.

CASE STUDY

THE MICROSOFT CASE

A particularly important and controversial antitrust case was the U.S. government's suit against the Microsoft Corporation, filed in 1998. The case certainly did not lack drama. It pitted one of the world's richest men (Bill Gates) against one of the world's most powerful regulatory agencies (the U.S. Justice Department). Testifying for the government was a prominent economist (MIT professor Franklin Fisher). Testifying for Microsoft was another prominent economist (MIT professor Richard Schmalensee). At stake was the future of one of the world's most valuable companies (Microsoft) in one of the economy's fastest-growing industries (computer software).

A central issue in the Microsoft case involved tying—in particular, whether Microsoft should be allowed to integrate its Internet browser into its Windows operating system. The government claimed that Microsoft was bundling these two products together to expand its market power in computer operating systems into the unrelated market of Internet browsers. Allowing Microsoft to incorporate such products into its operating system, the government argued, would deter other software companies from entering the market and offering new products.

Microsoft responded by pointing out that putting new features into old products is a natural part of technological progress. Cars today include CD players and air conditioners, which were once sold separately, and cameras come with built-in flashes. The same is true with operating systems. Over time, Microsoft has added many features to Windows that were previously stand-alone products. This has made computers more reliable and easier to use because consumers can be confident that the pieces work together. The integration of Internet technology, Microsoft argued, was the natural next step.

AP PHOTO/LAURA RAUCH

"Me? A monopolist? Now just wait a minute . . ."

One point of disagreement concerned the extent of Microsoft's market power. Noting that more than 80 percent of new personal computers used a Microsoft operating system, the government argued that the company had substantial monopoly power, which it was trying to expand. Microsoft replied that the software market is always changing and that Microsoft's Windows was constantly being challenged by competitors, such as the Apple Mac and Linux operating systems. It also argued that the low price it charged for Windows—about $50, or only 3 percent of the price of a typical computer—was evidence that its market power was severely limited.

Like many large antitrust suits, the Microsoft case became a legal morass. In November 1999, after a long trial, Judge Penfield Jackson ruled that Microsoft had great monopoly power and that it had illegally abused that power. In June 2000, after hearings on possible remedies, he ordered that Microsoft be broken up into two companies—one that sold the operating system and one that sold applications software. A year later, an appeals court overturned Jackson's breakup order and handed the case to a new judge. In September 2001, the Justice Department announced that it no longer sought a breakup of the company and wanted to settle the case quickly.

A settlement was finally reached in November 2002. Microsoft accepted some restrictions on its business practices, and the government accepted that a browser would remain part of the Windows operating system. But the settlement did not end Microsoft's antitrust troubles. In recent years, the company has contended with several private antitrust suits, as well as suits brought by the European Union alleging a variety of anticompetitive behaviors. ●

QuickQuiz *What kind of agreement is illegal for businesses to make? • Why are the antitrust laws controversial?*

IN THE NEWS

Europe versus Google

Google may be the next big target for antitrust regulators.

EU Files Formal Antitrust Charges against Google

The European Commission took direct aim at Google Inc. Wednesday, charging the Internet-search giant with skewing results to favor its comparison-shopping service. But the formal complaint may only be the opening salvo in a broader assault that prompts big changes at Google.

European antitrust chief Margrethe Vestager said she continues to examine other domains, such as travel and local services, where Google is accused of favoring its own services over those of others. She also opened a second front, intensifying a separate probe of Google's conduct with its Android mobile-operating system.

If history is a guide, the European case against Google will grow. The bloc's last big case against a U.S. tech firm began with charges against Microsoft Corp. in 2000 related to computer servers. The commission later added charges against Microsoft for bundling its media player, and Web browser, with its Windows operating system.

The charges could lead to billions of euros in fines and requirements for Google to change its business practices. Microsoft ultimately paid €2.2 billion ($2.3 billion). But people inside and outside Microsoft say the case also altered the company's culture, making it less brash and more cautious.

"There are certain things you know you can't do that other companies can do," said Jean-François Bellis, a lawyer who represented Microsoft against the EU. Being labeled "dominant," as the EU labeled Google on Wednesday, means executives now must worry about pleasing regulators, as well as users.

Inside Google on Wednesday, "the amount of concern over [antitrust enforcement] is enormous," said one person close to the company....

The complaint marked the first time a regulator has filed formal antitrust charges against Google. U.S. regulators closed their own investigation into Google's search practices two years ago after the company agreed to voluntary changes.

That European regulators decided to move against Google when their U.S. counterparts held back reflects in part the company's higher market share on the continent, but also different legal standards. Unlike the U.S., European antitrust law protects competitors, as well as consumers. ■

Source: *The Wall Street Journal*, April 15, 2015.

17-4 Conclusion

Oligopolies would like to act like monopolies, but self-interest drives them toward competition. Where oligopolies end up on this spectrum depends on the number of firms in the oligopoly and how cooperative the firms are. The story of the prisoners' dilemma shows why oligopolies can fail to maintain cooperation, even when cooperation is in their best interest.

Policymakers regulate the behavior of oligopolists through the antitrust laws. The proper scope of these laws is the subject of ongoing debate. Although price fixing among competing firms clearly reduces economic welfare and should be illegal, some business practices that appear to reduce competition may have legitimate if subtle purposes. As a result, policymakers need to be careful when they use the substantial powers of the antitrust laws to place limits on firm behavior.

CHAPTER QuickQuiz

1. The key feature of an oligopolistic market is that
   a. each firm produces a different product from other firms.
   b. a single firm chooses a point on the market demand curve.
   c. each firm takes the market price as given.
   d. a small number of firms are acting strategically.
2. If an oligopolistic industry organizes itself as a cooperative cartel, it will produce a quantity of output that is _______ the competitive level and _______ the monopoly level.
   a. less than, more than
   b. more than, less than
   c. less than, equal to
   d. equal to, more than
3. If an oligopoly does not cooperate and each firm chooses its own quantity, the industry will produce a quantity of output that is _______ the competitive level and _______ the monopoly level.
   a. less than, more than
   b. more than, less than
   c. less than, equal to
   d. equal to, more than
4. As the number of firms in an oligopoly grows large, the industry approaches a level of output that is _______ the competitive level and _______ the monopoly level.
   a. less than, more than
   b. more than, less than
   c. less than, equal to
   d. equal to, more than
5. The prisoners' dilemma is a two-person game illustrating that
   a. the cooperative outcome could be worse for both people than the Nash equilibrium.
   b. even if the cooperative outcome is better than the Nash equilibrium for one person, it might be worse for the other.
   c. even if cooperation is better than the Nash equilibrium, each person might have an incentive not to cooperate.
   d. rational, self-interested individuals will naturally avoid the Nash equilibrium because it is worse for both of them.
6. The antitrust laws aim to
   a. facilitate cooperation among firms in oligopolistic industries.
   b. encourage mergers to take advantage of economies of scale.
   c. discourage firms from moving production facilities overseas.
   d. prevent firms from acting in ways that reduce competition.

SUMMARY

- Oligopolists maximize their total profits by forming a cartel and acting like a monopolist. Yet, if oligopolists make decisions about production levels individually, the result is a greater quantity and a lower price than under the monopoly outcome. The larger the number of firms in the oligopoly, the closer the quantity and price will be to the levels that would prevail under perfect competition.
- The prisoners' dilemma shows that self-interest can prevent people from maintaining cooperation, even when cooperation is in their mutual interest. The logic of the prisoners' dilemma applies in many situations, including arms races, common-resource problems, and oligopolies.
- Policymakers use the antitrust laws to prevent oligopolies from engaging in behavior that reduces competition. The application of these laws can be controversial, because some behavior that can appear to reduce competition may in fact have legitimate business purposes.

KEY CONCEPTS

oligopoly, p. 337
game theory, p. 338
collusion, p. 339
cartel, p. 339
Nash equilibrium, p. 340
prisoners' dilemma, p. 342
dominant strategy, p. 343

QUESTIONS FOR REVIEW

1. If a group of sellers could form a cartel, what quantity and price would they try to set?
2. Compare the quantity and price of an oligopoly to those of a monopoly.
3. Compare the quantity and price of an oligopoly to those of a competitive market.
4. How does the number of firms in an oligopoly affect the outcome in the market?
5. What is the prisoners' dilemma, and what does it have to do with oligopoly?
6. Give two examples other than oligopoly that show how the prisoners' dilemma helps to explain behavior.
7. What kinds of behavior do the antitrust laws prohibit?

PROBLEMS AND APPLICATIONS

1. A large share of the world supply of diamonds comes from Russia and South Africa. Suppose that the marginal cost of mining diamonds is constant at $1,000 per diamond and the demand for diamonds is described by the following schedule:

Price	Quantity
$8,000	5,000 diamonds
7,000	6,000
6,000	7,000
5,000	8,000
4,000	9,000
3,000	10,000
2,000	11,000
1,000	12,000

   a. If there were many suppliers of diamonds, what would be the price and quantity?
   b. If there were only one supplier of diamonds, what would be the price and quantity?
   c. If Russia and South Africa formed a cartel, what would be the price and quantity? If the countries split the market evenly, what would be South Africa's production and profit? What would happen to South Africa's profit if it increased its production by 1,000 while Russia stuck to the cartel agreement?
   d. Use your answers to part (c) to explain why cartel agreements are often not successful.

2. Some years ago, the *New York Times* reported that "the inability of OPEC to agree last week to cut production has sent the oil market into turmoil . . . [leading to] the lowest price for domestic crude oil since June 1990."
   a. Why were the members of OPEC trying to agree to cut production?
   b. Why do you suppose OPEC was unable to agree on cutting production? Why did the oil market go into "turmoil" as a result?
   c. The newspaper also noted OPEC's view "that producing nations outside the organization, like Norway and Britain, should do their share and cut production." What does the phrase "do their share" suggest about OPEC's desired relationship with Norway and Britain?

3. This chapter discusses companies that are oligopolists in the market for the goods they sell. Many of the same ideas apply to companies that are oligopolists in the market for the inputs they buy.
   a. If sellers who are oligopolists try to increase the price of goods they sell, what is the goal of buyers who are oligopolists?
   b. Major league baseball team owners have an oligopoly in the market for baseball players. What is the owners' goal regarding players' salaries? Why is this goal difficult to achieve?
   c. Baseball players went on strike in 1994 because they would not accept the salary cap that the owners wanted to impose. If the owners were already colluding over salaries, why did they feel the need for a salary cap?

4. Consider trade relations between the United States and Mexico. Assume that the leaders of the two countries believe the payoffs to alternative trade policies are as follows:

Mexico's Decision / United States's Decision	Low Tariffs	High Tariffs
Low Tariffs	U.S. gains $25 billion; Mexico gains $25 billion	U.S. gains $30 billion; Mexico gains $10 billion
High Tariffs	U.S. gains $10 billion; Mexico gains $30 billion	U.S. gains $20 billion; Mexico gains $20 billion

   a. What is the dominant strategy for the United States? For Mexico? Explain.
   b. Define *Nash equilibrium.* What is the Nash equilibrium for trade policy?
   c. In 1993, the U.S. Congress ratified the North American Free Trade Agreement, in which the United States and Mexico agreed to reduce trade barriers simultaneously. Do the perceived payoffs shown here justify this approach to trade policy? Explain.
   d. Based on your understanding of the gains from trade (discussed in Chapters 3 and 9), do you think that these payoffs actually reflect a nation's welfare under the four possible outcomes?

5. Synergy and Dynaco are the only two firms in a specific high-tech industry. They face the following payoff matrix as they decide upon the size of their research budget:

Dynaco's Decision / Synergy's Decision	Large Budget	Small Budget
Large Budget	Synergy gains $20 million; Dynaco gains $30 million	Synergy gains zero; Dynaco gains $70 million
Small Budget	Synergy gains $30 million; Dynaco gains zero	Synergy gains $40 million; Dynaco gains $50 million

   a. Does Synergy have a dominant strategy? Explain.
   b. Does Dynaco have a dominant strategy? Explain.
   c. Is there a Nash equilibrium for this scenario? Explain. (*Hint:* Look closely at the definition of Nash equilibrium.)

6. You and a classmate are assigned a project on which you will receive one combined grade. You each want to receive a good grade, but you also want to avoid hard work. In particular, here is the situation:
   - If both of you work hard, you both get an A, which gives each of you 40 units of happiness.
   - If only one of you works hard, you both get a B, which gives each of you 30 units of happiness.
   - If neither of you works hard, you both get a D, which gives each of you 10 units of happiness.
   - Working hard costs 25 units of happiness.

   a. Fill in the payoffs in the following decision box:

Classmate's Decision / Your Decision	Work	Shirk
Work	You: ; Classmate:	You: ; Classmate:
Shirk	You: ; Classmate:	You: ; Classmate:

   b. What is the likely outcome? Explain your answer.
   c. If you get this classmate as your partner on a series of projects throughout the year, rather than only once, how might that change the outcome you predicted in part (b)?
   d. Another classmate cares more about good grades: She gets 50 units of happiness for a B and 80 units of happiness for an A. If this classmate were your partner (but your preferences were unchanged), how would your answers to parts (a) and (b) change? Which of the two classmates would you prefer as a partner? Would she also want you as a partner?

7. A case study in the chapter describes a phone conversation between the presidents of American Airlines and Braniff Airways. Let's analyze the game between the two companies. Suppose that each company can charge either a high price for tickets or a low price. If one company charges $300, it earns low profit if the other company also charges $300 and high profit if the other company charges $600. On the other hand, if the company charges $600, it earns very low profit if the other company charges $300 and medium profit if the other company also charges $600.
   a. Draw the decision box for this game.
   b. What is the Nash equilibrium in this game? Explain.
   c. Is there an outcome that would be better than the Nash equilibrium for both airlines? How could it be achieved? Who would lose if it were achieved?

8. Two athletes of equal ability are competing for a prize of $10,000. Each is deciding whether to take a dangerous performance-enhancing drug. If one athlete takes the drug and the other does not, the one who takes the drug wins the prize. If both or neither take the drug, they tie and split the prize. Taking the drug imposes health risks that are equivalent to a loss of X dollars.
   a. Draw a 2 × 2 payoff matrix describing the decisions the athletes face.
   b. For what *X* is taking the drug the Nash equilibrium?
   c. Does making the drug safer (that is, lowering X) make the athletes better or worse off? Explain.
9. Little Kona is a small coffee company that is considering entering a market dominated by Big Brew. Each company's profit depends on whether Little Kona enters and whether Big Brew sets a high price or a low price:

Little Kona \ Big Brew	High Price	Low Price
Enter	Brew makes $3 million; Kona makes $2 million	Brew makes $1 million; Kona loses $1 million
Don't Enter	Brew makes $7 million; Kona makes zero	Brew makes $2 million; Kona makes zero

   a. Does either player in this game have a dominant strategy?
   b. Does your answer to part (a) help you figure out what the other player should do?
   c. What is the Nash equilibrium? Is there only one?
   d. Big Brew threatens Little Kona by saying, "If you enter, we're going to set a low price, so you had better stay out." Do you think Little Kona should believe the threat? Why or why not?
   e. If the two firms could collude and agree on how to split the total profits, what outcome would they pick?

To find additional study resources, visit cengagebrain.com, and search for "Mankiw."

PART VI

The Economics of Labor Markets

CHAPTER

18

The Markets for the Factors of Production

When you finish school, your income will be determined largely by what kind of job you take. If you become a computer programmer, you will earn more than if you become a gas station attendant. This fact is not surprising, but it is not obvious why it is true. No law requires that computer programmers be paid more than gas station attendants. No ethical principle says that programmers are more deserving. What then determines which job will pay you the higher wage?

Your income, of course, is a small piece of a larger economic picture. In 2015, the total income of all U.S. residents (a statistic called *national income*) was about $16 trillion. People earned this income in various ways. Workers earned about two-thirds of it in the form of wages and fringe benefits. The rest went to landowners and to the owners of

capital—the economy's stock of equipment and structures—in the form of rent, profit, and interest. What determines how much goes to workers? To landowners? To the owners of capital? Why do some workers earn higher wages than others, some landowners higher rental income than others, and some capital owners greater profit than others? Why, in particular, do computer programmers earn more than gas station attendants?

The answers to these questions, like most in economics, hinge on supply and demand. The supply and demand for labor, land, and capital determine the prices paid to workers, landowners, and capital owners. To understand why some people have higher incomes than others, therefore, we need to look more deeply at the markets for the services they provide. That is our job in this and the next two chapters.

factors of production the inputs used to produce goods and services

This chapter provides the basic theory for the analysis of factor markets. As you may recall from Chapter 2, the **factors of production** are the inputs used to produce goods and services. Labor, land, and capital are the three most important factors of production. When a computer firm produces a new software program, it uses programmers' time (labor), the physical space on which its offices are located (land), and an office building and computer equipment (capital). Similarly, when a gas station sells gas, it uses attendants' time (labor), the physical space (land), and the gas tanks and pumps (capital).

In many ways factor markets resemble the markets for goods and services we analyzed in previous chapters, but they are different in one important way: The demand for a factor of production is a *derived demand*. That is, a firm's demand for a factor of production is derived from its decision to supply a good in another market. The demand for computer programmers is inseparably linked to the supply of computer software, and the demand for gas station attendants is inseparably linked to the supply of gasoline.

In this chapter, we analyze factor demand by considering how a competitive, profit-maximizing firm decides how much of any factor to buy. We begin our analysis by examining the demand for labor. Labor is the most important factor of production, because workers receive most of the total income earned in the U.S. economy. Later in the chapter, we will see that our analysis of the labor market also applies to the markets for the other factors of production.

The basic theory of factor markets developed in this chapter takes a large step toward explaining how the income of the U.S. economy is distributed among workers, landowners, and owners of capital. Chapter 19 builds on this analysis to examine in more detail why some workers earn more than others. Chapter 20 examines how much income inequality results from the functioning of factor markets and then considers what role the government should and does play in altering the income distribution.

18-1 The Demand for Labor

Labor markets, like other markets in the economy, are governed by the forces of supply and demand. This is illustrated in Figure 1. In panel (a), the supply and demand for apples determine the price of apples. In panel (b), the supply and demand for apple pickers determine the price, or wage, of apple pickers.

As we have already noted, labor markets are different from most other markets because labor demand is a derived demand. Most labor services, rather than being final goods ready to be enjoyed by consumers, are inputs into the production of other goods. To understand labor demand, we need to focus on the firms

The basic tools of supply and demand apply to goods and to labor services. Panel (a) shows how the supply and demand for apples determine the price of apples. Panel (b) shows how the supply and demand for apple pickers determine the wage of apple pickers.

FIGURE 1

The Versatility of Supply and Demand

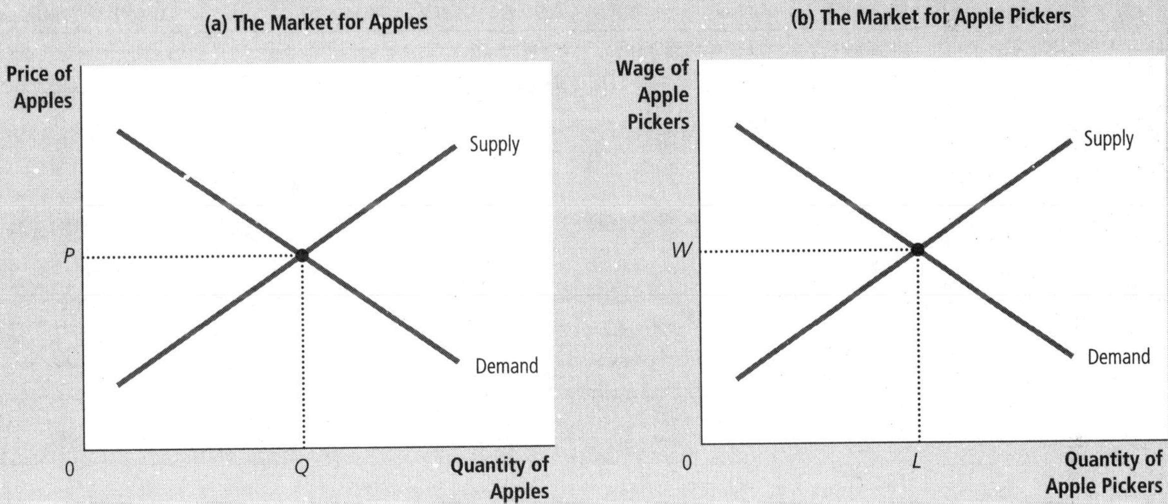

that hire the labor and use it to produce goods for sale. By examining the link between the production of goods and the demand for labor to make those goods, we gain insight into the determination of equilibrium wages.

18-1a The Competitive Profit-Maximizing Firm

Let's look at how a typical firm, such as an apple producer, decides what quantity of labor to demand. The firm owns an apple orchard and each week decides how many apple pickers to hire to harvest its crop. After the firm makes its hiring decision, the workers pick as many apples as they can. The firm then sells the apples, pays the workers, and keeps what is left as profit.

We make two assumptions about our firm. First, we assume that our firm is *competitive* both in the market for apples (where the firm is a seller) and in the market for apple pickers (where the firm is a buyer). A competitive firm is a price taker. Because there are many other firms selling apples and hiring apple pickers, a single firm has little influence over the price it gets for apples or the wage it pays apple pickers. The firm takes the price and the wage as given by market conditions. It only has to decide how many apples to sell and how many workers to hire.

Second, we assume that the firm is *profit-maximizing*. Thus, the firm does not directly care about the number of workers it employs or the number of apples it produces. It cares only about profit, which equals the total revenue from the sale of apples minus the total cost of producing them. The firm's supply of apples and its demand for workers are derived from its primary goal of maximizing profit.

18-1b The Production Function and the Marginal Product of Labor

To make its hiring decision, a firm must consider how the size of its workforce affects the amount of output produced. In our example, the apple producer must consider how the number of apple pickers affects the quantity of apples it can harvest and

TABLE 1

How the Competitive Firm Decides How Much Labor to Hire

(1) Labor L	(2) Output Q	(3) Marginal Product of Labor $MPL = \Delta Q / \Delta L$	(4) Value of the Marginal Product of Labor $VMPL = P \times MPL$	(5) Wage W	(6) Marginal Profit $\Delta Profit = VMPL - W$
0 workers	0 bushels				
		100 bushels	$1,000	$500	$500
1	100				
		80	800	500	300
2	180				
		60	600	500	100
3	240				
		40	400	500	−100
4	280				
		20	200	500	−300
5	300				

sell. Table 1 gives a numerical example. Column (1) shows the number of workers. Column (2) shows the quantity of apples the workers harvest each week.

production function
the relationship between the quantity of inputs used to make a good and the quantity of output of that good

These two columns of numbers describe the firm's ability to produce apples. Recall that economists use the term **production function** to describe the relationship between the quantity of the inputs used in production and the quantity of output from production. Here the "input" is the apple pickers and the "output" is the apples. The other inputs—the trees themselves, the land, the firm's trucks and tractors, and so on—are held fixed for now. This firm's production function shows that if the firm hires 1 worker, that worker will pick 100 bushels of apples per week. If the firm hires 2 workers, the 2 workers together will pick 180 bushels per week. And so on.

Figure 2 graphs the data on labor and output presented in Table 1. The number of workers is on the horizontal axis, and the amount of output is on the vertical axis. This figure illustrates the production function.

marginal product of labor
the increase in the amount of output from an additional unit of labor

One of the *Ten Principles of Economics* introduced in Chapter 1 is that rational people think at the margin. This idea is the key to understanding how firms decide what quantity of labor to hire. To take a step toward this decision, column (3) in Table 1 shows the **marginal product of labor**, the increase in the amount of output produced by an additional unit of labor. When the firm increases the number of workers from 1 to 2, for example, the amount of apples produced rises from 100 to 180 bushels. Therefore, the marginal product of the second worker is 80 bushels.

diminishing marginal product
the property whereby the marginal product of an input declines as the quantity of the input increases

Notice that as the number of workers increases, the marginal product of labor declines. That is, the production process exhibits **diminishing marginal product**. At first, when only a few workers are hired, they can pick the low-hanging fruit. As the number of workers increases, additional workers have to climb higher up the ladders to find apples to pick. Hence, as more and more workers are hired, each additional worker contributes less to the production of apples. For this reason, the production function in Figure 2 becomes flatter as the number of workers rises.

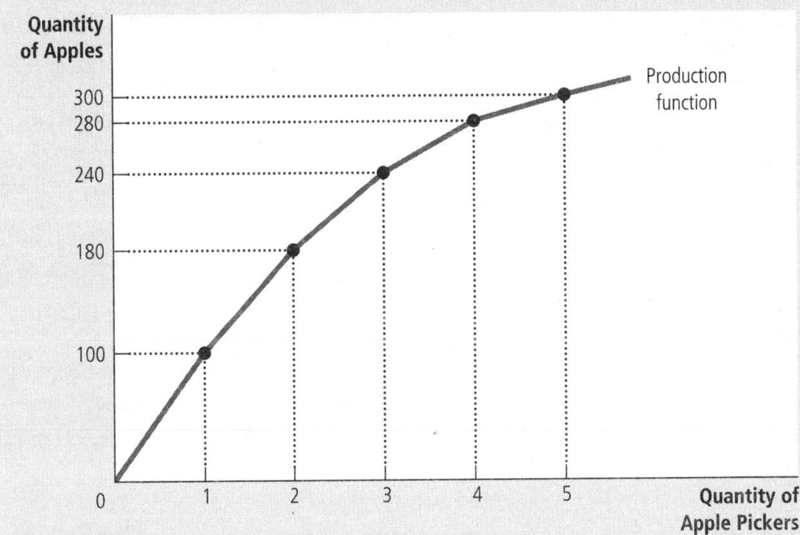

FIGURE 2

The Production Function
The production function shows how an input into production (apple pickers) influences the output from production (apples). As the quantity of the input increases, the production function gets flatter, reflecting the property of diminishing marginal product.

18-1c The Value of the Marginal Product and the Demand for Labor

Our profit-maximizing firm is concerned not about apples themselves but rather about the money it can make by producing and selling them. As a result, when deciding how many workers to hire to pick apples, the firm considers how much profit each worker will bring in. Because profit is total revenue minus total cost, the profit from an additional worker is the worker's contribution to revenue minus the worker's wage.

To find the worker's contribution to revenue, we must convert the marginal product of labor (which is measured in bushels of apples) into the *value* of the marginal product (which is measured in dollars). We do this using the price of apples. To continue our example, if a bushel of apples sells for $10 and if an additional worker produces 80 bushels of apples, then the worker produces $800 of revenue.

The **value of the marginal product** of any input is the marginal product of that input multiplied by the market price of the output. Column (4) in Table 1 shows the value of the marginal product of labor in our example, assuming the price of apples is $10 per bushel. Because the market price is constant for a competitive firm while the marginal product declines with more workers, the value of the marginal product diminishes as the number of workers rises. Economists sometimes call this column of numbers the firm's *marginal revenue product:* It is the extra revenue the firm gets from hiring an additional unit of a factor of production.

value of the marginal product
the marginal product of an input times the price of the output

Now consider how many workers the firm will hire. Suppose that the market wage for apple pickers is $500 per week. In this case, as you can see in Table 1, the first worker that the firm hires is profitable: The first worker yields $1,000 in revenue, or $500 in profit. Similarly, the second worker yields $800 in additional revenue, or $300 in profit. The third worker produces $600 in additional revenue, or $100 in profit. After the third worker, however, hiring workers is unprofitable. The fourth worker would yield only $400 of additional revenue. Because the worker's wage is $500, hiring the fourth worker would mean a $100 reduction in profit. Thus, the firm hires only 3 workers.

Figure 3 graphs the value of the marginal product. This curve slopes downward because the marginal product of labor diminishes as the number of workers

FIGURE 3

The Value of the Marginal Product of Labor

This figure shows how the value of the marginal product (the marginal product times the price of the output) depends on the number of workers. The curve slopes downward because of diminishing marginal product. For a competitive, profit-maximizing firm, this value-of-marginal-product curve is also the firm's labor-demand curve.

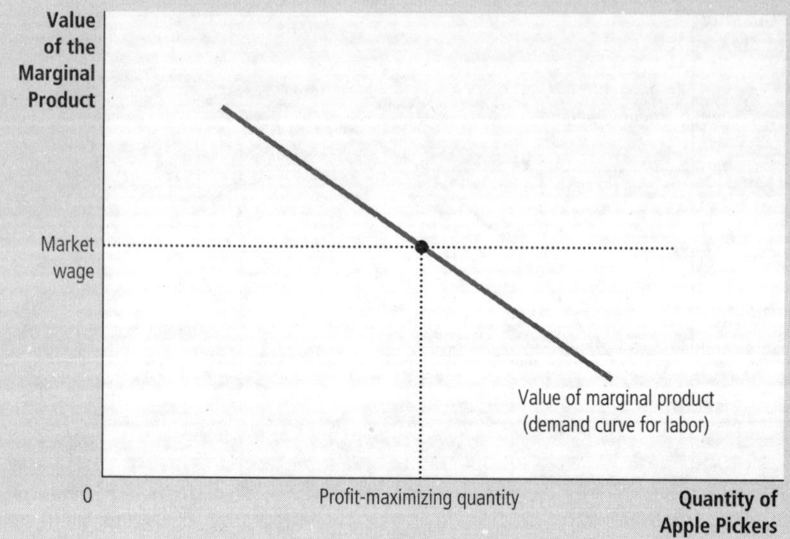

rises. The figure also includes a horizontal line at the market wage. To maximize profit, the firm hires workers up to the point where these two curves cross. Below this level of employment, the value of the marginal product exceeds the wage, so hiring another worker increases profit. Above this level of employment, the value of the marginal product is less than the wage, so the marginal worker is unprofitable. Thus, *a competitive, profit-maximizing firm hires workers up to the point at which the value of the marginal product of labor equals the wage.*

Now that we understand the profit-maximizing hiring strategy for a competitive firm, we can offer a theory of labor demand. Recall that a firm's labor-demand curve tells us the quantity of labor that a firm decides to hire at any given wage. Figure 3 shows that the firm makes that decision by choosing the quantity of labor at which the value of the marginal product equals the wage. As a result, *the value-of-marginal-product curve is the labor-demand curve for a competitive, profit-maximizing firm.*

18-1d What Causes the Labor-Demand Curve to Shift?

We now understand that the labor-demand curve reflects the value of the marginal product of labor. With this insight in mind, let's consider a few of the things that might cause the labor-demand curve to shift.

The Output Price The value of the marginal product is marginal product times the price of the firm's output. Thus, when the output price changes, the value of the marginal product changes, and the labor-demand curve shifts. An increase in the price of apples, for instance, raises the value of the marginal product of each worker who picks apples and, therefore, increases labor demand from the firms that supply apples. Conversely, a decrease in the price of apples reduces the value of the marginal product and decreases labor demand.

Technological Change Between 1960 and 2015, the output a typical U.S. worker produced in an hour rose by 195 percent. Why? The most important reason is

FYI

Input Demand and Output Supply: Two Sides of the Same Coin

In Chapter 14, we saw how a competitive, profit-maximizing firm decides how much of its output to sell: It chooses the quantity of output at which the price of the good equals the marginal cost of production. We have just seen how such a firm decides how much labor to hire: It chooses the quantity of labor at which the wage equals the value of the marginal product. Because the production function links the quantity of inputs to the quantity of output, you should not be surprised to learn that the firm's decision about input demand is closely linked to its decision about output supply. In fact, these two decisions are two sides of the same coin.

To see this relationship more fully, let's consider how the marginal product of labor (*MPL*) and marginal cost (*MC*) are related. Suppose an additional worker costs \$500 and has a marginal product of 50 bushels of apples. In this case, producing 50 more bushels costs \$500; the marginal cost of a bushel is \$500/50, or \$10. More generally, if W is the wage, and an extra unit of labor produces *MPL* units of output, then the marginal cost of a unit of output is $MC = W / MPL$.

This analysis shows that diminishing marginal product is closely related to increasing marginal cost. When the apple orchard grows crowded with workers, each additional worker adds less to the production of apples (*MPL* falls). Similarly, when the apple firm is producing a large quantity of apples, the orchard is already crowded with workers, so it is more costly to produce an additional bushel of apples (*MC* rises).

Now consider our criterion for profit maximization. We determined earlier that a profit-maximizing firm chooses the quantity of labor so that the value of the marginal product ($P \times MPL$) equals the wage (W). We can write this mathematically as

$$P \times MPL = W.$$

If we divide both sides of this equation by *MPL*, we obtain

$$P = W / MPL.$$

We just noted that W / MPL equals marginal cost, *MC*. Therefore, we can substitute to obtain

$$P = MC.$$

This equation states that the price of the firm's output equals the marginal cost of producing a unit of output. Thus, *when a competitive firm hires labor up to the point at which the value of the marginal product equals the wage, it also produces up to the point at which the price equals marginal cost.* Our analysis of labor demand in this chapter is just another way of looking at the production decision we first saw in Chapter 14. ■

technological progress: Scientists and engineers are constantly figuring out new and better ways of doing things. This has profound implications for the labor market. Advances in technology typically raise the marginal product of labor, which in turn increases the demand for labor and shifts the labor-demand curve to the right.

It is also possible for technological change to reduce labor demand. The invention of a cheap industrial robot, for instance, could conceivably reduce the marginal product of labor, shifting the labor-demand curve to the left. Economists call this *labor-saving* technological change. History suggests, however, that most technological progress is instead *labor-augmenting*. For example, a carpenter with a nail gun is more productive than a carpenter with only a hammer. Labor-augmenting technological advance explains persistently rising employment in the face of rising wages: Even though wages (adjusted for inflation) increased by 165 percent from 1960 to 2015, firms nonetheless more than doubled the amount of labor they employed.

The Supply of Other Factors The quantity of one factor of production that is available can affect the marginal product of other factors. The productivity of apple pickers depends, for instance, on the availability of ladders. If the supply of ladders declines, the marginal product of apple pickers will decline as well, reducing the demand for apple pickers. We consider the linkage among the factors of production more fully later in the chapter.

QuickQuiz *Define* marginal product of labor *and* value of the marginal product of labor. • *Describe how a competitive, profit-maximizing firm decides how many workers to hire.*

18-2 The Supply of Labor

Having analyzed labor demand in detail, let's turn to the other side of the market and consider labor supply. A formal model of labor supply is included in Chapter 21, where we develop the theory of household decision making. Here we informally discuss the decisions that lie behind the labor-supply curve.

18-2a The Trade-off between Work and Leisure

One of the *Ten Principles of Economics* in Chapter 1 is that people face trade-offs. Probably no trade-off in a person's life is more obvious or more important than the trade-off between work and leisure. The more hours you spend working, the fewer hours you have to watch TV, browse social media, enjoy dinner with friends, or pursue your favorite hobby. The trade-off between labor and leisure lies behind the labor-supply curve.

Another of the *Ten Principles of Economics* is that the cost of something is what you give up to get it. What do you give up to get an hour of leisure? You give up an hour of work, which in turn means an hour of wages. Thus, if your wage is $15 per hour, the opportunity cost of an hour of leisure is $15. And when you get a raise to $20 per hour, the opportunity cost of enjoying leisure goes up.

"I really didn't enjoy working five days a week, fifty weeks a year for forty years, but I needed the money."

The labor-supply curve reflects how workers' decisions about the labor-leisure trade-off respond to a change in that opportunity cost. An upward-sloping labor-supply curve means that an increase in the wage induces workers to increase the quantity of labor they supply. Because time is limited, more work means less leisure. That is, workers respond to the increase in the opportunity cost of leisure by taking less of it.

It is worth noting that the labor-supply curve need not be upward-sloping. Imagine you got that raise from $15 to $20 per hour. The opportunity cost of leisure is now greater, but you are also richer than you were before. You might decide that with your extra wealth you can now afford to enjoy more leisure. That is, at the higher wage, you might choose to work fewer hours. If so, your labor-supply curve would slope backward. In Chapter 21, we discuss this possibility in terms of conflicting effects on your labor-supply decision (called the *income* and *substitution effects*). For now, we ignore the possibility of backward-sloping labor supply and assume that the labor-supply curve is upward-sloping.

18-2b What Causes the Labor-Supply Curve to Shift?

The labor-supply curve shifts whenever people change the amount they want to work at a given wage. Let's now consider some of the events that might cause such a shift.

Changes in Tastes In 1950, 34 percent of women were employed at paid jobs or looking for work. By 2015, that number had risen to 57 percent. Although there are many explanations for this development, one of them is changing tastes, or attitudes toward work. Sixty-five years ago, it was the norm for women to stay at home and raise their children. Today, the typical family size is smaller, and more mothers choose to work. The result is an increase in the supply of labor.

Changes in Alternative Opportunities The supply of labor in any one labor market depends on the opportunities available in other labor markets. If the wage earned by pear pickers suddenly rises, some apple pickers may choose to switch occupations, causing the supply of labor in the market for apple pickers to fall.

Immigration Movement of workers from region to region, or country to country, is another important source of shifts in labor supply. When immigrants come to the United States, for instance, the supply of labor in the United States increases and the supply of labor in the immigrants' home countries falls. In fact, much of the policy debate about immigration centers on its effect on labor supply and, thereby, equilibrium wages in the labor market.

QuickQuiz *Who has a greater opportunity cost of enjoying leisure—a janitor or a brain surgeon? Explain. Can this help explain why doctors work such long hours?*

18-3 Equilibrium in the Labor Market

So far we have established two facts about how wages are determined in competitive labor markets:

- The wage adjusts to balance the supply and demand for labor.
- The wage equals the value of the marginal product of labor.

At first, it might seem surprising that the wage can do both of these things at once. In fact, there is no real puzzle here, but understanding why there is no puzzle is an important step toward understanding wage determination.

Figure 4 shows the labor market in equilibrium. The wage and the quantity of labor have adjusted to balance supply and demand. When the market is in this equilibrium, each firm has bought as much labor as it finds profitable at the equilibrium wage. That is, each firm has followed the rule for profit maximization: It has hired workers until the value of the marginal product equals the wage. Hence, the wage must equal the value of the marginal product of labor once it has brought supply and demand into equilibrium.

ASK THE EXPERTS

Immigration

"The average US citizen would be better off if a larger number of highly educated foreign workers were legally allowed to immigrate to the US each year."

What do economists say?

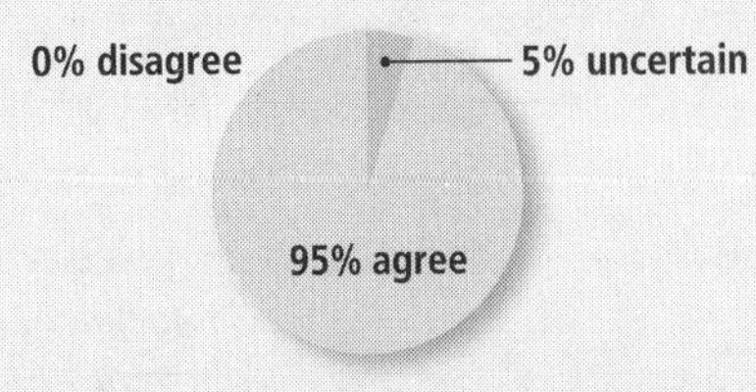

"The average US citizen would be better off if a larger number of low-skilled foreign workers were legally allowed to enter the US each year."

What do economists say?

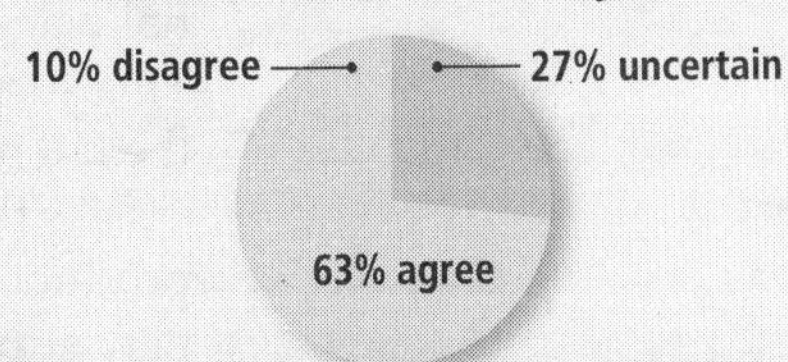

"Unless they were compensated by others, many low-skilled American workers would be substantially worse off if a larger number of low-skilled foreign workers were legally allowed to enter the US each year."

What do economists say?

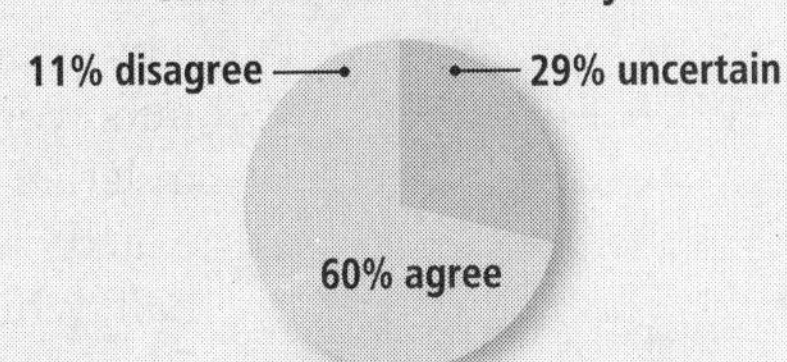

Source: IGM Economic Experts Panel, February 12, 2013, December 10, 2013.

FIGURE 4

Equilibrium in a Labor Market
Like all prices, the price of labor (the wage) depends on supply and demand. Because the demand curve reflects the value of the marginal product of labor, in equilibrium workers receive the value of their marginal contribution to the production of goods and services.

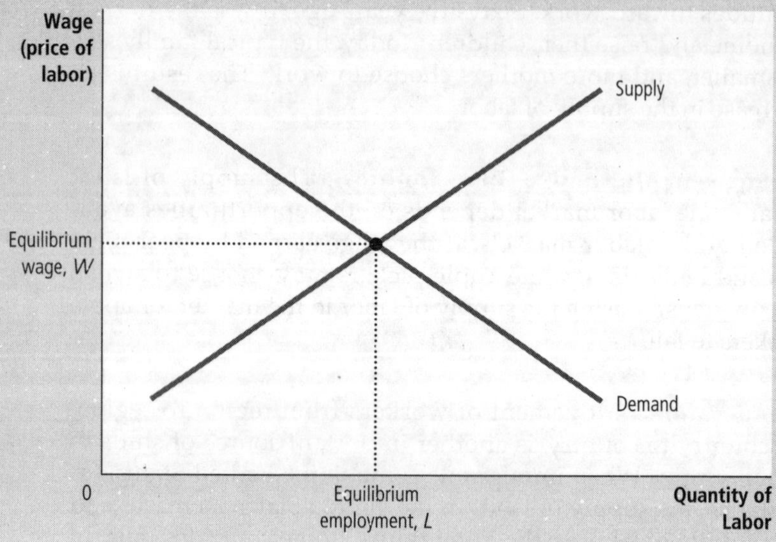

This brings us to an important lesson: *Any event that changes the supply or demand for labor must change the equilibrium wage and the value of the marginal product by the same amount because these must always be equal.* To see how this works, let's consider some events that shift these curves.

18-3a Shifts in Labor Supply

Suppose that immigration increases the number of workers willing to pick apples. As Figure 5 shows, the supply of labor shifts to the right from S_1 to S_2. At the initial wage W_1, the quantity of labor supplied now exceeds the quantity demanded. This surplus of labor puts downward pressure on the wage of apple pickers, and the fall in the wage from W_1 to W_2 makes it profitable for firms to hire more workers. As the number of workers employed in each apple orchard rises, the marginal product of a worker falls, and so does the value of the marginal product. In the new equilibrium, both the wage and the value of the marginal product of labor are lower than they were before the influx of new workers.

An episode from Israel, studied by MIT economist Joshua Angrist, illustrates how a shift in labor supply can alter the equilibrium in a labor market. During most of the 1980s, many thousands of Palestinians regularly commuted from their homes in the Israeli-occupied West Bank and Gaza Strip to jobs in Israel, primarily in the construction and agriculture industries. In 1988, however, political unrest in these occupied areas induced the Israeli government to take steps that, as a by-product, reduced this supply of workers. Curfews were imposed, work permits were checked more thoroughly, and a ban on overnight stays of Palestinians in Israel was enforced more rigorously. The economic impact of these steps was exactly as theory predicts: The number of Palestinians with jobs in Israel fell by half, while those who continued to work in Israel enjoyed wage increases of about 50 percent. With a reduced number of Palestinian workers in Israel, the value of the marginal product of the remaining workers was much higher.

When considering the economics of immigration, keep in mind that the economy consists not of a single labor market but rather a variety of labor markets for

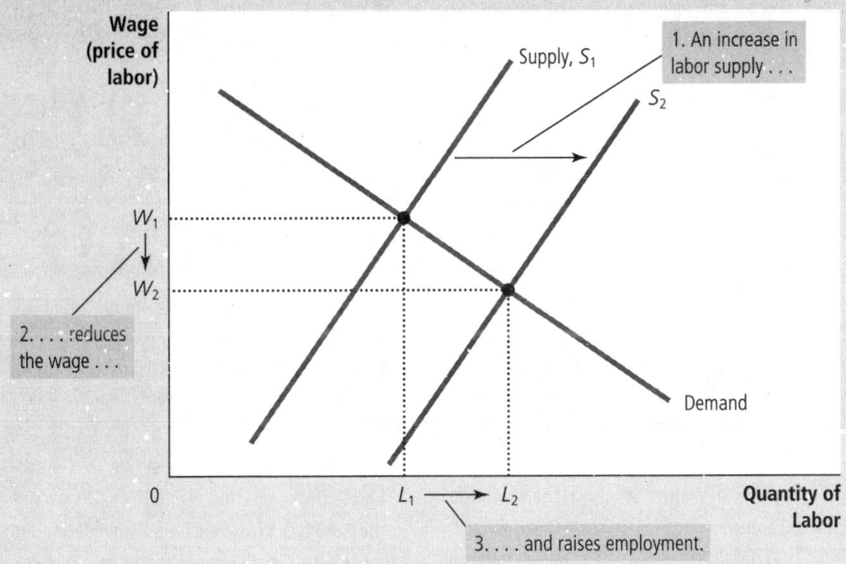

FIGURE 5

A Shift in Labor Supply

When labor supply increases from S_1 to S_2, perhaps because of an immigration wave of new workers, the equilibrium wage falls from W_1 to W_2. At this lower wage, firms hire more labor, so employment rises from L_1 to L_2. The change in the wage reflects a change in the value of the marginal product of labor: With more workers, the added output from an extra worker is smaller.

different kinds of workers. A wave of immigration may lower wages in those labor markets in which the new immigrants seek work, but it could have the opposite effect in other labor markets. For example, if the new immigrants look for jobs as apple pickers, the supply of apple pickers increases and the wage of apple pickers declines. But suppose the new immigrants are physicians who use some of their income to buy apples. In this case, the wave of immigration increases the *supply* of physicians but increases the *demand* for apples and thus apple pickers. As a result, the wages of physicians decline, and the wages of apple pickers rise. The linkages among various markets—sometimes called *general equilibrium effects*—make analyzing the full effect of immigration more complex than it first appears.

18-3b Shifts in Labor Demand

Now suppose that an increase in the popularity of apples causes their price to rise. This price increase does not change the marginal product of labor for any given number of workers, but it does raise the *value* of the marginal product. With a higher price for apples, hiring more apple pickers is now profitable. As Figure 6 shows, when the demand for labor shifts to the right from D_1 to D_2, the equilibrium wage rises from W_1 to W_2 and equilibrium employment rises from L_1 to L_2. Once again, the wage and the value of the marginal product of labor move together.

This analysis shows that prosperity for firms in an industry is often linked to prosperity for workers in that industry. When the price of apples rises, apple producers make greater profit and apple pickers earn higher wages. When the price of apples falls, apple producers earn smaller profit and apple pickers earn lower wages. This lesson is well known to workers in industries with highly volatile prices. Workers in oil fields, for instance, know from experience that their earnings are closely linked to the world price of crude oil.

From these examples, you should now have a good understanding of how wages are set in competitive labor markets. Labor supply and labor demand together determine the equilibrium wage, and shifts in the supply or demand curve

IN THE NEWS

The Economics of Immigration

Here is an interview with Pia Orrenius, a senior economist at the Federal Reserve Bank of Dallas who studies immigration.

Q: What can you tell us about the size of the immigrant population in the United States?

A: Immigrants make up about 13.3 percent of the overall population, which means about 42 million foreign-born live in the United States. The commonly accepted 2014 estimate for the unauthorized portion of the foreign-born population is 11.3 million. Immigrants come from all parts of the world, but we've seen big changes in their origins. In the 1950s and 1960s, 75 percent of immigrants were from Europe. Today, over 80 percent are from Latin America and Asia. Inflows are also much larger today, with 1 million to 2 million newcomers entering each year, although levels were significantly depressed in the aftermath of the Great Recession of 2007–2009, when the housing bust led to a significant decline in illegal immigration.

What's interesting about the United States is how our economy has been able to absorb immigrants and put them to work. U.S. immigrants are much more likely to be working compared with immigrants in other developed countries. This is partly because we don't set high entry-level wages or have cumbersome hiring and firing rules. In this type of flexible system, there are more job openings. Workers have more opportunities. Of course, entry-level wages are also lower, but immigrants at least get their foot in the door.

Being in the workforce allows immigrants to interact with the rest of society. They learn the language faster, pay taxes and become stakeholders.

Q: Where do immigrants fit into the U.S. economy?

A: U.S. immigrants are diverse in economic terms. We rely on them to fill both high- and low-skilled jobs. Some immigrants do medium-skilled work, but more than anything else they're found on the low and the high ends of the education distribution.

The economic effects of immigration are positive, but the fiscal impact depends on the group. We have a very important group of high-skilled immigrants. We rely on them to fill high-level jobs in health and STEM [science, technology, engineering, and mathematics] occupations. Each year, over one-third of Ph.D.s in science and engineering are awarded to students who were born abroad. Moreover, research shows that foreign-born workers in STEM fields are more innovative and entrepreneurial than their U.S.-born counterparts, which boosts productivity growth.

High-skilled immigration also contributes positively to government finances. People tend to focus on undocumented or low-skilled immigrants when discussing immigration and often do not recognize the tremendous contributions of high-skilled immigrants.

FIGURE 6

A Shift in Labor Demand

When labor demand increases from D_1 to D_2, perhaps because of an increase in the price of the firm's output, the equilibrium wage rises from W_1 to W_2 and employment rises from L_1 to L_2. The change in the wage reflects a change in the value of the marginal product of labor: With a higher output price, the added output from an extra worker is more valuable.

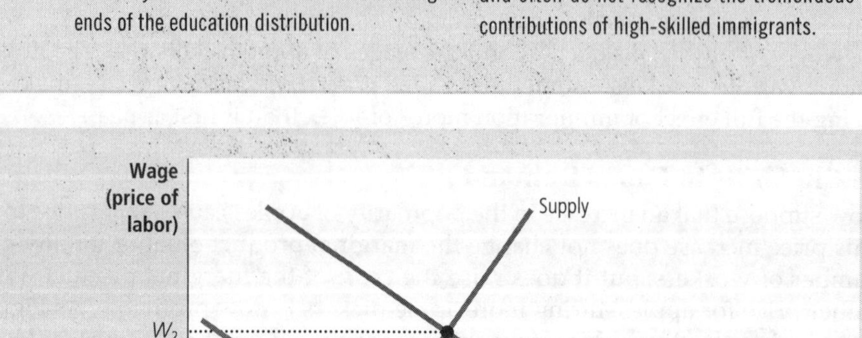

Q: What about the low-skilled immigration?

A: With low-skilled immigration, the economic benefits of the added labor, such as lower prices for consumers and higher returns to capital, have to be balanced against the fiscal impact, which is likely negative. The fiscal impact is the difference between what families contribute in taxes and what they use up in the form of publicly provided services.

What makes the fiscal issue more difficult is the distribution of the burden. The federal government reaps much of the revenue from immigrants who work and pay employment taxes. State and local governments realize less of that benefit and have to pay more of the costs associated with low-skilled immigration—usually education and health expenses.

Q: Does it matter whether the immigration is legal or not?

A: Illegal immigration has helped fuel the U.S. economy for many years. Five percent of the U.S. workforce is made up of unauthorized workers—the outcome of decades of robust labor demand and, until recently, lax enforcement. Nevertheless, from an economic and fiscal perspective, it makes more sense to differentiate among immigrants of various

COURTESY OF FEDERAL RESERVE BANK OF DALLAS, SOUTHWEST ECONOMY, MARCH/APRIL 2006

Pia Orrenius

skill levels than it does to focus on legal status.

The economic benefits of low-skilled immigrants aren't typically going to depend on how they entered the United States. Unauthorized immigrants may pay less in taxes, but they're also ineligible for most public programs. Lacking legal status doesn't mean these immigrants have a worse fiscal impact. In fact, a low-skilled unauthorized immigrant likely creates less fiscal burden than a low-skilled legal immigrant because the undocumented get almost no government benefits.

Q: How does immigration affect jobs and earnings for the native-born population?

A: Labor economists have looked long and hard at this question, namely how immigration has affected the wages of Americans, particularly the low-skilled who lack a high school degree. One reason we worry about this is that the real wages of less-educated U.S. men have been falling since the late 1970s.

The studies tend to show that little of the decline is due to immigration. The consensus seems to be that wages overall are about 1 to 3 percent lower today as a result of immigration, although some scholars find larger effects for low-skilled workers. Still, labor economists think it's a bit of a puzzle that they haven't been able to systematically identify larger adverse wage effects.

The reason may be the way the economy is constantly adjusting to the inflow of immigrants. On a geographical basis, for example, a large influx of immigrants into an area tends to encourage an inflow of physical capital or a change in technology or production processes which puts new workers to use. So you have an increase in labor supply, but you also have an increase in labor demand, and the wage effects are ameliorated. ■

Source: This interview, updated for this edition by Dr. Orrenius, was originally published in *Southwest Economy*, March/April 2006.

for labor cause the equilibrium wage to change. At the same time, profit maximization by the firms that demand labor ensures that the equilibrium wage always equals the value of the marginal product of labor.

CASE STUDY

PRODUCTIVITY AND WAGES

One of the *Ten Principles of Economics* in Chapter 1 is that our standard of living depends on our ability to produce goods and services. We can now see how this principle works in the market for labor. In particular, our analysis of labor demand shows that wages equal productivity as measured by the value of the marginal product of labor. Put simply, highly productive workers are highly paid, and less productive workers are less highly paid.

This lesson is key to understanding why workers today are better off than workers in previous generations. Table 2 presents some data on growth in productivity and growth in real wages (that is, wages adjusted for inflation). From 1960 to 2015, productivity as measured by output per hour of work grew about 2.0 percent per year. Real wages grew at 1.8 percent—almost the same rate. With a growth rate of 2 percent per year, productivity and real wages double about every 35 years.

Productivity growth varies over time. Table 2 also shows the data for three shorter periods that economists have identified as having very different

TABLE 2

Productivity and Wage Growth in the United States

Time Period	Growth Rate of Productivity	Growth Rate of Real Wages
1960–2015	2.0%	1.8%
1960–1973	2.7	2.7
1973–1995	1.4	1.2
1995–2015	2.1	1.8

Source: Bureau of Labor Statistics.

productivity experiences. Around 1973, the U.S. economy experienced a significant slowdown in productivity growth that lasted until 1995. The cause of this productivity slowdown is yet to be fully explained, but the link between productivity and real wages is exactly as standard theory predicts. The slowdown in productivity growth from 2.7 to 1.4 percent per year coincided with a slowdown in real wage growth from 2.7 to 1.2 percent per year.

Productivity growth picked up again about 1995, and many observers hailed the arrival of the "new economy." This productivity acceleration is most often attributed to the spread of computers and information technology. As theory predicts, growth in real wages picked up as well. From 1995 to 2015, productivity grew by 2.1 percent per year and real wages grew by 1.8 percent per year.

The bottom line: Both theory and history confirm the close connection between productivity and real wages. ●

QuickQuiz *How does immigration of workers affect labor supply, labor demand, the marginal product of labor, and the equilibrium wage?*

FYI

Monopsony

On the preceding pages, we built our analysis of the labor market with the tools of supply and demand. In doing so, we assumed that the labor market was competitive. That is, we assumed that there were many buyers and sellers of labor, so each buyer or seller had a negligible effect on the wage.

Yet that assumption doesn't always apply. Imagine that the labor market in a small town is dominated by a single, large employer. That employer can exert a large influence on the going wage, and it can use its market power to alter the outcome in the labor market. Such a market in which there is a single buyer is called a *monopsony*.

A monopsony (a market with one buyer) is in many ways similar to a monopoly (a market with one seller). Recall from Chapter 15 that a monopoly firm produces less of the good than would a competitive firm; by reducing the quantity offered for sale, the monopoly firm moves along the product's demand curve, raising the price and also its profit. Similarly, a monopsony firm in a labor market hires fewer workers than would a competitive firm; by reducing the number of jobs available, the monopsony firm moves along the labor supply curve, reducing the wage it pays and raising its profit. Thus, both monopolists and monopsonists reduce economic activity in a market below the socially optimal level. In both cases, the existence of market power distorts the outcome and causes deadweight losses.

This book does not present the formal model of monopsony because monopsonies are rare. In most labor markets, workers have many possible employers, and firms compete with one another to attract workers. In this case, the model of supply and demand is the best one to use. ■

18-4 The Other Factors of Production: Land and Capital

We have seen how firms decide how much labor to hire and how these decisions determine workers' wages. At the same time that firms are hiring workers, they are also deciding about other inputs to production. For example, our apple-producing firm might have to choose the size of its apple orchard and the number of ladders for its apple pickers. We can think of the firm's factors of production as falling into three categories: labor, land, and capital.

The meaning of the terms *labor* and *land* is clear, but the definition of *capital* is somewhat tricky. Economists use the term **capital** to refer to the stock of equipment and structures used for production. That is, the economy's capital represents the accumulation of goods produced in the past that are being used in the present to produce new goods and services. For our apple firm, the capital stock includes the ladders used to climb the trees, the trucks used to transport the apples, the buildings used to store the apples, and even the trees themselves.

capital
the equipment and structures used to produce goods and services

18-4a Equilibrium in the Markets for Land and Capital

What determines how much the owners of land and capital earn for their contribution to the production process? Before answering this question, we need to distinguish between two prices: the purchase price and the rental price. The *purchase price* of land or capital is the price a person pays to own that factor of production indefinitely. The *rental price* is the price a person pays to use that factor for a limited period of time. It is important to keep this distinction in mind because, as we will see, these prices are determined by somewhat different economic forces.

Having defined these terms, we can now apply the theory of factor demand that we developed for the labor market to the markets for land and capital. Because the wage is the rental price of labor, much of what we have learned about wage determination applies also to the rental prices of land and capital. As Figure 7 illustrates,

FIGURE 7

The Markets for Land and Capital

Supply and demand determine the compensation paid to the owners of land, as shown in panel (a), and the compensation paid to the owners of capital, as shown in panel (b). The demand for each factor, in turn, depends on the value of the marginal product of that factor.

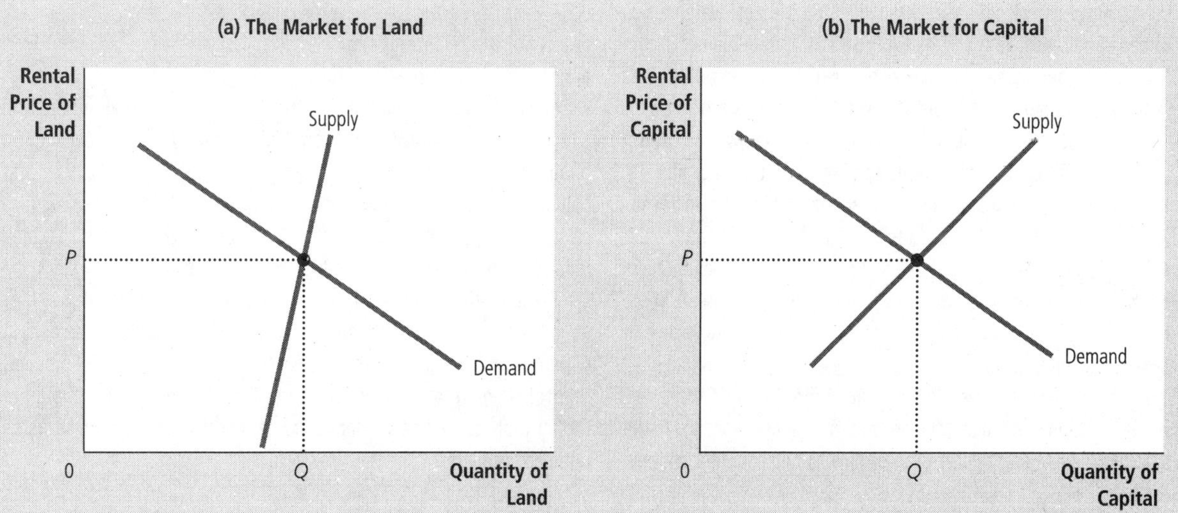

the rental price of land, shown in panel (a), and the rental price of capital, shown in panel (b), are determined by supply and demand. Moreover, the demand for land and capital is determined just like the demand for labor. That is, when our apple-producing firm is deciding how much land and how many ladders to rent, it follows the same logic as when deciding how many workers to hire. For both land and capital, the firm increases the quantity hired until the value of the factor's marginal product equals the factor's price. Thus, the demand curve for each factor reflects the marginal productivity of that factor.

We can now explain how much income goes to labor, how much goes to landowners, and how much goes to the owners of capital. As long as the firms using the factors of production are competitive and profit-maximizing, each factor's rental price must equal the value of the marginal product for that factor. *Labor, land, and capital each earn the value of their marginal contribution to the production process.*

Now consider the purchase price of land and capital. The rental price and the purchase price are related: Buyers are willing to pay more for a piece of land or capital if it produces a valuable stream of rental income. And as we have just seen, the equilibrium rental income at any point in time equals the value of that factor's marginal product. Therefore, the equilibrium purchase price of a piece of land or capital depends on both the current value of the marginal product and the value of the marginal product expected to prevail in the future.

FYI

What Is Capital Income?

Labor income is an easy concept to understand: It is the paycheck that workers get from their employers. The income earned by capital, however, is less obvious.

In our analysis, we have been implicitly assuming that households own the economy's stock of capital—ladders, drill presses, warehouses, and so on—and rent it to the firms that use it. Capital income, in this case, is the rent that households receive for the use of their capital. This assumption simplified our analysis of how capital owners are compensated, but it is not entirely realistic. In fact, firms usually own the capital they use, and therefore, they receive the earnings from this capital.

These earnings from capital, however, are paid to households eventually in a variety of forms. Some of the earnings are paid in the form of interest to those households that have lent money to firms. Bondholders and bank depositors are two examples of recipients of interest. Thus, when you receive interest on your bank account, that income is part of the economy's capital income.

In addition, some of the earnings from capital are paid to households in the form of dividends. Dividends are payments by a firm to the firm's stockholders. A stockholder is a person who has bought a share in the ownership of the firm and, therefore, is entitled to a portion of the firm's profits.

A firm does not have to pay out all its earnings to households in the form of interest and dividends. Instead, it can retain some earnings within the firm and use these earnings to buy additional capital. Unlike dividends, these retained earnings do not yield a direct cash payment to the firm's stockholders, but the stockholders benefit from them nonetheless. Because retained earnings increase the amount of capital the firm owns, they tend to increase future earnings and, thereby, the value of the firm's stock.

These institutional details are interesting and important, but they do not alter our conclusion about the income earned by the owners of capital. Capital is paid according to the value of its marginal product, regardless of whether this income is transmitted to households in the form of interest or dividends or whether it is kept within firms as retained earnings. ■

18-4b Linkages among the Factors of Production

We have seen that the price paid for any factor of production—labor, land, or capital—equals the value of the marginal product of that factor. The marginal product of any factor, in turn, depends on the quantity of that factor that is available. Because of diminishing marginal product, a factor in abundant supply has a low marginal product and thus a low price, and a factor in scarce supply has a high marginal product and a high price. As a result, when the supply of a factor falls, its equilibrium price rises.

When the supply of any factor changes, however, the effects are not limited to the market for that factor. In most situations, factors of production are used together in a way that makes the productivity of each factor depend on the quantities of the other factors available for use in the production process. Therefore, when some event changes the supply of any one factor of production, it will typically affect not only the earnings of that factor but also the earnings of all the other factors as well.

For example, suppose a hurricane destroys many of the ladders that workers use to pick apples from the orchards. What happens to the earnings of the various factors of production? Most obviously, when the supply of ladders falls, the equilibrium rental price of ladders rises. Those owners who were lucky enough to avoid damage to their ladders now earn a higher return when they rent out their ladders to the firms that produce apples.

Yet the effects of this event do not stop at the ladder market. Because there are fewer ladders with which to work, the workers who pick apples have a smaller marginal product. Thus, the reduction in the supply of ladders reduces the demand for the labor of apple pickers, and this shift in demand causes the equilibrium wage to fall.

This story shows a general lesson: *An event that changes the supply of any factor of production can alter the earnings of all the factors*. The change in earnings of any factor can be found by analyzing the impact of the event on the value of the marginal product of that factor.

CASE STUDY

THE ECONOMICS OF THE BLACK DEATH

In 14th-century Europe, the bubonic plague wiped out about one-third of the population within a few years. This event, called the *Black Death*, provides a grisly natural experiment to test the theory of factor markets that we have just developed. Consider the effects of the Black Death on those who were lucky enough to survive. What do you think happened to the wages earned by workers and the rents earned by landowners?

To answer this question, let's examine the effects of a reduced population on the marginal product of labor and the marginal product of land. With a smaller supply of workers, the marginal product of labor rises. (This is diminishing marginal product working in reverse.) Thus, we would expect the Black Death to raise wages.

Because land and labor are used together in production, a smaller supply of workers also affects the market for land, the other major factor of production in medieval Europe. With fewer workers available to farm the land, an additional unit of land produced less additional output. In other words, the marginal product of land fell. Thus, we would expect the Black Death to lower rents.

In fact, both predictions are consistent with the historical evidence. Wages approximately doubled during this period, and rents declined 50 percent or more.

BETTMANN/CORBIS

Workers who survived the plague were lucky in more ways than one.

The Black Death led to economic prosperity for the peasant classes and reduced incomes for the landed classes. ●

QuickQuiz *What determines the income of the owners of land and capital? • How would an increase in the quantity of capital affect the incomes of those who already own capital? How would it affect the incomes of workers?*

18-5 Conclusion

This chapter has explained how labor, land, and capital are compensated for the roles they play in the production process. The theory developed here is called the *neoclassical theory of distribution*. According to the neoclassical theory, the amount paid to each factor of production depends on the supply and demand for that factor. The demand, in turn, depends on that particular factor's marginal productivity. In equilibrium, each factor of production earns the value of its marginal contribution to the production of goods and services.

The neoclassical theory of distribution is widely accepted. Most economists begin with the neoclassical theory when trying to explain how the U.S. economy's $16 trillion of income is distributed among the economy's various members. In the following two chapters, we consider the distribution of income in more detail. As you will see, the neoclassical theory provides the framework for this discussion.

Even at this point, you can use the theory to answer the question that began this chapter: Why are computer programmers paid more than gas station attendants? It is because programmers can produce a good of greater market value than can gas station attendants. People are willing to pay dearly for a good computer game, but they are willing to pay little to have their gas pumped and their windshield washed. The wages of these workers reflect the market prices of the goods they produce. If people suddenly got tired of using computers and decided to spend more time driving, the prices of these goods would change, and so would the equilibrium wages of these two groups of workers.

CHAPTER QuickQuiz

1. Approximately what percentage of U.S. national income is paid to workers, as opposed to owners of capital and land?
   a. 25 percent
   b. 45 percent
   c. 65 percent
   d. 85 percent
2. If firms are competitive and profit-maximizing, the demand curve for labor is determined by
   a. the opportunity cost of workers' time.
   b. the value of the marginal product of labor.
   c. offsetting income and substitution effects.
   d. the value of the marginal product of capital.
3. A bakery operating in competitive markets sells its output for $20 per cake and hires labor at $10 per hour. To maximize profit, it should hire labor until the marginal product of labor is
   a. 1/2 cake per hour.
   b. 2 cakes per hour.
   c. 10 cakes per hour.
   d. 15 cakes per hour.
4. A technological advance that increases the marginal product of labor shifts the labor-________ curve to the ________.
   a. demand, left
   b. demand, right
   c. supply, left
   d. supply, right

5. Around 1973, the U.S. economy experienced a significant ________ in productivity growth, coupled with a(n) ________ in the growth of real wages.
   a. acceleration, acceleration
   b. acceleration, slowdown
   c. slowdown, acceleration
   d. slowdown, slowdown

6. A storm destroys several factories, thereby reducing the stock of capital. What effect does this event have on factor markets?
   a. Wages and the rental price of capital both rise.
   b. Wages and the rental price of capital both fall.
   c. Wages rise and the rental price of capital falls.
   d. Wages fall and the rental price of capital rises.

SUMMARY

- The economy's income is distributed in the markets for the factors of production. The three most important factors of production are labor, land, and capital.
- The demand for factors, such as labor, is a derived demand that comes from firms that use the factors to produce goods and services. Competitive, profit-maximizing firms hire each factor up to the point at which the value of the factor's marginal product equals its price.
- The supply of labor arises from individuals' trade-off between work and leisure. An upward-sloping labor-supply curve means that people respond to an increase in the wage by working more hours and enjoying less leisure.
- The price paid to each factor adjusts to balance the supply and demand for that factor. Because factor demand reflects the value of the marginal product of that factor, in equilibrium each factor is compensated according to its marginal contribution to the production of goods and services.
- Because factors of production are used together, the marginal product of any one factor depends on the quantities of all factors that are available. As a result, a change in the supply of one factor alters the equilibrium earnings of all the factors.

KEY CONCEPTS

factors of production, p. 362
production function, p. 364
marginal product of labor, p. 364
diminishing marginal product, p. 364
value of the marginal product, p. 365
capital, p. 375

QUESTIONS FOR REVIEW

1. Explain how a firm's production function is related to its marginal product of labor, how a firm's marginal product of labor is related to the value of its marginal product, and how a firm's value of marginal product is related to its demand for labor.
2. Give two examples of events that could shift the demand for labor, and explain why they do so.
3. Give two examples of events that could shift the supply of labor, and explain why they do so.
4. Explain how the wage can adjust to balance the supply and demand for labor while simultaneously equaling the value of the marginal product of labor.
5. If the population of the United States suddenly grew because of a large wave of immigration, what would happen to wages? What would happen to the rents earned by the owners of land and capital?

PROBLEMS AND APPLICATIONS

1. Suppose that the president proposes a new law aimed at reducing healthcare costs: All Americans are required to eat one apple daily.
   a. How would this apple-a-day law affect the demand and equilibrium price of apples?
   b. How would the law affect the marginal product and the value of the marginal product of apple pickers?
   c. How would the law affect the demand and equilibrium wage for apple pickers?
2. Show the effect of each of the following events on the market for labor in the computer manufacturing industry.
   a. Congress buys personal computers for all U.S. college students.
   b. More college students major in engineering and computer science.
   c. Computer firms build new manufacturing plants.
3. Suppose that labor is the only input used by a perfectly competitive firm. The firm's production function is as follows:

Days of Labor	Units of Output
0 days	0 units
1	7
2	13
3	19
4	25
5	28
6	29
7	29

   a. Calculate the marginal product for each additional worker.
   b. Each unit of output sells for $10. Calculate the value of the marginal product of each worker.
   c. Compute the demand schedule showing the number of workers hired for all wages from zero to $100 a day.
   d. Graph the firm's demand curve.
   e. What happens to this demand curve if the price of output rises from $10 to $12 per unit?
4. Smiling Cow Dairy can sell all the milk it wants for $4 a gallon, and it can rent all the robots it wants to milk the cows at a capital rental price of $100 a day. It faces the following production schedule:

Number of Robots	Total Product
0	0 gallons
1	50
2	85
3	115
4	140
5	150
6	155

   a. In what kind of market structure does the firm sell its output? How can you tell?
   b. In what kind of market structure does the firm rent robots? How can you tell?
   c. Calculate the marginal product and the value of the marginal product for each additional robot.
   d. How many robots should the firm rent? Explain.
5. The nation of Ectenia has 20 competitive apple orchards, all of which sell apples at the world price of $2 per apple. The following equations describe the production function and the marginal product of labor in each orchard:

$$Q = 100L - L^2$$
$$MPL = 100 - 2L,$$

where Q is the number of apples produced in a day, L is the number of workers, and MPL is the marginal product of labor.
   a. What is each orchard's labor demand as a function of the daily wage W? What is the market's labor demand?
   b. Ectenia has 200 workers who supply their labor inelastically. Solve for the wage W. How many workers does each orchard hire? How much profit does each orchard owner make?
   c. Calculate what happens to the income of workers and orchard owners if the world price doubles to $4 per apple.
   d. Now suppose the price is back at $2 per apple, but a hurricane destroys half the orchards. Calculate how the hurricane affects the income of each worker and of each remaining orchard owner. What happens to the income of Ectenia as a whole?

6. Your enterprising uncle opens a sandwich shop that employs 7 people. The employees are paid $12 per hour, and a sandwich sells for $6. If your uncle is maximizing his profit, what is the value of the marginal product of the last worker he hired? What is that worker's marginal product?
7. Leadbelly Co. sells pencils in a perfectly competitive product market and hires workers in a perfectly competitive labor market. Assume that the market wage rate for workers is $150 per day.
   a. What rule should Leadbelly follow to hire the profit-maximizing amount of labor?
   b. At the profit-maximizing level of output, the marginal product of the last worker hired is 30 boxes of pencils per day. Calculate the price of a box of pencils.
   c. Draw a diagram of the labor market for pencil workers (as in Figure 4 of this chapter) next to a diagram of the labor supply and demand for Leadbelly Co. (as in Figure 3). Label the equilibrium wage and quantity of labor for both the market and the firm. How are these diagrams related?
   d. Suppose some pencil workers switch to jobs in the growing computer industry. On the side-by-side diagrams from part (c), show how this change affects the equilibrium wage and quantity of labor for both the pencil market and for Leadbelly. How does this change affect the marginal product of labor at Leadbelly?
8. Policymakers sometimes propose laws requiring firms to give workers certain fringe benefits, such as health insurance or paid parental leave. Let's consider the effects of such a policy on the labor market.
   a. Suppose that a law required firms to give each worker $3 of fringe benefits for every hour that the worker is employed by the firm. How does this law affect the marginal profit that a firm earns from each worker at a given cash wage? How does the law affect the demand curve for labor? Draw your answer on a graph with the cash wage on the vertical axis.
   b. If there is no change in labor supply, how would this law affect employment and wages?
   c. Why might the labor-supply curve shift in response to this law? Would this shift in labor supply raise or lower the impact of the law on wages and employment?
   d. As discussed in Chapter 6, the wages of some workers, particularly the unskilled and inexperienced, are kept above the equilibrium level by minimum-wage laws. What effect would a fringe-benefit mandate have for these workers?
9. Some economists believe that the U.S. economy as a whole can be modeled with the following production function, called the *Cobb–Douglas production function*:

$$Y = AK^{1/3}L^{2/3},$$

   where Y is the amount of output, K is the amount of capital, L is the amount of labor, and A is a parameter that measures the state of technology. For this production function, the marginal product of labor is

$$MPL = (2/3)\, A(K/L)^{1/3}.$$

   Suppose that the price of output P is 2, A is 3, K is 1,000,000, and L is 1,000. The labor market is competitive, so labor is paid the value of its marginal product.
   a. Calculate the amount of output produced Y and the dollar value of output PY.
   b. Calculate the wage W and the real wage W/P. (Note: The wage is labor compensation measured in dollars, whereas the real wage is labor compensation measured in units of output.)
   c. Calculate the labor share (the fraction of the value of output that is paid to labor), which is $(WL)/(PY)$.
   d. Calculate what happens to output Y, the wage W, the real wage W/P, and the labor share $(WL)/(PY)$ in each of the following scenarios:
      i. Inflation increases P from 2 to 3.
      ii. Technological progress increases A from 3 to 9.
      iii. Capital accumulation increases K from 1,000,000 to 8,000,000.
      iv. A plague decreases L from 1,000 to 125.
   e. Despite many changes in the U.S. economy over time, the labor share has been relatively stable. Is this observation consistent with the Cobb–Douglas production function? Explain.

To find additional study resources, visit cengagebrain.com, and search for "Mankiw."

CHAPTER

Earnings and Discrimination

19

In the United States today, the typical physician earns about $200,000 a year, the typical police officer about $60,000, and the typical fast-food cook about $20,000. These examples illustrate the large differences in earnings in our economy. These differences explain why some people live in mansions, ride in limousines, and vacation on the French Riviera, while other people live in small apartments, ride the bus, and vacation in their own backyards.

Why do earnings vary so much from person to person? Chapter 18, which developed the basic neoclassical theory of the labor market, offers an answer to this question. There we saw that wages are governed by labor supply and labor demand. Labor demand, in turn, reflects the marginal productivity of labor. In equilibrium, each worker is paid the value of her marginal contribution to the economy's production of goods and services.

This theory of the labor market, though widely accepted by economists, is only the beginning of the story. To understand the wide variation in earnings that we observe, we must go beyond this general framework and examine more precisely what determines the supply and demand for different types of labor. That is our goal in this chapter.

19-1 Some Determinants of Equilibrium Wages

Workers differ from one another in many ways, as do jobs. In this section, we consider how the characteristics of workers and jobs affect labor supply, labor demand, and equilibrium wages.

ROBERT MANKOFF/ THE NEW YORKER COLLECTION/ WWW.CARTOONBANK.COM

"On the one hand, I know I could make more money if I left public service for the private sector, but, on the other hand, I couldn't chop off heads."

compensating differential a difference in wages that arises to offset the nonmonetary characteristics of different jobs

19-1a Compensating Differentials

When a worker is deciding whether to take a job, the wage is only one of many job attributes that the worker takes into account. Some jobs are easy, fun, and safe, while others are hard, dull, and dangerous. The better the job as gauged by these nonmonetary characteristics, the more people there are who are willing to do the job at any given wage. In other words, the supply of labor for easy, fun, and safe jobs is greater than the supply of labor for hard, dull, and dangerous jobs. As a result, "good" jobs will tend to have lower equilibrium wages than "bad" ones.

For example, imagine you are looking for a summer job in a local beach community. Two kinds of jobs are available. You can take a job as a beach-badge checker, or you can take a job as a garbage collector. The beach-badge checkers take leisurely strolls along the beach during the day and check to make sure the tourists have bought the required beach permits. The garbage collectors wake up before dawn to drive dirty, noisy trucks around town to pick up garbage. Which job would you want? If the two jobs paid the same wage, most people would prefer the badge-checker job. To induce people to become garbage collectors, the town has to offer higher wages to garbage collectors than to beach-badge checkers.

Economists use the term **compensating differential** to refer to a difference in wages that arises from nonmonetary characteristics of different jobs. Compensating differentials are prevalent in the economy. Here are some examples:

- Coal miners are paid more than other workers with similar levels of education. Their higher wage compensates them for the dirty and dangerous nature of coal mining, as well as the long-term health problems that coal miners experience.
- Workers who work the night shift at factories are paid more than similar workers who work the day shift. The higher wage compensates them for having to work at night and sleep during the day, a lifestyle that most people find undesirable.
- Professors are paid less than lawyers and doctors, who have similar amounts of education. The higher wages of lawyers and doctors compensate them for missing out on the great intellectual and personal satisfaction that professors' jobs offer. (Indeed, teaching economics is so much fun that it is surprising economics professors are paid anything at all!)

19-1b Human Capital

As we discussed in the previous chapter, the word *capital* usually refers to an economy's stock of equipment and structures. The capital stock includes the farmer's tractor, the manufacturer's factory, and the teacher's chalkboard. The essence of capital is that it is a factor of production that itself has been produced.

There is another type of capital that, while less tangible than physical capital, is just as important to the economy's production. **Human capital** is the accumulation of investments in people. The most important type of human capital is education. Like all forms of capital, education represents an expenditure of resources at one time to raise productivity in the future. But unlike an investment in other forms of capital, an investment in education is tied to a specific person, and this linkage is what makes it human capital.

human capital
the accumulation of investments in people, such as education and on-the-job training

Not surprisingly, workers with more human capital earn more on average than those with less human capital. College graduates in the United States, for example, earn almost twice as much as those with only a high school diploma. This large difference has been documented in many countries around the world. It tends to be even larger in less developed countries, where educated workers are in scarce supply.

From the perspective of supply and demand it is easy to see why education raises wages. Firms—the demanders of labor—are willing to pay more for highly educated workers because these workers have higher marginal products. Workers—the suppliers of labor—are willing to pay the cost of becoming educated only if there is a reward for doing so. In essence, the difference in wages between highly educated workers and less educated workers may be considered a compensating differential for the cost of becoming educated.

CASE STUDY

THE INCREASING VALUE OF SKILLS

"The rich get richer, and the poor get poorer." Like many adages, this one is not always true, but it has been in recent years. Many studies have documented that the earnings gap between workers with high skills and workers with low skills has increased over the past several decades.

Table 1 presents data on the average earnings of college graduates and of high school graduates without any additional education. These data show the increase in the financial reward from education. In 1974, a man on average earned 42 percent more with a college degree than without one; by 2014, this figure had risen to 81 percent. For a woman, the reward for attending college rose from a 35 percent increase in earnings in 1974 to a 71 percent increase in 2014. The incentive to stay in school is as great today as it has ever been.

Why has the gap in earnings between skilled and unskilled workers widened in recent years? No one knows for sure, but economists have proposed two hypotheses to explain this trend. Both hypotheses suggest that the demand for skilled labor has risen over time relative to the demand for unskilled labor. The shift in demand has led to a corresponding change in the wages of both groups, which in turn has led to greater inequality.

TABLE 1

Average Annual Earnings by Educational Attainment
College graduates have always earned more than workers without the benefit of college, but the salary gap has grown even larger over the past few decades.

	1974	2014
Men		
High school, no college	$52,521	$46,688
College graduates	$74,801	$84,567
Percent extra for college grads	+42%	+81%
Women		
High school, no college	$30,185	$34,394
College graduates	$40,831	$58,894
Percent extra for college grads	+35%	+71%

Note: Earnings data are adjusted for inflation and are expressed in 2014 dollars. Data apply to full-time, year-round workers age 18 and over. Data for college graduates exclude workers with additional schooling beyond college, such as a master's degree or Ph.D.

Source: U.S. Census Bureau and author's calculations.

The first hypothesis is that international trade has altered the relative demand for skilled and unskilled labor. In recent years, the amount of trade with other countries has increased substantially. As a percentage of total U.S. production of goods and services, imports have risen from 8 percent in 1974 to 17 percent in 2014, and exports have risen from 8 percent in 1974 to 14 percent in 2014. Because unskilled labor is plentiful and cheap in many foreign countries, the United States tends to import goods produced with unskilled labor and export goods produced with skilled labor. Thus, when international trade expands, the domestic demand for skilled labor rises and the domestic demand for unskilled labor falls.

ASK THE EXPERTS

Inequality and Skills

"One of the leading reasons for rising U.S. income inequality over the past three decades is that technological change has affected workers with some skill sets differently than others."

What do economists say?

Source: IGM Economic Experts Panel, January 24, 2012.

The second hypothesis is that changes in technology have altered the relative demand for skilled and unskilled labor. Consider, for instance, the introduction of computers. Computers raise the demand for the skilled workers who can use them and reduce the demand for the unskilled workers whose jobs are replaced by them. For example, many companies now rely more on computer databases, and less on filing cabinets, to keep business records. This change raises the demand for computer programmers and reduces the demand for filing clerks. Thus, as more firms use computers, the demand for skilled labor rises and the demand for unskilled labor falls. Economists call this phenomenon *skill-biased technological change.*

Economists debate the importance of trade, technology, and other forces on the changing distribution of wages. There is likely not a single answer as to why income inequality has increased. Increasing international trade and skill-biased technological change may share responsibility for the changes we have observed in recent decades. In the next chapter, we discuss the issue of increasing inequality in more detail. ●

IN THE NEWS

Schooling as a Public Investment

An economist makes the case for increased spending.

Throw More Money at Education

By Noah Smith

It's become almost conventional wisdom that throwing more money at public education doesn't produce results. But what if conventional wisdom is wrong?

A new paper from economists C. Kirabo Jackson, Rucker Johnson and Claudia Persico suggests that it is. To disentangle correlation from causation, they look at periods from 1955 through 1985 when courts ordered governments to spend more on schools, from kindergarten through 12th grade. They then track how students in those areas did, up through 2011. The result is a very detailed long-term picture of the effect of spending more money on education.

The economists find that spending works. Specifically, they find that a 10 percent increase in spending, on average, leads children to complete 0.27 more years of school, to make wages that are 7.25 percent higher and to have a substantially reduced chance of falling into poverty. These are long-term, durable results. Conclusion: throwing money at the problem works.

Here's the hitch: The authors find that the benefits of increased spending are much stronger for poor kids than for wealthier ones. So if you, like me, are in the upper portion of the U.S. income distribution, you may be reading this and thinking: "Why should I be paying more for some poor kid to be educated?" After all, why should one person pay the cost while another reaps the benefits?

Well, let me try to answer that. There are several good reasons.

First, if you're an upper-income American, you probably do derive some direct benefit. When poor Americans become better workers, it doesn't just boost their wages. It also boosts the profitability of the companies where they work. If you own stock in such a company (and I hope you do), the value of those shares will go up if American worker productivity increases.

There might be even bigger, though less direct, effects from having a more-educated populace. The more industries can use U.S. workers instead of Chinese workers, the more industries will base their production in the U.S. This will feed local economies, boosting the profits of stores and other service businesses. That also feeds into your stock portfolio.

If you own your own business, you might need to hire some low-income people. If those people are better readers, better at doing simple math, more efficient at everyday tasks, and just more productive in general, that cuts down on the time and money you need to spend fixing their mistakes.

Next, having more educated poor people makes for a better civil society. Suppose you live in, say, Chicago, or some other city that hasn't enjoyed as big a drop in crime as New York or Los Angeles. I bet you don't enjoy having to worry about driving or walking through unsafe neighborhoods. I also bet you would like to walk around downtown without fear of getting mugged. It might also be nice not to have to live behind the isolating walls of a gated community.

One way to reduce crime, of course, is to pay for more police and increase incarceration rates. But another way is to improve education. Economists Lance Lochner and Enrico Moretti found in 2003 that education decreases crime. An educated populace is a well-socialized populace. There is also the fact that better education leads to higher wages for poor people, reducing the incentive for them to engage in crime.

At the risk of sounding grandiose, let me go even further: Education is really the difference between a cohesive society and a collection of people who happen to live next to each other. This was understood well by Fukuzawa Yukichi, Japan's version of Ben Franklin. After Japan opened up to the West in the mid-1800s, Fukuzawa volunteered for Japan's first diplomatic mission to the U.S. He returned convinced that universal education was the key to transforming Japan into the equal of the Western nations. His ideas were influential, and Japan to this day has one of the world's best education systems.

Detractors of our public education system point out that the U.S. already spends as much on public education as many other developed countries—5.5 percent of gross domestic product, compared with only 3.5 percent in Japan, 4.9 percent in Canada, 5 percent in South Korea and 5.9 percent in Finland. Many view increased education spending as a giveaway to powerful and greedy teachers' unions.

But maybe the U.S. spends more because it *needs* to spend more. The U.S. has more inequality and more poor people than those countries. Just as some countries naturally need to spend more on health care than others, the U.S. might naturally need more education spending.

The argument for more education spending, of course, isn't at odds with the need to make our schools more efficient. Education-reform movements such as charter schools—which are also effective mainly for poor kids—don't clash with the idea of higher spending. We can do both, and each may help the other.

So this is one problem the U.S. really should consider throwing more money at. ■

Mr. Smith is an economics professor at Stony Brook University.

Source: *Bloomberg View*, January 23, 2015.

19-1c Ability, Effort, and Chance

Why do major league baseball players get paid more than minor league players? Certainly, the higher wage is not a compensating differential. Playing in the major leagues is not a less pleasant job than playing in the minor leagues; in fact, the opposite is true. The major leagues do not require more years of schooling or more experience. To a large extent, players in the major leagues earn more because they have greater natural ability.

Natural ability is important for workers in all occupations. Because of heredity and upbringing, people differ in their physical and mental attributes. Some people are strong, others weak. Some people are smart, others less so. Some people are outgoing, others awkward in social situations. These and many other personal characteristics determine how productive workers are and, therefore, play a role in determining the wages they earn.

Closely related to ability is effort. Some people work hard; others are lazy. We should not be surprised to find that those who work hard are more productive and earn higher wages. To some extent, firms reward hard work directly by paying people based on what they produce. Salespeople, for instance, are often paid a percentage of the sales they make. At other times, hard work is rewarded less directly in the form of a higher annual salary or a bonus.

Chance also plays a role in determining wages. If a person attended a trade school to learn how to repair televisions with vacuum tubes and then found this skill made obsolete by the invention of solid-state electronics, she would end up earning a low wage compared to others with similar years of training. The low wage of this worker is due to chance—a phenomenon that economists recognize but do not shed much light on.

How important are ability, effort, and chance in determining wages? It is hard to say because these factors are difficult to measure. But indirect evidence suggests that they are very important. When labor economists study wages, they relate a worker's wage to those variables that can be measured, such as years of schooling, years of experience, age, and job characteristics. All of these measured variables affect a worker's wage as theory predicts, but they account for less than half of the variation in wages in our economy. Because so much of the variation in wages is left unexplained, omitted variables—including ability, effort, and chance— must play an important role.

CASE STUDY

THE BENEFITS OF BEAUTY

People differ in many ways, one of which is physical attractiveness. The actress Emma Stone, for instance, is a beautiful woman. In part for this reason, her movies attract large audiences. Not surprisingly, the large audiences mean a large income for Ms. Stone.

How prevalent are the economic benefits of beauty? Labor economists Daniel Hamermesh and Jeff Biddle tried to answer this question in a study published in the December 1994 issue of the *American Economic Review.* Hamermesh and Biddle examined data from surveys of individuals in the United States and Canada. The interviewers who conducted the survey were asked to rate each respondent's physical appearance. Hamermesh and Biddle then examined how much the wages of the respondents depended on the standard determinants—education, experience, and so on—and how much they depended on physical appearance.

Hamermesh and Biddle found that beauty pays. People who are deemed more attractive than average earn 5 percent more than people of average looks, and people of average looks earn 5 to 10 percent more than people considered less attractive than average. Similar results were found for men and women.

What explains these differences in wages? There are several ways to interpret the "beauty premium."

One interpretation is that good looks are a type of innate ability determining productivity and wages. Some people are born with the physical attributes of a movie star; other people are not. Good looks are useful in any job in which workers present themselves to the public—such as acting, sales, and waiting on tables. In this case, an attractive worker is more valuable to the firm than an unattractive worker. The firm's willingness to pay more to attractive workers reflects its customers' preferences.

A second interpretation is that reported beauty is an indirect measure of other types of ability. How attractive a person appears depends on more than just heredity. It also depends on dress, hairstyle, personal demeanor, and other attributes that a person can control. Perhaps a person who successfully projects an attractive image in a survey interview is more likely to be an intelligent person who succeeds at other tasks as well.

A third interpretation is that the beauty premium is a type of discrimination, a topic to which we return later. ●

JENNA BLAKE/CORBIS

Good looks pay.

19-1d An Alternative View of Education: Signaling

Earlier we discussed the human-capital view of education, according to which schooling raises workers' wages because it makes them more productive. Although this view is widely accepted, some economists have proposed an alternative theory, which emphasizes that firms use educational attainment as a way of sorting between high-ability and low-ability workers. According to this alternative view, when people earn a college degree, for instance, they do not become more productive, but they do *signal* their high ability to prospective employers. Because it is easier for high-ability people to earn a college degree than it is for low-ability people, more high-ability people get college degrees. As a result, it is rational for firms to interpret a college degree as a signal of ability.

The signaling theory of education is similar to the signaling theory of advertising discussed in Chapter 16. In the signaling theory of advertising, the advertisement itself contains no real information, but the firm signals the quality of its product to consumers by its willingness to spend money on advertising. In the signaling theory of education, schooling has no real productivity benefit, but the worker signals her innate productivity to employers by her willingness to spend years at school. In both cases, an action is being taken not for its intrinsic benefit but because the willingness to take that action conveys private information to someone observing it.

Thus, we now have two views of education: the human-capital theory and the signaling theory. Both views can explain why more educated workers tend to earn more than less educated ones. According to the human-capital view, education makes workers more productive; according to the signaling view, education is correlated with natural ability. But the two views have radically different predictions for the effects of policies that aim to increase educational attainment. According to the human-capital view, increasing educational levels for all workers would raise all workers' productivity and thereby their wages. According to the signaling view, education does not enhance productivity, so raising all workers' educational levels would not affect wages.

Most likely, the truth lies somewhere between these two extremes. The benefits of education are probably a combination of the productivity-enhancing effects of human capital and the productivity-revealing effects of signaling. The relative size of these two effects is an open question.

19-1e The Superstar Phenomenon

Although most actors earn little and often take jobs as waiters to support themselves, Robert Downey, Jr., earns millions of dollars for each film he makes. Similarly, while most people who play tennis do it as a hobby, Maria Sharapova earns millions on the pro tour. Downey and Sharapova are superstars in their fields, and their great public appeal is reflected in astronomical incomes.

Why do Downey and Sharapova earn so much? It is not surprising that incomes differ within occupations. Good carpenters earn more than mediocre carpenters, and good plumbers earn more than mediocre plumbers. People vary in ability and effort, and these differences lead to differences in income. Yet the best carpenters and plumbers do not earn the many millions that are common among the best actors and athletes. What explains the difference?

To understand the tremendous incomes of Downey and Sharapova, we must examine the special features of the markets in which they sell their services. Superstars arise in markets that have two characteristics:

- Every customer in the market wants to enjoy the good supplied by the best producer.
- The good is produced with a technology that makes it possible for the best producer to supply every customer at low cost.

If Robert Downey, Jr., is the best actor around, then everyone will want to see his next movie; seeing twice as many movies by an actor half as talented is not a good substitute. Moreover, it is *possible* for everyone to enjoy a performance by Robert Downey, Jr. Because it is easy to make multiple copies of a film, Downey can provide his service to millions of people simultaneously. Similarly, because tennis matches are broadcast on television, millions of fans can enjoy the extraordinary athletic skills of Maria Sharapova.

We can now see why there are no superstar carpenters and plumbers. Other things being equal, everyone prefers to employ the best carpenter, but a carpenter, unlike a movie actor, can provide her services to only a limited number of customers. Although the best carpenter will be able to command a somewhat higher wage than the average carpenter, the average carpenter will still be able to earn a good living.

19-1f Above-Equilibrium Wages: Minimum-Wage Laws, Unions, and Efficiency Wages

Most analyses of wage differences among workers are based on the equilibrium model of the labor market—that is, wages are assumed to adjust to balance labor supply and labor demand. But this assumption does not always apply. For some workers, wages are set above the level that brings supply and demand into equilibrium. Let's consider three reasons this might be so.

One reason for above-equilibrium wages is minimum-wage laws, as we first saw in Chapter 6. Most workers in the economy are not affected by these laws because their equilibrium wages are well above the legal minimum. But for some workers, especially the least skilled and experienced, minimum-wage laws raise wages above the level they would earn in an unregulated labor market.

A second reason that wages might rise above their equilibrium level is the market power of labor unions. A **union** is a worker association that bargains with employers over wages and working conditions. Unions often raise wages above the level that would prevail in their absence, perhaps because they can threaten to withhold labor from the firm by calling a **strike.** Studies suggest that union workers earn about 10 to 20 percent more than similar, nonunion workers.

union
a worker association that bargains with employers over wages and working conditions

strike
the organized withdrawal of labor from a firm by a union

A third reason for above-equilibrium wages is based on the theory of **efficiency wages.** This theory holds that a firm can find it profitable to pay high wages because doing so increases the productivity of its workers. In particular, high wages may reduce worker turnover, increase worker effort, and raise the quality of workers who apply for jobs at the firm. If this theory is correct, then some firms may choose to pay their workers more than they would normally earn.

efficiency wages
above-equilibrium wages paid by firms to increase worker productivity

Above-equilibrium wages, whether caused by minimum-wage laws, unions, or efficiency wages, have similar effects on the labor market. In particular, pushing a wage above the equilibrium level raises the quantity of labor supplied and reduces the quantity of labor demanded. The result is a surplus of labor, or unemployment. The study of unemployment and the public policies aimed to deal with it is usually considered a topic within macroeconomics, so it goes beyond the scope of this chapter. But it would be a mistake to ignore these issues completely when analyzing earnings. Although most wage differences can be understood while maintaining the assumption of equilibrium in the labor market, above-equilibrium wages play a role in some cases.

QuickQuiz *Define* compensating differential *and give an example. • Give two reasons why more educated workers earn more than less educated workers.*

19-2 The Economics of Discrimination

Another source of differences in wages is discrimination. **Discrimination** occurs when the marketplace offers different opportunities to similar individuals who differ only by race, ethnic group, sex, age, or other personal characteristics. Discrimination reflects some people's prejudice against certain groups in society. Discrimination is an emotionally charged topic that often generates heated debate, but economists try to study the topic objectively to separate myth from reality.

discrimination
the offering of different opportunities to similar individuals who differ only by race, ethnic group, sex, age, or other personal characteristics

19-2a Measuring Labor-Market Discrimination

How much does discrimination in labor markets affect the earnings of different groups of workers? This question is important, but answering it is not easy.

There is no doubt that different groups of workers earn substantially different wages, as Table 2 demonstrates. The median black man in the United States is paid 20 percent less than the median white man, and the median black woman is paid 17 percent less than the median white woman. The differences by sex are also significant. The median white woman is paid 21 percent less than the median white man, and the median black woman is paid 18 percent less than the median

TABLE 2

Median Annual Earnings by Race and Sex

	White	Black	Percent by Which Earnings Are Lower for Black Workers
Men	$51,022	$40,719	20%
Women	$40,439	$33,533	17%
Percent by Which Earnings Are Lower for Women Workers	21%	18%	

Note: Earnings data are for the year 2014 and apply to full-time, year-round workers aged 14 and over. Individuals who report more than one race are excluded from these data.

Source: U.S. Census Bureau.

black man. Taken at face value, these differentials look like evidence that employers discriminate against blacks and women.

Yet there is a potential problem with this inference. Even in a labor market free of discrimination, different people have different wages. People differ in the amount of human capital they have and in the kinds of work they are able and willing to do. The wage differences we observe in an economy are, to some extent, attributable to the determinants of equilibrium wages we discussed in the preceding section. Simply observing differences in wages among broad groups—whites and blacks, men and women—does not prove that employers discriminate.

Consider, for example, the role of human capital. In 2014, among men aged 25 and older, 32 percent of the white population had a college degree, compared with 20 percent of the black population. Among women aged 25 and older, 32 percent of the white population had a college degree, compared with 24 percent of the black population. Thus, at least some of the difference between the wages of whites and the wages of blacks can be traced to differences in educational attainment.

Moreover, human capital may be more important in explaining wage differentials than years of schooling suggest. Historically, public schools in predominantly black areas have been of lower quality—as measured by expenditure, class size, and so on—than public schools in predominantly white areas. If we could measure the quality as well as the quantity of education, the differences in human capital among these groups would appear even larger.

Human capital acquired in the form of job experience can also help explain wage differences. In particular, women are more likely to interrupt their careers to raise children. Among the population aged 25 to 44 (when many people have children at home), only about 75 percent of women are in the labor force, compared to about 90 percent of men. As a result, female workers, especially at older ages, tend to have less job experience than male workers.

Yet another source of wage differences is compensating differentials. Men and women do not always choose the same type of work, and this fact may help explain some of the earnings differential between men and women. For example, women are more likely to be secretaries, and men are more likely to be truck drivers. The relative wages of secretaries and truck drivers depend in part on the working conditions of each job. Because these nonmonetary aspects are hard to measure, it is difficult to gauge the practical importance of compensating differentials in explaining the wage differences that we observe.

In the end, the study of wage differences among groups does not establish any clear conclusion about the prevalence of discrimination in U.S. labor markets. Most economists believe that some of the observed wage differentials are attributable to discrimination, but there is no consensus about how much. The only conclusion about which economists are in consensus is a negative one: Because the differences in average wages among groups in part reflect differences in human capital and job characteristics, they do not by themselves say anything about how much discrimination there is in the labor market.

Of course, differences in human capital among groups of workers may also reflect a kind of discrimination. The less rigorous curriculums historically offered to female students, for instance, can be considered a discriminatory practice. Similarly, the inferior schools historically available to black students may be traced to prejudice on the part of city councils and school boards. But this kind of discrimination occurs long before the worker enters the labor market. In this case, the disease is political, even if the symptom is economic.

CASE STUDY

IS EMILY MORE EMPLOYABLE THAN LAKISHA?

Although measuring the extent of discrimination from labor-market outcomes is hard, some compelling evidence for the existence of such discrimination comes from a creative "field experiment." Economists Marianne Bertrand and Sendhil Mullainathan answered more than 1,300 help-wanted ads run in Boston and Chicago newspapers by sending in nearly 5,000 fake résumés. Half of the résumés had names that were common in the African-American community, such as Lakisha Washington or Jamal Jones. The other half had names that were more common among the white population, such as Emily Walsh and Greg Baker. Otherwise, the résumés were similar. The results of this experiment were published in the *American Economic Review* in September 2004.

The researchers found large differences in how employers responded to the two groups of résumés. Job applicants with white names received about 50 percent more calls from interested employers than applicants with African-American names. The study found that this discrimination occurred for all types of employers, including those who claimed to be an "Equal Opportunity Employer" in their help-wanted ads. The researchers concluded that "racial discrimination is still a prominent feature of the labor market." ●

19-2b Discrimination by Employers

Let's now turn from measurement to the economic forces that lie behind discrimination in labor markets. If one group in society receives a lower wage than another group, even after controlling for human capital and job characteristics, who is to blame for this differential?

The answer is not obvious. It might seem natural to blame employers for discriminatory wage differences. After all, employers make the hiring decisions that determine labor demand and wages. If some groups of workers earn lower wages than they should, then it seems that employers are responsible. Yet many economists are skeptical of this easy answer. They believe that competitive, market economies provide a natural antidote to employer discrimination. That antidote is called the profit motive.

Imagine an economy in which workers are differentiated by their hair color. Blondes and brunettes have the same skills, experience, and work ethic. Yet because of discrimination, employers prefer to hire workers with brunette hair. Thus, the demand for blondes is lower than it otherwise would be. As a result, blondes earn a lower wage than brunettes.

How long can this wage differential persist? In this economy, there is an easy way for a firm to beat out its competitors: It can hire blonde workers. By hiring blondes, a firm pays lower wages and thus has lower costs than firms that hire brunettes. Over time, more and more "blonde" firms enter the market to take advantage of this cost advantage. The existing "brunette" firms have higher costs and, therefore, begin to lose money when faced with the new competitors. These losses induce the brunette firms to go out of business. Eventually, the entry of blonde firms and the exit of brunette firms cause the demand for blonde workers to rise and the demand for brunette workers to fall. This process continues until the wage differential disappears.

Put simply, business owners who care only about making money are at an advantage when competing against those who also care about discriminating. As a result, firms that do not discriminate tend to replace those that do. In this way, competitive markets have a natural remedy for employer discrimination.

CASE STUDY

SEGREGATED STREETCARS AND THE PROFIT MOTIVE

In the early 20th century, streetcars in many southern cities were segregated by race. White passengers sat in the front of the streetcars, and black passengers sat in the back. What do you suppose caused and maintained this discriminatory practice? And how was this practice viewed by the firms that ran the streetcars?

In a 1986 article in the *Journal of Economic History*, economic historian Jennifer Roback looked at these questions. Roback found that the segregation of races on streetcars was the result of laws that required such segregation. Before these laws were passed, racial discrimination in seating was rare. It was far more common to segregate smokers and nonsmokers.

Moreover, the firms that ran the streetcars often opposed the laws requiring racial segregation. Providing separate seating for different races raised the firms' costs and reduced their profits. One railroad company manager complained to the city council that, under the segregation laws, "the company has to haul around a good deal of empty space."

Here is how Roback describes the situation in one southern city:

> The railroad company did not initiate the segregation policy and was not at all eager to abide by it. State legislation, public agitation, and a threat to arrest the president of the railroad were all required to induce them to separate the races on their cars. . . . There is no indication that the management was motivated by belief in civil rights or racial equality. The evidence indicates their primary motives were economic; separation was costly. . . . Officials of the company may or may not have disliked blacks, but they were not willing to forgo the profits necessary to indulge such prejudice.

The story of southern streetcars illustrates a general lesson: Business owners are usually more interested in making profits than in discriminating against a particular group. When firms engage in discriminatory practices, the ultimate source of the discrimination often lies not with the firms themselves but elsewhere. In this particular case, the streetcar companies segregated whites and blacks because discriminatory laws, which the companies opposed, required them to do so. ●

19-2c Discrimination by Customers and Governments

The profit motive is a strong force acting to eliminate discriminatory wage differentials, but there are limits to its corrective abilities. Two important limiting factors are customer preferences and government policies.

To see how customer preferences for discrimination can affect wages, consider again our imaginary economy with blondes and brunettes. Suppose that restaurant owners discriminate against blondes when hiring waiters. As a result, blonde waiters earn lower wages than brunette waiters. In this case, a restaurant can open up with blonde waiters and charge lower prices. If customers care only about the quality and price of their meals, the discriminatory firms will be driven out of business, and the wage differential will disappear.

On the other hand, it is possible that customers prefer being served by brunette waiters. If this discriminatory preference is strong, the entry of blonde restaurants need not succeed in eliminating the wage differential between brunettes and blondes. That is, if customers have discriminatory preferences, a competitive market is consistent with a discriminatory wage differential. An economy with such discrimination would contain two types of restaurants. Blonde restaurants would hire blondes, have lower costs, and charge lower prices. Brunette restaurants would hire brunettes, have higher costs, and charge higher prices. Customers who did not care about the hair color of their waiters would be attracted to the lower prices at the blonde restaurants. Bigoted customers would go to the brunette restaurants and would pay for their discriminatory preference in the form of higher prices.

Another way for discrimination to persist in competitive markets is for the government to mandate discriminatory practices. If, for instance, the government passed a law stating that blondes could wash dishes in restaurants but could not work as waiters, then a wage differential could persist in a competitive market. The example of segregated streetcars in the previous case study is one example of government-mandated discrimination. Similarly, before South Africa abandoned its formal policy of racial segregation called apartheid in 1990, blacks were prohibited from working in some jobs. Discriminatory governments pass such laws to suppress the normal equalizing force of free and competitive markets.

To sum up: *Competitive markets contain a natural remedy for employer discrimination. The entry of firms that care only about profit tends to eliminate discriminatory wage differentials. These wage differentials persist in competitive markets only when customers are willing to pay to maintain the discriminatory practice or when the government mandates it.*

CASE STUDY

DISCRIMINATION IN SPORTS

As we have seen, measuring discrimination is often difficult. To determine whether one group of workers is discriminated against, a researcher must correct for differences in the productivity between that group and other workers in the economy. Yet in most firms, it is difficult to measure a particular worker's contribution to the production of goods and services.

One type of firm in which such measurements are easier is the sports team. Professional teams have many objective measures of productivity. In baseball, for instance, we can measure a player's batting average, the frequency of home runs, the number of stolen bases, and so on.

Studies of sports teams suggest that racial discrimination has, in fact, been common and that much of the blame lies with customers. One study, published in the *Journal of Labor Economics* in 1988, examined the salaries of basketball players and found that black players earned 20 percent less than white players of comparable ability. The study also found that attendance at basketball games was larger for teams with a greater proportion of white players. One interpretation of these facts is that, at least at the time of the study, customer discrimination made black players less profitable than white players for team owners. In the presence of such customer discrimination, a discriminatory wage gap can persist, even if team owners care only about profit.

A similar situation once existed for baseball players. A study using data from the late 1960s showed that black players earned less than comparable white players. Moreover, fewer fans attended games pitched by blacks than games pitched by whites, even though black pitchers had better records than white pitchers. Studies of more recent salaries in baseball, however, have found no evidence of discriminatory wage differentials.

Another study, published in the *Quarterly Journal of Economics* in 1990, examined the market prices of old baseball cards. This study found similar evidence of discrimination. The cards of black hitters sold for 10 percent less than the cards of comparable white hitters, and the cards of black pitchers sold for 13 percent less than the cards of comparable white pitchers. These results suggest customer discrimination among baseball fans. ●

QuickQuiz *Why is it hard to establish whether a group of workers is being discriminated against? • Explain how profit-maximizing firms tend to eliminate discriminatory wage differentials. • How might a discriminatory wage differential persist?*

19-3 Conclusion

In competitive markets, workers earn a wage equal to the value of their marginal contribution to the production of goods and services. There are, however, many things that affect the value of the marginal product. Firms pay more for workers who are more talented, more diligent, more experienced, and more educated because these workers are more productive. Firms pay less to those workers against whom customers discriminate because these workers contribute less to revenue.

The theory of the labor market we have developed in the last two chapters explains why some workers earn higher wages than other workers. The theory does not say that the resulting distribution of income is equal, fair, or desirable in any way. That is the topic we take up in Chapter 20.

CHAPTER QuickQuiz

1. Ted leaves his job as a high school math teacher and returns to school to study the latest developments in computer programming, after which he takes a higher-paying job at a software firm. This is an example of
   a. a compensating differential.
   b. human capital.
   c. signaling.
   d. efficiency wages.
2. Marshall and Lily work at a local department store. Marshall, who greets customers as they arrive, is paid less than Lily, who cleans the bathrooms. This is an example of
   a. a compensating differential.
   b. human capital.
   c. signaling.
   d. efficiency wages.
3. Barney runs a small manufacturing company. He pays his employees about twice as much as other firms in the area, even though he could pay less and still recruit all the workers he wants. He believes that higher wages make his workers more loyal and hard-working. This is an example of
   a. a compensating differential.
   b. human capital.
   c. signaling.
   d. efficiency wages.
4. A business consulting firm hires Robin because she was a math major in college. Her new job does not require any of the mathematics she learned, but the firm believes that anyone who can graduate with a math degree must be very smart. This is an example of
   a. a compensating differential.
   b. human capital.
   c. signaling.
   d. efficiency wages.
5. Measuring to what extent discrimination affects labor market outcomes is difficult because
   a. data on wages are crucial but not readily available.
   b. firms misreport the wages they pay to hide discriminatory practices.
   c. workers differ in their attributes and the types of jobs they have.
   d. the same minimum-wage law applies to workers in all groups.
6. The forces of competition in markets with free entry and exit tend to eliminate wage differentials that arise from discrimination by
   a. employers.
   b. customers.
   c. government.
   d. all of the above.

SUMMARY

- Workers earn different wages for many reasons. One reason is that wage differentials play a role compensating workers for job attributes. Other things being equal, workers in hard, unpleasant jobs are paid more than workers in easy, pleasant jobs.
- Workers with more human capital are paid more than workers with less human capital. The return to accumulating human capital is high and has increased over the past several decades.
- Although years of education, experience, and job characteristics affect earnings as theory predicts, much variation in earnings cannot be explained by things that economists can easily measure. The unexplained variation in earnings is largely attributable to natural ability, effort, and chance.
- Some economists have suggested that more educated workers earn higher wages not because education raises productivity but because workers with high natural ability use education as a way to signal their high ability to employers. If this signaling theory is correct, then increasing the educational attainment of all workers would not raise the overall level of wages.
- Wages are sometimes pushed above the level that brings supply and demand into balance. Three explanations of above-equilibrium wages are minimum-wage laws, unions, and efficiency wages.
- Some differences in earnings are attributable to discrimination based on race, sex, or other factors. Measuring the amount of discrimination is difficult, however, because one must correct for differences in human capital and job characteristics.

- Competitive markets tend to limit the impact of discrimination on wages. If the wages of a group of workers are lower than those of another group for reasons not related to marginal productivity, then nondiscriminatory firms will be more profitable than discriminatory firms. Profit-maximizing behavior, therefore, can reduce discriminatory wage differentials. Discrimination persists in competitive markets, however, if customers are willing to pay more to discriminatory firms or if the government passes laws requiring firms to discriminate.

KEY CONCEPTS

compensating differential, p. 384
human capital, p. 385
union, p. 391
strike, p. 391
efficiency wages, p. 391
discrimination, p. 391

QUESTIONS FOR REVIEW

1. Why are coal miners paid more than other workers with similar amounts of education?
2. In what sense is education a type of capital?
3. How might education raise a worker's wage without raising the worker's productivity?
4. What conditions lead to highly compensated superstars? Would you expect to see superstars in dentistry? In music? Explain.
5. Give three reasons a worker's wage might be above the level that balances supply and demand.
6. What difficulties arise in deciding whether a group of workers has a lower wage because of discrimination?
7. Do the forces of economic competition tend to exacerbate or ameliorate discrimination based on race?
8. Give an example of how discrimination might persist in a competitive market.

PROBLEMS AND APPLICATIONS

1. College students sometimes work as summer interns for private firms or the government. Many of these positions pay little or nothing.
   a. What is the opportunity cost of taking such a job?
   b. Explain why students are willing to take these jobs.
   c. If you were to compare the earnings later in life of workers who had worked as interns and those who had taken summer jobs that paid more, what would you expect to find?
2. As explained in Chapter 6, a minimum-wage law distorts the market for low-wage labor. To reduce this distortion, some economists advocate a two-tiered minimum-wage system, with a regular minimum wage for adult workers and a lower, "subminimum" wage for teenage workers. Give two reasons a single minimum wage might distort the labor market for teenage workers more than it would the market for adult workers.
3. A basic finding of labor economics is that workers who have more experience in the labor force are paid more than workers who have less experience (holding constant the amount of formal education). Why might this be so? Some studies have also found that experience at the same job (called *job tenure*) has an extra positive influence on wages. Explain why this might occur.
4. At some colleges and universities, economics professors receive higher salaries than professors in some other fields.
   a. Why might this be true?

b. Some other colleges and universities have a policy of paying equal salaries to professors in all fields. At some of these schools, economics professors have lighter teaching loads than professors in some other fields. What role do the differences in teaching loads play?

5. Imagine that someone offered you a choice: You could spend four years studying at the world's best university, but you would have to keep your attendance there a secret. Or you could be awarded an official degree from the world's best university, but you couldn't actually attend. Which choice do you think would enhance your future earnings more? What does your answer say about the debate over signaling versus human capital in the role of education?

6. When recording devices were first invented more than 100 years ago, musicians could suddenly supply their music to large audiences at low cost. How do you suppose this development affected the income of the best musicians? How do you suppose it affected the income of average musicians?

7. A current debate in education is whether teachers should be paid on a standard pay scale based solely upon their years of training and teaching experience, or whether part of their salary should be based upon their performance (called "merit pay").
   a. Why might merit pay be desirable?
   b. Who might be opposed to a system of merit pay?
   c. What is a potential challenge of merit pay?
   d. A related issue: Why might a school district decide to pay teachers significantly more than the salaries offered by surrounding districts?

8. When Alan Greenspan (who would later become chairman of the Federal Reserve) ran an economic consulting firm in the 1960s, he primarily hired female economists. He once told the *New York Times*, "I always valued men and women equally, and I found that because others did not, good women economists were cheaper than men." Is Greenspan's behavior profit-maximizing? Is it admirable or despicable? If more employers were like Greenspan, what would happen to the wage differential between men and women? Why might other economic consulting firms at the time not have followed Greenspan's business strategy?

To find additional study resources, visit cengagebrain.com, and search for "Mankiw."

Income Inequality and Poverty

CHAPTER 20

The great British Prime Minister Winston Churchill once summarized alternative economic systems as follows: "The inherent vice of capitalism is the unequal sharing of blessings. The inherent virtue of socialism is the equal sharing of miseries." Churchill's quip draws attention to two important facts. First, nations that use market mechanisms to allocate resources usually achieve greater prosperity than those that do not. This is the result of Adam Smith's invisible hand in action. Second, the prosperity that market economies produce is not shared equally. Incomes can differ greatly between those at the top and those at the bottom of the economic ladder. The gap between rich and poor is a fascinating and important topic of study—for the comfortable rich, for the struggling poor, and for the aspiring and worried middle class.

From the previous two chapters, you should have some understanding about why different people have different incomes. A person's earnings depend on the supply and demand for that person's labor, which in turn depend on natural ability, human capital, compensating differentials, discrimination, and so on. Because labor earnings make up about two-thirds of the total income in the U.S. economy, the factors that determine wages are also largely responsible for determining how the economy's total income is distributed among the various members of society. In other words, they determine who is rich and who is poor.

In this chapter, we discuss the distribution of income—a topic that raises some fundamental questions about the role of economic policy. One of the *Ten Principles of Economics* introduced in Chapter 1 is that governments can sometimes improve market outcomes. This possibility is particularly important when considering the distribution of income. The invisible hand of the marketplace allocates resources efficiently but does not necessarily allocate them fairly. As a result, many economists—though not all—believe that the government should redistribute income to achieve greater equality. In doing so, however, the government runs into another of the *Ten Principles of Economics*: People face trade-offs. When the government enacts policies to make the distribution of income more equal, it distorts incentives, alters behavior, and makes the allocation of resources less efficient.

Our discussion of the distribution of income proceeds in three steps. First, we assess how much inequality there is in our society. Second, we consider some different views about the role that government should play in altering the distribution of income. Third, we discuss various public policies aimed at helping society's poorest members.

20-1 The Measurement of Inequality

We begin our study of the distribution of income by addressing four questions of measurement:

- How much inequality is there in our society?
- How many people live in poverty?
- What problems arise in measuring the amount of inequality?
- How often do people move between income classes?

ROBERT MANKOFF/ THE NEW YORKER COLLECTION/ WWW.CARTOONBANK.COM

"As far as I'm concerned, they can do what they want with the minimum wage, just as long as they keep their hands off the maximum wage."

These measurement questions are the natural starting point from which to discuss public policies aimed at changing the distribution of income.

20-1a U.S. Income Inequality

Imagine that you lined up all the families in the economy according to their annual income. Then you divided the families into five equal groups, called *quintiles*. Table 1 shows the income ranges for each quintile, as well as for the top 5 percent. You can use this table to find where your family lies in the income distribution.

For examining differences in the income distribution over time, economists find it useful to present the income data as in Table 2. This table shows the share of total income that each group of families received in selected years. In 2014, the bottom quintile received 3.6 percent of all income and the top quintile received 48.9 percent of all income. In other words, even though all the quintiles include the same number of families, the top quintile has more than thirteen times as much income as the bottom quintile.

Group	Annual Family Income
Bottom Quintile	$29,100 and below
Second Quintile	$29,101–$52,697
Middle Quintile	$52,698–$82,032
Fourth Quintile	$82,033–$129,006
Top Quintile	$129,007 and above
Top 5 percent	$230,030 and above

TABLE 1

The Distribution of Income in the United States: 2014

Source: U.S. Bureau of the Census.

Year	Bottom Quintile	Second Quintile	Middle Quintile	Fourth Quintile	Top Quintile	Top 5%
2014	3.6%	9.2%	15.1%	23.2%	48.9%	20.8%
2010	3.8	9.4	15.4	23.5	47.9	20.0
2000	4.3	9.8	15.4	22.7	47.7	21.1
1990	4.6	10.8	16.6	23.8	44.3	17.4
1980	5.3	11.6	17.6	24.4	41.1	14.6
1970	5.4	12.2	17.6	23.8	40.9	15.6
1960	4.8	12.2	17.8	24.0	41.3	15.9
1950	4.5	12.0	17.4	23.4	42.7	17.3
1935	4.1	9.2	14.1	20.9	51.7	26.5

TABLE 2

Income Inequality in the United States

This table shows the percentage of total before-tax income received by families in each fifth of the income distribution and by those families in the top 5 percent.

Source: U.S. Bureau of the Census.

The last column in the table shows the share of total income received by the very richest families. In 2014, the top 5 percent of families received 20.8 percent of all income, which was greater than the total income of the poorest 40 percent.

Table 2 also shows the distribution of income in various years beginning in 1935. At first glance, the distribution of income appears to have been remarkably stable over time. Throughout the past several decades, the bottom quintile has received about 4 to 5 percent of income, while the top quintile has received about 40 to 50 percent of income. Closer inspection of the table reveals some trends in the degree of inequality. From 1935 to 1970, the distribution gradually became more equal. The share of the bottom quintile rose from 4.1 to 5.4 percent, and the share of the top quintile fell from 51.7 to 40.9 percent. In more recent years, this trend has reversed itself. From 1970 to 2014, the share of the bottom quintile fell from 5.4 to 3.6 percent, and the share of the top quintile rose from 40.9 to 48.9 percent.

In Chapter 19, we discussed some explanations for this recent rise in inequality. Increases in international trade with low-wage countries and changes in technology have tended to reduce the demand for unskilled labor and raise the demand for skilled labor. As a result, the wages of unskilled workers have fallen relative to the wages of skilled workers, and this change in relative wages has increased inequality in family incomes.

20-1b Inequality around the World

How does the amount of inequality in the United States compare to that in other countries? This question is interesting, but answering it is problematic. For some countries, data are not available. Even when they are, not every country collects data in the same way; for example, some countries collect data on individual incomes, whereas other countries collect data on family incomes, and still others collect data on expenditure and use it as a crude measure of income. As a result, whenever we find a difference between two countries, we can never be sure whether it reflects a true difference in the economies or merely a difference in the way data are collected.

With this warning in mind, consider Figure 1, which compares inequality in twenty major countries. The inequality measure used here is the *quintile ratio*, which is the income of the richest quintile divided by the income of the poorest quintile. The most equality is found in Sweden, where the top quintile receives 3.7 times as much income as the bottom quintile. The least equality is found in South Africa, where the top group receives 28.5 times as much income as the bottom group. All countries have significant disparities between rich and poor, but the degree of inequality varies substantially around the world.

When countries are ranked by inequality, the United States ends up with more inequality than the typical country. The United States has substantially greater income disparity than most other economically advanced countries, such as Japan and Germany. But it has a more equal income distribution than some developing countries, such as South Africa and Brazil. The United States has about the same degree of inequality as China, the world's most populous nation.

FIGURE 1

Inequality around the World

This figure shows the ratio of the income of the richest quintile to the income of the poorest quintile. Among these nations, Sweden and Pakistan have the most equal distribution of economic well-being, while South Africa and Brazil have the least equal.

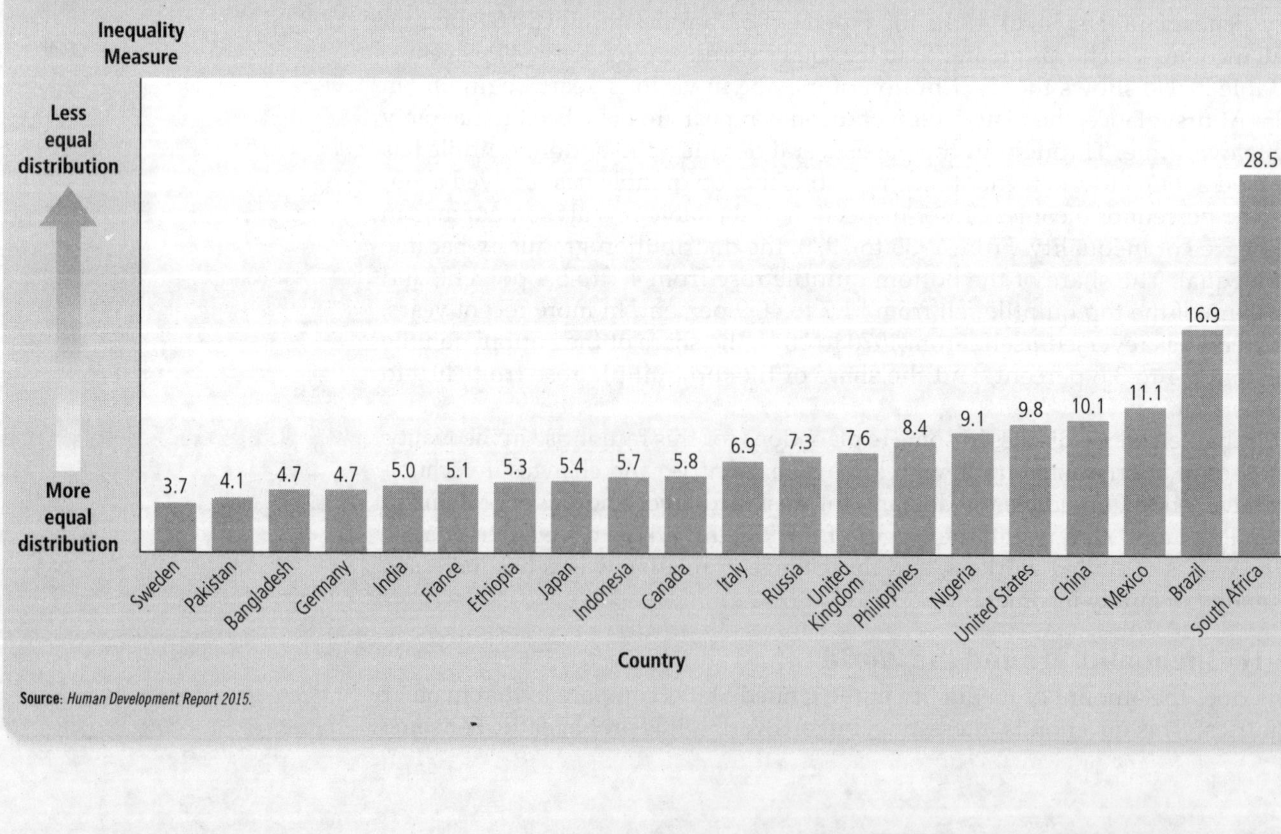

Source: *Human Development Report 2015.*

20-1c The Poverty Rate

A commonly used gauge of the distribution of income is the poverty rate. The **poverty rate** is the percentage of the population whose family income falls below an absolute level called the **poverty line**. The poverty line is set by the federal government at roughly three times the cost of providing an adequate diet. This line depends on family size and is adjusted every year to account for changes in the level of prices.

poverty rate
the percentage of the population whose family income falls below an absolute level called the poverty line

poverty line
an absolute level of income set by the federal government for each family size below which a family is deemed to be in poverty

To get some idea about what the poverty rate tells us, consider the data for 2014. In that year, the median family in the United States had an income of $66,632, and the poverty line for a family of four was $24,230. The poverty rate was 14.8 percent. In other words, 14.8 percent of the U.S. population were members of families with incomes below the poverty line for their family size.

Figure 2 shows the poverty rate since 1959, when the official data begin. You can see that the poverty rate fell from 22.4 percent in 1959 to a low of 11.1 percent in 1973. This decline is not surprising, as average income in the economy (adjusted for inflation) rose more than 50 percent during this period. Because the poverty line is an absolute rather than a relative standard, more families are pushed above the poverty line as economic growth pushes the entire income distribution upward. As John F. Kennedy once put it, a rising tide lifts all boats.

Since the early 1970s, however, the economy's rising tide has left some boats behind. Despite continued growth in average income, the poverty rate has not declined below the level reached in 1973. This lack of progress in reducing poverty in recent decades is closely related to the increasing inequality we saw in Table 2. Although economic growth has raised the income of the typical family, the increase in inequality has prevented the poorest families from sharing in this greater economic prosperity.

Poverty is an economic malady that affects all groups within the population, but it does not affect all groups with equal frequency. Table 3 shows the poverty rates for several groups, and it reveals three striking facts:

- Poverty is correlated with race. Blacks and Hispanics are more than twice as likely to live in poverty as whites.

FIGURE 2

The Poverty Rate
The poverty rate measures the percentage of the population with incomes below an absolute level called the poverty line.

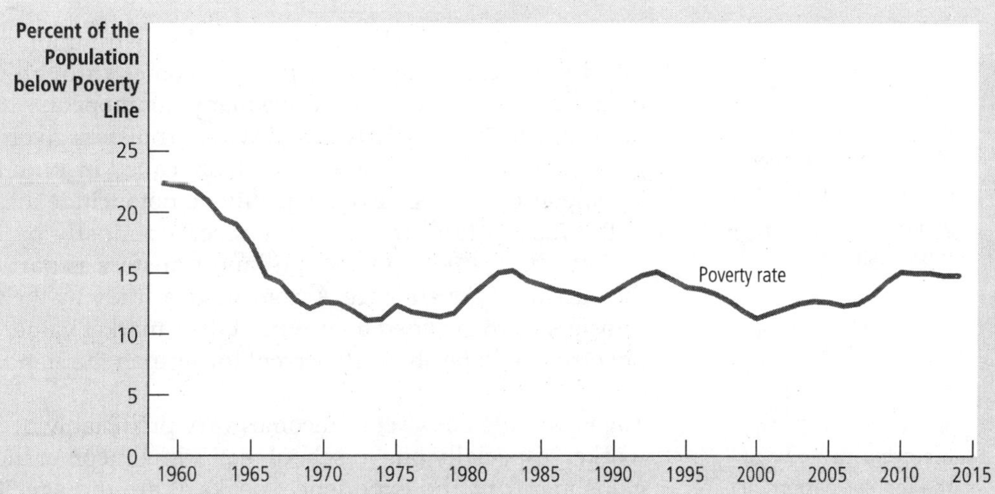

Source: U.S. Bureau of the Census.

Group	Poverty Rate
All persons	14.8%
White, not Hispanic	10.1
Black	26.2
Hispanic	23.6
Asian	12.0
Children (under age 18)	21.1
Elderly (over age 64)	10.0
Married-couple families	6.2
Female household, no spouse present	33.1

TABLE 3

Who Is Poor?
This table shows that the poverty rate varies greatly among different groups within the population.

Source: U.S. Bureau of the Census. Data are for 2014.

- Poverty is correlated with age. Children are more likely than average to be members of poor families, and the elderly are less likely than average to be poor.
- Poverty is correlated with family composition. Families headed by a single mother are about five times as likely to live in poverty as families headed by a married couple.

These three facts have described American society for many years, and they show which people are most likely to be poor. These effects also work together: Almost half the children in black and Hispanic female-headed households live in poverty.

20-1d Problems in Measuring Inequality

Although data on the income distribution and the poverty rate give us some idea about the degree of inequality in our society, interpreting these data is not always straightforward. The data are based on households' annual incomes. What people care about, however, is not their incomes but their ability to maintain a good standard of living. For at least three reasons, data on the income distribution and the poverty rate give an incomplete picture of inequality in living standards.

In-Kind Transfers Measurements of the distribution of income and the poverty rate are based on families' *monetary* income. Through various government programs, however, the poor receive many nonmonetary items, including free food, housing vouchers, and medical services. Transfers given to the poor in the form of goods and services rather than cash are called **in-kind transfers**. Standard measurements of the degree of inequality do not include these in-kind transfers.

in-kind transfers
transfers to the poor given in the form of goods and services rather than cash

Because in-kind transfers are received mostly by the poorest members of society, the failure to include in-kind transfers as part of income greatly affects the measured poverty rate. According to a study by the Census Bureau, if in-kind transfers were included in income at their market value, the number of families in poverty would be about 10 percent lower than the standard data indicate.

The Economic Life Cycle Incomes vary predictably over people's lives. A young worker, especially one in school, has a low income. Income rises as the worker gains maturity and experience, peaks at around age 50, and then falls sharply when the worker retires at around age 65. This regular pattern of income variation is called the **life cycle**.

life cycle
the regular pattern of income variation over a person's life

Because people can borrow and save to smooth out life cycle changes in income, their standard of living in any year depends more on lifetime income than on that year's income. The young often borrow, perhaps to go to school or to buy a house, and then repay these loans later when their incomes rise. People have their highest saving rates when they are middle-aged. Because people can save in anticipation of retirement, the large declines in incomes at retirement need not lead to similar declines in the standard of living. This normal life cycle pattern causes inequality in the distribution of annual income, but it does not necessarily represent true inequality in living standards.

Transitory versus Permanent Income Incomes vary over people's lives not only because of predictable life cycle variation but also because of random and transitory forces. One year a frost kills off the Florida orange crop, and Florida orange growers see their incomes fall temporarily. At the same time, the Florida frost drives up the price of oranges, and California orange growers see their incomes temporarily rise. The next year the reverse might happen.

Just as people can borrow and save to smooth out life cycle variation in income, they can also borrow and save to smooth out transitory variation in income. To the extent that a family saves in good years and borrows (or depletes its savings) in bad years, transitory changes in income need not affect its standard of living. A family's ability to buy goods and services depends largely on its **permanent income**, which is its normal, or average, income.

permanent income
a person's normal income

To gauge inequality of living standards, the distribution of permanent income is more relevant than the distribution of annual income. Many economists believe that people base their consumption on their permanent income; as a result, inequality in consumption is one gauge of inequality of permanent income. Because permanent income and consumption are less affected by transitory changes in income, they are more equally distributed than is current income.

CASE STUDY

ALTERNATIVE MEASURES OF INEQUALITY

A 2008 study by Michael Cox and Richard Alm of the Federal Reserve Bank of Dallas shows how different measures of inequality lead to dramatically different results. Cox and Alm compared American households in the top fifth of the income distribution to those in the bottom fifth to see how far apart they are.

According to Cox and Alm, the richest fifth of U.S. households in 2006 had an average income of $149,963, while the poorest fifth had an average income of $9,974. Thus, the top group had about 15 times as much income as the bottom group.

The gap between rich and poor shrinks a bit if taxes are taken into account. Because the tax system is progressive, the top group paid a higher percentage of its income in taxes than did the bottom group. Cox and Alm found that the richest fifth had 14 times as much after-tax income as the poorest fifth.

The gap shrinks more if one looks at consumption rather than income. Households having an unusually good year are more likely to be in the top group and are likely to save a high fraction of their incomes. Households having an unusually bad year are more likely to be in the bottom group and are more likely to consume out of their savings. According to Cox and Alm, the consumption of the richest fifth was only 3.9 times as much as the consumption of the poorest fifth.

The consumption gap becomes smaller still if one corrects for differences in the number of people in the household. Because larger families are more likely to have two earners, they are more likely to find themselves near the top of the income distribution. But they also have more mouths to feed. Cox and Alm reported that households in the top fifth had an average of 3.1 people, while those in the bottom fifth had an average of 1.7 people. As a result, consumption per person in the richest fifth of households was only 2.1 times consumption per person in the poorest fifth.

These data show that inequality in material standards of living is much smaller than inequality in annual income. ●

20-1e Economic Mobility

People sometimes speak of "the rich" and "the poor" as if these groups consisted of the same families year after year. But this is not at all the case. Economic mobility, the movement of people between income classes, is significant in the U.S. economy. Movements up the income ladder can be due to good luck or hard work, and movements down the ladder can be due to bad luck or laziness. Some of this mobility reflects transitory variation in income, while some reflects more persistent changes in income.

Because family income changes over time, temporary poverty is more common than the poverty rate suggests, but persistent poverty is less common. In a typical 10-year period, about one in four families falls below the poverty line in at least one year. Yet fewer than 3 percent of families are poor for 8 or more years. Because it is likely that the temporarily poor and the persistently poor face different problems, policies that aim to combat poverty need to distinguish between these groups.

Another way to gauge economic mobility is the persistence of economic success from generation to generation. Economists who have studied this topic find that having an above-average income carries over from parents to children, but the persistence is far from perfect, indicating substantial mobility among income classes. If a father earns 20 percent above his generation's average income, his son will most likely earn 8 percent above his generation's average income. There is only a small correlation between the income of a grandfather and the income of his grandson.

One result of this intergenerational economic mobility is that the U.S. economy is filled with self-made millionaires (as well as with heirs who have squandered the fortunes they inherited). According to one study, about four out of five millionaires made their money on their own, often by starting and building a business or by climbing the corporate ladder. Only one in five millionaires inherited his fortune.

QuickQuiz *What does the poverty rate measure? • Describe three potential problems in interpreting the measured poverty rate.*

20-2 The Political Philosophy of Redistributing In

We have just seen how the economy's income is distributed and have considered some of the problems in interpreting measured inequality. This discussion was *positive* in the sense that it merely described the world as it is. We now turn to the *normative* question facing policymakers: What should the government do about economic inequality?

This question is not just about economics. Economic analysis alone cannot tell us whether policymakers should try to make our society more egalitarian. Our views on this question are, to a large extent, a matter of political philosophy. Yet because the government's role in redistributing income is central to so many debates over economic policy, let's digress from economic science to consider a bit of political philosophy.

20-2a Utilitarianism

utilitarianism
the political philosophy according to which the government should choose policies to maximize the total utility of everyone in society

utility
a measure of happiness or satisfaction

A prominent school of thought in political philosophy is **utilitarianism**. The founders of utilitarianism are the English philosophers Jeremy Bentham (1748–1832) and John Stuart Mill (1806–1873). To a large extent, the goal of utilitarians is to apply the logic of individual decision making to questions concerning morality and public policy.

The starting point of utilitarianism is the notion of **utility**—the level of happiness or satisfaction that a person receives from his circumstances. Utility is a measure of well-being and, according to utilitarians, is the ultimate objective of all public and private actions. The proper goal of the government, they claim, is to maximize the sum of utility achieved by everyone in society.

The utilitarian case for redistributing income is based on the assumption of *diminishing marginal utility*. It seems reasonable that an extra dollar of income provides a poor person with more additional utility than an extra dollar would provide to a rich person. In other words, as a person's income rises, the extra well-being derived from an additional dollar of income falls. This plausible assumption, together with the utilitarian goal of maximizing total utility, implies that the government should try to achieve a more equal distribution of income.

The argument is simple. Imagine that Peter and Paul are the same, except that Peter earns $80,000 and Paul earns $20,000. In this case, taking a dollar from Peter to pay Paul will reduce Peter's utility and raise Paul's utility. But because of diminishing marginal utility, Peter's utility falls by less than Paul's utility rises. Thus, this redistribution of income raises total utility, which is the utilitarian's objective.

At first, this utilitarian argument might seem to imply that the government should continue to redistribute income until everyone in society has exactly the same income. Indeed, that would be the case if the total amount of income—$100,000 in our example—were fixed. But in fact, it is not. Utilitarians reject complete equalization of incomes because they accept one of the *Ten Principles of Economics* presented in Chapter 1: People respond to incentives.

To take from Peter to pay Paul, the government must pursue policies that redistribute income. The U.S. federal income tax and welfare system are examples. Under these policies, people with high incomes pay high taxes, and people with low incomes receive income transfers. These income transfers are phased out: As a person earns more, he receives less from the government. Yet when Peter faces a higher income tax rate and Paul faces a system of phased-out transfers, both have less incentive to work hard, because each gets to keep only a fraction of any additional earnings. As they both work less, society's income falls, and so does total utility. The utilitarian government has to balance the gains from greater equality against the losses from distorted incentives. To maximize total utility, therefore, the government stops short of making society fully egalitarian.

A famous parable sheds light on the utilitarian's logic. Imagine that Peter and Paul are thirsty travelers trapped at different places in the desert. Peter's oasis has a lot of water; Paul's has only a little. If the government could transfer water from one oasis to the other without cost, it would maximize total utility from water by equalizing the amount in the two places. But suppose that the government has only a leaky bucket. As it tries to move water from one place to the other, some of the water is lost in transit. In this case, a utilitarian government might still try to move some water from Peter to Paul, depending on the size of Paul's thirst and the size of the bucket's leak. But with only a leaky bucket at its disposal, a utilitarian government will stop short of trying to reach complete equality.

20-2b Liberalism

liberalism
the political philosophy according to which the government should choose policies deemed just, as evaluated by an impartial observer behind a "veil of ignorance"

A second way of thinking about inequality might be called **liberalism**. Philosopher John Rawls develops this view in his book *A Theory of Justice*. This book was first published in 1971, and it quickly became a classic in political philosophy.

Rawls begins with the premise that a society's institutions, laws, and policies should be just. He then takes up the natural question: How can we, the members of society, ever agree on what justice means? It might seem that every person's point of view is inevitably based on his particular circumstances—whether he is talented or less talented, diligent or lazy, educated or less educated, born to a wealthy family or a poor one. Could we ever *objectively* determine what a just society would look like?

To answer this question, Rawls proposes the following thought experiment. Imagine that before any of us is born, we all get together in the beforelife (the pre-birth version of the afterlife) for a meeting to design the rules that will govern society. At this point, we are all ignorant about the station in life each of us will end up filling. In Rawls's words, we are sitting in an "original position" behind a "veil of ignorance." In this original position, Rawls argues, we can choose a just set of rules for society because we must consider how those rules will affect every person. As Rawls puts it, "Since all are similarly situated and no one is able to design principles to favor his particular conditions, the principles of justice are the result of fair agreement or bargain." Designing public policies and institutions in this way allows us to be objective about what policies are just.

Rawls then considers what public policy designed behind this veil of ignorance would try to achieve. In particular, he considers what income distribution a person would consider fair if that person did not know whether he would end up at the top, bottom, or middle of the distribution. Rawls argues that a person in the original position would be chiefly concerned about the possibility of being at the *bottom* of the income distribution. In designing public policies, therefore, we should aim to raise the welfare of the worst-off person in society. That is, rather than maximizing the sum of everyone's utility, as a utilitarian would do, Rawls would strive to maximize the minimum utility. Rawls's rule is called the **maximin criterion**.

maximin criterion
the claim that the government should aim to maximize the well-being of the worst-off person in society

Because the maximin criterion emphasizes the least fortunate person in society, it justifies public policies aimed at equalizing the distribution of income. By transferring income from the rich to the poor, society raises the well-being of the least fortunate. The maximin criterion would not, however, lead to a completely egalitarian society. If the government promised to equalize incomes completely, people would have no incentive to work hard, society's total income would fall substantially, and the least fortunate person would be worse off. Thus, the maximin criterion still allows disparities in income because such disparities can improve incentives and thereby raise society's ability to help the poor. Nonetheless, because Rawls's philosophy puts weight on only the least fortunate members of society, it calls for more income redistribution than does utilitarianism.

social insurance
government policy aimed at protecting people against the risk of adverse events

Rawls's views are controversial, but the thought experiment he proposes has much appeal. In particular, this thought experiment allows us to consider the redistribution of income as a form of **social insurance**. That is, from the perspective of the original position behind the veil of ignorance, income redistribution is like an insurance policy. Homeowners buy fire insurance to protect themselves from the risk of their house burning down. Similarly, when we as a society choose policies that tax the rich to supplement the incomes of the poor, we are all insuring ourselves against the possibility that we might have been members of poor families. Because people generally dislike risk, we should be happy to have been born into a society that provides us this insurance.

It is not at all clear, however, that rational people behind the veil of ignorance would truly be so risk averse that they would follow the maximin criterion. Indeed, because a person in the original position might end up anywhere in the distribution of outcomes, he might treat all possible outcomes equally when designing public policies. In this case, the best policy behind the veil of ignorance would be to maximize the average utility of members of society, and the resulting notion of justice would be more utilitarian than Rawlsian.

20-2c Libertarianism

A third view of inequality is called **libertarianism**. The two views we have considered so far—utilitarianism and liberalism—both view the total income of society as a shared resource that a social planner can freely redistribute to achieve some social goal. By contrast, libertarians argue that society itself earns no income—only individual members of society earn income. According to libertarians, the government should not take from some individuals and give to others to achieve any particular distribution of income.

libertarianism
the political philosophy according to which the government should punish crimes and enforce voluntary agreements but not redistribute income

For instance, philosopher Robert Nozick writes the following in his famous 1974 book *Anarchy, State, and Utopia*:

> We are not in the position of children who have been given portions of pie by someone who now makes last minute adjustments to rectify careless cutting. There is no *central* distribution, no person or group entitled to control all the resources, jointly deciding how they are to be doled out. What each person gets, he gets from others who give to him in exchange for something, or as a gift. In a free society, diverse persons control different resources, and new holdings arise out of the voluntary exchanges and actions of persons.

Whereas utilitarians and liberals try to judge what amount of inequality is desirable in a society, Nozick denies the validity of this very question.

The libertarian alternative to evaluating economic *outcomes* is to evaluate the *process* by which these outcomes arise. When the distribution of income is achieved unfairly—for instance, when one person steals from another—the government has the right and duty to remedy the problem. But as long as the process determining the distribution of income is just, the resulting distribution is fair, no matter how unequal.

Nozick criticizes Rawls's liberalism by drawing an analogy between the distribution of income in society and the distribution of grades in a course. Suppose you were asked to judge the fairness of the grades in the economics course you are now taking. Would you imagine yourself behind a veil of ignorance and choose a grade distribution without knowing the talents and efforts of each student? Or would you ensure that the process of assigning grades to students is fair without regard for whether the resulting distribution is equal or unequal? For the case of grades at least, the libertarian emphasis on process over outcomes is compelling.

Libertarians conclude that equality of opportunities is more important than equality of incomes. They believe that the government should enforce individual rights to ensure that everyone has the same opportunity to use his talents and achieve success. Once these rules of the game are established, the government has no reason to alter the resulting distribution of income.

QuickQuiz *Petra earns more than Paula. Someone proposes taxing Petra to supplement Paula's income. How would a utilitarian, a liberal, and a libertarian each evaluate this proposal?*

20-3 Policies to Reduce Poverty

As we have just seen, political philosophers hold various views about what role the government should take in altering the distribution of income. Political debate among the larger population of voters reflects a similar disagreement. Despite these continuing debates, most people believe that, at the very least, the government should try to help those most in need. According to a popular metaphor, the government should provide a "safety net" to prevent any citizen from falling too far.

Poverty is one of the most difficult problems that policymakers face. Poor families are more likely than the overall population to experience homelessness, drug dependence, health problems, teenage pregnancy, illiteracy, unemployment, and low educational attainment. Members of poor families are more likely both to commit crimes and to be victims of crimes. Although it is hard to separate the causes of poverty from the effects, there is no doubt that poverty is associated with various economic and social ills.

Suppose that you were a policymaker in the government and your goal was to reduce the number of people living in poverty. How would you achieve this goal? Here we examine some of the policy options that you might consider. Each of these options helps some people escape poverty, but none of them is perfect, and deciding upon the best combination to use is not easy.

20-3a Minimum-Wage Laws

Laws setting a minimum wage that employers can pay workers are a perennial source of debate. Advocates view the minimum wage as a way of helping the working poor without any cost to the government. Critics view it as hurting those it is intended to help.

The minimum wage is easily understood using the tools of supply and demand, as we first saw in Chapter 6. For workers with low levels of skill and experience, a high minimum wage forces the wage above the level that balances supply and demand. It therefore raises the cost of labor to firms and reduces the quantity of labor that those firms demand. The result is higher unemployment among those groups of workers affected by the minimum wage. Those workers who remain employed benefit from a higher wage, but those who might have been employed at a lower wage are worse off.

The magnitude of these effects depends crucially on the elasticity of labor demand. Advocates of a high minimum wage argue that the demand for unskilled labor is relatively inelastic so that a high minimum wage depresses employment only slightly. Critics of the minimum wage argue that labor demand is more elastic, especially in the long run when firms can adjust employment and production more fully. They also note that many minimum-wage workers are teenagers from middle-class families so that a high minimum wage is imperfectly targeted as a policy for helping the poor.

20-3b Welfare

One way for the government to raise the living standards of the poor is to supplement their incomes. The primary way the government does this is through the welfare system. **Welfare** is a broad term that encompasses various government programs. Temporary Assistance for Needy Families (TANF) is a program that assists families with children and no adult able to support the family. In a typical family receiving such assistance, the father is absent and the mother is at home raising small children. Another welfare program is Supplemental Security Income (SSI), which provides assistance to the poor who are sick or disabled. Note that for both of these welfare programs, a poor person cannot qualify for assistance simply by having a low income. He must also establish some additional "need," such as small children or a disability.

welfare
government programs that supplement the incomes of the needy

A common criticism of welfare programs is that they create incentives for people to become "needy." For example, these programs may encourage families to break up, for many families qualify for financial assistance only if the father is absent. The programs may also encourage illegitimate births, for many poor, single women qualify for assistance only if they have children. Because poor, single mothers are such a large part of the poverty problem and because welfare programs seem to raise the number of poor, single mothers, critics of the welfare system assert that these policies exacerbate the very problems they are supposed to cure. As a result of these arguments, the welfare system was revised in a 1996 law that limited the amount of time recipients could stay on welfare.

How severe are these potential problems with the welfare system? No one knows for sure. Proponents of the welfare system point out that being a poor, single mother on welfare is a difficult existence at best, and they do not believe that many people would choose such a life if it were not thrust upon them. Moreover, trends over time do not support the view that the decline of the two-parent family is largely a symptom of the welfare system, as the system's critics sometimes claim. Since the early 1970s, welfare benefits (adjusted for inflation) have declined, yet the percentage of children living with only one parent has risen.

20-3c Negative Income Tax

Whenever the government chooses a system to collect taxes, it affects the distribution of income. This is clearly true in the case of a progressive income tax, whereby high-income families pay a larger percentage of their income in taxes than do low-income families. As we discussed in Chapter 12, equity across income groups is an important goal in the design of a tax system.

negative income tax
a tax system that collects revenue from high-income households and gives subsidies to low-income households

Many economists have advocated supplementing the income of the poor using a **negative income tax**. According to this policy, every family would report its income to the government. High-income families would pay a tax based on their incomes. Low-income families would receive a subsidy. In other words, they would "pay" a "negative tax."

For example, suppose the government used the following formula to compute a family's tax liability:

$$\text{Taxes owed} = (\tfrac{1}{3} \text{ of income}) - \$10{,}000.$$

In this case, a family that earned $60,000 would pay $10,000 in taxes, and a family that earned $90,000 would pay $20,000 in taxes. A family that earned $30,000 would owe nothing. And a family that earned $15,000 would "owe" –$5,000. In other words, the government would send this family a check for $5,000.

Under a negative income tax, poor families would receive financial assistance without having to demonstrate need. The only qualification required to receive assistance would be a low income. Depending on one's point of view, this feature can be either an advantage or a disadvantage. On the one hand, a negative income tax does not encourage illegitimate births and the breakup of families, as critics of the welfare system believe current policy does. On the other hand, a negative income tax would subsidize not only the unfortunate but also those who are simply lazy and, in some people's eyes, undeserving of government support.

One actual tax provision that works much like a negative income tax is the Earned Income Tax Credit (EITC). This credit allows poor working families to receive income tax refunds greater than the taxes they paid during the year. Because the EITC applies only to the working poor, it does not discourage recipients from working, as other antipoverty programs may. For the same reason, however, it also does not help alleviate poverty due to unemployment, sickness, or other inability to work.

20-3d In-Kind Transfers

Another way to help the poor is to provide them directly with some of the goods and services they need to raise their living standards. For example, charities provide the needy with food, clothing, shelter, and toys at Christmas. The government gives poor families food through the Supplemental Nutrition Assistance Program, or SNAP. This program, which replaced a similar one called food stamps, gives low-income families a plastic card, like a debit card, that can be used to buy food at stores. The government also gives many poor people healthcare through a program called Medicaid.

Is it better to help the poor with these in-kind transfers or with direct cash payments? There is no clear answer.

Advocates of in-kind transfers argue that such transfers ensure that the poor get what they need most. Among the poorest members of society, alcohol and drug addiction is more common than it is in society as a whole. By providing the poor with food and shelter, society can be more confident that it is not helping to support such addictions. This is one reason in-kind transfers are more politically popular than cash payments to the poor.

Advocates of cash payments, on the other hand, argue that in-kind transfers are inefficient and disrespectful. The government does not know what goods and services the poor need most. Many of the poor are ordinary people down on their luck. Despite their misfortune, they are in the best position to decide how to raise their own living standards. Rather than giving the poor in-kind transfers of goods and services that they may not want, it may be better to give them cash and allow them to buy what they think they need most.

20-3e Antipoverty Programs and Work Incentives

Many policies aimed at helping the poor can have the unintended effect of discouraging the poor from escaping poverty on their own. To see why, consider the following example. Suppose that a family needs an income of \$20,000 to maintain a reasonable standard of living. And suppose that, out of concern for the poor, the government promises to guarantee every family that income. Whatever a family earns, the government makes up the difference between that income and \$20,000. What effect would you expect this policy to have?

The incentive effects of this policy are obvious: Any person who would make under \$20,000 by working has little incentive to find and keep a job. For every dollar that the person would earn, the government would reduce the income supplement by a dollar. In effect, the government taxes 100 percent of additional earnings. An effective marginal tax rate of 100 percent is surely a policy with a large deadweight loss.

The adverse effects of this high effective tax rate can persist over time. A person discouraged from working loses the on-the-job training that a job might offer. In addition, his children miss the lessons learned by observing a parent with a full-time job, and this may adversely affect their own ability to find and hold a job.

The antipoverty program we have been discussing is hypothetical, but it is not as unrealistic as it might first appear. Welfare, Medicaid, SNAP, and the EITC are all programs aimed at helping the poor, and they are all tied to family income. As a family's income rises, the family becomes ineligible for these programs. When all these programs are taken together, it is common for families to face effective marginal tax rates that are very high. Sometimes the effective marginal tax rates even exceed 100 percent so that poor families are worse off when they earn more. By trying to help the poor, the government discourages those families from working. According to critics of antipoverty programs, these programs alter work attitudes and create a "culture of poverty."

It might seem that there is an easy solution to this problem: Reduce benefits to poor families more gradually as their incomes rise. For example, if a poor family loses 30 cents of benefits for every dollar it earns, then it faces an effective marginal tax rate of 30 percent. This effective tax reduces work effort to some extent, but it does not eliminate the incentive to work completely.

The problem with this solution is that it greatly increases the cost of programs to combat poverty. If benefits are phased out gradually as a poor family's income rises, then families just above the poverty level will also be eligible for substantial benefits. The more gradual the phase-out, the more families are eligible, and the more the program costs. Thus, policymakers face a trade-off between burdening the poor with high effective marginal tax rates and burdening taxpayers with costly programs to reduce poverty.

There are various other ways to reduce the work disincentive of antipoverty programs. One is to require any person collecting benefits to accept a government-provided job—a system sometimes called *workfare*. Another possibility is to provide benefits for only a limited period of time. This route was taken in the 1996 welfare reform bill, which imposed a 5-year lifetime limit on welfare recipients. When President Clinton signed the bill, he explained his policy as follows: "Welfare should be a second chance, not a way of life."

QuickQuiz *List three policies aimed at helping the poor, and discuss the pros and cons of each.*

20-4 Conclusion

People have long reflected on the distribution of income in society. Plato, the ancient Greek philosopher, concluded that in an ideal society the income of the richest person would be no more than four times the income of the poorest person. Although the measurement of inequality is difficult, it is clear that our society has much more inequality than Plato recommended.

One of the *Ten Principles of Economics* discussed in Chapter 1 is that governments can sometimes improve market outcomes. There is little consensus, however, about how this principle should be applied to the distribution of income. Philosophers and policymakers today do not agree on how much income inequality is desirable, or even whether public policy should aim to alter the distribution of income. Much of public debate reflects this disagreement. Whenever taxes are raised, for instance, lawmakers argue over how much of the tax hike should fall on the rich, the middle class, and the poor.

Another of the *Ten Principles of Economics* is that people face trade-offs. This principle is important to keep in mind when thinking about economic inequality. Policies that penalize the successful and reward the unsuccessful reduce the incentive to succeed. Thus, policymakers face a trade-off between equality and efficiency. The more equally the pie is divided, the smaller the pie becomes. This is the one lesson concerning the distribution of income about which almost everyone agrees.

CHAPTER QuickQuiz

1. In the United States today, the poorest fifth of the population earns about _____ percent of all income, while the richest fifth earns about _____ percent.
   a. 2, 70
   b. 4, 50
   c. 6, 35
   d. 8, 25
2. When income inequality is compared across nations, one finds that the United States is
   a. the most equal nation in the world.
   b. more equal than most nations but not the most equal.
   c. less equal than most nations but not the least equal.
   d. the least equal nation in the world.
3. A utilitarian believes that the redistribution of income from the rich to the poor is worthwhile as long as
   a. the worst-off members of society benefit from it.
   b. those contributing to the system are in favor of it.
   c. each person's income, after taxes and transfers, reflects his marginal product.
   d. the distortionary effect on work incentives is not too large.
4. Rawls's thought experiment of the "original position" behind the "veil of ignorance" is meant to draw attention to the fact that
   a. most of the poor do not know how to find better jobs and escape poverty.
   b. the station of life each of us was born into is largely a matter of luck.
   c. the rich have so much money that they don't know how to spend it all.
   d. outcomes are efficient only if everyone begins with equal opportunity.
5. A negative income tax is a policy under which
   a. individuals with low income get transfers from the government.
   b. the government raises tax revenue without distorting incentives.
   c. everyone pays less than under a conventional income tax.
   d. some taxpayers are on the wrong side of the Laffer curve.
6. If the benefits from an antipoverty program are phased out as an individual's income increases, then the program will
   a. encourage greater work effort from the poor.
   b. lead to an excess supply of labor among unskilled workers.
   c. increase the effective marginal tax rate that the poor face.
   d. cost the government more than a program that benefits everyone.

SUMMARY

- Data on the distribution of income show a wide disparity in U.S. society. The richest fifth of families earns more than twelve times as much income as the poorest fifth.
- Because in-kind transfers, the economic life cycle, transitory income, and economic mobility are so important for understanding variation in income, it is difficult to gauge the degree of inequality in our society using data on the distribution of income in a single year. When these other factors are taken into account, they tend to suggest that economic well-being is more equally distributed than is annual income.
- Political philosophers differ in their views about the role of government in altering the distribution of income. Utilitarians (such as John Stuart Mill) would choose the distribution of income that maximizes the sum of utility of everyone in society. Liberals (such as John Rawls) would determine the distribution of income as if we were behind a "veil of ignorance" that prevented us from knowing our stations in life. Libertarians (such as Robert Nozick) would have the government enforce individual rights to ensure a fair process but then would not be concerned about inequality in the resulting distribution of income.
- Various policies aim to help the poor—minimum-wage laws, welfare, negative income taxes, and in-kind transfers. While these policies help alleviate poverty, they also have unintended side effects. Because financial assistance declines as income rises, the poor often face very high effective marginal tax rates, which discourage poor families from escaping poverty on their own.

KEY CONCEPTS

poverty rate, p. 406
poverty line, p. 406
in-kind transfers, p. 407
life cycle, p. 407
permanent income, p. 408
utilitarianism, p. 410
utility, p. 410
liberalism, p. 411
maximin criterion, p. 411
social insurance, p. 411
libertarianism, p. 412
welfare, p. 414
negative income tax, p. 414

QUESTIONS FOR REVIEW

1. Does the richest fifth of the U.S. population earn closer to three, six, or twelve times the income of the poorest fifth?
2. What has happened to the income share of the richest fifth of the U.S. population over the past 40 years?
3. What groups in the U.S. population are most likely to live in poverty?
4. When gauging the amount of inequality, why do transitory and life cycle variations in income cause difficulties?
5. How would a utilitarian, a liberal, and a libertarian each determine how much income inequality is permissible?
6. What are the pros and cons of in-kind (rather than cash) transfers to the poor?
7. Describe how antipoverty programs can discourage the poor from working. How might you reduce this disincentive? What are the disadvantages of your proposed policy?

PROBLEMS AND APPLICATIONS

1. Table 2 shows that income inequality in the United States has increased since 1970. Some factors contributing to this increase were discussed in Chapter 19. What are they?
2. Table 3 shows that the percentage of children in families with income below the poverty line far exceeds the percentage of the elderly in such families. How might the allocation of government money across different social programs have contributed to this phenomenon?
3. This chapter discusses the importance of economic mobility.
   a. What policies might the government pursue to increase economic mobility *within* a generation?
   b. What policies might the government pursue to increase economic mobility *across* generations?
   c. Do you think we should reduce spending on current welfare programs to increase spending on programs that enhance economic mobility? What are some of the advantages and disadvantages of doing so?
4. Consider two communities. In one community, ten families have incomes of $100,000 each and ten families have incomes of $20,000 each. In the other community, ten families have incomes of $200,000 each and ten families have incomes of $22,000 each.
   a. In which community is the distribution of income more unequal? In which community is the problem of poverty likely to be worse?
   b. Which distribution of income would Rawls prefer? Explain.
   c. Which distribution of income do you prefer? Explain.
   d. Why might someone have the opposite preference?
5. This chapter uses the analogy of a "leaky bucket" to explain one constraint on the redistribution of income.
   a. What elements of the U.S. system for redistributing income create the leaks in the bucket? Be specific.
   b. Do you think that Republicans or Democrats generally believe that the bucket used for redistributing income is leakier? How does that belief affect their views about the amount of income redistribution that the government should undertake?
6. Suppose there are two possible income distributions in a society of ten people. In the first distribution, nine people have incomes of $30,000 and one person has an income of $10,000. In the second distribution, all ten people have incomes of $25,000.
   a. If the society had the first income distribution, what would be the utilitarian argument for redistributing income?
   b. Which income distribution would Rawls consider more equitable? Explain.
   c. Which income distribution would Nozick consider more equitable? Explain.
7. The poverty rate would be substantially lower if the market value of in-kind transfers were added to family income. The largest in-kind transfer is Medicaid, the government health program for the poor. Let's say the program costs $10,000 per recipient family.
   a. If the government gave each recipient family a $10,000 check instead of enrolling them in the Medicaid program, do you think that most of these families would spend that money to purchase health insurance? Why? (Recall that the poverty level for a family of four is about $23,000.)
   b. How does your answer to part (a) affect your view about whether we should determine the poverty rate by valuing in-kind transfers at the price the government pays for them? Explain.
   c. How does your answer to part (a) affect your view about whether we should provide assistance to the poor in the form of cash transfers or in-kind transfers? Explain.
8. Consider two of the income security programs in the United States: Temporary Assistance for Needy Families (TANF) and the Earned Income Tax Credit (EITC).
   a. When a woman with children and very low income earns an extra dollar, she receives less in TANF benefits. What do you think is the effect of this feature of TANF on the labor supply of low-income women? Explain.
   b. The EITC provides greater benefits as low-income workers earn more income (up to a point). What do you think is the effect of this program on the labor supply of low-income individuals? Explain.
   c. What are the disadvantages of eliminating TANF and allocating the savings to the EITC?

To find additional study resources, visit cengagebrain.com, and search for "Mankiw."

PART VII

Topics for Further Study

The Theory of Consumer Choice

CHAPTER 21

When you walk into a store, you are confronted with thousands of goods that you might buy. Because your financial resources are limited, however, you cannot buy everything that you want. You therefore consider the prices of the various goods offered for sale and buy a bundle of goods that, given your resources, best suits your needs and desires.

In this chapter, we develop a theory that describes how consumers make decisions about what to buy. Thus far in this book, we have summarized consumers' decisions with the demand curve. As we have seen, the demand curve for a good

reflects consumers' willingness to pay for that good. When the price rises, consumers are willing to pay for fewer units, so the quantity demanded falls. We now look more deeply at the decisions that lie behind the demand curve. The theory of consumer choice presented in this chapter provides a more complete understanding of demand, just as the theory of the competitive firm in Chapter 14 provides a more complete understanding of supply.

One of the *Ten Principles of Economics* discussed in Chapter 1 is that people face trade-offs. The theory of consumer choice examines the trade-offs that people face as consumers. When a consumer buys more of one good, she can afford less of other goods. When she spends more time enjoying leisure and less time working, she has lower income and therefore lower consumption. When she spends more of her income in the present and saves less of it, she reduces the amount she will be able to consume in the future. The theory of consumer choice examines how consumers facing these trade-offs make decisions and how they respond to changes in their environment.

After developing the basic theory of consumer choice, we apply it to three questions about household decisions. In particular, we ask:

- Do all demand curves slope downward?
- How do wages affect labor supply?
- How do interest rates affect household saving?

At first, these questions might seem unrelated. But as we will see, we can use the theory of consumer choice to address each of them.

21-1 The Budget Constraint: What the Consumer Can Afford

Most people would like to increase the quantity or quality of the goods they consume—to take longer vacations, drive fancier cars, or eat at better restaurants. People consume less than they desire because their spending is *constrained*, or limited, by their income. We begin our study of consumer choice by examining this link between income and spending.

To keep things simple, we examine the decision facing a consumer who buys only two goods: pizza and Pepsi. Of course, real people buy thousands of different kinds of goods. Assuming there are only two goods greatly simplifies the problem without altering the basic insights about consumer choice.

We first consider how the consumer's income constrains the amount she spends on pizza and Pepsi. Suppose the consumer has an income of $1,000 per month and spends her entire income on pizza and Pepsi. The price of a pizza is $10, and the price of a liter of Pepsi is $2.

The table in Figure 1 shows some of the many combinations of pizza and Pepsi that the consumer can buy. The first row in the table shows that if the consumer spends all her income on pizza, she can eat 100 pizzas during the month, but she would not be able to buy any Pepsi at all. The second row shows another possible consumption bundle: 90 pizzas and 50 liters of Pepsi. And so on. Each consumption bundle in the table costs exactly $1,000.

The graph in Figure 1 illustrates the consumption bundles that the consumer can choose. The vertical axis measures the number of liters of Pepsi, and the horizontal axis measures the number of pizzas. Three points are marked on this

FIGURE 1

The Consumer's Budget Constraint

The budget constraint shows the various bundles of goods that the consumer can buy for a given income. Here the consumer buys bundles of pizza and Pepsi. The table and graph show what the consumer can afford if her income is $1,000, the price of pizza is $10, and the price of Pepsi is $2.

Number of Pizzas	Liters of Pepsi	Spending on Pizza	Spending on Pepsi	Total Spending
100	0	$1,000	$ 0	$1,000
90	50	900	100	1,000
80	100	800	200	1,000
70	150	700	300	1,000
60	200	600	400	1,000
50	250	500	500	1,000
40	300	400	600	1,000
30	350	300	700	1,000
20	400	200	800	1,000
10	450	100	900	1,000
0	500	0	1,000	1,000

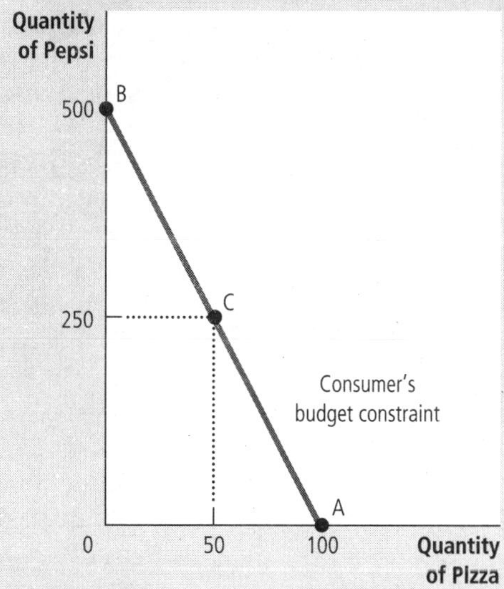

figure. At point A, the consumer buys no Pepsi and consumes 100 pizzas. At point B, the consumer buys no pizza and consumes 500 liters of Pepsi. At point C, the consumer buys 50 pizzas and 250 liters of Pepsi. Point C, which is exactly at the middle of the line from A to B, is the point at which the consumer spends an equal amount ($500) on pizza and Pepsi. These are only three of the many combinations of pizza and Pepsi that the consumer can choose. All the points on the line from A to B are possible. This line, called the **budget constraint**, shows the consumption bundles that the consumer can afford. In this case, it shows the trade-off between pizza and Pepsi that the consumer faces.

budget constraint
the limit on the consumption bundles that a consumer can afford

The slope of the budget constraint measures the rate at which the consumer can trade one good for the other. Recall that the slope between two points is calculated as the change in the vertical distance divided by the change in the horizontal distance ("rise over run"). From point A to point B, the vertical distance is 500 liters, and the horizontal distance is 100 pizzas. Thus, the slope is 5 liters per pizza. (Actually, because the budget constraint slopes downward, the slope is a negative number. But for our purposes we can ignore the minus sign.)

Notice that the slope of the budget constraint equals the *relative price* of the two goods—the price of one good compared to the price of the other. A pizza costs five times as much as a liter of Pepsi, so the opportunity cost of a pizza is 5 liters of Pepsi. The budget constraint's slope of 5 reflects the trade-off the market is offering the consumer: 1 pizza for 5 liters of Pepsi.

QuickQuiz *Draw the budget constraint for a person with income of $1,000 if the price of Pepsi is $5 and the price of pizza is $10. What is the slope of this budget constraint?*

21-2 Preferences: What the Consumer Wants

Our goal in this chapter is to understand how consumers make choices. The budget constraint is one piece of the analysis: It shows the combinations of goods the consumer can afford given her income and the prices of the goods. The consumer's choices, however, depend not only on her budget constraint but also on her preferences regarding the two goods. Therefore, the consumer's preferences are the next piece of our analysis.

21-2a Representing Preferences with Indifference Curves

The consumer's preferences allow her to choose among different bundles of pizza and Pepsi. If you offer the consumer two different bundles, she chooses the bundle that best suits her tastes. If the two bundles suit her tastes equally well, we say that the consumer is *indifferent* between the two bundles.

Just as we have represented the consumer's budget constraint graphically, we can also represent her preferences graphically. We do this with indifference curves. An **indifference curve** shows the various bundles of consumption that make the consumer equally happy. In this case, the indifference curves show the combinations of pizza and Pepsi with which the consumer is equally satisfied.

indifference curve
a curve that shows consumption bundles that give the consumer the same level of satisfaction

Figure 2 shows two of the consumer's many indifference curves. The consumer is indifferent among combinations A, B, and C because they are all on the same curve. Not surprisingly, if the consumer's consumption of pizza is reduced, say, from point A to point B, consumption of Pepsi must increase to keep her equally happy. If consumption of pizza is reduced again, from point B to point C, the amount of Pepsi consumed must increase yet again.

The slope at any point on an indifference curve equals the rate at which the consumer is willing to substitute one good for the other. This rate is called the **marginal rate of substitution** (*MRS*). In this case, the marginal rate of substitution measures how much Pepsi the consumer requires to be compensated for a one-unit reduction in pizza consumption. Notice that because the indifference curves are not straight lines, the marginal rate of substitution is not the same at all points on a given indifference curve. The rate at which a consumer is willing to trade one good for the other depends on the amounts of the goods she is already consuming. In other words, the rate at which a consumer is willing to trade pizza

marginal rate of substitution
the rate at which a consumer is willing to trade one good for another

FIGURE 2

The Consumer's Preferences

The consumer's preferences are represented with indifference curves, which show the combinations of pizza and Pepsi that make the consumer equally satisfied. Because the consumer prefers more of a good, points on a higher indifference curve (I_2) are preferred to points on a lower indifference curve (I_1). The marginal rate of substitution (*MRS*) shows the rate at which the consumer is willing to trade Pepsi for pizza. It measures the quantity of Pepsi the consumer must be given in exchange for 1 pizza.

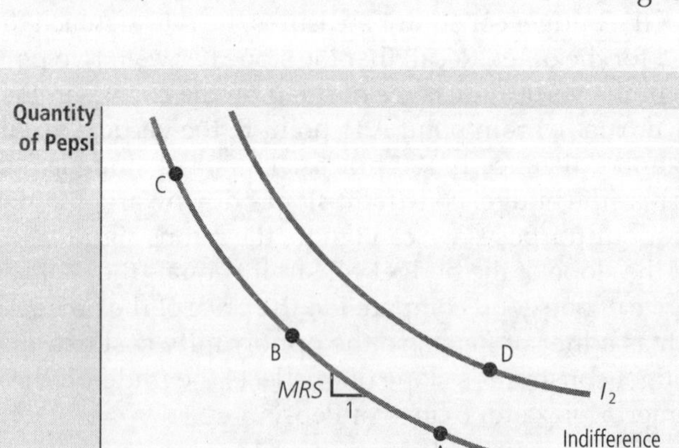

for Pepsi depends on whether she is hungrier or thirstier, which in turn depends on her current consumption of pizza and Pepsi.

The consumer is equally happy at all points on any given indifference curve, but she prefers some indifference curves to others. Because she prefers more consumption to less, higher indifference curves are preferred to lower ones. In Figure 2, any point on curve I_2 is preferred to any point on curve I_1.

A consumer's set of indifference curves gives a complete ranking of the consumer's preferences. That is, we can use the indifference curves to rank any two bundles of goods. For example, the indifference curves tell us that point D is preferred to point A because point D is on a higher indifference curve than point A. (That conclusion may be obvious, however, because point D offers the consumer both more pizza and more Pepsi.) The indifference curves also tell us that point D is preferred to point C because point D is on a higher indifference curve. Even though point D has less Pepsi than point C, it has more than enough extra pizza to make the consumer prefer it. By seeing which point is on the higher indifference curve, we can use the set of indifference curves to rank any combination of pizza and Pepsi.

21-2b Four Properties of Indifference Curves

Because indifference curves represent a consumer's preferences, they have certain properties that reflect those preferences. Here we consider four properties that describe most indifference curves:

- *Property 1: Higher indifference curves are preferred to lower ones.* People usually prefer to consume more rather than less. This preference for greater quantities is reflected in the indifference curves. As Figure 2 shows, higher indifference curves represent larger quantities of goods than lower indifference curves. Thus, the consumer prefers being on higher indifference curves.
- *Property 2: Indifference curves are downward-sloping.* The slope of an indifference curve reflects the rate at which the consumer is willing to substitute one good for the other. In most cases, the consumer likes both goods. Therefore, if the quantity of one good is reduced, the quantity of the other good must increase for the consumer to be equally happy. For this reason, most indifference curves slope downward.
- *Property 3: Indifference curves do not cross.* To see why this is true, suppose that two indifference curves did cross, as in Figure 3. Then, because point A

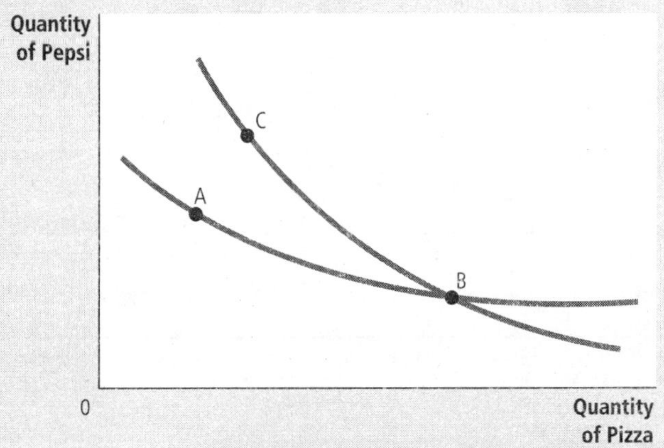

FIGURE 3

The Impossibility of Intersecting Indifference Curves

A situation like this can never happen. According to these indifference curves, the consumer would be equally satisfied at points A, B, and C, even though point C has more of both goods than point A.

is on the same indifference curve as point B, the two points would make the consumer equally happy. In addition, because point B is on the same indifference curve as point C, these two points would make the consumer equally happy. But these conclusions imply that points A and C would also make the consumer equally happy, even though point C has more of both goods. This contradicts our assumption that the consumer always prefers more of both goods to less. Thus, indifference curves cannot cross.

- *Property 4: Indifference curves are bowed inward.* The slope of an indifference curve is the marginal rate of substitution—the rate at which the consumer is willing to trade off one good for the other. The marginal rate of substitution (*MRS*) usually depends on the amount of each good the consumer is currently consuming. In particular, because people are more willing to trade away goods that they have in abundance and less willing to trade away goods of which they have little, the indifference curves are bowed inward toward the graph's origin. As an example, consider Figure 4. At point A, because the consumer has a lot of Pepsi and only a little pizza, she is very hungry but not very thirsty. To induce the consumer to give up 1 pizza, she has to be given 6 liters of Pepsi: The *MRS* is 6 liters per pizza. By contrast, at point B, the consumer has little Pepsi and a lot of pizza, so she is very thirsty but not very hungry. At this point, she would be willing to give up 1 pizza to get 1 liter of Pepsi: The *MRS* is 1 liter per pizza. Thus, the bowed shape of the indifference curve reflects the consumer's greater willingness to give up a good that she already has a lot of.

21-2c Two Extreme Examples of Indifference Curves

The shape of an indifference curve reveals the consumer's willingness to trade one good for the other. When the goods are easy to substitute for each other, the indifference curves are less bowed; when the goods are hard to substitute, the

FIGURE 4

Bowed Indifference Curves
Indifference curves are usually bowed inward. This shape implies that the marginal rate of substitution (*MRS*) depends on the quantity of the two goods the consumer is currently consuming. At point A, the consumer has little pizza and much Pepsi, so she requires a lot of extra Pepsi to induce her to give up one of the pizzas: The *MRS* is 6 liters of Pepsi per pizza. At point B, the consumer has much pizza and little Pepsi, so she requires only a little extra Pepsi to induce her to give up one of the pizzas: The *MRS* is 1 liter of Pepsi per pizza.

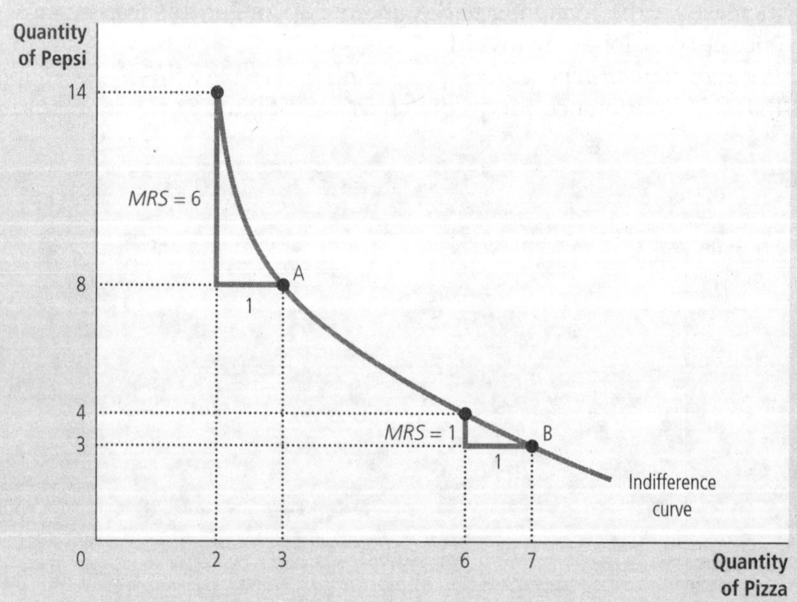

indifference curves are very bowed. To see why this is true, let's consider the extreme cases.

Perfect Substitutes Suppose that someone offered you bundles of nickels and dimes. How would you rank the different bundles?

Most likely, you would care only about the total monetary value of each bundle. If so, you would always be willing to trade 2 nickels for 1 dime. Your marginal rate of substitution between nickels and dimes would be a fixed number: $MRS = 2$, regardless of the number of nickels and dimes in the bundle.

We can represent your preferences for nickels and dimes with the indifference curves in panel (a) of Figure 5. Because the marginal rate of substitution is constant, the indifference curves are straight lines. In this extreme case of straight indifference curves, we say that the two goods are **perfect substitutes**.

perfect substitutes
two goods with straight-line indifference curves

Perfect Complements Suppose now that someone offered you bundles of shoes. Some of the shoes fit your left foot, others your right foot. How would you rank these different bundles?

In this case, you might care only about the number of pairs of shoes. In other words, you would judge a bundle based on the number of pairs you could assemble from it. A bundle of 5 left shoes and 7 right shoes yields only 5 pairs. Getting 1 more right shoe has no value if there is no left shoe to go with it.

We can represent your preferences for right and left shoes with the indifference curves in panel (b) of Figure 5. In this case, a bundle with 5 left shoes and 5 right shoes is just as good as a bundle with 5 left shoes and 7 right shoes. It is also just as good as a bundle with 7 left shoes and 5 right shoes. The indifference curves, therefore, are right angles. In this extreme case of right-angle indifference curves, we say that the two goods are **perfect complements**.

perfect complements
two goods with right-angle indifference curves

When two goods are easily substitutable, such as nickels and dimes, the indifference curves are straight lines, as shown in panel (a). When two goods are strongly complementary, such as left shoes and right shoes, the indifference curves are right angles, as shown in panel (b).

FIGURE 5

Perfect Substitutes and Perfect Complements

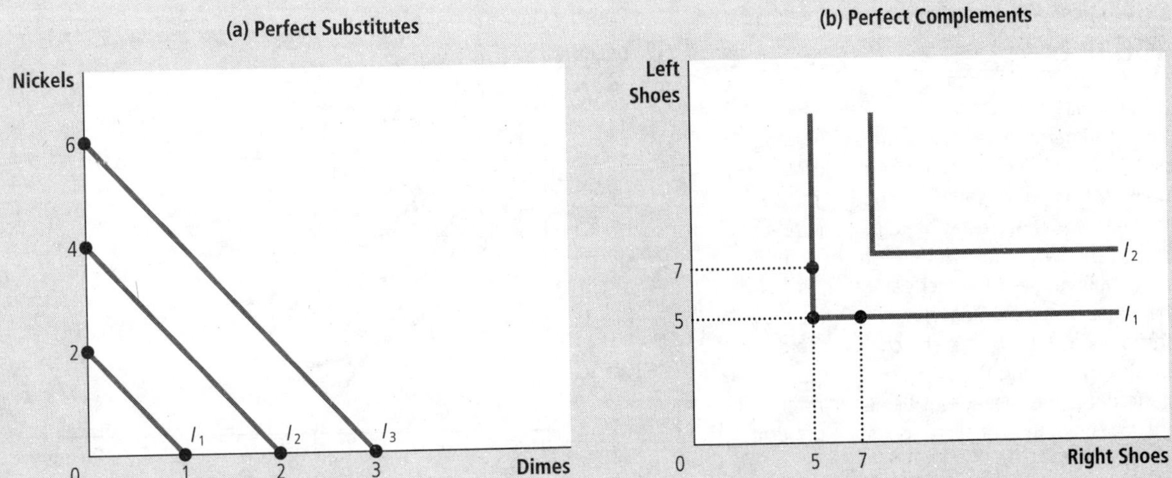

In the real world, of course, most goods are neither perfect substitutes (like nickels and dimes) nor perfect complements (like right shoes and left shoes). More typically, the indifference curves are bowed inward, but not so bowed that they become right angles.

QuickQuiz *Draw some indifference curves for pizza and Pepsi. Explain the four properties of these indifference curves.*

21-3 Optimization: What the Consumer Chooses

The goal of this chapter is to understand how a consumer makes choices. We have the two pieces necessary for this analysis: the consumer's budget constraint (how much she can afford to spend) and the consumer's preferences (what she wants to spend it on). Now we put these two pieces together and consider the consumer's decision about what to buy.

21-3a The Consumer's Optimal Choices

Once again, consider our pizza and Pepsi example. The consumer would like to end up with the best possible combination of pizza and Pepsi for her—that is, the combination on her highest possible indifference curve. But the consumer must also end up on or below her budget constraint, which measures the total resources available to her.

Figure 6 shows the consumer's budget constraint and three of her many indifference curves. The highest indifference curve that the consumer can reach (I_2 in the figure) is the one that just barely touches her budget constraint. The point at which this indifference curve and the budget constraint touch is called the *optimum*. The consumer would prefer point A, but she cannot afford that point because it lies above her budget constraint. The consumer can afford point B, but that point is on a lower indifference curve and, therefore, provides the consumer less satisfaction. The optimum represents the best combination of pizza and Pepsi available to the consumer.

FIGURE 6

The Consumer's Optimum

The consumer chooses the point on her budget constraint that lies on the highest indifference curve. At this point, called the optimum, the marginal rate of substitution equals the relative price of the two goods. Here the highest indifference curve the consumer can reach is I_2. The consumer prefers point A, which lies on indifference curve I_3, but she cannot afford this bundle of pizza and Pepsi. By contrast, point B is affordable, but because it lies on a lower indifference curve, the consumer does not prefer it.

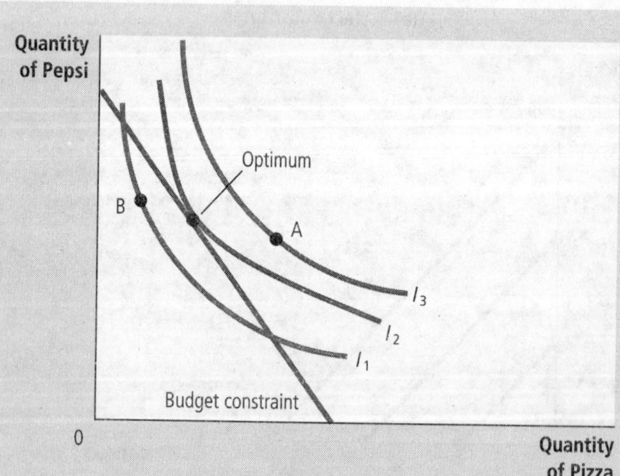

Notice that, at the optimum, the slope of the indifference curve equals the slope of the budget constraint. We say that the indifference curve is *tangent* to the budget constraint. The slope of the indifference curve is the marginal rate of substitution between pizza and Pepsi, and the slope of the budget constraint is the relative price of pizza and Pepsi. Thus, *the consumer chooses consumption of the two goods so that the marginal rate of substitution equals the relative price.*

In Chapter 7, we saw how market prices reflect the marginal value that consumers place on goods. This analysis of consumer choice shows the same result in another way. In making her consumption choices, the consumer takes the relative price of the two goods as given and then chooses an optimum at which her marginal rate of substitution equals this relative price. The relative price is the rate at which the *market* is willing to trade one good for the other, whereas the marginal rate of substitution is the rate at which the *consumer* is willing to trade one good for the other. At the consumer's optimum, the consumer's valuation of the

FYI

Utility: An Alternative Way to Describe Preferences and Optimization

We have used indifference curves to represent the consumer's preferences. Another common way to represent preferences is with the concept of *utility*. Utility is an abstract measure of the satisfaction or happiness that a consumer receives from a bundle of goods. Economists say that a consumer prefers one bundle of goods to another if one provides more utility than the other.

Indifference curves and utility are closely related. Because the consumer prefers points on higher indifference curves, bundles of goods on higher indifference curves provide higher utility. Because the consumer is equally happy with all points on the same indifference curve, all these bundles provide the same utility. You can think of an indifference curve as an "equal-utility" curve.

The *marginal utility* of any good is the increase in utility that the consumer gets from an additional unit of that good. Most goods are assumed to exhibit *diminishing marginal utility*: The more of the good the consumer already has, the lower the marginal utility provided by an extra unit of that good.

The marginal rate of substitution between two goods depends on their marginal utilities. For example, if the marginal utility of good X is twice the marginal utility of good Y, then a person would need 2 units of good Y to compensate for losing 1 unit of good X, and the *MRS* equals 2. More generally, the marginal rate of substitution (and thus the slope of the indifference curve) equals the marginal utility of one good divided by the marginal utility of the other good.

Utility analysis provides another way to describe consumer optimization. Recall that, at the consumer's optimum, the marginal rate of substitution equals the ratio of prices. That is,

$$MRS = P_X/P_Y.$$

Because the marginal rate of substitution equals the ratio of marginal utilities, we can write this condition for optimization as

$$MU_X/MU_Y = P_X/P_Y.$$

Now rearrange this expression to become

$$MU_X/P_X = MU_Y/P_Y.$$

This equation has a simple interpretation: At the optimum, the marginal utility per dollar spent on good X equals the marginal utility per dollar spent on good Y. If this equality did not hold, the consumer could increase utility by spending less on the good that provided lower marginal utility per dollar and more on the good that provided higher marginal utility per dollar.

When economists discuss the theory of consumer choice, they sometimes express the theory using different words. One economist might say that the goal of the consumer is to maximize utility. Another economist might say that the goal of the consumer is to end up on the highest possible indifference curve. The first economist would conclude that at the consumer's optimum, the marginal utility per dollar is the same for all goods, whereas the second would conclude that the indifference curve is tangent to the budget constraint. In essence, these are two ways of saying the same thing. ■

two goods (as measured by the marginal rate of substitution) equals the market's valuation (as measured by the relative price). As a result of this consumer optimization, market prices of different goods reflect the value that consumers place on those goods.

21-3b How Changes in Income Affect the Consumer's Choices

Now that we have seen how the consumer makes a consumption decision, let's examine how this decision responds to changes in the consumer's income. To be specific, suppose that income increases. With higher income, the consumer can afford more of both goods. The increase in income, therefore, shifts the budget constraint outward, as in Figure 7. Because the relative price of the two goods has not changed, the slope of the new budget constraint is the same as the slope of the initial budget constraint. That is, an increase in income leads to a parallel shift in the budget constraint.

The expanded budget constraint allows the consumer to choose a better combination of pizza and Pepsi, one that is on a higher indifference curve. Given the shift in the budget constraint and the consumer's preferences as represented by her indifference curves, the consumer's optimum moves from the point labeled "initial optimum" to the point labeled "new optimum."

Notice that, in Figure 7, the consumer chooses to consume more Pepsi and more pizza. The logic of the model does not require increased consumption of both goods in response to increased income, but this situation is the most common. As you may recall from Chapter 4, if a consumer wants more of a good when her income rises, economists call it a **normal good**. The indifference curves in Figure 7 are drawn under the assumption that both pizza and Pepsi are normal goods.

normal good
a good for which an increase in income raises the quantity demanded

FIGURE 7

An Increase in Income
When the consumer's income rises, the budget constraint shifts outward. If both goods are normal goods, the consumer responds to the increase in income by buying more of both of them. Here the consumer buys more pizza and more Pepsi.

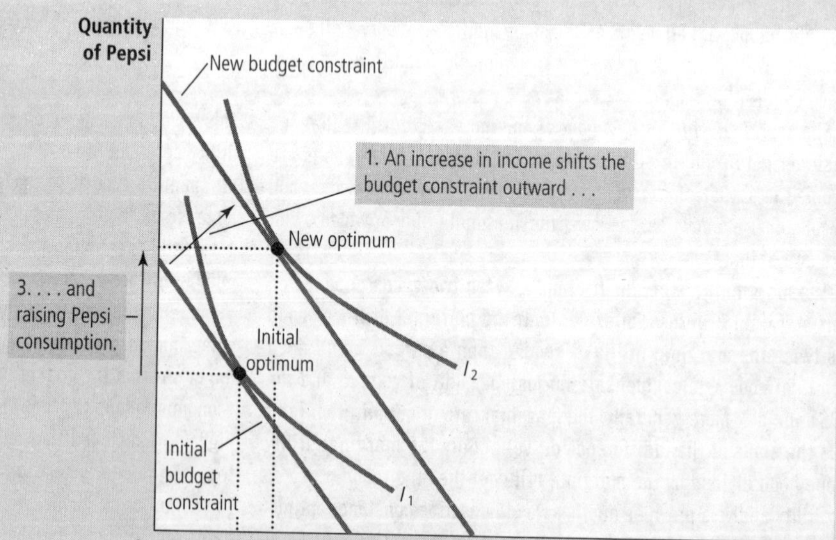

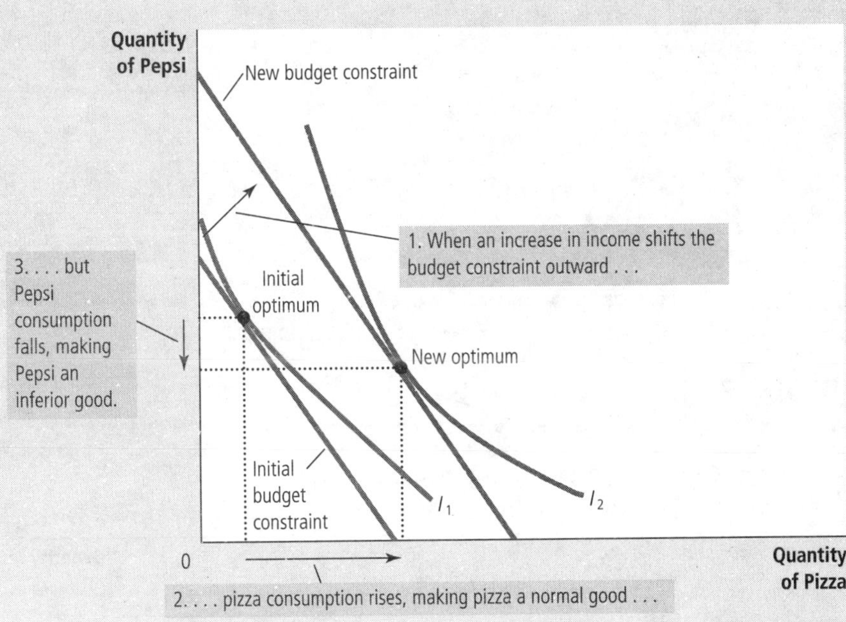

FIGURE 8

An Inferior Good
A good is inferior if the consumer buys less of it when her income rises. Here Pepsi is an inferior good: When the consumer's income increases and the budget constraint shifts outward, the consumer buys more pizza but less Pepsi.

Figure 8 shows an example in which an increase in income induces the consumer to buy more pizza but less Pepsi. If a consumer buys less of a good when her income rises, economists call it an **inferior good**. Figure 8 is drawn under the assumption that pizza is a normal good and Pepsi is an inferior good.

inferior good
a good for which an increase in income reduces the quantity demanded

Although most goods in the world are normal goods, there are some inferior goods as well. An example is bus rides. As income increases, consumers are more likely to own cars or take taxis and less likely to ride the bus. Bus rides, therefore, are an inferior good.

21-3c How Changes in Prices Affect the Consumer's Choices

Let's now use this model of consumer choice to consider how a change in the price of one of the goods alters the consumer's choices. Suppose, in particular, that the price of Pepsi falls from $2 to $1 per liter. It is no surprise that the lower price expands the consumer's set of buying opportunities. In other words, a fall in the price of any good shifts the budget constraint outward.

Figure 9 considers more specifically how the fall in price affects the budget constraint. If the consumer spends her entire $1,000 income on pizza, then the price of Pepsi is irrelevant. Thus, point A in the figure stays the same. Yet if the consumer spends her entire income of $1,000 on Pepsi, she can now buy 1,000 liters rather than only 500. Thus, the endpoint of the budget constraint moves from point B to point D.

Notice that in this case the outward shift in the budget constraint changes its slope. (This differs from what happened previously when prices stayed the same but the consumer's income changed.) As we have discussed, the slope of the budget constraint reflects the relative price of pizza and Pepsi. Because the price of Pepsi has fallen to $1 from $2, while the price of pizza has remained $10, the consumer can now trade a pizza for 10 rather than 5 liters of Pepsi. As a result, the new budget constraint has a steeper slope.

FIGURE 9

A Change in Price
When the price of Pepsi falls, the consumer's budget constraint shifts outward and changes slope. The consumer moves from the initial optimum to the new optimum, which changes her purchases of both pizza and Pepsi. In this case, the quantity of Pepsi consumed rises, and the quantity of pizza consumed falls.

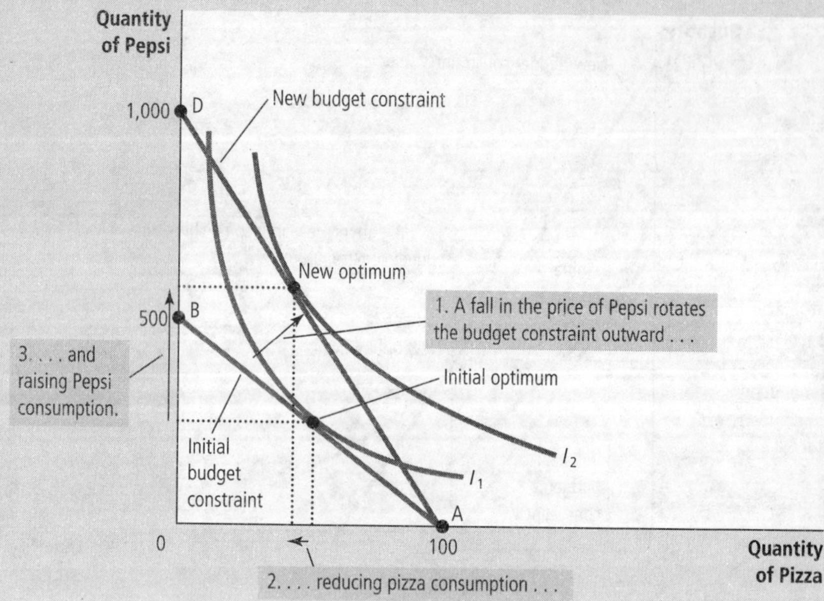

How such a change in the budget constraint alters the consumption of both goods depends on the consumer's preferences. For the indifference curves drawn in this figure, the consumer buys more Pepsi and less pizza.

21-3d Income and Substitution Effects

income effect
the change in consumption that results when a price change moves the consumer to a higher or lower indifference curve

substitution effect
the change in consumption that results when a price change moves the consumer along a given indifference curve to a point with a new marginal rate of substitution

The impact of a change in the price of a good on consumption can be decomposed into two effects: an **income effect** and a **substitution effect**. To see what these two effects are, consider how our consumer might respond when she learns that the price of Pepsi has fallen. She might reason in the following ways:

- "Great news! Now that Pepsi is cheaper, my income has greater purchasing power. I am, in effect, richer than I was. Because I am richer, I can buy both more pizza and more Pepsi." (This is the income effect.)
- "Now that the price of Pepsi has fallen, I get more liters of Pepsi for every pizza that I give up. Because pizza is now relatively more expensive, I should buy less pizza and more Pepsi." (This is the substitution effect.)

Which statement do you find more compelling?

In fact, both of these statements make sense. The decrease in the price of Pepsi makes the consumer better off. If pizza and Pepsi are both normal goods, the consumer will want to spread this improvement in her purchasing power over both goods. This income effect tends to make the consumer buy more pizza and more Pepsi. Yet at the same time, consumption of Pepsi has become less expensive relative to consumption of pizza. This substitution effect tends to make the consumer choose less pizza and more Pepsi.

Now consider the result of these two effects working at the same time. The consumer certainly buys more Pepsi because the income and substitution effects both act to increase purchases of Pepsi. But for pizza, the income and substitution effects work in opposite directions. As a result, whether the consumer buys more

Good	Income Effect	Substitution Effect	Total Effect
Pepsi	Consumer is richer, so she buys more Pepsi.	Pepsi is relatively cheaper, so consumer buys more Pepsi.	Income and substitution effects act in the same direction, so consumer buys more Pepsi.
Pizza	Consumer is richer, so she buys more pizza.	Pizza is relatively more expensive, so consumer buys less pizza.	Income and substitution effects act in opposite directions, so the total effect on pizza consumption is ambiguous.

TABLE 1

Income and Substitution Effects When the Price of Pepsi Falls

or less pizza is not clear. The outcome could go either way, depending on the sizes of the income and substitution effects. Table 1 summarizes these conclusions.

We can interpret the income and substitution effects using indifference curves. *The income effect is the change in consumption that results from the movement to a new indifference curve. The substitution effect is the change in consumption that results from moving to a new point on the same indifference curve with a different marginal rate of substitution.*

Figure 10 shows graphically how to decompose the change in the consumer's decision into the income effect and the substitution effect. When the price of Pepsi falls, the consumer moves from the initial optimum, point A, to the new optimum, point C. We can view this change as occurring in two steps. First, the consumer moves *along* the initial indifference curve, I_1, from point A to point B. The consumer

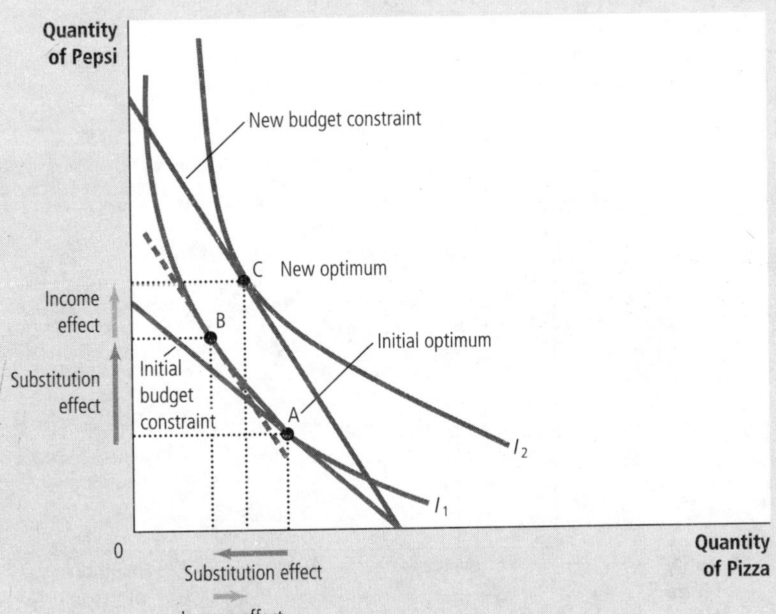

FIGURE 10

Income and Substitution Effects

The effect of a change in price can be broken down into an income effect and a substitution effect. The substitution effect—the movement along an indifference curve to a point with a different marginal rate of substitution—is shown here as the change from point A to point B along indifference curve I_1. The income effect—the shift to a higher indifference curve—is shown here as the change from point B on indifference curve I_1 to point C on indifference curve I_2.

is equally happy at these two points, but at point B, the marginal rate of substitution reflects the new relative price. (The dashed line through point B is parallel to the new budget constraint and thus reflects the new relative price.) Next, the consumer *shifts* to the higher indifference curve, I_2, by moving from point B to point C. Even though point B and point C are on different indifference curves, they have the same marginal rate of substitution. That is, the slope of the indifference curve I_1 at point B equals the slope of the indifference curve I_2 at point C.

The consumer never actually chooses point B, but this hypothetical point is useful to clarify the two effects that determine the consumer's decision. Notice that the change from point A to point B represents a pure change in the marginal rate of substitution without any change in the consumer's welfare. Similarly, the change from point B to point C represents a pure change in welfare without any change in the marginal rate of substitution. Thus, the movement from A to B shows the substitution effect, and the movement from B to C shows the income effect.

21-3e Deriving the Demand Curve

We have just seen how changes in the price of a good alter the consumer's budget constraint and, therefore, the quantities of the two goods that she chooses to buy. The demand curve for any good reflects these consumption decisions. Recall that a demand curve shows the quantity demanded of a good for any given price. We can view a consumer's demand curve as a summary of the optimal decisions that arise from her budget constraint and indifference curves.

For example, Figure 11 considers the demand for Pepsi. Panel (a) shows that when the price of a liter falls from $2 to $1, the consumer's budget constraint shifts outward. Because of both income and substitution effects, the consumer increases her purchases of Pepsi from 250 to 750 liters. Panel (b) shows the demand curve

FIGURE 11

Deriving the Demand Curve

Panel (a) shows that when the price of Pepsi falls from $2 to $1, the consumer's optimum moves from point A to point B, and the quantity of Pepsi consumed rises from 250 to 750 liters. The demand curve in panel (b) reflects this relationship between the price and the quantity demanded.

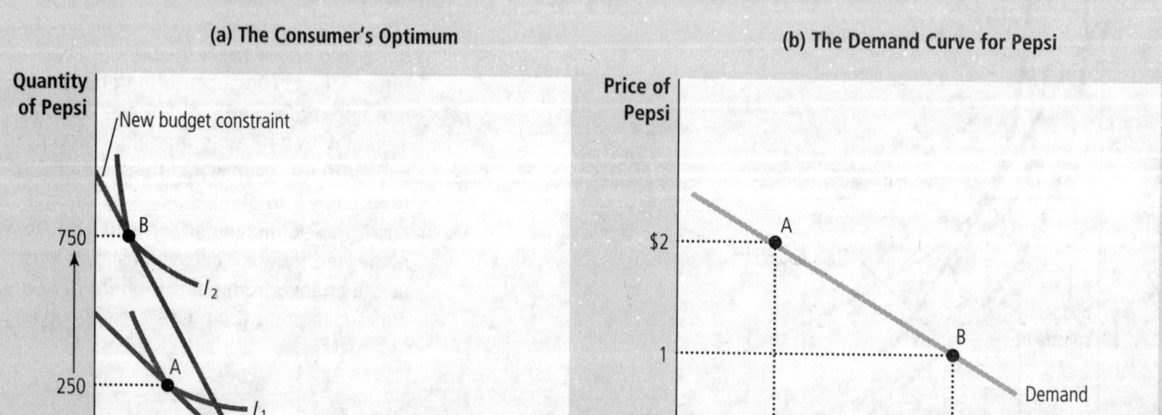

that results from this consumer's decisions. In this way, the theory of consumer choice provides the theoretical foundation for the consumer's demand curve.

It may be comforting to know that the demand curve arises naturally from the theory of consumer choice, but this exercise by itself does not justify developing the theory. There is no need for a rigorous, analytic framework just to establish that people respond to changes in prices. The theory of consumer choice is, however, useful in studying various decisions that people make as they go about their lives, as we see in the next section.

QuickQuiz *Draw a budget constraint and indifference curves for pizza and Pepsi. Show what happens to the budget constraint and the consumer's optimum when the price of pizza rises. In your diagram, decompose the change into an income effect and a substitution effect.*

21-4 Three Applications

Now that we have developed the basic theory of consumer choice, let's use it to shed light on three questions about how the economy works. These three questions might at first seem unrelated. But because each question involves household decision making, we can address it with the model of consumer behavior we have just developed.

21-4a Do All Demand Curves Slope Downward?

Normally, when the price of a good rises, people buy less of it. This typical behavior, called the *law of demand*, is reflected in the downward slope of the demand curve.

As a matter of economic theory, however, demand curves can sometimes slope upward. In other words, consumers can sometimes violate the law of demand and buy *more* of a good when the price rises. To see how this can happen, consider Figure 12. In this example, the consumer buys two goods—meat and potatoes.

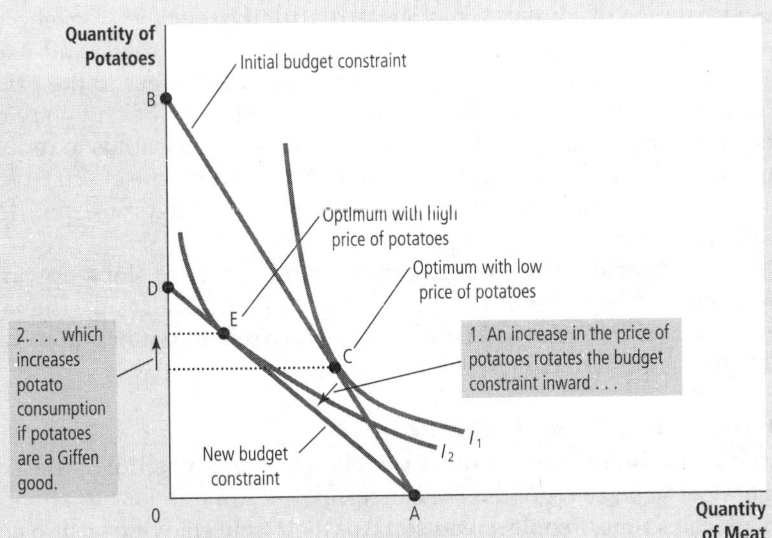

FIGURE 12

A Giffen Good

In this example, when the price of potatoes rises, the consumer's optimum shifts from point C to point E. In this case, the consumer responds to a higher price of potatoes by buying less meat and more potatoes.

Initially, the consumer's budget constraint is the line from point A to point B. The optimum is point C. When the price of potatoes rises, the budget constraint shifts inward and is now the line from point A to point D. The optimum is now point E. Notice that a rise in the price of potatoes has led the consumer to buy a larger quantity of potatoes.

Why is the consumer responding in this strange way? In this example, potatoes are a strongly inferior good; that is, potatoes are a good that a person buys a lot less of when her income rises and a lot more of when her income falls. In Figure 12, the increase in the price of potatoes makes the consumer poorer; that is, the higher price puts her on a lower indifference curve. Because she is poorer and potatoes are an inferior good, the income effect makes her want to buy less meat and more potatoes. At the same time, because the potatoes have become more expensive relative to meat, the substitution effect makes the consumer want to buy more meat and fewer potatoes. If the income effect is much larger than the substitution effect, as it is in this example, the consumer responds to the higher price of potatoes by buying less meat and more potatoes.

Giffen good
a good for which an increase in the price raises the quantity demanded

Economists use the term **Giffen good** to describe a good that violates the law of demand. (The term is named for economist Robert Giffen, who first noted this possibility.) In this example, potatoes are a Giffen good. Giffen goods are inferior goods for which the income effect dominates the substitution effect. Therefore, they have demand curves that slope upward.

CASE STUDY

THE SEARCH FOR GIFFEN GOODS

Have any actual Giffen goods ever been observed? Some historians suggest that potatoes were a Giffen good during the Irish potato famine of the 19th century. Potatoes were such a large part of people's diet that when the price of potatoes rose, the change had a large income effect. People responded to their reduced living standard by cutting back on the luxury of meat and buying more of the staple food of potatoes. Thus, it is argued that a higher price of potatoes actually raised the quantity of potatoes demanded.

A study by Robert Jensen and Nolan Miller, published in the *American Economic Review* in 2008, produced similar but more concrete evidence for the existence of Giffen goods. These two economists conducted a field experiment for five months in the Chinese province of Hunan. They gave randomly selected households vouchers that subsidized the purchase of rice, a staple in local diets, and used surveys to measure how consumption of rice responded to changes in the price. They found strong evidence that poor households exhibited Giffen behavior. Lowering the price of rice with the subsidy voucher caused households to reduce their consumption of rice, and removing the subsidy had the opposite effect. Jensen and Miller wrote, "To the best of our knowledge, this is the first rigorous empirical evidence of Giffen behavior."

Thus, the theory of consumer choice allows demand curves to slope upward, and sometimes that strange phenomenon actually occurs. As a result, the law of demand we first saw in Chapter 4 is not completely reliable. It is safe to say, however, that Giffen goods are very rare. ●

21-4b How Do Wages Affect Labor Supply?

So far, we have used the theory of consumer choice to analyze how a person allocates income between two goods. We can apply the same theory to analyze how a person allocates time. People spend some of their time enjoying leisure and some of it working so they can afford to buy consumption goods. The essence of the time-allocation problem is the trade-off between leisure and consumption.

Consider the decision facing Kayla, a freelance software designer. Kayla is awake for 100 hours per week. She spends some of this time enjoying leisure—playing *Minecraft*, watching *The Bachelor* on television, and reading this textbook. She spends the rest of this time at her computer developing software. For every hour she works developing software, she earns \$50, which she spends on consumption goods—food, clothing, and music downloads. Her hourly wage of \$50 reflects the trade-off Kayla faces between leisure and consumption. For every hour of leisure she gives up, she works one more hour and gets \$50 of consumption.

Figure 13 shows Kayla's budget constraint. If she spends all 100 hours enjoying leisure, she has no consumption. If she spends all 100 hours working, she earns a weekly consumption of \$5,000 but has no time for leisure. If she works a 40-hour week, she enjoys 60 hours of leisure and has weekly consumption of \$2,000.

Figure 13 uses indifference curves to represent Kayla's preferences for consumption and leisure. Here consumption and leisure are the two "goods" between which Kayla is choosing. Because Kayla always prefers more leisure and more consumption, she prefers points on higher indifference curves to points on lower ones. At a wage of \$50 per hour, Kayla chooses a combination of consumption and leisure represented by the point labeled "optimum." This is the point on the budget constraint that is on the highest possible indifference curve, I_2.

Now consider what happens when Kayla's wage increases from \$50 to \$60 per hour. Figure 14 illustrates two possible outcomes. In each case, the budget constraint, shown in the left graphs, shifts outward from BC_1 to BC_2. In the process, the budget constraint becomes steeper, reflecting the change in relative price: At the higher wage, Kayla earns more consumption for every hour of leisure that she gives up.

Kayla's preferences, as represented by her indifference curves, determine how her choice regarding consumption and leisure responds to the higher wage. In both panels, consumption rises. Yet the response of leisure to the change in the

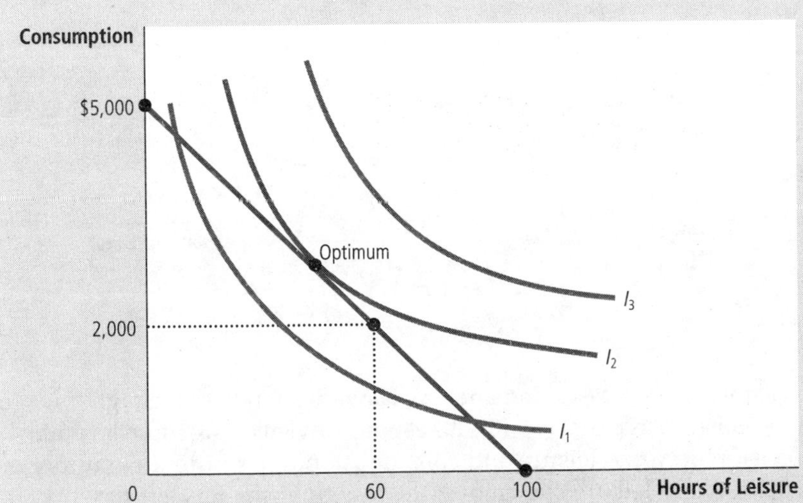

FIGURE 13

The Work-Leisure Decision
This figure shows Kayla's budget constraint for deciding how much to work, her indifference curves for consumption and leisure, and her optimum.

FIGURE 14

An Increase in the Wage

The two panels of this figure show how a person might respond to an increase in the wage. The graphs on the left show the consumer's initial budget constraint, BC_1, and new budget constraint, BC_2, as well as the consumer's optimal choices over consumption and leisure. The graphs on the right show the resulting labor-supply curve. Because hours worked equal total hours available minus hours of leisure, any change in leisure implies an opposite change in the quantity of labor supplied. In panel (a), when the wage rises, consumption rises and leisure falls, resulting in a labor-supply curve that slopes upward. In panel (b), when the wage rises, both consumption and leisure rise, resulting in a labor-supply curve that slopes backward.

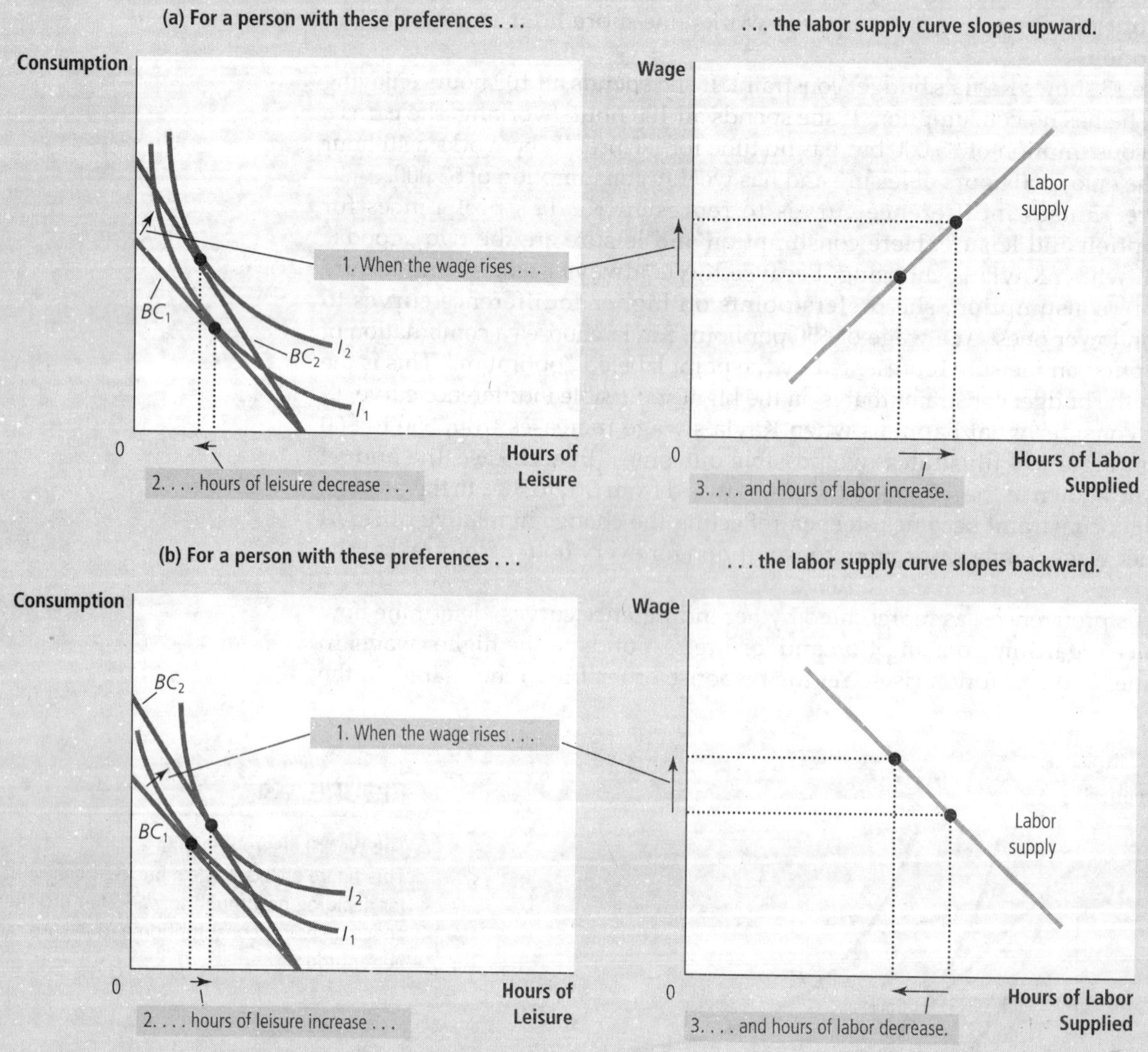

wage is different in the two cases. In panel (a), Kayla responds to the higher wage by enjoying less leisure. In panel (b), Kayla responds by enjoying more leisure.

Kayla's decision between leisure and consumption determines her supply of labor because the more leisure she enjoys, the less time she has left to work. In each panel of Figure 14, the right graph shows the labor-supply curve implied by Kayla's decision. In panel (a), a higher wage induces Kayla to enjoy less leisure and work more, so the labor-supply curve slopes upward. In panel (b), a higher wage induces Kayla to enjoy more leisure and work less, so the labor-supply curve slopes "backward."

At first, the backward-sloping labor-supply curve is puzzling. Why would a person respond to a higher wage by working less? The answer comes from considering the income and substitution effects of a higher wage.

Consider first the substitution effect. When Kayla's wage rises, leisure becomes more expensive relative to consumption, and this encourages Kayla to substitute away from leisure and toward consumption. In other words, the substitution effect induces Kayla to work more in response to higher wages, which tends to make the labor-supply curve slope upward.

Now consider the income effect. When Kayla's wage rises, she moves to a higher indifference curve. She is now better off than she was. As long as consumption and leisure are both normal goods, she tends to want to use this increase in well-being to enjoy both higher consumption and greater leisure. In other words, the income effect induces her to work less, which tends to make the labor-supply curve slope backward.

In the end, economic theory does not give a clear prediction about whether an increase in the wage induces Kayla to work more or less. If the substitution effect is greater than the income effect, she works more. If the income effect is greater than the substitution effect, she works less. The labor-supply curve, therefore, could be either upward- or backward-sloping.

CASE STUDY

INCOME EFFECTS ON LABOR SUPPLY: HISTORICAL TRENDS, LOTTERY WINNERS, AND THE CARNEGIE CONJECTURE

The idea of a backward-sloping labor-supply curve might at first seem like a mere theoretical curiosity, but in fact it is not. Evidence indicates that the labor-supply curve, considered over long periods, does indeed slope backward. A hundred years ago, many people worked six days a week. Today, five-day workweeks are the norm. At the same time that the length of the workweek has been falling, the wage of the typical worker (adjusted for inflation) has been rising.

Here is how economists explain this historical pattern: Over time, advances in technology raise workers' productivity and, thereby, the demand for labor. This increase in labor demand raises equilibrium wages. As wages rise, so does the reward for working. Yet rather than responding to this increased incentive by working more, most workers choose to take part of their greater prosperity in the form of more leisure. In other words, the income effect of higher wages dominates the substitution effect.

Further evidence that the income effect on labor supply is strong comes from a very different kind of data: winners of lotteries. Winners of large prizes in the lottery see large increases in their incomes and, as a result, large outward shifts in their budget constraints. Because the winners' wages have not changed, however, the *slopes* of their budget constraints remain the same. There is, therefore, no substitution effect. By examining the behavior of lottery winners, we can isolate the income effect on labor supply.

The results from studies of lottery winners are striking. Of those winners who win more than \$50,000, almost 25 percent quit working within a year and another 9 percent reduce the number of hours they work. Of those winners who win more than \$1 million, almost 40 percent stop working. The income effect on labor supply of winning such a large prize is substantial.

GETTY IMAGES NEWS/GETTY IMAGES

"No more 9 to 5 for me."

Similar results were found in a 1993 study, published in the *Quarterly Journal of Economics,* of how receiving a bequest affects a person's labor supply. The study found that a single person who inherits more than $150,000 is four times as likely to stop working as a single person who inherits less than $25,000. This finding would not have surprised the 19th-century industrialist Andrew Carnegie. Carnegie warned that "the parent who leaves his son enormous wealth generally deadens the talents and energies of the son, and tempts him to lead a less useful and less worthy life than he otherwise would." That is, Carnegie viewed the income effect on labor supply to be substantial and, from his paternalistic perspective, regrettable. During his life and at his death, Carnegie gave much of his vast fortune to charity. ●

21-4c How Do Interest Rates Affect Household Saving?

An important decision that every person faces is how much income to consume today and how much to save for the future. We can use the theory of consumer choice to analyze how people make this decision and how the amount they save depends on the interest rate their savings will earn.

Consider the decision facing Saul, a worker planning for retirement. To keep things simple, let's divide Saul's life into two periods. In the first period, Saul is young and working. In the second period, he is old and retired. When young, Saul earns $100,000. He divides this income between current consumption and saving. When he is old, Saul will consume what he has saved, including the interest that his savings have earned.

Suppose the interest rate is 10 percent. Then for every dollar that Saul saves when young, he can consume $1.10 when old. We can view "consumption when young" and "consumption when old" as the two goods that Saul must choose between. The interest rate determines the relative price of these two goods.

Figure 15 shows Saul's budget constraint. If he saves nothing, he consumes $100,000 when young and nothing when old. If he saves everything, he consumes nothing when young and $110,000 when old. The budget constraint shows these and all the intermediate possibilities.

FIGURE 15

The Consumption-Saving Decision
This figure shows the budget constraint for a person deciding how much to consume in the two periods of his life, the indifference curves representing his preferences, and the optimum.

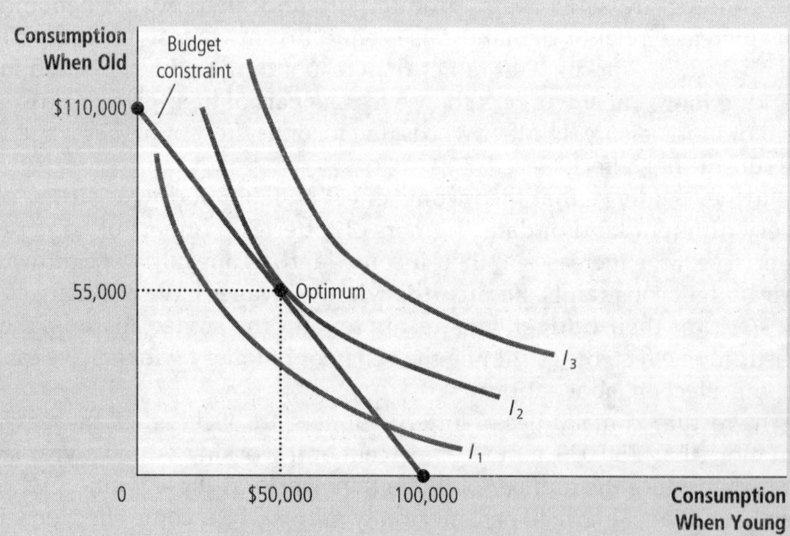

Figure 15 uses indifference curves to represent Saul's preferences for consumption in the two periods. Because Saul prefers more consumption in both periods, he prefers points on higher indifference curves to points on lower ones. Given his preferences, Saul chooses the optimal combination of consumption in both periods of life, which is the point on the budget constraint that is on the highest possible indifference curve. At this optimum, Saul consumes $50,000 when young and $55,000 when old.

Now consider what happens when the interest rate increases from 10 to 20 percent. Figure 16 shows two possible outcomes. In both cases, the budget constraint shifts outward and becomes steeper. At the new, higher interest rate, Saul gets more consumption when old for every dollar of consumption that he gives up when young.

The two panels show the results given different preferences by Saul. In both cases, consumption when old rises. Yet the response of consumption when young to the change in the interest rate is different in the two cases. In panel (a), Saul responds to the higher interest rate by consuming less when young. In panel (b), Saul responds by consuming more when young.

Saul's saving is his income when young minus the amount he consumes when young. In panel (a), an increase in the interest rate reduces consumption when young, so saving must rise. In panel (b), an increase in the interest rate induces Saul to consume more when young, so saving must fall.

The case shown in panel (b) might at first seem odd: Saul responds to an increase in the return to saving by saving less. But this behavior is not as peculiar as it might seem. We can understand it by considering the income and substitution effects of a higher interest rate.

FIGURE 16

An Increase in the Interest Rate

In both panels, an increase in the interest rate shifts the budget constraint outward. In panel (a), consumption when young falls, and consumption when old rises. The result is an increase in saving when young. In panel (b), consumption in both periods rises. The result is a decrease in saving when young.

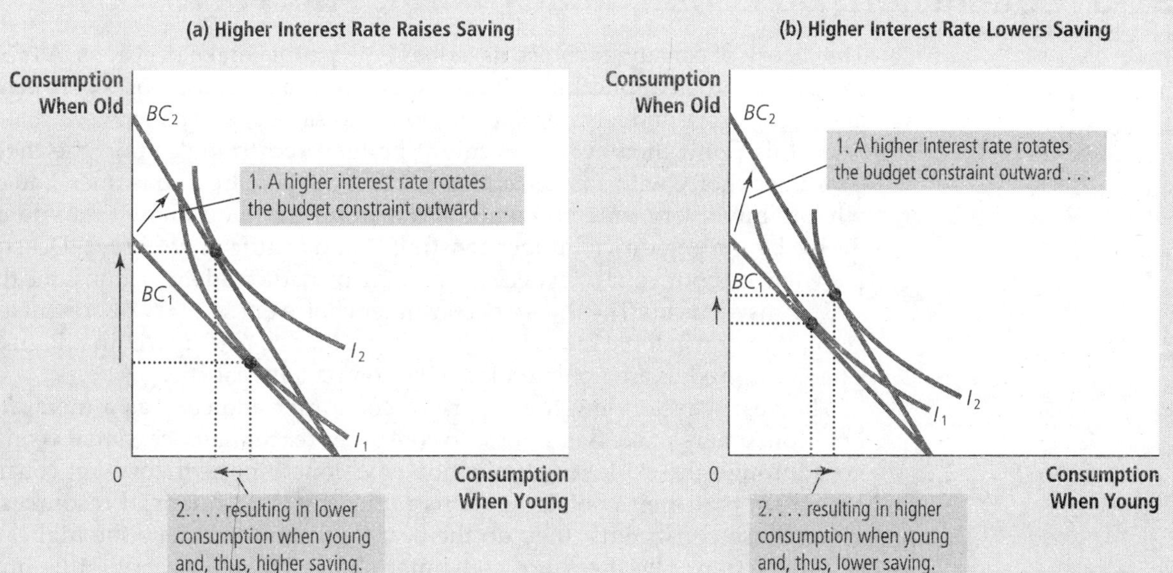

Consider first the substitution effect. When the interest rate rises, consumption when old becomes less costly relative to consumption when young. Therefore, the substitution effect induces Saul to consume more when old and less when young. In other words, the substitution effect induces Saul to save more.

Now consider the income effect. When the interest rate rises, Saul moves to a higher indifference curve. He is now better off than he was. As long as consumption in both periods consists of normal goods, he tends to want to use this increase in well-being to enjoy higher consumption in both periods. In other words, the income effect induces him to save less.

The result depends on both the income and substitution effects. If the substitution effect of a higher interest rate is greater than the income effect, Saul saves more. If the income effect is greater than the substitution effect, Saul saves less. Thus, the theory of consumer choice says that an increase in the interest rate could either encourage or discourage saving.

This ambiguous result is interesting from the standpoint of economic theory, but it is disappointing from the standpoint of economic policy. It turns out that an important issue in tax policy hinges in part on how saving responds to interest rates. Some economists have advocated reducing the taxation of interest and other capital income, arguing that such a policy change would raise the after-tax interest rate that savers can earn and thereby encourage people to save more. Other economists have argued that because of offsetting income and substitution effects, such a tax change might not increase saving and could even reduce it. Unfortunately, research has not led to a consensus about how interest rates affect saving. As a result, there remains disagreement among economists about whether changes in tax policy aimed to encourage saving would, in fact, have the intended effect.

QuickQuiz *Explain how an increase in the wage can potentially decrease the amount that a person wants to work.*

21-5 Conclusion: Do People Really Think This Way?

The theory of consumer choice describes how people make decisions. As we have seen, it has broad applicability. It can explain how a person chooses between pizza and Pepsi, work and leisure, consumption and saving, and so on.

At this point, however, you might be tempted to look upon the theory of consumer choice with some skepticism. After all, you are a consumer. You decide what to buy every time you walk into a store. And you know that you do not decide by writing down budget constraints and indifference curves. Doesn't this knowledge about your own decision making provide evidence against the theory?

The answer is no. The theory of consumer choice does not try to present a literal account of how people make decisions. It is a model. And as we first discussed in Chapter 2, models are not intended to be completely realistic.

The best way to view the theory of consumer choice is as a metaphor for how consumers make decisions. No consumer (except an occasional economist) goes through the explicit optimization envisioned in the theory. Yet consumers are aware that their choices are constrained by their financial resources. And given those constraints, they do the best they can to achieve the highest level of satisfaction. The theory of consumer choice tries to describe this implicit, psychological process in a way that permits explicit, economic analysis.

Just as the proof of the pudding is in the eating, the test of a theory is in its applications. In the last section of this chapter, we applied the theory of consumer choice to three practical issues about the economy. If you take more advanced courses in economics, you will see that this theory provides the framework for much additional analysis.

CHAPTER QuickQuiz

1. Emilio buys pizza for $10 and soda for $2. He has income of $100. His budget constraint will experience a parallel outward shift if which of the following events occur?
   a. The price of pizza falls to $5, the price of soda falls to $1, and his income falls to $50.
   b. The price of pizza rises to $20, the price of soda rises to $4, and his income remains the same.
   c. The price of pizza falls to $8, the price of soda falls to $1, and his income rises to $120.
   d. The price of pizza rises to $20, the price of soda rises to $4, and his income rises to $400.
2. At any point on an indifference curve, the slope of the curve measures the consumer's
   a. income.
   b. willingness to trade one good for the other.
   c. perception of the two goods as substitutes or complements.
   d. elasticity of demand.
3. Matthew and Susan are both optimizing consumers in the markets for shirts and hats, where they pay $100 for a shirt and $50 for a hat. Matthew buys 4 shirts and 16 hats, while Susan buys 6 shirts and 12 hats. From this information, we can infer that Matthew's marginal rate of substitution is _____ hats per shirt, while Susan's is _____.
   a. 2, 1
   b. 2, 2
   c. 4, 1
   d. 4, 2
4. Darius buys only lobster and chicken. Lobster is a normal good, while chicken is an inferior good. When the price of lobster rises, Darius buys
   a. less of both goods.
   b. more lobster and less chicken.
   c. less lobster and more chicken.
   d. less lobster, but the impact on chicken is ambiguous.
5. If the price of pasta increases and a consumer buys more pasta, we can infer that
   a. pasta is a normal good and the income effect is greater than the substitution effect.
   b. pasta is a normal good and the substitution effect is greater than the income effect.
   c. pasta is an inferior good and the income effect is greater than the substitution effect.
   d. pasta is an inferior good and the substitution effect is greater than the income effect.
6. The labor-supply curve slopes upward if
   a. leisure is a normal good.
   b. consumption is a normal good.
   c. the income effect on leisure is greater than the substitution effect.
   d. the substitution effect on leisure is greater than the income effect.

SUMMARY

- A consumer's budget constraint shows the possible combinations of different goods she can buy given her income and the prices of the goods. The slope of the budget constraint equals the relative price of the goods.
- The consumer's indifference curves represent her preferences. An indifference curve shows the various bundles of goods that make the consumer equally happy. Points on higher indifference curves are preferred to points on lower indifference curves. The slope of an indifference curve at any point is the consumer's marginal rate of substitution—the rate at which the consumer is willing to trade one good for the other.
- The consumer optimizes by choosing the point on her budget constraint that lies on the highest indifference curve. At this point, the slope of the indifference curve (the marginal rate of substitution between the goods) equals the slope of the budget constraint (the relative price of the goods), and the consumer's valuation of the two goods (measured by the marginal rate of substitution) equals the market's valuation (measured by the relative price).

- When the price of a good falls, the impact on the consumer's choices can be broken down into an income effect and a substitution effect. The income effect is the change in consumption that arises because a lower price makes the consumer better off. The substitution effect is the change in consumption that arises because a price change encourages greater consumption of the good that has become relatively cheaper. The income effect is reflected in the movement from a lower to a higher indifference curve, whereas the substitution effect is reflected by a movement along an indifference curve to a point with a different slope.
- The theory of consumer choice can be applied in many situations. It explains why demand curves can potentially slope upward, why higher wages could either increase or decrease the quantity of labor supplied, and why higher interest rates could either increase or decrease saving.

KEY CONCEPTS

budget constraint, p. 427
indifference curve, p. 428
marginal rate of substitution, p. 428
perfect substitutes, p. 431
perfect complements, p. 431
normal good, p. 434
inferior good, p. 435
income effect, p. 436
substitution effect, p. 436
Giffen good, p. 440

QUESTIONS FOR REVIEW

1. A consumer has income of $3,000. Wine costs $3 per glass, and cheese costs $6 per pound. Draw the consumer's budget constraint with wine on the vertical axis. What is the slope of this budget constraint?
2. Draw a consumer's indifference curves for wine and cheese. Describe and explain four properties of these indifference curves.
3. Pick a point on an indifference curve for wine and cheese, and show the marginal rate of substitution. What does the marginal rate of substitution tell us?
4. Show a consumer's budget constraint and indifference curves for wine and cheese. Show the optimal consumption choice. If the price of wine is $3 per glass and the price of cheese is $6 per pound, what is the marginal rate of substitution at this optimum?
5. A person who consumes wine and cheese gets a raise, so her income increases from $3,000 to $4,000. Show what happens if both wine and cheese are normal goods. Next, show what happens if cheese is an inferior good.
6. The price of cheese rises from $6 to $10 per pound, while the price of wine remains $3 per glass. For a consumer with a constant income of $3,000, show what happens to consumption of wine and cheese. Decompose the change into income and substitution effects.
7. Can an increase in the price of cheese possibly induce a consumer to buy more cheese? Explain.

PROBLEMS AND APPLICATIONS

1. Maya divides her income between coffee and croissants (both of which are normal goods). An early frost in Brazil causes a large increase in the price of coffee in the United States.
   a. Show the effect of the frost on Maya's budget constraint.
   b. Show the effect of the frost on Maya's optimal consumption bundle assuming that the substitution effect outweighs the income effect for croissants.
   c. Show the effect of the frost on Maya's optimal consumption bundle assuming that the income effect outweighs the substitution effect for croissants.
2. Compare the following two pairs of goods:
   - Coke and Pepsi
   - Skis and ski bindings

   a. In which case are the two goods complements? In which case are they substitutes?
   b. In which case do you expect the indifference curves to be fairly straight? In which case do you expect the indifference curves to be very bowed?
   c. In which case will the consumer respond more to a change in the relative price of the two goods?

3. You consume only soda and pizza. One day, the price of soda goes up, the price of pizza goes down, and you are just as happy as you were before the price changes.
   a. Illustrate this situation on a graph.
   b. How does your consumption of the two goods change? How does your response depend on income and substitution effects?
   c. Can you afford the bundle of soda and pizza you consumed before the price changes?

4. Carlos consumes only cheese and crackers.
   a. Could cheese and crackers both be inferior goods for Carlos? Explain.
   b. Suppose that cheese is a normal good for Carlos while crackers are an inferior good. If the price of cheese falls, what happens to Carlos's consumption of crackers? What happens to his consumption of cheese? Explain.

5. Jacob buys only milk and cookies.
   a. In year 1, Jacob earns $100, milk costs $2 per quart, and cookies cost $4 per dozen. Draw Jacob's budget constraint.
   b. Now suppose that all prices increase by 10 percent in year 2 and that Jacob's salary increases by 10 percent as well. Draw Jacob's new budget constraint. How would Jacob's optimal combination of milk and cookies in year 2 compare to his optimal combination in year 1?

6. State whether each of the following statements is true or false. Explain your answers.
   a. "All Giffen goods are inferior goods."
   b. "All inferior goods are Giffen goods."

7. A college student has two options for meals: eating at the dining hall for $6 per meal, or eating a Cup O' Soup for $1.50 per meal. Her weekly food budget is $60.
   a. Draw the budget constraint showing the trade-off between dining hall meals and Cups O' Soup. Assuming that she spends equal amounts on both goods, draw an indifference curve showing the optimum choice. Label the optimum as point A.
   b. Suppose the price of a Cup O' Soup now rises to $2. Using your diagram from part (a), show the consequences of this change in price. Assume that our student now spends only 30 percent of her income on dining hall meals. Label the new optimum as point B.
   c. What happened to the quantity of Cups O' Soup consumed as a result of this price change? What does this result say about the income and substitution effects? Explain.
   d. Use points A and B to draw a demand curve for Cup O' Soup. What is this type of good called?

8. Consider your decision about how many hours to work.
   a. Draw your budget constraint assuming that you pay no taxes on your income. On the same diagram, draw another budget constraint assuming that you pay a 15 percent income tax.
   b. Show how the tax might lead to more hours of work, fewer hours, or the same number of hours. Explain.

9. Anya is awake for 100 hours per week. Using one diagram, show Anya's budget constraints if she earns $12 per hour, $16 per hour, and $20 per hour. Now draw indifference curves such that Anya's labor-supply curve is upward-sloping when the wage is between $12 and $16 per hour and backward-sloping when the wage is between $16 and $20 per hour.

10. Draw the indifference curve for someone deciding how to allocate time between work and leisure. Suppose the wage increases. Is it possible that the person's consumption would fall? Is this plausible? Discuss. (*Hint*: Think about income and substitution effects.)

11. Economist George Stigler once wrote that, according to consumer theory, "if consumers do not buy less of a commodity when their incomes rise, they will surely buy less when the price of the commodity rises." Explain this statement using the concepts of income and substitution effects.

12. Five consumers have the following marginal utility of apples and pears:

	Marginal Utility of Apples	Marginal Utility of Pears
Claire	6	12
Phil	6	6
Haley	6	3
Alex	3	6
Luke	3	12

The price of an apple is $1, and the price of a pear is $2. Which, if any, of these consumers are optimizing over their choice of fruit? For those who are not, how should they change their spending?

To find additional study resources, visit cengagebrain.com, and search for "Mankiw."

CHAPTER

22

Frontiers of Microeconomics

Economics is a study of the choices that people make and the resulting interactions they have with one another. As the preceding chapters demonstrate, the field has many facets. Yet it would be a mistake to think that all the facets we have seen make up a finished jewel, perfect and unchanging. Like all scientists, economists are always looking for new areas to study and new phenomena to explain. This final chapter on microeconomics offers an assortment of three topics at the discipline's frontier to show how economists are trying to expand their understanding of human behavior and society.

The first topic is the economics of *asymmetric information*. In many different situations, some people are better informed than others, and the imbalance in information affects the choices they make and how they deal with one another.

Thinking about this asymmetry can shed light on many aspects of the world, from the market for used cars to the custom of gift giving.

The second topic we examine in this chapter is *political economy*. Throughout this book, we have seen many examples in which markets fail and government policy can potentially improve matters. But "potentially" is a necessary qualifier: Whether this potential is realized depends on how well our political institutions work. The field of political economy uses the tools of economics to understand the functioning of government.

The third topic in this chapter is *behavioral economics*. This field brings some insights from psychology into the study of economic issues. It offers a view of human behavior that is more subtle and complex than the one found in conventional economic theory, a view that may be more realistic.

This chapter covers a lot of ground. To do so, it offers not full helpings of these three topics but, instead, a taste of each. One goal of this chapter is to show a few of the directions economists are heading in their effort to expand knowledge of how the economy works. Another is to whet your appetite for more courses in economics.

22-1 Asymmetric Information

"I know something you don't know." This statement is a common taunt among children, but it also conveys a deep truth about how people sometimes interact with one another. Many times in life, one person knows more about what is going on than another. A difference in access to knowledge that is relevant to an interaction is called an *information asymmetry*.

Examples abound. A worker knows more than his employer about how much effort he puts into his job. A seller of a used car knows more than the buyer about the car's condition. The first is an example of a *hidden action*, whereas the second is an example of a *hidden characteristic*. In each case, the uninformed party (the employer, the car buyer) would like to know the relevant information, but the informed party (the worker, the car seller) may have an incentive to conceal it.

Because asymmetric information is so prevalent, economists have devoted much effort in recent decades to studying its effects. Let's discuss some of the insights that this study has revealed.

22-1a Hidden Actions: Principals, Agents, and Moral Hazard

moral hazard
the tendency of a person who is imperfectly monitored to engage in dishonest or otherwise undesirable behavior

agent
a person who is performing an act for another person, called the principal

principal
a person for whom another person, called the agent, is performing some act

Moral hazard is a problem that arises when one person, called the **agent**, is performing some task on behalf of another person, called the **principal**. If the principal cannot perfectly monitor the agent's behavior, the agent tends to undertake less effort than the principal considers desirable. The phrase *moral hazard* refers to the risk, or "hazard," of inappropriate or otherwise "immoral" behavior by the agent. In such a situation, the principal tries various ways to encourage the agent to act more responsibly.

The employment relationship is the classic example. The employer is the principal, and the worker is the agent. The moral-hazard problem is the temptation of imperfectly monitored workers to shirk their responsibilities. Employers can respond to this problem in various ways:

- *Better monitoring*. Employers may plant hidden video cameras to record workers' behavior. The aim is to catch irresponsible actions that might occur when supervisors are absent.

- *High wages*. According to *efficiency-wage theories* (discussed in Chapter 19), some employers may choose to pay their workers a wage above the level that balances supply and demand in the labor market. A worker who earns an above-equilibrium wage is less likely to shirk because if he is caught and fired, he might not be able to find another high-paying job.
- *Delayed payment*. Firms can delay part of a worker's compensation, so if the worker is caught shirking and is fired, he suffers a larger penalty. One example of delayed compensation is the year-end bonus. Similarly, a firm may choose to pay its workers more later in their lives. Thus, the wage increases that workers get as they age may reflect not just the benefits of experience but also a response to moral hazard.

Employers can use any combination of these various mechanisms to reduce the problem of moral hazard.

There are also many examples of moral hazard beyond the workplace. A homeowner with fire insurance will likely buy too few fire extinguishers because the

FYI

Corporate Management

Much production in the modern economy takes place within corporations. Like other firms, corporations buy inputs in markets for the factors of production and sell their output in markets for goods and services. Also like other firms, they are guided in their decisions by the objective of profit maximization. But a large corporation has to deal with some issues that do not arise in, say, a small family-owned business.

What is distinctive about a corporation? From a legal standpoint, a corporation is an organization that is granted a charter recognizing it as a separate legal entity, with its own rights and responsibilities distinct from those of its owners and employees. From an economic standpoint, the most important feature of the corporate form of organization is the separation of ownership and control. One group of people, called the shareholders, own the corporation and share in its profits. Another group of people, called the managers, are employed by the corporation to make decisions about how to deploy the corporation's resources.

The separation of ownership and control creates a principal-agent problem. In this case, the shareholders are the principals and the managers are the agents. The chief executive officer and other managers, who are in the best position to know the available business opportunities, are charged with the task of maximizing profits for the shareholders. But ensuring that they carry out this task is not always easy. The managers may have goals of their own, such as taking life easy, having a plush office and a private jet, throwing lavish parties, or presiding over a large business empire. The managers' goals may not always coincide with the shareholders' goal of profit maximization.

The corporation's board of directors is responsible for hiring and firing the top management. The board monitors the managers' performance, and it designs their compensation packages. These packages often include incentives aimed at aligning the interests of shareholders with the interests of management. Managers might be given bonuses based on performance or options to buy the company's stock, which are more valuable if the company performs well.

Note, however, that the directors are themselves agents of the shareholders. The existence of a board overseeing management only shifts the principal-agent problem. The issue then becomes how to ensure that the board of directors fulfills its own legal obligation of acting in the best interest of the shareholders. If the directors become too friendly with management, they may not provide the required oversight.

The corporation's principal-agent problem became big news around 2005. The top managers of several prominent companies, including Enron, Tyco, and WorldCom, were found to be engaging in activities that enriched themselves at the expense of their shareholders. In these cases, the actions were so extreme as to be criminal, and the corporate managers were not just fired but also sent to prison. Some shareholders sued the directors for failing to monitor management sufficiently.

Fortunately, criminal activity by corporate managers is rare. But in some ways, it is only the tip of the iceberg. Whenever ownership and control are separated, as they are in most large corporations, there is an inevitable tension between the interests of shareholders and the interests of management. ■

homeowner bears the cost of the extinguisher while the insurance company receives much of the benefit. A family may live near a river with a high risk of flooding because the family enjoys the scenic views, while the government bears the cost of disaster relief after a flood. Many regulations are aimed at addressing the problem: An insurance company may require homeowners to buy fire extinguishers, and the government may prohibit building homes on land with high risk of flooding. But the insurance company does not have perfect information about how cautious homeowners are, and the government does not have perfect information about the risk that families undertake when choosing where to live. As a result, the problem of moral hazard persists.

22-1b Hidden Characteristics: Adverse Selection and the Lemons Problem

adverse selection
the tendency for the mix of unobserved attributes to become undesirable from the standpoint of an uninformed party

Adverse selection is a problem that arises in markets in which the seller knows more about the attributes of the good being sold than the buyer does. In such a situation, the buyer runs the risk of being sold a good of low quality. That is, the "selection" of goods sold may be "adverse" from the standpoint of the uninformed buyer.

The classic example of adverse selection is the market for used cars. Sellers of used cars know their vehicles' defects while buyers often do not. Because owners of the worst cars are more likely to sell them than are the owners of the best cars, buyers are worried about getting a "lemon." As a result, many people avoid buying vehicles in the used car market. This lemons problem can explain why a used car only a few weeks old sells for thousands of dollars less than a new car of the same type. A buyer of the used car might surmise that the seller is getting rid of the car quickly because the seller knows something about it that the buyer does not.

A second example of adverse selection occurs in the labor market. According to another efficiency-wage theory, workers vary in their abilities, and they know their own abilities better than do the firms that hire them. When a firm cuts the wage it pays, the more talented workers are more likely to quit, knowing they will be able to find employment elsewhere. Conversely, a firm may choose to pay an above-equilibrium wage to attract a better mix of workers.

A third example of adverse selection occurs in markets for insurance. For example, buyers of health insurance know more about their own health problems than do insurance companies. Because people with greater hidden health problems are more likely to buy health insurance than are other people, the price of health insurance reflects the costs of a sicker-than-average person. As a result, people with average health may observe the high price of insurance and decide not to buy it.

When markets suffer from adverse selection, the invisible hand does not necessarily work its magic. In the used car market, owners of good cars may choose to keep them rather than sell them at the low price that skeptical buyers are willing to pay. In the labor market, wages may be stuck above the level that balances supply and demand, resulting in unemployment. In insurance markets, buyers with low risk may choose to remain uninsured because the policies they are offered fail to reflect their true characteristics. Advocates of government-provided health insurance sometimes point to the problem of adverse selection as one reason not to trust the private market to provide the right amount of health insurance on its own.

22-1c Signaling to Convey Private Information

Although asymmetric information is sometimes a motivation for public policy, it also motivates some individual behavior that otherwise might be hard to explain.

Markets respond to problems of asymmetric information in many ways. One of them is **signaling**, which refers to actions taken by an informed party for the sole purpose of credibly revealing his private information.

signaling
an action taken by an informed party to reveal private information to an uninformed party

We have seen examples of signaling in previous chapters. As we saw in Chapter 16, firms may spend money on advertising to signal to potential customers that they have high-quality products. As we saw in Chapter 19, students may earn college degrees merely to signal to potential employers that they are high-ability individuals, rather than to increase their productivity. These two examples of signaling (advertising, education) may seem very different, but below the surface, they are much the same: In both cases, the informed party (the firm, the student) uses the signal to convince the uninformed party (the customer, the employer) that the informed party is offering something of high quality.

What does it take for an action to be an effective signal? Obviously, it must be costly. If a signal were free, everyone would use it and it would convey no information. For the same reason, there is another requirement: The signal must be less costly, or more beneficial, to the person with the higher-quality product. Otherwise, everyone would have the same incentive to use the signal, and the signal would reveal nothing.

Consider again our two examples. In the advertising case, a firm with a good product reaps a larger benefit from advertising because customers who try the product once are more likely to become repeat customers. Thus, it is rational for the firm with a good product to pay for the cost of the signal (advertising), and it is rational for the customer to use the signal as a piece of information about the product's quality. In the education case, a talented person can get through school more easily than a less talented one. Thus, it is rational for the talented person to pay for the cost of the signal (education), and it is rational for the employer to use the signal as a piece of information about the person's talent.

The world is replete with instances of signaling. Magazine ads sometimes include the phrase "as seen on TV." Why does a firm selling a product in a magazine choose to stress this fact? One possibility is that the firm is trying to convey its willingness to pay for an expensive signal (a spot on television) in the hope that you will infer that its product is of high quality. For the same reason, graduates of elite schools are always sure to put that fact on their résumés.

CASE STUDY

GIFTS AS SIGNALS

A man is debating what to give his girlfriend for her birthday. "I know," he says to himself, "I'll give her cash. After all, I don't know her tastes as well as she does, and with cash, she can buy anything she wants." But when he hands her the money, she is offended. Convinced he doesn't really love her, she breaks off the relationship.

What's the economics behind this story?

In some ways, gift giving is a strange custom. As the man in our story suggests, people typically know their own preferences better than others do, so we might expect everyone to prefer cash to in-kind transfers. If your employer substituted merchandise of his choosing for your paycheck, you would likely object to this means of payment. But your reaction is very different when someone who (you hope) loves you does the same thing.

One interpretation of gift giving is that it reflects asymmetric information and signaling. The man in our story has private information that the girlfriend would like to know: Does he really love her? Choosing a good gift for her is a signal of his love. Certainly, the act of picking out a gift, rather than giving cash, has the

MONKEY BUSINESS IMAGES/SHUTTERSTOCK.COM

"Now we'll see how much he loves me."

right characteristics to be a signal. It is costly (it takes time), and its cost depends on private information (how much he loves her). If he really loves her, choosing a good gift is easy because he is thinking about her all the time. If he doesn't love her, finding the right gift is more difficult. Thus, giving a gift that suits his girlfriend is one way for him to convey the private information of his love for her. Giving cash shows that he isn't even bothering to try.

The signaling theory of gift giving is consistent with another observation: People care most about the custom when the strength of affection is most in question. Thus, giving cash to a girlfriend or boyfriend is usually a bad move. But when college students receive a check from their parents, they are less often offended. The parents' love is less likely to be in doubt, so the recipient probably won't interpret the cash gift as a signal of insufficient affection. ●

22-1d Screening to Uncover Private Information

When an informed party takes actions to reveal private information, the phenomenon is called signaling. When an uninformed party takes actions to induce the informed party to reveal private information, the phenomenon is called **screening**.

screening
an action taken by an uninformed party to induce an informed party to reveal information

Some screening is common sense. A person buying a used car may ask that it be checked by an auto mechanic before the sale. A seller who refuses this request reveals his private information that the car is a lemon. The buyer may decide to offer a lower price or to look for another car.

Other examples of screening are more subtle. For example, consider a firm that sells car insurance. The firm would like to charge a low premium to safe drivers and a high premium to risky drivers. But how can it tell them apart? Drivers know whether they are safe or risky, but the risky ones won't admit it. A driver's history is one piece of information (which insurance companies in fact use), but because of the intrinsic randomness of car accidents, history is an imperfect indicator of future risk.

The insurance company might be able to sort out the two kinds of drivers by offering different insurance policies that would induce the drivers to separate themselves. One policy would have a high premium and cover the full cost of any accidents that occur. Another policy would have low premiums but would have, say, a $1,000 deductible. (That is, the driver would be responsible for the first $1,000 of damage, and the insurance company would cover the remaining risk.) Notice that the deductible is more of a burden for risky drivers because they are more likely to have an accident. Thus, with a large enough deductible, the low-premium policy with a deductible would attract the safe drivers, while the high-premium policy without a deductible would attract the risky drivers. Faced with these two policies, the two kinds of drivers would reveal their private information by choosing different insurance policies.

22-1e Asymmetric Information and Public Policy

We have examined two kinds of asymmetric information: moral hazard and adverse selection. And we have seen how individuals may respond to the problem with signaling or screening. Now let's consider what the study of asymmetric information suggests about the proper scope of public policy.

The tension between market success and market failure is central in microeconomics. We learned in Chapter 7 that the equilibrium of supply and demand is efficient in the sense that it maximizes the total surplus that society can obtain in a market. Adam Smith's invisible hand seemed to reign supreme. This conclusion was then tempered with the study of externalities (Chapter 10), public goods (Chapter 11), imperfect competition (Chapters 15 through 17), and poverty

(Chapter 20). In those chapters, we saw that government can sometimes improve market outcomes.

The study of asymmetric information gives us a new reason to be wary of markets. When some people know more than others, the market may fail to put resources to their best use. People with high-quality used cars may have trouble selling them because buyers will be afraid of getting a lemon. People with few health problems may have trouble getting low-cost health insurance because insurance companies lump them together with those who have significant (but hidden) health problems.

Asymmetric information may call for government action in some cases, but three facts complicate the issue. First, as we have seen, the private market can sometimes deal with information asymmetries on its own using a combination of signaling and screening. Second, the government rarely has more information than the private parties. Even if the market's allocation of resources is not ideal, it may be the best that can be achieved. That is, when there are information asymmetries, policymakers may find it hard to improve upon the market's admittedly imperfect outcome. Third, the government is itself an imperfect institution—a topic we take up in the next section.

QuickQuiz *A person who buys a life insurance policy pays a certain amount per year and receives for his family a much larger payment in the event of his death. Would you expect buyers of life insurance to have higher or lower death rates than the average person? How might this be an example of moral hazard? Of adverse selection? How might a life insurance company deal with these problems?*

22-2 Political Economy

As we have seen, markets left on their own do not always reach a desirable allocation of resources. When we judge the market's outcome to be either inefficient or inequitable, there may be a role for the government to step in and improve the situation. Yet before we embrace an activist government, we need to consider one more fact: The government is also an imperfect institution. The field of **political economy** (sometimes called the field of public choice) uses the methods of economics to study how government works.

political economy
the study of government using the analytic methods of economics

22-2a The Condorcet Voting Paradox

Most advanced societies rely on democratic principles to set government policy. When a city is deciding between two locations to build a new park, for example, we have a simple way to choose: The majority gets its way. Yet for most policy issues, the number of possible outcomes far exceeds two. A new park could be placed in many possible locations. In this case, as the 18th-century French political theorist Marquis de Condorcet famously noted, democracy might run into some problems trying to choose the best outcome.

For example, suppose there are three possible outcomes, labeled A, B, and C, and there are three voter types with the preferences shown in Table 1. The mayor of our town wants to aggregate these individual preferences into preferences for society as a whole. How should he do it?

At first, he might try some pairwise votes. If he asks voters to choose first between B and C, voter types 1 and 2 will vote for B, giving B the majority. If he then asks voters to choose between A and B, voter types 1 and 3 will vote for A, giving A the majority. Observing that A beats B, and B beats C, the mayor might conclude that A is the voters' clear choice.

But wait: Suppose the mayor then asks voters to choose between A and C. In this case, voter types 2 and 3 vote for C, giving C the majority. That is, under pairwise majority voting, A beats B, B beats C, and C beats A. Normally, we expect preferences to exhibit a property called *transitivity*: If A is preferred to B, and B is preferred to C, then we would expect A to be preferred to C. The **Condorcet paradox** is that democratic outcomes do not always obey this property. Pairwise voting might produce transitive preferences for society in some cases, but as our example in the table shows, it cannot be counted on to do so.

Condorcet paradox the failure of majority rule to produce transitive preferences for society

One implication of the Condorcet paradox is that the order in which things are voted on can affect the result. If the mayor suggests choosing first between A and B and then comparing the winner to C, the town ends up choosing C. But if the voters choose first between B and C and then compare the winner to A, the town ends up with A. And if the voters choose first between A and C and then compare the winner to B, the town ends up with B.

The Condorcet paradox teaches two lessons. The narrow lesson is that when there are more than two options, setting the agenda (that is, deciding the order in which items are voted on) can have a powerful influence over the outcome of a democratic election. The broad lesson is that majority voting by itself does not tell us what outcome a society really wants.

22-2b Arrow's Impossibility Theorem

Since political theorists first noticed Condorcet's paradox, they have spent much energy studying existing voting systems and proposing new ones. For example, as an alternative to pairwise majority voting, the mayor of our town could ask each voter to rank the possible outcomes. For each voter, we could give 1 point for last place, 2 points for second to last, 3 points for third to last, and so on. The outcome that receives the most total points wins. With the preferences in Table 1, outcome B is the winner. (You can do the arithmetic yourself.) This voting method is called a *Borda count* for the 18th-century French mathematician and political theorist, Jean-Charles de Borda, who devised it. It is often used in polls that rank sports teams.

Is there a perfect voting system? Economist Kenneth Arrow took up this question in his 1951 book *Social Choice and Individual Values*. Arrow started by defining what a perfect voting system would be. He assumes that individuals in society have preferences over the various possible outcomes: A, B, C, and so on. He then assumes that society wants a voting system to choose among these outcomes that satisfies several properties:

TABLE 1

The Condorcet Paradox
If voters have these preferences over outcomes A, B, and C, then in pairwise majority voting, A beats B, B beats C, and C beats A.

	Voter Type		
	Type 1	Type 2	Type 3
Percent of electorate	35	45	20
First choice	A	B	C
Second choice	B	C	A
Third choice	C	A	B

- *Unanimity:* If everyone prefers A to B, then A should beat B.
- *Transitivity:* If A beats B, and B beats C, then A should beat C.
- *Independence of irrelevant alternatives:* The ranking between any two outcomes A and B should not depend on whether some third outcome C is also available.
- *No dictators:* There is no person who always gets his way, regardless of everyone else's preferences.

These all seem like desirable properties of a voting system. Yet Arrow proved, mathematically and incontrovertibly, that *no voting system can satisfy all these properties.* This amazing result is called **Arrow's impossibility theorem**.

Arrow's impossibility theorem
a mathematical result showing that, under certain assumed conditions, there is no scheme for aggregating individual preferences into a valid set of social preferences

The mathematics needed to prove Arrow's theorem is beyond the scope of this book, but we can get some sense of why the theorem is true from a couple of examples. We have already seen the problem with the method of majority rule. The Condorcet paradox shows that majority rule fails to produce a ranking of outcomes that always satisfies transitivity.

As another example, the Borda count fails to satisfy the independence of irrelevant alternatives. Recall that, using the preferences in Table 1, outcome B wins with a Borda count. But suppose that suddenly C disappears as an alternative. If the Borda count method is applied only to outcomes A and B, then A wins. (Once again, you can do the arithmetic on your own.) Thus, eliminating alternative C changes the ranking between A and B. This change occurs because the result of the Borda count depends on the number of points that A and B receive, and the number of points depends on whether the irrelevant alternative, C, is also available.

Arrow's impossibility theorem is a deep and disturbing result. It doesn't say that we should abandon democracy as a form of government. But it does say that no matter what voting system society adopts for aggregating the preferences of its members, it will in some way be flawed as a mechanism for social choice.

22-2c The Median Voter Is King

Despite Arrow's theorem, voting is how most societies choose their leaders and public policies, often by majority rule. The next step in studying government is to examine how governments run by majority rule work. That is, in a democratic society, who determines what policy is chosen? In some cases, the theory of democratic government yields a surprisingly simple answer.

Let's consider an example. Imagine that society is deciding how much money to spend on some public good, such as the army or the national parks. Each voter has his own most preferred budget, and he always prefers outcomes closer to his most preferred value to outcomes farther away. Thus, we can line up voters from those who prefer the smallest budget to those who prefer the largest. Figure 1 is an example. Here there are 100 voters, and the budget size varies from zero to $20 billion. Given these preferences, what outcome would you expect democracy to produce?

median voter theorem
a mathematical result showing that if voters are choosing a point along a line and each voter wants the point closest to his most preferred point, then majority rule will pick the most preferred point of the median voter

According to a famous result called the **median voter theorem**, majority rule will produce the outcome most preferred by the *median voter*. The median voter is the voter exactly in the middle of the distribution. In this example, if you take the line of voters ordered by their preferred budgets and count 50 voters from either end of the line, you will find that the median voter wants a budget of $10 billion. By contrast, the average preferred outcome (calculated by adding the preferred outcomes and dividing by the number of voters) is $9 billion, and the modal outcome (the one preferred by the greatest number of voters) is $15 billion.

FIGURE 1

The Median Voter Theorem: An Example

This bar chart shows how 100 voters' most preferred budgets are distributed over five options, ranging from zero to $20 billion. If society makes its choice by majority rule, the median voter, who here prefers $10 billion, determines the outcome.

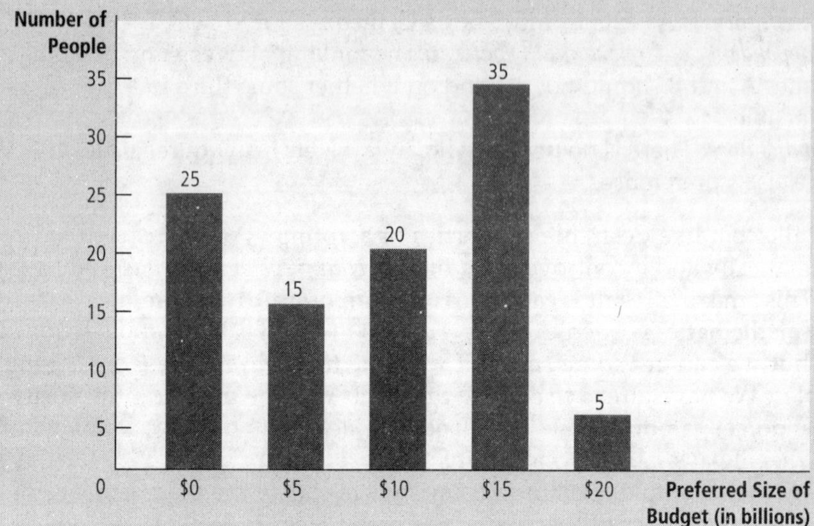

The median voter rules the day because his preferred outcome beats any other proposal in a two-way race. In our example, more than half the voters want $10 billion or more, and more than half want $10 billion or less. If someone proposes, say, $8 billion instead of $10 billion, everyone who prefers $10 billion or more will vote with the median voter. Similarly, if someone proposes $12 billion instead of $10 billion, everyone who wants $10 billion or less will vote with the median voter. In either case, the median voter has more than half the voters on his side.

What about the Condorcet voting paradox? It turns out that when the voters are picking a point along a line and each voter aims for his own most preferred point, the Condorcet paradox cannot arise. The median voter's most preferred outcome beats all challengers.

One implication of the median voter theorem is that if two political parties are each trying to maximize their chance of election, they will both move their positions toward the median voter. Suppose, for example, that the Democratic Party advocates a budget of $15 billion, while the Republican Party advocates a budget of $10 billion. The Democratic position is more popular in the sense that $15 billion has more proponents than any other single choice. Nonetheless, the Republicans get more than 50 percent of the vote: They will attract the 20 voters who want $10 billion, the 15 voters who want $5 billion, and the 25 voters who want zero. If the Democrats want to win, they will move their platform toward the median voter. Thus, this theory can explain why the parties in a two-party system are similar to each other: They are both moving toward the median voter.

Another implication of the median voter theorem is that minority views are not given much weight. Imagine that 40 percent of the population want a lot of money spent on the national parks and 60 percent want nothing spent. In this case, the median voter's preference is zero, regardless of the intensity of the minority's view. Rather than reaching a compromise that takes everyone's preferences into account, majority rule looks only to the person in the exact middle of the distribution. Such is the logic of democracy.

22-2d Politicians Are People Too

When economists study consumer behavior, they assume that consumers buy the bundle of goods and services that gives them the greatest level of satisfaction.

When economists study firm behavior, they assume that firms produce the quantity of goods and services that yields the greatest level of profits. What should they assume when they study people involved in the practice of politics?

Politicians also have objectives. It would be nice to assume that political leaders are always looking out for the well-being of society as a whole, that they are aiming for an optimal combination of efficiency and equality. Nice, perhaps, but not realistic. Self-interest is as powerful a motive for political actors as it is for consumers and firm owners. Some politicians, motivated by a desire for reelection, are willing to sacrifice the national interest to solidify their base of voters. Others are motivated by simple greed. If you have any doubt, you should look at the world's poor nations, where corruption among government officials is a common impediment to economic development.

This book is not the place to develop a theory of political behavior. But when thinking about economic policy, remember that this policy is made not by a benevolent king (or even by benevolent economists) but by real people with their own all-too-human desires. Sometimes they are motivated to further the national interest, but sometimes they are motivated by their own political and financial ambitions. We shouldn't be surprised when economic policy fails to resemble the ideals derived in economics textbooks.

"Isn't that the real genius of democracy? . . . The VOTERS are ultimately to blame."

QuickQuiz *A public school district is deciding on the school budget and the resulting student–teacher ratio. A poll finds that 20 percent of the voters want a ratio of 9:1, 25 percent want a ratio of 10:1, 15 percent want a ratio of 11:1, and 40 percent want a ratio of 12:1. If the district uses majority-rule voting, what outcome would you expect the district to end up with? Explain.*

22-3 Behavioral Economics

Economics is a study of human behavior, but it is not the only field that can make that claim. The social science of psychology also sheds light on the choices that people make in their lives. The fields of economics and psychology usually proceed independently, in part because they address a different range of questions. But recently, a field called **behavioral economics** has emerged in which economists are making use of basic psychological insights. Let's consider some of these insights here.

22-3a People Aren't Always Rational

Economic theory is populated by a particular species of organism, sometimes called *Homo economicus*. Members of this species are always rational. As firm owners, they maximize profits. As consumers, they maximize utility (or equivalently, pick the point on the highest indifference curve). Given the constraints they face, they rationally weigh all the costs and benefits and always choose the best possible course of action.

Real people, however, are *Homo sapiens*. Although in many ways they resemble the rational, calculating people assumed in economic theory, they are far more complex. They can be forgetful, impulsive, confused, emotional, and shortsighted. These imperfections of human reasoning are the bread and butter of psychologists, but until recently, economists have neglected them.

Herbert Simon, one of the first social scientists to work at the boundary of economics and psychology, suggested that humans should be viewed not as rational maximizers but as *satisficers*. Instead of always choosing the best course of action, they make decisions that are merely good enough. Similarly, other economists have suggested that humans are only "near rational" or that they exhibit "bounded rationality."

behavioral economics
the subfield of economics that integrates the insights of psychology

Studies of human decision making have tried to detect systematic mistakes that people make. Here are a few of the findings:

- *People are overconfident*. Imagine that you were asked some numerical questions, such as the number of African countries in the United Nations, the height of the tallest mountain in North America, and so on. Instead of being asked for a single estimate, however, you were asked to give a 90 percent confidence interval—a range such that you were 90 percent confident the true number falls within it. When psychologists run experiments like this, they find that most people give ranges that are too small: The true number falls within their intervals far less than 90 percent of the time. That is, most people are too sure of their own abilities.
- *People give too much weight to a small number of vivid observations.* Imagine that you are thinking about buying a car of brand X. To learn about its reliability, you read *Consumer Reports*, which has surveyed 1,000 owners of car X. Then you run into a friend who owns car X, and he tells you that his car is a lemon. How do you treat your friend's observation? If you think rationally, you will realize that he has only increased your sample size from 1,000 to 1,001, which does not provide much new information. But because your friend's story is so vivid, you may be tempted to give it more weight in your decision making than you should.
- *People are reluctant to change their minds.* People tend to interpret evidence to confirm beliefs they already hold. In one study, subjects were asked to read and evaluate a research report on whether capital punishment deters crime. After reading the report, those who initially favored the death penalty said they were more certain of their view, and those who initially opposed the death penalty also said they were more certain of their view. The two groups interpreted the same evidence in exactly opposite ways. This behavior is sometimes called *confirmation bias*.

Think about decisions you have made in your own life. Do you exhibit some of these traits?

A hotly debated issue is whether deviations from rationality are important for understanding economic phenomena. An intriguing example arises in the study of 401(k) plans, the tax-advantaged retirement savings accounts that some firms offer their workers. In some firms, workers can choose to participate in the plan by filling out a simple form. In other firms, workers are automatically enrolled and can opt out of the plan by filling out a simple form. It turns out many more workers participate in the second case than in the first. If workers were perfectly rational maximizers, they would choose the optimal amount of retirement saving, regardless of the default offered by their employer. In fact, workers' behavior appears to exhibit substantial inertia. Understanding their behavior seems easier once we abandon the model of rational man.

Why, you might ask, is economics built on the rationality assumption when psychology and common sense cast doubt on it? One answer is that the assumption, even if not exactly true, may be true enough that it yields reasonably accurate models of behavior. For example, when we studied the differences between competitive and monopoly firms, the assumption that firms rationally maximize profit yielded many important and valid insights. Incorporating complex psychological deviations from rationality into the story might have added realism, but it also would have muddied the waters and made those insights harder to find. Recall from Chapter 2 that economic models are not meant to replicate reality but are supposed to show the essence of the problem at hand.

Another reason economists often assume rationality may be that economists are themselves not rational maximizers. Like most people, they are overconfident and reluctant to change their minds. Their choice among alternative theories of human behavior may exhibit excessive inertia. Moreover, economists may be content with a theory that is not perfect but is good enough. The model of rational man may be the theory of choice for a satisficing social scientist.

22-3b People Care about Fairness

Another insight about human behavior is best illustrated with an experiment called the *ultimatum game*. The game works like this: Two volunteers (who are otherwise strangers to each other) are told that they are going to play a game and could win a total of $100. Before they play, they learn the rules. The game begins with a coin toss, which is used to assign the volunteers to the roles of player A and player B. Player A's job is to propose a division of the $100 prize between himself and the other player. After player A makes his proposal, player B decides whether to accept or reject it. If he accepts it, both players are paid according to the proposal. If player B rejects the proposal, both players walk away with nothing. In either case, the game then ends.

Before proceeding, stop and think about what you would do in this situation. If you were player A, what division of the $100 would you propose? If you were player B, what proposals would you accept?

Conventional economic theory assumes in this situation that people are rational wealth maximizers. This assumption leads to a simple prediction: Player A should propose that he gets $99 and player B gets $1, and player B should accept the proposal. After all, once the proposal is made, player B is better off accepting it as long as he gets something out of it. Moreover, because player A knows that accepting the proposal is in player B's interest, player A has no reason to offer him more than $1. In the language of game theory (discussed in Chapter 17), the 99–1 split is the Nash equilibrium.

Yet when experimental economists ask real people to play the ultimatum game, the results differ from this prediction. People in player B's role usually reject proposals that give them only $1 or a similarly small amount. Anticipating this, people in the role of player A usually propose giving player B much more than $1. Some people will offer a 50–50 split, but it is more common for player A to propose giving player B an amount such as $30 or $40, keeping the larger share for himself. In this case, player B usually accepts the proposal.

What's going on here? The natural interpretation is that people are driven in part by some innate sense of fairness. A 99–1 split seems so wildly unfair to many people that they reject it, even to their own detriment. By contrast, a 70–30 split is still unfair, but it is not so unfair that it induces people to abandon their normal self-interest.

Throughout our study of household and firm behavior, the innate sense of fairness has not played any role. But the results of the ultimatum game suggest that perhaps it should. For example, in Chapters 18 and 19, we discussed how wages were determined by labor supply and labor demand. Some economists have suggested that the perceived fairness of what a firm pays its workers should also enter the picture. Thus, when a firm has an especially profitable year, workers (like player B) may expect to be paid a fair share of the prize, even if the standard equilibrium does not dictate it. The firm (like player A) might well decide to give workers more than the equilibrium wage for fear that the workers might otherwise try to punish the firm with reduced effort, strikes, or even vandalism.

22-3c People Are Inconsistent over Time

Imagine some dreary task, such as doing your laundry, shoveling snow off your driveway, or filling out your income tax forms. Now consider the following questions:

1. Would you prefer (A) to spend 50 minutes doing the task right now or (B) to spend 60 minutes doing the task tomorrow?
2. Would you prefer (A) to spend 50 minutes doing the task in 90 days or (B) to spend 60 minutes doing the task in 91 days?

When asked questions like these, many people choose B for question 1 and A for question 2. When looking ahead to the future (as in question 2), they minimize the amount of time spent on the dreary task. But faced with the prospect of doing the task immediately (as in question 1), they choose to put it off.

In some ways, this behavior is not surprising: Everyone procrastinates from time to time. But from the standpoint of the theory of rational man, it is puzzling. Suppose that in response to question 2, a person chooses to spend 50 minutes in 90 days. Then, when the 90th day arrives, we allow him to change his mind. In effect, he then faces question 1, so he opts for doing the task the next day. But why should the mere passage of time affect the choices he makes?

Many times in life, people make plans for themselves, but then they fail to follow through. A smoker promises himself that he will quit, but within a few hours of smoking his last cigarette, he craves another and breaks his promise. A person trying to lose weight promises that he will stop eating dessert, but when the waiter brings the dessert cart, the diet goes out the window. In both cases, the desire for instant gratification induces the decision maker to abandon his past plans.

Some economists believe that the consumption–saving decision is an important instance in which people exhibit this inconsistency over time. For many people, spending provides a type of instant gratification. Saving, like passing up the cigarette or the dessert, requires a sacrifice in the present for a reward in the distant future. And just as many smokers wish they could quit and many overweight individuals wish they ate less, many consumers wish they saved more of their income. According to one survey, 76 percent of Americans said they were not saving enough for retirement.

An implication of this inconsistency over time is that people should try to find ways to commit their future selves to following through on their plans. A smoker trying to quit may throw away his cigarettes, and a person on a diet may put a lock on the refrigerator. What can a person who saves too little do? He should find some way to lock up his money before he spends it. Some retirement accounts, such as 401(k) plans, do exactly that. A worker can agree to have some money taken out of his paycheck before he ever sees it. The money is deposited in an account that can be used before retirement only with a penalty. Perhaps that is one reason these retirement accounts are so popular: They protect people from their own desires for instant gratification.

QuickQuiz *Describe at least three ways in which human decision making differs from that of the rational individual of conventional economic theory.*

22-4 Conclusion

This chapter examined the frontier of microeconomics. You may have noticed that we sketched out ideas rather than fully developing them. This is no accident. One reason is that you might study these topics in more detail in advanced courses. Another reason is that these topics remain active areas of research and, therefore, are still being fleshed out.

To see how these topics fit into the broader picture, recall the *Ten Principles of Economics* from Chapter 1. One principle states that markets are usually a good way to organize economic activity. Another principle states that governments can sometimes improve market outcomes. As you study economics, you can more fully appreciate the truth of these principles as well as the caveats that go with them. The study of asymmetric information should make you more wary of market outcomes. The study of political economy should make you more wary of government solutions. And the study of behavioral economics should make you wary of any institution that relies on human decision making, including both the market and the government.

If there is a unifying theme to these topics, it is that life is messy. Information is imperfect, government is imperfect, and people are imperfect. Of course, you knew this long before you started studying economics, but economists need to understand these imperfections as precisely as they can if they are to explain, and perhaps even improve, the world around them.

CHAPTER QuickQuiz

1. Because Elaine has a family history of significant medical problems, she buys health insurance, whereas her friend Jerry, who has a healthier family, goes without. This is an example of
   a. moral hazard.
   b. adverse selection.
   c. signaling.
   d. screening.
2. George has a life insurance policy that pays his family $1 million if he dies. As a result, he does not hesitate to enjoy his favorite hobby of bungee jumping. This is an example of
   a. moral hazard.
   b. adverse selection.
   c. signaling.
   d. screening.
3. Before selling anyone a health insurance policy, the Kramer Insurance Company requires that applicants undergo a medical examination. Those with significant preexisting medical problems are charged more. This is an example of
   a. moral hazard.
   b. adverse selection.
   c. signaling.
   d. screening.
4. The Condorcet paradox illustrates Arrow's impossibility theorem by showing that pairwise majority voting
   a. is inconsistent with the principle of unanimity.
   b. leads to social preferences that are not transitive.
   c. violates the independence of irrelevant alternatives.
   d. makes one person in effect a dictator.
5. Two political candidates are vying for town mayor, and the key issue is how much to spend on the annual Fourth of July fireworks. Among the 100 voters, 40 want to spend $30,000, 30 want to spend $10,000, and 30 want to spend nothing at all. What is the winning position on this issue?
   a. $10,000
   b. $15,000
   c. $20,000
   d. $30,000
6. The experiment called the ultimatum game illustrates that people
   a. are overconfident in their own abilities.
   b. play the Nash equilibrium in strategic situations.
   c. care about fairness, even to their own detriment.
   d. make inconsistent decisions over time.

SUMMARY

- In many economic transactions, information is asymmetric. When there are hidden actions, principals may be concerned that agents suffer from the problem of moral hazard. When there are hidden characteristics, buyers may be concerned about the problem of adverse selection among the sellers. Private markets sometimes deal with asymmetric information with signaling and screening.
- Although government policy can sometimes improve market outcomes, governments are themselves imperfect institutions. The Condorcet paradox shows that majority rule fails to produce transitive preferences for society, and Arrow's impossibility theorem shows that no voting system will be perfect. In many situations, democratic institutions will produce the outcome desired by the median voter, regardless of the preferences of the rest of the electorate. Moreover, the individuals who set government policy may be motivated by self-interest rather than the national interest.
- The study of psychology and economics reveals that human decision making is more complex than is assumed in conventional economic theory. People are not always rational, they care about the fairness of economic outcomes (even to their own detriment), and they can be inconsistent over time.

KEY CONCEPTS

moral hazard, p. 452
agent, p. 452
principal, p. 452
adverse selection, p. 454
signaling, p. 455
screening, p. 456
political economy, p. 457
Condorcet paradox, p. 458
Arrow's impossibility theorem, p. 459
median voter theorem, p. 460
behavioral economics, p. 461

QUESTIONS FOR REVIEW

1. What is moral hazard? List three things an employer might do to reduce the severity of this problem.
2. What is adverse selection? Give an example of a market in which adverse selection might be a problem.
3. Define *signaling* and *screening* and give an example of each.
4. What unusual property of voting did Condorcet notice?
5. Explain why majority rule respects the preferences of the median voter rather than the average voter.
6. Describe the ultimatum game. What outcome from this game would conventional economic theory predict? Do experiments confirm this prediction? Explain.

PROBLEMS AND APPLICATIONS

1. Each of the following situations involves moral hazard. In each case, identify the principal and the agent and explain why there is asymmetric information. How does the action described reduce the problem of moral hazard?
   a. Landlords require tenants to pay security deposits.
   b. Firms compensate top executives with options to buy company stock at a given price in the future.
   c. Car insurance companies offer discounts to customers who install antitheft devices in their cars.
2. Suppose that the Live-Long-and-Prosper Health Insurance Company charges $5,000 annually for a family insurance policy. The company's president suggests that the company raise the annual price to $6,000 to increase its profits. If the firm followed this suggestion, what economic problem might arise? Would the firm's pool of customers tend to become more or less healthy on average? Would the company's profits necessarily increase?
3. A case study in this chapter describes how a boyfriend can signal his love to a girlfriend by giving an appropriate gift. Do you think saying "I love you" can also serve as a signal? Why or why not?

4. The health insurance reform signed into law by President Obama in 2010 included the following two provisions:
   i. Insurance companies must offer health insurance to everyone who applies and charge them the same price regardless of a person's preexisting health condition.
   ii. Everyone must buy health insurance or pay a penalty for not doing so.
   a. Which of these policies taken on its own makes the problem of adverse selection worse? Explain.
   b. Why do you think the policy you identified in part (a) was included in the law?
   c. Why do you think the other policy was included in the law?

5. Ken walks into an ice-cream parlor.

   Waiter: "We have vanilla and chocolate today."
   Ken: "I'll take vanilla."
   Waiter: "I almost forgot. We also have strawberry."
   Ken: "In that case, I'll take chocolate."

   What standard property of decision making is Ken violating? (*Hint*: Reread the section on Arrow's impossibility theorem.)

6. Three friends are choosing a restaurant for dinner. Here are their preferences:

	Rachel	Ross	Joey
First choice	Italian	Italian	Chinese
Second choice	Chinese	Chinese	Mexican
Third choice	Mexican	Mexican	French
Fourth choice	French	French	Italian

   a. If the three friends use a Borda count to make their decision, where do they go to eat?
   b. On their way to their chosen restaurant, they see that the Mexican and French restaurants are closed, so they use a Borda count again to decide between the remaining two restaurants. Where do they decide to go now?
   c. How do your answers to parts (a) and (b) relate to Arrow's impossibility theorem?

7. Three friends are choosing a TV show to watch. Here are their preferences:

	Chandler	Phoebe	Monica
First choice	*Empire*	*Supergirl*	*Homeland*
Second choice	*Supergirl*	*Homeland*	*Empire*
Third choice	*Homeland*	*Empire*	*Supergirl*

   a. If the three friends try using a Borda count to make their choice, what would happen?
   b. Monica suggests a vote by majority rule. She proposes that first they choose between *Empire* and *Supergirl*, and then they choose between the winner of the first vote and *Homeland*. If they all vote their preferences honestly, what outcome would occur?
   c. Should Chandler agree to Monica's suggestion? What voting system would he prefer?
   d. Phoebe and Monica convince Chandler to go along with Monica's proposal. In round one, Chandler dishonestly says he prefers *Supergirl* over *Empire*. Why might he do this?

8. Five roommates are planning to spend the weekend in their dorm room watching movies, and they are debating how many movies to watch. Here is their willingness to pay:

	Quentin	Spike	Ridley	Martin	Steven
First film	$14	$10	$8	$4	$2
Second film	12	8	4	2	0
Third film	10	6	2	0	0
Fourth film	6	2	0	0	0
Fifth film	2	0	0	0	0

   Buying a DVD costs $15, which the roommates split equally, so each pays $3 per movie.
   a. What is the efficient number of movies to watch (that is, the number that maximizes total surplus)?
   b. From the standpoint of each roommate, what is the preferred number of movies?
   c. What is the preference of the median roommate?
   d. If the roommates held a vote on the efficient outcome versus the median voter's preference, how would each person vote? Which outcome would get a majority?
   e. If one of the roommates proposed a different number of movies, could his proposal beat the winner from part (d) in a vote?
   f. Can majority rule be counted on to reach efficient outcomes in the provision of public goods?

9. Two ice-cream stands are deciding where to set up along a 1-mile beach. The people are uniformly located along the beach, and each person sitting on the beach buys exactly 1 ice-cream cone per day from the nearest stand. Each ice-cream seller wants the maximum number of customers. Where along the beach will the two stands locate? Of which result in this chapter does this outcome remind you?

10. The government is considering two ways to help the needy: giving them cash or giving them free meals at soup kitchens.
   a. Give an argument, based on the standard theory of the rational consumer, for giving cash.
   b. Give an argument, based on asymmetric information, for why the soup kitchen may be better than the cash handout.
   c. Give an argument, based on behavioral economics, for why the soup kitchen may be better than the cash handout.

To find additional study resources, visit cengagebrain.com, and search for "Mankiw."

Glossary

A

ability-to-pay principle the idea that taxes should be levied on a person according to how well that person can shoulder the burden

absolute advantage the ability to produce a good using fewer inputs than another producer

accounting profit total revenue minus total explicit cost

adverse selection the tendency for the mix of unobserved attributes to become undesirable from the standpoint of an uninformed party

agent a person who is performing an act for another person, called the principal

Arrow's impossibility theorem a mathematical result showing that, under certain assumed conditions, there is no scheme for aggregating individual preferences into a valid set of social preferences

average fixed cost fixed cost divided by the quantity of output

average revenue total revenue divided by the quantity sold

average tax rate total taxes paid divided by total income

average total cost total cost divided by the quantity of output

average variable cost variable cost divided by the quantity of output

B

behavioral economics the subfield of economics that integrates the insights of psychology

benefits principle the idea that people should pay taxes based on the benefits they receive from government services

budget constraint the limit on the consumption bundles that a consumer can afford

business cycle fluctuations in economic activity, such as employment and production

C

capital the equipment and structures used to produce goods and services

cartel a group of firms acting in unison

circular-flow diagram a visual model of the economy that shows how dollars flow through markets among households and firms

club goods goods that are excludable but not rival in consumption

Coase theorem the proposition that if private parties can bargain without cost over the allocation of resources, they can solve the problem of externalities on their own

collusion an agreement among firms in a market about quantities to produce or prices to charge

common resources goods that are rival in consumption but not excludable

comparative advantage the ability to produce a good at a lower opportunity cost than another producer

compensating differential a difference in wages that arises to offset the nonmonetary characteristics of different jobs

competitive market a market with many buyers and sellers trading identical products so that each buyer and seller is a price taker

complements two goods for which an increase in the price of one leads to a decrease in the demand for the other

Condorcet paradox the failure of majority rule to produce transitive preferences for society

constant returns to scale the property whereby long-run average total cost stays the same as the quantity of output changes

consumer surplus the amount a buyer is willing to pay for a good minus the amount the buyer actually pays for it

corrective tax a tax designed to induce private decision makers to take into account the social costs that arise from a negative externality

cost the value of everything a seller must give up to produce a good

cost–benefit analysis a study that compares the costs and benefits to society of providing a public good

cross-price elasticity of demand a measure of how much the quantity demanded of one good responds to a change in the price of another good, computed as the percentage change in quantity demanded of the first good divided by the percentage change in price of the second good

D

deadweight loss the fall in total surplus that results from a market distortion, such as a tax

demand curve a graph of the relationship between the price of a good and the quantity demanded

demand schedule a table that shows the relationship between the price of a good and the quantity demanded

diminishing marginal product the property whereby the marginal product of an input declines as the quantity of the input increases

discrimination the offering of different opportunities to similar individuals who differ only by race, ethnic group, sex, age, or other personal characteristics

diseconomies of scale the property whereby long-run average total cost rises as the quantity of output increases

dominant strategy a strategy that is best for a player in a game regardless of the strategies chosen by the other players

E

economic profit total revenue minus total cost, including both explicit and implicit costs

economics the study of how society manages its scarce resources

economies of scale the property whereby long-run average total cost falls as the quantity of output increases

efficiency the property of a resource allocation of maximizing the total surplus received by all members of society

efficiency wages above-equilibrium wages paid by firms to increase worker productivity

efficient scale the quantity of output that minimizes average total cost

elasticity a measure of the responsiveness of quantity demanded or quantity supplied to a change in one of its determinants

equality the property of distributing economic prosperity uniformly among the members of society

equilibrium a situation in which the market price has reached the level at which quantity supplied equals quantity demanded

equilibrium price the price that balances quantity supplied and quantity demanded

equilibrium quantity the quantity supplied and the quantity demanded at the equilibrium price

excludability the property of a good whereby a person can be prevented from using it

explicit costs input costs that require an outlay of money by the firm

exports goods produced domestically and sold abroad

externality the uncompensated impact of one person's actions on the well-being of a bystander

F

factors of production the inputs used to produce goods and services

fixed costs costs that do not vary with the quantity of output produced

free rider a person who receives the benefit of a good but avoids paying for it

G

game theory the study of how people behave in strategic situations

Giffen good a good for which an increase in the price raises the quantity demanded

H

horizontal equity the idea that taxpayers with similar abilities to pay taxes should pay the same amount

human capital the accumulation of investments in people, such as education and on-the-job training

I

implicit costs input costs that do not require an outlay of money by the firm

imports goods produced abroad and sold domestically

incentive something that induces a person to act

income effect the change in consumption that results when a price change moves the consumer to a higher or lower indifference curve

income elasticity of demand a measure of how much the quantity demanded of a good responds to a change in consumers' income, computed as the percentage change in quantity demanded divided by the percentage change in income

indifference curve a curve that shows consumption bundles that give the consumer the same level of satisfaction

inferior good a good for which, other things being equal, an increase in income leads to a decrease in demand

inflation an increase in the overall level of prices in the economy

in-kind transfers transfers to the poor given in the form of goods and services rather than cash

internalizing the externality altering incentives so that people take into account the external effects of their actions

L

law of demand the claim that, other things being equal, the quantity demanded of a good falls when the price of the good rises

law of supply the claim that, other things being equal, the quantity supplied of a good rises when the price of the good rises

law of supply and demand the claim that the price of any good adjusts to bring the quantity supplied and the quantity demanded for that good into balance

liberalism the political philosophy according to which the government should choose policies deemed just, as evaluated by an impartial observer behind a "veil of ignorance"

libertarianism the political philosophy according to which the government should punish crimes and enforce voluntary agreements but not redistribute income

life cycle the regular pattern of income variation over a person's life

lump-sum tax a tax that is the same amount for every person

M

macroeconomics the study of economywide phenomena, including inflation, unemployment, and economic growth

marginal change a small incremental adjustment to a plan of action

marginal cost the increase in total cost that arises from an extra unit of production

marginal product the increase in output that arises from an additional unit of input

marginal product of labor the increase in the amount of output from an additional unit of labor

marginal rate of substitution the rate at which a consumer is willing to trade one good for another

marginal revenue the change in total revenue from an additional unit sold

marginal tax rate the amount by which taxes increase from an additional dollar of income

market a group of buyers and sellers of a particular good or service

market economy an economy that allocates resources through the decentralized decisions of many firms and households as they interact in markets for goods and services

market failure a situation in which a market left on its own fails to allocate resources efficiently

market power the ability of a single economic actor (or small group of actors) to have a substantial influence on market prices

maximin criterion the claim that the government should aim to maximize the well-being of the worst-off person in society

median voter theorem a mathematical result showing that if voters are choosing a point along a line and each voter wants the point closest to his most preferred point, then majority rule will pick the most preferred point of the median voter

microeconomics the study of how households and firms make decisions and how they interact in markets

monopolistic competition a market structure in which many firms sell products that are similar but not identical

monopoly a firm that is the sole seller of a product without any close substitutes

moral hazard the tendency of a person who is imperfectly monitored to engage in dishonest or otherwise undesirable behavior

N

Nash equilibrium a situation in which economic actors interacting with one another each choose their best strategy given the strategies that all the other actors have chosen

natural monopoly a type of monopoly that arises because a single firm can supply a good or service to an entire market at a lower cost than could two or more firms

negative income tax a tax system that collects revenue from high-income households and gives subsidies to low-income households

normal good a good for which, other things being equal, an increase in income leads to an increase in demand

normative statements claims that attempt to prescribe how the world should be

O

oligopoly a market structure in which only a few sellers offer similar or identical products

opportunity cost whatever must be given up to obtain some item

P

perfect complements two goods with right-angle indifference curves

perfect substitutes two goods with straightline indifference curves

permanent income a person's normal income

political economy the study of government using the analytic methods of economics

positive statements claims that attempt to describe the world as it is

poverty line an absolute level of income set by the federal government for each family size below which a family is deemed to be in poverty

poverty rate the percentage of the population whose family income falls below an absolute level called the poverty line

price ceiling a legal maximum on the price at which a good can be sold

price discrimination the business practice of selling the same good at different prices to different customers

price elasticity of demand a measure of how much the quantity demanded of a good responds to a change in the price of that good, computed as the percentage change in quantity demanded divided by the percentage change in price

price elasticity of supply a measure of how much the quantity supplied of a good responds to a change in the price of that good, computed as the percentage change in quantity supplied divided by the percentage change in price

price floor a legal minimum on the price at which a good can be sold

principal a person for whom another person, called the agent, is performing some act

prisoners' dilemma a particular "game" between two captured prisoners that illustrates why cooperation is difficult to maintain even when it is mutually beneficial

private goods goods that are both excludable and rival in consumption

producer surplus the amount a seller is paid for a good minus the seller's cost of providing it

production function the relationship between the quantity of inputs used to make a good and the quantity of output of that good

production possibilities frontier a graph that shows the combinations of output that the economy can possibly produce given the available factors of production and the available production technology

productivity the quantity of goods and services produced from each unit of labor input

profit total revenue minus total cost

progressive tax a tax for which high-income taxpayers pay a larger fraction of their income than do low-income taxpayers

property rights the ability of an individual to own and exercise control over scarce resources

proportional tax a tax for which high-income and low-income taxpayers pay the same fraction of income

public goods goods that are neither excludable nor rival in consumption

Q

quantity demanded the amount of a good that buyers are willing and able to purchase

quantity supplied the amount of a good that sellers are willing and able to sell

R

rational people people who systematically and purposefully do the best they can to achieve their objectives

regressive tax a tax for which high-income taxpayers pay a smaller fraction of their income than do low-income taxpayers

rivalry in consumption the property of a good whereby one person's use diminishes other people's use

S

scarcity the limited nature of society's resources

screening an action taken by an uninformed party to induce an informed party to reveal information

shortage a situation in which quantity demanded is greater than quantity supplied

signaling an action taken by an informed party to reveal private information to an uninformed party

social insurance government policy aimed at protecting people against the risk of adverse events

strike the organized withdrawal of labor from a firm by a union

substitutes two goods for which an increase in the price of one leads to an increase in the demand for the other

substitution effect the change in consumption that results when a price change moves the consumer along a given indifference curve to a point with a new marginal rate of substitution

sunk cost a cost that has already been committed and cannot be recovered

supply curve a graph of the relationship between the price of a good and the quantity supplied

supply schedule a table that shows the relationship between the price of a good and the quantity supplied

surplus a situation in which quantity supplied is greater than quantity demanded

T

tariff a tax on goods produced abroad and sold domestically

tax incidence the manner in which the burden of a tax is shared among participants in a market

total cost the market value of the inputs a firm uses in production

total revenue the amount paid by buyers and received by sellers of a good, computed as the price of the good times the quantity sold

Tragedy of the Commons a parable that illustrates why common resources are used more than is desirable from the standpoint of society as a whole

transaction costs the costs that parties incur during the process of agreeing to and following through on a bargain

U

union a worker association that bargains with employers over wages and working conditions

utilitarianism the political philosophy according to which the government should choose policies to maximize the total utility of everyone in society

utility a measure of happiness or satisfaction

V

value of the marginal product the marginal product of an input times the price of the output

variable costs costs that vary with the quantity of output produced

vertical equity the idea that taxpayers with a greater ability to pay taxes should pay larger amounts

W

welfare government programs that supplement the incomes of the needy

welfare economics the study of how the allocation of resources affects economic well-being

willingness to pay the maximum amount that a buyer will pay for a good

world price the price of a good that prevails in the world market for that good

SUGGESTIONS FOR
Summer Reading

f you enjoyed the economics course that
ou just finished, you might like to read more
about economic issues in the following books.

aron Acemoglu and James A. Robinson

hy Nations Fail: The Origins of Power,
rosperity, and Poverty

New York: Crown Publishing, 2012)

n economist and political scientist argue that stablishing the right institutions is the key to conomic success.

bijit Banerjee and Esther Duflo

oor Economics

New York: Public Affairs, 2011)

wo prominent development economists offer eir proposal on how to fight global poverty.

oram Bauman and Grady Klein

he Cartoon Introduction to Economics

New York: Hill and Wang, 2010)

asic economic principles, with humor.

en S. Bernanke

he Courage to Act: A Memoir
f a Crisis and Its Aftermath

New York: Norton, 2015)

former chair of the Federal Reserve offers his ke on what we learned from the financial crisis at shook the world in 2008 and 2009.

William Breit and Barry T. Hirsch

Lives of the Laureates

(Cambridge, MA: MIT Press, 2009)

Twenty-three winners of the Nobel Prize in Economics offer autobiographical essays about their life and work.

Bryan Caplan

The Myth of the Rational Voter: Why Democracies Choose Bad Policies

(Princeton, NJ: Princeton University Press, 2008)

An economist asks why elected leaders often fail to follow the policies that economists recommend.

Angus Deaton

The Great Escape: Health, Wealth, and the Origins of Inequality

(Princeton, NJ: Princeton University Press, 2013)

The 2015 Nobel laureate in economics discusses why the world is now a vastly richer place than it was in the past and why some people have been left behind.

Avinash Dixit and Barry Nalebuff

The Art of Strategy: A Game Theorist's Guide to Success in Business and Life

(New York: Norton, 2008)

This introduction to game theory discusses how all people—from corporate executives to criminals under arrest—should and do make strategic decisions.